The Coptic Encyclopedia

Editors and Consultants

The Coptic Encyclopedia

Aziz S. Atiya
EDITOR IN CHIEF

Volume 3

Macmillan Publishing Company
NEW YORK
Collier Macmillan Canada
TORONTO
Maxwell Macmillan International
NEW YORK · OXFORD · SINGAPORE · SYDNEY

Macmillan Publishing Company
866 Third Avenue, New York, NY 10022

Collier Macmillan Canada, Inc.
1200 Eglinton Avenue East, Suite 200, Don Mills, Ontario M3C 3N1

Library of Congress Catalog Card No.: 90-23448

Printed in the United States of America

printing number
1 2 3 4 5 6 7 8 9 10

Library of Congress Cataloging-in-Publication Data

The Coptic encyclopedia / Aziz S. Atiya, editor-in-chief.
p. cm.
Includes bibliographical references and index.
ISBN 0-02-897025-X (set)
1. Coptic Church—Dictionaries. 2. Copts—Dictionaries.
I. Atiya, Aziz S., 1898– .
BX130.5.C66 1991 90-23448
281′.7′03—dc20 CIP

The preparation of this volume was made possible in part by a grant from the National Endowment for the Humanities, an independent federal agency.

Photographs on pages 567, 736, 754, 755, 790, 791, 876–878, 1284, 1311, and 2168 are reproduced courtesy of the Metropolitan Museum of Art. Photography by the Egyptian Expedition.

C

(continued)

CROSS WITH TAPERS. *See* Liturgical Insignia.

CROSS VAULT. *See* Architectural Elements of Churches: Vault.

CRUET. *See* Liturgical Instruments.

CRUM, WALTER EWING (1865–1944), English Coptologist. He studied Egyptology in Paris under Gaston MASPERO and in Berlin under Adolf ERMAN, specializing in Coptic. He held no public office, but devoted all his life to Coptic studies. Crum worked in nearly all branches of Coptology, published thousands of papyri and ostraca, and in 1939 completed almost single-handedly the standard *Coptic Dictionary* (Oxford, 1939; reprinted 1962). He was elected fellow of the British Academy in 1931 and was awarded honorary degrees by the universities of Oxford and Berlin. His festschrift, *Coptic Studies in Honor of Walter Ewing Crum* (1950, pp. vii–xi), contains his complete bibliography. His notebooks and papers are kept in the Griffith Institute at Oxford, and his correspondence is in the British Museum (Add. MSS 45 681–90). He died in Bath.

BIBLIOGRAPHY

Bell, H. I. "Bibliography." *Journal of Egyptian Archaeology* 25 (1939):134–38; 30 (1944):65–66.

Coptic Studies in Honor of Walter Ewing Crum. The Byzantine Institute, Thomas Whittemore, Founder. Boston, 1950.

Dawson, W. R., and E. P. Uphill. *Who Was Who in Egyptology,* pp. 72ff. London, 1972.

MARTIN KRAUSE

CRUSADES, COPTS AND THE. To understand the position of the Copts vis-à-vis the movement of the Crusading expeditions from the West against the Muslim Middle Eastern countries, one must go back to the time of the last ecumenical council of CHALCEDON in 451. The reason for this inquiry is to elucidate Coptic feelings toward those Western nations as a result of their theological arguments over the single or dual nature of Jesus Christ, the problem of his divinity and humanity. In other words, this was the problem of MONOPHYSITISM against the conception of dyophysitism. The theological background of this problem is complex, but the differences between the Copts and their Western peers at this meeting, which the Copts ultimately considered to be out of the ecumenical movement, led to an irreparable breach between the two sets of delegations. Whereas the Copts clung firmly to the union of the two natures of God, the Western delegation swung toward the idea of dyophysitism. The Copts became alienated from the West as totally heretical, while the Western delegation was condemned by the Copts as equally heretical. The Coptic sources and the history of subsequent patriarchs indicate Coptic bitterness against the Dyophysitic West. They could never forgive the Western delegation for the deposition of DIOSCORUS I (444–458) and for his being exiled to Gangra because of his firm stand against his adversaries on Coptic monophysitism. While Dioscorus was regarded in the West as a heretic, the Copts considered him one of their prominent saints and continued glorifying him until the beginning of the Crusades in the eleventh century.

The Copts in principle could never have condoned this new movement of their old antagonists against the countries of the Middle East, whatever their motives might have been. In the meantime, the Crusaders from the West against Islam could not envisage any possibility of a united front with the Eastern Christians, even assuming that they were aware of their existence in these Muslim countries, which is somewhat doubtful after the lapse of more than five centuries since Chalcedon. In fact, the sources, both Western and Eastern, show beyond a shadow of doubt that the Copts had never forgotten Chalcedon, which they continued to curse, while the West became almost oblivious of the events of 451. Nevertheless, the conquest of Jerusalem in 1099 and the appropriation of the Holy Sepulcher by the Franks led the new Latin kingdom of Jerusalem to prohibit all Eastern Christians, the Copts included, from approaching the holy places because of their heretical views. To the pious Copts this was a very serious decision, since it impeded them from the performance of their annual pilgrimage to the Holy Land, where walking in the steps of Jesus was part and parcel of the fulfillment of the dictates of their Orthodox faith. In other words, the Western War of the Cross turned out to be a hostile movement against the Christians of the East, the Copts included.

This situation naturally turned the Copts against the Crusades, despite their precarious position within the Islamic kingdom, where they suffered even more persecution and financial imposts as a result of a movement that they hardly favored. Even in the mild reigns of men like the Ayyubid sultan al-Kāmil, they had to bear most of the brunt of financing the Muslim defense.

The HISTORY OF THE PATRIARCHS by SĀWĪRUS IBN AL-MUQAFFA' includes most of the details of these financial imposts in the course of the biographies of the contemporary patriarchs. Nevertheless, one example is quoted from the biography of MACARIUS II (1102–1128), the sixty-ninth Coptic patriarch, which touches the crusading campaign of 1106 by King Baldwin of the Latin kingdom of Jerusalem against al-Faramā on the frontier of Fatimid Egypt. Al-Muqaffa' eloquently expresses Coptic feelings toward the Crusades and his loyalty toward the Fatimid caliphate. He writes:

> And in Abīb of the year eight hundred and thirty-four of the Martyrs, and it was the fifteenth year of the patriarchate of the saintly father Abbā (Anbā) Macarius (Maqārah) the Patriarch, Baldwin (Bardwīl) the leader of the Franks (al-Faranj) arrived with a great army at al-Faramā, and he pillaged it and he burned it, and he determined upon a sudden attack against Cairo (Miṣr). Then he fell sick, and on the third day his sickness became serious, and he commanded his companions to carry him and to return to Syria (al-Shām). Then they carried him and returned, and when they reached al-'Arīsh, he died there. Then they cut open his belly and they salted him, as he had commanded them. And they returned with him to Jerusalem (al-Quds). And it happened, when news of their arrival at al-Faramā reached the noble Lord al-Afḍal, he raised a great army (to oppose) them. When Baldwin (Bardwīl), their leader, died, and they returned, the army pursued them to Syria (al-Shām), and returned, and God protected us against their deeds. We asked Him whose Name (is) great, to perpetuate His mercy and His grace; and to inspire us to give thanks to Him and to cause us not to forget the remembrance of Him through His goodness and glory. And when it was the Sunday of the half of (the month of) Kiyahk (in the) year five hundred and eleven of the Tax Year (*al-Kharājiyyah*) and it (was) the end of the month of Ramaḍān of the year five hundred and fifteen of the lunar (year), on the morrow of which would be the *fiṭr* (fast breaking), the noble Lord al-Afḍal rode from his house to Cairo (Miṣr) which is called the House of the King (*Dār al-Mulk*) and he went up to Cairo (al-Qāhirah) the protected, and he entered into the noble Castle, and he sat before our Sire al-Amir bi-Aḥkāmillāh [*History of the Patriarchs,* Vol. 3, pt. 1, pp. 35–36].

The sum total of this purely Coptic record is the outspoken feeling of loyalty to the Fatimid rulers of the country and the recognition by the Coptic community of the protection God granted them against the invaders.

Even at the time when Saladin was applying so much pressure on the Coptic community during the patriarchate of MARK III (1167–1189), the Copts looked upon the reconquest of the city of Jerusalem in 1187 with excitement. It opened the gates of the holy places before them and removed the barrier of the Frankish kingdom, which had interrupted their relations with the sister church of Antioch. In other words, the disappearance of Frankish rule from the holy places and their return to the Muslim kingdom was a blessing to the Eastern Christians.

This situation lasted even beyond the fall of ʿAkkā in 1291 and the total extermination of the Latin kingdom of Jerusalem. Since that date, and even before it, the perennial raids of the shadowy hosts of the Crusade on Egyptian industrial towns situated on the Mediterranean littoral proved to be mere hit-and-run raids after the pillaging of such coastal towns as Damietta in 1249, where the pillage of the textile factories included mainly those possessed by Coptic craftsmen.

A new chapter in the Crusades began in the fourteenth century when Philippe de Mézières, the French chancellor of the kingdom of Cyprus, established a new military order called the Order of the Passion of Jesus Christ. This was under the leadership of King Peter I of Cyprus, who conducted a multinational army against the city of Alexandria in 1365. They were incapable of penetrating Egyptian territory beyond that city, but the havoc, destruction, and pillage thereof was extensive. The city had a strong Coptic community, which suffered equally with the Muslim inhabitants at the hands of these invaders. This happened during the reign of the Mamluk sultan Shaʿbān (1363–1377), a boy of eleven under the tutelage of the atabeg Yalbogha, who was unable to marshal enough manpower to save Alexandria. Both Muslims and Copts were massacred. Mosques and churches were sacked or burned. Sources mention the story of a crippled old Coptic woman who saved some of the treasured relics of her church by ceding all her possessions to the marauding Crusaders and thereby deflecting their passage from her Coptic church. The ships of the retreating pillagers were so heavily laden with prisoners and other booty that the sailors had to throw much back into the sea, and Egyptian divers had to work hard in salvaging what they could for a long time after 1365. This expedition and the Cypriot holocaust of Alexandria provided an eloquent demonstration of the place of the Copts in the history of the Crusades.

It is clear that the Copts were excluded from the Muslim armies of defense because they paid the poll tax (JIZYAH) as a fee toward the employment of their substitutes in the armed forces. But it is definitely established by Muslim and Coptic sources that Islamized Copts did not only join the Islamic hosts but reached the highest ministerial positions, controlling the finances and very structure of the forces that fought the Crusaders. Doubtless those Islamized Copts must have played a prominent role in the extermination of the Frankish Latin kingdom of Jerusalem.

BIBLIOGRAPHY

Atiya, A. S. *The Crusade in the Later Middle Ages.* London, 1938.

______. *Crusade, Commerce, and Culture.* Bloomington, Ind., 1962.

Runciman, S. *A Story of the Crusades,* 3 vols. Cambridge, 1951–1954.

AZIZ S. ATIYA

CRYPT. *See* Architectural Elements of Churches.

CRYPTOGRAPHY. *See Appendix.*

CRYPTOPHONEME. *See Appendix.*

CUPS, BASINS, CAULDRONS, BUCKETS. *See* Metalwork, Coptic.

CURZON, ROBERT (1810–1873), English scholar and traveler. He was born in Harringworth and visited Egypt, Syria, and Palestine in 1833–1834 on a research tour of monastic libraries, looking for manuscripts, of which he amassed a fine collection. He also collected Egyptian antiquities. His travels are described in his *Visits to Monasteries of the Levant* (New York, 1849); a privately printed catalog of his collection, limited to fifty copies, was issued in 1849 as *Catalogue of Materials for Writing: Early Writings on Tablets and Stones, Rolled and Other Manuscripts and Oriental Manuscript Books, in the Library of the Hon. Robert Curzon at Parham* *in the County of Sussex.* His own copy of this catalog, with many notes and letters from others inserted, is in the Department of Manuscripts of the British Museum; his collection of Oriental manuscripts was presented to the museum. He died at Parham Park, Sussex.

BIBLIOGRAPHY

"Curzon, Robert." *Dictionary of National Biography,* Vol. 5, pp. 354–55. London, 1908.
Dawson, W. R., and E. P. Uphill. *Who Was Who in Egyptology, p. 74.* London, 1972.

AZIZ S. ATIYA

CYCLE, one of a group of works in Coptic literature dealing with episodes in the life of one or more specific characters, mostly saints and martyrs.

There are two basic types of cycle: homiletic and hagiographical. The difference lies simply in the different literary forms used, with the homiletic cycles being made up of texts produced in the form of homilies, and the hagiographical cycles being in the form of Passions of martyrs.

The hagiographical cycles (see HAGIOGRAPHY) are the better known (just as they have also been known for a longer time), especially because of the studies of E. AMÉLINEAU and later those of H. Delehaye. The homiletic cycles are coming to be recognized only today. Until now, the individual texts have often been falsely attributed to the more famous fathers of the fourth and fifth centuries, and broadly based study is needed in order to gather them together again and date them with reasonable accuracy.

For both types the first criterion for recognizing the unity of a cycle (at any specific point in the tradition) is content, that is, on the basis solely of the characters mentioned and the events described. Where this criterion reveals a unified narrative, the works in question can be described as forming part of a specific cycle.

Recognition of a cycle does not necessarily entail attributing the various works to one single author nor even to a group of contemporary authors or to one specific time. However, it is still the first step toward solving these questions. We shall therefore list the more important or recognizable cycles, referring the reader to the specific entries in this *Encyclopedia* for detailed information on the individual works; only after this shall we speak of attributing dates and authors.

One further word of warning is needed. From an objective viewpoint these homilies are recognizable only by means of the titles they bear in manuscripts. It should be borne in mind that these titles are frequently far from accurate indications of the true content of the homilies in question. Even when we use these titles, we shall therefore always add a short note on the actual content.

Homiletic Cycles

Cycle of Athanasius Athanasius was always considered a central figure not only in the Egyptian tradition in general but also (after CHALCEDON) in the specifically Coptic tradition. He was seen both as the founder of the Egyptian church as a well-defined autochthonous entity and as the champion of orthodoxy, of which the Egyptian church then became the depositary.

Coptic literary tradition therefore devoted great attention to Athanasius, creating around him a web of events based on historically attested episodes, which soon gave way to a complex, but still fairly unified, legend. This legend included two exiles, one in lonely, barbarian lands, the other in the Egyptian desert, where he was hidden by some monks; relations with barbarian peoples who were converted to Christianity; and struggles with the emperor Constans, an Arian, resulting in attempts to kill the saint.

Most of these episodes were already included in the Coptic *History of the Church* (perhaps fifth century) in the chapter relating to Athanasius. They were later recalled in various works having Athanasius as the subject or attributed to him. Of the former category, two have been preserved: the *Life of Athanasius* (this manuscript lacks its beginning; ed. Orlandi, 1968; papyrus manuscript now in Turin, and some codices from the White Monastery) and the *Encomium of Athanasius* attributed to CYRIL I of Alexandria.

The texts whose authorship was credited directly to Athanasius are mostly homilies of a moral nature, although they do contain certain autobiographical allusions to the legendary events of his life. In *On Murder and Michael the Archangel,* Athanasius speaks of his exile, of a stay in the convent of Pachomius, and of another stay with an anchorite (Pierpont Morgan Library, New York, M602, unpublished; Italian translation in Orlandi, 1981). In *To the Isaurians, Exegesis of Luke 11:5–9,* Athanasius speaks of friendship, a visit to the convent of Pachomius, and an episode at the Council of Nicaea (Pierpont Morgan Library, M577, unpublished; Italian translation in Orlandi, 1981). The Pierpont Morgan Library also holds a manuscript of *On Pentecost and the Parable of the Rich Man and the Poor Man* (MS M595, unpublished). The homily *Exegesis of Leviticus 21:9ff. and on the End of the World* is very important because it can be dated fairly precisely, since it refers to the Arab domination of Egypt in the form of prophecy. Certain details enable us to deduce that the homily dates to the second half of the seventh century (cf. Orlandi, 1981).

Cycle of Cyril of Jerusalem This cycle seems to have its source in an interest in Jerusalem and in a certain type of apocrypha that claimed to originate there (for other details, see the article on CYRIL OF JERUSALEM). It consists of several homilies that were to be added to the eighteen authentic *Catecheses* as numbers 19, 20, and 21, and of certain other additional texts (cf. Orlandi, 1974; Campagnano, 1980). *On the Passion* (divided into two homilies) comments on the relevant passage from John's gospel, but includes other excursuses, among them one on the Virgin (which will be considered in connection with the following homilies). *In Praise of the Cross* includes many legendary episodes from the time of the crucifixion and from later times (Constantine and Eusignius, Constantius and the luminous Cross, etc.). *On the Virgin* includes a description of the childhood of the Virgin and the Dormition.

Other homilies would appear to have been added to this cycle at a later stage: two further ones *On the Passion*, and another also entitled *On the Passion*, which in fact contains an apocryphon with a revelation of the Risen Jesus to the disciples.

Cycle of Theophilus Among the Copts, Theophilus of Alexandria was known as a great destroyer of pagan monuments. His legend was based, in fact, on passages from the Greek church historians echoed in the Coptic history of the church. The legend tells of the discovery of great treasures in the ruins of various temples that Theophilus destroyed, treasures he used, with the consent of the emperor Theodosius, for the construction or embellishment of churches in honor of different saints.

Insofar as we are able to reconstruct it from the works that have come down to us, his cycle was made up of the following: a homily on the destruction of the shrine of Serapis (Serapeum) and the construction of the Martyrium of Saint John the Baptist; a homily on the building of the church of the Virgin on Mount Kos (Qusqām); a homily on the building of the church for the relics of the Three Saints of Babylon; and a homily on the building of a church in honor of the archangel Raphael on the island of Patres. (For all these homilies, see THEOPHILUS of Alexandria.)

Cycle of John Chrysostom and Demetrius In later Coptic tradition, JOHN CHRYSOSTOM's fame was linked to his fight with the Empress EUDOXIA, after which (leaving aside the action of Theophilus of Alexandria) he died in exile. The cycle developed around this theme would seem to have its basis in an anonymous homily, *The Life of John Chrysostom;* this homily has links with a homily *In Honor of the Archangel Michael,* attributed to Eustathius of Thrace, and another, *In Honor of the Twenty-four Elders,* attributed to PROCLUS OF CONSTANTINOPLE, both of which refer to the same events, with novelistic variations. According to all these texts, John was supposed to have spent at least part of his exile in Thrace, where he converted the pagan population.

The theme was enlarged with the introduction of one DEMETRIUS OF ANTIOCH, the bishop by whom John Chrysostom claims to have been consecrated presbyter. A homily *In Honor of the Martyr Victor* attributed to John himself refers to him, and he is also personally credited with various homilies of a hagiographical nature, which, however, are not directly connected with the cycle.

Cycle of Basil of Caesarea A fairly large number of authentic homilies of BASIL THE GREAT were translated into Coptic in the "classical" period of translations (see LITERATURE, COPTIC). Later, however, there was an effort to present the figure of Basil as defender of Christianity against the barbarians, probably as propaganda against the Arab domination.

A number of homilies (only two of which have come down to us) were thus produced, set in the region of Lazica (Georgia, although the name is probably used to indicate an imaginary area) and celebrating the liberation of the region from the Sarmatian barbarians with the help of the archangel Michael.

Cycle of Evodius of Rome According to tradition, which must also have been recorded in the Coptic history of the church (though the relevant passage is lost), Peter's successor in Rome was Linus. However, the Copts attributed at least three homilies to an Evodius of Rome, a figure based on the Evodius who was Peter's successor in Antioch, and who therefore personally knew the apostles and possibly Jesus.

The content of these homilies (see EVODIUS) included older apocryphal narratives that had circulated without any named author, so that some ancient authority was needed for them. The first deals with the Passion and includes an interesting episode about the Jews in Rome at the time of Claudius; the second deals with the Dormition of the Virgin; and the third deals with the apostles.

Hagiographical Cycles

The development of the Egyptian hagiographic literature from Passions of single martyrs (originally in Greek) to cycles including many Passions of different martyrs referring to one another (probably produced directly in Coptic) is described in the article HAGIOGRAPHY. We mention here the hagiographic cycles that were more productive, to place them beside their homiletical counterpart described above.

The *Cycle of Victor, Claudius, and Cosmas and Damian* seems to be the earliest, and to have been based on Greek legendary Passions common in Egypt in the fifth and sixth centuries. The authors of the cycle gave a special impression of the court of Diocletian in Antioch that introduces the subsequent cycles.

One of them is the *Cycle of the Theodores,* where around the well-known figures of the martyrs Theodore the General and Theodore Anatolius, the Copts produced a story about the war between Diocletian and the Persians, the capturing of a Persian prince, and the treachery of the bishop of Antioch.

This led to the legend of the "Egyptian" Diocletian (formerly named Agrippidas) and the family of the Christian general Basilides, with his friends and relatives. This is the most widespread cycle, to which the following Passions belong: Anatolius, Apoli, Besamon, Epima, Christodorus, Eusebius, Justus, Macarius, Camul, Ter, and Erai.

Finally, a cycle was composed around the person of Julius the "commentator," the scribe who assisted at trials of martyrs and took note of their deeds and words. Probably his name was used simply to bring together a group of Passions that at first did not share any common feature. They are Are, Didymus, Heraclides, Macrobius, Nahrou, Panesneu, and Shenufe.

Conclusion

For many of the general problems about the production and characteristics of the cycles, the reader is referred to the article LITERATURE, COPTIC. Here we will say something on the probable period in which the cycles were written. The content and form of many of these cycles presuppose a cultural background and a literary style typical of the period of the bishop DAMIANUS (late sixth century). But since there was no need during this period for anyone to produce false texts, we must place these works in a somewhat later time, when the Arab dominion determined the appropriate circumstances for creating such falsifications. We can see the beginning of this process in some homilies by Constantine of Asyūṭ and its advancement in the homily *On the Arab Invasion* (probably mid-seventh century) attributed to Athanasius.

We note also that in the late libraries (notably that from Tin, now in Turin, and that from the White Monastery) the codices written from the eighth century on contain the works belonging to the cycles not in their proper order but as single entities, in the order of the later synaxarial readings.

We can therefore designate an interval from the mid-seventh century to the mid-eighth century as the most logical time for the composition of these cycles. This, of course, is a simplification, since there are reasons to think that the individual texts were produced in many ways and circumstances; but taken as such it can clarify many of the problems posed by those texts.

BIBLIOGRAPHY

Campagnano, A., ed. *Ps. Cirillo di Gerusalemme. Omelie copte sulla Passione, sulla Croce e sulla Vergine.* Testi e Documenti per lo Studio dell'Antichità. Serie Copta 65. Milan, 1980.

Orlandi, T. *Testi copti: 1. Encomio di Atanasio. 2. Vita di Atanasio.* Testi e documenti per lo Studio dell'Antichità 21. Milan, 1968.

______. "Patristica copta e patristica greca." *Vetera Christianorum* 10 (1973):327–41.

______. *Omelie copte.* Turin, 1981.

TITO ORLANDI

CYMBALS. *See* Music, Coptic: Musical Instruments.

CYPRIAN THE MAGICIAN. The legend of Cyprian the Magician (perhaps mid-fourth century with further development at a later period) tells how a young man in Antioch approaches Cyprian so that with magic he can win the love of the Christian virgin Justina. But all the magical arts are frustrated by prayer and by the sign of the cross made by Justina. Thereupon the magician becomes a convert and burns his magical books. He first becomes a presbyter and then bishop of Antioch, while Justina assumes the leadership of a house for Christian virgins. In DIOCLETIAN's persecution of the Christians (other emperors, too, are mentioned in various versions), both Justina and the converted magician die as martyrs in Nicomedia. In the East the figure of Cyprian of Carthage and this fictitious converted magician have been fused (cf. Forget, CSCO 47, in Scriptores Arabici 3, pp. 33f.; CSCO 78, Scriptores Arabici 12, pp. 37f. [Latin translation]).

There are three important texts in which the legend is found: (1) *Conversio Justinae et Cypriani* (around 350), which relates the history of the conversion of Justina and Cyprian; (2) *Confessio seu paenitentia Cypriani* (which follows the *Conversio* chronologically), which presents discourses and the life story of Cyprian in autobiographical form, including his initiation into numerous magical arts, his conversion, his confession of faults, his penitence, and his baptism; (3) *Martyrium Cypriani et Justinae* (end of the fourth or beginning of the fifth century). A clue to the dating is the sermon preached by GREGORY OF NAZIANZUS in 379 on the feast of Cyprian of Carthage (14 September) in Constantinople, in which the story of the Antiochene Cyprian's conversion has already left its coloring on that of the Carthaginian (Or. 24 [PG 35, cols. 1169–93]).

The texts, originally in Greek, were translated into Latin and into Oriental languages (Syrian, Coptic, Arabic, Ethiopic). There is a survey of the surviving Coptic items in Bilabel and Grohmann (1934, pp. 37f.). Bilabel and Grohmann published supplements to the older editions of O. von Lemm (1899) and W. E. Crum (1905), especially the edition and translation of the Pierpont Morgan Manuscript 609 (*Conversio and Martyrium*). The Arabic prayers of Cyprian and the conjuring-book of Cyprian are in the Heidelberg University Library.

BIBLIOGRAPHY

Amore, A. "Cipriano, Giustina e Teoctisto." *Bibliotheca Sanctorum* 3 (1963):1281–85.

Baumeister, T. "C. v. Antiochia." In *Lexikon des Mittelalters,* Vol. 3, pp. 402f. Munich and Zurich, 1984.

Bilabel, F., and A. Grohmann. "Studien zu Kyprian dem Magier." *Griechische, koptische und arabische Texte zur Religion und religiösen Literatur in Ägyptens Spätzeit,* pp. 32–325. Veröffentlichungen aus den badischen Papyrus-Sammlungen 5. Heidelberg, 1934.

Crum, W. E. *Catalogue of the Coptic Manuscripts in the British Museum,* pp. 151f., no. 331. London, 1905.

Delehaye, H. "Cyprien d'Antioche et Cyprien de Carthage." *Analecta Bollandiana* 39 (1921):314–32.

Krestan, L., and A. Hermann. "Cyprianus II" (Magier). *Reallexikon für Antike und Christentum* 3 (1957):467–77.

Lemm, O. von. "Sahidische Bruchstücke der Legende von Cyprian von Antiochien." *Mémoires de l'Académie impériale des Sciences de St. Pétersbourg,* ser. 8, Vol. 4, no. 6 (1899).

O'Leary, DeL. E. *The Saints of Egypt,* p. 115. London/New York, 1937.

THEOFRIED BAUMEISTER

CYRENAICA. *See* Pentapolis.

CYRIACUS, Bishop of al-Bahnasā (Oxyrhynchus), assumed author of eight homilies. We have no historical evidence of either the existence of this person or the period in which he lived. On the latter, opinions greatly diverge: G. Graf (1944–1953, Vol. 1, p. 475) thinks that if one accepts what is said by the Ethiopian *Book of Aksum* (Conti-Rossini, 1909–1910, CSCO 54, p. 5 [text], and 58, p. 5 [trans.]), Cyriacus would have had to have lived in the first half of the sixth century or the works that are attributed to him would be of the Islamic period. But Graf thought that the dating of these works to the eleventh century was without foundation.

E. Galtier, who published the *Martyrdom of Pilate* (1912, p. 41), believed, while admitting his ignorance, that Cyriacus dated to the fourteenth century at the latest. G. Giamberardini (1974–1978, Vol. 2, p. 53) placed him in the eighth century, but did not support his own conclusion and remained hesitant about being too definite. P. Sbath (1938, no. 444, p. 57) indicated in laconic fashion the fifteenth century.

No serious study of Cyriacus' vocabulary and syntax permits one to say if the Arabic text (there is no extant Coptic text) is a simple translation from the Coptic or an original composition in Arabic. Nothing in these works reveals the period in which he wrote. It is possible that any one of these works is in fact a redaction of an earlier document. Thus, of his two homilies on the flight of the Holy Family into Egypt, the first gives the impression of taking up the one attributed to the patriarch THEOPHILUS or that of ZACHARIAS of Sakhā, while the second appears to be a plagiarizing of the first, the legend of the flight of the Holy Family into Egypt having crystallized at first around al-ASHMŪNAYN (there is evidence of it from the fifth century) and then later having extended to al-Quṣiyyah (Qusqām).

One difficulty remains. What is the true spelling of his name? Were there perhaps two persons with this name? The name is often spelled H(e)ryāq(u)s, which is read Cyriaqus; but one may ask if the name was not Heraklios, which through a copyist's error could have become H(e)ryākaios. The confusion of *a* with *l* in writing is easy, while that of *k* with *h* is not attested. One can see how the Arabic spelling H(i)ryākus was arrived at. This corruption of the name Heraklios is not inconceivable, for it is found in the episcopal lists (Munier, 1943, p. 16, l. 25; cf. p. 17, l. 35).

If this hypothesis is correct, it would indicate that there was a celebrated bishop named Heraklios before, or at the beginning of, the Islamic epoch to whom certain late homilies were attributed.

Given the paucity of the documentation on Cyriacus, the simplest course is to enumerate here, one after another, the homilies attributed to him in the manuscript tradition:

1. Homily on the miracles wrought by the Holy Family at Pi-Jesus (i.e., at Dayr al-Jarnūs): Graf, 1944–1953, Vol. 1, p. 232; Giamberardini, 1974–1978, Vol. 2, pp. 56–63, an analysis of the homily; an edition without translation in *Al-La'āli' al-Saniyyah fī al-Mayāmir wa-al-ʿAjā'ib al-Maryamiyyah* ("Precious pearls in the Marian sermons and miracles"), Cairo, 1966, pp. 79–91.
2. Homily on the coming of the Holy Family to al-Qūṣiyyah: Graf, 1944–1953, Vol. 1, p. 233; Giamberardini, 1974–1978, Vol. 2, pp. 63–72, an analysis of the homily; edition without translation in *Al-La'āli'*, pp. 71–78.
3. Homily on the Compassion of Mary at Golgotha and at the tomb: Graf, 1944–1953, Vol. 1, p. 247; Giamberardini, 1974–1978, Vol. 2, pp. 72–85, an analysis of the homily; edition without translation in *Al-La'āli'*, pp. 92–110). E. Galtier calls attention to two Garshuni manuscripts in Paris (BN Syr. 232, 233). These manuscripts appear to be of Syro-Jacobite origin.
4. Homily on the Assumption of Mary: Vat. Arab. 170; analysis by A. van Lantschoot, 1946, pp. 509–511.
5. Homily on the Resurrection and on the martyrdom of Pilate: Graf, 1944–1953, Vol. 1, p. 239; edition and translation by Galtier, 1912, pp. 42–103. See also the edition and translation of the Ethiopic text by M. A. van den Oudenrijn, 1959. In fact, the Sanhedrin member Gamaliel speaks in the first person (Acts 5:34–39; 22:3); the text attributed to Cyriacus of al-Bahnasā is perhaps only a reworking.
6. Homily on Saint VICTOR, son of Romanos: unpublished; Graf, 1944–1953, Vol. 1, p. 476. In his *Inventaire des manuscrits de Dayr Abū Maqār* (1986, p. 55, no. 380; compare p. 64, no. 414), Zanetti seems to say that the same panegyric on Saint Victor is sometimes put under the name of DEMETRIUS OF ANTIOCH, an author still not identified.
7. On the martyrs of Isnā: Sbath, 1938, no. 444, p. 57. (Perhaps this was the same sermon as that attributed to John, bishop of Asyūṭ, edited and translated by A. Khater, 1981.) The whereabouts of the manuscript is not known.
8. Homily on Saint Justus: contained in a manuscript of the Monastery of Saint Antony (DAYR ANBĀ ANṬŪNIYŪS near the Red Sea): Hist. 112, fols. 41v–108r.

Mention should be made of the Ethiopic version of several of these texts. The two Marian homilies (1 and 2) seem to exist in an Ethiopic version: British Library Ethiop. 209, 211, 216, 217, 263, 341; Vatican Ethiop. 151.

The homily on the Compassion of Mary (3) also exists in an Ethiopic version: National Library, Paris, Ethiop. 104. The Ethiopic version of homily 5 has already been mentioned. The homily on Saint Victor is also extant in an Ethiopic version: British Library Ethiop. 247, 254, and 306.

There is an Ethiopic anaphora of Mary that is attributed to Cyriacus of al-Bahnasā: S. Euringer, "Die äthiopische Anaphora unserer Herrin Maria," *Oriens Christianus* 34 (1937):63–102, 248–62.

BIBLIOGRAPHY

Conti-Rossini, K. *Documenta ad illustrandam historiam,* Vol. 1, *Liber Axumae.* CSCO 54 [text] and 58 [trans.]. Paris and Leipzig, 1909–1910.

Euringer, S. "Die äthiopische Anaphora unserer Herrin Maria." *Oriens Christianus* 34 (1937):63–102, 248–62.

Galtier, E. *Mémoires et fragments inédits.* Mémoires de l'Institut français d'Archéologie orientale 27. Cairo, 1912.

Giamberardini, G. *Il culto mariano in Egitto,* 3 vols. Jerusalem, 1974–1978.

Khater, A. *Martyres des citoyens d'Esna.* Cairo and Jerusalem, 1981. *La'ālī' al-Saniyyah fī 'al-Mayāmir wa-al-'ajā'ib al-maryamiyyah, al-.* Cairo, 1966.

Lantschoot, A. van. "L'Assomption de la sainte vierge chez les Coptes." *Gregorianum* 27 (1946):493–526.

Munier, H. *Recueil des listes épiscopales de l'église copte.* Cairo, 1943.

Oudenrijn, M. A. van. *Gamaliel: Äthiopische Texte zur Pilatus-literatur.* Fribourg, Switzerland, 1959.

Sbath, P. *Al-Fihris (Catalogue de manuscrits arabes).* Cairo, 1938.

Zanetti, U. *Les Manuscrits de Dair Abu Maqar.* Inventaire Cahiers d'orientalisme 11. Geneva, 1986.

RENÉ-GEORGES COQUIN

CYRIACUS AND JULITTA, SAINTS, a son and his mother who were martyred under DIOCLETIAN (feast day: 15 Abīb). Cyriacus and Julitta came from Iconium (modern Konya, Turkey), but were killed at Tarsus in Cilicia. It appears that the text of their Passion, which is partially related to that of Saint George, was well known. It is mentioned in the *Decretum Gelasianum,* although the Greek text is unavailable. There is a Latin version (*Acta Sanctorum,* 4 June, pp. 24–28), as well as Syriac, Armenian, and Arabic versions (cf. Bibliotheca Hagiographica Orientalis, pp. 193–94). In Coptic, only a few fragments have survived (Michigan University Library, Inv. 554); however, these seem to bear witness to the existence of the entire text (ed. Husselman, 1965).

Julitta, a Christian woman from Iconium, had fled to Tarsus to escape the persecution of the governor Alexander. However, she finds him in Tarsus as well. After she refuses to offer sacrifice, she asks the governor to have her three-year-old son Cyriacus brought, saying that he would offer sacrifice to the gods he recognized. Cyriacus also refuses to offer sacrifice, whereupon both mother and son are severely tortured in various ways. In the midst of torture, the child pronounces a prayer of a vaguely Gnostic flavor, which is found in the Coptic, Arabic, and Syriac versions, but not in the Latin. After various miracles, both are beheaded.

The prayer appears to be the most important passage of the text. This prayer has been studied in detail by Gressmann (1921). Apart from the *Passio* of George, it is related to the "hymn of the pearl" in the *Acts of Thomas.* However, in Gressmann's opinion the prayer is of Jewish, not Gnostic origin.

BIBLIOGRAPHY

Dillmann, A. *Über die apokryphen Märtyrergeschichte des Cyriacus mit Julitta und des Georgius.* Sitzungsberichte der Königlichen Preussischen Akademie der Wissenschaften zu Berlin 12–13, pp. 339–56. Berlin, 1887.

Gressmann, H. "Das Gebet des Kyriakos." *Zeitschrift für die neutestamentliche Wissenschaft* 20 (1921):23–35.

Husselman, E. M. "The Martyrdom of Cyriacus and Julitta in Coptic." *Journal of the American Research Center in Egypt* 4 (1965):79–86.

TITO ORLANDI

CYRIL I, SAINT, or Cyril of Alexandria, twenty-fourth patriarch of the See of Saint Mark (412–444), who is reckoned one of the greatest prelates of Christian antiquity (feast day: 3 Abīb). Cyril spent his early years at Dayr Anbā Maqār in the Nitrian Valley, which had become noted as a center of theological studies. After five years of intensive study in that monastery, Cyril was summoned to Alexandria by his uncle, the reigning patriarch THEOPHILUS, and was ordained a presbyter. He distinguished himself as an eloquent preacher, and his name became widely known in the capital. At the death of his uncle, he automatically became a candidate for succession to the throne of Saint Mark against another local rival, the archdeacon Timotheus, who had the support of the government. Nevertheless, only three days after Theophilus' death, Cyril was enthroned on the archiepiscopal seat of Saint Mark, despite the strong opposition of the prefect, Orestes, who was regarded as a strong competitor of Cyril in influence in Alexandria. The rivalry between the two potentates in the capital, the one heading the church and the other the local prefecture, flared up repeatedly in the following years. From the early years of his accession, Cyril proved himself to be a man of strong personality, unusual ability, and profound theological scholarship, a match for the tempestuous events that marked his thirty-two-year reign.

Immediately on his accession, he declared spiritual warfare on several fronts, both at Rome and in other areas beyond his frontiers. At home, he had under his command an army of dedicated and self-effacing followers known as *Parabolani,* that is, "those who disregarded their own lives" in the service of the church. The *Parabolani* were monks from adjacent monasteries who made themselves available for any drastic action.

One of Cyril's first actions was to confirm the rejection of Novatianism by DIONYSIUS I, the fourteenth patriarch. The organization of Novatianists was a residue of a movement that originated in Rome after the Decian persecution of 249–250. Its founder, Novatian, initially espoused a lenient system of approach toward readmission to church communion of persons who had apostatized in the course of a Christian persecution. Later, during a papal election in which he was a losing candidate and which he ended by becoming a rival bishop of Rome, Novatian reverted to a rigorist policy regarding the apostates. Novatian was later martyred by Valerian. His legacy, however, survived him. His followers, though perfectly orthodox in their profession, persisted in keeping his rigorist policy even though they functioned under a sentence of excommunication until the fifth century, when Cyril tried to destroy their Alexandrian branch. While closing their headquarters and laying his hand on their secret treasure, Cyril dispossessed their bishop Theopemptus, and left him an impecunious and powerless nonentity.

In the meantime, Cyril continued to inspire the *Parabolani* with mortal hatred for Neoplatonist philosophy, which was taught in the Alexandrian Museon. At that time, the leader of the Neoplatonist school was Hypatia, at whose feet both pagan and Christian pupils studied philosophy. She was also highly esteemed by the prefect Orestes. Though avowedly a Christian baptized by a bishop of Constantinople, Orestes was accused by the *Parabolani* of being a pagan and a firm supporter of the pagan Hypatia, after whose blood they thirsted. Thus, in 415 they encountered Hypatia in her chariot, attacked her, dragged her to the Caesarian church where they murdered her, and took her mutilated corpse to a place called Cinaron where they burnt it. This tragedy aroused public feeling, and some followers of Orestes went as far as to accuse Cyril of indirectly inspiring the crime. Though it would be a mistake to involve Cyril in this act, the hostility of the patriarch to Neoplatonism must have been the starting point of all the trouble that precipitated this ungodly crime inside a godly institution during the holy season of Lent.

On another front, Cyril's hostility to the Jewish community in Alexandria was reciprocated by the Jews, who began to plot against the archbishop and the church. At one point, rumors circulated that the church of Alexander had been set on fire by Jews. When the Christians hastened to save their sanctuary, the Jewish plotters fell upon them and slew some of their number. Cyril did not let the occurrence pass without response. He and his monastic bodyguard, which was beefed up by monks from Wadī al-Naṭrūn, descended one morning on the synagogues in the city, took possession of them, and the Jews were expelled from the capital. Orestes was powerless in the face of such lawlessness sponsored by Cyril's armed monks and the *Parabolani*. He could only complain to Emperor Theodosius II (408–450), who was himself just a youngster of fourteen, and Cyril had no difficulty in facing the imperial court with a case about the Jewish sacrilege. In the end, the matter was laid to rest, but the hostility toward the prefect remained. One day Orestes' chariot was assailed by the monks in the streets of Alexandria, and a monk by the name of Ammonius hurled a stone at Orestes, seriously wounding him. Consequently, the prefect's men seized Ammonius and tortured him to death. Cyril considered this a crime and gave the dead monk a martyr's funeral. However, this affair was allowed to sink into oblivion as a minor incident. The fact remains that Cyril was a implacable fighter, not merely a saintly head of a religious institution, and his warfare was not confined to Egypt.

In the field of foreign policies, Cyril inherited his uncle's hostility to Saint JOHN CHRYSOSTOM, though in the end Cyril was persuaded to accept John Chrysostom's name in the Alexandrian diptych. The greatest conflict of Cyril's career was directed toward the patriarch of the Byzantine capital, NESTORIUS. The subject of the conflict was Christology. The discord between the two prelates was Nestorius' rejection of the term THEOTOKOS (Mother of God) in regard to the Virgin MARY, whom he designated only as Mother of Jesus in the flesh. This led to the inference of the dual nature of Jesus, which precipitated another round of metaphysical warfare between the two patriarchs. Cyril wrote a corrective letter to Nestorius without avail. Consequently, he addressed himself directly to Theodosius II, Empress EUDOXIA, and the emperor's sister, PULCHERIA, whose interest in religious matters was well known. The imperial family was, on the whole, disenchanted with these quarrels within the church and began to contemplate the possibility of holding an ecumenical council to settle the disputes and restore order and unity within the empire.

In the meantime, Cyril contacted the bishop of Rome, Celestine I (422–432), regarding the irregularities committed by Nestorius. It happened at the time that Nestorius had received the Pelagian enemies (see PELAGIANISM) of Celestine with honor, and this naturally stirred up the wrath of the bishop of Rome against the patriarch of Constantinople. Celestine was more than willing to listen to Cyril's complaint against Nestorius, whom he condemned in a council at Rome, while Cyril was encouraged to hurl twelve anathemas from Alexandria against his peer at Constantinople. Nestorius at once answered by casting twelve counteranathemas at his adversary. Thus the stage was set for another phase in the war between the two prelates, and only an ecumenical council could settle their differences.

The imperial decision was made to hold that council at EPHESUS in the year 431, and the summons to that meeting was issued jointly by Theodosius II in the East and Valentinian III in the West. This was the third ecumenical council, the other two being NICAEA in 325 and CONSTANTINOPLE in 381. Nestorius arrived at Ephesus with sixteen of his bishops and an armed bodyguard headed by the commander of the imperial guard. Cyril came by sea with fifty bishops, and he was surrounded by an army of devotees, the *Parabolani,* and some monks. These were said to have included the great SHENUTE in their number, though this report is unconfirmed by the sources and must be quoted with caution. On Cyril's side was the bishop of Ephesus, Memnon, who mustered another body of forty suffragans from Asia and twelve from Pamphylia. Celestine was able to send two Roman bishops and a priest who openly upheld Cyril's cause. With such a host of supporters, Cyril did not hesitate to open the session. Nestorius abstained from attendance because he still awaited the episcopal contingent from Antioch under the leadership of his old friend John, bishop of Antioch. Later, John arrived together with forty-two Antiochene bishops, and immediately Nestorius held his own rival council. Cyril's gathering of approximately two hundred bishops unanimously condemned Nestorius and anathematized him, and the Nestorian rivals independently and unanimously anathematized both Cyril and Memnon, also deposing them. The two parties rushed their verdicts to the emperor, who unwittingly signed both deposition edicts, and all the leaders found themselves under arrest.

However, after much maneuvering and diplomatic intrigue, the Cyrillian party succeeded in recovering its freedom, and Cyril returned to Alexandria, where his loyal congregation gave him a hero's welcome. Nestorius remained incarcerated in his old cloister at Antioch. For the next two years, numerous dispatches were exchanged between Cyril and the authorities and leading churchmen. The result was his total reconciliation with them, even with John of Antioch, thus leaving Nestorius a solitary victim to face a grim future. Nestorius was a sorry figure in 453. He was manhandled in his forced retirement and then was carried into exile first to Petra and afterward to the Egyptian oasis of the Western Desert, where he died at an unknown date after 439. According to the Coptic SYNAXARION, his death occurred at the city of Akhmīm in Upper Egypt in the year 440; however, this information is not corroborated by other sources.

In 439, Cyril was at the peak of his power in the universal church. He wrote to the then reigning bishop of Rome, Sixtus III, that peace was restored, and he signed a declaration possibly prepared by Theodoret of Cyrrhus confessing the divine maternity of Mary. He never halted his theological warfare against all supporters of Nestorianism. While he condemned THEODORUS OF MOPSUESTIA, the old mentor of Nestorius, he refrained from an open clash with him in order to avoid the revival of the Christological controversy. Cyril died on 27 June 444; the Coptic church commemorates him on 3 Abīb.

Like Athanasius, Cyril left behind him a tremendous number of theological studies and works of exegesis, homiletics, and apologetics. A meticulous theologian, he seems to have devoted more attention to the essence of his arguments than to the elegance of his style. Nevertheless, it is worthy of note that his indiscriminate use of the terms *physis* (nature) and *hypostasis* (substance) resulted in the Chalcedonian confusion, which led to the establishment of the so-called Monophysite doctrine. Cyril's apology against JULIAN THE APOSTATE is a document of historical interest. His numerous epistles are documents of the highest importance for the ecclesiastical historian. His twenty-nine paschal homilies defined the date of Easter. His extended liturgy, practiced in full mainly in monasteries, presumably reflects older texts ascribed to Saint Mark's Anaphora. On the whole, Cyril's theology was regarded by subsequent generations as the key to orthodoxy, though some theologians tend to differ on its interpretation. At his death, the Alexandrian church occupied a position of undisputed leadership in the whole of the Christian world.

Cyril's massive writings have been the subject of several editions since the sixteenth century. In 1546 at Basel, George of Trebizond published all available material of his works in four volumes. In 1573 and 1605, Gentianus Hervetus reproduced his works at Paris in two majestic volumes. From 1859 to 1864 John Aubert, canon of Laon and master of its college in Paris, published Cyril's works in ten volumes.

Cyril's immense literary heritage has been analyzed in works on patrology. A selected list of his works follows:

A. Commentaries on the Old Testament

1. *De adoratione et cultu in spiritu et veritate.*
2. *Glaphyra* (thirteen books, of which seven are devoted to Genesis; three to Exodus; and one to each of Leviticus, Numbers, and Deuteronomy).
3. *Commentary on Isaiah* (consisting of five *biblia* (books), of which some are divided into *logoi* (principles), others into *tomoi* (dogmatic pronouncements).
4. *Commentary on Minor Prophets.*

B. Commentaries on the New Testament

1. *Commentary on the Gospel of Saint John* (consisting of twelve books subdivided into numerous chapters).
2. *Commentary on the Gospel of Saint Luke* (containing homilies on Luke; a Syriac version of the sixth or seventh century preserves at least 156 such homilies).
3. *Commentary on the Gospel of Saint Matthew* (covering twenty-eight chapters of which only fragments remain).

C. Dogmatic-polemical works against the Arians

1. *Thesaurus de sancta et consubstantiali Trinitate* (mainly reproducing Athanasius, *Contra Arianos*).
2. *De sancta et consubstantiali Trinitate* (seven dialogues with Hermias).

D. Dogmatic-polemical works against Nestorius

1. *Adversus Nestorii blasphemias* (history of Nestorian blasphemies; five tomes).
2. *De recta fide* (consisting of three memoranda refuting Nestorianism, one to Emperor Theodosius II, another to his younger sisters Arcadia and Marina, and the third to his elder sister Pulcheria and his wife Eudoxia).
3. *Twelve Anathemas against Nestorius* (consisting of three apologies, two refuting accusations of Apollinarianism and monophysitism, and a third in defense of the anathemas by quoting the Scriptures).
4. *Apologeticus ad imperatorum* (submitted to Theodosius II after Cyril's release and return to Alexandria).
5. *Scholia de incarnatione Unigeniti* (defining the *hypostasis* union as against mixture or external association).
6. *Adversus nolentes confiteri sanctam Virginem esse Deiparam* (treatise against those who do not acknowledge that Mary is the Mother of God).
7. *Contra Diodorum et Theodorum* (treatise against Diodore of Tarsus and Theodore of Mopsuestia, mentors of Nestorius).
8. *Quod unus sit Christus* (dialogue on unity of person in Christ, one of Cyril's last anti-Nestorian works).

E. *The Apology Against Julian* (dedicated to Theodosius II, consisting of thirty books refuting Julian the Apostate's work *Against the Galileans* written in 363, and the survival of paganism in Egypt).

F. *Paschal Letters* (twenty-nine *Homiliae Paschales* addressed to churches of Egypt, fixing date of Easter and dealing with Christological controversies, the refutation of paganism, and the establishment of Jewish infidelity).

G. *Sermons* (twenty-two *Homiliae diversae* to distinguish them from the *Homiliae Paschales* of which eight date from the summer of 431 during the Council of Ephesus. Of the remaining homilies, the most famous is the Marian Sermon delivered at Saint Mary's Church in Ephesus).

H. *Letters* (eighty-eight letters; PG 77, cols. 10–390; some surviving in Coptic, Syriac, and Armenian versions; these are important documents on church history and ecclesiastical doctrine and law).

I. *Liturgical Work* (Cyril's liturgy reflecting Saint Mark's has been confirmed by the discovery of several papyrus fragments at DAYR AL-BALĀ'YZAH in Asyūṭ relating to a third-century Coptic Euchologion and the Anaphora of Saint Mark probably used at the time of Athanasius and preserved by Cyril).

Cyril's fame spread during his lifetime and after his death. His contemporary, Pope Celestine I of Rome, described him on several occasions as *homo fidei catholicae defensor* (defender of the faith), *vir apostolicus* (apostolic man), and *probatissimus sacerdos* (upright priest). After his decease, he became renowned in the Eastern churches as the ultimate authority in all Christological subjects. He was called the "Seal of the Fathers" by the seventh-century ecclesiastical authority Anastasius Sinaita. In 1882, the Sacred Congregation of Rites dubbed him Doctor of the Church. To this day he is considered the "Pillar of the Faith" in the Coptic church.

BIBLIOGRAPHY

Standard editions of Cyril's works in 10 volumes by J. Aubert (Paris, 1859–1864); also in PG 68–77. Many of Cyril's works have also been edited by P. E. Pusy in 7 volumes (Oxford, 1868–1877). E. Schwartz edited numerous epistles of Cyril in *Acta Conciliorum Oecumenicorum* 10. Berlin, 1922.

Atiya, A. S. *A History of Eastern Christianity*. London, 1968.

Bell, H. I. "Anti-Semitism in Alexandria." *Journal of Roman Studies* 31 (1941):1–18.

Campenhausen, H. von. *Griechische Kirchenväter*, pp. 133–64. Stuttgart, 1955.

Franses, D. "Cyrille au Concile d'Ephèse." *Studia Catholica* (1931):369–98.

Harnack, A. von. *History of Dogma*, 7 vols., trans. N. Buchanan. London, 1897–1899.

Hefele, K. J. von. *History of the Christian Councils*. 5 vols. Eng. trans. from German by W. R. Clarke. Edinburgh, 1871–1896.

Juaye, H. du Manoir de. *Dogme et spiritualité chez saint Cyrille d'Alexandrie*. Paris, 1944.

Kopallik, J. *Cyrillus von Alexandrien, eine Biographie nach den Quellen bearbeitet*. Mayence, 1881.

Kyrilliana. Etudes variées à l'occasion du XVe centenaire de saint Cyrille d'Alexandrie A.D. 444–1944. Cairo, 1947.

LeNain de Tillemont, Louis S. *Mémoires pour servir à l'histoire ecclésiastique des dix premiers siècles*, 16 vols. Brussels, 1693–1712.

Liébaert, J. "St. Cyrille d'Alexandrie et la culture antique." *Mélanges des Sciences religieuses* 12 (1955):5–26.

Maspéro, J. "Horapollon et la fin du paganisme Egyptien." *Bulletin de l'Institut français d'Archéologie orientale* 11 (1914):163–95.

Nau, F. "Cyril and Nestorius." *Revue de l'Orient chrétien* 15 (1910):365–91; 16 (1911):1–54.

Papadopoulos, C. Ὁ ἅγιος Κύριλλος Ἀλεξανδρείας. Alexandria, 1933.

Percoli-Ridolfini, F. "La controversia tra Cirillo d'Alessandria e Giovanni d'Antiochia nell' epistolario di Andrea da Samosata." *Rivista degli Studi Orientali* 29 (1954):187–217.

Praechter, K. "Hypatia." In *Realenzyklopedie der klassischen Altertumswissenschaft*, Vol. 9, pp. 242–49. Stuttgart, 1916.

Quasten, J. *Patrology*, 3 vols. Utrecht and Antwerp, 1975.

Rehrmann, A. *Die Christologie des hl. Cyrillus von Alexandrien*. Hildesheim, 1902.

Remondon, R. "L'Egypte et la suprème résistance au christianisme." *Didaskaleion* 51 (1952):116–28.

Rucker, J. "Cyrillus von Alexandrien und Timotheus Aelurus in der alten armenischen Christenheit." *Handes Ansorya, Monatschrift für armenische Philologie* (1927):699–71.

AZIZ S. ATIYA

CYRIL II, sixty-seventh patriarch of the See of Saint Mark (1078–1092). Cyril was a monk of the Monastery of Saint Macarius (DAYR ANBĀ MAQĀR), and his original name was George (Jirjā). Nothing is known about his secular life or his date of birth beyond the fact that he was a native of the province of Beheira when he joined his monastery. After the death of Patriarch CHRISTODOULUS, a large body of bishops, a number of the clergymen of Cairo and Alexandria, and some ARCHONS went to the Monastery of Saint Macarius in search of a candidate. The episcopal delegation included Quzmān, bishop of Nūsā; John, bishop of Sakhā, known as Ibn al-Ẓālim; Mark, bishop of Abū Ṣīr; Mercurius, bishop of Maṣīl; Gabriel, bishop of Basṭah (al-Khandaq); Khayāl, bishop of Quṭūr; Theodorus (Tadrus), bishop of Khirbitā; George (Jirjā), bishop of Ibṭū; John (Yuḥannā), bishop of Atrīb; Mark (Murqus), bishop of al-Balyanā; Peter (Buṭrus), bishop of al-Bahnasā; Macarius (Maqārah), bishop of al-Qays; and Mīnā, bishop of al-Baynayn. They deliberated for two months, without coming to a decision. Hence, accompanied by the archdeacon of Saint Macarius, they moved to a neighboring monastery, DAYR YUḤANNIS KAMA, where they selected a saintly man by the name of Bisūs. But he protested that he was a common man unfit for that dignity and began banging his chest with a stone until he was almost dead. So the delegation moved back to the Monastery of Saint Macarius, where they discovered a middle-aged monk of great sanctity by the name of George, on whom they settled as their candidate. They took him against his will, clothed him with the patriarchal garb, and named him Cyril (Kyrillos). Then they took him to Alexandria, where he was formally consecrated. He then went to Cairo to pay homage to the caliph, al-Mustanṣir, where he was received with honor. Later he called on his vizier, Badr al-Jamālī, who issued a special decree for his administration to execute all the patriarchal wishes. The position of the church thus became secure, after the hardships it had sustained under Caliph al-ḤĀKIM.

Cyril began his reign with the exchange of synodical epistles with his spiritual brother, Dionysius, patriarch of Antioch. Then he started to fill vacant dioceses with bishops. He refrained from demanding simony (CHEIROTONIA), unlike most of his predecessors. Nevertheless, he did come to an understanding with the new bishops that they should share their income with him. Apparently this did not suit a number of bishops, who began a rebellious movement by submitting complaints against Cyril to Badr al-Jamālī. Consequently, Badr ordered the patriarch to convene a general council of his bishops to settle their differences. The HISTORY OF THE PATRIARCHS (Vol. 2, pt. 3, pp. 214–15) gives a very rare list of forty-seven bishops who attended, including twenty-two from Lower Egypt and a similar number from Upper Egypt, in addition to the bishops of Miṣr, Giza, and al-Khandaq. This meeting took place in A.M. 802/A.D. 1086, and resulted in the revision of the Coptic legal system, which the patriarch reported to Badr al-Jamālī, who seems to have supported Cyril and requested the bishops to obey him.

The *History of the Patriarchs* (Vol. 2, pt. 2, pp. 187ff.) lists a series of encounters between Cyril and Badr al-Jamālī, which makes clear that the position of the church was secure and peaceful in al-Mustanṣir's caliphate. When it came to financial considerations, however, the government imposed the land tax of the KHARAJ, without the slightest diminution. Thus, the church was taxed 4,000 dinars per annum, and this was divided evenly among the bishops of Lower Egypt and those of Upper Egypt. Furthermore, the poll tax, or JIZYAH, was imposed on all Christians at the rate of, in the language of the time, one dinar and a third and a quarter, per person. There were also extraordinary financial imposts arising from unusual situations. Perhaps the most significant example of this occurred when all Alexandrians, Copts, Muslims, and Jews alike, were subjected to a tremendous fine of 12,000 dinars as a penalty for their complicity with al-Afḍal's son, who in 1085 had revolted against his father and fortified himself in the capital city.

Relations with the Christian kingdom of NUBIA were complex. While the country was ecclesiastically under Cyril II, the Islamic administration had parallel interests in the country, and Cyril's influence was supportive of Egypt's general position in Nubia. Furthermore, it is known that the Nubian king, Solomon, abdicated his throne to a nephew and retired to Egypt for worship in its sacred wilderness. Although Solomon was later seized by the Fatimid agents and taken to Cairo, Badr al-Jamālī treated him with deference, as a guest rather than a prisoner, and placed him in one of the state palaces. When he died shortly afterward, he was buried in Saint George's Monastery at al-Khandaq with all the Coptic funerary celebrations.

Relations with Ethiopia during Cyril's reign began with the consecration of Sawīros as archbishop of the diocese. He was a vigorous middle-aged politician besides being an ecclesiastic, and he conferred with Badr al-Jamālī over the Egyptian policy toward Ethiopia. Badr al-Jamālī sought two things in Ethiopia: the building of some mosques for its Muslim inhabitants and the assurance of safe conduct for Egyptian merchants. He granted the archbishop some funds for the building of mosques, and Sawīros sanctioned the restoration of seven mosques, which the Ethiopian Christians had destroyed. Moreover, Egyptian merchants in Ethiopia continued to be subjected to seizure and pillage. Badr al-Jamālī summoned Cyril II, whom he openly rebuked and requested to act sternly with his Abyssinian coreligionists. This was a serious problem for Cyril. Participating in the deliberations was the Coptic archon Abū al-Malīḥ Mīnā ibn Zakariyyā, who was an important functionary in the Islamic administration of the country. It was decided to strengthen the position of Sawīros by dispatching two bishops to the Ethiopian court—Mark (Murqus), bishop of Awsīm and Giza, and Theodorus (Tadrus), bishop of Sinjār—in an attempt to rectify this situation. Apparently no satisfactory solution was reached, but the story is indicative of the position of the Coptic patriarchate in these international relations.

After a reign lasting fourteen years and three months, Cyril II died in Cairo on 12 Ba'ūnah and was temporarily buried in the Church of Saint Michael on the island of Rodah. His remains were later transferred to the monastery of Saint Macarius in Wādī al-Naṭrūn in the Western Desert.

BIBLIOGRAPHY

Amélineau, E. *Géographie de l'Egypte à l'époque copte.* Paris, 1893.

Lane-Poole, S. *The Mohammadan Dynasties.* London, 1894.

______. *History of Egypt in the Middle Ages.* London, 1901.

SUBHI Y. LABIB

CYRIL III IBN LAQLAQ, seventy-fifth patriarch of the See of Saint Mark (1235–1243). Cyril, known as Ibn Laqlaq before his investiture, was called Dawūd ibn Yuḥannā ibn Laqlaq al-Fayyūmī, indicating that he was originally a native of the city of al-Fayyūm in Upper Egypt. His date of birth is unknown, and his ascension to the throne of Saint Mark in peculiar circumstances came to pass after an interregnum of nineteen years, during which the patriarchal seat remained vacant.

In the end, Dawūd, who was well connected with the Ayyubid administration through Ibn al-Mīqāṭ, the Coptic chief scribe of the sultan, prevailed on the caliph to issue a special decree appointing him patriarch without any regard to the normal democratic Coptic procedure used to choose the head of the church. This aroused fierce opposition in Coptic circles, and a procession was to go to the citadel where Sultan al-Kāmil (1218–1238) resided and to protest against such an appointment. Since the appointment decree was issued by al-ʿĀdil (1200–1218) without consulting the Copts, it was decided to keep that decree in abeyance until a council of bishops, clergy, and Coptic ARCHONS had reviewed the situation. At last, however, Dawūd was able to manipulate the council and emerge as the winner.

Cyril III needed large funds, partly to enable him to pay the caliphal court for its support of his case. He raised the money by applying the simoniacal practice of CHEIROTONIA and by the sale of the empty episcopal seats to the highest bidders. Many of these seats had fallen vacant during the long interregnum. This practice alarmed the community of the faithful, who protested against the practices. The rebellious congregation found a leader for their opposition movement in the person of a monk named ʿImād (Ḥāmid) of Dayr Anbā Maqār. The movement was further strengthened by a Coptic archon named Saniy al-Dawlah ibn al-Thuʿbān, who insisted that Cyril was pope only by bribery and corruption, and he raised serious doubts about the legality of Cyril's ordination. In light of these circumstances, it was decided to hold a general council of the clergy and the archons to look into the situation and make recommendations. The Islamic administration of the country favored the suggestion, and Sultan al-Malik al-Ṣāliḥ Najm al-Dīn Ayyūb (1239–1249) took the initiative and summoned that council where, according to al-MAQRĪZĪ, the Islamic historian of the Copts, the patriarch was sharply criticized. Nevertheless, Cyril, who prevailed upon the Coptic scribes of the administration while bribing the caliphal court with 12,000 dinars, was able to swing the verdict in his favor. In this way, the opposition to the patriarchal party was stifled, and Cyril was able to hold his own and rule the church in his way and in relative peace until his death in 1243. His reign lasted seven years, nine months, and ten days, and he was buried in Dayr al-Shamʿ at Giza.

It is noteworthy that the HISTORY OF THE PATRIARCHS curtailed his biography to a single page and that Coptic authors of the period, such as ABŪ AL-MAKĀRIM, the famous thirteenth-century historian of the churches and monasteries in Egypt, overlooked his name completely. In fact, Cyril is better remembered for an edificatory work entitled *Book of the Master and the Pupil,* which consists of fifty-five discourses of a moralistic character.

He was a contemporary of the sultans al-Kāmil (1218–1238), al-ʿĀdil II (1238–1239), and al-Ṣāliḥ Najm al-Dīn (1239–1249), thus being contemporaneous with the decline and fall of the Ayyubid dynasty. After his death, the throne of Saint Mark remained vacant for more than seven years before the community found a successor in the person of ATHANASIUS III.

BIBLIOGRAPHY

Atiya, A. S. *Crusade, Commerce and Culture.* Bloomington, Ind., 1962.

Lane-Poole, S. *The Mohammedan Dynasties.* London, 1894.

______. *History of Egypt in the Middle Ages.* London, 1901.

Runciman, S. *History of the Crusades,* 3 vols. Cambridge, 1951–1954.

SUBHI Y. LABIB

CYRIL IV, 110th Patriarch of the See of Saint Mark (1854–1861). He was born Dawūd Tūmās Bāshūt in 1816 at Najʿ Abū Zaqālī, near Akhmīm in Upper Egypt. At the age of twenty-two he entered St. Antony's monastery (DAYR ANBĀ ANṬŪNIYŪS), becoming its abbot at the age of twenty-four by virtue of his good character and charitable disposition. Throughout his life he displayed a deep love for learning and keen enthusiasm to improve the condition of monasteries and churches, as well as a great interest in the laity, which later earned for him the title "Cyril the Father of Reform." He was brought to the attention of PETER VII, who appreciated his outstanding qualities.

In 1851 reports of friction and dissent between the Ethiopian clergy and the Coptic Metropolitan "Anbā Salāma" were received by the Patriarch, who was requested to intervene in person. As the journey was too arduous for him, he delegated Father Dāwūd for this delicate task. His sojourn in Ethiopia extended to eighteen months, and he was able to achieve some success. But before he could finally accomplish his mission he was recalled by the Patriarch who had suddenly fallen ill. Two and a half months before Father Dāwūd arrived in Cairo on 17 July 1852, the Patriarch had already passed away, having recommended Father Dāwūd to succeed him.

Father Dāwūd's absence in Ethiopia and the lack of news about him led to a split of opinion among the clergy. Some members supported him, but others were in favor of appointing the bishop of Akhmīm. When Father Dāwūd eventually appeared in Cairo, the majority agreed to submit his name to the khedive Abbās I for ratification. The latter, however, was in the habit of consulting fortune-tellers and astrologers before committing himself to any important decision, and in this case he was strongly warned, at his risk, against approving Father Dāwūd. The situation reached an impasse as both sections of the community stuck to their positions. Two months later they agreed to a recommendation made by the Armenian Bishop in Cairo, to promote Father Dāwūd to the rank of Metropolitan of Cairo as a conciliatory measure, for a probationary period, after which he would be elevated to the Patriarchate, should he prove himself capable of shouldering that high responsibility. Final agreement as to his suitability was reached fourteen months later, and approval was secured from Khedive Abbās. He assumed his responsibilities as Patriarch in the summer of 1854, on 11 Bā'ūnah 1570 A.M.

Cyril IV now devoted all his energies toward implementing a radical reform program. His name became synonymous with educational reform and the introduction of modern schools. He established a new school for boys and another school for girls (a daring and revolutionary step at the time) in 1855 at al-Darb al-Wāsi' district in Cairo, two others at Ḥārāt al-Saqqāyīn in the district of 'Abdīn also in Cairo, a school at Manṣūrah and another under St. Antony's monastery in the valley at BŪSH. He paid special attention to the teaching of Arabic, Coptic, and foreign languages. He put the curricula under his own personal supervision and visited the schools regularly to encourage both teachers and students. He was convinced that reform can be attained only through a sound system of education.

With equal far-sightedness, Cyril IV realized the necessity of having a printing press at the Patriarchate to supply schools with the right textbooks at a reasonable price, and also to reprint the precious manuscripts that were stored in various churches and monasteries. He therefore gave orders for the purchase of a press from Europe, and obtained permission from Khedive SA'ĪD to admit four Coptic students as apprentices at the Būlāq Government Press. They were to receive their salaries from the patriarch himself.

It is related that when the press arrived in Alexandria, Cyril IV was away in St. Antony's monastery, but he asked his Vicar to welcome the arrival of the press at the railway station with an organized and jubilant procession to the seat of the Patriarchate. The clergy would take part and the deacons sing. Some persons, who could not understand the significance of such a reception, belittled the whole matter and criticized the Patriarch. He told them that had he been present at the time, he would have danced in the procession as David had danced in front of the Ark of the Covenant.

In September 1856 he was called upon once again to undertake an important official mission to Ethiopia on behalf of Khedive Sa'īd, who delegated him to negotiate a solution to the thorny problem of the two countries' common borders. Emperor Theodorus gave the patriarch a warm welcome, but very shortly afterwards news came that Sa'īd was threatening to invade Ethiopia. The Emperor could not but think that the Coptic Patriarch was the cat's paw in a joint conspiracy. He flew into a rage and commanded his men to burn the Patriarch alive, and only the intervention of the Queen saved his life. The emperor was eventually convinced of the patriarch's innocence and his good intentions, and set him at liberty. After eighteen months' absence Cyril arrived back in Egypt. As soon as he set foot on Egyptian soil he knelt down and kissed the ground in gratitude to God for his safe return. On 13 February 1858, the Copts came out to welcome their beloved Patriarch back to Cairo. Cyril IV resumed his effort during the rest of his pontificate to consolidate the ties between the Coptic Church and other Orthodox churches. He built new churches and restored the cathedral building in Cairo. He took the restoration as an opportunity to teach his people a lesson on the sin of excessive attachment to religious pictures and images. He even collected a number of icons from old church buildings and burnt them in the presence of a large crowd.

Cyril IV died in 1861 at the relatively early age of forty-five. The events surrounding his death are rather obscure, and some sources contend that he was poisoned. Nevertheless, he is remembered as one of the great patriarchs of the Coptic Church.

BIBLIOGRAPHY

Butcher, E.L. *The Story of the Church in Egypt*. London, 1897.

Jirjis Philūthāwus ʿAwaḍ. *Dhikrā Muṣliḥ ʿAẓīm, al-Anbā Kīrullus al-Rābiʿ, Abī-al Iṣlāḥ al-Qibṭī*. Cairo, 1911.

Tawfiq, I. *Nawābigh al-Aqbāṭ wa-Mashāhīruhum fī-al Qarn al-Tāsiʿ ʿAshar* (Outstanding Copts of the Nineteenth Century). Cairo, 1910.

Ya'qūb Nakhlah, R. *Tārīkh al-Ummah al-Qibṭiyyah*. Cairo, 1899.

MOUNIR SHOUCRI

CYRIL V, 112th patriarch of the See of Saint Mark (1874–1927). He was born at the village of Tizmant in Banī Suef Province, in 1824, and was known as Ḥannā al-Nāsikh (the calligrapher) because of his beautiful handwriting. At the age of twenty he entered DAYR AL-BARĀMŪS in Wādī al-Naṭrūn. He was elevated to the priesthood and ultimately became abbot of his monastery. DEMETRIUS II appointed him HEGUMENOS at the Cairo Cathedral, but, at the request of his fellow monks in his old monastery, Cyril was allowed to return to the Barāmūs monastery.

After Demetrius' death the papal seat remained vacant for five years. Eventually, Ḥannā was chosen for the position and was enthroned on 1 November 1874.

During the interregnum Vicar General Metropolitan Murqus of Beheirah province, who aspired to occupy the papal seat, drew up a plan for the establishment of the COMMUNITY COUNCIL to assist the clergy in conducting church affairs. At the outset, the new patriarch functioned harmoniously in cooperation with the council, but it was not long before a rift developed not only between the clergy and the secular party but also between the members of the council.

In 1883, under the chairmanship of BOUTROS GHĀLĪ the laity obtained a khedivial decree to have the council established by law. The patriarch became more and more dissatisfied with it, and its meetings were eventually suspended. It met again in 1891, but did not continue for long. A third council was formed in 1892, but the gap had grown wider between the two sides, which led the council to ask the government to have the patriarch removed to al-Barāmūs monastery. The council then elected the bishop of Sanabū as papal deputy. The patriarch excommunicated the said bishop. The bulk of the people were thus divided, and some of them even kept away from churches. Petitions continued to be sent to the government; and when a new cabinet was formed, the council finally agreed that their wisest course was to submit to the patriarch and ask for his recall. Cyril V returned to Cairo in a triumphal procession, with huge numbers of cheering Muslims and Christians to welcome him back.

The council was consequently dissolved and a four-member committee was formed by the patriarch, but before long it was abolished, and the fourth council was formed in 1906. It continued to discharge its duties until 1912 when its jurisdiction was redefined and curtailed. Its powers were restored in 1927 when the patriarch died, at the age of 103, after having occupied the papal seat for almost fifty-three years.

During his pontificate the CLERICAL COLLEGE was established in Cairo in 1894. Also operated were a school for boys in Alexandria, the Tawfiq schools in Cairo, the ʿAbbasiyyah Coptic College for Girls, as well as churches, hospitals, and benevolent societies. He paid two visits to the Sudan, in 1904 and 1909, during which he established the Khartoum bishopric and church.

He had good relations with the khedive of Egypt, the sultan of Turkey, the emperors of Ethiopia, and the czar of Russia, by all of whom he was awarded the highest official decorations. He was also appointed member of the National Legislative Assembly. By virtue of his long life he was contemporaneous with all the members of the MUḤAMMAD ʿALĪ DYNASTY from its founder down to King Fouad.

MOUNIR SHOUCRI

CYRIL VI, 116th patriarch of the See of Saint Mark (1959–1971). He was born ʿĀzir Yūsuf ʿAṭā in 1902 at Ṭūkh al-Naṣārā, in the Minūfiyyah Province, to a devout family who later moved to Alexandria, where he completed his education.

Cyril VI (left) with the Ethiopian Anbā Basilios, who was ordained in 1959. *Courtesy Aziz S. Atiya collection.*

At the age of twenty-five, he retreated to al-Barāmūs Monastery (DAYR AL-BARĀMŪS), where he was held in high esteem by all its monks. In 1931 JOHN XIX ordained him priest at the monastery, with the name of Mīnā. Later on he lived as a hermit in a deserted windmill on the eastern slopes of the Muqaṭṭam hills overlooking Cairo. In 1959 he was elected patriarch.

One of his earliest achievements, barely twenty days after his enthronement, was to reestablish relations between the Coptic and Ethiopian churches. He sent a delegation to Emperor HAILE SELASSIE to inform him of his intention, and to request him to send a deputation to attend the discussions in Cairo. The outcome of the talks was a decision to raise the office of metropolitan of Ethiopia to the rank of patriarch catholicos, and to choose its occupant in accordance with the traditions of the See of Saint Mark. He was to be selected from the Ethiopian monks no higher than HEGUMENOS, and to be finally consecrated by the pope of Alexandria. Consequently, it was agreed that the then metropolitan, Anbā Basilios, be elevated to the newly established catholicate. After Basilios' death, the bishop of Harar, Anbā Theophilos, was sent to Alexandria for consecration as patriarch catholicos. In October 1960, Cyril VI paid a pastoral visit to Ethiopia so as to further strengthen the relations between the two churches.

In January 1965 Cyril presided over the Oriental Orthodox Conference convened by Emperor Haile Selassie in Addis Ababa. It was attended by Mār Ighnaṭius Yaʿqūb III, patriarch of Antioch and the East; Anbā Vaskim I, the Armenian catholicos (USSR); Anbā Khorin, the Caelician catholicos (Lebanon); the Syrian catholicos in Judea; Anbā Basilios, the Ethiopian catholicos; and Anbā Theophilos, bishop of Harar.

The conference adopted various resolutions confirming its adherence to the Orthodox faith based on the Holy Bible and the sacred tradition received from Saint Mark. It also stressed the urgent need for the proper reconciliation between the church and the individual, the study of family problems, and the respect of the sanctity of marriage.

Cyril VI noticed that certain Copts, by merely converting to a sister church, the Syrian Orthodox Church, could obtain grounds for the dissolution of marriage. Consequently, in 1965, he issued a joint declaration with the Syrian patriarch, Mār Ighnaṭius Yaʿqūb III, stressing the unity of the two churches.

On the ecumenical front he took steps to bring the Church of Alexandria into the mainstream of Christendom by means of active participation in world conferences. This brought about various fruitful results, such as membership in the World Council of Churches and the Middle East Council of Churches. It also led to the exchange of pastoral visits among the heads of Orthodox, Catholic, Episcopal, and Protestant churches.

The recognition of the unique place of the Church of Alexandria was made abundantly clear in 1968 when Cyril VI welcomed 172 delegates from around the world, who came to participate with the Coptic church in celebrating the 1,900th anniversary of the martyrdom of Saint MARK, its founder and patron. On 25 June 1968, together with President Nasser and Emperor Haile Selassie, he laid the foundation stone for the largest cathedral in Africa, to which were brought the rest of Saint Mark's holy relics from Venice, which were buried in the crypt of what is known now as Anbā Ruways Cathedral.

On the domestic front Cyril VI achieved far-reaching successes in reform. He was fully aware of the responsibility of the church toward every individual, especially the needy and unemployed. He established the Bishopric of Social Services to help such people to help themselves through vocational and technical training. Thousands of families benefited from this organization by making use of their natural talents.

To settle the question of the administration of *waqfs* (land and property endowed to the church) Cyril VI was instrumental in the promulgation of Laws 1433 and 962 (1960 and 1966, respectively), whereby such endowments were brought under the sole authority of a well-organized administration.

Being first and foremost a monk and fully aware of the deep attachment a monk should have toward his own monastery, without which link there could be no real spiritual growth, Cyril issued a papal order in August 1960 by which monks were required to return to their own monasteries. This measure helped to restore the essence of Egyptian monasticism to its basic purpose. His interest in monastic life manifested itself in the establishment of a new monastery, DAYR MĀR MĪNĀ, at Maryūt (Mareotis) to the west of Alexandria, a spot where monastic life flourished in the early centuries of Christianity. Together with this monastery, he built a magnificent cathedral where he chose to be buried.

He encouraged church building throughout Egypt; at least forty churches in Cairo and Alexandria alone were constructed in his lifetime.

During Cyril's reign, beginning on 2 April 1968, repeated apparitions of the VIRGIN MARY were seen at the Church of Zaytūn. This was an occasion of tremendous spiritual uplift to countless men and women of piety. That event also attracted much attention throughout the Christian world. Cyril VI died on 9 March 1971 after a life of piety and inspiration to his flock.

MOUNIR SHOUCRI

CYRIL, ANAPHORA OF SAINT. *See* Anaphora of Saint Cyril.

CYRIL OF ALEXANDRIA. *See* Cyril I, Saint.

CYRIL OF ALEXANDRIA, PSEUDO-. *See* Pseudo-Cyril of Alexandria.

CYRIL OF JERUSALEM, bishop of Jerusalem (c. 350–387) due to the efforts of the Arianite faction. However, because his doctrine was substantially anti-Arian, he was repeatedly exiled by the Arian emperors Constantius (357–362) and Valens (367–378).

The Egyptian tradition recognized him as orthodox and regarded his character and work with favor. Consequently, the Copts accorded him a prominent position both as historic and as a literary figure. In Coptic history, the episode involving the appearance of the shining cross upon Golgotha has become especially well known. This story appears in Greek in a letter attributed to Cyril (PG 33, cols. 1165–76), and in various ecclesiastical histories (Socrates 2.28; Sozomen 4.5; Philostorgius 3.26). In Coptic we find this event recorded in the HISTORIA ECCLESIASTICA, with a mention of the letter cited above, and in a homily, *De cruce,* likewise attributed to Cyril (ed. Compagnano, 1980, par. 106). Further, on 12 Bashans, the Copto-Arabic SYNAXARION celebrates this appearance of the cross (ed. Forget, 1954, Vol. 2, p. 116), in which both the letter of Cyril and the section from the *Historia ecclesiastica* are cited. Therefore, it is quite probable that such a letter might have existed in Coptic.

In Coptic literature, a translation of his *Catecheses* (cf. Orlandi, 1974, pp. 56–76) was adopted at a very early date. However, since only a few fragments taken from Book 6—polemic, Gnostic, and/or Manichaean—remain, we are not certain if the translation is complete. There is certainly enough evidence for us to assume that his *Mystagogical Catecheses* never existed in Coptic.

Later, a series of homilies was attributed to Cyril. These are of diverse character, but some of them may be classified together as one of the literary CYCLES typical of the late period of Coptic literature. As such, they are spurious. The others, which stand isolated, are probably spurious as well, but a few might be traced to Greek originals of the fourth and fifth centuries.

The "isolated" pseudo-Cyrillian homilies are as follows:

1. *De passione I* and *II.* These two homilies form one unit, which is an exegesis of the Passion as narrated in John 13–20. These homilies have been transmitted to us in numerous codices, of which the principal ones are in the Pierpont Morgan Library, New York (M594 and M595); there are also four fragmentary codices from the White Monastery that are as yet unedited.
2. *De Passione.* This late apocryphal work on the Passion is attributed to the apostles. Under the guise of a homily, it presents a story about the discovery of an ancient manuscript long forgotten in a building of Jerusalem. It is transmitted in a manuscript in the Pierpont Morgan Library (M610); this text also remains unedited.

Homilies that refer to one another in some way to form the "Cyrillian Cycle" are as follows:

1. *De passione* (*a* and *b,* ed. Campagnano, 1980) is in fact two homilies, the contents of which—like the isolated homilies *De passione*—form one unit. Here the exegesis of the Passion is based on no particular gospel but contains citations taken from all four.
2. *De cruce* (ed. Campagnano, 1980). This text incorporates into one unit several episodes derived from earlier manuscripts, such as the miracle of

Isaac the Samaritan and the cross; the miracle of Cleophas and Rufas (relatives of the Virgin Mary); the recovery of the cross through the efforts of Helena and the story of Eusignius; and the episode of the shining cross.

3. *In Mariam Virginem* (ed. Campagnano, 1980). This work is built around the well-known apocryphal work of the *Dormitio Virginis,* but in a version somewhat different from the version, for example, in pseudo-Evodius of Rome. The work also includes a section directed against heretics of Gnostic tendencies.

BIBLIOGRAPHY

Campagnano, A. *Ps. Cirillo di Gerusaleme, Omelie copte sulla passione, sulla Croce e sulla Vergine.* Testi e documenti per lo studio dell'antichità, Serie Copta 65. Milan, 1980.

Orlandi, T. "Cirillo di Gerusalemme nella letteratura copta." *Vetera Christianorum* 9 (1972):93–100.

———. *Koptische Papyri theologischen Inhalts* (*Papiri copti di contenuto teologica*). Österreichische Nationalbibliothek, n.s. 9, pp. 56–79. Vienna, 1974.

TITO ORLANDI

CYRUS, SAINT. *See* Saints, Coptic.

CYRUS AL-MUQAWQAS, Byzantine bishop of Phasis in the region of the Caucasus until 631, when Emperor Heraclius decided to assign him the more important diocese of Egypt, with the express command to curb the obstinate Coptic community and bring its members to Chalcedonian obedience. In 451 the Copts had opposed the Council of CHALCEDON and were never reconciled to its deposition of their native patriarch DIOSCORUS and his exile.

In order to enable Cyrus to force the religious unity of the empire on the dissident Monophysite sect in Egypt if an attempt at a peaceful resolution failed, the new bishop was appointed in a triple capacity that would allow him to use force to attain his aim: besides being Byzantine patriarch of Alexandria, he was made civil viceroy of Egypt and military commander of the imperial forces in the country. With combined powers, Cyrus became a virtual dictator, abusing his authority in the treatment of the Coptic hierarchy and the Coptic people in his attempt to force Chalcedonian obedience upon them, while the Arabs were gathering at the gates of Egypt in readiness for their invasion of this Byzantine colony.

Apparently Cyrus was mistakenly thought by the Arabs to be a Copt. They corrupted his name in Arabic sources as al-Muqawqas and regarded him as the head of that nation, *'azīm al-Qibṭ,* the great one of the Copts. The details of this corruption in the sources have been accumulated by A. Grohmann (1987, Vol. 6, pp. 712–15). The Prophet Muḥammad is said to have addressed him a special epistle, possibly apocryphal but recorded by Ibn 'Abd al-Hakam, whereby he invited him to espouse his new religion even before the ARAB CONQUEST OF EGYPT.

Contrary to Arab understanding, Cyrus was, of course, no Copt, but rather one of the worst oppressors of the Copts throughout his tenure (631–642). Though it is doubtful whether Heraclius condoned the brutality of his agent, Cyrus knew no limits in his persecution of the Copts to attain the unity of the church. Here he failed miserably to bridge the gap between Constantinople and Alexandria. With the support of Serjius, the Byzantine patriarch, and the approval of Pope Honorius of Rome, Heraclius devised a new edict in a final attempt to persuade the Copts to obedience. This edict is known as the Ecthesis, whereby all churches in the eastern empire were forbidden to use the term "energies" in speaking of the Person of Christ and asserted that the two natures of the Lord were united in a single will; it thus substituted MONOTHELETISM for MONOPHYSITISM. But the imperial ruse for rapprochement with the Copts did not work. As a result, the exasperated Cyrus inaugurated one of the fiercest persecutions of the Copts in history. The native pope Benjamin I, thirty-eighth patriarch of the Coptic church, seems to have anticipated troubles with the advent of Cyrus in 631, for he took refuge in the Coptic monasteries of Wādī al-Naṭrūn, moving continuously from one monastery to another to dodge his pursuers. In the meantime, the Coptic hierarchy, to quote the HISTORY OF THE PATRIARCHS, became subjected to infinite harassment by Cyrus, who was like "a wolf devouring the flock and never satiated." In his description of this sordid situation, Alfred Butler says "that the Coptic Church was smitten and torn asunder, but it never yielded" (1978, p. 191). Mīnā, the patriarch's brother, was seized and tortured to make him divulge the hiding place of Benjamin, to no avail. When they failed either to make him talk about the patriarchal concealment or accept the Chalcedonian formula, they bundled him in a sack full of stones and cast him in the middle of the Nile, where he drowned.

While these humiliations and tortures were in progress, the Arabs were starting their invasion of Egypt under the leadership of ʿAmr ibn al-ʿĀṣ. In the circumstances, the Copts could do nothing but stand aside and watch the invaders annihilate their persecutors in a series of battles from Bilbeis to Aeliopolis, to the siege and surrender of the fort of Babylon, thus opening the road across the Delta for a speedy march toward the capital, Alexandria. On the way, the Coptic farmers furnished the Arab hosts with sorely needed provisions, which ensured their unopposed progress. The bewildered and powerless Cyrus, who managed to escape to the capital, decided to negotiate a treaty of peaceful surrender to save Alexandria from total destruction; it was signed on 8 November 641. The terms of the treaty have been preserved in the chronicle of JOHN OF NIKIOU and may be summarized here as the final chapter in the life of Cyrus, who was permitted to leave the country with his Byzantine troops.

The first article of the treaty concerned the payment of a tribute by able-bodied persons at the rate of two dinars, thus yielding a total of approximately 12 million gold dinars (Butler, 1978, p. 321). Other articles stipulated the cessation of all resistance and gave permission for the Byzantine army to depart by sea with its possessions, on condition that no Byzantine forces should return to Egyptian shores or attempt the recovery of the country. Other articles decreed that the Arabs should desist from interference with Christian churches and that Jews should desist from interference with Christian churches and that Jews should be allowed to remain unharmed in Alexandria. Finally, a fixed number of Byzantine hostages were to be retained by the invaders until the complete evacuation of the Byzantine forces and the fulfillment of the terms of the treaty.

It was then that ʿAmr reported to the caliph the seizure of the great capital in the following terms: "I have taken a city of which I can but say that it contains 4,000 palaces, 4,000 baths, 400 theaters, 12,000 sellers of green vegetables and 40,000 tributary Jews" (Butler, 1978, p. 368).

Nevertheless, the treaty was broken in 645 when a Byzantine general by the name of Manuel succeeded in the temporary recapture of the city. In the following year, the Arabs, perhaps with the help of treachery inside the walls, were able to force their way through an open gate and exterminate its military occupants, who failed to escape by sea. In this way, the fate of Egypt was sealed for all time and the Copts became separated from Western Christendom by a permanent Islamic occupation of Egypt.

BIBLIOGRAPHY

Butler, A. *The Treaty of Miṣr in Ṭabari.* Oxford, 1913.

——. *The Arab Conquest of Egypt,* ed. P. M. Fraser. Oxford, 1978.

Caetani, L. *Annali dell'islam,* Vol. 4. Milan, 1911.

Grohmann, A. "Al-Muḳawḳas." In *Encyclopedia of Islam,* Vol. 6, pp. 712–15. Leiden, 1987.

Lane-Poole, S. "The First Mohammadan Treaty with Christians." *Proceedings of the Royal Irish Academy* 24 (1902–1904).

——. *A History of Egypt in the Middle Ages.* London, 1925.

AZIZ S. ATIYA

D

DAFF. *See* Music, Coptic: Musical Instruments.

DAHLAK, town in Egypt, the location of which is unknown. The patriarch Cyril II (1078–1092) fled to Dahlak when conflicts within the church and threats of Muslim encroachment forced him to seek refuge. However, the Muslim authority in Dahlak captured him, took his money, and returned him to the amir al-Guyus in Cairo.

BIBLIOGRAPHY

Timm, S. *Das christlich-koptische Ägypten in arabischer Zeit,* pt. 2, p. 492. Wiesbaden, 1984.

RANDALL STEWART

DAHSHŪR, town located on the left bank of the Nile about 15 miles (23 km) south of Giza. The importance of the town in ancient Egypt is evidenced by the pyramids of the Fourth Dynasty (2575–2465 B.C.), Twelfth Dynasty (1991–1783), and Thirteenth Dynasty (1783–1640) that still exist at the site.

Although there are no references in Coptic or Christian-Arabic literature to a Christian community in Dahshūr in the pre-Arabic period, *The Churches and Monasteries of Egypt* speaks of a Church of the Virgin Mary in the town that was renovated in the time of Patriarch ISAAC (686–689) and Bishop Gregory of al-Qays. This suggests that Dahshūr knew Christianity in the Byzantine era. Parts of the Church of the Virgin Mary were taken to build a mosque in IṬFĪḤ in 1139 (*The Churches,* fol. 54a). Elsewhere the author says there was a Church of Moses with an accompanying monastery in the district of Dahshūr. Neither the church nor the monastery existed as such in his day; the church had been converted into a mosque and the Nile had flooded the monastery (*The Churches,* fol. 53a).

BIBLIOGRAPHY

Timm, S. *Das christlich-koptische Ägypten in arabischer Zeit,* pt. 2, pp. 495–97. Wiesbaden, 1984.

RANDALL STEWART

DALĀṢ, town in middle Egypt located some 8 miles (13 km) north of Banī Suef. Dalāṣ was home to a bishop at least as early as the Decian persecutions of 250 when Chaeremon, bishop of Neilopolis/Dalāṣ, fled for safety from his bishopric and was never heard from again (Eusebius *Ecclesiastical History* 6.42.3).

Monasticism also had an early beginning in Dalāṣ. The "mountain of Tilodj [Dalāṣ]" was the home of Saint ANTONY for a time and monks from TABENNĒSĒ came to the monastery of Tilodj/Dalāṣ to learn about Antony after the death of PACHOMIUS (Lefort, 1952, pp. 174, 177).

Though we have no certain attestation of a bishop in Dalāṣ in the Arabic period, the fact that the town is mentioned in medieval Copto-Arabic scales and lists of Egyptian bishops is an indication that it was still a bishopric in the Middle Ages (see Munier, 1943, p. 64).

BIBLIOGRAPHY

Amélineau, E. *La Géographie de l'Egypte à l'époque copte,* pp. 138. Paris, 1893.
Lefort, L. T. *S. Pachomii Vitae Sahidice Scriptae.*

CSCO 99–100, *Scriptores Coptici* 9–10. Louvain, 1952.
Munier, H. *Recueil des listes épiscopales de l'église copte*. Cairo, 1943.
Timm, S. *Das christlich-koptische Ägypten in arabischer Zeit*, pt. 2, pp. 498–502. Wiesbaden, 1984.

RANDALL STEWART

DALMATIC. *See* Costume, Civil.

DAMALLŪ, town in the Delta in the province of Minūfiyyah. The only reference to Damallū in Christian-Arabic literature is in the HISTORY OF THE PATRIARCHS, where it is related that during the patriarchate of CYRIL II (1078–1092) a bedouin entered the Church of Saint George in Damallū and attacked the icon of the saint, whereupon Saint George slew him.

BIBLIOGRAPHY

Timm, S. *Das christlich-koptische Ägypten in arabischer Zeit*, pt. 2, p. 505. Wiesbaden, 1984.

RANDALL STEWART

DAMANHŪR, today an important town, the capital of the Beheira, the western province of the Delta. The origin of its name has been well established: it is "the city of Horus," a name that suggests that it was made famous by a temple of Horus in the pharaonic period (see Černý, 1976, p. 354). In the numerous Greek papyri from the third century B.C. to the fourth century A.D., the town is designated Hermopolis Mikra, or the Lower, to distinguish it from Hermopolis Magna (today al-Ashmūnayn) in Middle Egypt.

Damanhūr is documented as the seat of a bishop from the fourth century. In 325, Melitius appointed an Agathammon as bishop of the "Chora [district] of the Alexandrians," Damanhūr probably being the capital of what formed the region thus described. It is also probable that alongside this Melitian bishop there was a partisan of Saint Athanasius and that this was before Dracontius, the Catholic titular of this see in 354. He was followed by one Isidorus the Confessor and then by the famous Dioscorus, at first a priest of the desert of Nitria, who was counted among the Tall Brothers (see AMMONIUS OF KELLIA), who incurred the wrath of the patriarch THEOPHILUS (385–412) for their attachment to the teachings of ORIGEN. Dioscorus, it appears, became bishop between 390 and 394. Later this bishopric was not further mentioned.

Without doubt the hagiographical texts speak of Damanhūr, but such references are deceptive, for this bishopric existed in the period of the hagiographer, not in that of the martyrs whose lives he is tracing. Thus, at 14 Ba'ūnah the Coptic SYNAXARION speaks of four martyrs, one of whom was a native of Damanhūr, but the author adds "in the diocese of (A)būṣīr," which indicates that, the town of Damanhūr having declined, its bishopric at the date of the composition of the second part of the Synaxarion (perhaps thirteenth century) no longer had a titular, but was united with that of Abūṣīr.

The name of a titular of Damanhūr only reappears under the eleventh-century patriarchate of CYRIL II.

An anonymous bishop of Damanhūr is cited along with the bishop of Fuwwah around 1238 as being among the opponents of CYRIL III IBN LAQLAQ. Bishop Yusāb of Damanhūr is known as a contemporary of YUḤANNĀ, bishop of Samannūd, and of the patriarch ATHANASIUS III (Graf, 1944–1953, Vol. 2, p. 378). Around 1299, a bishop of Damanhūr was present at the preparation of the CHRISM. Then this bishopric was joined to that of Laqqānah, a single titular assuming the functions of the two dioceses, for the number of Christians had continued to decrease (Munier, 1943, p. 36). Yusāb's successor, Mark, took part in the preparation of the chrism in 1320 (Munier, 1943, pp. 36, 49). Mark is listed as being present at the 1330 preparation of the chrism (Munier, p. 40), but his see is described not as being the town of Damanhūr but as the province of Beheira. This Mark was designated bishop of Damanhūr, but in 1330 and 1342 the same Mark is described as bishop of Beheira. Unfortunately, the records of the preparation of the chrism, which mention the bishops and the bishoprics of the time, at least to the extent that the bishops were able to participate in the ceremony, survive only for the thirteenth and fourteenth centuries.

The traveler J. M. Vansleb, who was in Egypt in 1672 and 1673, drew up a list of the ancient bishoprics, in which he included "Demonhor, in Greek Hermou the lower," but in his list of "the bishoprics which are presently in Egypt," where he counts seventeen, that of "Béhéiré" appears (1677, pp. 19, 27).

In the middle of the nineteenth century, the presence of one Sarapammon, bishop of Beheira and al-Minūfiyyah, is attested (Muyser, 1944, p. 169). A certain number of celebrated monastic sites were attached to this bishopric: the desert of Nitria, since one of its priests became bishop of this see; KELLIA, which was a kind of annex to it; and, finally, Scetis (Wādī al-Naṭrūn), called Wādī Habīb in the Middle Ages. There is some doubt about a monastery for women called that "of Apa Jeremias," mentioned in the life of Abbā Daniel (Clugnet, 1900, p. 68), but it is thought that the reference is to Hermopolis Magna in Middle Egypt (Drew-Bear, 1979, p. 132).

In 1912, S. Clarke, in drawing up a review of the state of the Coptic church as an appendix to his *Christian Antiquities in the Nile Valley* (pp. 199–216), listed the churches and monasteries of Egypt, following the register of the patriarchate, and placed a bishopric at Damanhūr, having for its territory the province of Beheira. However, O. H. E. Burmester (1967, p. 6), in drawing up the list of the present episcopal sees, placed the churches of Damanhūr under the jurisdiction of the diocese of Gharbiyyah and Beheira, with the bishop's residence at Ṭanṭā.

All the same, Meinardus (1977, p. 68) spoke of an episcopal see of Beheira, Maryūṭ, and the Pentapolis, with Damanhūr as its "monastery of origin." This expression appears to have been retained from the first edition (1965), which mentioned the monastery of origin of the prelate; here it seems rather to indicate Damanhūr as the residence of the bishop.

BIBLIOGRAPHY

Burmester, O. H. E. *The Egyptian or Coptic Church.* Cairo, 1967.

Černý, J. *Coptic Etymological Dictionary.* Cambridge, 1976.

Clarke, S. *Christian Antiquities in the Nile Valley.* Oxford, 1912.

Clugnet, L. "Vie et récits de l'abbé Daniel." *Revue de l'orient chrétien* 5 (1900):49–73, 254–71, 370–406, 535–64.

Drew-Bear, M. *Le Nome hermopolite.* American Studies in Papyrology 21. Missoula, Mont., 1979.

Evelyn-White, H. G. *The Monasteries of the Wadi 'n Natrūn*, Pt. 2, *The History of the Monasteries of Nitria and Scetis.* New York, 1932.

Graf, G. *Catalogue des manuscrits arabes chrétiens, conservés au Caire.* Studi e testi 63. Vatican City, 1934.

Le Quien, M. *Oriens Christianus,* 3 vols. Paris, 1740; repr. Graz, 1958.

Meinardus, O. *Christian Egypt, Ancient and Modern.* Cairo, 1965; 2nd ed. 1977.

Munier, H. *Recueil des listes épiscopales de l'église copte.* Cairo, 1943.

Muyser, J. *Contribution à l'étude des listes episcopales de l'église copte.* Cairo, 1944.

Vansleb, J. M. *Histoire de l'église d'Alexandrie.* Paris, 1677.

RENÉ-GEORGES COQUIN

DAMANHŪRĪ, SHAYKH AHMAD, AL- (full name: Aḥmad ibn 'Abd al-Mun'im ibn Yūsuf ibn Sayyām al-Damanhūrī) (1689/1690–1778), Egyptian Muslim scholar. He moved from Beheira to the university al-Azhar as a young man without means, studied there, and obtained the qualification to teach for all four schools of law, for which he also gave opinions. He was unsociable and spent most of his lifetime in private studies. After the death of the *shaykh* al-Ḥifnī (1767) he succeeded him as director of al-Azhar and thereby became the highest Muslim scholar in Egypt. Among the political leaders, he was feared for his incorruptibility and rigidity; the Muslim lower classes venerated him for his love of justice.

In addition to his program of study, a work with the heading *Iqāmat al-Ḥujjah al-Bāhirah 'alā Hadm Kanā'is Miṣr wa-al-Qāhirah* ("Presentation of the Clear Proof for the Necessary Destruction of the Churches of Old and New Cairo") is preserved. It was written at the beginning of the year 1739 as an answer to an inquiry concerning the legality of the churches in Old and New Cairo. This inquiry was evoked by the construction of a church near the Darb al-Ḥīn, which greatly irritated the Muslims. After a historical introduction that demonstrates that Old Cairo was conquered by force and that the New Cairo was founded by Muslims at a later date, Damanhūrī examines in four chapters the commentaries of the four schools of law on the existence, maintenance, and restoration of old churches and the construction of new churches. He comes to the conclusion that even if there are some points of divergence among the various schools, the case of Old and New Cairo is quite clear. According to the great majority of Muslim legal authorities, the existence of churches in both cities is illegal, and therefore they must be demolished.

These *fatāwā* (legal opinions) of Damanhūrī are examples of an interpretation of law that became prevalent among the *'ulamā'* (Muslim scholars) in the thirteenth century A.D. From the eighteenth century, several *fatāwā* with similar tendencies are known, but some others also emerged that showed more tolerance by permitting the restoration of the older churches.

BIBLIOGRAPHY

Jabartī, al-. *Ajā'ib al-Āthār fī al-Tarājim wa-al-Akbār,* Vol. 2, pp. 25–27. Būlāq, A.H. 1297/A.D. 1879–1880.

Perlmann, M. *Shaykh Damanhūrī on the Churches of Cairo (1739).* Berkeley and Los Angeles, 1975.

HARALD MOTZKI

DAMANHŪR AL-WAḤSH, town located in the middle of the Delta about 4.5 miles (7 km) southwest of Zifta in the province of Minufiyyah.

It is probable that Damanhūr al-Waḥsh was the birthplace of the martyrs Cyrus and John (see MARTYRS, COPTIC). The SYNAXARION commemorates Cyrus, John, Ptolemaeus, and Filya on 14 Ba'ūnah and states that they were from Damanhūr in the diocese of Būṣīr to the west of the Nile (Amélineau, 1893, p. 7, n. 9). After the martyrs were killed by being dragged behind a horse from Qarṭasā to Damanhūr and then beheaded, the inhabitants of Ṣā buried John's body and built a memorial church for him. The citizens of Damanhūr cared for the bodies of the other three martyrs. The Damanhūr mentioned in connection with Qarṭasā whose inhabitants buried Cyrus's companions must be the well-known Damanhūr in the western Delta, but the Damanhūr in the diocese of Busir that is mentioned as the birthplace of Cyrus appears to be the town in the mid-Delta that is now known as Damanhūr al-Waḥsh. If this identification is correct, we have a witness for Christianity in Damanhūr al-Waḥsh in the fourth century.

A passage in the writings of al-MAQRĪZĪ indicates that Christianity in Damanhūr al-Waḥsh lived on into the Middle Ages. Al-Maqrīzī reports that when many churches in Cairo and elsewhere were destroyed in 1320, two churches in Damanhūr were also ruined.

BIBLIOGRAPHY

Amélineau, E. *La Géographie de l'Egypte à l'époque copte,* pp. 113–16. Paris, 1893.

Timm, S. *Das christlich-koptische Ägypten in arabischer Zeit,* pt. 2, pp. 516–17. Wiesbaden, 1984.

RANDALL STEWART

DAMIAN, thirty-fifth patriarch of the See of Saint Mark (569–605). (Some sources list the beginning of his reign as 578.) He was contemporary to four Byzantine emperors, Justin II (565–578), Tiberius II (578–582), Maurice (582–602), and Phocas (602–610). During their reigns, the Byzantine rulers were distracted from the imposition of the Chalcedonian profession of faith on Egypt by the Persian wars in the east and the Barbarian inroads in the north. Inasmuch as Alexandria remained essentially a Melchite fortress, the national patriarchs resided in neighboring Coptic monasteries.

Damian was of Syrian origin, his father and brother being officials at Edessa. He had long been a monk at SCETIS when PETER IV brought him as deacon and secretary to his headquarters at the ENATON monastery. On Peter's death Damian was elected and consecrated to the patriarchate.

The early years of Damian's pontificate were consumed by burning problems of an ecclesiastical nature with Antioch. Jacob Baradaeus, the missionary prelate from Antioch, departed for Alexandria to confer with Damian on the problem of PAUL THE BLACK, the Egyptian patriarch of Antioch, who seemed to be in error doctrinally. But Jacob died en route and his party disintegrated. Damian attempted to install another person as patriarch of Antioch whose orthodoxy was assured. But he and his party were compelled to flee from Antioch before secretly consecrating a rival candidate.

Then the scene of events moved to Constantinople, where the Arab Christian prince al-Nu'man ibn al-Mundhir (al-Mundaras of Christian sources) called an inconclusive conference to solve the Antiochene problem. Thus Damian returned home and gave up the attempt to establish the ecumenical precedence of Alexandria. He ultimately broke off communion with Peter Callinicus, the next patriarch of Antioch. He accused him of tritheism, whose formula of three persons sharing a common godhead was suspected to introduce a fourth principle, thus giving rise to the new term Tetradite. The ensuing schism between the Copts and the Syrians persisted beyond Damian's reign until the concordat of 616, concluded between ANASTASIUS, his successor, and Athanasius, patriarch of Antioch.

Meanwhile Bishop Longinus, failing to secure support for his candidate for Alexandria, Theodorus, returned to Nubia. An effort was made to replace him, but he was locally supported, and after an adventurous desert journey planted the church among the Alaudae further south (probably near Khartoum). The Nubian church, thus established, was long an important ally of the Coptic church.

Within Egypt, Damian's administration was both vigorous and successful. He took residence at the Enaton monastery in the western Delta, but paid frequent visits to Alexandria. He managed to exterminate the remaining schismatic vestiges of the Melitians (see MELITIAN SCHISM) and the ACEPHALOI, which had plagued the peace of the church for decades. Thus he left behind him a well-organized and united church.

Damian's teaching on the Incarnation and the Trinity was clearly expounded in his letter to Jacob Baradaeus together with the clergy and people of Antioch, in which he repudiated Paul the Black. This document has been preserved in a Syriac version (Michael Syrus, 10.14) and is inscribed in Coptic on the walls of the monastery of Saint Epiphanius (DAYR EPIPHANIUS) at Thebes. It has also been adapted as a discourse on the Logos in the HISTORY OF THE PATRIARCHS (Vol. 1, pt. 2, p. 474) by omitting the Syrian references at the beginning and replacing the epistolary conclusion with a homiletic one, including prayers for the emperor and a doxology. Essentially this document must have been prepared at Enaton Monastery for general circulation among the Egyptian clergy.

After a life abounding in fasts, prayers, and struggles against all manner of heretical teachings and schisms for thirty-six years, Damian died on 28 Ba'ūnah (*History of the Patriarchs*, Vol. 1, pt. 2, p. 478), on which day he is commemorated annually by the Coptic church.

BIBLIOGRAPHY

Bréhier, L.; P. de Labriole; G. Bardy; and G. de Plinval. "De la mort de Théodose à l'avènement de Grégoire le Grand." In *Histoire de l'église,* ed. A. Fliche and V. Martin, Vol. 4, pp. 490–93. Paris, 1937.

Frend, W. H. C. *The Rise of the Monophysite Movement,* pp. 341–42. Cambridge, 1972.

Hardy, E. R. *Christian Egypt,* pp. 152–54, 162, 169–71, 178. New York, 1952.

Jülicher, A. "Die Liste der alexandrinischen Patriarchen im 6. und 7. Jahrhundert." In *Festgabe Karl Mueller.* Tübingen, 1922.

Maspéro, J. *Histoire des Patriarches d'Alexandrie,* chap. 9. Paris, 1923.

Syrus, Michael. *Chronique de Michel le Syrien* X, ed. and trans. J.-B. Chabot, Vol. 2, pp. 13–22. Paris, 1901.

Timothy of Constantinople. *De Receptione Haereticorum.* In PG 86, pp. 11–74.

Winlock, H. E., and W. E. Crum. *The Monastery of Epiphanius at Thebes,* pt. 2, pp. 148–52, 331–42. New York, 1926.

E. R. HARDY

DAMRŪ, village 10.5 miles (17 km) north of Maḥallah al-Kubrā in the Gharbiyyah province and 13 miles (21 km) west of Manṣūrah in the Province of Daqahliyyah that served as cell or residence of the Coptic patriarchs for almost 100 years, from 975 to about 1061. The name of this village is mentioned sixteen times in the HISTORY OF THE PATRIARCHS. In the days of al-ʿAzīz (975–996), Macarius, the secretary of the synod, advised PHILOTHEUS, the sixty-third patriarch (979–1003), to move the patriarchal residence from Alexandria to Damrū, where Menas, the bishop of Ṭanah and the brother of Macarius, lived. Bishop Menas had what was called a good dwelling-place at Damrū, which made it attractive for the patriarch to accept the suggestion of the synod's secretary. The patriarchal quarters were quite extensive, for the patriarch used to receive and entertain guests, whose usual custom it was to sit and drink with him.

ZACHARIAS, the sixty-fourth patriarch (1004–1032), also took up his residence at Damrū, where he frequently entertained bishops, priests, monks, and laymen. He built the "Great Church," that is, the patriarchal cathedral. Damrū rose rapidly in importance and seems to have been inhabited entirely by Christians. SHENUTE II, the sixty-fifth patriarch (1032–1046), also resided at Damrū and completed the construction of the "Great Church," where he was buried. The fourth and last patriarch to reside at Damrū was CHRISTODOULUS, the sixty-sixth patriarch (1047–1077). During his patriarchate, Damrū increased even more in importance and size, so that it was known as the "Second Constantinople" with seventeen churches, most of which were restored.

In the latter part of the reign of Christodoulus, some 40,000 Berber horsemen and their attendants invaded the Nile Delta and went to Damrū and took the patriarch from his residence and plundered all that was in it. The patriarch then took temporary refuge in Alexandria and subsequently transferred the patriarchal residence to Cairo. Most if not all of the churches and the patriarchal residence were destroyed. Those buildings that survived the devastations of the Berbers were probably destroyed by the Ghuzz, who, during the patriarchate of CYRIL II (1078–1092) took possession of the Province of Gharbiyyah.

The present Damrū comprises the three villages of Kafr Damrū, Shubrā Nabāt or Shubra Damrū, and Damrū Khammārah. These three villages, of which Kafr Damrū is the southernmost, appear as a single unit without visible boundaries. Within these three villages, there are no archaeological or architectural traces of the former churches. Just north of the limit of Damrū al-Khammārah there is the Muslim cemetery on a slight elevation. Many of the tombs are constructed with burned bricks, and the villagers maintain that the bricks belonged to the ancient baths that were the property of a king. This may have been the bathing place that is referred to in the *History of the Patriarchs.*

BIBLIOGRAPHY

Amélineau, E. *La Géographie de l'Egypte à l'epoque copte,* p. 302. Paris, 1886.

Meinardus, O. "Damrua (Gharbiyah): Past and Present." *Bulletin de la Société de géographie d'Egypte* 38 (1965):195–99.

Munier, H. *Recueil des listes épiscopales de l'église copte,* p. 26. Cairo, 1943.

OTTO MEINARDUS

DANCERS. *See* Mythological Subjects in Coptic Art.

DANDARAH, ancient town on the west bank of the Nile. Up to the Roman period it was the chief site for the worship of Hathor (Aphrodite), the goddess of heaven and of love. As early as the Old Kingdom a shrine existed here. The present temple, however, had its origin in the late Ptolemaic and early Roman period. It is one of the best preserved Egyptian temples. Christianity had already gained a foothold here at the end of the third century. Since the first quarter of the fourth century Dandarah has been known as the seat of a bishop.

Church of Dandarah near the *Mammisi* of the Temple of Hathor. Fifth century. *Courtesy P. Brice.*

All that remains of the old town today is a shapeless field of potsherds out of which juts the impressive precinct of the Hathor temple. It is not known when the town was abandoned. ABŪ AL-MAKĀRIM (at the beginning of the thirteenth century), who normally speaks only of churches, mentions the town only in respect to the temple and the holy lake. Thus the site might already have been abandoned in the thirteenth century. At any rate, it is inserted in the lists of bishops down to the fourteenth century (Timm, 1984, Vol. 2, p. 545), although the last bishops were presumably only titular bishops.

Whether the Hathor temple or sections of it were converted into a Christian church has not been ascertained. Only M. Jullien speaks of the insertion of a church in the pronaos of the temple (Munier, 1940, p. 162). But extensive remains of a church are preserved between the two birth houses (*Mammisi*) on the northwest corner of the inner precinct of the temple. This church is one of the most beautiful of Egyptian churches; the regularity of its ground plan and the balanced proportions are only seldom encountered. The entrances are found at the west end of both long sides. Across small anterooms one enters the narthex situated rather deep inside the building and bordered on the west side by a series of rooms. Here are the stairs as well as accommodations for a couple of liturgical side chambers. In no other Egyptian building was a solution of this kind repeated. The naos has three aisles and is provided with a western return aisle. The side walls contain semicircular niches. They are decorated with flanking columns and sculptured niche heads, and in their location they correspond exactly to the intercolumnia of the rows of columns. The sanctuary has the plan of a triconch as is the case in the two monastery churches of Suhāj, DAYR ANBĀ SHINŪDAH and DAYR ANBĀ BISHOI. The main conch in the east was provided with niches and an inner circle of columns. Moreover, the general regularity of the formation points to the fact that here for the first time a cupola was constructed over the center. The stones required for vaulting were cut in the neighboring Roman *Mammisi* where today a drawing of the triconch is preserved on the floor (Monneret de Villard, 1925, p. 49). Both the side chambers of the sanctuary are gamma-shaped in order to lead around the side conchs of the triconch. Judging by the stone sculpture of the building, especially the design of the heads of the niches, the church could have been built about the middle of the sixth century. It belongs to the small number of Egyptian examples of

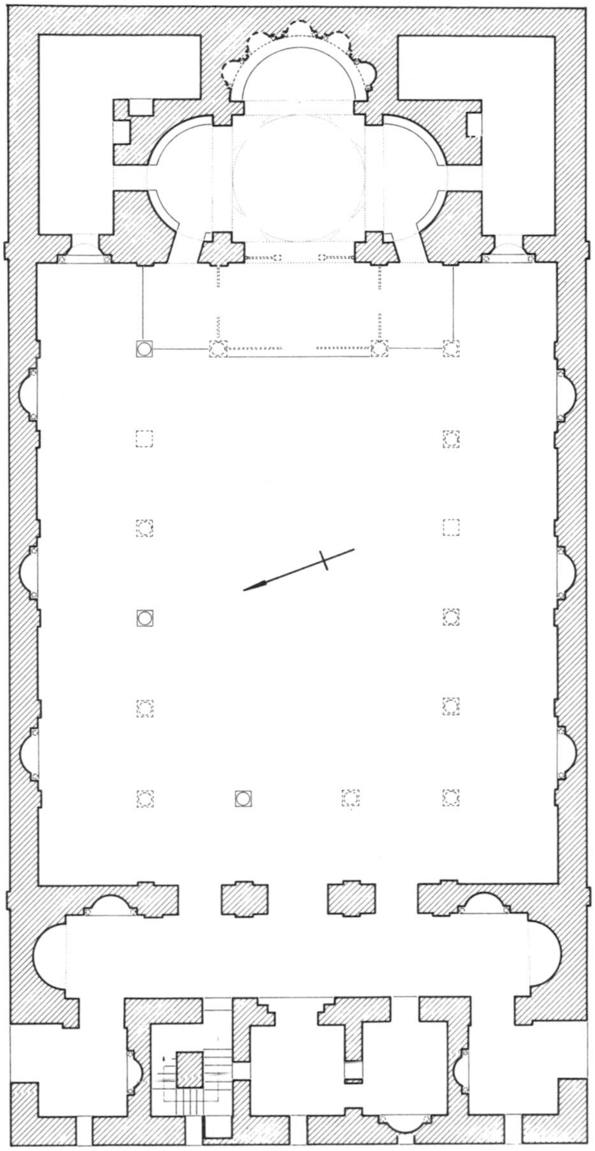

Plan of the church near the *Mammisi* at Dandarah. *Courtesy Peter Grossmann.*

architectural sculpture produced specifically for the buildings in which they are now found. Only the great columns and capitals in the nave were reused from older buildings.

BIBLIOGRAPHY

Daumas, F. *Dendara et le temple d'Hathor.* Cairo, 1969.

Grossmann, P. "Esempi d'architettura paleocristiana in Egitto dal V al VII secolo." *Corsi Ravenna* 28 (1981):170–72.

Johann Georg. *Streifzüge durch die Kirchen und Klöster Ägyptens,* pp. 52–53. Leipzig and Berlin, 1914.

Monneret de Villard, U. *Les Couvents près de Sohâg,* Vol. 1, pp. 47–49. Milan, 1925.

Munier, H. "Les Monuments coptes d'après le père Michel Jullien." *Bulletin de la Société d'archéologie copte* 6 (1940):141–68.

Timm, S. *Das christlich-koptische Ägypten in arabischer Zeit,* Vol. 2, pp. 543–48. Wiesbaden, 1984.

PETER GROSSMANN

DANÈL. *See* Ethiopian Prelates.

DANIEL IN THE LION'S DEN. *See* Biblical Subjects in Coptic Art.

DANIEL AND MOSES, two hermits whose lives have come down to us in two witnesses of the Sahidic recension of the Arabic Synaxarion. One is a complete manuscript for the first half of the year, preserved at Luxor, the other a fragment of the same Synaxarion consisting of four leaves (Troupeau, 1974, Vol. 2, pp. 67–68). Both are still unpublished.

Daniel and Moses were brothers and natives of the village called al-ʿArīsh, near Armant, in Upper Egypt. They were peasants, possessing some lands and living by their labor in the fields, gardens, and vineyards. When each turned thirty-five, they married "according to the law," the Synaxarion notes. Daniel had three sons, named Isaac, Jacob, and Lazarus; Moses had a single son named Peter. Later they decided to abandon everything and embrace the monastic life, placing themselves under the direction of Anbā Jacob, about whom no details are given. They lived at first in monasteries, then became hermits on the left bank at Qūṣ: Daniel in the mountain of Banhadab, Moses in a mountain in the neighborhood of Ṭūkh. The text relates as a salient fact from the life of Daniel the vision that he had near the ramparts of Jēme on the left bank at Luxor. In this vision he saw a troop of demons armed like barbarians with bows and arrows. He dispersed them by turning toward the east, by making the sign of the cross, and invoking the help of God. Then the demons changed into weeping old women. This story recalls the most ancient monastic texts, although here the demons are not in the desert but on the outskirts of a town.

This notice in the Synaxarion of Upper Egypt is of particular interest as it shows that these two monks did not abandon their family cares. Each of them, in fact, had children who caused them suffering. Two of Daniel's sons had the idea, "contrary to the canons of the Church," as the story emphasizes, of becoming eunuchs. One of them died as a result; the other "fell into temptation." The father's grief was such that he had to abandon his eremitic life for a while. Moses was scarcely more fortunate, for his son became mad very young, and he kept him in his own cave, enduring alone the presence of the sick man. The author presents these family trials as acts of virtue and asceticism, which is rare in the hagiographic texts, the monks rather fleeing from concern for their progeny.

Both Daniel and Moses lived for more than forty years in the wilderness, persevering in their forbearance and in their exercises as hermits. Their feast day is 9 Amshīr.

BIBLIOGRAPHY

Coquin, R.-G. "Le Synaxaire des Coptes. Un nouveau témoin de la recension de Haute Egypte." *Analecta Bollandiana* 96 (1978):351–65.

Troupeau, G. *Catalogue des manuscrits arabes,* Vol. 2, pt. 1, *Manuscrits chrétiens.* Paris, 1974.

RENÉ-GEORGES COQUIN

DANIEL OF SCETIS, SAINT, HEGUMENOS

DANIEL OF SCETIS, SAINT, HEGUMENOS who lived in the sixth century. The text of his life has come down in Coptic and Ethiopic. It is made up of fourteen episodes, which were originally separate. Eleven are, in fact, found scattered in Greek in collections of *Apophthegmata* (sayings of the Fathers) and *Gerontika* (anecdotes of the old monks), and correspondingly in Syriac and Arabic. The Coptic text is found in Bohairic and in only one codex.

Internal examination of the texts leads one to deduce that various anecdotes, some of them concerning other monks of the same name, were collected around the historical figure of one Daniel of Scetis, who lived in the first half of the sixth century. Even the anecdotes concerning the "real" Daniel are not always true. Examples include the stories of the noblewoman Anastasia who, in order to escape from court life, seeks refuge at Scetis in men's clothing; the monk Marcus who as a penance pretends to be mad and is recognized by Daniel; the visit to a convent of nuns in the south, where Daniel discovers the injustice and ill treatment being inflicted on one nun; and Daniel's refusal to support Tomus of Lyons when Justinian orders him to do so.

The historical information to be drawn from these episodes is exclusively of a chronological and confessional nature, enabling us to date his life to the first half of the sixth century and to conclude that he was one of the prominent figures in anti-Chalcedonian Egyptian monasticism. Nothing can be assumed about the actual events of his life.

BIBLIOGRAPHY

Cauwenbergh, P. van. *Etude sur les moines d'Egypte.* Paris, 1914.

Clugnet, L.; F. Nau; and I. Guidi. *Vie (et récits) de l'Abbé Daniel le Scetiote (VIe Siècle).* Bibliothèque Hagiographique Orientale 1. Paris, 1901.

Evelyn-White, H. G. *The Monasteries of the Wadi 'n Natrūn,* Pt 1, *New Coptic Texts from the Monastery of Saint Macarius.* New York, 1926.

Garitte, G. "Daniel de Scète." In *Dictionnaire d'histoire et de géographie ecclésiastique,* Vol. 14, cols. 70–72. Paris, 1912ff.

Guidi, I. "Vie et récits de l'abbé Daniel de Scété (VI Siècle). III. Texte copte publié et traduit." *Revue de l'Orient chrétien* 5 (1900):535–64; 6 (1901):51–53.

TITO ORLANDI

DAPHNE. *See* Mythological Subjects in Coptic Art.

DAQĀDŪS, village in the province of Daqahliyyah. A medieval list of Egyptian church locations also says that the village of Daqādūs was the site of a Church of Mary, the mother of Jesus. From the order of the place-names in the list it is reasonable to deduce that Daqādūs was located in the Delta. Hence it is probable that modern Daqādūs, located about one-half mile northeast of Mīt Ghamr on the east arm of the Nile, is the village mentioned in the list.

Although there are no records to indicate when Christianity established a foothold in Daqādūs, the Coptic church in the modern city was built over a medieval church and one of the manuscripts (no. 27) housed in the church is dated to 1332.

[*See also:* Pilgrimages.]

BIBLIOGRAPHY

Amélineau, E. *La Géographie de l'Egypte à l'époque copte,* pp. 65–66. Paris, 1893.

Timm, S. *Das christlich-koptische Ägypten in arabischer Zeit,* pt. 2, pp. 555–56. Wiesbaden, 1984.

RANDALL STEWART

DAQAHLAH, village in Egypt located in the northeast part of the Delta about 5.5 miles (8.5 km) south of Fāriskūr in the province of Daqahliyyah.

The first reference to Daqahlah in Christian-Arabic literature is in the HISTORY OF THE PATRIARCHS where it is related that a great famine afflicted Egypt in the first years of Moorish rule in the tenth century. Many towns that were without a bishop because of the depopulation of the land had to be joined to episcopal sees that were still occupied. In addition, colophons in two tenth-century Coptic manuscripts attest to the presence of Christians in Daqahlah at this early date. The name of the town also appears in a medieval Copto-Arabic list of Egyptian bishoprics (Munier, 1943, pp. 49–55).

BIBLIOGRAPHY

Amélineau, E. *La Géographie de l'Egypte à l'époque copte,* pp. 509–510. Paris, 1893.

Munier, H. *Recueil des listes épiscopales de l'église copte.* Cairo, 1943.

Timm, S. *Das christlich-koptische Ägypten in arabischer Zeit,* pt. 2, pp. 556–58. Wiesbaden, 1984.

RANDALL STEWART

DARAJ AL-HAYKAL. *See* Architectural Elements of Churches: Sanctuary.

DARESSY, GEORGES EMILE JULES (1864–1938), French Egyptologist. Daressy was born at Sourdon. He studied at the Ecole des Hautes Etudes from 1881 to 1885. He went to Egypt as a member of the Mission archéologique française du Caire, later becoming its director. He was made assistant keeper at the Bulāq Museum in 1887. He was a member of the Institut d'Egypte (from 1894), and secretary general (1917); chevalier of the Legion of Honor; and commander of the Order of the Nile. He retired in France in 1923. He made a few contributions to Coptic studies, a list of which can be found in *A Coptic Bibliography* (Kammerer, 1950, 1969).

BIBLIOGRAPHY

Kammerer, W., comp. *A Coptic Bibliography.* Ann Arbor, Mich., 1950; repr., New York, 1969.

AZIZ S. ATIYA

DATING. Broadly speaking, the dating of Coptic monuments and artifacts is one of the thorniest problems in this archaeological field.

The most varied forces seem to have combined to make any attempt at dating impossible, or at least subject to caution. The most substantial reason for this is the oppressed condition into which the Copts were plunged first under Roman and then under Byzantine occupation. This was further accentuated under Muslim rule, and the progressive reduction of the Copts to the position of a minority on the periphery of official life did nothing to ease it. The vitality that enabled them under the most intractable circumstances to produce works in various fields of Christian religious literature and of art was in many cases stifled. This situation, together with the separation of the Copts from the Christian world since the time of the Council of CHALCEDON (451), deprived them of every means of defense or of resort to outside protection. Hence, the quality of their works could not reach the heights normally fostered by an environment of luxury or at least by a free environment. In this respect they were, artistically speaking, very poor relations indeed, when compared with other manifestations of art on Egyptian soil, namely, pharaonic, Alexandrian, Byzantine, and Muslim art.

Because of the unmistakable progressive dwindling in the number of Copts from the time of the Muslim domination and the pronounced deterioration in their social status, there was a total cessation after the twelfth century of any art of their own, however modest. In our own day there has been the scorn heaped on Coptic art both by art lovers and by archaeologists, though this prejudice is now beginning to be challenged.

During the centuries of Muslim domination, the maintenance of the monuments (churches and monasteries) was subject to great difficulties. Most of them, having been secularized, were soon in ruins. They were pillaged, with their reliefs, stone by stone, for the construction of houses and even of mosques, causing the loss of their paintings. Many were abandoned and simply fell into ruin where they stood. Seekers after *sebakh*—organic matter connected with the habitat—did not disdain these ruins, and dispersed them with everything they contained: objects, tombs, furnishings, fabrics, et cetera, to enrich the cultivated soil. Further, the *Book of the Buried Pearl,* which advised digging behind a wall painting that was supposed to hide a treasure, was somewhat responsible for innumerable destructions of Coptic frescoes. Another unexpected factor contributed more intentionally, though indirectly, to the disappearance of Coptic remains: Awed by the prestige of the pharaonic monuments, archaeologists used to see in Coptic monuments a hint of deeper and older layers that might yield more promising discoveries. They thus did not hesitate to sacrifice valuable Coptic artifacts that were little appreciated in favor of those that interested them more. What remains standing has been subjected to the ravages of time and of successive transformations, restorations, and recoveries to such a degree that they cannot be cleared without damaging, and even destroying, the original layer.

Given the extent of such upheavals, inflicted on almost all the sites and involving no less serious damage to the objects, one wonders what indications of dating can be left, since dating is related to the preservation of the soil and of the layers that should contain, according to their level, evidences of their chronological sequence.

Explicit datings do exist. Among the Christians, they are established from the third century in relation to the "year of Diocletian" (29 August 284); his name was replaced in the eleventh century by that of "the Martyrs," sometimes—from the eighth to the tenth century—conjoined with the "age of the Saracens" (that is "of the Hegira"). Unfortunately, relative dating by indictions (the fifteen-year cycles instituted by Constantine in 313) does not have any absolute reference. At any rate, the presence of these datings is restricted to inscriptions on stone, mostly those on funerary stelae. Even in this context they are rare.

One can approximate a dating through the coexistence of objects from the same site or of objects in the same style, with items that are explicitly dated, especially coins, or with some other item in use at a given period. But the upheavals to which the soil has been subjected in the course of time and under the impact of weathering do not always make it possible to discern any assured basis there.

The carbon-14 dating method has been disappointing, because the Coptic period in the history of Egypt is relatively close to our own; moreover, it can be used only with items that are subject to change and doomed to destruction.

In most instances, we are reduced to assigning dates to objects either because of archaeological landmarks relating to iconography or because of common stylistic features that, through one item or another, may extend to other groups of objects or representations. For example, A, which can be dated from one of these items, is a legitimate basis for dating B, which also has a feature in common with A though otherwise differing from it. B in turn may make us aware of an item or a feature of A that relates it to C, so that C—which to all appearances lacks any common characteristics with A—may nevertheless, like B, be considered contemporary with A.

It should be noted that iconography itself has very little value for dating other than the dates of the appearance or disappearance of some theme. Its chronology depends on other data provided either by some explicit dating or by the characteristics of the style of an age.

Despite these approximations, the margin of doubt is relatively narrow. When all is said, Coptic archaeology is like history, the certainty of which is far more the product of an accumulation of reliable indications than of dates or facts that are recorded with certainty. Unfortunately, such an accumulation is more difficult and more delicate to make for Coptic art than for most other types of art.

BIBLIOGRAPHY

Bourguet, P. du. *L'Art Copte*, p. 166. Collection L'Art dans le monde. Paris, 1968.

______. *Catalogue des étoffes coptes* [Louvre], Vol. I: *Introduction*. Paris, 1964.

PIERRE DU BOURGUET, S.J.

DAUMAS, FRANÇOIS (1915–1984), French Egyptologist. He was born at Castelnau-le-Lez, near Montpellier. He was the son of François Daumas, who had participated as a draftsman-artist in the excavations of Jean MASPÉRO at BĀWĪṬ in 1913. A student of Gustave Lefebvre and Pierre LACAU, young Daumas was a resident of the Institut français d'Archéologie orientale du Caire (1946–1950) and later became its director (1959–1969). He occupied the chair of Egyptology and ancient Oriental history at the University of Lyons (1954–1959). After his return from Cairo in 1969, he held the chair of Egyptology at the Université Paul Valéry in Montpellier, where he created a new center of Egyptological studies and served as its director (1969–1978). Although primarily an Egyptologist, he dedicated part of his teaching and research to Coptic language and archaeology. With Antoine Guillaumont, he directed the French excavations conducted on the Coptic monastic site of KELLIA (1964–1969), as well as the first publication produced about this research (*Kellia I, Kom 219*, Cairo, 1969). To him must also be credited the publication of the posthumous work of Emile CHASSINAT (whose labors Daumas continued at Dandarah), *Le manuscrit magique copte no. 42573 du Musée égyptien du Caire* (Cairo, 1955), to which he added an appendix dealing with the identification of certain technical terms.

ANTOINE GUILLAUMONT

DAVID AT THE COURT OF SAUL. *See* Biblical Subjects in Coptic Art.

DAYR, word that seems to be borrowed from Syriac, like the greater part of the characteristic terms that form the lexical stock of the Christian Arabs, and linked by the classical dictionaries to the root "d w r," which suggests the idea of moving around in a circle. C. Brockelmann derives the Syriac word *dayra* from the Akkadian. However that may be, the word in Syriac describes a habitation in general, but may designate a sheepfold. It took on the specific sense of "monastery" (of cenobites). It seems that it was also used to describe any dwelling place of Christians. The Coptic word *raoue*, which means "a town quarter, a neighborhood," was also translated into Arabic by *dayr*, which leads one to suppose that the word had a fairly generic sense. The term *dayr* thus does not necessarily describe a habitation specifically of monks.

BIBLIOGRAPHY

Coquin, R. G. *Le Livre de la consécration du sanctuaire de Benjamin*. Bibliothèque d'études coptes 13. Cairo, 1975.

Crum, W. E. *A Coptic Dictionary*. Oxford, 1939; 2nd ed., 1962.

RENÉ-GEORGES COQUIN

DAYR, AL-, town located some 12 miles (20 km) northeast of Khargah, at the foot of the Jabal Ghanāyim. The site of al-Dayr includes a Roman fortress, a well, a pagan cemetery, and a small temple of baked bricks, later converted to a chapel in the Christian period. This monument, which consists of a vestibule and two vaulted chambers, is full of Coptic or Greco-Coptic graffiti, of which some are very late. Among the drawings can be seen a cross and a fine text dating from the year A.M. 576 (860), as well as two travelers' graffiti, one of Yohannes, son of Phoibammon, the other of Aron, son of Kyros, come from Kerameion (Madāmūd), evidently by the trail from Luxor.

BIBLIOGRAPHY

Bock, W. de. *Matériaux pour servir à l'archéologie de l'Egypte chrétienne*, pp. 1–6, fig. 6, pls. 1–2. St. Petersburg, 1901.

Naumann, R. "Bauwerke der Oase Khargeh." *Mitteilungen des deutschen archäologischen Instituts—Abteilung Kairo* 8 (1939):15–16, fig. 7.

GUY WAGNER

DAYR ABĪRŪN, on the testimony of ABŪ ṢĀLIḤ THE ARMENIAN, who is the only one to mention it (fol. 92; 1895, p. 257), a monastery in the district of Būṣir Qūrīdus (an abbreviation of Dioscurides), today called Būṣīr al-Malaq, on the left bank of the Nile, at the same latitude as DAYR AL-MAYMŪN.

The name attested by Abū Ṣāliḥ could be that of the martyr Piroou, whose name is sometimes corrupted in Arabic into Abīrūm or even Abīrūn. He is listed at 3 Abīb in the SYNAXARION (Forget, 1905–1926, Vols. 67 [text], p. 212, and 90 [trans.], pp. 208–210). Abū Ṣāliḥ adds that the last Umayyad caliph, Marwān II, came to this monastery before being killed not far from there. The site of the monastery is therefore linked with that of the death of Marwān in 750. Abū Ṣāliḥ places this event at Būsīr Qūrīdus, as do the historians al-Makīn and Ibn Zawlāq and the geographer Yāqūt (Abbott, 1937, p. 53; Ibn Duqmāq, 1893, Vol. 5, p. 2); however, in another passage (fol. 77a; 1895, p. 221), where he is following the information given in the Life of the patriarch Khā'īl I, he indicates that Marwān was killed at Cleopatra, the town founded by Alexander, which is now al-Ashmūnayn. This Life, which forms part of the HISTORY OF THE PATRIARCHS, first relates that a Syrian stylite predicted the death of Marwān II, saying that he would be killed at Abū Abīs, at Cleopatra (*History of the Patriarchs*, PO 5, 1909, p. 156; Evetts erroneously corrects Abū Abīs to Arsinoë), and then places the defeat and death of the caliph at the Mountain of Abāh (or Bābah, in the oldest manuscript) to the west of Cleopatra, but without indicating which Cleopatra is intended (ibid., p. 186). At least three are known, not to mention the place-name Cleopatris, which could have been confused by the copyists. A little further on (p. 187), the narrator indicates again that Marwān was taken prisoner at Dāwatūn, but the very variable ways of writing this name in the manuscripts make its location uncertain. The *History of the Patriarchs* thus seems to take account of divergent testimonies, but only Abū Ṣāliḥ identifies the Cleopatra of which the *History* speaks with the town of the same name near al-Ashmūnayn.

BIBLIOGRAPHY

Abbott, N. *The Monasteries of the Fayyūm.* Studies in Ancient Oriental Civilization 16. Chicago, 1937.

Ibn Duqmāq. *Kitāb al-Intiṣār,* ed. C. Vollers. Cairo, 1893; repr. Beirut, 1966.

Maspéro, J., and G. Wiet. *Matériaux pour servir à la géographie de l'Egypte.* Mémoire de l'Institut français d'Archéologie orientale 36. Cairo, 1919.

RENÉ-GEORGES COQUIN
MAURICE MARTIN, S.J.

DAYR ABŪ ANŪB, or Nūb, vanished monastery mentioned only by ABŪ ṢĀLIḤ THE ARMENIAN (1895, p. 252). He indicates that Dayr Abū Anūb (Apa Nob) was situated to the north of al-Ashmūnayn and that it contained the bodies of sixty-three monks martyred in A.M. 781/A.D. 1065–1066. They had been killed by a certain black named Ḥaffāz under the caliphate of al-Mustanṣir Billāh, in the patriarchate of CHRISTODOULUS, at the time of troubles in Upper Egypt. Abū Ṣāliḥ is the only one to mention this event. Neither the HISTORY OF THE PATRIARCHS nor the Muslim historians speak of it. The same historian later speaks of several churches, but it does not seem that these were in the monastery.

Ramzī (1953–1963, Vol. 1, p. 259) gives an account following another document of a Dayr Banūb in the district of al-Ashmūnayn, but it is not known if it is the same monastery.

BIBLIOGRAPHY

Ramzī, M. *Al-Qāmūs al-Jughrāfī lil-Bilād al Miṣrīyyah,* 3 vols. Cairo, 1953–1968.

RENÉ-GEORGES COQUIN
MAURICE MARTIN, S.J.

DAYR ABŪ BIFĀM (Asyūṭ). ABŪ ṢĀLIḤ THE ARMENIAN placed this monastery in the region of Asyūṭ, without further specification (fols. 60^{v}, 90^{r}; 1895, pp. 56, 114 [text], 179, 251 [trans.]). He does indicate that it was called Dayr al-Tinādah, the last word being no doubt the transcription of the Coptic *heneete* with the feminine article meaning "the monastery." Abū Ṣāliḥ reports as well that the body of Saint Abū Bifām was deposited there. The geographer Yāqūt also identifies it as Abū Bifām (1866–1873, Vol. 2, p. 649).

AL-MAQRĪZĪ distinguishes two monasteries of the same name, the one "below Dayr Karfūnah, in the *ḥāgir* [i.e., the pebbly ground between the cultivated land and the mountain] of Asyūṭ," or, according to the context, near Dayr Durunkah or Udrunkah on the left bank of the Nile. He places the other monastery near Ṭimā (1853, Vol. 2, pp. 506, 507; 1845, pp. 42–43, 103, 105; both of these editions erroneously give the name as Abū Baghām, as does the editor of Abū Ṣāliḥ).

Al-Maqrīzī adds that Saint Abū Bifām was a soldier martyred under Diocletian and celebrated on 2 Kiyahk. The martyr in question must be the saint mentioned by the SYNAXARION and by several Coptic and Arabic manuscripts—a soldier at the *castrum* (camp) of Aprahat near Antinoë (ANTINOOPOLIS) who was martyred at Asyūṭ and buried near there. His feast is on 1 Ba'ūnah, a date different from that reported by al-Maqrīzī.

No existing monastery in the region bears the name Abū Bifām.

BIBLIOGRAPHY

Crum, W. E. *The Monastery of Epiphanius,* Vol. 1, pp. 109–110. New York, 1926.

Yāqūt. *Geographisches Wörterbuch* (Mu'jam al-Buldān), 6 vols., ed. F. Wüstenfeld. Leipzig, 1866–1873.

RENÉ-GEORGES COQUIN
MAURICE MARTIN, S.J.

DAYR ABŪ BIFĀM (Samālūṭ). ABŪ ṢĀLIḤ THE ARMENIAN (fol. 88^{a}; 1895, pp. 111–12 [text], 247–48 [trans.]) mentions "a monastery of SAMĀLŪṬ in [the district of] al-ASHMŪNAYN and a church in the name of the martyr Abū Bifām." (It is necessary to correct the reading of B. T. A. Evetts, who writes the name consistently as Abū Baghām; Bifām is a variant of PHOIBAMMON.) The author describes this monastery as being surrounded by a wall and possessing a mill, an oven, an oil press, a large and lofty keep, and a garden with date palms and other trees. The caliphs had endowed it with twenty *feddans* (acres) of black earth. One of the Ghuzz or Kurds took possession of it in A.H. 569/A.D. 1173–1174, turned the church into a mosque, took over the garden and the *feddans,* and lived in the keep, but he died within the year, which prevented him from realizing the whole of his design.

Abū Ṣāliḥ is the only one known to have mentioned a Dayr Abū Bifām at Samālūṭ. AL-MAQRĪZĪ (1853) mentions two monasteries dedicated to Abū Bifām (Phoibammon), one near ASYŪṬ, in the region of DURUNKAH (or Udrunkah), on the west bank, and the other more to the south, before Ṭimā, or about 12 miles (40 km) from the first. The SYNAXARION recognizes two martyrs by the name of Phoibammon: the one celebrated on 27 Ṭūbah was martyred at Ṭimā, and the one celebrated on 1 Ba'ūnah died and was buried near Asyūṭ.

No monastery of this name is now known in the region of Samālūṭ.

RENÉ-GEORGES COQUIN

DAYR ABŪ BIFĀM (Ṭimā). Al-MAQRĪZĪ (1853, Vol. 2, p. 507; 1845, pp. 43 [text], 105 [trans.]) refers to a Monastery of Abū Bifām (the two editions wrongly give the name as Abū Baghām) situated outside Ṭimā on the left bank of the Nile, about 12 miles (20 km) from ABŪ TĪJ. Today no existing monastery in the region bears this name.

However, the SYNAXARION, in its Upper Egypt recension, mentions at 27 Ṭūbah the martyrdom of Saint PHOIBAMMON, stating that he was beheaded to the west of Ṭimā and that a martyrium was constructed for him there, where numerous miracles were accomplished (Basset, 1916, pp. 711–26; Forget, 1905, pp. 420–28, and 1922, pp. 419–30); one should read at the end in these two editions "at Dimnū, in the land of Akhmīm"). The notice about the martyr Saint Olympius for 30 Ṭūbah in the single manuscript of Luxor states that he was buried at Salamūn, to the west of Ṭimā in the land of Qāw, and that his church is situated between that of Phoibammon and that of Pecosh. The monastery of which al-Maqrīzī speaks must therefore have been at Salamūn, a village also situated on the left bank, near Ṭimā. S. Clarke's list (p. 212, no. 26) shows a church dedicated to Abū Bifām at Ṭimā and another to Olympius (in Arabic, Abū Limbah).

This Saint Phoibammon is different from the one buried near Asyūṭ (DAYR ABŪ BIFĀM at Asyūṭ) and celebrated on 1 Ba'ūnah, although the edition of the Synaxarion by 'Abd al-Masīḥ Mīkhā'īl and Armānyūs Ḥabashī Shaṭa al-Birmāwī (1973, Vol. 2, pp. 285–86) confuses them with one another, to the point of ignoring the one in Asyūṭ.

BIBLIOGRAPHY

Crum, W. E. *The Monastery of Epiphanius at Thebes,* Vol. 1, pp. 101–110. New York, 1926.

RENÉ-GEORGES COQUIN

DAYR ABŪ DARAJ. About 45 miles (68 km) to the southwest of Suez and about 160 yards from the police station known as Bi'r Abū Daraj, and 18 miles (28 km) from 'Ayn Sukhnah—that is to say, on the road that runs along the Red Sea—are the ruins of the Dayr Abū Daraj. These include several elements of different age and origin. There are, first of all, Nabataean traces, this road being the one taken by the Nabataeans, and the square tower appears to be of Roman and military origin.

Some authors have wished to see here Ptolemaic ruins. Hermits seem indeed to have installed themselves there, and there is no doubt that several hermitages were grouped around a well and a church. The renown of Saint Antony, whose monastery is not far distant (about 37 miles, or 60 km, as the crow flies), and the water supply attracted the hermits. A small monastery or center for the assembly of the hermits on Saturdays and Sundays was constructed there.

In 1717, C. Sicard (1982; his source is unclear) saw there the Monastery of John Climacus (*daraj* means "steps," whence the association with the saint's work, by the title of *klimax,* for *klimax* means "ladder"; Vol. 1, p. 42). It was in the twentieth century that archaeologists became interested in the site and described it. Wilkinson mentioned it in 1823, but his notes were not to be published until more than a century later (Littmann, 1953, p. 27). The site is described by several authors: Scaife (1936, pp. 63–64), Meredith (1952, p. 106), Fontaine (1955–1956, pp. 53–83), Martin (1966–1971), and Meinardus (1965, pp. 364–65; 1977, pp. 509–510)

BIBLIOGRAPHY

Fontaine, A. L. "Les Ruines du bir Abou Darag sur le golfe de Suez." *Bulletin de la Société d'etudes historiques et géographiques de l'isthme de Suez* 6 (1955–1956):55–83.

Littmann, E. "Nabatean Inscriptions from Egypt." *Bulletin of the School of Oriental and African Studies* 15 (1953):1–28.

Martin, M. P. "Les Ermitages d'Abou Darag." *Bulletin de la Sociéte d'Archéologie copte* 18 (1966):139–45.

______. "Abou Darag dans la montagne de Saint Antoine." *Bulletin de l'Institut français d'Archéologie orientale* 70 (1971):173–89.

Meinardus, O. *Christian Egypt, Ancient and Modern.* Cairo, 1965; 2nd ed., 1977.

Meredith, D. "The Roman Remains in the Eastern Desert of Egypt." *Journal of Egyptian Archaeology* 38 (1952):94–111.

Scaife, C. H. O. "Further Notes on Myos Hormos . . . and Some Ruins at Abou Darag." *Bulletin of the Faculty of Arts* (Cairo) 4 (1936):63–64.

Sicard, C. *Oeuvres,* 3 vols., ed. M. Martin and S. Sauneron. Bibliothèque d'étude 83–85. Cairo, 1982.

RENÉ-GEORGES COQUIN
MAURICE MARTIN, S.J.

DAYR ABŪ FĀNAH. [*This entry discusses Dayr Abū Fānah from two perspectives: recorded history and architecture, including recent and important diggings there.*]

History

This monastery is situated to the northwest of al-ASHMŪNAYN, beyond the Baḥr Yūsuf and about 2 miles (3 km) from Qaṣr Hūr, at the edge of the Libyan desert. Today one can see only the church, of the basilica type, deeply sunk into the sand in the center of a vast mound that no doubt conceals the ruins of the monastery. Its decoration won for it the sobriquet Monastery of the Crosses. Local tradition places the hermitage of the founder beyond the monastery, at the foot of a rocky ridge where the remains of a fairly large construction of baked brick are still visible. The neighboring *koms* (mounds) perhaps conceal isolated cells or hermitages of the type at Kellia and Isnā.

The Coptic text of the APOPHTHEGMATA PATRUM, and it alone, has preserved a sequence of sayings attributed to "abba Bane, who lived in the mountain of Houôr" (Chaine, 1960, nos. 244–49).

ABŪ ṢĀLIḤ THE ARMENIAN (fol. 89[a]; *The Churches . . .,* pp. 112 [text], 249 [trans.]) speaks only of a church dedicated to Abū Fānah not in the region of al-Ashmūnayn but in that of al-Khuṣūṣ, that is to say, to the north of Asyūṭ, on the right bank. It cannot therefore be the same site as that of the monastery.

The HISTORY OF THE PATRIARCHS mentions the monastery twice: first in connection with THEODOSIUS, a monk of Dayr Abū Fānah who was elected patriarch in 1294, and second, with regard to the childhood of the patriarch MATTHEW I, on which the judgment of Ibrāhīm, superior of the monastery, is reported (Vol. 3, pt. 3, pp. 134, 137 [text], 230, 237 [trans.]).

Al-MAQRĪZĪ (1853, Vol. 2, p. 505; 1845, pp. 41 [text], 101 [trans.]) situated the monastery very exactly "to the north of Banī Khālid" and "in the province of Minyā." He noted that it was built of stone and was a fine piece of architecture and that it formerly sheltered a thousand monks but that no more than two remained.

A life of Saint Abū Fānah is preserved in at least two manuscripts (Graf, Vol. 1 (1944), p. 533, and Vol. 2 (1947), p. 504; see also Kāmil Ṣāliḥ Nakhlah, 1942). E. F. Jomard (1821, Vol. 4, pp. 327–29) gives the state of the monastery and its plan at the time of Napoleon's expedition.

G. Maspero (1891, p. 511) speculates that the *kom* perhaps conceals a temple of Osiris. (See also Daressy, 1920, pp. 153–58, and 1917, p. 197.) The Arabic life (National Library, Paris, Arabe 153, fol. 216[r]) situates the hermitage of Abū Fānah "in the mountain, to the west of the village called Būṣīr."

BIBLIOGRAPHY

Chaine, M., ed. *Apophthegmata Patrum,* Bibliothèque d'études coptes 6. Cairo, 1960.

Daressy, G. "Abousir d'Achmounein." *Annales du Service des Antiquités de l'Egypte* 19 (1920):153–58.

______. "Indicateur topographique du 'Livre des Perles enfouies et du mystère précieux.'" *Bulletin de l'Institut français d'Archéologie orientale* 13 (1917):175–230.

Jomard, E. F. "Environs d'Hermopolis, Deyr Abou-Fâneh. . . ." In *Description de l'Egypte,* Vol. 5, §9, pp. 327–29, ed. M. Jomard. Paris, 1821.

Jullien, M. "Quelques anciens couvents de l'Egypte." *Mission Catholique* 35 (1903):212–14.

Kamil Salīḥ Nakhlah. "Summary of the Life of Saint Abū Fānāh." In *Risālat Nahḏat al-Kanā'is* 3 (1942): 16–18, 52–54. Cairo, 1942.

Leroy, J. *Les Peintures des couvents du désert d'Esna,* pl. 2, p. xv, and n. 3. Mémoires publiés par les membres de l'Institut français d'Archéologie orientale 94. Cairo, 1975.

Martin, M. *La Laure de deir al-Dik à Antinoë.* Bibliothèque d'études coptes 8. Cairo, 1971.

______. "Notes inédites du P. Jullien sur trois monastères chrétiens d'Egypte." *Bulletin de l'Institut français de Archéologie orientale* 72 (1972):120–24 and pl. 22.

Maspero, G. "Notes au jour le jour." *Proceedings of the Society of Biblical Archeology* 13 (1891):298–315; 407–437; 496–525.

Meinardus, O. *Christian Egypt, Ancient and Modern.* Cairo, 1965, pp. 262–63; 2nd ed., 1977, pp. 364–66.

Monneret de Villard, U. *Les Couvents près de Sohag,* p. 62, n. 2. Milan, 1925; this gives a short bibliography and reproduces Jomard's plan (fig. 95).

Munier, H. "Les Monuments coptes d'après les explorations du Père Michel Jullien." *Bulletin de la Société d'Archéologie copte* 6 (1940):141–68, esp. 147–52.

______. "Chronique (1941) IV: Deir Abū Fāna." *Bulletin de la Société d'Archéologie copte* 7 (1941):88.

Sicard, C. *Oeuvres*, ed. M. Martin, Vol. 2, pp. 100–101. Cairo and Paris, 1982.

RENÉ-GEORGES COQUIN
MAURICE MARTIN, S. J.

Architecture

Of the extant buildings, only part of the church from the sixth century now rises above the ground. It is used occasionally even today for divine service and is for this reason surrounded by a staircase construction and protective brick walls intended to hold back the sand. Whereas the outer walls of the church are still well preserved, the interior has been altered through the insertion of thick brick columns and several new partition walls. In shape, the sanctuary is a triconch; however, its individual members are given unequal treatment. The eastern apse is semicircular and adorned with a circle of engaged columns. The transverse space in front of it is narrower and has a simple rectangular shape.

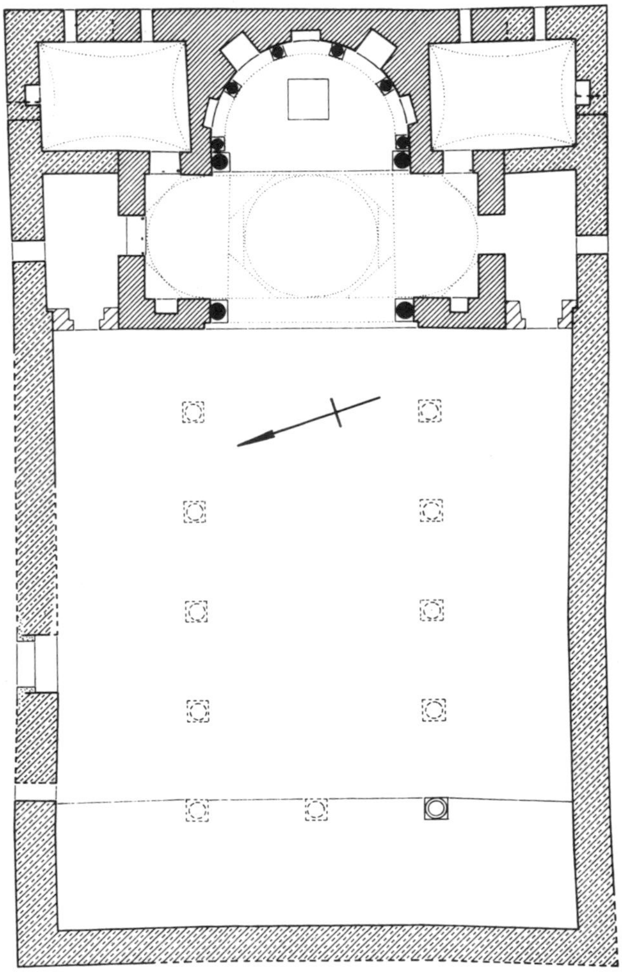

Plan of the sixth-century church at Dayr Abū Fānah. *Courtesy Peter Grossmann.*

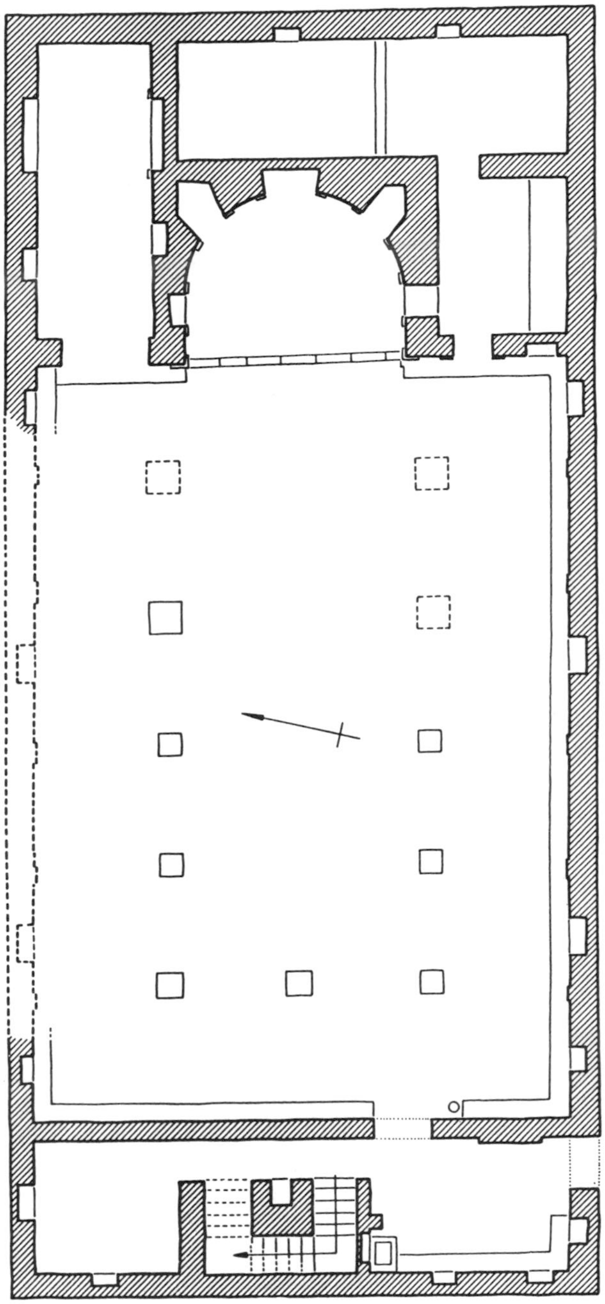

Plan of the three-aisled basilica discovered at Dayr Abū Fānah in 1987. *Courtesy Peter Grossmann.*

Strangely, the triconch at first stood alone (Grossmann, 1982, fig. 25). This fact reveals that a change of plan took place with regard to the lateral chambers of the sanctuary. In the original plan, these were designed to enclose the triconch on both sides. During the completion of the church, however, the connections with the rear parts were walled up to produce two separate rooms. At the west end of the church the usual return aisle is found. The entrance is on the north side. There was no western entrance. Of the original furnishings, various remains of paintings on the west wall and at the western end of the north wall have been preserved. The painting in the apse is of more recent date. Still surviving are a few column capitals, which are not original to the building. The cornice over the primary triumphal arch is original, and this ensures the dating of the edifice to the sixth century.

Other buildings belonging to the monastery are visible north of the church. In 1987 an Austrian mission excavating in this area discovered another three-aisled basilica, datable to the sixth century. It has a tripartite narthex with traces of stairs in the middle and the usual return aisle. The apse has several wall niches flanked with pilasters. Its floor is raised one step above the floor level of the nave. The lateral pastophoria are arranged in such a way that they encircle the apse on three sides.

To the south of this new church and among other buildings, some very broad halls have been unearthed, similar to those until now known only from Bāwīṭ. The larger one is furnished, as in Bāwīṭ, with a relatively small apse in the longer eastern wall. Probably these halls were used as prayer halls for the regular service hours. The other buildings might be understood mainly as lodging houses for the accommodation of the monks. Traces for the location of the refectory have not yet been recognized.

BIBLIOGRAPHY

Adli, S. "Several Churches in Upper Egypt." In *Mitteilungen des Deutschen Archäologischen Instituts—Abteilung Kairo* 36 (1980):8–9, fig. 6.

Buschhausen, H. "Die Ausgrabungen von Dayr Abū Fāna in Mittelägypten im Jahre 1987." *Jahrbuch der Österreichischen Byzantinistik* 38 (1988):353–62.

Grossmann, P. *Mittelalterliche Langhauskuppelkirchen und verwandte Typen in Oberägypten,* p. 78, fig. 25. Glückstadt, 1982.

Jomard, E. F., ed. "Environs d'Hermopolis, Dayr Abou Fâneh." In *Description de l'Egypte,* Vol. 4, pp. 326ff., 2nd ed. Paris, 1821.

Martin, M. "Notes inédites du P. Jullien sur trois monastères chrétiens d'Egypte." *Bulletin de l'Institut français d'Archéologie orientale* 71 (1972):119–24.

Timm, S. *Das christlich-koptische Ägypten in arabischer Zeit,* Vol. 2, pp. 573–74. Wiesbaden, 1984.

PETER GROSSMANN

DAYR ABŪ ḤALBĀNAH. This monastery is mentioned only by ABŪ ṢĀLIḤ THE ARMENIAN (1895, p. 243). He states that it is to the east of AKHMĪM and that a spring there flows from the mountain and runs into a basin. It may be remarked that to the east of Akhmīm there is today a large wadi called Wādī al-Jilbānah, whose name may correspond to that attested by Abū Ṣāliḥ. This could be so if the copyist has forgotten a diacritical point under the letter *j*, the latter having the same form as the *ḥ* and being distinguished from it only by a point placed below the letter. It must be noted that al-Qalqashandī at 3 Baramhāt in the Coptic calendar (Coquin, 1975–1976, pp. 398–99) records that there was a cult of a saint by this nick-name (Jilbānah—given perhaps because he fed himself on wild beans for which the word is *julbānah*; see Jomard, Vol. 17, p. 88). One would be tempted to identify Dayr Abū Ḥalbānah either with Dayr Mār Jirjis (which, however, is to the south of Akhmīm) or with Dayr al-ʿAdhrā' (which is less than 2 miles [3 km] from the beginning of Wādī Abū Jilbānah). In the eighteenth century a traveler, Alexis Bert, a major in the Army of the Orient, said he saw near Akhmīm what he called "Deir Halaouba-Come" (Couyat, 1911, pp. 139–84). Could Dayr Abū Ḥalbānah be seen in this badly spelled name? This nearby spring, which runs into a basin, resembles a site called DAYR AL-SABʿAT JIBĀL (Monastery of the Seven Mountains) by al-Maqrīzī (1853, Vol. 2, p. 504).

All the same, European travelers since the eighteenth century have described a site to the east of Akhmīm that strangely resembled that noted by Abū Ṣāliḥ and that they called "Dermadoud" (Dayr Ma'dud or Dayr al-Madwid; cf. Lucas, 1719, Vol. 2, p. 362, and Pococke, 1743–1745, Vol. 1, p. 78); Maspero (1886, pp. 232–42) described the state of the site in 1880–1886. Meinardus gave a more recent description of its state (1965, p. 298; 1977, p. 410).

It seems then that we may identify Abū Ṣāliḥ's Dayr Abū Ḥalbānah with the Dayr al-Ma'dūdī.

BIBLIOGRAPHY

Coquin, R.-G. "Le Calendrier copte des fêtes de saints chez al-Qalqashandi." *Parole de l'Orient* 6–7 (1975–1976):387–411. Vols. 6–7 are also *Mélanges Graffin* (Studies presented to Prof. Fr. Graffin).

Couyat, J. "Dayr Abu Halbanah." From the notes of Alexis Bert, Chef de bataillon d'artillerie dans l'armée d'Orient. *Bulletin de l'Institut français d'Archéologie orientale* 9 (1911):137–84.

Jomard, E. F. *Description de l'Egypte,* Vols. 11–17, *Etat moderne.* 2nd ed., Paris, 1822.

Lucas, P. *Troisième voyage du sieur Paul Lucas fait en 1714.* Rouen, 1719.

Maspero, G. "Rapport à l'Institut egyptien sur les fouilles et travaux exécutés en Egypte en 1885–86." *Bulletin de l'Institut d'Egypte* (2nd ser.) 7 (1886):232–42.

Meinardus, O. *Christian Egypt, Ancient and Modern.* Cairo, 1965; 2nd ed., 1977.

Pococke, R. *A Description of the East and Some Other Countries.* London, 1743–1745.

RENÉ-GEORGES COQUIN

DAYR ABŪ ḤINNIS (Mallawī). [*This entry consists of two articles: the history of Dayr Abū Ḥinnis, and its buildings. The first part seeks to reconcile ancient records referring to the dayr with existing ruins. The second part examines a present-day church and its incorporation of the earlier church, as well as a quarry cavern that was once used for a church.*]

History

The name of Dayr Abū Ḥinnis generally designates a Christian village; an ancient basilica, which today serves as the parish church; and the great LAURA with a rock-cut church in the mountains. The whole is situated on the right bank of the Nile, to the southeast of the ruins of Antinoë (Al-Shaykh Abādah). A map of the site is given by J. Clédat (1902, p. 45); the plan of the caves in the mountain is supplied by M. Martin (1971, p. 67).

As for many other Christian sites in Egypt, it is difficult to reconcile the archaeological data with the information in surviving documents. The fourth-century HISTORIA MONACHORUM IN AEGYPTO (1971, pp. 44–45) speaks of an ascetic living in the desert of ANTINOOPOLIS in a cavern very difficult to reach. PALLADIUS, who lived at Antinoë from 406 to 410, mentions in the *Historia lausiaca* the large number of monks and hermits living in the caves (1898–1904, Vol. 2, pp. 151–54). He also mentions the martyrium of Saint COLLUTHUS. This same martyrium is cited several times in Coptic texts, as in the reports relating to Saint Claude of Antioch (Godron, pp. 642, 650, 654). Abū Ṣāliḥ (fol. 86b; 1895, pp. 110 [text], 244 [trans.]) mentions at Antinoë only the monastery of Saint Colluthus with the body of the martyr.

Al-MAQRĪZĪ (1853, Vol. 2, p. 503; 1845, pp. 38 [text], 93 [trans.]) speaks of Dayr Abū al-Niʿnāʿ, outside of Anṣinā (Antinoë), forming part of the most ancient constructions in the town. Its church was in the *qaṣr* (tower), not on the ground, and was dedicated to JOHN COLOBOS (the Dwarf; in Arabic, al-Qaṣīr), whose feast is on 20 Bābah. Al-Maqrīzī reports the legend of the coming of John Colobos to Antinoë when he fled from SCETIS before the Mazices in 407. But documents indicate that John Colobos took refuge not in Antinoë but at al-Qulzūm (CLYSMA). H. G. Evelyn-White has advanced the hypothesis that the reference to John might be to JOHN KAMĀ, who died in 859 (1932, pp. 157–58 and 307, n. 3). The true identity of the Saint John to whom this church of Abū Ḥinnis is dedicated is still uncertain.

J. Doresse wanted to include this site in what he called "the independent monastic movement" of Middle Egypt (1952, pp. 390–95; 1970, pp. 7–29). But the most celebrated saints of this independent monastic movement do not appear in the published inscriptions.

The major archaeological sites of Dayr Abū Ḥinnis are the laura in the mountain and the church of the village (see below).

The church and the cells established in ancient quarries have been described by travelers such as Vansleb (1677, pp. 384–86; 1678, pp. 230–32); Sicard (1982, Vol. 2, pp. 83–86); Granger (1745, pp. 128–29); Jomard (1821, Vol. 4, pp. 272–75); and Jullien (1894, pp. 495–96).

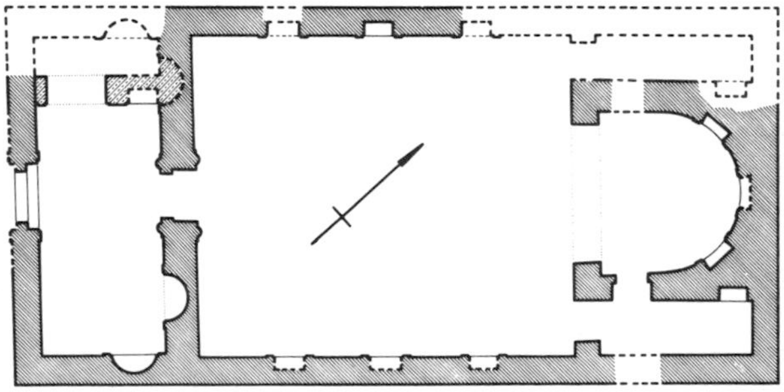

Plan of the village church at Dayr Abū Ḥinnis. *Courtesy Peter Grossmann.*

H. Leclerq (1903–1953, Vol. 1, col. 2351) thinks that the rock-cut church is the martyrium of Saint Colluthus about which the Greek and Coptic texts and Abū Ṣāliḥ speak. If this is correct, the very extensive laura (see Martin, 1971, pp. 66–69) could, along with Saint Menas in the Mareotis region, provide us with one of the best examples in Egypt of these more or less stable establishments of free monks, "sarabaïtes," living by preference on the outskirts of towns and in the service of the martyria (see Frend, 1969, pp. 542–49 and Février, 1974, pp. 39–61).

In the village church, in the north annex of the sanctuary, an ancient offering-table, today placed as an altar stone, was once used as a funerary stela. It has often been published and translated, the best study being that of M. Cramer (1941, pp. 5–7; photograph by Peter Grossmann, 1971, pl. 37, c). The very numerous inscriptions, Coptic, Syriac, Greek, and Arabic, have been published more or less completely.

BIBLIOGRAPHY

Clédat, J. "Notes archéologiques et philologiques." *Bulletin de l'Institut français d'Archéologie orientale* 2 (1902):49–67.

Cramer, M. *Die Totenklage bei den Kopten.* Vienna and Leipzig, 1941.

Crum, W. E. *Coptic Monuments,* p. 76, no. 8321. Cairo, 1902.

Daressy, G. "Renseignements sur la provenance des stèles coptes du Musée du Caire." *Annales du Service des Antiquités de l'Egypte* 13 (1914):266–71.

Doresse, J. "Recherches d'archéologie copte: Les monastères de moyenne Egypte." *Comptes rendus de l'Académie des inscriptions et belles lettres* (1952):390–95.

______. "Monastères de moyenne Egypte." *Bulletin de la Société française d'egyptologie* 59 (1970):7–29.

Evelyn-White, H. G. *The Monasteries of the Wadi'n Natrun,* Vol. 2. New York, 1932.

Fenoyl, M. "Une Inscription funéraire bilingue." *Bulletin de la Société d'archéologie copte* 17 (1964):57–61.

Février, A. "La Ville, le désert." In *Les Mystiques du désert dans l'Islam, le Judaïsme et le Christianisme.* Gordes, 1975.

Frend, W. H. C. "Circumcelliones and Monks." *Journal of Theological Studies* 20, pt. 2, new ser. (1969):542–49.

Galtier, E. "Coptica-arabica. Coptica." *Bulletin de l'Institut français d'Archéologie orientale* 5 (1906):87–164; pp. 112–15 for the stela from Dayr Abū Ḥinnis.

Godron, G. *Textes coptes relatifs à saint Claude d'Antioche.* In PO 35, fascicule 4 [n. 166]. Turnhout, 1970.

Granger, Sieur. *Relation du voyage fait en Egypte, par le sieur Granger, en l'année 1730.* Cairo, 1745.

Jarry, J. "Les Inscriptions syriaques de Deir Abu Hennes en Moyenne Egypte." *Bulletin de l'Institut français d'Archéologie orientale* 68 (1969):121–31.

______. "Nouvelles inscriptions coptes, grecques, arabes et syriaques de Deir Abou Hennes." *Bulletin de la Société d'Archéologie copte* 21 (1971–1973):52–78.

Jomard, E. F. "Description d'Antinoë." In *Description de l'Egypte.* Antiquités 4. Paris, 1821.

Jullien, M. "Les Grottes de la Basse Thebaïde." *Missions catholiques* (1894):495–96.

Leclerq, H. "Antinoë." In *Dictionnaire d'archéologie chrétienne et liturgie,* Vol. 1, col. 2351. Paris, 1903.

Lefebvre, G. *Recueil des inscriptions grecques-chrétiennes d'Egypte,* pp. 41–43. Cairo, 1907.

Mallon, A. "Epigraphie copte." In *Dictionnaire d'archéologie chrétienne et liturgie,* Vol. 3., cols. 2855–58. Paris, 1914.

Martin, M. *La Laure de Deir al-Dîk à Antinoë.* Bibliothèque d'études coptes 8. Cairo, 1971.

Meinardus, O. *Christian Egypt, Ancient and Modern.* Cairo, 1965, pp. 266–67; 2nd ed., 1977, pp. 372–73.

Sayce, A. H. "Coptic and Early Christian Inscriptions in Upper Egypt." *Proceedings of the Society of Biblical Archaeology* 8 (1886):175–91.

Sicard, C. *Oeuvres,* 3 vols., ed. M. Martin and S. Sauneron. Bibliothèque d'étude 83–85. Cairo, 1982.

Vansleb, J. *Nouvelle Relation en forme de journal d'un voyage fait en Egypte en 1672 et 1673.* Paris, 1677. Translated as *The Present State of Egypt.* London, 1678.

RENÉ-GEORGES COQUIN
MAURICE MARTIN, S. J.

Buildings

In the small church in the middle of the present-day village have been preserved substantial elements of a foundation that may be assigned to the late fifth century. The naos, approached by a narthex, had a single aisle (Clarke's often reprinted reconstruction with two rows of columns [1912, p. 185, pl. 56] is to be rejected) and correspondingly ends—to preserve the spatial proportions—in a relatively wide apse, on either side of which there is room only for comparatively small side chambers. The side walls of the church were provided with niches framed by pilasters. There are more niches in the narthex and in the apse. Today the church has been greatly modified by various alterations and internal additions. The naos has been split by two thick cross walls into three sections covered by domed and half-domed vaults. The northern-apse side room has been widened into a second *haykal* (altar room), and a baptistery added on the other side of the north wall. The women's area (BAYT AL-NIṢĀ'), which occupies the entire south side and to which large parts of the south wall were sacrificed, was erected in the twentieth century. Similarly, the semicircular external buttresses on both sides of the entrance derive from a later period.

There is a second small church in the midst of several hermit caves above the village of Abū Ḥīnnis, on the slope of the eastern desert plateau. In the literature it carries the peculiar designation "subterranean church." It is an originally shapeless quarry cavern that was built up for use as a church with the aid of some mud brick walls. This cave deserves attention because of the numerous inscriptions and paintings contained in it. The latter, in contrast to other Christian paintings in Egypt, constitute an imposing pictorial program with extensive presentation of scenes, such as is not very common elsewhere. According to J. CLÉDAT (1902, p. 47), the paintings belong to the sixth century.

[*See also:* Christian Subjects in Coptic Art.]

BIBLIOGRAPHY

Clarke, S. *Christian Antiquities in the Nile Valley,* pp. 181–87. Oxford, 1912.

Clédat, J. "Notes archéologiques et philologiques." *Bulletin de l'Institut français d'Archéologie orientale* 2 (1902):41–70.

Grossmann, P. "Neue Untersuchungen in der Kirche von Dair Abu Hinnis in Mittelägypten." *Mitteilungen des Deutschen Archäologischen Instituts, Abteilung Kairo* 27 (1971):157–71.

———. "Frühchristliche Baukunst in Ägypten." *Spätantike und frühes Christentum. Propyläen Kunstgeschichte,* Suppl. 1 (1977):243, fig. 73.

Timm, S. *Das christlich-koptische Ägypten in arabischer Zeit,* Vol. 2, pp. 577–85. Wiesbaden, 1984.

PETER GROSSMANN

DAYR ABŪ ISḤĀQ, a monastery, the church of which has been rebuilt, situated at the edge of the desert on the right bank between two villages called 'Arab Miṭīr and 'Arab al-'Awāmir in the district of Abnūb. It is surrounded by a Christian cemetery.

One cannot with complete certainty identify it with the monastery of Isaac of which a Coptic manuscript speaks (Kuhn, 1978, p. 1). A certain number of parchment leaves that come from there prove that the monastery was in use down to the eighteenth century (Burmester, 1975, Vol. 1, pp. 290, 294, 296–301).

The Christian cemetery proves that this place played an important role in the Byzantine period (Kamal, 1903, p. 83). This is explained by its proximity to al-Khuṣus, which was an important center of the Coptic community in the Middle Ages. S. Clarke names the church in his list of churches and attaches it to al-Hammān (1912, p. 210, no. 20). O. Meinardus (1965, pp. 280–81; 1977, pp. 389–90) describes its present state. He also indicates that a *mawlid* (pilgrimage) takes place there in the month of May.

It is not known which Isaac is intended. Probably it was a local saint whose Life has not come down rather than Saint Isaac of Difre, the martyr commemorated on 6 Bashans.

BIBLIOGRAPHY

Burmester, O. *Koptische Handschriften, Vol. 1, Die Handschriftenfragmente der Staats- und Universitätsbibliothek Hamburg,* Pt. 1. Wiesbaden, 1975.

Clarke, S. *Christian Antiquities in the Nile Valley.* London, 1912.

Kamāl, A. "Rapport sur la nécropole d'Arab el-Borg." *Annales du Service des antiquités de l'Egypte* 3 (1903):80–84.

Kuhn, K. H. *A Panegyric on Apollo, Archimandrite, of the Monastery of Isaac by Stephen, Bishop of Heracleopolis Magna.* CSCO 394. Louvain, 1978.

Meinardus, O. F. A. *Christian Egypt, Ancient and Modern.* Cairo, 1965; 2nd ed., 1977.

RENÉ-GEORGES COQUIN
MAURICE MARTIN, S.J.

DAYR ABŪ ISḤĀQ (Fayyūm). *See* Dayr al-Ḥammām.

DAYR ABŪ JA'RĀN. *See* Monasteries of the Fayyūm.

DAYR ABŪ AL-LĪF, also called the Monastery of Andrew, who was a friend of Pisentius and superior of the neighboring monastery Dayr al-Salīb.

His Life is contained in two manuscripts in the National Library, Paris (Arabe 4793, 4882), but it has not yet been published. It is not known if Abū Līf was simply a surname of Saint Andrew. A Muslim *shaykh* bears this name at QŪṢ, although it is not possible to say whether or not these two appellations designate the same person (Garcin, 1976, p. 34, n. 3).

However that may be, there is a monastery called Dayr Abū al-Līf on the left bank of the Nile about 150 feet (50 m) from Dayr al-Ṣalīb, of which Andrew was the superior (O'Leary, 1930, pp. 430–40, 462; Crum, 1926, Vol. 1, pp. 114–15).

BIBLIOGRAPHY

Crum, W. E. *The Monastery of Epiphanius at Thebes,* Vol. 1. New York, 1926.

Garcin, J.-C. *Un Centre musulman de la Haute-Egypte médiévale: Qūs.* Textes arabes et études islamiques 6. Cairo, 1976.

O'Leary, De L. *The Arabic Life of Pisentius.* PO 22. Paris, 1930.

RENÉ-GEORGES COQUIN
MAURICE MARTIN, S.J.

DAYR ABŪ LĪFAH. The ruins of this monastery are situated 1.25 miles (2 km) northwest of Qaṣr al-Sāghah, on the southeastern spur of the Jabal Qaṭrānī mountain chain, approximately 8 miles (13 km) north of Lake Qarūn. Among the seven Coptic inscriptions that Henri MUNIER and André Pochan discovered at this monastery, there were two with dates, A.M. 402/A.D. 686 and A.M. 574/A.D. 858. This means that we have definite evidence of its occupancy by Coptic monks between the seventh and ninth centuries. Apart from the archaeological evidence, the first literary reference to this monastery is a fifteenth-century manuscript published in 1907 by Aḥmad Kamāl under the title *Le Livre des perles enfouies.* In the Middle Ages the monastery was also known as the Dayr Abū Banūkh. In the seventeenth century, Dayr Abū Līfah, though in ruins, was still well known to the inhabitants of the Fayyūm, as recorded by J. M. VANSLEB. By 1966 the southern part of the monastery, which was hewn out of the soft sandstone, had broken away. The only remains of the monastery are two caves that are cut into the rock. The first cave is situated 16 feet (5 m), and the second cave 40 feet (12 m), below the summit of the mountain. Either earthquakes or rain must have caused the collapse of the southern section of the monastery, entailing a considerable fall of rock and leaving no more than the northernmost caves in situ. There is good reason to believe that the last vestiges of Dayr Abū Līfah will eventually disappear as more and more of the mountain collapses.

BIBLIOGRAPHY

Bittel, Kurt. "Kasr el Sagha." *Mitteilungen des deutschen Instituts für ägyptische Altertumskunde in Kairo* 5 (1934):1–10 and 4 pl.

Brown, R. H. *The Fayum and Lake Moeris,* p. 52. London, 1892.

Caton-Thompson, G. *The Desert Fayum,* Vol. 1, p. 81; Vol. 2, pl. 86, p. 6. London, 1934.

Kamāl, Aḥmad. *Le Livre des perles enfouies,* p. 178. Cairo, 1907.

Meinardus, O. "Dair Abū Līfā Revisited." *Bulletin de la Société d'archéologie copte* 19 (1970):177–80.

Munier, H. "Le Deir Abou-Lifa." *Bulletin de la société d'archéologie copte* 3 (1937):1–5.

Vansleb, J. M. *Nouvelle Relation en forme de journal d'un voyage fait en Egypte 1672 et 1673,* p. 268. Paris, 1677.

OTTO F. A. MEINARDUS

DAYR ABŪ MAQRŪFAH and DAYR AL-JANĀDLAH. [*This article is composed of two parts. The first describes the location and history of the dayr. The second delves into the architecture as revealed in the archaeological remnants.*]

History

These two villages are on the border between the cultivated land and the desert, on the left bank of the Nile, about 7.5 miles (12 km) south of ABŪ TĪJ, in the province of ASYŪṬ. These two villages now form a single agglomeration under the name of Dayr al-Janādlah. The first appears to be the older, since it is the only one mentioned in the surviving documents: the *State of the Provinces* (A.H. 777/A.D. 1375) and the histories by ABŪ ṢĀLIḤ THE ARMENIAN and al-MAQRĪZĪ.

In the rocky cliff about half a mile south of WĀDĪ SARJAH is the Monastery of the Virgin with its two churches, built into old quarries. The old church dedicated to the Virgin contains an altar dedicated to Abū Maqrūfah (Macrobius). It also contains paintings of personages that are scarcely legible.

One hour's walk away, in the mountain, there is also a small LAURA called Dayr Maqrūfiyus.

The Dayr Abū Maqrūfah is mentioned by Ibn Duqmaq (1893, Vol. 5, p. 24) and by Abū Ṣāliḥ (*The Churches . . .*, fol. 90[a], 1895, pp. 114 [text], 252 [trans.]). Abū Ṣāliḥ seems guilty of double confusion, for he indicates that the church is dedicated to Saint Sergius, perhaps because of the neighboring Wādī Sarjah, and situates the monastery east of Asyūṭ. Al-Maqrīzī (1853, Vol. 2, p. 507; 1845, pp. 43 [text], 104–105 [trans.]) is more precise. According to him, the name Abū Maqrūfah is that of the neighboring village. The monastery is dug in the lower part of the mountain with a number of caves, is dedicated to the Virgin, and has no water supply. This corresponds to the present situation. At the foot of the *dayr* there is a large, deep well of fine cut stone.

A more recent description is given by M. Jullien (1903, pp. 237–38; see also Clarke, 1912, pp. 171–74). However, the plan of the church hewn out of rock (pl. 52, fig. 1) appears erroneous, for there is no room for the right-hand chapel to the southeast.

The cemeteries at the edge of the village and at the foot of the Dayr al-ʿAdhrā' were excavated by W. M. Flinders Petrie in 1907, and the stelae found were published by him (1909, pl. 54, no. 13; 1907, pl. 39–40). The saints invoked on these funerary stelae are Thomas, Peter, Joseph, Anup, and Pamun; oddly, the name of Macrobius is not there. The first might be the founder of the monastery Wādī Sarjah.

The saint who gave his name to the village and to the laura in the mountain is Macrobius, disciple of Moses of Abydos, and is mentioned very briefly in the SYNAXARION for 7 Baramūdah (Forget, 1953–1954, Vol. 67, p. 64 [text]; vol. 90, p. 65 [trans.]). The text of manuscript C (National Library, Paris, Arabe 4780, from DAYR AL-MUḤARRAQ) reads: "Today went to his rest the great saint Macrobius, son of the prince of the town of Qāw, who lived in the mountain of Wādī Sarjah." The edition of the Synaxarion by the *qummuṣ* ʿAbd al-Masīḥ Mīkhā'īl and the *qummuṣ* Armāniyūs Ḥabashī Shaṭā al-Birmāwī (1935–1937) gives a more developed notice.

BIBLIOGRAPHY

Clarke, S. *Christian Antiquities in the Nile Valley.* Oxford, 1912.

Ibn Duqmāq, *Kitāb al-intiṣār. Description de l'Egypte,* ed. C. Vollers, pts. 4 and 5. Cairo, 1893; repr. Beirut, n.d.

Johann Georg, Duke of Saxony. *Neueste Streifzüge durch Kirchen und Klöster Ägyptens,* pp. 8–10, fig. 10–15. Leipzig and Berlin, 1931.

Jullien, M. "Quelques anciens couvents de l'Egypte." *Mission catholiques* 35 (1903): 188–90; 198–202; 212–14; 237–40; 250–52; 257–58; 274–76; 283–84.

Meinardus, O. *Christian Egypt, Ancient and Modern.* Cairo, 1965, pp. 287–88; 2nd ed., 1977, pp. 397–98.

Petrie, W. M. F. *Gizeh and Rifeh.* London, 1907.

______. *Memphis,* Vol. 1. London, 1909.

RENÉ-GEORGES COQUIN

Architecture

The old church dedicated to Abū Maqrūfah in Dayr al-Janādlah (Clarke, 1912, p. 171) was dismantled some time in the mid-twentieth century. About 1.25 miles (2 km) to the southwest, on a mountain slope in the area of an extensive pre-Christian hillside quarry, lies a walled ecclesiastical precinct of the same name. It is uninhabited today and contains two churches and some unpretentious living quarters. Both churches have been regarded as modern (built in 1865, according to Meinardus, 1965), although included in the older one is a quarry cave that was already serving as a church in the early Christian period. Some of the furnishings of this older church are visible on the ceiling and the walls of the cave. The erection of a few brick walls and perhaps also some round columns or pillars presumably gave it the appearance of a basilica. The central section of the cave, where more of the ceiling has been hollowed out, assumed the role of the nave. The side walls are virtually parallel and contain a number of niches hewn out of the rock. Their upper border is provided with a gable-shaped piece such as is known particularly from the niches of the church of the Shenute monastery (DAYR ANBĀ SHINŪDAH) at Suhāj. The rock walls are plastered. In several places extensive fragments of painting are preserved, though severely blackened by smoke. There is not a trace of the original sanctuary, which, according to the generally required eastern direction, would have been positioned in the area at the cave entrance and must have been built of bricks. Like the rest of the rooms, the apse is modern. The *hijāb* (screen) erected in front is made up of different varieties of early Christian decorated stones (tomb stelae and fragments of friezes). It is possible that some of these were used in the original church. In all probability, this church belonged to a community of monks who made their homes in the neighboring quarry caves. It is to be dated to the seventh century.

BIBLIOGRAPHY

Clarke, S. *Christian Antiquities in the Nile Valley,* pp. 171ff., pl. 52.1. Oxford, 1912.

Johann Georg, Duke of Saxony. *Neueste Streifzüge durch die Kirchen und Klöster Ägyptens,* pp. 8ff. Leipzig and Berlin, 1931.

Meinardus, O. F. A. *Christian Egypt, Ancient and Modern,* pp. 287–88. Cairo, 1965.

PETER GROSSMANN

DAYR ABŪ MATTĀ (Dākhlah Oasis), the ruins of a church lying on a small hill, immediately beside the road about 12.5 miles (20 km) north of Mūt. Despite its construction in simple mud bricks, it has been preserved remarkably well. The outer walls are still standing in part to a considerable height, and on all sides several large windows can be seen. The interior forms a three-aisled BASILICA (wrongly described by Mills [1981, p. 185] as a nine-roomed structure), and as in the churches in the Nile Valley it is provided with a return aisle. The sanctuary has the form of a triconch with gamma-shaped side rooms laid around the two lateral apses. Whether there were two further columns or pillars in front of the opening of the triumphal arch, as is the case in the other examples of this type in the Nile Valley, was not investigated during the excavations in the church, but because of its small size it seems that the answer must be negative. In any case, an additional triumphal arch set up with the aid of such columns would also have had to be provided with stout buttresses at the sides. Chronologically, the church is probably to be assigned to the late sixth century. An outer portico (not on the plan) was later added on the east side.

The remaining constructions in the neighborhood of the church have the character of monastic buildings. Several layers of settlement can be distinguished. The remains of a KEEP (*jawsaq*) can be seen immediately west of the church.

[*See also:* Architectural Elements of Churches.]

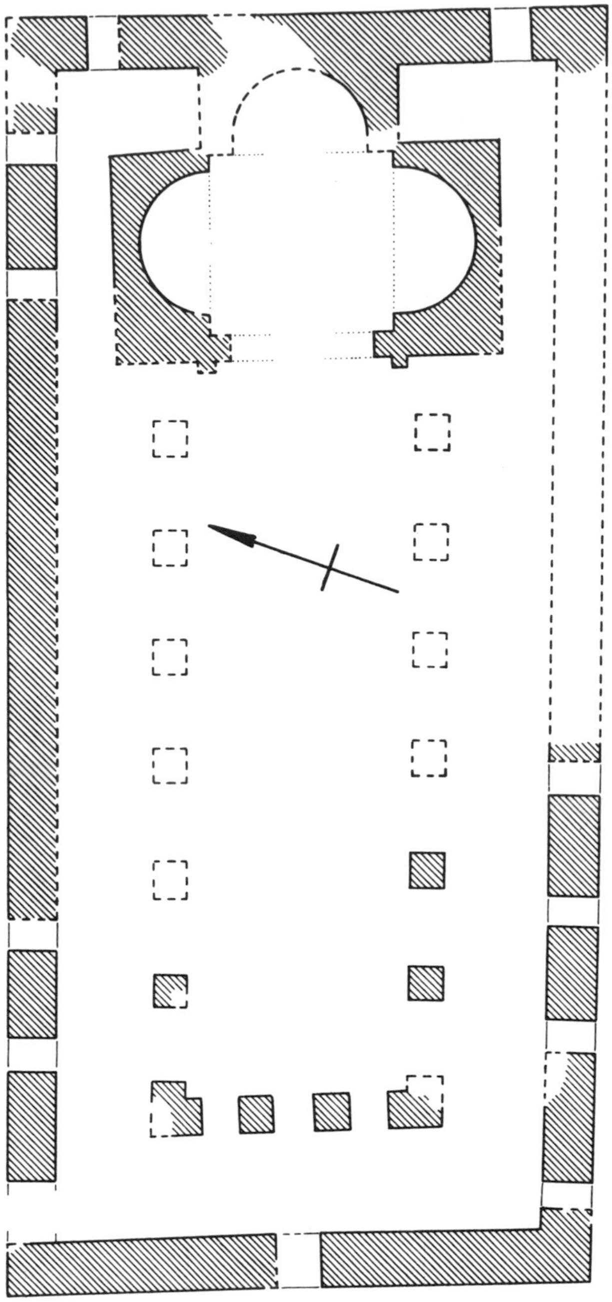

Plan of the church at Dayr Abū Mattā. *Courtesy Peter Grossmann.*

BIBLIOGRAPHY

Mills, A. J. "The Dakhlah Oasis Project." *Journal of the Society for the Study of Egyptian Antiquities* 11 (1981):185.

Winlock, H. E. *El Dakhleh Oasis,* p. 24, pl. 10. New York, 1936.

PETER GROSSMANN

DAYR ABŪ MĪNĀ (Maryūt). When a recluse in a mill on the Muqaṭṭam hills, Abūnā Mīnā al-Barāmūsī, was enthroned as Pope CYRIL VI (1959–1971) and the 116th patriarch of the See of Saint Mark, he was able to realize his old dream of renewing the older monastery of Saint Menas in the western desert of Mareotis (Maryūt) in the neighborhood of Alexandria. Since the excavations of that ancient monastery were in progress, Cyril VI could select an area for his new foundation nearer the Alexandria-Cairo desert road within reach of the original terrain. He had to settle the project with the authorities since this was a military region, and special dispensation for work within these precincts was necessary. An area of 130 acres was earmarked for this enterprise. On 25 November 1960, the pope started building a church dedicated to Saint Samuel. He included a row of cells to accommodate new monks, together with structures for a growing library and some lodgings for pilgrims. In the course of 1961, the pope laid the foundation for a monumental cathedral in the name of Saint Menas (ABŪ MĪNĀ).

After his death in 1971, the pope's remains were transported from DAYR MĀR MĪNĀ in Old Cairo to his new foundation in the desert of Mareotis. The remains of his close disciple Bishop SAMUEL, who was assassinated with President Anwar al-Sadat on 6 October 1981, were placed beside those of Cyril VI. Thus the great mentor and his follower are now entombed in a traditional pilgrimage area.

MOUNIR SHOUCRI

DAYR ABŪ MŪSĀ (Mīsas). The Coptic texts of MOSES OF ABYDOS give us some information about his monastery. Moses established himself first of all in proximity to the temples of Abydos, at a place called Pehke; then he went off toward the south wishing to escape the importuning crowds attracted by his miracles. But he was arrested by a vision and constrained to return north; he halted a mile from Pehke, and there, it seems, founded his monastery. Like PACHOMIUS, he began by constructing an enclosure wall and then two wells, one of them for passing strangers. It is said that he founded a community of women, and archaeologists have discovered in the temple of Seti I some graffiti that show that a community of women lived there, the most recent of them going back to the tenth century (Crum, in Murray, 1904, pp. 38–43).

ABŪ ṢĀLIḤ THE ARMENIAN, at the beginning of the thirteenth century, wrote of the monastery of Moses but called it that of Banī Mūsā, which is no doubt a fault of his source or of the copyists (1895, pp. 231–32). He noted that the monastery was restored by its abbot al-Ṣafī, who surrounded it with an enclosing wall; that it was provided with a *sāqyah* (waterwheel); and finally that the body of the saint was there. Abū Ṣāliḥ knew that the real titular saint was Moses, but he did not indicate the precise site of the monastery; he contented himself with saying "to the west of the Nile," which is vague. Abū Ṣāliḥ related to this monastery a miracle that occurred under the patriarch CHRISTODOULUS. The columns of the church oozed, thus announcing a famine. But the HISTORY OF THE PATRIARCHS relates this event to the monastery of MOSES THE BLACK in Wādī al-Naṭrūn, not to that of Moses of Abydos (1959, Vol. 2, pt. 3, pp. 189–90 [text], 289–90 [trans.]).

Al-MAQRĪZĪ (1853, Vol. 2, p. 507) made reference to a monastery in this region in his list of the monasteries of Egypt but called it that of Bū Mīsas or Bū Mīsīs (Moses). He added but little, saying that it was a large monastery and that Moses was a native of al-Balyanā, which links up with the prophecy of SHENUTE attributed to him by the author of the Coptic life.

It was not until 1718 that a traveler, C. SICARD, mentioned the monasteries of Abydos. He names three: one to the south of the Memnonion, of which he mentions the enclosure wall and the waterwheel (Abū Ṣāliḥ's *sāqyah*) but which he calls that of Pachomius; one which he calls that "of the abbot Moses, to the west of the village, at the foot of Mt. Afodos," which is the present Dayr Mūsā, also called DAYR SITT DIMYANAH; and one to the south of that of the abbot Moses, but entirely in ruins (1982, Vol. 3, pp. 65–68). There is some chance that the first is the one that Moses founded at Abydos. In 1731 the traveler Granger spoke of Abydos, but not of the Monastery of Moses (1845, pp. 38–39).

In the early twentieth century Lefebvre spoke of "a long quadrilateral of which only the walls of unbaked brick emerge" and noted that the inhabitants call it the "Monastery of the Greeks" (1911, Vol. 4, p. 239).

The modern description of the monastery that bears the name of Moses and of Sitt Dimyānah to the northwest of Shūnat al-Zabīb is given by O. Meinardus (1965, p. 302; 1977, pp. 413–14).

BIBLIOGRAPHY

Granger, (Sieur). *Relation du voyage fait en Egypte, par le sieur Granger, en l'année 1730*. Paris, 1845.

Lefebvre, G. "Egypte chrétienne." *Annales du Service des antiquités de l'Egypte* 11 (1911):238–50.

Meinardus, O. *Christian Egypt, Ancient and Modern*. Cairo, 1965; 2nd ed., 1977.

Murray, M. A. *The Osireion at Abydos.* London, 1904.

Sicard, C. *Oeuvres,* Vol. 3, ed. S. Sauneron and M. Martin. Bibliothèque d'étude 85. Cairo, 1982.

RENÉ-GEORGES COQUIN
MAURICE MARTIN, S.J.

DAYR ABŪ MŪSĀ AL-ʿASWAD. The Monastery of MOSES THE BLACK, dedicated to Our Lady, is situated opposite DAYR AL-BARĀMŪS in the wilderness of Wādī Habīb in the Western Desert. Though the precise date of its foundation is unknown, it is presumably one of the early monasteries in this area, perhaps from the fourth or fifth century.

It is mentioned in subsequent centuries by numerous authors. In the eleventh century, the Coptic writer and deacon Mawhūb ibn Manṣūr ibn Mufarrij recorded its existence as an independent unit; but al-MAQRĪZĪ (1970) in the fifteenth century confused it with the neighboring Dayr al-Barāmūs. However, E. AMÉLINEAU, in his famous Coptic geography of Egypt, listed it as one of seven monasteries in that region.

Abū Mūsā al-ʿAswad, or Moses the Black, is known to have been a fourth-century Abyssinian slave who became a highwayman involved in robberies and murders. Later he was reformed and became a monk of SCETIS, living as a solitary in a cave hewn in the rock opposite Dayr al-Barāmūs. Eventually other monks congregated around his cave and built their own cells, which constituted the aforementioned monastic laura. According to Mawhūb, the area was sparsely inhabited by monks, who possibly preferred the security of the better protected Dayr al-Barāmūs. The number of monks was also depleted by the Black Death of 1349 and the famine of 1374. The Monastery of Moses the Black was utterly abandoned and fell into ruin.

BIBLIOGRAPHY

Amélineau, E. *La Géographie de l'Egypte à l'époque copte.* Paris, 1893.

Burmester, O. H. E. *A Guide to the Monasteries of Wādī'n-Naṭrūn.* Cairo, n.d.

Evelyn-White, H. G. *The Monasteries of the Wādī'n-Naṭrūn,* 3 vols. New York, 1926–1933.

Meinardus, O. F. A. *Christian Egypt, Ancient and Modern.* Cairo, 1965; 2nd ed., 1977

FAYEK ISHAK

DAYR ABŪ MŪSHĀ. Al-MAQRĪZĪ mentions a Dayr Mūshā (1853, Vol. 2, p. 507), which he places "outside ASYŪṬ, to the south of this town, built in the name of Thomas, the apostle of India, in the middle of the gardens, near Rīfah. In the days of the Nile [flood] one can reach it only by boat."

The geographical situation is clear, for the village called Mūshā still exists to the south of Shutb (Upselis), to the east of Rīfah, on the left bank. Under its Coptic name, Pmoushe, it is known as the place of the martyrdom of Victor of Shū (as in the typicon of the White Monastery, DAYR ANBĀ SHINŪDAH, and the recension of the SYNAXARION from Upper Egypt at 5 Kiyahk). The Synaxarion (Basset, 1905, p. 380) specifies that this village of Shū is to the east of the village of Ibsīdiyyah, where ABŪ ṢĀLIḤ THE ARMENIAN (1895, p. 251) places a monastery. Al-Maqrīzī (1853, pp. 518–19) situates at Mūshā a church named for Victor, built above a bath. This Victor of Shū was martyred at Mūshā, being thrown into the roaring furnace of a bath. This church still exists (Clarke, 1912, p. 210, no. 9), but not the Monastery of Thomas. This was perhaps the one placed in Ibsīdiyyah by Abū Ṣāliḥ (1895, p. 252).

BIBLIOGRAPHY

Clarke, S. *Christian Antiquities in the Nile Valley.* London, 1912.

RENÉ-GEORGES COQUIN
MAURICE MARTIN, S.J.

DAYR ABŪ AL-NIʿNĀ. *See* Dayr Abū Ḥinnis.

DAYR ABŪ QARQŪRAH, monastery discovered in 1948 in ruins at Ḥilwān by the author, who had been conducting First and Second Dynasty necropolis excavations in the neighborhood of that town. This area is supposed to have been in the proximity of the old dynastic Egyptian capital of Iwnu. While digging the popular cemetery of that early period, the author came upon what remained of this monastery, which was known only from early medieval literature on Coptic churches and monasteries by the twelfth-century writer ABŪ AL-MAKĀRIM, wrongly ascribed to Abū Ṣāliḥ the Armenian. The writer states that during the reign of ʿAbd-al-ʿAziz ibn Marwān, Umayyad viceroy of Egypt (685–706), a monastery by the name of Dayr Abū Qarqar or Qarqūrah, possibly an Arabic corruption of the Coptic Gregorios, existed between Shahrān and Ḥilwān a few miles south of Cairo on the right bank of the Nile. The writer associates that monastery with a bishop of al-Qays, a district at Banī Mazār in the province of Minyā in Middle Egypt, whose name was Gregorios. There is a lacuna in the manuscript of that work that makes it difficult for us to define the specific particulars or foundation date of that monastery. But Abū al-Makārim states that it was restored and extended during the regency of ʿAbdal-ʿAzīz ibn Marwān by his servants, who were Melchites, for the fortieth patriarch of the See of Saint Mark, JOHN III (677–686). The work was performed in the name of Saint George.

There is no doubt that this monastery was in a very fine state of preservation in the seventh century. It is known that in the year 692, a plague broke out in Egypt and spread to the capital al-Fusṭāṭ (Old Cairo), which was the Umayyad viceroy's seat. For this reason, ʿAbd-al-ʿAzīz ibn Marwān left the capital and went south toward Ḥilwān and, according to the historians al-Shābushtī and Abū al-Makārim, ʿAbd-al-ʿAzīz resided as a guest for a while in that monastery. As he seemed to like the area, he ordered the construction of his own palace there for permanent residence, which gave Ḥilwān royal status. A bath built in that region by ʿAbd-al-ʿAzīz around that date was discovered during the modern restoration of the city in 1872.

This Coptic monastery must have been one of the largest on record in Egypt. Its excavation has revealed the enormous number of sixty-six rooms or monastic cells. The court in the middle of the structure was a vast space, divisible into three sections. In the north part existed an orchard, and still visible are the holes or ditches in the soil that were prepared for filling with Nile silt to fertilize trees. Portions of the irrigation aqueducts, where the monks used burnt bricks taken from the tombs of the ancient Egyptian cemetery, are still to be seen. In the south part, there was a large reservoir where the monks stored water. Next to that reservoir was a structure of strange design by which earthenware jars were fitted into holes resembling pigeonholes in the walls. The purpose of that structure is uncertain. Throughout the floors of the monastery buildings we may witness traces of piping and drainage canals. In the south also is to be found the remains of a moderately sized church. Beyond the church still farther south was situated a cemetery where thirty-six graves were excavated and found to contain skeletons in a bad state of preservation. No special items of value were found in these tombs except perhaps tomb 1, where an ivory was found that showed traces of Coptic letters.

From the nature of pottery and glass fragments found on the site one can establish that the monastery was of Byzantine origin. What is certain is that it was heavily populated with monks at the time of the ARAB CONQUEST OF EGYPT.

The excavation has revealed little in the way of objects of art. However, a Coptic earthenware lamp and a Coptic copper cross were found in the debris. Also a few bronze and copper coins were recovered, but not identified. Perhaps the most important objects of historical importance discovered in the whole excavation were four gold dinars, two dated 698, a third dated 699, and a fourth 700. It must be assumed that the monastery remained inhabited until the eighth century. Afterward it fell into decay, and its contents were collected by treasure hunters over the subsequent centuries.

[*See also* Ḥilwān.]

BIBLIOGRAPHY

Atiya, A. S. "Some Egyptian Monasteries According to the Unpublished Manuscript of al-Shābushti's *Kitāb al Diyārāt*." *Bulletin de la Societé d'archéologie copte,* Vol. 5. Cairo, 1939.

Shābushtī, Abū-al-Ḥasan ʿAlī ibn Muḥammad al-. *Al-Diyārāt,* ed. Korkis ʿAwwād. Baghdad, 1951.

Zaki Yusef Saad. *The Excavations at Helwan.* Norman, Okla.; 1969.

ZAKI YUSEF SAAD

DAYR ABŪ SARABĀM (near Minyā). The most explicit of the ancient authors regarding this monastery is without doubt al-MAQRĪZĪ (1853, Vol. 2, p. 518), for he described "in the district of Dayrūṭ a church near the town, as well as a monastery named after the monk Serapion, who lived in the time of Shenute and was elected bishop." It may be a case of this monastery, since a confusion of spelling is possible in Arabic between Sarabām and Serapion. The name does not appear to be attested elsewhere in relation to Dayrūṭ and Dayrūṭ al-Sharīf.

Yāqūt, in the thirteenth century, also called the village Darwāt Sarabām (1870–1873, Vol. 2, p. 570). ABŪ ṢĀLIḤ (1895, p. 222) also called it Darwāt al-Sarabām, but he does not mention any monastery.

E. QUATREMÈRE (1812, p. 13) contented himself with citing al-Maqrīzī. G. MASPERO (1919, p. 197) referred to E. F. Jomard's description (1821). The monastery was described by the latter (Vol. 4, p. 187) as a small deserted monastery now serving as a cemetery, to the northeast and very close to Dayrūṭ al-Sharīf (Clarke, 1912, p. 208, no. 12). In the maps of the *Survey of Egypt* (1907) the monastery is called Abū Suryān Monastery and situated less than a mile to the east of Dayrūṭ.

BIBLIOGRAPHY

Amélineau, E. *La Géographie de l'Egypte à l'époque copte*. Paris, 1893.

Clarke, S. *The Christian Antiquities in the Nile Valley*. London, 1912.

Jomard, E. F. *Description de l'Egypte*, Vol. 4. Paris, 1821.

Maspero, G. "Notes au jour le jour." *Proceedings of the Society of Biblical Archaeology* 13 (1891):298–315, 407–37, 496–525; 14 (1892):170–204; 305–27; 20 (1898):123–44.

Maspéro, G., and G. Wiet. *Matériaux pour servir à la géographie d'Egypte*, p. 87. Mémoires de l'Institut français d'Archéologie orientale 36. Cairo, 1919.

Quatremère, E. *Observations sur quelques points de la géographie de l'Egypte*. Paris, 1812.

Survey of Egypt. Cairo, 1907. Contains maps of Egypt.

Yāqūt ibn ʿAbd Allāh al-Ḥamawī. *Kitāb Muʿjam al-Buldān*, 10 vols. Cairo, 1956–1957.

______. *Jacūt's Geographisches Wörterbuch*, 6 vols., ed. F. Wüstenfeld. Leipzig, 1866–1873. Repr. Tehran, 1965; Beirut, 4 vols., 1955–1957.

RENÉ-GEORGES COQUIN
MAURICE MARTIN, S.J.

DAYR ABŪ SAYFAYN (Akhmīm). *See* Akhmīm.

DAYR ABŪ SAYFAYN (Nag Hammadi). *See* Dayr Anbā Palaemon.

DAYR ABŪ SAYFAYN (Old Cairo), Christian enclosure that derives its name from the great church dedicated to Abū Sayfayn (Father of Two Swords), an epithet given to Saint MERCURIUS of Caesarea. The complex also has churches of Saint SHENUTE and the Virgin Mary, as well as a convent of nuns dedicated to Saint Mercurius.

The HISTORY OF THE PATRIARCHS, in discussing the patriarch MARK VII, (1745–1769) mentions "the monastery of the great martyr Philopator Mercurius, Father of the Two Swords."

A. J. Butler (1884, pp. 75–76) reported that "half a mile beyond Mari Mina lies the walled enclosure or dair of Abu's-Sifain, so called after the principal though not the most ancient church within it." M. JULLIEN (1891, p. 224) wrote about "the Coptic quarter of Abou Seyfeyn," indicating that it was a small town surrounded by ramparts not far from the mosque. P. Casanova (1919, pp. 192–98) said that "under the name of deir Abou-s Seifain there is in the centre of the ancient Fustāt a quite important group of buildings." M. Simaykah (1937, p. 75) spoke of "Deir Aboul Sefein."

Dayr Abū Sayfayn is situated north of Qaṣr al-Shamʿ in the old city of Miṣr (Old Cairo) in Jāmiʿ ʿAmr Street, near the railway to Hilwān and northwest of the mosque of ʿAmr ibn al-ʿĀṣ. In 1672, J. Vansleb (1677, p. 131) wrote that "near the Kasr esh Schamma, on the Cairo side, is the domain of the Coptic patriarch, called in Arabic Haret il Batrak; it is separated from this castle by a high rampart by which it is surrounded."

The construction of an enclosure around Dayr Abū Sayfayn was probably undertaken in the course of the twelfth century by a certain Ibn Abū al-Faḍā'il ibn Farūj. Butler (1884, pp. 75–76) remarked that "at the low square doorway of the enclosure one sees, swung back on its hinges, a ponderous door, plated with bands of iron and studded over with flattened bolt-heads. This iron casing stands out six inches from the wooden frame or backing, and fits closely into the doorway. A short dim passage leads by a turn to the left to Al ʿAdra; straight onwards it emerges from a sort of tunnel into a street about eight yards long, on one side of which are high dwelling-houses, on the other the churches of Anba Shanūdah and Abu-s-Sifain."

Thus, the entrance gate of Dayr Abū Sayfayn was down to Butler's time on the west side. Simaykah (1937, p. 75) said that the ring of high ramparts surrounding Dayr Abū Sayfayn had formerly only a single entrance on the west side, noting that "recently a new gate on the south side is used." The door of sycamore wood reinforced by bands of iron was transferred to the Coptic Museum in Old Cairo; in the inventory of the museum it bears the number 688 (ibid., pp. 19–20, 75; see also Coquin, 1974, p. 34).

Between the churches of Saint Mercurius and Saint Shenute one notices an ancient mosque, very confined and today no longer in use. It is probably the mosque of Ibn al-Ḥāmid. Butler, in a sketch of Dayr Abū Sayfayn placed opposite the title page, drew attention to the crescent of the mosque, situated between the two churches, while Jullien, in a view of the *dayr* taken from the south, noted three crescents surmounting three cupolas (see Casanova, 1919, p. 193).

BIBLIOGRAPHY

Butler, A. J. *The Ancient Coptic Churches of Egypt*, Vol. 1. Oxford, 1884.

Casanova, P. *Essai de reconstitution topographique de la ville d'al Foustat ou Misr.* Mémoires publiés par les membres de l'Institut français d'Archéologie orientale 35. Cairo, 1919.

Coquin, C. *Les Edifices chrétiens du Vieux-Caire*, Vol. 1, *Bibliographie et topographie historiques.* Bibliothèque d'études coptes 11. Cairo, 1974.

Jomard, M. "Description de la ville et de la citadelle du Caire." In *Description de l'Egypte moderne*, Vol. 18, pt. 2. Paris, 1829.

Jullien, M. *L'Egypte: Souvenirs bibliques et chrétiens.* Lille, 1891.

Simaykah, M. H. *Guide sommaire du Musée copte et des principales églises du Caire.* Cairo, 1937.

Vansleb, J.-M. *Nouvelle Relation en forme de journal d'un voyage fait en Egypt en 1672 et 1673.* Paris, 1677.

CHARALAMBIA COQUIN

DAYR ABŪ AL-SAYFAYN or Mār Buqṭūr (Qūṣ), the only surviving monastery to the southeast of the town of QŪṢ, from which it is about 7 miles (12 km) distant. It is surrounded by an enclosure wall and contains a Christian cemetery. It is situated some way out of the village of Ḥijāzah. This village, and hence the monastery, is at the starting point of the ancient southern track from Qūṣ to ʿAidhāb on the Red Sea. Starting from Qūṣ, there were two tracks that joined at Laqīṭah, round about a well and some palm trees. One will find the line of this track in Garcin, *Un Centre musulman de la Haute-Egypte médiévale, Quṣ* (1976, pp. 6, 208). In the Middle Ages the trade in spices coming to the West passed by this route. Murray's study points out some "Coptic ruins" (p. 146), which is the site described in *Mémoires sur l'Egypte* (Vol. 3, pp. 232, 273). A little after Laqīṭah is listed a place "dayr Ḥamāmah." Perhaps this is an ancient monastery.

We have no written evidence on this Dayr Abū al-Sayfayn. In addition to a central church dedicated to Saint Mercurius (Abū al-Sayfayn, the "Father of the Two Swords," designates Saint Mercurius), it contains three other churches, one of which is consecrated to Saint Victor, whence the name Dayr Mār Buqṭūr often given to the monastery. The principal church contains an altar dedicated to Saint PACHOMIUS, and ABŪ ṢĀLIḤ at the beginning of the thirteenth century (1895, p. 230) mentions a monastery of Saint Pachomius in the region of Qūṣ. ʿAbd al-Masīḥ Salīb noted it under the name Dayr Mār Buqṭūr and remarks that worship was conducted by the clergy of Qūṣ (1932, p. 179).

Its present state is described by Meinardus (1965, pp. 306–307; 2nd ed., 1977, p. 420).

BIBLIOGRAPHY

ʿAbd al-Masīḥ Ṣalīb al-Masʿūdī al Baramūsī. *Kitāb Tuḥfat al-Saʾilīn fī Dhikr Adyirat Ruhbān al-Miṣriyyīn.* Cairo, 1932.

Garcin, J. C. *Un centre musulman de la Haute Egypte médiévale, Qūṣ.* Textes arabes et études islamiques 6. Cairo, 1976.

Meinardus, O. F. A. *Christian Egypt, Ancient and Modern.* Cairo, 1st ed. 1965; 2nd ed. 1977.

Mémoires sur l'Egypte publiés pendant les campagnes du général Bonaparte, 4 vols. Paris, 1800–1803.

Murray, G. W. "The Roman Roads and Stations in the Eastern Desert." *Journal of Egyptian Archeology* 2 (1925).

RENÉ-GEORGES COQUIN
MAURICE MARTIN, S.J.

DAYR ABŪ AL-SAYFAYN (Ṭamwayh). The village of Ṭamwayh is situated on the left bank of the Nile, 16 miles (25 km) to the south of Cairo. It is rich in Christian artifacts (see Amélineau, 1893, pp. 477–78).

The first mention of the Monastery of Abū al-Sayfayn (Saint MERCURIUS) appears to be that of al-Shābushtī (1939, pp. 20, 27) at the end of the tenth century or beginning of the eleventh.

At the beginning of the thirteenth century ABŪ ṢĀLIḤ (1895, pp. 177, 197–98) gave the same approximate geographical situation as al-Shābushtī, whom he quotes: "opposite Ḥulwān." In reality, this town is to the southeast of Ṭamwayh. He indicated that the church was destroyed by the troops of Caliph al-Saffāḥ, who was pursuing Marwān II in 750, and was restored in the years 1102–1130. Abū Ṣāliḥ adds that in the church is the body of Saint PAPHNŪTIUS, anchorite and superior of this monastery and celebrated on 15 Amshīr, although Abū Ṣāliḥ states that the DAYR AL-SHAM' possessed his relics. In the time of Abū Ṣāliḥ, the monastery was well populated with monks.

This monastery was also mentioned by the Arab geographer Yāqūt in 1200 (1870–1873, Vol. 2, p. 674).

Al-MAQRĪZĪ (1893, Vol. 2, p. 504) reproduced what Yāqūt wrote, in particular about the vocalization of the name Ṭamwayh. In fact, it is written Tammūh, closer to the Coptic system. He also cited al-Shābushtī, who described the monastery as one of the most beautiful places in Egypt. Al-Maqrīzī named Saint George as the patron of the monastery, no doubt confusing it with a church dedicated to this saint and pointed out by Abū Ṣāliḥ (1895, p. 198) as in the district of Ṭamwayh.

The *History of the Patriarchs* (Vol. 3, pt. 3, pp. 179 [text], 318 [trans.]) mentions the restoration of the monastery of Abū al-Sayfayn during the patriarchate of Demetrius II (1862–1870).

Several travelers have mentioned it: Norden (1795–1798, Vol. 2, p. 19, pl. 28); Pococke (1743, pl. 7, plan of greater Cairo), who called it the church of the village of "Abouenemora"; and Brown (1800, p. 258), who called it the monastery of "Abou Nemrus." Abū al-Nimrus is a village to the north of Ṭamwayh (Ramzī, 1954–1968, Vol. 2, pt. 3, p. 3; cf. Amélineau, 1893, under "Ponmonros," pp. 361–62). S. Clarke (1912, p. 205, no. 8) attached it to the bishopric of the Fayyūm and Giza.

The monastery, like many others, became a Christian village (Meinardus, 1965, p. 241; 1977, p. 347).

BIBLIOGRAPHY

Amélineau, E. *La Géographie de l'Égypte à l'époque copte*. Paris, 1893.

Browne, W. G. *Nouveau voyage dans l'Haute-Egypte*. Paris, 1800.

Clarke, S. *Christian Antiquities in the Nile Valley*. Oxford, 1912.

Meinardus, O. *Christian Egypt, Ancient and Modern*. Cairo, 1965; 2nd ed. 1977.

Norden, F. *Voyage d'Egypte et de Nubie*, 3 vols., ed. L. Langlès. Paris, 1795–1798.

Pococke, R. *A Description of the East and Some Other Countries*, Vol. 1. London, 1743.

Ramzī, M. *Al-Qāmūs al-Jughrāfī lil-Bilād al Miṣrīyyah*, 3 vols. Cairo, 1953–1968.

Shābushtī, al-. "Some Egyptian Monasteries," ed. A. S. Atiya. *Bulletin de la Société d'archéologie copte* 5 (1939):1–28.

Yāqūt ibn 'Abd Allāh al-Hamawī. *Kitāb Mu'jam al-Buldān*, 10 vols. Cairo, 1956–1957.

———. *Jacūt's Geographisches Wörterbuch*, 6 vols., ed. F. Wüstenfeld. Leipzig, 1866–1873. Repr. Tehran, 1965, Beirut, 4 vols., 1955–1957.

MAURICE MARTIN, S.J.
RENÉ-GEORGES COQUIN

DAYR ABŪ SHINŪDAH. *See* Monasteries of the Fayyūm.

DAYR AL-ABYAD (Armant). *See* Dayr al-Maṭmar.

DAYR AL-ABYAD (Suhāj). *See* Dayr Anbā Shinūdah (Suhāj).

DAYR AL-'ADAWIYYAH. The ancient authors speak of this *dayr* only as a church. At the beginning of the thirteenth century ABŪ ṢĀLIḤ (1895, pp. 136–37, n. 5) situated al-'Adawiyyah at Minyat al-Sudān, which al-Idrisi places 15 miles (24 km) from Miṣr on the way to Upper Egypt. The village of this name at this place has disappeared.

Abū Ṣāliḥ (p. 137) described a church called al-Martūtī (Syriac for "Our Lady"). The place is said to be that of a temple of the Israelites in Egypt and one of the abodes of the Holy Family in their flight from Herod. Abū Ṣāliḥ, it appears, is the only one to mention al-'Adawiyyah on the itinerary of the FLIGHT INTO EGYPT. This church was restored under Caliph al-Amir (1101-1131).

A certain Jew was baptized in this church during the caliphate of al-Fa'iz, according to Abū Ṣāliḥ. The same historian mentioned the restoration in 1186 of a church adjacent to al-Martūtī. It appears that he confused this al-Martūtī with the church of the same name at Damanhūr Shubrā, to which the body of Saint John of Sanhūt was transported.

Abū Ṣāliḥ gives an account of a monastery of the Nestorians, the church of which was transformed into a mosque in the caliphate of al-Ḥākim. This was probably DAYR AL-NASṬŪR.

Al-MAQRĪZĪ (d. 1441; 1893, Vol. 2, p. 517) mentioned that "the church of Mary in the district of al-'Adawiyyah toward the south is ancient, but already in ruins."

In the seventeenth century people spoke of it as the Monastery of the Holy Virgin at al-'Adawiyyah (National Library, Paris, Arabic MS 319; Troupeau, 1972, Vol. 1, p. 278). Travelers have given accounts of the site (Vansleb, 1671, p. 203; Norden, 1795–1798, Vol. 1, pl. 28).

Sawīrus ibn al-Muqaffaʿ (1970, Vol. 3, pt. 3, pp. 162, 165, 168 [text], 282, 288, 292–293 [trans.]) mentioned under the patriarch JOHN XVI a restoration of the church and the death of the patriarch MARK VII at the church. Under the patriarch DEMETRIUS II (1862–1870) a tower was built in the monastery of ʿAdawiyyah (ibid., pp. 179 [text], 318 [trans.]).

Several manuscripts of the Coptic Patriarchate were written for the church of ʿAdawiyyah or even at ʿAdawiyyah, in the eighteenth century (Simaykah and ʿAbd al-Masīh, 1942, Vol. 2, pt. 1, nos. 73, 341, 825, 832).

BIBLIOGRAPHY

Amélineau, E. *La Géographie de l'Egypte à l'époque copte.* Paris, 1893.

Nordon, F. S. *Voyage d'Egypte et de Nubie,* 3 vols. ed. L. Langlès. Paris, 1795–1798.

Troupeau, G. *Catalogue des manuscrits arabes,* Vol. 1. Paris, 1972.

Vansleb, J. M. *Relazione dello stato presente dell'Egitto.* Paris, 1671.

RENÉ-GEORGES COQUIN
MAURICE MARTIN, S.J.

DAYR AL-ʿADHRĀʾ (Akhmīm), one of a group of three small monasteries near the village of al-Hawāwīsh, to the northeast of AKHMĪM on the edge of the desert. This village is situated about 3 miles (5 km) from Akhmīm. About a mile from the village is the Monastery of the Martyrs (DAYR AL-SHUHADĀ). Dayr al-ʿAdhrā' is to be found about half a mile to the south of this monastery. It is not known to ancient writers or travelers. A description is given by Meinardus (1965, pp. 297–98; 1977, pp. 409–410).

The enclosure wall has semicircular buttresses on its eastern and western sides. The church is built by the south and east walls. North and west of the church are a number of monastic buildings, including quarters for monks and visitors, as well as work and storage areas. The church is a late-medieval hall church (*Hallenkirche*) with columns. Rectangular corner chambers flank three sanctuaries. The western part of the church is five bays wide and two bays deep. The bays are divided by columns and are domed. The dome over the bay in front of the central sanctuary rests on squinches; the others

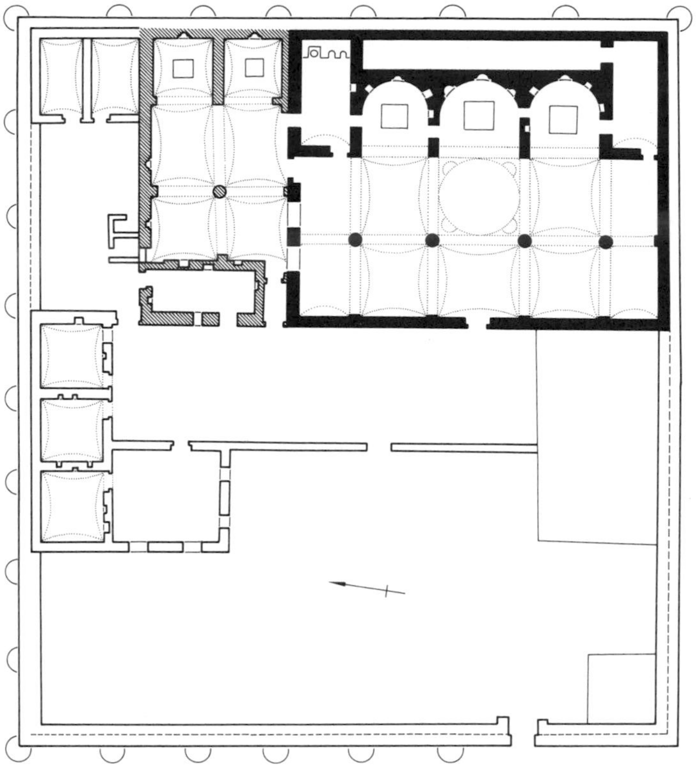

Plan of Dayr Al-ʿAdhrā' near Akhmim. *Courtesy Peter Grossmann.*

rest on pendentives. Additional chapels have been added to the north side. The church belongs to a local group marked by two peculiarities. One is that the deep sanctuaries have straight sides leading to semicircular ends. Other examples with this feature are the two churches of ABŪ SAYFAYN, and Sitt Dimyānah in the town of Akhmīm (probably dating to the sixteenth century), as well as the church of DAYR MĀR JIRJIS AL-ḤADĪDĪ. The second peculiarity is the construction of vaulted corridors behind the sanctuaries, also found at DAYR AL-MALĀK MĪKHĀ'ĪL, Sitt Dimyānah, and Dayr Mār Jirjis al-Ḥadīdī. All the original sanctuaries have five niches. The central sanctuary screen is badly inlaid. The side ones are painted. The church was restored in 1980, and fresh plaster and whitewash obscure construction details. Before repainting, the brickwork was apparently painted in red-and-black patterns (Clarke, 1912, fig. 31), a type of decoration found also at the above-mentioned churches in and around Akhmīm.

BIBLIOGRAPHY

Clarke, S. *Christian Antiquities in the Nile Valley,* pp. 144–45, pl. 42, no. 2. Oxford, 1912.

Grossmann, P. *Mittelalterliche Langhauskuppelkir-*

chen und verwandte Typen in Oberägypten, p. 196 et passim. Glückstadt, 1982.
Meinardus, O. F. A. *Christian Egypt, Ancient and Modern*. Cairo, 1965; 2nd ed., 1977.
Timm, S. *Das christlich-koptische Ägypten in arabischer Zeit*, Vol. 2, pp. 636–37. Wiesbaden, 1984.

SHELA MCNALLY

DAYR AL-ʿADHRĀʾ (Asyūṭ). Maps mention a Dayr al-ʿAdhrāʾ (Monastery of the Virgin) at Banī Riḍah in the outskirts northeast of Abnūb (right bank, to the north of Asyūṭ).

ABŪ ṢĀLIḤ does not speak of it. Al-MAQRĪZĪ (1853, Vol. 2, p. 517) indicates only a "church of Mary in the district of al-Khuṣūṣ." Vansleb (1677, p. 361; 1678, p. 217) gave an account of the Monastery of the Holy Virgin at Abnūb.

Today this is a completely modern church in the middle of a Christian quarter (Meinardus, 1965, pp. 279–80; 1977, p. 388).

BIBLIOGRAPHY

Meinardus, O. *Christian Egypt, Ancient and Modern*. Cairo, 1965; 2nd ed., 1977.
Vansleb, J. M. *Nouvelle Relation en forme de journal d'un voyage fait en Egypte en 1672 et 1673*. Paris, 1677. Translated as *The Present State of Egypt*. London, 1678.

RENÉ-GEORGES COQUIN
MAURICE MARTIN, S.J.

DAYR AL-ʿADHRĀʾ (near Bayaḍ al-Naṣārā), monastery of uncertain origin, first described by G. Wilkinson (1843, Vol. 2, p. 19). The monastery is not mentioned by the ancient authors, and neither J. Vansleb nor C. Sicard spoke of it, although they must have crossed the Nile from Banī Suef and landed not far from Bayaḍ al-Naṣārā to go to the Monastery of Saint Antony on the Red Sea.

Wilkinson (1843, Vol. 2, p. 19) is the first to speak of a *dayr* at this place; Clarke (1912, p. 206, no. 6) mentioned only a church dedicated to the Holy Virgin, and not a *dayr* (monastery). The present church dates only from 1963 (Meinardus, 1965, p. 254; 1977, p. 357); it contains some ancient elements, including a Greek inscription engraved on a granite column above the baptistery (Van Rengen and Wagner, 1984, pp. 348–53). These elements probably came from an excavated ancient *kom* adjacent to the church.

This monastery is the object of pilgrimages by the Copts of the region (Viaud, 1979, p. 44).

BIBLIOGRAPHY

Clarke, S. *Christian Antiquities in the Nile Valley*. London, 1912.
Meinardus, O. *Christian Egypt, Ancient and Modern*. Cairo, 1965; 2nd ed., 1977.
Van Rengen, W., and G. Wagner. "Une Dédicace à Valerius Titinianus, fils du préfet des vigiles Valerius Titanianus." *Chronique d'Egypte* (Brussels) 59, fasc. 118 (1984):348–53.
Viaud, G., after the notes of Jacob Muyser. *Les Pèlerinages coptes en Egypte*. Cairo, 1979.
Wilkinson, G. *Modern Egypt and Thebes: A Description of Egypt*, 2 vols. London, 1843. Repr. Wiesbaden, 1981.

RENÉ-GEORGES COQUIN
MAURICE MARTIN, S. J.

DAYR AL-ʿADHRĀʾ (near Bilbays). *See* Dayr Mart Maryam.

DAYR AL-ʿADHRĀʾ (Fayyūm). ABŪ ṢĀLIḤ THE ARMENIAN (fol. 73a; 1895, p. 209) placed in the neighborhood of Saylah, to the west of the Fayyūm, a monastery bearing the name of the Virgin and equipped with a tower of refuge that had been restored. He is the only author who mentions a monastery in the region other than the DAYR AL-IKHWAH. Al-Nābulsī (1899) indicates only a single monastery to the south of the town of Siyalah.

N. Abbott (1937, p. 57, n. 150) hypothesized that this Dayr al-ʿAdhrāʾ (Monastery of the Virgin) was "in all probability a Theotokos duplicate of the monastery of the Brothers at Siyalah [Dayr al-Ikhwah]," as was the case at SCETIS in the first half of the sixth century. In fact, besides the original monasteries of al-Barāmūs, JOHN COLOBUS, and Bishoi, three other monasteries were mentioned: "the Virgin of Baramus," "the Virgin of John Colobus," and "the Virgin of Bishoy."

EVELYN-WHITE (1932, pp. 232–35) thought that these duplicate monasteries were founded by Severian monks driven from their monasteries by Julianists, who dedicated their new monasteries to the THEOTOKOS to affirm the reality of the Incarnation. Evelyn-White's hypothesis seems to be derived from historical facts, but that of Abbott seems gratuitous, since the monastery at Siyalah dedicated to the Virgin was not called that of "the Virgin of the Brothers."

BIBLIOGRAPHY

Abbott, N. *The Monasteries of the Fayyūm.* Studies in Ancient Oriental Civilization 16. Chicago, 1937.

Abū ʿUtmān ibn Ibrahim al-Nābulsī. *Tarʾikh al-Fayyūm wa bilādihi,* ed. B. Moritz. Cairo, 1899.

Evelyn-White, H. G. *The Monasteries of the Wadi'n Natrūn,* Pt. 2, *The History of the Monasteries of Nitria and Scetis.* New York, 1932.

Salmon, G. "Répertoire géographique de la province du Fayyoum d'après le Kitāb Tārikh al-Fayyoūm d'an-Nāboulsi." *Bulletin de l'Institut français d'archéologie orientale* 1 (1901):29–77.

RENÉ-GEORGES COQUIN

DAYR AL-ʿADHRĀʾ, also called Dayr al-Bakarah, monastery located near Jabal al-Ṭayr, a modern village on the east bank of the Nile in the domain of an old monastery that was inhabited by monks down to the end of the nineteenth century. The church belonging to it was accommodated in a rock tomb evidently deriving from the late imperial period. Of this tomb there survived a peristyle, which is still surrounded today on three sides by columns hewn out of the rock. These later served as the naos of the church, with a richly decorated western entrance in the axis of the southern portico and an additional anteroom on the south side. Substantially less regular are the rooms on the east, which, at the time of its conversion into a church, were probably first wrought out of the rock in their present form. It is significant that in the middle of the altar area there is a hollow space leading deeper. This rebuilding can hardly have taken place before the seventh century. The upper interior structures belong to modern times, including the galleries and a spatial reorganization in the sanctuary. At this time a couple of additional pillars were set up in front of the altar area. The staircase approach from above in the southeast corner, described by earlier visitors (Noroff, 1840, and Curzon, 1881), is no longer in existence.

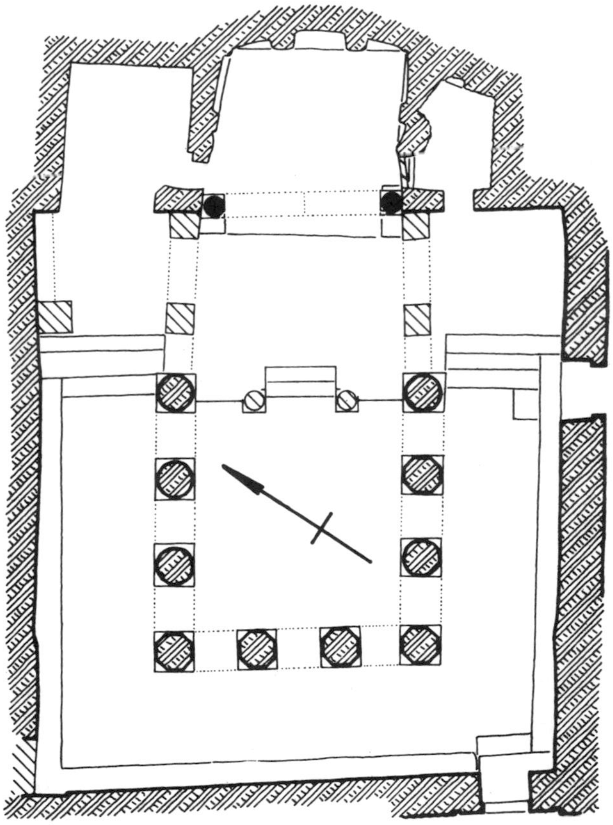

Plan of the church, with columns and rooms hewn out of the rock, which was converted from a tomb. *Courtesy Peter Grossmann.*

BIBLIOGRAPHY

Butler, A. J. *The Ancient Coptic Churches of Egypt,* Vol. 1, pp. 348–51. Oxford, 1884. Repr. 1970.

Curzon, R. *Visits to Monasteries in the Levant,* pp. 114–22. London, 1881.

Noroff, A. *Voyage en Egypte et en Nubie en 1834–1835,* Vol. 2. Petersburg, 1840. French trans. by O. V. Volkoff, *Le Monde copte* 11 (1985):42–44.

PETER GROSSMANN

DAYR AL-ʿADHRĀʾ (Qifṭ). *See* Monasteries of the Upper Ṣaʿīd.

DAYR AL-ʿADHRĀʾ (Samālūṭ). This Monastery of the Virgin is also called Dayr al-Bakarah (Monastery of the Pulley) or Dayr Jabal al-Ṭayr (Monastery of the Mountain of the Bird), from the name of the mountain that dominates the Nile at that point and on which the monastery is perched opposite Samālūṭ, on the right bank of the river. The first name derives from the fact that provisions and visitors were hoisted by means of a pulley across a crevasse that runs the height of the cliff. At the end of the tenth or beginning of the eleventh century al-Shābūshtī (pp. 23, 28) noted this monastery for its picturesque character and reported the legend of the birds that came in a group on the day of the monastery's festival. They remained there until one of them caught its beak in the crevasse and could not pull it out. In the list of the places through which the Holy Family passed, the *History of the Patriarchs* (1959, Vol. 2, pt. 3, pp. 227 [text], 361 [trans.]) mentioned the Jabal al-Kaff.

At the beginning of the thirteenth century ABŪ ṢĀLIḤ (1895, pp. 217–19) gave it the name Jabal al-Kaff (Mountain of the Palm) because, according to legend, at the time of the FLIGHT INTO EGYPT, the mountain prostrated itself before Jesus, and when he raised it up, his palm remained graven in the rock. He also indicated that the church is hollowed into the mountain, but that there are two churches, an upper and a lower. He adds that the Frankish Crusaders in 1168 carried off the part of the rock on which the palm of Jesus was engraved and took it away to Syria. The monastery and its church were dedicated to the Holy Virgin.

Al-MAQRĪZĪ (d. 1441), indicating that access to the monastery could also be gained from the north by a staircase hollowed into the rock, contented himself with quoting al-Shābūshtī and the legend of the birds (1853, Vol. 2, pp. 503–504).

In 1597 a monk-priest of the monastery named Gabriel was one of the delegation sent by the patriarch GABRIEL VIII (1586–1601) to Pope Clement VIII to present the Act of Union between the Coptic and Roman churches (Buri, 1931; Graf, 1951, Vol. 4, pp. 120–22; see also DAYR AL-MUḤARRAQ, near ASYŪṬ).

The site is noted by all the travelers because it was picturesque (Vansleb, 1677, p. 357; 1678, pp. 214–15; Lucas, 1719, Vol. 2, pp. 158–60). Unfortunately this monastery has had little attention from archaeologists. The plan of the church was drawn up by Curzon (1849, pp. 121–28); it was reproduced by A. G. Butler (1884, pp. 348–50), U. Monneret de Villard (1925, Vol. 1, no. 105), and A. Badawy (1947, pp. 372–73). This plan appears seriously deficient; for example, it ignores the richly decorated west door, which could go back to the fifth or sixth century, according to E. Pauty (1942, pp. 87–88).

The apse of the church, hewn into the rock, recalls the rock churches of the region of Antinoë (ANTINOOPOLIS). It may have been originally fitted up in a quarry, across which the vault was later thrown, which would explain Abū Ṣāliḥ's remark about the upper and lower churches. The traces of the ancient buildings and the way of access from the north indicated by al-Maqrīzī, marked by numerous pilgrim crosses carved in the rock, have also not been examined. C. Butler (Palladius, 1898–1904, Vol. 1, p. 222) places here the community of Pithirion, but this is not very likely, for the Jabal al-Ṭayr is too far to the south and close to Achoris (TIHNĀH AL-JABAL).

Doresse (1970, p. 13) situates here the memorial of the monk Abū Fīs, whose name the town of Minyā formerly bore (Minia Abū Fis). A church there was dedicated to this saint (Abū Ṣāliḥ, 1895, pp. 223–24). The present state of the monastery is given by O. Meinardus (1965, pp. 362–64; 1977, pp. 258–59).

BIBLIOGRAPHY

Badawy, A. *Les Premières églises d'Egypte jusqu'au siècle de St. Cyrille,* in *Kyrilliana,* pp. 321–80. Cairo, 1947.

Buri, V. "L'unione della chiesa copta con Roma sotto Clemente VIII." Orientalia Christiana 23, 2, no. 72 (1931):101–264.

Butler, A. G. *The Ancient Coptic Churches of Egypt,* 2 vols. Oxford, 1884.

Curzon, R. *Visit to Monasteries in the Levant.* New York, 1849. London, 1865.

Doresse, J. "Monastères coptes de moyenne Egypte." *Bulletin de la Société française d'égyptologie* 59 (1970):7–29.

Lucas, Paul. *Troisième Voyage du Sieur Paul Lucas fait en MDCCXIV par ordre de Louis XIV dans la Turquie, l'Asie, la Sourie, la Palestine, la haute et basse Egypte,* Vol. 3. Rouen, 1719.

Maspero, J., and G. Wiet. "Matériaux pour servir à la géographie d'Egypte." *Mémoires de l'Institut française d'Archéologie orientale* 36 (1919): passim.

Meinardus, O. *Christian Egypt, Ancient and Modern.* Cairo, 1965; 2nd ed., 1977.

Monneret de Villard, U. *Les Couvents près de Sohāg,* Vol. 1. Milan, 1925.

Pauty, E. "Chronique." *Bulletin de la Société d'archéologie copte* 7 (1941):87–88.

Shābūshtī, al-. "Some Egyptian Monasteries," ed. A. S. Atiya. *Bulletin de la Société d'archéologie copte* 5 (1939):1–28.

Vansleb, J. M. *Nouvelle Relation en forme de journal d'un voyage fait en Egypte en 1672 et 1673.* Paris, 1677. Translated as *The Present State of Egypt.* London, 1678.

RENÉ-GEORGES COQUIN
MAURICE MARTIN, S.J.

DAYR AL-AḤMAR (Giza). This monastery was mentioned in the beginning of the thirteenth century by ABŪ ṢĀLIḤ THE ARMENIAN (1895, p. 177), who spoke of a church dedicated to Saint Michael called Dayr al-Aḥmar (Red Monastery). He added that it was on the edge of the Nile and that it contained a church dedicated to Saints COSMAS AND DAMIAN. He situated this church at Ṭamūh. It is probably the same church, given the rarity of the dedication. It was restored at a period earlier than Abū Ṣāliḥ. The author clearly distinguished it from the great synagogue of the Jews, which was also situated at Ṭamūh.

Al-MAQRĪZĪ (1853, Vol. 2, p. 504) spoke of the monastery of Saints Cosmas and Damian at Ṭamūh and equally of the synagogue of the Jews at the same place.

Unfortunately, the village of Ṭamūh no longer exists. There is, though, a church of Saints Cosmas and Damian in the region, at Manyal Shīḥah (Clarke, 1912, p. 205, no. 6). This Dayr al-Aḥmar then was at Manyal Shīḥah. This identification was proposed by J. Muyser (1952, p. 179, n. 15). Ramzī advanced the same hypothesis (1953–1968, Vol. 2, pt. 3, pp. 20–21).

BIBLIOGRAPHY

Clarke, S. *Christian Antiquities in the Nile Valley.* London, 1912.

Muyser, J. "Un 'Psali' copte pour la première heure du Samedi de la joie." *Le Muséon* 65 (1952):175–84.

Ramzī, M. *Al-Qāmūs al-Jughrāfī lil-Bilād al Miṣriyyah,* 3 vols. Cairo, 1953–1968.

RENÉ-GEORGES COQUIN
MAURICE MARTIN, S.J.

DAYR AL-AḤMAR (Suhāj). *See* Dayr Anbā Bishoi (Suhāj).

DAYR AL-ʿAJAMIYYIN (Fayyūm). *See* Monasteries of the Fayyūm.

DAYR AL-AMĪR TADRŪS (Cairo). *See* Babylon.

DAYR AL-AMĪR TADRŪS (Jabal Abū Fūdah). This small monastery is placed almost in the middle of the Abū Fūdah massif and at the same latitude as the town of Banī Shiqīr, situated on the left bank of the Nile. It is built on the terrace of an ancient hypogeum that has been transformed into a church. Other tombs, today vanished, had been fitted up as cells by hermits. It has been described by G. LEGRAIN (1900, p. 12) and G. MASPERO (1914, pp. 19–28). The latter wrongly called it Dayr al-Bakarah (Monastery of the Pulley), which would be more appropriate for DAYR MĀR MĪNĀ, which is 3 miles (5 km) farther south. S. Clarke, in his list of churches (1912, p. 209, no. 4), designates it as dependent on the town of Banī Shiqīr.

BIBLIOGRAPHY

Clarke, S. *Christian Antiquities in the Nile Valley.* Oxford, 1912.

Legrain, G. "Notes archéologiques prises au gebel Abū Fūda." *Annales du Service des antiquités de l'Egypte* 1 (1900):2–14.

Maspero, G. *Ruines et paysages d'Egypte.* Paris, 1914.

RENÉ-GEORGES COQUIN
MAURICE MARTIN, S.J.

DAYR AL-AMĪR TADRŪS (Luxor). This small monastery is situated on the stony part of the left bank of the Nile, opposite the town of Luxor, at the foot of the Libyan Mountains about 550 yards (500 m) from Madīnat Hābū. It perhaps occupies the site, famous in the Middle Ages, of a church dedicated to the same saint, Theodore (Winlock and Crum, 1926, Vol. 1, pp. 5, 177).

However that may be, the present buildings are modern. The oldest witness appears to be Lepsius (1852, p. 259) who spoke of it at some length but called it that of Saint Donadeus. It was also mentioned by S. Clarke (1912, p. 216, no. 6), who also gave the plan of the church (p. 116, pl. 34, frankly incomplete).

The church and the neighboring cemetery for a long time served the Christians of the region. It was to the priest who ministered to this church that the manuscript of the Synaxarion from Upper Egypt belonged (Coquin, 1978).

Meinardus (1965, p. 319; 1977, p. 433) gave a good description of its modern state. About 1980 some nuns attempted to revive the monastic life there.

BIBLIOGRAPHY

Clarke, S. *Christian Antiquities in the Nile Valley.* Oxford, 1912.

Coquin, R.-G. "Le Synaxaire des Coptes: Un Nouveau témoin de la recension de Haute-Egypte." *Analecta Bollandiana* 96 (1978):351–65.

Lepsius, R. *Letters from Egypt . . . 1844–45*. London, 1852.
Winlock, H. E., and W. E. Crum. *The Monastery of Epiphanius at Thebes*, 2 vols. New York, 1926.

RENÉ-GEORGES COQUIN
MAURICE MARTIN, S.J.

DAYR AL-AMĪR TADRŪS (Munā al-Amīr). This monastery bears a portion of the Arabic name of THEODORUS OF SHOTEP, al-Amīr Tadrūs al-Shuṭbī. After Theodorus' martyrdom by fire, his remains were saved at great expense by a rich Christian woman, who transported them to Egypt after the Edict of Milan in 312 and buried them in a spot where a church was later built and where in the fourth century Dayr al-Amīr Tadrūs was founded at Munā al-Amīr around that church.

Situated on the west bank of the Nile, opposite Maʿādī and Maʿṣarat Ḥulwān, this ancient monastery lies in the neighborhood of the modern district of al-Ḥawamdiyyah, adjacent to the village of Mūnā al-Amīr.

The area of the monastery is especially fitted for monastic life with its salubrious atmosphere, as well as with the agricultural produce of its arable soil. In reality, a number of other monasteries are known to have emerged in that area on both banks of the Nile. Within a short distance on the west bank to the north arose DAYR APA JEREMIAH at Saqqara. Nearby, DAYR ABŪ SAYFAYN was founded at another early date, but both seem to have started dwindling in the fourteenth century. On the east bank at a much later date, the laura of Saint BARSŪM THE NAKED (al-ʿIryān) came into existence.

It is interesting that Pope CYRIL V (1874–1927) selected the site of Dayr al-Amīr Tadrūs for occasional retirement and established there his summer resort. He was probably attracted to the area not only by its proximity to the patriarchal seat in Cairo but also by the very survival of the church where such sacred remains were buried.

Originally the monastery occupied an extensive tract surrounded by a massive stone wall. With the gradual encroachment of farmers on its arable soil, the wall disappeared. The archaeological remains have shrunk to mere fractions of the ancient structures, which include, besides the traces of monastic cells, the great church at which Pope Cyril built his summer resort and which became a place of pilgrimage for pious Copts of that region.

The church entrance is reached by descending a few steps to about a yard below the actual ground level. Apparently as the silt accumulated through the centuries, it raised the ground level around the church. Inside its sanctuary, the church contains three altars inlaid with mother-of-pearl and embellished by icons of different periods. The ICONOSTASIS is made of artistic arabesque woodwork. Within the sanctuary are the remains of three martyrs, of whom the youngest, Saint Cyriacus, was three years old. The other two famous saints are Saint MERCURIUS (Abū Sayfayn) and Saint THEODORUS (al-Amīr Tadrūs), whose feast day is 20 Abīb. However, the sanctification of the church itself is celebrated on 20 Hātūr. According to al-Makārim, the church was restored by Abū al-Yumn ibn al-Bazzāz, most probably in the course of the twelfth century.

Other visible remains to the west of the church comprise the cemetery where bishops and monks were buried. To the east of the church is the modern patriarchal summer residence and an ancient well used by the monks in bygone days when the Nile ran low. An inner stone wall, approximately 4 yards high, surrounds these structures.

During the Middle Ages, the eparchy of Munā al-Amīr comprised the adjacent towns north of Memphis to Giza, together with Maʿādī and Ṭurah east of the river. This eparchy is known to have existed for three centuries, until the sixteenth century, when it was incorporated into the more recent eparchy of Awsīm, whose seat was consequently moved to the city of Giza, where it has remained to the present day. Evidently all this may be considered an offshoot of the much older Memphytic eparchy of ancient times.

BIBLIOGRAPHY

Abū al-Makārim, Saʿd-Allāh ibn Jirjis ibn Masʿūd. *Tārīkh al-Kanā'is wa-al-Adyirah*, 5 vols., ed. Samūʾīl al-Suryānī. Cairo, 1984.
Mājid al-Quss Tādrus. "Dayr al-Amīr Tadrūs al-Shuṭbī." *Majallat Madāris al-Aḥad* nos. 3–4 (1986):50–52.

AZIZ S. ATIYA

DAYR ANBĀ ABSHĀY (Abū Tīj). The monastery appears to have left no trace, and its existence is known only from literary sources. At the end of the eleventh century the HISTORY OF THE PATRIARCHS (Vol. 2, pt. 3, p. 228 [text], p. 362 [transl.]) mentions to the south of Abū Tīj the bodies of the holy martyrs Abū Bīshah and Bīsah "in coffins in their church."

ABŪ ṢĀLIḤ THE ARMENIAN seems to have borrowed

this phrase from the *History of the Patriarchs,* for he mentioned the same saints in the same location and alluded to the coffins containing the relics (1895, fol. 91a [text]; p. 253 [trans.] is wrong: he thought the reference was to PACHOMIUS and SHENUTE).

A manuscript of the Arabic SYNAXARION of the Copts deriving from DAYR AL-MUḤARRAQ copies a manuscript dating from 1770 (National Library, Paris, Arabe 4780; cf. Troupeau, 1974, Vol. 2, p. 30) and mentions these two martyrs at 26 Ba'ūnah, without specifying the place. According to the encomium of Moses, bishop of Qāw (Antaeopolis; it is thus that we should read the printed text), the martyrs Abshāy and Peter, his companion, were venerated in their *dayr* in the land of their origin (Būhā) opposite Qāw, but on the left bank of the Nile. See the Arabic version of this encomium, published several times (Sirat, 1976, p. 70).

The Ethiopian Synaxarion indicates the martyrdom of these two saints at 5 Sané (Ba'ūnah) and mentions the church at Būhā (Guidi, p. 557). The Arabic Synaxarion of ʿAbd al-Masīh Mīkhā'īl and Armānyūs Ḥabashī Shaṭā al-Birmāwī (1935–1936) puts the martyrdom of the saints at 5 Ba'ūnah and indicates that their bones are at Ṣidfā, a town near Būhā. Muyser (1944, p. 176, n. 1) indicates the location of Būhā, but seems to think that the village is still in existence.

BIBLIOGRAPHY

Guidi, I., ed. *Le Synaxaire éthiopien.* PO 1, pt. 5. Paris, 1905.

Moses, Bishop of Qaw. *Sirat al Anbā Abshai wa al-Anbā Butrus.* Cairo, 1976.

Muyser, J. "Ermite pérégrinant et pélerin infatigable." *Bulletin de la Société d'Archéologie copte* 9 (1944):159–236.

Troupeau, G. *Catalogue des manuscrits arabes.* Paris, 1972–1985.

Vansleb, J. M. *Nouvelle Relation en forme de journal d'un voyage fait en Egypte en 1672 et 1673.* Paris, 1677. Translated as *The Present State of Egypt.* London, 1678.

RENÉ-GEORGES COQUIN
MAURICE MARTIN, S. J.

DAYR ANBĀ ABSHĀY, monastery that still exists on the right bank of the Nile at the edge of the desert less than half a mile east of the town of al-Ṭūd. A church was discovered in the course of archaeological excavations in the Ptolemaic temple (Vercoutter, 1952, pp. 83–84; Drioton, 1937).

The present monastery is of late construction, but one may conjecture that it occupies the site of a more ancient monastery, mentioned "to the east" of (al-) Ṭūd in the sixth and seventh centuries by the Sahidic recension of the Coptic SYNAXARION. The neighboring cemetery has been the object of excavations (Maspero, 1884, p. 185; 1886, p. 71). These excavations have revealed bodies, perhaps that of Bishop Pisentius, and vestments (Vercoutter, 1947, pp. 217ff.). The site was noted by J. Doresse (1949, p. 342), and O. Meinardus also mentioned it (1965, p. 322; 1977, pp. 436–37), but these two authors think that the church has been shifted from the temple of al-Ṭūd to its present site.

The summary of the life of Saint Abshay (in Coptic no doubt Pshoi) is preserved in the Sahidic recension of the Coptic Synaxarion at 25 Kiyahk. This saint was surnamed al-Qabrīn or al-Qubrayn, the meaning of which is not clear. He died at "the ford" or "the crossroads" or "the watering place" of Ṭūd (the Arabic word can have these three meanings).

BIBLIOGRAPHY

Doresse, J. "Monastères coptes aux environs d'Armant en Thébaïde." *Analecta Bollandiana* 67 (1949):327–49.

Drioton, E. "La Découverte d'un trésor en Haute-Egypte." *Revue des conférences françaises en Orient* (1937):2.

Maspero, G. "Trois Années de fouilles dans les tombeaux de Thèbes et de Memphis." In *Mémoires de la Mission archéologique française du Caire,* Vol. 1, pp. 133–242. Paris, 1884.

______. "Premier rapport à l'Institut d'Egypte sur les fouilles exécutées en Egypte de 1881 à 1885." *Bulletin de l'Institut d'Egypte* 6 (1885):3–91.

______. *Etudes de mythologie et d'archéologie égyptiennes,* 4 vols. Paris, 1893–1900.

Meinardus, O. *Christian Egypt, Ancient and Modern.* Cairo, 1965; 2nd ed., 1977.

Vercoutter, J. "Tôd, 1946–1949: Rapport succinct des fouilles." *Bulletin de l'Institut français d'Archéologie orientale* 50 (1952):69–87.

______. "Le Deir copte de Tôd et les remplois de Thoutmosis III." *Annales du Service des antiquités de l'Egypte* 47 (1947):217–22.

Winlock, H. E., and W. E. Crum. *The Monastery of Epiphanius at Thebes,* 2 vols. New York, 1926.

RENÉ-GEORGES COQUIN
MAURICE MARTIN, S.J.

DAYR ANBĀ ANṬŪNIYŪS. [*This entry consists of several parts. They are the history and chronology of the monastery; the layout of the monastery* *and a brief description of the major church of Saint Antony; a description of the wall paintings; and a description of the area in which the monastery is located. Each section uses a variety of recent as well as early sources.*]

History

The Monastery of Saint Antony is situated 30 miles (45 km) southwest of the Red Sea lighthouse of Rās Za'farānah (100 miles, or 290 km, from Cairo via Suez) at the foot of the south end of the Jalālah mountain range.

After the death of Saint ANTONY, a monastic settlement was established in the reign of JULIAN THE APOSTATE (361–363), which included merely the most necessary buildings—a church, cells, a kitchen, and a bakehouse. During the fifth century the monastery served as a place of refuge for some monks of the Wādī al-Naṭrūn monasteries, which were sacked several times. In the seventh and eighth centuries the monastery was occupied by Melchite monks. Saint John the Almoner, Melchite patriarch of Alexandria from 609 to 620, supplied a certain Anastasius, HEGUMENOS of the monastery, with large sums of money and ordered him to redeem the captives taken by the Persians. Around 790, Coptic monks removed the relics of Saint JOHN COLOBOS (the Short) from the monastery and transferred them to Wādī al-Naṭrūn. In the eleventh century the survivors of the army of Naṣr al-Dawlah pillaged the Monastery of Saint Antony and killed many of the monks. During the patriarchate of JOHN VI (1189–1216) the monastery was inhabited by Coptic monks and supplied candidates for the Ethiopian office of *abūna*. In the thirteenth century the monastery was surrounded by a fortified wall. A large garden contained palm trees, apple and pear trees, beds of vegetables, and three springs of perpetually flowing water. Major repairs and renovations were executed during the twelfth and thirteenth centuries. In the fourteenth and fifteenth centuries the monastery was visited by Ogier VIII (1395), Ghillebert de Lannoy (1429), and Dettlof Heinkel (1436). At the Council of Florence (1438–1445), John, the *hegumenos* of the Monastery of Saint Antony, represented the Coptic church. In the latter part of the fifteenth century the monastery and its library were destroyed by bedouins who lived in the monastery as servants. During the first half of the sixteenth century, Patriarch GABRIEL VII sent twenty monks of the Syrian monastery of the Wādī al-Naṭrūn to the Monastery of Saint Antony to assist in the rebuilding.

After the restoration, an Ethiopian community lived for some time together with Egyptian monks at the monastery. Pilgrims and travelers of the sixteenth and seventeenth centuries included Dom Franciscus (1520), Cassian (1617), Bernadus (1626), Coppin (1638), Monceaux and Laisné (1667–1675), J. M. VANSLEB (1672), and de Maillet (1692). In the seventeenth century the monastery was used by the Capuchin fathers as a language school for the preparation of their missionaries.

Eighteenth-century travelers provided much information. For example, P. Lucas (1714) was sent by Louis XIV for study purposes; an anonymous traveler (1716) sketched the monastery; and C. Sicard and J. S. Assemani (1716) secured volumes for the Vatican Library. Granger (1730) noticed and recorded twenty-five monks in the monastery, and Sarqis (1765) scratched his name in Armenian on the north wall of the Church of the Holy Virgin.

In the latter part of the eighteenth century, the monastery underwent major restorations. In 1766 the Church of Saint Mark was rebuilt and in 1783 IBRAHĪM AL-JAWHARĪ renovated the walls.

Nineteenth-century travelers were H. Tattam (1893), who examined the library, and Archimandrite Porfirij Uspenskij (1850), who worked for the union of the Russian and the Coptic churches. In 1859 Callinicus, the Greek Orthodox patriarch of Alexandria, visited the monastery. G. Chester (1873), G. Schweinfurth (1877), and M. Jullien (1883) added considerably to our knowledge by their descriptions and observations.

The leadership of the Monastery of Saint Antony was especially notable during the seventeenth, eighteenth, and nineteenth centuries. Twelve Antonian monks ascended the patriarchal throne, and for almost 300 years they determined the history of the Coptic church.

The Church of Saint Antony and the old south wall belong to the few remains dating to the period prior to the rebuilding of the monastery in the sixteenth century. The wall paintings in the sanctuary, the nave, the narthex, and the chapel fall into the period of the restoration of the church by the sons of Ghālib in 1232. This church is used during the winter. From April to October, the liturgy is celebrated in the Church of the Apostles, east of the Church of Saint Antony. This church has three altars, dedicated to Saint George, the Apostles, and Saint Dimyānah. For fifteen days during Lent, the liturgy is celebrated in the Church of Saint Mark, which was used by the Catholic missionaries during the seventeenth century. The Church of the Holy Virgin is used only during the fifteen days prior to the Feast of the Assumption of the Virgin. The Chapel of Saint Michael is located on the top floor of the keep. In addition to these five churches, there are two churches named after Saint Paul the Theban, both of which are under construction. The library contains three collections of manuscripts and printed books. The spring of Saint Antony supplies the community with water. The walls enclose an area of 18 feddans (about 17 acres), of which 10 feddans belong to the garden.

BIBLIOGRAPHY

Chester, G. "Notes on the Coptic Dayrs of the Wady Natroun and on the Dayr Antonios in the Eastern desert." *Archaeological Journal* 30 (1873):105–116.

Cogordan, G. *Relations du voyage fait au couvent de Saint-Antoine au mois de Novembre de l'an mille neuf cent un.* Paris, 1903.

Coppin, J. *Relations des voyage faits dans la Turquie, la Thébaïde, et la Barbarie,* p. 307. Lyons, 1720.

Daumas, F., and F. Jomier. "Deir Antonios." *Bulletin de la Société historique et géographique de l'Isthme de Suez* 6 (1960).

Doresse, H. "Les Monastères de saint Antoine et de saint Paul." *Comptes rendus de l'Académie des inscriptions et belles-lettres* (1951):268ff.

Elias, R. "Le Couvent St. Antoine." *Collège de la Sainte Famille* 48 (1963):21ff.

Fedden, H. R. "A Study of the Monastery of St. Anthony in the Eastern Desert." *University of Egypt, Faculty of Arts Bulletin* 5 (1937):1–60.

Johann Georg, Duke of Saxony. *Neue Streifzüge durch die Kirchen und Klöster Ägyptens,* pp. 32–43. Berlin, 1930.

Leroy, J. *Moines et monastères du Proche Orient.* Paris, 1957.

Lewis, A. S. "Hidden Egypt." *Century Magazine* 68 (1904):745–58.

Lucas, P. *Voyage du Sieur Paul Lucas fait en 1714,* Vol. 3, p. 149. Rouen, 1744.

Meinardus, O. *Monks and Monasteries of the Egyptian Deserts,* pp. 31–88. Cairo, 1960.

______. "The Collection of Coptica in the Qaṣr of the Monastery of St. Antony." *Bulletin de la Société d'archéologie copte* 18 (1964).

Piankoff, A. "Les Peintures de la petite chapelle au monastère de Saint Antoine." *Les Cahiers Coptes* 12 (1956):7–16.

______. "Peintures au monastère de Saint Antoine." *Bulletin de la Société d'archéologie copte* 14 (1956):151–63.

Platt, (Miss). *Journal of a Tour Through Egypt,* Vol. 2, p. 93. London, 1842.

Pococke, R. *A Description of the East,* p. 128. London, 1743.

Schweinfurth, G. *Auf unbetretenen Wegen,* p. 185. Hamburg, 1922.

Sicard, C. *Lettres édifiantes et curieuses,* Vol. 3, p. 280. Paris, 1845.

Strothmann, R. *Die koptische Kirche in der Neuzeit,* p. 31. Tübingen, 1932.

Vansleb, J. M. *Nouvelle relation en forme de journal d'un voyage fait en Egypte en 1672 et 1673,* p. 302. Paris, 1677.

Wilkinson, G. *Modern Egypt and Thebes,* Vol. 2, pp. 381ff. London, 1843.

OTTO MEINARDUS

Chronology

With the present state of documentation, one can only set out a few landmarks in the history of Dayr Anbā Anṭūniyūs, while awaiting the publication of a serious archaeological study of the monastery.

401: Postumian appears to be the first author to attest the existence of the Monastery of Saint Antony. He said, "Duo beati Antonii monasteria adii, quae hodieque ab eius discipulis incoluntur" (I came to two monasteries of the blessed Antony, where his disciples dwell today; Sulpicius Severus, 1866, p. 17).

Beginning of seventh century: Anastasius, *hegumenos* of Saint Antony, is delegated by the Melchite patriarch John the Almoner to ransom the prisoners of the Persians at Jerusalem (Delehaye, 1927, pp. 23–24).

Before 622: Jews resident in Tomei, near Bilbeis, are baptized at the Monastery of Saint Antony (Griveau, 1908, p. 298).

Before 690: Menas, future bishop of Tmuis, and KHĀ'ĪL I, future Coptic patriarch (744), are monks at Saint Antony (Evelyn-White, 1932, p. 284).

End of ninth century: Two monks of the monastery of Saint Antony go begging in Ethiopia (*History of the Patriarchs*).

1064–1065: A note is written in the Vatican Manuscript Coptic 66, fol. 194v (Hebbelynck and van Lantschoot, 1937, p. 484).

1070: The letters of Saint Antony are translated from Coptic into Arabic at his monastery (Garitte, 1939, p. 29).

Toward 1160: MURQUS IBN QANBAR is exiled to Saint Antony.

1204–1205: Vatican Manuscript Coptic 9 is written at Saint Antony (Hebbelynck-van Lantschoot, 1937, pp. 29f.).

1209–1210: Isaac, monk of Saint Antony, becomes *abūna* of Ethiopia.

1232–1233: The mural frescoes of the Church of Saint Antony are painted, according to an inscription in the church (Coquin and Laferrière, 1978, p. 282).

1235 or 1245: Syrian monks live at Saint Antony to a date unknown (Evelyn-White, 1932, pp. 317, n. 4; 389–90).

1270: Gabriel is monk at Saint Antony, according to the Ethiopian SYNAXARION at 11 Hamle (Evelyn-White, 1932, p. 391). He writes a note in Vatican Manuscript Coptic 9, fol. lr (Hebbelynck and van Lantschoot, 1937, pp. 31–32) when he becomes patriarch under the name of GABRIEL III.

1283–1284: Gabriel al-Durunki, priest-monk of the Monastery of Saint Antony, copies the Kacmarcik manuscript (Samir, 1978, pp. 85–90).

1378: The patriarch MATTHEW I, monk at Abū Fānah and then at Saint Antony, is elected patriarch.

1386: MURQUS AL-ANṬŪNI dies as a saint.

1393: A Syrian monk copies in Garshūni the manuscript in the National Library, Paris, Syrian 191 (cf. Zotenberg, 1874, p. 133).

1395–1396: The Seigneur d'Anglure visits the monasteries of Saint Antony and Saint Paul (D'Anglure, 1878, pp. 70–72).

1396: This is the date of the manuscript Vatican Arabic 123, written at Saint Antony (Hanssens, 1972, p. 470).

Toward 1397: Symeon translates into Ge'ez the Arabic Synaxarion of the Copts (Guidi, 1911, p. 742) and *A Life of Saint Basilides* (Peeters, 1922, p. 248).

1422: Ghillebert de Lannoy visits the monastery and notes the presence of fifty monks (de Lannoy, 1878, pp. 69–70).

1440: Andrew, abbot of Saint Antony, is present at the Council of Florence (Alberigo, 1962, pp. 545, 558).

Before 1441: AL-MAQRĪZĪ speaks of the monasteries of Saint Antony and Saint Paul.

1466: GABRIEL I, monk of Saint Antony, is named patriarch.

Toward 1484: The monastery is pillaged and the monks are massacred by the bedouin (Coquin and Laferrière, 1978, pp. 278–79).

1506: The patriarch JOHN XIII in the manuscript Vatican Coptic 9 says that the monastery has been pillaged and that the manuscript in question has been recovered from the bedouin who had carried it off (Coquin and Laferrière, 1978, p. 278).

1512: Jean Thenaud (1884, p. 81) says that the Monastery of Saint Antony has been in ruins for seven years.

1540: The patriarch GABRIEL VII restores the Monastery of Saint Antony with some monks from Wādī al-Naṭrūn (Coquin and Laferrière, 1978, p. 317).

1547: Bellon du Mans (1970, fol. 128a–b) speaks of the monastery as inhabited by monks.

1561: An Ethiopian monk writes a treatise on penitence at the monastery (Cerulli, 1943, Vol. 2, p. 419).

1638–1639: Coppin (1971, pp. 227ff.) pays a visit to the Monastery of Saint Antony and states that the Monastery of Saint Paul is still in ruins.

1650–1651: MARK VI, monk of Saint Antony, is chosen to be patriarch.

1665: A. Gonzales (1977, Vol. 1, p. 33, and Vol. 2, p. 654) notes that some Franciscans are studying Arabic at the Monastery of Saint Antony and that the Monastery of Saint Paul is still uninhabited.

1672: J. Vansleb visits Saint Antony (1677, p. 289; 1678, pp. 177–202).

1676: A monk of Saint Antony is elected patriarch under the name of JOHN XVI. He repeoples the Monastery of Saint Paul in 1701, after an interruption of 119 years (Kāmil Ṣāliḥ Nakhlah, 1954, Pt. 4, p. 146).

1716: C. Sicard (1982, Vol. 1, pp. 24–27) visits the monasteries of Saint Antony and Saint Paul.

1730: Granger (1745, pp. 106ff.) visits the Monastery of Saint Antony.

1766: The church of Saint Mark is built through the attentions of Mu'allim (meaning "teacher" but here a title of respect) Ḥasab-Allāh al-Bayāḍī (Simaykah, 1930, Vol. 2, p. 112); Vansleb (1678, p. 184) points out the tomb of this saint, situated in his church in the middle of the garden.

1769: The successor of Mark in the see of Alexandria is a monk of Saint Antony.

1771: The Church of the Holy Apostles Peter and Paul is (re)constructed through the attentions of Mu'allim Lutfallah Chakir (Simaykah, 1930, p. 110); in 1673 Vansleb (1677, pp. 183–84) had given an account of a church dedicated to the apostles Peter and Paul.

1796: MARK VIII, 108th patriarch of Alexandria, is also a monk of Saint Antony.

1805: The monks suffer from extreme want because of the interruption of the caravans coming from Cairo (Arabic Manuscript Bibl. 164 colophon, according to Simaykah, 1930, p. 114).

1809: A monk of Saint Antony is elected patriarch under the name of PETER VII.

1854: CYRIL IV, *hegumenos* of the Monastery of Saint Antony, is named patriarch of Alexandria. He enlarges the precincts to the south and west (Simaykah, 1930, p. 114).

The precious library that was long preserved in the keep is now in a special building. According to Simaykah (1930, Vol. 2, p. 112), the 1,438 manuscripts may be divided into five groups as follows: biblical (294), theological (254), historical (193), ecclesiastical sciences (655), and miscellaneous (42). There must be added 124 printed books. The library contains also the treasures of the monastery (Meinardus, 1961).

BIBLIOGRAPHY

Alberigo, J.; P. P. Ioannou; C. Leonardi; and P. Prodi. *Conciliorum oecumenicorum decreta*. Freiburg, 1962.

Anglure, Ogier d'. *Le Saint voyage de Jherusalem du seigneur d'Anglure*, ed. François Bonnardot and A. Longnon. Paris, 1878.

Bellon du Mans, P. *Voyage en Egypte*, ed. S. Sauneron. Cairo, 1970.

Cerulli, E. *Etiopi in Palestina*, Vol. 2. Rome, 1943.

Coppin, J. *Les Voyages faits en Egypte*, ed. S. Sauneron. Cairo, 1971.

Coquin, R.-G., and P. Laferrière. "Les Inscriptions pariétales de l'ancienne église du monastère de St. Antoine, dans le désert oriental." *Bulletin de l'Institut français d'Archéologie orientale* 78 (1978):266–321.

Delehaye, H. "Une Vie inédite de St. Jean l'Aumônier." *Analecta Bollandiana* 45 (1927):5–74.

Evelyn-White, H. G. *The Monasteries of the Wadi'n Natrūn*, pt. 2, *The History of the Monasteries of Nitria and Scetis*. New York, 1932.

Fedden, H. R. "A Study of the Monastery of Saint Antony in the Eastern Desert." *Bulletin of the Faculty of Arts of the University of Egypt* 5, no. 1 (1937):1–60.

Garitte, G. "A Propos des lettres de St. Antoine, l'ermite." *Le Muséon* 52 (1939):11–31.

Gonzales, A. *Le Voyage en Egypte*, Vols. 1–2, ed. Institut français d'Archéologie orientale. Cairo, 1977.

Granger, Sieur. *Relation du voyage fait en Egypte en l'année 1730*. Paris, 1745.

Griveau, R. "Histoire de la conversion des juifs, habitants de la ville de Tomei en Egypte." *Revue de l'orient chrétien* 13 (1908):298–313.

Guidi, I., ed. "The Ethiopic Senkassar." *Journal of the Royal Asiatic Society* 43 (1911):739–58.

Hanssens, J. M. "Un Traité copte du XIVe siècle sur l'Eucharistie." *Orientalia Christiana* 38 (1972):467–72.

Hebbelynck, A., and A. van Lantschoot. *Codices Coptici Vaticani*, Vol. 1. Vatican City, 1937.

Jullien, M. "Voyage dans le désert de la Basse Thébaïde, aux couvents de St. Antoine et St. Paul." *Missions Catholique* 16 (1884).

______. *L'Egypte, souvenirs bibliques et chrétiens*. Lille, 1891.

Kāmil Ṣāliḥ Nākhlāh. *Silsilat Tarīkh al-Bābāwāt Batārikat al-Kursī al-Iskandarī*. Pt. 4. Cairo, 1954.

Khalil, Samir. "Le Codex Kacmarcik et sa version arabe de la liturgie alexandrine." *Orientalia Christiana* 44, no. 1 (1978):74–106.

Lannoy, G. de. *Oeuvres*, ed. C. Potvin and J. C. Houzeau. Louvain, 1878.

Meinardus, O. *Monks and Monasteries of the Egyptian Desert*. Cairo, 1961.

______. *Christian Egypt, Ancient and Modern*. Cairo, 1965; 2nd ed., 1977.

______. "The Collection of Coptica in the Qasr of St. Anthony." *Bulletin de la Société d'archéologie copte* 18 (1965–1966):251–54.

Peeters, P. "Traductions et traducteurs dans l'hagiographie orientale à l'époque byzantine." *Analecta Bollandiana* 40 (1922):241–98.

Sicard, C. *Oeuvres*, Vol. 1, ed. M. Martin. Bibliothèque d'étude 83. Cairo, 1982.

Simaykah, M. *Guide du Musée copte*, Vol. 2 (in Arabic). Cairo, 1930.

Thenaud, J. *Le Voyage d'outremer*, ed. C. Schefer. Paris, 1884.

Vansleb, J. M. *Nouvelle relation en forme de journal d'un voyage fait en Egypte en 1672 et 1673*. Paris, 1677. Translated as *The Present State of Egypt*. London, 1678.

Zotenberg, H. *Catalogues des manuscrits syriaques et sabéens (Mandaites) de la Bibliothèque nationale*. Paris, 1874.

RENÉ-GEORGES COQUIN
MAURICE MARTIN, S.J.

General Layout of the Monastery

The present monastery at the foot of the southern Jalālah plateau takes in an extensive area surrounded by a high wall, of which large parts in the south and west were added only in 1854. However,

General view of Dayr Anbā Anṭūniyūs from the south, showing the mountains of al-Jalālah al-Baḥriyyah in the north. *Courtesy French Institute of Oriental Archaeology, Cairo.*

the older, northeastern section of the monastery seems to have been in existence in its present form for a much longer period. It also contains within it all the buildings that gradually took shape.

The monastery has a number of churches, but of these only the Church of Saint Antony (also called the Old Church or the Great Church) has any historical significance. The Church of Saint Peter and Saint Paul, occasionally mentioned by older travelers, was torn down in 1772 and replaced at that time by a new building with the same name. The latest church, which is situated some way to the north because the axis of the building deviated from the required east-west orientation, has not yet been dedicated and serves as a library. Only the

Old wall and back wall (new extension), Dayr Anbā Anṭūniyūs. *Courtesy Father Martin, College of the Holy Family, Cairo.*

smaller of the two keeps of the monastery lays claim to a somewhat advanced age. Whether it is to be identified with the tower mentioned by ABŪ AL-MAKĀRIM at the beginning of the thirteenth century is uncertain. As usual, entrance was effected by means of a retractable bridge that originally led from the roof of a small building situated opposite. Today the later tower stands on this spot, so that now one must climb up inside it to the corresponding height. The residential quarters of the monks consist of elongated multistory building units arranged like streets in a settlement. When Vansleb (1677, pp. 300–302) visited the monastery in 1672, the monks lived separately, scattered about in small, low houses. This way of living corresponds to the original form of the anchorite settlements, as excavations in KELLIA and ABŪ MĪNĀ prove. At the same time, it is much closer to the ideal of the anchorite way of life, because the anchorite monks,

Inside the walls of Dayr Anbā Anṭūniyūs, with the library on the far left and only the cupolas of the Church of al-Rusul on the far right. *Courtesy French Institute of Oriental Archaeology, Cairo.*

View of Dayr Anbā Anṭūniyūs taken from the Hermitage of Paul the Simple (disciple of Anbā Anṭūniyūs). *Courtesy Father Martin, College of the Holy Family, Cairo.*

Grain mill, Dayr Anbā Anṭūniyūs. *Courtesy French Institute of Oriental Archaeology, Cairo.*

in contrast to the cenobite monks accommodated in communal buildings, could prosecute and carry through their own personal development much more effectively. The fact that the settled area is surrounded by a wall is only a formality based on the security necessary to protect their own treasures and is not adopted from cenobite monasticism. The monastery's water supply was maintained by a perennial running spring at the foot of the western plateau. It was incorporated into the monastery area by a surrounding wall only in 1854.

Finally, on a terrace slightly elevated above the monastery is a small cave where Saint Antony is thought to have once lived. It is entered by a long corridor and has an altar inside (Meinardus, 1961, pp. 65, 88).

Of the numerous churches in the monastery, only the Church of Saint Antony deserves some attention. It was built at the beginning of the thirteenth century and is still largely intact. Typically, it belongs to the long, single-nave domed churches that appeared in the Fatimid period and that have a naos made up of two successive bays. The present entrance is situated on the northern side of the western domed bay. In the east there is a *khūrus* (room between naos and sanctuary) in the south wall, in which remains of a burial are preserved. According to local tradition, Saint Antony was once buried here, but this could not have been his original burial place. The actual sanctuary consists of three sanctuaries arranged side by side, connected to each other by open arches. They all have their own cupolas. The altars appear to be original. Finally, at a slightly later period a small PAREKKLESION dedicated to the four beasts of the Apocalypse was added to the west end of the south wall. The quality of its construction is very modest. To connect it with the Church of Saint Antony, a large opening was effected in the south wall of the western domed naos chamber.

BIBLIOGRAPHY

Fedden, H. R. "A Study of the Monastery of Saint Antony in the Eastern Desert." *Bulletin of the Faculty of Arts of the University of Egypt* 5, no. 1 (1937):1–60.

Grossmann, P. *Mittelalterliche Langhauskuppelkirchen und verwandte Typen in Oberägypten.* Glückstadt, 1982.

Meinardus, O. *Monks and Monasteries of the Egyptian Deserts,* pp. 29–88. Cairo, 1961.

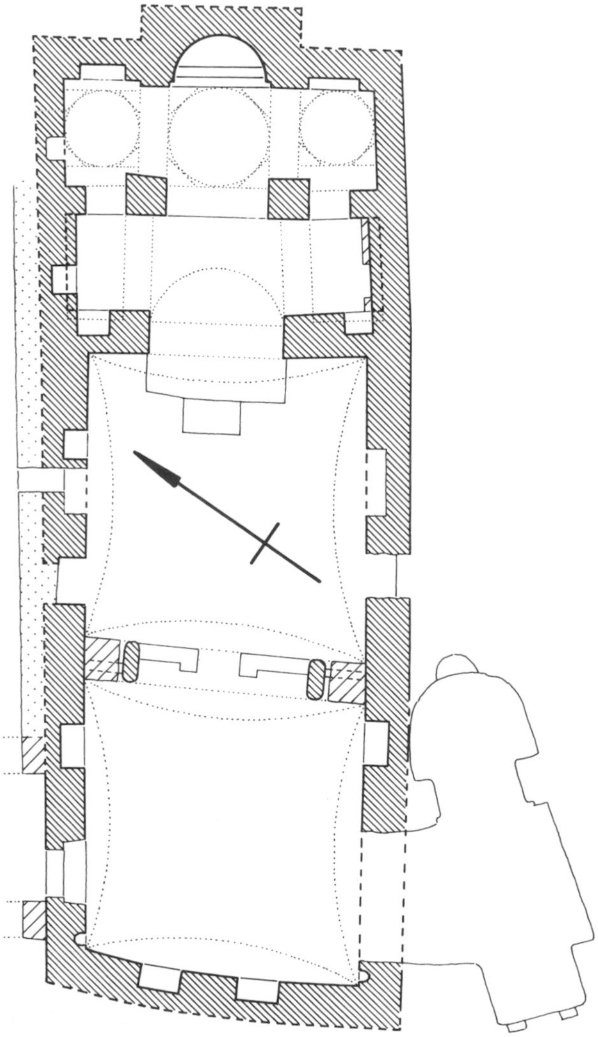

Plan of the Church of Saint Antony, Dayr Anbā Anṭūniyūs. *Courtesy Peter Grossmann.*

Vansleb, J. M. *Nouvelle relation en forme de journal d'un voyage fait en Egypte en 1672 et 1673.* Paris, 1677. Translated as *The Present State of Egypt.* London, 1678.

PETER GROSSMANN

Wall Paintings

Since the Old Church of the Monastery of Saint Antony had been lavishly decorated by wall paintings in different styles that are still partly visible, several expeditions visited this monastery with the purpose of publishing the murals. From the first expeditions, directed in 1930–1931 by Thomas Whittemore, some results are known by small publications from A. Piankoff. After World War II, J. Doresse visited Saint Antony's, and later, in the 1970s, J. Leroy did so. After 1981 the work of Leroy was carried on by Paul van Moorsel. Thanks to the studies of so many predecessors and an epigraphical study by R.-G. Coquin and P.-H. Laferrière, one can draft the following hypothesis: After the building of this church a group of about twenty men (priests and monks) ordered a certain Theodorus, who called himself a son of Bishop Gabriel of Aṭfīḥ (Aphroditopolis), to paint this church and perhaps also the adjoining chapel, dedicated to the Four Living Creatures. According to inscriptions, Theodorus must have been at work here about 1232–1233.

Sacrifice of Abraham. Painting at Dayr Anbā Anṭūniyūs. Ca. A.D. 1232–1233. *Courtesy Kees Crena de Iongh.*

Inscription below the painting of the Sacrifice of Abraham at Dayr Anbā Anṭūniyūs giving the name of "Painter Theodorus." Ca. A.D. 1232–1233. *Courtesy Kees Crena de Iongh.*

Of his work, huge parts are still preserved. In the sanctuary the cupola is decorated by the bust of a *pantokrator,* surrounded by angels and Cherubim and Seraphim, adored by eight other angelic figures, while the twenty-four priests from the book of Revelation join the celestial liturgy. Still above the main altar, four scenes from the Old Testament are represented: the seraph cleaning Isaiah's lips, the sacrifice of Melchizedek, the sacrifice of Abraham, and the sacrifice of Jephthah. The main apse is, as usual, decorated with the double theme in two zones: above, an enthroned Christ and, below, an enthroned Virgin with child, both assisted by angelic beings. Portraits of several patriarchs of Alexandria, of SEVERUS OF ANTIOCH, and of an anonymous patriarch in the same sanctuary are interesting for the history of the liturgical vestments in Egypt. Still from the hand of Theodorus are portraits of six prophets and the horse-riding saints, MERCURIUS and GEORGE. These riders decorate, together with the popular scene of the Three HEBREWS in the furnace and with Abraham, Isaac, and Jacob, the lower part of the *khūrus,* the upper part being (re)painted later.

The eastern part of the nave has been decorated by Theodorus with portraits of the Holy Virgin

Sacrifice of Jephthah's daughter. Painting at Dayr Anbā Anṭūniyūs. Ca. A.D. 1232–1233. *Courtesy Kees Crena de Iongh.*

(again an enthroned Virgin with child) and monks, the western part with portraits of riders and four other standing saints. It is interesting to see how Pachomius and Shenute share the company of Saint Antony, Paul the Hermit, Kaau, Barsūm the Syrian, Arsenius, Samuel of Qalamūn, Paul the Simple, Isaac, Moses the Black, Pisentius, and the founders of the great monasteries in SCETIS and, of course, of monks whose names are lost now. Their portraits provide information about monastic vestments. Apart from Kaau Thouan, Athom, and Piro, the saints portrayed in the western part of the church (obviously the part reserved for the laymen) are all military men: Saints George (again), Sisinnius, Theodorus Stratelates, Menas, Victor, Claudius Theodorus the Oriental and two unidentified figures, Menas and Victor being painted like courtiers, the others in battle dress, fighting (like Saints Mercurius and George in the above-mentioned *khūrus*) personifications of evil. The chapel of the Four Living Creatures shows above a lavishly decorated cross an enthroned Christ, being a part of a classical *deisis* (with the Holy Virgin and the Baptist), enriched by a scene of the Four Creatures standing in the attitude of acclamation of the Lord.

Later, probably in the fourteenth century, work from Theodorus in this western part of the nave and in the upper part of the *khūrus* as well, disappeared behind the products of a new master. At the east wall of the *khūrus,* this man painted two scenes connected with the resurrection of Christ (the women at Christ's tomb and his meeting with the two women named Mary) and two pairs of archangels at different places in the church.

Although parts of the secco murals are lost and sometimes "restored," the work of Theodorus can be considered complete, more complete than so many other cycles in Coptic mural painting. Being a painter of a mediocre style, Theodorus betrays the great influence of Coptic medieval iconography, while the new master fits in the fourteenth-century trend that has been more inspired in Christian Egypt by Byzantine painters.

BIBLIOGRAPHY

Coquin, R.-G., and P.-H. Laferrière. "Les Inscriptions pariétales de l'ancienne église du monastère de S. Antoine dans le désert oriental." *Bulletin de l'Institut français d'Archéologie orientale* 78 (1978):267–321.

Doresse, J. "Nouvelles études sur l'art copte, les monastères de Saint-Antoine et de Saint-Paul." *Comptes rendus des séances de l'Académie des inscriptions et belles-lettres* (1951):268–74.

Scene of the "Chairete." Work of the new master, Dayr Anbā Anṭūniyūs. Fourteenth century (?). *Courtesy Kees Crena de Iongh.*

———. "Deux Monastères coptes oubliés, Saint-Antoine et Saint-Paul, dans le désert de la Mer rouge." *Revue des arts* 2 (1952):3–14.

Leroy, J. "Le Programme décoratif de l'église de Saint-Antoine du désert de la Mer rouge." *Bulletin de l'Institut français d'Archéologie orientale* 76 (1976):347–79.

Moorsel, P. van. "Les Travaux de la mission de peintures coptes à Saint-Antoine." *Bulletin de la Société français d'Egyptologie* 97 (1983):16–29.

Nelson, R. S. "An Icon at Mt. Sinai and Christian Painting in Muslim Egypt During the Thirteenth and Fourteenth Centuries." *Art Bulletin* 65 (1983):201–218.

Piankoff, A. "Peintures au monastère de Saint-Antoine." *Bulletin de la Société d'archéologie copte* 14 (1950–1957):151–63.

———. "Thomas Whittemore, Les Cahiers coptes." *Les Cahiers coptes* 7–8 (1954):19–24.

———. "Deux Peintures de saints militaires au monastère de Saint-Antoine." *Les Cahiers coptes* 10 (1956):17–25.

PAUL VAN MOORSEL

Region of Dayr Anbā Anṭūniyūs

The personality of Saint Antony attracted many hermits, the ruins of whose hermitages are still to be seen. Apart from the two dependencies of Būsh and Dayr al-Maymūn, which represent the outer desert of the ancient texts, and the two monasteries of Saint Antony and Saint Paul, which are the inner desert, the hermits installed themselves either in the wadis flowing into Wādī ʿAraba or on the mountain between the Monastery of Saint Antony and CLYSMA (Qulzum).

The hermitages that are found in the wadis coming down from the Jalālah plateau in the north, opposite the monastery of Saint Antony, are those in the Wādī Natfah; those in Wādī Hannebah; the most important hermitage, called Dayr Bakhīt; and those in Wādī ʿArabah, halfway between the Nile Valley and the Monastery of Saint Antony, ʿAyn Bardah. They have been described by F. Bissey and R. Chabot-Morisseau (1953–1954); A. L. Fontaine (1953–1954); and R. Fourteau (1900).

The best known, 42 miles (68 km) from Suez on the road of Saint Antony, is without doubt Dayr Abū Daraj, one cell of which contains Coptic inscriptions. It has been described by E. Brown (1974); A. L. Fontaine (1955–1956); and J. Jarry (1971–1973).

In Egypt, Saint Antony appears to be little venerated. His name appears rarely in the list of invocations of the monks. *The Life of Antony*, by Athanasius, is meagerly represented in Coptic, and the monasteries and churches dedicated to him are not very numerous. Al-Maqrīzī drew attention to a church in the district of Bayāḍ to the north of Iṭfīḥ. A *topos* (memorial site) of Saint Antony is noted in the province of al-Ashmūnayn (Garitte, 1943, p. 347). A monastery was dedicated to Saint Antony in the region of Qifṭ.

BIBLIOGRAPHY

Bissey, F., and R. Chabot-Morisseau, "Notes de voyages sur l'ouadi Arabah: Ruines de constructions chrétiennes dans les Branches est et ouest de l'ouadi Hannaka." *Bulletin de la Société d'études historiques et géographiques de l'Isthme de Suez* 5 (1953–1954):155–60.

Brown, E. "Voyage en Egypte (1673–1674)." *Bulletin de l'Institut français d'Archéologie copte* (1974):261.

Fontaine, A. L. "Explorations dans l'ouadi Arabah, Ayn Barda, ses vestiges d'habitations anciens." *Bulletin de la Société d'études historiques et géographiques de l'Isthme de Suez* 5 (1953–1954):159ff.

———. "Les Ruines du bir Abou Darag sur le golfe de Suez." *Bulletin de la Société d'études historiques et Géographiques de l'Isthme de Suez* 6 (1955–1956):55ff.

———. "Le Monachisme copte et la montagne de St. Antoine." *Bulletin de l'Institut des études coptes* 1 (1958):3–33.

Fourteau, R. "Voyage dans la partie septentrionale du désert arabique." *Bulletin de la Société khediviale de Geographie*, ser. 5, 9 (1900):517–33.

Garitte, G. "Panégyrique de St. Antoine par Jean, évêque d'Hermopolis." *Orientalia Christiana Periodica* 9 (1943):100–134, 330–65.

Jarry, J. "Nouvelles Inscriptions coptes, grecques, arabes et syriaques." *Bulletin de la Société d' archéologie copte* 21 (1971–1973):55–81.

Littman, E. "Nabatean Inscriptions from Egypt." *Bulletin of the School of Oriental and African Studies* 15 (1953):1–28.

Martin, M. "Abou Darag dans la montagne de St. Antoine." *Bulletin de l'Institut français d'Archéologie orientale* 70 (1971):173–89.

Meredith, D. "The Roman Remains at the Eastern Desert of Egypt." *Journal of Egyptian Archeology* 38 (1952):94–111.

Scaipe, C. H. O. "Further Notes on Myos Hormos and Some Ruins at Abu Darag." *Bulletin of the Faculty of Arts of the University of Egypt,* 4 (1936):63–64.

Sicard, C. *Oeuvres,* Vol. 1, *Lettres et relations,* ed. M. Martin. Cairo, 1982.

RENÉ-GEORGES COQUIN
MAURICE MARTIN, S.J.

DAYR ANBĀ ANṬŪNIYŪS (Qifṭ). *See* Monasteries of the Upper Ṣaʿīd.

DAYR ANBĀ BĀKHŪM (Abydos). The Coptic Life of MOSES OF ABYDOS says clearly that the saint founded his monastery to the south of the temple of Bēs, which is none other than the Memnonion of Strabo (i.e., the funerary temple of Seti I). The present Dayr Mūsā, also called DAYR SITT DIMYANAH, which is to the northwest of the temple of Osiris, can hardly be the monastery founded by Moses.

ABŪ ṢĀLIḤ THE ARMENIAN (1895, pp. 231–32) and al-MAQRĪZĪ (1854, Vol. 2, p. 507) also spoke of the monastery of Moses near al-BALYANĀ, but did not indicate its exact position in relation to the pharaonic temples.

C. SICARD (1982, Vol. 3, p. 68) related that at this site he saw the ruins of a monastery called the Monastery of Pachomius, or Dayr Anbā Bākhūm: "To the south of the Memnonion there appear the ruins of a monastery of Saint Pachomius, about 100 paces square, with a dried-up well with a wheel." The Coptic Life of Moses mentions explicitly the digging of a well.

At the beginning of this century G. Lefebvre (1911, Vol. 4, p. 239) saw at the same place the ruins of a monastery, "a long quadrilateral, of which only the brick walls emerge," but he remarked that the locals call it the Monastery of the Greeks. The Jesuit Sicard, who passed quickly through these places, may have confused DAYR AL-RŪMĪ and Dayr Anbā Bākhūm.

No doubt no one will ever know the truth. If Moses called his monastery that of Pachomius, it would prove beyond any doubt what the Coptic texts seem to show—that he did indeed intend to remain within the Pachomian tradition.

BIBLIOGRAPHY

Lefebvre, G. "Egypte chrétienne, IV." *Annales du Service des antiquités de l'Egypte* 11 (1911):230–50.

Sicard, C. *Oeuvres,* Vol. 3, ed. S. Sauneron and M. Martin. Bibliothèque d'étude 85. Cairo, 1982.

RENÉ-GEORGES COQUIN
MAURICE MARTIN, S. J.

DAYR ANBĀ BĀKHŪM (Barjanūs). ABŪ ṢĀLIḤ THE ARMENIAN (1895, p. 243) is the only ancient author to mention this *dayr.* He placed the village of Barjanūs in the district of Ṭaḥā (al-Aʿmidah). In the Arabic versions of this Life the place-name (Coptic: "percoush") is transcribed Brgūsh (National Library, Paris, Arabe 4787, fols. 196r–229r; Saint Antony, Hist. 67, fols. 2r–29v; Abū Maqār, Hag. 19, fols. 110r–131v).

The *History of the Patriarchs* (Vol. 2, pt. 1, pp. 32 [text], 45 [trans.]) related that about 866 the monasteries of Apa SHENUTE, of al-Qalamūn, and of Saint PACHOMIUS in the nome of Ṭaḥā (al-Aʿmidah) near the village of Barjanūs were destroyed by the troops of al-Muʿtazz and al-Mustaʿīn. Unfortunately the name of the village is not certain in the Arabic texts, for it is written without any diacritical points (Brjwas). Renaudot, who used the Paris manuscripts in his *Historia* (1713, p. 310), transcribed the name of the village Birhowas.

The monastery is also named, it seems, in *Les Miracles de St. Ptolemée* (Leroy, PO 5, pp. 782, 801). It appears that the monastery disappeared very early, for no author mentions it after Abū Ṣāliḥ.

M. Ramzī (1953–1968, Vol. 2, pt. 3, p. 236) attempted to identify it with the *kom* (mound) of al-Rāhib, but there is nothing to prove that the ruins of the monastery there discovered are those of Dayr Anbā Bakhūm.

BIBLIOGRAPHY

Amélineau, E. *Monuments pour servir à l'histoire d'Egypte chrétienne.* Mémoires publiés par les membres de la Mission archéologique française au Caire 4. Paris, 1886–1888.

Leroy, L. *Les Miracles de St. Ptolemée,* pp. 779–806. PO 5. Paris, 1910.

Ramzī, M. *Al-Qāmūs al-Jughrāfī lil-Bilād al-Miṣrīyyah,* 3 vols. Cairo, 1953–1968.

Renaudot, E. *Historia Patriarcharum Alexandrinorum.* Paris, 1713.

RENÉ-GEORGES COQUIN
MAURICE MARTIN, S. J.

DAYR ANBĀ BĀKHŪM, a small monastery on the Nile's left bank, near Medamud, about 5 miles (8 km) from the ruins of the temples of Karnak and close to the present Luxor airport, to the north of this town.

The first to name it, although he said nothing very precise, appears to have been C. SICARD, in

1718 (1982, Vol. 1, p. 58). It was described at the beginning of the twentieth century by M. JULLIEN (1903, p. 283). S. CLARKE (1912, pp. 120–21) gave the plan of it and inserted it into his final list of the churches of Egypt (p. 215, no. 22). Johann Georg (1914, pp. 54–55; 1930, p. 48) noted it in his wanderings.

A local legend was reported by G. LEGRAIN (1914, pp. 37–43); this legend can only hold good for a nineteenth-century reconstruction of the monastery, since the latter is mentioned by Sicard, as has been said. The *dayr* was also noted by 'ABD AL-MASĪḤ ṢALĪB (1932, p. 180), who remarked that it was served by the clergy of Luxor and that it is ancient. Its present situation was given by O. Meinardus (1965, pp. 307–308; 1977, p. 421).

BIBLIOGRAPHY

'Abd al-Masīḥ Ṣalīb al-Masū'dī al-Bāramūsī. *Kitāb Tuḥfat al-Sā'ilīn fī Dhikr Adyirat Ruhbān al-Misriyyin.* Cairo, 1932.

Clarke, S. *Christian Antiquities in the Nile Valley.* Oxford, 1912.

Johann Georg, Prince of Saxony. *Streifzüge durch die Kirchen und Klöster Ägyptens.* Leipzig, 1914.

______. *Neue Streifzüge durch die Kirchen und Klöster Ägyptens.* Leipzig and Berlin, 1930.

Jullien, M. "Quelques anciens couvents de l'Egypte." *Missions catholiques* 35 (1903):188–90, 198–202, 212–14, 237–40, 250–52, 257–58, 274–76, 283–84.

Legrain, G. *Louqsor sans les pharaons.* Paris and Brussels, 1914.

Meinardus, C. *Christian Egypt, Ancient and Modern.* Cairo, 1965; 2nd ed. 1977.

Sicard, C. *Oeuvres,* ed. S. Sauneron and M. Martin, 3 vols. Bibliothèque d'étude 83–85. Cairo, 1982.

RENÉ-GEORGES COQUIN
MAURICE MARTIN, S. J.

DAYR ANBĀ BĀKHŪM (Qūṣ). *See* Monasteries of the Upper Ṣa'īd.

DAYR ANBĀ BĀKHŪM (al-Ṣawām'ah Sharq). [*Two parts, history and architecture, make up this article on Dayr Anbā Bākhūm.*]

History

In the small town of al-Sawām'ah Sharq, 5 miles (8 km) north of AKHMĪM, is a church dedicated to Saint Bākhūm (PACHOMIUS) and his sister Dālūshām, martyrs under DIOCLETIAN.

The first author to mention this church was the Jesuit C. SICARD. He spoke briefly of the church (the monastery had no doubt disappeared) in his famous *Parallèle géographique* (1982, Vol. 3, pp. 38–39). Although the inhabitants of the place told him that this Pachomius was a martyr, Sicard believed that he was the Pachomius who shaped Egyptian cenobitism. Granger also mentioned this monastery some years later, but called it Deir Habouba-Comé (1745, p. 98).

A panegyric by Abraham, bishop of Qifṭ (the date of which is unknown), on the titular saints of this *dayr,* Anbā Bākhūm and his sister Dālūshām, has been published by Nabīl al-Manqabādī (1969, pp. 4–11) after a manuscript preserved in this church. It is now evident that the titular saint of this monastery is not Palamon, the disciple of Saint Pachomius, the founder of the cenobitic life.

All that remains of the ancient monastery is the church, which has, moreover, been reconstructed on the foundations of the old one (Meinardus, 1965, p. 195; 1977, p. 401). This church is mentioned by S. Clarke in his list of the churches (1912, p. 213, no. 19).

BIBLIOGRAPHY

Clarke, S. *Christian Antiquities in the Nile Valley.* London, 1912.

Granger, Sieur. *Relation du voyage fait en Egypte en l'annee 1730.* Paris, 1745.

Manqabadi, Nabil al-. *Min Diyarat al-Abā.* Cairo, 1969.

Meinardus, O. *Christian Egypt, Ancient and Modern.* Cairo, 1965; 2nd ed., 1977.

Sicard, C. *Oeuvres,* Vol. 3, ed. S. Sauneron and M. Martin. Bibliothèque d'étude 85. Cairo, 1982.

Timm, S. *Das christlich-koptische Ägypten in arabischer Zeit,* Vol. 2. Wiesbaden, 1984.

RENÉ-GEORGES COQUIN
MAURICE MARTIN, S. J.

Architecture

Of this monastery only the church has survived. It is dedicated to the famous Saint Pachomius, founder of cenobite monasticism, and his sister, whose icon is in the church. Timm (1984, p. 655) identifies this monastery with the Pachomian foundation at Tsē in the region of Shmin, the ancient name for Akhmīm.

The church has passed through three building

periods. An early basilican church with a triconch sanctuary was transformed during the Middle Ages into a smaller centralized structure, which has been slightly enlarged in more recent times. The eastern and southern apses still survive, together with a square room between them in the southeast corner. The apses contain niches with angled gables (crowns with broken tympanum) similar to those in the churches of DAYR ANBĀ SHINŪDAH and DAYR ANBĀ BISHOI at Suhāj on the other side of the Nile, causing P. Grossmann (1980) to date this church to the seventh century. Such dating makes it the oldest surviving church in the Akhmīm area and possibly an influence on DAYR ANBĀ BISĀDAH, south of Akhmīm. The basic shape of the original nave and aisles is indicated by the remains of four of the piers that supported the original wooden roof. Two are embedded in the heavier piers between the present nave and choir, and one in the west wall. The foundation of the fourth can be seen in the courtyard that now occupies much of the space of the original aisles and nave.

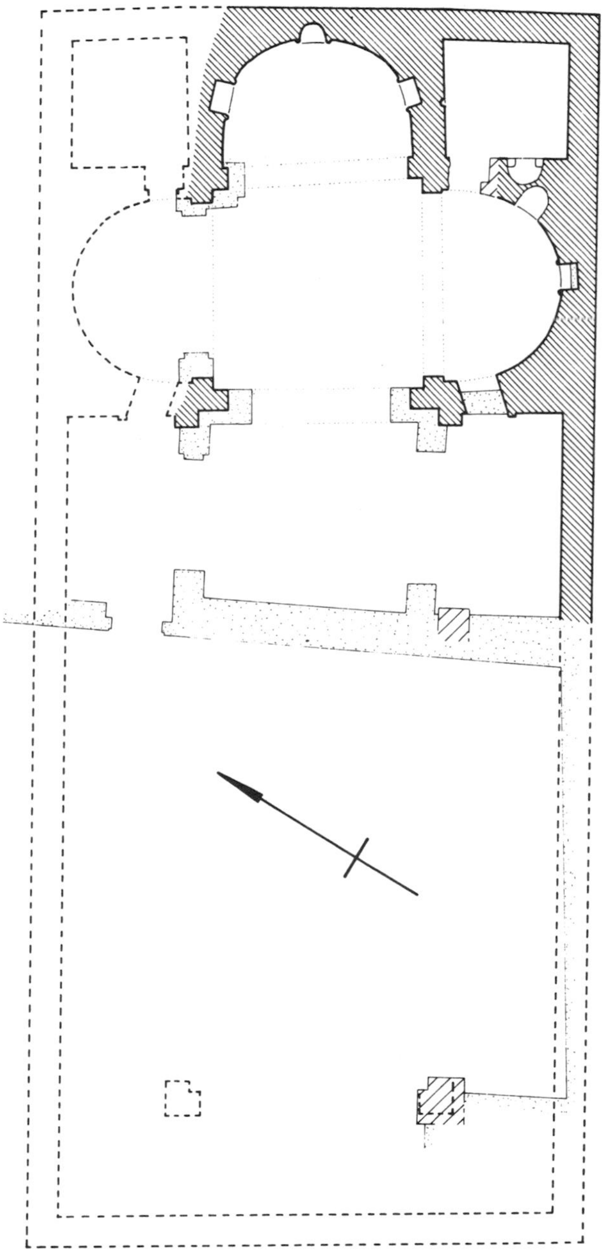

Plan of the church surviving at Dayr Anbā Bākhūm, near al-Sawām'ah Sharq. *Courtesy Peter Grossmann.*

Over the entrance to this courtyard is a block with a pharaonic inscription, possibly retained from the first building phase, since use of spolia (capitals reused from older buildings) became less common later. A marble altar table in the present southern sanctuary, the original eastern conch, is of an early type illustrated by A. J. Butler (1884, Vol. 2, p. 8).

When the church was cut down to a centralized building, large piers had to be built around two of the small original piers in order to support domes. More recently, three rooms have been built at the north, and a column has been added to support the new domes. The dome in front of the southern sanctuary is supported by brackets and squinches. The other units are covered by domes on pendentives.

BIBLIOGRAPHY

Butler, A. J. *The Ancient Coptic Churches of Egypt*, 2 vols. Oxford, 1884.

Grossmann, P. "Survey Arbeiten im Raum von Ahmīm." *Archiv für Orientforschung* 27 (1980):304–306.

Meinardus, O. *Christian Egypt, Ancient and Modern*, p. 295. Cairo, 1965.

Timm, S. *Das christlich-koptische Ägypten in arabischer Zeit*, Vol. 2, pp. 653–57. Wiesbaden, 1984.

SHELA MCNALLY

DAYR ANBĀ BĪḌĀBĀ, a monastery-village 1.25 miles (2 km) west of Nag Hammadi and south of Bahjūrah. It is mentioned in the recension of the Coptic SYNAXARION from Upper Egypt at 13 Kiyahk, the feast day of the saint, who was bishop of the town of QŪṢ (cf. Coquin, 1978, p. 361).

L. T. Lefort believed that this was the monastery of Tmoushons (BAKHĀNIS), founded by Saint PACHOMIUS, but that is not very probable, for the placename Tmoushons survives in the Arabic Bakhānis, or Makhānis, which is to the north of Farshūṭ or about 8 miles north of Dayr Anbā Bīḏābā (Lefort, 1939, pp. 399–401).

The monastery was pointed out by J. VANSLEB (1677, p. 413; 1678, p. 247) and by M. JULLIEN (1901, p. 253), who calls it Deir n'Nassara. Its present state was described by O. Meinardus (1965, p. 302; 1977, p. 435).

BIBLIOGRAPHY

Coquin, R.-G. *Le Synaxaire des Coptes: Un Nouveau témoin de la recension de Haute Egypte*. Analecta Bollandiana 96 (1978):351–65.

Jullien, M. "A la recherche de Tabenne et des autres monastères fondés par St. Pachôme." *Etudes* 89 (1901):238–58.

Lefort, L. T. "Les Premiers monastères pachômiens: Exploration topographique." *Le Muséon* 52 (1939):379–407.

Meinardus, O. *Christian Egypt, Ancient and Modern*. Cairo, 1965; 2nd ed., 1977.

Vansleb, J. M. *Nouvelle relation en forme de journal d'un voyage fait en Egypte en 1672 et 1673*. Paris, 1677. Translated as *The Present State of Egypt*. London, 1678.

RENÉ-GEORGES COQUIN
MAURICE MARTIN, S.J.

DAYR ANBĀ BISĀDAH.

[*This monastery is discussed in two parts: history and architectural layout.*]

History

This monastery, on the right bank of the Nile in the village of al-Aḥāywah Sharq, about 11 miles (18 km) south of Akhmīm, preserves the memory and the relics of a martyr bishop in the fourth century, PSOTE. He was bishop of the town of Psoi/Ptolemais, which at least in the Byzantine era was the place of residence, along with Antinoë (ANTINOOPOLIS), of the *dux*, the military and also civil chief of the province of the Thebaid, whose powers extended as far as Aswan. The life of this bishop has come down to us in Latin, a rare thing, and this text, which does not present the embellishments of too many saints' lives, says that he was buried to the east of the town of Psoi. There is every reason to believe that the present monastery was built over the tomb of this bishop, for the monastery, which still exists and is frequented as a place of pilgrimage (Muyser and Viaud, 1979, p. 59), is in fact situated in the stony area on the right bank of the Nile, opposite al-Manshiyyah, a small town that perpetuates the ancient Psoi or Ptolemais Hermou of the Hellenistic period.

The recension of the Coptic SYNAXARION from Upper Egypt, which no doubt summarizes a more ancient Coptic text, indicates the antiquity of the monastery. A panegyric of Saint Claudius, attributed to the patriarch SEVERUS OF ANTIOCH, mentions on the right bank and to the south of Abydos the monastery of the martyr bishop Psote. If the manuscripts that have handed down this text are of the ninth century, the tradition that they transmit is certainly older, but the date of the foundation of this monastery cannot be fixed with certainty (Godron, PO 35, p. 500).

This monastery was provided with an enclosure and is a true cenobium. The present buildings, according to local tradition, are of the thirteenth century, but include ancient elements.

Al-MAQRĪZĪ did not fail to point it out (1853, Vol. 2, p. 504; correct the Bulāq edition and read Absādah instead of Abshādah). Some travelers drew attention to it from the eighteenth century on. R. Pococke (1743–1745, p. 81) mentioned it, calling it Embabsag, but the description and location that he gave do not lend themselves to any confusion. Likewise, M. JULLIEN (1903, pp. 274–76, with three photos) gave a good description of it (cf. Martin, 1972, pp. 127–28). Martin's information is more precise than that published by H. Munier (1940, pp. 155–56). O. Meinardus (1965, pp. 299–300; 1977, pp. 411–12) furnished an exact description.

BIBLIOGRAPHY

Godron, G. *Texte coptes relatifs à saint Claude d'Antioche*. In PO 35. Turnhout, 1970.

Jullien, M. "Quelques anciens couvents de l'Egypte." *Missions catholiques* 35 (1903):188–90; 198–202; 212–14; 237–40; 250–52; 257–58; 274–76; 283–84.

Martin, M. "Notes inédites du P. Jullien sur trois monastères chrétiens d'Egypte: Dêr Abou Fâna, le couvent des 'sept montagnes,' Dêr amba Bisâda." *Bulletin de l'Institut français d'Archéologie orientale* 71 (1972):119–28.

Meinardus, O. *Christian Egypt, Ancient and Modern*. Cairo, 1965; 2nd ed., 1977.

Munier, H. "Les Monuments coptes d'après les explorations du Père Michel Jullien." *Bulletin de la Société d'archéologie copte* 6 (1940):141–68.

Muyser, J., and G. Viaud. *Les Pèlerinages coptes en Egypte*. Cairo, 1979.

Orlandi, T. *Il dossier copto del Martire Psote.* Testi e documenti per lo studio dell'antichità 61. Milan, 1978.

Pococke, R. *A Description of the East and Some Other Countries.* London, 1743–1745.

RENÉ-GEORGES COQUIN
MAURICE MARTIN, S. J.

Architecture

A walled enclosure contains the priest's house, some minor structures, and, on the east, the church. It has an elaborate doorway surmounted by a small stone slab with a cross in relief and surrounded by lozenge-shaped bricks, some combined to form stars. This doorway opens into an irregularly shaped narthex that belongs to a secondary building period. Behind the narthex lies the oldest part, the remains of a triconch. There is no visible evidence as to whether the church was originally centralized, like the church of DAYR MĀR TUMĀS, north of Akhmīm, or naved and later truncated, like DAYR ANBĀ BĀKHŪM, also near Akhmīm.

What remains is the eastern apse, a short stretch of the wall of the southern side apse, and, between them, an irregularly shaped room that formed the corner of the first church. This room contains a tomb said to be of Anbā Bisādah. The original stone doorway into the room survives. It has a carved lintel, and traces of carving remain on the southern jamb. The plan of the church could be early Christian, but the poor construction caused P. Grossmann (1980, p. 306) to suggest a later date. O. Meinardus records a traditional thirteenth-century date. The additions to the church show some relationship to the plans of DAYR ABŪ SAYFAYN, DAYR SITT DIMYANAH (both in Akhmīm), and DAYR MĀR JIRJIS AL-ḤADĪDĪ, but were executed in a more asymmetrical manner and include a number of unusual features. Four more sanctuaries have been added, two north of the main sanctuary and two south of the room containing Anbā Bisādah's grave. A solid wooden iconastasis stands in front of each altar. There are single bays in front of each of the two northern sanctuaries and double bays in front of each of the southern sanctuaries. Beyond the sanctuaries on each side are corridors. The one on the south turns back to a well at the east. Further to the east are a row of rooms. One, accessible from the room containing Anbā Bisādah's tomb, contains a baptismal font. The others, accessible only from above, have been used for burial. In the southwest

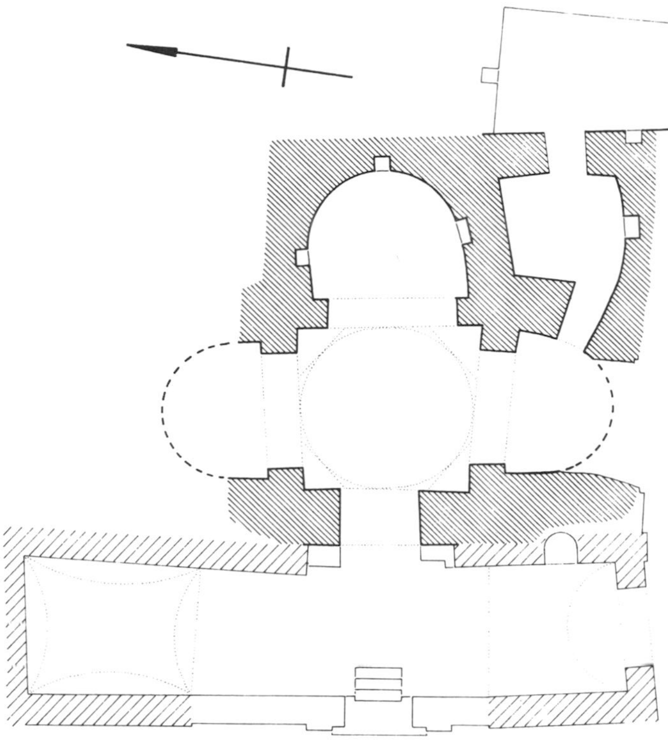

Plan of the remains of the church at Dayr Anbā Bisādah. *Courtesy Peter Grossmann.*

corner of the church a stairway leads to an upper room for women worshipers, screened off from the rest of the church by a brick wall pierced with irregular openings. There is a small, granite LAQQĀN to the right of the church door. Whitewashing obscures further structural details of the interior.

The earliest visible structure may belong to the early medieval period.

BIBLIOGRAPHY

Grossman, P. "SurveyArbeiten im Raum von Ahmīm." *Archiv für Orientforschung* 27 (1980):304–306.

Meinardus, O. *Christian Egypt, Ancient and Modern,* pp. 299–300. Cairo, 1965.

Munier, H. "Les Monuments coptes d'après les explorations du Père Michel Jullien." *Bulletin de la Société d'archéologie copte* 6 (1940):141–68.

Timm, S. *Das christlich-koptische Ägypten in arabischer Zeit,* Vol. 2, pp. 660–61. Wiesbaden, 1984.

SHELA MCNALLY

DAYR ANBĀ BISHOI (Barshah-Minyā). *See* Dayr al-Barshah.

DAYR ANBĀ BISHOI (Scetis). [*This article encompasses two main topics: history and architecture of Dayr Anbā Bishoi. Subtitles under the architectural section are the church, the refectories, and the* jawsaq.]

History

This is one of the surviving ancient monasteries in SCETIS (modern Wādī al-Naṭrūn). There is no historically reliable information on its foundation, but on the basis of what little is known of the earliest monastic establishments in Scetis, it may be surmised that it grew from a settlement, or laura, of anchorites whose forerunners had gathered around the desert father Bishoi (in medieval Arabic sources, Bīshāy) from whom the monastery has taken its name. The settlement probably came into being later than those of DAYR AL-BARAMŪS and Dayr Abū Maqār, but before the death of MACARIUS THE EGYPTIAN, around 390.

According to the various recensions of the Life of Bishoi, whose author claims to be JOHN COLOBOS (the Short), Bishoi's companion during their earlier years in Scetis, the two of them eventually parted company. John stayed in the place where they had most recently lived, while Bishoi moved to a cave 2 miles to the north. Dayr Anbā Bishoi is, in fact, about 2 Roman miles northwest of the ruins of the former Monastery of John the Short, but the association and then separation of John and Bishoi in the legend may be no more than an etiological reflection of that topographic reality. After a barbarian raid, which may be the historical raid through Scetis in 407, Bishoi, according to the Arabic recension of the legend, fled to a spot near the city of Antinoë (ANTINOOPOLIS) and spent the rest of his life there. When he died, his body was taken to Antinoë, where it was to remain for the next four centuries.

In Scetis the monastic settlement to which his memory and his name were attached was quickly revived, but historical information on its subsequent history is very scarce. It obviously shared in the general vicissitudes of monastic establishments in Scetis through the centuries.

Dayr Anbā Bishoi was founded between 535 and 580. During that period the Theodosian monks, who adhered to the Christological doctrine of SEVERUS OF ANTIOCH, were in opposition to the Gaianite monks, who adhered to the doctrinal position of JULIAN of Halicarnassus. Since the Gaianites were in temporary control of the existing monasteries, the Theodosian monks established their own monasteries dedicated to the Virgin Mother as counterparts.

It is not known how long any of the monasteries remained in Gaianite control, but it is certain, from the colophons of certain Syrian manuscripts from the middle of the ninth century, that the present DAYR AL-SURYĀN was originally the counterpart Monastery of the Virgin Mother of God of Anbā Bishoi. After a period of general desolation in Scetis resulting from a particularly serious barbarian raid probably in the late sixth century and from the troubled times that preceded the Arab conquest of Egypt, both Dayr Anbā Bishoi and its counterpart were rebuilt in the reign of the Coptic patriarch BENJAMIN I (622–661). At the time of another general reconstruction in Scetis during the reign of the patriarch YŪSĀB I (830–849), after yet another barbarian destruction around 817, the body of Anbā Bishoi was at last transported from its resting place in Antinoë to the monastery in Scetis that bears his name.

For greater protection, the enclosure walls of Dayr Anbā Bishoi, like those surrounding the other monasteries in Wādī al-Naṭrūn, were fortified sometime before the end of the ninth century. Unlike the monasteries of Abū Maqār and of John the Short, Dayr Anbā Bishoi seems to have had no large outlying cells, or "dwellings" (in reality small monasteries in themselves), dependent upon it. In the statistical list of the monasteries of Wādī al-Naṭrūn drawn up in 1088, there are forty monks listed for the Monastery of Bishoi, more than the numbers listed for the communities of JOHN KAMA and Baramūs and the small "Cave of Moses." However, the number is less than those listed for the Monastery of the Syrians and considerably less than the numbers given for the monasteries of Abū Maqār and of John the Short, which are, however, surely inflated by inclusion of all the monks living in the cells and dwellings dependent on those two monasteries. By 1330 the buildings of Dayr Anbā Bishoi were on the verge of collapse because of the damage done by termites in the woodwork. In that year the patriarch BENJAMIN II intervened personally to assure the monastery's reconstruction as a cooperative project of the monks of various houses, in order to save the community from dispersion. In the late Middle Ages and as recently as the nineteenth century, Dayr Anbā Bishoi was at times called the White Monastery, which can lead to its confusion with the White Monastery of Shenute west of Suhāj in Upper Egypt.

Visitors to Wādī al-Naṭrūn in the seventeenth century consistently noted that the church of Dayr Anbā Bishoi was in the best condition of all the churches in the region, but the number of monks living in the monastery was very low. C. Sicard discovered only three or four in 1712; there were twelve when General Andréossy visited in 1799, and thirteen when Sir Gardner Wilkinson was there in 1843. In 1976 there were thirty-two monks of the community, twenty-two of them in the monastery and ten in its dependency at Kafr Dawūd in the Delta or elsewhere (Meinardus, 1977, p. 67). The Coptic patriarchs GABRIEL VIII and MACARIUS III were monks of Dayr Anbā Bishoi.

BIBLIOGRAPHY

Evelyn-White, H. G. *The Monasteries of the Wadi'n Natrūn,* Pt. 2, *The History of the Monasteries of Nitria and Scetis,* esp. pp. 111–15, 158–60, 232–35, 302, 360–61, 395–96, 418–25, 432–33, 435. New York, 1932.

Meinardus, O. F. A. *Monks and Monasteries of the Egyptian Deserts,* esp. pp. 236–38 (for the recent period not covered by Evelyn-White). Cairo, 1961.

______. "Zur monastischen Erneuerung in der koptischen Kirche." *Oriens Christianus* 61 (1977):59–70.

AELRED CODY, O.S.B.

Architecture

The walled area of the monastery forms an asymmetrical rectangle enclosing all the buildings. The only entrance is situated at the western end of the north wall. It consists of the usual lofty gateway and an inner gatehouse, the best of its kind preserved in the Wādī al-Naṭrūn (Evelyn-White, 1933, p. 139). The church and most of the remaining buildings, including the monks' cells, stand in the southern half of the walled area. The northern half (apart from the great *jawsaq,* or keep, of the monastery) is in the main taken over by gardens.

The Church

The present-day church is a conglomerate of different buildings, renovations, and extensions that are disentangled only with difficulty. According to Evelyn-White (1933, p. 142), the oldest remains of the church do not predate the great destruction of the monastery between 830 and 849. However, one can, with a great degree of certainty, reconstruct the ground plan of the new building erected after-

The main church at Dayr Anbā Bishoi. *Courtesy Father Martin, College of the Holy Family, Cairo.*

ward. It had a three-aisled naos with a western return aisle; a broad, deep *khūrus,* the like of which is encountered almost universally in buildings from the eighth century on, especially in monastic architecture; and a tripartite sanctuary. The latter consisted originally of a large square altar room (*haykal*) and two very narrow adjoining side chambers (Evelyn-White, 1933, fig. 13). At a later period the southern side chamber was expanded into a second altar room.

Presumably in the eleventh century a *parekklesion* dedicated to Abū Iskhīrūn was added on the south side; it repeated in principle the form of the main church, though on a reduced scale. Its almost square naos, approximately 20 feet (6 m) wide, could only have had a single nave and probably always had a cupola (in contrast to the assumption of Evelyn-White). Other extensions and renovations were carried out only after the eleventh or twelfth century.

The Refectories

Evelyn-White mentioned only one refectory, the latest of all of them. It is found to the west of the complex of churches from which it is separated by a narrow vaulted passageway. It is an elongated single-aisle building that is subdivided by transverse arches into five domed bays of equal size. A further domed bay made up the kitchen. The main entrance is situated in the center opposite the western entrance of the church. A table, about 3 feet wide, stands inside and occupies the entire length of the refectory.

The monastery has two additional refectories of an older type. The smaller of these may be seen in the southwestern corner building of the main church. It was transformed later into the Chapel of Mār Jirjis (Evelyn-White, 1933, p. 161). The room contains a sturdy square central pillar from which arches radiate on all four sides and divide the room into four domed bays.

A third refectory, which is likewise abandoned, is found in the southeastern corner of the monastery and is now used as a storeroom. Its architectural plan is the same as the building on the site of the present-day chapel of Mār Jirjis, but is considerably larger and is subdivided by four square pillars into nine bays. In the rooms bordering on the north are the bakery and the mill.

Church of al-ʿAdhrā. *Courtesy The Metropolitan Museum of Art, New York.*

The *Jawsaq*

The *jawsaq* of Dayr Anbā Bishoi is one of the largest and most finely executed towers of Wādī al-Naṭrūn. It is a few years older in date than the one in the Monastery of Macarius (DAYR ANBĀ MAQĀR). Its architectural layout shows the usual schema of all the towers in Wādī al-Naṭrūn. It is two (originally three, according to Evelyn-White) floors high and can be entered by a drawbridge, in the present instance leading out from the tower gate of the monastery wall onto the first floor. Inside there is a long, straight corridor. In front, on the right, lie the stairs, and at the farthest end, the bathrooms. The rooms on the left of the corridor are two rows deep. It was originally intended to fit out the first floor as a church (Grossmann, 1982, pp. 213ff., fig. 81), but this intention was never fulfilled. The present-day Church of Saint Michael on the second floor is later in origin and was built only after the loss of the original second floor. The *jawsaq* dates to the late thirteenth century.

BIBLIOGRAPHY

Evelyn-White, H. G. *The Monasteries of the Wâdî 'n-Natrûn*, Pt. 3, *The Architecture and Archaeology*, pp. 131–65. New York, 1933.

Grossmann, P. *Mittelalterliche Langhauskuppelkirchen und verwandte Typen in Oberägypten*, pp. 213ff. Glückstadt, 1982.

PETER GROSSMANN

Dayr Anbā Bishoi. Roof of the old refectory in the foreground. *Courtesy Father Martin, College of the Holy Family, Cairo.*

DAYR ANBĀ BISHOI (Suhāj). [*The entry concerning this renowned monastery consists of three parts. The first section deals with the history, as anciently recorded and as given by visiting scholars in more recent times. Since only the church is still standing, the second section describes the architectural sculpture of the church itself and of older surrounding walls. The last part admits to little present information on the layout of the area, and details the architectural structure of the church.*]

History

This famous monastery stands about 2 miles (3 km) to the north of DAYR ANBĀ SHINŪDAH. As with Anbā Shinūdah, nothing remains but the church, which is built of red bricks and thus gives the monastery the popular nickname Dayr al-Aḥmar (the Red Monastery). It is not known if Anbā Bishoi was the founder or only the holy anchorite in honor of whom the monastery was built.

It will be noted that in the typika (calendars) of the neighboring Monastery of Anbā Shinūdah, Anbā Bishoi is called only "anchorite," not archimandrite. What is known of him is supplied by the Sahidic recension of the Coptic SYNAXARION at 5 Amshīr. Anbā Shinūdah, at the age of only five years, was entrusted by his father to Anbā PJOL (Bājul in Arabic), his maternal uncle, who lived as a hermit on the "mountain" of Atrīb. He had a companion who was called Pshoi (in Arabic, Bishoi). The latter was also named Peter. This detail is also found in a sermon of JOHN OF SHMŪN in the sixth or seventh century (Orlandi, 1968, p. 18). All three built cells (not "celliers" as Basset translates, for the word *khizānah* is given as the equivalent of *ri*, cell, by Crum, 1939), which were still in existence when this recension was compiled. Near their cells they built a church that they called the *raghāmah*. This strange word is found three times in the Arabic life of Shinūdah, and in the three cases it is the Coptic parallel *toou* (mountain or desert) that is thus rendered (Amélineau, 1886–1888, Vol. 4, pp. 418, 437, 474). One might then think that this church was in some sense that "of the mountain." In fact, the archaeologist V. de Bock found a cave containing inscriptions and drawings of monks or hermits about 2 miles (3 km) to the south of the DAYR ANBĀ SHINŪDAH. One wonders if these are the ruins of this first church (de Bock, 1901, pp. 68–69; Jullien, 1903, pp. 257–58). W. M. F. Petrie also points out the ruins of a monastery of brick at the foot of the mountain. The monks of that monastery seem to have decorated the neighboring rock tombs (Crum, 1907–1908, p. 72).

What was the name of the place where Anbā Pjol and his nephew Anbā Shinūdah and Anbā Pshoi lived in harmony? The Coptic Life of Shinūdah, written by his disciple and successor Anbā Besa (in Arabic, Wīṣā), describes Pshoi as "he of the mountain of Psoou." This expression cannot indicate his place of birth, for another passage and the Synaxarion cited above report that he was born at Psone (in Greek, Psonis, and in Arabic, Basūnah, a village still in existence; cf. Ramzī, 1953–1968, Vol. 2, pt. 4, p. 124). It can only designate, especially preceded by "mountain," the place where he lived. Thus it is probable that the place where the present Monastery of Anbā Bishoi stands was originally called the "mountain" or the "desert" (the Coptic word has both senses) of Psoou. Unfortunately, the formula is missing in the Arabic version of the Life of Anbā Shinūdah, and in the notice in the Synaxarion. Anbā Psoi's place of retreat was then the parallel of Atrīb, where Anbā Shinūdah had chosen to live and which is immortalized by the "White Monastery."

Shinūdah, in a passage in his works that his editor J. Leipoldt has entitled "On the Subject of the Life of the Monks," stated precisely the extent of his monastery: "Our domain is from the valley which is to the north of the village of Triphois northward to the valley which is to the south of the dwelling of our father, the aged Apa Pshoi, the place where he first lived in the desert." It is thus clear that the site of the Red Monastery is the site where Anbā Pshoi lived.

This monastery always remained in the shadow of its celebrated neighbor, so much so that its history is somewhat eclipsed by it. This fact explains the lack of historical documents. Two inscriptions pointed out by V. de Bock (1901, p. 66, figs. 78–79) and dated by A. Mallon, who described them according to de Bock, would date from the ninth or tenth century. It seems that they have disappeared. From what one can understand of them (apparently de Bock did not know Coptic, and photography had not made the progress it has since made), they commemorated gifts made to the monastery by one Kolthe (Colluthus) and his son Paul (Mallon, 1914, Vol. 3, col. 2870). In 1973 R.-G. Coquin did not obtain permission to go and collect the inscriptions at the Monastery of Anbā Bishoi.

However, a colophon dated A.M. 807/A.D. 1091 indicates that the copyist was one Raphael, at first monk of the Monastery of Apa Pshoi (the name is followed by an apposition that appears to qualify not Pshoi but the monastery that bears his name: ⲡϩⲩⲛⲁϯⲟⲛ ⲛ̄ⲛⲁⲅⲅⲉⲗⲟⲥ). It might be asked if this is learned Hellenization of the Coptic word ϩⲉⲛⲉⲉⲧⲉ, as A. van Lantschoot (1929, Vol. 1, pp. 127–31) suggests. In this case, it would mean "angelic monastery"; but it is not known from where this designation might have come and then passed to the neighboring Monastery of Anbā Shinūdah. These transfers of monks were nothing unusual, for an inscription published by W. E. Crum (1904, p. 559), but which in part fell along with the plaster in 1973, mentions a director (*archigos*) of the Monastery of Anbā Shinūdah who had at first been a monk in the Monastery of Moses, no doubt that of Abydos.

One should note a monk of the Monastery of Anbā Shinūdah, the painter Mercurius, who left his name in the monastery of Pshoi by an inscription dated 1017/1301 (the best reproduction is given by

Monneret de Villard, 1925, Vol. 2, fig. 221), just as the painter did in 1315–1316 at Isnā (cf. Coquin, 1975, pp. 275ff.) and at Aswan (cf. Clédat, 1915, p. 15).

ABŪ ṢĀLIḤ THE ARMENIAN seems to have mentioned this monastery, if we trust the published Arabic text: "Dayr Abū B sh w n h, possessor of the monastery of Akhmīm," but his editor, B. T. A. Evetts, unfortunately translated this proper name as "Pachomius" and did not notice that this is the same formula as in the recension of the Synaxarion of the Copts from Lower Egypt, from which Abū Ṣāliḥ probably borrowed it. One may believe that this is a case of a copyist's error in Abū Ṣāliḥ's only manuscript and correct slightly to read B(i)sh(oi)h. It is enough to think that the copyist placed not two points below the letter but a single point above, thus transforming a *y* into an *n*. This similarity of formula may be an indication for dating this recension of the Synaxarion.

There is no evidence from the thirteenth to the fifteenth century, when al-MAQRĪZĪ mentioned this monastery in his catalog of the monasteries of Egypt. He knew the two names, the primitive one that the Copts knew well and the popular one, for he calls it "Red Monastery also called monastery of Abū Bishāi." He knew that it was three hours' travel (no doubt on foot) north of the White Monastery and that it was built of red bricks; he also said that this Abū Bishāi was a contemporary of Shenute and that the latter was his pupil (no doubt confusing Bishoi with Pjol). Finally, he believed that there was another monastery bearing his name in the desert of Scetis, thus confusing the Pshoi of Akhmīm and the one of Scetis.

From the seventeenth century on, there was the evidence of the European travelers. The first appears to have been J. VANSLEB (1677, pp. 372–77; 1678, pp. 225–26), who visited it in 1673. He noted that the two monasteries, the White and the Red, were neighbors; for him "an hour's journey" separated them (no doubt he made the passage mounted). He remarked that the architecture of the two churches was similar and that both were ruined, although he noted the beauty of the capitals. According to the life of the saint that he had read, Anbā Bishoi had been a thief before becoming a hermit. Vansleb may have confused him with MOSES THE BLACK. Vansleb was the only one to give this detail.

C. SICARD (1982, Vol. 2, pp. 225, 270) contented himself with mentioning it in relation to Shenoute; R. POCOCKE (1743–1745, Vol. 1, pp. 79–80) spoke of it and even drew up a plan, although not very exactly. Granger (1745, pp. 95–96) mentioned it, and F. L. Norden (1795–1798, Vol. 2, p. 70) did likewise. V. Denon (1802, Vol. 1, pp. 157ff.) spoke of it, and from him one learns that in his time (about 1798) the Red Monastery was burned down by the Mamluks.

In the nineteenth century one must mention the works of A. J. Butler (1884, Vol. 1, pp. 357–59). From the beginning of the twentieth century come the notes of M. JULLIEN (1903, pp. 257–58) and S. CLARKE (1912, pp. 151–61 and pl. 49–52). O. Meinardus spoke of it several times (1969–1970, pp. 111–17; 1974–1975, pp. 79–86; 1981, pp. 148–62). He gave a good description of it in *Christian Egypt, Ancient and Modern* (1965, pp. 293–94; 1977, pp. 404–405).

It is appropriate to mention Monneret de Villard's study *Les Couvents près de Sohag* (1925) and Walters's synthetic study *Monastic Archaeology in Egypt* (1974).

'Abd al-Masīḥ (1924, p. 171) noted that people visit the Monastery of Anbā Bishoi on 8 Abīb each year, but it seems that this is a confusion with the saint of the same name in Scetis, whose feast in fact falls on 8 Abīb.

BIBLIOGRAPHY

'Abd al-Masīḥ Ṣalīb al-Masū'dī al-Bāramūsī. *Tuḥfat al-Sā'ilīn fī Dhikr Adyirat Ruhbān al-Miṣriyyīn.* Cairo, 1924.

Amélineau, E. *Monuments pour servir à l'histoire de l'Egypte chrétienne aux IVe, Ve, VIe et VIIe siècles.* Mémoires de la Mission archéologique française du Caire 4. Paris, 1886–1888.

Bock, V. de. *Matériaux pour servir à l'archéologie de l'Egypte chrétienne.* St. Petersburg, 1901.

Butler, A. J. *The Ancient Coptic Churches,* 2 vols. Oxford, 1884.

Clarke, S. *Christian Antiquities in the Nile Valley.* Oxford, 1912.

Clédat, J. "Les Inscriptions de Saint-Siméon." *Recueil de Travaux* 37 (1915):41–57.

Coquin, R.-G. "Les Inscriptions pariétales des monastères d'Esna: Dayr al-Suhadā', Dayr al-Fakhūrī." *Bulletin de l'Institut français d'archéologie orientale* 75 (1975):241–84.

Crum, W. E. "Inscriptions from Shenute's Monastery." *Journal of Theological Studies* 5 (1904):552–69.

______. "Coptic Studies." In F. L. Griffith, *Archaeological Report* (1907–1908).

______. *A Coptic Dictionary.* Oxford, 1939.

Denon, V. *Voyages dans la Haute et la Basse Egypte pendant les campagnes du général Bonaparte.* Paris, 1802.

Granger, Sieur. *Relation d'un voyage fait en Egypte en l'année 1730.* Paris, 1745.

Jullien, M. "Quelques anciens couvents de l'Egypte." *Missions catholiques* 35 (1903):188–90, 198–202, 212–14, 237–40, 250–52, 257–58, 274–76, 283–84.

Lantschoot, A. van. *Recueil des colophons des manuscrits chrétiens d'Egypte,* Vol. 1, *Les Colophons coptes des manuscrits sahidiques.* Bibliothèque du Muséon 1. Louvain, 1929.

Mallon, A. "Copte (épigraphie)." In *Dictionnaire d'archéologie chrétienne et de liturgie,* Vol. 3, cols. 2819–86. Paris, 1914.

Meinardus, O. *Christian Egypt, Ancient and Modern.* Cairo, 1965; 2nd ed., 1977.

______. "Some Lesser Known Wall-Paintings in the Red Monastery." *Bulletin de la Société d'archéologie copte* 20 (1969–1970):111–17.

______. "The Semi-domes of the Red Monastery at Sohâg." *Bulletin de la Société d'archéologie copte* 22 (1974–1975):79–86.

______. "Die Nischen-fresken im roten Kloster bei Sohagin." *Oriens Christianus* 65 (1981):148–62.

Monneret de Villard, U. *Les Couvents près de Sohâg (Deir el-Abiad et Deir el-Aḥmar),* 2 vols. Milan, 1925–1926.

Norden, F. L. *Voyage d'Egypte et de Nubie,* 3 vols. Paris, 1795–1798.

Orlandi, T. *Studi Copti.* Testi e Documenti per lo Studio dell'Antichità 22. Milan, 1968.

Petrie, W. M. F. *Athribis.* Publication of the British School of Archaeology in Egypt 14. London, 1908.

Pococke, R. *A Description of the East and Some Other Countries,* 2 vols. in 3. London, 1743–1745.

Ramzī, M. *Al-Qāmūs al-Jughrāfī lil-Bilād al Miṣrīyyah,* 3 vols. Cairo, 1953–1968.

Sicard, C. *Oeuvres.* ed. M. Martin and S. Sauneron, 3 vols. Bibliothèque d'étude 83–85. Cairo, 1982.

Walters, C. C. *Monastic Archaeology in Egypt.* Warminster, 1974.

RENÉ-GEORGES COQUIN
MAURICE MARTIN, S.J.

Architectural Sculpture

The significant architectural sculpture of this church must be divided into two areas: the original decoration in the eastern part of the naos and in the triconch; and the older pieces of work contained in the medieval surrounding walls, some of them unintelligibly patched together.

The architectural sculpture contained in the east wall of the naos and in the triconch can without exaggeration be described as unique, in view of the unhappy situation regarding monuments handed down and preserved from early Christian Egypt. Here in the area of the sanctuary the most magnificent part of the architectural decoration of an imposing church has been preserved in situ in almost pristine condition. It is a representative ensemble that also allows insights into the relationship between homogeneity and variety of types and forms within a system of decoration.

The architectural decoration, especially in the triconch, was executed with markedly greater economy than in the more lavish church of Dayr Anbā Shinūdah at Suhāj, insofar as various parts of the building are decorated only with painting (e.g., entablatures, pediments, barrels and calottes, profiles and pilaster shafts of the majority of niches). This yields an interesting insight into the relative regard and rank accorded to sculpture and painting, for those parts of the building decorated only with painting are plainly used as a substitute for sculptured decoration (as an economy measure, so to speak) and are accordingly considered second-rate.

All the capitals are executed in stonework, as are the gables at particularly important positions (the side passages into the triconch). The dominant form is the Corinthian capital, fanning out in several types of varying profusion, which are ordered in accordance with the criteria of architectural composition (e.g., decidedly magnificent capitals on the pair of columns in the western opening of the triconch and corresponding pilaster capitals on the eastern end wall of the naos). The column capitals of the naos are slightly simpler, but well above average in their profusion of forms. Again somewhat simpler but likewise provided with two crowns of eight leaves each is the series of column capitals of the lower order in the triconch, where the capitals arranged in the middle axis of the conchs are emphasized by additional volutes. More-severely reduced column capitals, with only one leaf crown of eight leaves, appear in the upper level of the projecting order of the triconch, and capitals reduced to four corner leaves in the half-columns or pilasters of the wall niches. As a whole, different types of pilaster capitals correspond to the column capitals.

From a typological point of view, the niche heads and the gables over the passages essentially correspond to the stage of development evident in the church of Dayr Anbā Shinūdah, but in certain cases they go considerably further (the side passages to the triconch) and accordingly point to the second half of the fifth century as the date for the architectural decoration.

Contrary to older opinions, the two well-known

entrances, the north door and the south door of the surrounding walls, are neither homogeneous nor in situ. Essentially they do indeed contain decorated stone material that may derive from the time when the church was built, but it has been positioned with little understanding and, more often than not, misplaced. Evidently here architectural sculptures, which at least in part may derive from the original building of the church, have been inserted into the later brick walls at a time when the understanding of the relationships and associations of late classical architectural decoration had largely faded away.

BIBLIOGRAPHY

Monneret de Villard, U. *Les Couvents près de Sohâg,* 2 vols., pp. 121ff. Milan, 1925–1926.

HANS GEORG SEVERIN

Buildings

Up to the beginning of the twentieth century, clear remains of the surrounding wall were still visible in the south, west, and east. They enclosed an area that was about 500 feet (150 m) long in a north–south direction. Today these remains have been almost completely removed. On the east side, the boundary of the former monastic territory might even have been situated within the present-day village of Naj ʿAbū ʿAzīzah, which has continued to expand into the territory of the former monastery.

The buildings that used to stand within the monastery still wait to be uncovered. At present only the ruins of the church are visible, together with the *jawsaq* (keep) immediately in front of its southern entrance. As for the rest of the buildings attached to the church in the southwest and east, they are modern constructions, which have nothing much to do with the monastery itself.

In non-Coptic texts, the old church of the monastery bears the name "Red Monastery, Dayr al-Aḥmar," an expression best avoided because it gives rise to misleading information and pertains simply to its external appearance, as the outer walls were built with fired bricks. The spatial arrangement inside is reminiscent of the churches of Dayr Anbā Shinūdah. On the south side of the building was a row of ecclesiastical side rooms. In this case, however, they can be reconstructed only with difficulty because the dividing wall against the actual church is now almost completely missing. To the far southwest lay the staircase, while the present-day staircase in the east did not belong to the original structure. The large central main room could have had a western apse as in the church of Dayr Anbā Shinūdah.

The church itself was a galleried basilica with a western return aisle. There was no narthex. The sanctuary, however, is shaped like a triconch. With the exception of the central dome, which appears in the position of the original wooden ceiling, it still preserves all the standard features almost intact, including the inner applied columns and the vaulted semidomes. The side rooms of the sanctuary are gamma-shaped, built around the side conchs. Also in this building a front triumphal arch resting on high columns was placed in front of the triumphal arch at the entrance of the triconch at the level of the front steps of the presbytery. Unusually (as also in the church of DAYR ABŪ FĀNAH), the triconch in this building at first stood on its own. Judging by the decor, it is to be dated to the second half of the fifth century. The rows of columns in the nave, like the outer walls of the church and sanctuary, come from a later period, perhaps the end of the fifth or even sixth century.

The tower was constructed directly in front of the southern main entrance of the church and immediately assumed responsibility for the protection of the church. Its ground plan corresponds to the outline of the older keeps of other monasteries, having the staircase in the southwest and three rooms in the remaining quadrants. The ground level entry is unusual and is probably due to its special position in front of the church door. Presumably this tower dates to the ninth century.

BIBLIOGRAPHY

Bock, V. de. *Matériaux pour servir à l'archéologie de l'Egypte chrétienne,* pp. 61–67. St. Petersburg, 1901.

Clarke, S. *Christian Antiquities in the Nile Valley,* pp. 161–71. Oxford, 1912.

Evers, H. G., and R. Romero. "Rotes und Weisses Kloster bei Sohag: Probleme der Rekonstruktion." In *Christentum am Nil,* ed. K. Wessel, pp. 175–94. Recklinghausen, 1964.

Grossmann, P. "Die von Somers Clarke in Ober-Anṣinā entdeckten Kirchenbauten." *Mitteilungen des Deutschen Archäologischen Instituts, Abteilung Kairo* 24 (1969):156–60.

———. "Sohāg." *Archiv für Orientforschung* 25 (1974–1977):323–25.

Monneret de Villard, U. *Les Couvents près de Sohâg,* 2 vols. Milan, 1925–1926.

PETER GROSSMANN

DAYR ANBĀ BŪLĀ. [*This entry is composed of three parts. The first discusses chronological accounts regarding Dayr Anbā Būlā, as well as some details regarding the structures still standing. The second part recounts historical information and the holdings of the library. Part three gives details that have been revealed about the old church.*]

Chronology

The Monastery of Saint Paul (Anbā Būlā) is situated 26 miles (39 km) southwest of the Red Sea lighthouse station of Rās Zaʿfarānah. It marks the site to which Saint PAUL OF THEBES, at the age of sixteen, fled to escape the Decian persecution in the middle of the third century. Prior to his death in 343, he was visited by Saint ANTONY, upon whom he bestowed his tunic of palm leaves. The monastery was founded in memory of the first hermit (Saint JEROME) in the latter part of the fourth or the fifth century. Antoninus Martyr visited it between 560 and 570. According to an Ethiopian reference, GABRIEL II Ibn Turayk, the seventieth patriarch, was banished for three years to this monastery. ABŪ AL-MAKĀRIM stated that the monastery was totally dependent upon the Monastery of Saint Antony. In 1395 Ogier de Saint-Chéron counted sixty monks at the monastery being "of the same habit, rite and piety as the brotherhood of Saint Antony." In the first half of the fifteenth century, al-MAQRĪZĪ included the Monastery of Saint Paul as the seventh monastery in his list of eighty-six monasteries and called it the Dayr al-Numurah, or Monastery of the Tigers.

Reports about the monastery and its monks were given by the following travelers: Ogier de Saint Chéron (1395), Ghillebert de Lannoy (1421), Coppin (1638), Gerard (1639), De Maillet (1692), C. SICARD and J. S. Assemani (1716), Granger (1730), R. Pococke (1737), N. Savary (1777), P. Bruns (1791), A. Norov (1834), G. Wilkinson (1837), H. Tattam (1839), J. Bonomi (1840), P. Uspensky (1847), G. Schweinfurth (1878), M. JULLIEN (1883), A. S. Lewis (1904), F. Vignozzi da Seano (1908), Johann Georg, Duke of Saxony (1930), J. Doresse (1951), G. Giamberardini (1956), V. Taeckholm (1956), and J. Leroy (1957). For several centuries, the administration of the monastery was entrusted to the abbot of the Monastery of Saint Antony (DAYR ANBĀ ANṬŪNIYŪS), a situation that prevailed until the nineteenth century.

The monastery has four churches, of which three are situated in the ancient part. The Church of Saint Paul of Thebes is the spiritual center and occupies the cave in which Saint Paul is believed to have lived. Here, his relics are venerated. The inscription on the tomb reads: "Born in Alexandria in A.D. 228, died in the year A.D. 343." The walls are adorned with eighteenth-century paintings executed by a monk of the monastery and several fifteenth-century Gothic graffiti. The three altars are dedicated to the Twenty-four Elders (north), Saint Antony the Great (center), Saint Paul of Thebes (south). The divine liturgy is celebrated here during the months of January, February, and March. Close to the Church of Saint Paul, almost above it, is the Church of Abū Sayfayn (Saint Mercurius), built in the latter part of the eighteenth century. This church is used once a year during the week prior to Lent. The Church of the Holy Virgin Mary is situated on the third floor of the keep. The Church of Saint Michael, situated southwest of the Church of Saint Paul, is the largest and the main church of the monastery. The church has two sanctuaries; the northern altar is dedicated to the Archangel Michael, and the southern altar, to Saint John the Baptist. According to tradition, the icon of the Holy Virgin is attributed to Saint Luke the Evangelist, who painted it in A.D. 40. The sanctuary screen decoration shows the Twelve Apostles in robes of Coptic desert fathers. The library occupies a small room on the north side of this church. There are altogether thirty-two cells in the monastery. The water is supplied by two sources, the Spring of Saint Paul in the western part of the monastery and the Pool of Miriam, about 300 feet south of the monastery.

OTTO MEINARDUS

BIBLIOGRAPHY

Antoninus Placentinus. *Itinerarium,* ed. P. Geyer. Corpus Scriptorum Ecclesiasticorum Latinorum 39. Vienna, 1898.

Coppin, J. *Relation des voyages faits dans la Turquie, la Thébaide . . . ,* p. 313. Lyons, 1720.

Granger, Sieur. *Relation du voyage fait en Egypte,* p. 115. Paris, 1745.

Johann Georg, Duke of Saxony. *Neueste Streifzüge durch die Kirchen und Klöster Ägyptens,* p. 17. Berlin, 1930.

Jullien, M. *Voyage dans le désert de la Basse-Thébaïde aux couvents de St. Antoine et de St. Paul,* p. 61. Lyons, 1884.

Keimer, L. "Les Prosternations pénitentiaires des moines du couvent de St. Paul dans le désert de l'Est." *Les Cahiers coptes* 11 (1956):21.

Meinardus, O. "The Eighteenth-Century Wall-Paintings in the Church of St. Paul the Theban, Dair

Anbā Būlā." *Bulletin de la Société d'archéologie copte* 19 (1967–1968):181–97.
______. "The Monastery of St. Paul in the Eastern Desert." *Bulletin de la Sociéte de géographie d'Egypte* 34 (1961):81–109.
Tattam, Mrs. Henry. *Journal of a Tour Through Egypt, the Peninsula of Sinai, and the Holy Land,* Vol. 2, pp. 97–98. London, 1841.
Schweinfurth, G. *Auf unbetretenen Wegen in Ägypten,* p. 198. Hamburg, 1922.
Sicard, C. *Lettres édifiantes et curieuses,* Vol. 3, p. 300. Paris, 1845.
Strothmann, R. *Die koptische Kirche in der Neuzeit,* p. 4. Tübingen, 1932.

Historical Landmarks

If Paul of Thebes is a historical personage very different from the one presented by Saint Jerome (Delehaye, 1926, pp. 64–65), the origins of his monastery remain obscure. The first mention of the site appears to have been that of Postumian: "Ad eum etiam locum in quo beatissimus Paulus primus eremita est diversatus, accessi" (I was also going to the place in which the blessed hermit Paul dwelt) (Sulpicius Severus, *Dialogues* 1.17). Hence, at this period (401), in contrast with its neighbor, the Monastery of Saint Paul did not yet exist.

In 570 the anonymous pilgrim from Placentia noted only the spring (1898, p. 151).

In 1235 or 1245, the Monastery of Saint Paul was laid claim to by Syrian monks (Evelyn-White, 1932, pp. 317, n. 4, and 389–90).

In 1393 a Syrian monk copied a manuscript in Karshūnī, the colophon of which is reproduced in the Syriac manuscript (National Library, Paris, 191; cf. Sauget, 1983, p. 488).

In 1484 the monastery was pillaged by the bedouin; it remained in ruins for 119 years. It seems that the patriarch GABRIEL VII restored the monastery, but the bedouin plundered it a second time (Coquin and Laferrière, 1978, pp. 278, n. 2, and 279).

In 1638–1639 Coppin (1971, pp. 233ff.) paid a visit to the monastery and stated that the Monastery of Saint Paul was in ruins and uninhabited. In 1665 Gonzales (1977, Vol. 1, pt. 2, pp. 33, 654) confirmed that the monastery was still uninhabited.

In 1701 the patriarch JOHN XVI restored the monastery and repopulated it with the aid of Mark, *hegumenos* of the Monastery of Saint Antony.

C. Sicard (1982, Vol. 1, pp. 24–28) visited the monastery in 1716. In 1718 the *hegumenos* of Saint Paul was elected patriarch of Alexandria under the name of PETER VI. In 1726 his successor, JOHN XVII, was a monk of Saint Paul. In 1745 his successor, a monk of Saint Paul, became patriarch under the name of MARK VII.

The library, which is less important than that of the Monastery of Saint Antony, is described by Simaykah (1930, Vol. 2, p. 122) as containing the following classes and numbers of manuscripts: biblical (122), theological (99), historical (123), ecclesiastical sciences (411), and miscellaneous (9). These total 764 manuscripts, most dating from the fourteenth, seventeenth, and eighteenth centuries.

BIBLIOGRAPHY

Antoninus Placentinus. *Itinerarium,* ed. P. Geyer. CSEL 39. Vienna, 1898.
Coppin, J. *Les Voyages faits en Egypte,* ed. S. Sauneron. Cairo, 1971.
Coquin, R.-G., and J. H. Laferrière. "Les Inscriptions pariétales de l'ancienne église du monastère de St. Antoine dans le désert oriental." *Bulletin de l'Institut français d'Archéologie orientale* 78 (1978):267–321.
Delehaye, H. "La Personnalité historique de St. Paul." *Analecta Bollandiana* 44 (1926):64–69.
Evelyn-White, H. G. *The Monasteries of the Wadi'n Natrūn,* Pt. 2, *The History of the Monasteries of Nitria and Scetis.* New York, 1932.
Gonzales, A. *Le Voyage en Egypte,* 2 vols. Institut français d'Archéologie orientale. Cairo, 1977.
Nakhlah, Kamil Ṣāliḥ. *Silsilat Tarīkh al Bābawāt Batārikat al-Kursī al-Iskandarī,* Pt. 4. Dayr al-Suryan, 1954.
Sauget, J. M. "Trois recueils de discours de Grégoire de Nazianze en traduction arabe: Simples Réflexions sur leur structure." *Augustinianum* 23 (1983):487–515.
Sicard, C. *Oeuvres,* Vol. 1, ed. M. Martin. Bibliothèque d'étude 83. Cairo, 1982.
Simaykah, M. *Guide du Músee copte,* Vol. 2. Cairo, 1930 (in Arabic).
Sulpicius Severus. *Dialogues,* ed. C. Halm. CSEL 1. Vienna, 1886.

RENÉ-GEORGES COQUIN
MAURICE MARTIN, S.J.

The Old Church

Although the history of this church is still to be written, the hypothesis could be put forward that the room in which the relics of the saint are preserved belongs to the older parts. Unfortunately neither there nor in the adjoining *haykal* (sanctuary) have paintings been preserved. Visiting these parts must have been facilitated by a staircase with a

Central *haykal,* Dayr Anbā Būlā. Archangel. A.D. 1333–1334. *Courtesy Kees Crena de Iongh.*

narrow adjoining subterranean corridor. Nowadays this staircase descends from the Church of Saint Mercurius, which has been built over the relics of Saint Paul's. These four parts (the room for the relics, the adjoining sanctuary, the old staircase, and its corridor) have been cut into the rock and provide a kind of subterranean complex, as is the northern extension of this complex, being a large room with a flat roof. Before 1333–1334 at the northern side of the sanctuary adjoining the room with the saint's relics, a second sanctuary has been cut into the rock. From outside, domes indicate the existence of these older sanctuaries. Later, but before 1713–1714, the actual northernmost sanctuary must have been built, together with an adjoining room on its west side and with the actual narthex with the new staircase as the westernmost part, perhaps replacing older structures. These three rooms are covered with domes.

For the wall paintings, two dates have already been referred to in the hypothetical lines on the history of the church. The first one is A.M. 1050 (A.D. 1333–1334), given in an inscription near the enthroned Christ on the east wall from the central sanctuary. To this master, one may attribute as well the two archangels and the two cherubim or seraphim painted on the same level in the same sanctuary and the not well-preserved Christ between angels and stars above the entrance to the same sanctuary. The murals on the ground level—the Annunciation, the remains of an enthroned Virgin between two angels and of a standing John the Evangelist—are products of another medieval master. One of the two old masters must have been responsible for the portraits of monks like Arsenius, Shenute, and John in the old subterranean corridor leading to the old staircase. One of them must also have worked above the northern entrance to the room with Saint Paul's relics. According to inscriptions, the three Magi and probably Herod must have been there. The second date given by an inscription is that in the dome above the actual narthex, referring to the construction of this church by Pope John XVI of the Holy See of Saint Mark's, A.M. 1429 (A.D. 1713–1714). In those days a monk from Saint Paul's painted in all parts of the church more or less where the old paintings had disappeared or where new structures required new murals. By 1716, Sicard could give quite a negative judgment of this work, and unfortunately, it is these paintings that are considered indicative of the quality of the murals in Saint Paul's. The monk-painter of 1713–1714 often worked without preparing any background and without designing important parts of his figures, like the faces, with compasses, forget-

Arsenios, Dayr Anbā Būlā. Work of a medieval master. *Courtesy Kees Crena de Iongh.*

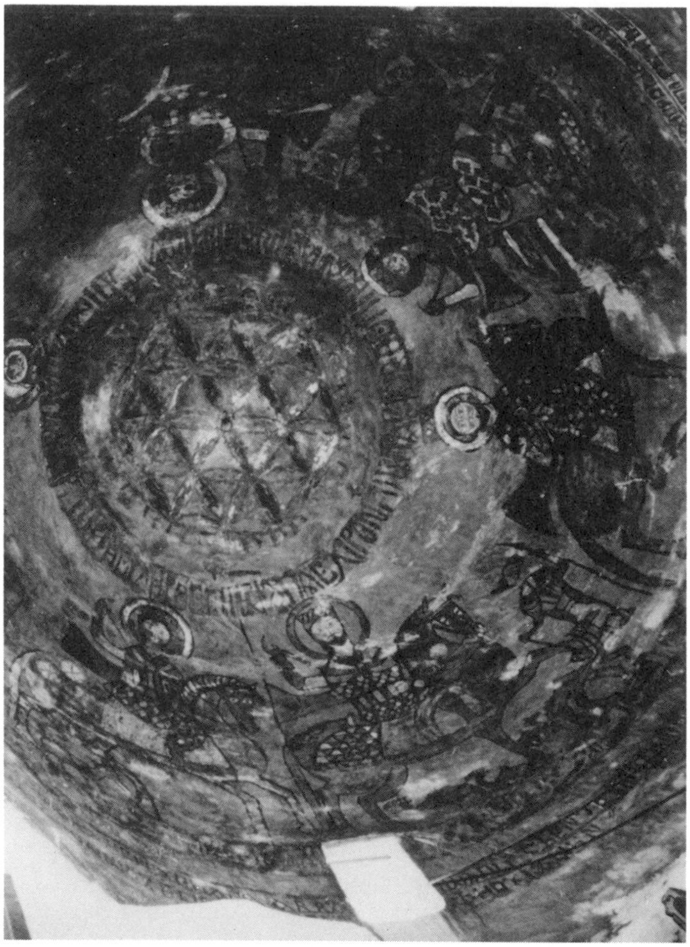

Martyr's Dome, Dayr Anbā Būlā. A.D. 1713. *Courtesy Kees Crena de Iongh.*

ting the ears, sometimes working in the sgraffito technique. His favorite colors were yellow, red, and green. This artist made a new row of saints in the old subterranean corridor near the old staircase (Saints John, Arsenius, Abib, Apollo, Samuel), the Holy Virgin between seraphim above the northern entrance to this corridor, three archangels and the scene of the Fiery Furnace nearby on the western wall of the room with the flat roof, and some portraits of monks in the same room. He also decorated the northernmost sanctuary of the Twenty-four Priests with a disputable figure of an enthroned Christ in Majesty, the dome and walls of the adjoining room on its west side (with four archangels and with Saints Marina, Irene, Kuriakos, Julietta, Paul, Anthony, and an unknown bishop), and the new narthex with the well-known horseback-riding martyrs. Although he was certainly not the best painter, this monk worked in a good Coptic tradition, being aware of iconographical rules. Unfortunately the many expeditions that have traveled to Saint Paul's Monastery (J. G. zu Sachsen, T. Whittemore, and J. Leroy) have not yet revealed all its art treasures.

BIBLIOGRAPHY

Adli, S. "Several Churches in Upper Egypt." *Mitteilungen des deutschen archäologischen Instituts* 16 (1980):7–8.

Butler, A. J. *The Ancient Coptic Churches of Egypt,* Vol. 1, pp. 346–47. Oxford, 1884; repr., 1970.

Leroy, J. "Le Programme décoratif de l'église de Saint-Paul du désert de la Mer rouge." *Bulletin de l'Institut français d'Archéologie orientale* 78 (1978):323–37.

Meinardus, O. *Monks and Monasteries of the Egyptian Deserts,* pp. 91–116. Cairo, 1961.

Schweinfürth, G. *Auf unbetretenen Wegen in Ägypten,* pp. 190–209. Hamburg, 1922.

PAUL VAN MOORSEL

DAYR ANBĀ DARYŪS, monastery mentioned in the Sahidic recension of the SYNAXARION in commemorating Anbā Yūnā (perhaps Jonas) at 2 Ṭūbah. The Synaxarion locates it near the town of Armant. Anbā Yūnā's uncle Victor, who prayed for the saint's birth and to whom he owed his vocation, was buried near the church of this monastery.

No archaeological investigation allows us to identify with certainty the Monastery of Anbā Daryūs, nor is it attested by any other written document. One may, it seems, say with E. Amélineau (1893, p. 125) that it was a true cenobium.

BIBLIOGRAPHY

Amélineau, E. *La Géographie de l'Egypte à l'époque copte.* Paris, 1893.

Doresse, J. "Monastères coptes aux environs d'Armant en Thébaïde." *Analecta Bollandiana* 67 (1949):327–49.

RENÉ-GEORGES COQUIN
MAURICE MARTIN, S.J.

DAYR ANBĀ HADRĀ. [*This entry consists of three articles:* History, Architecture, *and* Art.]

History

This monastery, although uninhabited since the twelfth century, is fairly well preserved and has aroused the enthusiasm of archaeologists.

It raises its imposing silhouette on the left bank

of the Nile at a latitude south of the island of Elephantine. It is above the mausoleum of the Aga Khan, the religious head of the Isma'ili sect, who died in 1957. The monastery was built in the seventh century, then rebuilt in the tenth, and destroyed in the twelfth century. The funerary stelae date from the sixth to the ninth centuries. It is said to have been founded to commemorate a holy recluse, Anbā Hadrā, who is celebrated on 12 Kiyahk and whose life is summarized in the Synaxarion of the Copts from Upper Egypt. He became bishop of Aswan in the time of the patriarch THEOPHILUS (385–412). Later the monastery was given the name of a local saint, Simeon. All travelers and archaeologists cite it under this name, but the Coptic sources always call it Anbā Hadrā.

Apart from the Synaxarion, which probably summarizes an older Coptic text, the most ancient witness appears to have been ABŪ ṢĀLIḤ (see Abū al-Makārim), at the beginning of the thirteenth century. Abū Ṣāliḥ spoke of it twice, the first time to tell of a church dedicated to Anbā Hadrā then on an island in the Nile and destroyed in his time. A little later he spoke of a monastery of this name that was on the left bank and was still occupied by monks. No doubt, he was speaking of two different sites or perhaps working from two sources, which he did not fully coordinate.

From the eighteenth century on, it was mentioned by travelers, E. F. Jomard (1809–1822, Vol. 1, p. 144) spoke of it, and M. Jullien (1903, pp. 283–84) noted it. Johann Georg (1913, pp. 60–67; 1930, p. 48) showed his interest in it and G. Maspero (1910, p. 193) paused there.

Unfortunately, the frescoes have not been systematically photographed. There remain only a *maiestas domini* (representation of Christ in majesty) and a fresco. This is the more regrettable in that today these paintings are almost invisible.

Happily the funerary stelae have been published several times, notably by U. Bouriant (1884, pp. 62–70) and J. Clédat (1908, pp. 224–29). They were conveniently brought together by H. Munier (1930–1931).

A Greek graffito attributed to a Nubian scribe is given by Griffith (1913, pp. 57–58).

BIBLIOGRAPHY

Bock, W. de. *Matériaux pour servir à l'archéologie chrétienne de l'Egypte.* St. Petersburg, 1901.

Bouriant, U. "Notice des monuments coptes du musée de Boulaq." *Recueil de travaux relatifs à la philologie et à l'archéologie égyptienne et assyrienne* 5 (1884):60–70.

______. "Notes de voyage, §19, le Deir amba Samāan en face d'Assouan." *Recueil de travaux relatifs à la philologie et à l'archéologie égyptienne et assyrienne* 15 (1893):176–89.

Budge, E. A. W. "Excavations made at Aswan, by Major-General Sir F. Grenfell During the Years 1885 and 1886." *Proceedings of the Society of Biblical Archaeology* 10 (1887–1888):4–40.

Clédat, J. "Notes d'archéologie copte: Assouan." *Annales du Service des antiquités de l'Egypte* 9 (1908):224–29.

Daressy, G. "Renseignements sur la provenance des stèles coptes du Musée du Caire." *Annales du Service des antiquités de l'Egypte* 13 (1914):266–71.

Denon, V. *Voyage dans la Haute et la Basse Egypte pendant les campagnes du géneral Bonaparte,* 2 vols. Paris, 1802.

Griffith, F. L. *The Nubian Texts of the Christian Period.* Berlin, 1913.

Johann Georg, Duke of Saxony. *Streifzüge durch die Kirchen und Klöster Ägyptens.* Leipzig, 1913.

______. *Neue Streifzüge durch die Kirchen und Klöster Ägyptens.* Leipzig and Berlin, 1930.

Jomard, E. F. "Description de Syène." In *Description de l'Egypte,* Vol. 1, *Antiquités,* pp. 143ff. Paris 1809–1822.

Jullien, M. "Quelques anciens couvents de l'Egypte." *Missions catholiques* 35 (1903):188–90; 198–202; 212–14; 237–40; 250–52; 257–58; 274–76; 283–84.

Maspero, G. "Premier rapport à l'Institut égyptien sur les fouilles exécutées en Egypte de 1881 à 1886." *Bulletin l'Institut d'Egypte* 6 (1886):3–91.

______. *Ruines et paysages d'Egypte.* Paris, 1910.

Monneret de Villard, U. "Descrizione generale di San Simeone presso Aswan." *Annales du Service des antiquités de l'Egypte* 26 (1926):211–45.

______. *Description générale du Monastère de St. Siméon à Aswan.* Milan, 1927.

______. *Il monastero di San Simeone presso Aswan,* 2 vols. Milan, 1927.

Morgan, J. de, et al. *Catalogue des monuments et inscriptions de l'Egypte antique,* 3 vols. Vienna, 1895–1909.

Munier, H. "Les Stèles coptes du monastère de saint Siméon à Assouan." *Aegyptus* 11 (1930–1931):257–300 and 433–84.

RENÉ-GEORGES COQUIN
MAURICE MARTIN, S.J.

Architecture

Dayr Anbā Hadrā lies about 4,000 feet (1200 m) from the riverbank in the region of the former hermitage of Anbā Hadrā. A few rock caves, some of

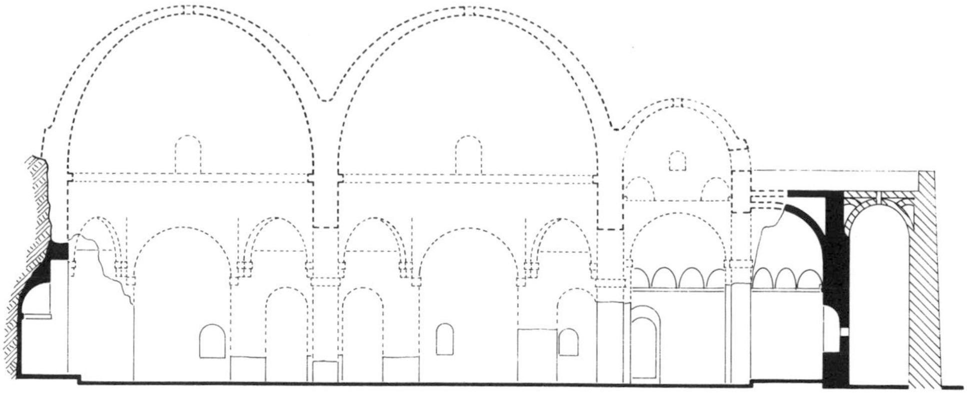

Projected elevation of Dayr Anbā Hadrā. *Courtesy Peter Grossmann.*

which contain wall paintings of the sixth or seventh century, can still be seen. These caves are, in fact, a string of rock tombs of the pharaonic period that were transformed into habitations. The high structures of stone and brick masonry of the *dayr,* however, belong to a refoundation of the monastery in the early eleventh century.

In its present shape the *dayr* is spread out on two natural terraces. Enclosed by a comparatively thin wall with a walkway for the lookout on top and several lookout towers at the corners, these terraces are joined into a coherent rectangular complex. In addition, each terrace has a gate with a towerlike structure attached to the front on the side opposite the other. As regards the internal arrangement, the lower terrace holds the church with the baptistery and several quarters for pilgrims. On the upper terrace the large living quarters, designed to serve also as a keep, make up the dominant building. Besides the monks' cells (chambers with six or more berths), it contains the refectory and the kitchen facilities. The mill and bakery as well as several storerooms lie outside the keep. On the upper terrace there are also numerous workshops. Deserving special attention among these are a pottery kiln situated in the upper southwest corner and several extensive laundering establishments. The latter suggest the existence of a dyer's establishment, indicating that probably the monastery kept its own flocks of sheep. A well or a cistern enabling the inhabitants to resist an extended siege has so far not been located.

Having lost its former domes, the monastery church is preserved only as a ruin. It was built in the first half of the eleventh century. Architecturally it belongs to the three-naved type of the octagon-domed church found most frequently in middle Byzantine architecture on the Greek mainland. It differs from the pure octagon-domed type by the fact that the nave was furnished with two domed bays instead of one behind the other. Thus, the church at Dayr Anbā Hadrā is at the same time an example of the domed oblong church, which appears in Egypt from the Fatimid period onward. The sanctuary in the proper meaning is only as broad as the domed area of the nave. The eastern niche (askīnah) here has a rectangular shape; it joins the *khūrus* to become the greater spatial form of a TRICONCH. On both sides the aisles continue along the sanctuary up to the east wall of the church. Originally the entrances to the church were found here. As the sanctuary was enlarged, occasioning the addition of a further zone of rooms to the east, the aisles were provided with open porticoes on each side. In a third phase, however, this form of access was abandoned once more, and the entrances were blocked. In this way were obtained two additional rooms, which could be entered only from within. In the northern room of these, the baptistery was installed.

BIBLIOGRAPHY

Clarke, S. *Christian Antiquities in the Nile Valley,* pp. 95ff. Oxford, 1912.

Clédat, J. "Les Inscriptions de Saint Siméon." *Recueil de travaux relatifs à la philologie et à l'archéologie égyptiennes et asyriennes* 37 (1915):41ff.

Grossmann, P. "Der christliche Baukunst in Ägypten." *Enchoria 8* (1978):97ff, table 19a, pl. 191.

______. *Mittelalterliche Langhauskuppelkirchen und verwandte Typen in Oberägypten.* Glückstadt, 1982.

Monneret de Villard, U. *Description générale du monastère de S. Siméon à Aswan.* Milan, 1927.

PETER GROSSMANN

Art

The decoration is exclusively pictorial. It is concentrated in the north wing of the church and to some extent in the keep. In the eastern conch of the sanctuary, the church shows Christ in a mandorla. He is enthroned, holding on one knee with his left hand a codex spanned by a cross and giving a benediction with his right hand, which passes beyond the ring of the mandorla. Each of two richly dressed angels leans on the mandorla with his right hand. The one on the right holds in his left hand a globe. Behind him is a personage of the same stature with a square nimbus. Below this fresco and separated from it by a decorative register, including an arcading between two pendentives, the decoration of which is destroyed, one can distinguish on the left the remains of a painting of small personages juxtaposed, each haloed and clothed in a white tunic.

In a niche on the west side, a fresco shows the Virgin standing full-face between two angels.

The grotto, which is situated at the western extremity of the north wing, has left some traces that are difficult to read. J. de Morgan (1894, p. 133) mentioned three walls occupied by a sequence of thirty-six figures in one register, which could be a part of the seventy-two disciples of Christ (Metzger, 1959, pp. 299–306). The ceiling is spanned by a series of meanders interrupted by large squares and octagons containing busts (de Bock, 1901, pl. 32.1).

In the castrum a painting, now destroyed, could still be seen at the time of de Morgan's investigation (1894, p. 134; de Bock, 1901, pl. 32.2). According to him, six personages stand out on the left against a red background, preceded by an archangel turned toward the enthroned Christ. The destruction of the continuation of the painting leads one to suppose a symmetrical group, which would complete the ensemble of the twelve apostles on either side of Christ.

BIBLIOGRAPHY

Bock, V. de. *Matériaux pour servir à l'archéologie de l'Egypte chrétienne.* St. Petersburg, 1901.

Metzger, B. M. "Seventy or Seventy-two Disciples?" *New Testament Studies* 5 (1959):299–306.

Morgan, J. de. "Service des antiquités de l'Egypte." *Catalogue des monuments et inscriptions,* ser. 1, Vol. 1. Vienna, 1894–1909.

Walters, C. C. *Monastic Archaeology in Egypt,* pp. 241, 311–13. Warminster, 1974.

PIERRE DU BOURGUET, S.J.

DAYR ANBĀ HELIAS (Naqādah), a rock church in the mountain three miles west of the small town of Naqādah, on the left bank of the Nile. Several texts deriving from the Theban region speak of a *topos* of Apa Elias. W. de Bock (1901, p. 83) discovered this church, and thought that it was identical with the *topos* of these texts. For these, the reader will find the essentials recorded by Winlock and Crum (1926, p. 113). Since the term *petra* (designating a monastery hollowed into the rock) evokes the site very well and it is read also on an ostracon containing the catalog of a monastic library, a connection has been made with this site (Coquin, 1975, pp. 207ff.).

BIBLIOGRAPHY

Bock, W. de. *Matériaux pour l'archéologie chrétienne d'Egypte.* St. Petersburg, 1901.

Bouriant, U. "Notes de voyage." *Recueil de travaux* 11 (1889):131–38.

Coquin, R.-G. "Le Catalogue de la bibliothèque du couvent de saint Elie du rocher." *Bulletin de l'Institut français d'Archéologie orientale* 75 (1975):207–239.

Kahle, P. *Bala'izah,* 2 vols. London, 1954.

Winlock, H. E., and W. E. Crum. *The Monastery of Epiphanius at Thebes,* 2 vols. New York, 1926.

RENÉ GEORGES COQUIN
MAURICE MARTIN, S.J.

DAYR ANBĀ HELIAS, twelfth-century Ethiopian monastery in Wādī al-Naṭrūn. In all the documents that concern this monastery, it is linked with the presence of Ethiopian monks. It is not that no other Ethiopian monks lived in other places in Wādī al-Naṭrūn, but this monastery appears to have been populated exclusively by Ethiopians.

The presence of Ethiopian monks in Egypt is attested at various places. In addition to the need for staging posts for their pilgrimage to Jerusalem, there was also the necessity of their continuing to lead the monastic life in the places where it had been born.

One question presents itself. Who actually was the Saint Elias under whose patronage this monastery came into being? In the second recension of the Ethiopian SYNAXARION, the oldest manuscript of which dates from 1581 (Colin, 1986, p. 323), a Saint Elias of Scetis is celebrated on 8 Yakatit, a feast that is missing in both the Coptic Synaxarion and the first recension of the Ethiopian, which dates from the end of the fourteenth century or the beginning of the fifteenth. It relates to the story of an interview between the emperor Theodosius, probably Theodosius II (408–450), and this holy monk. Hence, one may ask if the titular saint of this Ethiopian monastery was not this monk of Scetis, rather than the prophet. There is an English translation of this story by E. A. W. Budge (1976, p. 606). The manuscript of 1199 quoted below speaks for its part of "the great prophet Elias."

To what period can the foundation of this monastery be assigned? H. G. Evelyn-White, who examined this question, opts for the twelfth century. He remarked that a manuscript (1926, p. 273) notes that it was written for the Monastery of Saint Elias and the date of this gift is given as 1199. Besides, several manuscripts and fragments of multilingual Bibles come from Scetis, and the several languages of the text correspond to the nationalities then represented at Scetis: Armenian, Arabic, Coptic, Ethiopian, and Syriac. The manuscripts in question, now in the Ambrosian Library in Milan, have been dated to the twelfth century.

It is difficult to assign a precise date for the demise of this Ethiopian monastery's existence in Scetis. The monastery must still have been active in 1419, the date when a manuscript now in the National Library, Paris, was completed. The fifteenth-century Muslim historian al-MAQRĪZĪ mentioned this monastery, saying that it belonged to the Ethiopians and was in ruins. Since al-Maqrīzī died in 1441, the destruction of the Monastery of Saint Elias of the Ethiopians must therefore be established between 1419 and 1441.

BIBLIOGRAPHY

Budge, E. A. W. *The Book of the Saints of the Ethiopian Church.* 4 vols. Cambridge, 1928; repr. Hildesheim and New York, 1976.

Evelyn-White, H. G. *The Monasteries of the Wādī 'n Naṭrūn,* Vol. 1, *New Coptic Texts from the Monastery of Saint Macarius.* New York, 1926. Vol. 2, *The History of the Monasteries of Nitria and of Scetis.* New York, 1932. Repr. of all 3 vols., 1973.

Zotenberg, H. *Catalogue des manuscrits éthiopiens de la Bibliothèque nationale.* Paris, 1877.

RENÉ-GEORGES COQUIN

DAYR ANBĀ ḤIZIQYĀL,

DAYR ANBĀ ḤIZIQYĀL, monastery in Armant. The name of this monastery is given in two notices of saints by the recension of the SYNAXARION of the Copts from Upper Egypt, which provides an approximate indication of its geographical location. In the summary at 14 Kiyahk concerning one Ezekiel (Ḥiziqyāl), a native of Armant, whose parents were Christians, it is written that he became a monk in the district of his native town. He lived in the "inner" desert—that is, the most remote from the fertile valley. Since it was too distant from the town and infested by thieves, he moved closer to the town and installed himself "in the mountain," which means the stony plateau near the town. When he died, the people of the town instituted a pilgrimage to his church "until now," which means down to the period of the compilation of this recension of the Synaxarion (the twelfth or thirteenth century). It seems probable that a monastery was built over the tomb of Ezekiel.

There is also a reference to a Monastery of Anbā Ḥiziqyāl with reference to Anbā Yūnah (Jonas) in the Synaxarion at 2 Ṭūbah. Yūnah had a maternal uncle who brought about his birth through his prayers, on the condition that he should be offered at the age of three to the monastery, no doubt Dayr Anbā Ḥiziqyāl. This was done, and all his education was carried out by his uncle at the monastery.

The text says that this Dayr Anbā Ḥiziqyāl was remote from the cultivated lands, since it was "in the inner desert," but it does not specify if it was north or south of Armant. It appears that it was established on the left bank, as was Armant, although this is uncertain.

It does indeed seem that it is named in a Coptic document that speaks of a John, monk of the Monastery of Apa Ezekiel. According to the context, this text must be dated somewhere about 600. Hence, this monastery would have been founded largely before the ARAB CONQUEST OF EGYPT and would have survived down to the twelfth or thirteenth century.

There are no archaeological proofs for its identification, but J. Doresse (1949, p. 347) has suggested identifying it with the present DAYR AL-SĀQIYAH. This is only a working hypothesis.

BIBLIOGRAPHY

Doresse, J. "Monastères coptes aux environs d'Armant en Thébaïde." *Analecta Bollandiana* 67 (1949):327–49.

RENÉ-GEORGES COQUIN

DAYR ANBĀ MAQĀR. Rising on the desert horizon like a great fortress, the Monastery of Saint MACARIUS was originally the most remote and least accessible of the monasteries of Wādī al-Naṭrūn. It came into being around 360 when Saint Macarius

Dayr Anbā Maqār seen from the ruins of another monastery in the foreground. *Courtesy Father Martin, College of the Holy Family, Cairo.*

the Egyptian moved southward from the valley to escape the overcrowding of hermits. Here, at the age of sixty, he carved for himself a cell with a long subterranean vault in the rocky terrain, where he took refuge to avoid visitors. However, his followers grew in number and built their own cells of mud brick roofed with palm leaves around his cave. Dedicated to extreme poverty and silence, those hermits congregated only on Saturday and Sunday to listen to their mentor's sermon and to receive holy communion. Most of them spent their days reciting the scripture while doing manual labor. At the death of Macarius in 390, the settlement was well established, with some 2,400 monks in the area. The cell containing his remains became a shrine to perpetuate his name through the ages.

During the fifth century the monks sustained three invasions by desert barbarians who plundered everything in sight. Sometime before the third sack (444), the Tower of Palaemon (now disappeared) was constructed as a place of refuge. Also, the Church of Saint Macarius was begun, together with other buildings to serve as refectory, guesthouse, storerooms, and hospital for sick brothers. In 482 the emperor Zeno endowed the monastery and even dispatched two architects to supervise the construction of new buildings. Marble columns were used, and the discovery of numerous fragments of marble from these columns, their capitals, and some engravings attest to this. Legend says that the emperor's daughter, HILARIA, disguised as a young monk, joined the hermits and that Zeno made the endowment to commemorate this event and to demonstrate his appreciation for the desert fathers. Historians have it, too, that Zeno wished thereby to reassure himself of the loyalty and support of those holy men for his imperial throne.

During the following century, a new phase in the development of the monastery began by the construction of regular lauras (i.e., conglomerates of adjacent cells to house the monks instead of segregated caves for hermits).

Around 551, during the reign of the Coptic patriarch THEODOSIUS I, who had been exiled to Constantinople for some time, the Monastery of Saint Macarius became the occasional seat of the patriarchal throne as well as the center of church activity for many decades to come. From KHĀ'ĪL I to SHENUTE I the monastery monopolized the supply of prelates and also provided the church with many scholars. Its library grew to include a massive collection of manuscripts, now mostly scattered in museums throughout the world.

With the ARAB CONQUEST OF EGYPT (642), the general ʿAmr ibn al-ʿĀṣ pledged safe conduct to the monks and confirmed their revenues. Anbā Yu'annis was head of the monastery at that time, and under his aegis came the development of the *manshūbiyyas,* dwellings for groups of monks under the leadership of a single "father," or mentor, within a specific part of the building separated by a low wall from the remaining complex of structures. Notable instances may be traced in the wards of Anbā AGATHON THE STYLITE and Saint DOROTHEUS, where Saint JOHN KAMA received his training. In 800 the monk Epiphanius of Jerusalem visited the monastery and stated that it comprised a thousand *manshūbiyyas.*

This prosperous period soon changed when the poll tax imposed by the Muslim rulers was doubled

Old refectory of Dayr Anbā Maqār and Dayr Anbā Bishoi. Note the table and detail of the ceiling. *Courtesy Father Martin, College of the Holy Family, Cairo.*

in 704–705, and in 714–715 the monks were even branded. By 866, the financial burdens placed upon the monks became so heavy as to discourage monastic life. Also, marauding bedouins sacked the area repeatedly and thus forced the monks to erect high walls and strongholds to protect themselves. In fact, the patriarch Shenute I, during a visit in 870, personally supervised the building of these high walls around the church and subsidiary structures. This was the first concentration of buildings to form the nucleus of the present monastery.

During the eleventh century, chapels were being built and rebuilt, but in 1056 a terrible famine raged through Egypt, affecting the monastery greatly, and in 1069, invading Berbers again ravaged the place. Undiscouraged, the monks rebuilt the tower, the refectory, and the churches. According to the census of 1088, there were four hundred monks in the monastery.

But the fourteenth century witnessed the swift decline of this holy place. Beginning in 1346, two major disasters befell the monastery. First, the unprecedented persecution of the Copts begun by Sultan al-Ṣaliḥ ibn Qalawūn of the Baḥrī Mamluks resulted in the plunder of churches, the confiscation of Coptic properties, and the destruction of monasteries; the Coptic population was massacred or forcibly converted to Islam, bringing it to the edge of extinction. Second, the Black Death, which had scourged Egypt and its monasteries in 1348–1349,

Main church of Dayr Anbā Maqār. *Haykal* of Saint Mark. Detail: Luke. *Courtesy French Institute of Oriental Archaeology, Cairo.*

Main church of Dayr Anbā Maqār. *Haykal* of Saint Mark. Detail: Matthew. *Courtesy French Institute of Oriental Archaeology, Cairo.*

broke out again in 1374, and by 1388 the country was almost depopulated. The few remaining monks sought shelter within their monastery walls for protection from hunger and disease. Thereafter the Monastery of Saint Macarius remained substantially unchanged for centuries.

From the fourteenth century to the beginning of the twentieth, the monastery struggled against the human and natural elements of destruction, particularly ignorance. The gradual extinction of the language of the Copts, in which their early spiritual, liturgical, and theological history had been recorded, made the continuity of their tradition and the survival of their heritage very difficult. In addition, many manuscript robbers contributed to the depletion of the monastery library. Still worse, many stolen manuscripts were irrevocably lost when ships carrying them abroad foundered on the high seas.

However, toward the beginning of the twentieth century, signs of revival began to appear. Particularly since 1969, there has been an intense period of reconstruction. Today there are more than seventy monks in residence, mostly university graduates in almost all fields from medicine and engineering to the humanities and agronomy.

The monastery has a number of historic churches. The Church of Saint Macarius is noted for its three sanctuaries, those of Saint Macarius, Saint John the Baptist, and the Three Youths. After its

Sanctuary of Benjamin (first called the Sanctuary of Saint Macarius), Dayr Anbā Maqār. Doors. *Courtesy French Institute of Oriental Archaeology, Cairo.*

destruction in the sixth century by the Persians, the sanctuary of Saint Macarius was restored in 655 during the patriarchate of Saint BENJAMIN I, and for this reason it has sometimes been identified as the sanctuary of Benjamin. It is distinguished by its huge dome, 26 feet (8 m) in diameter, of which the lower part is decorated by portraits of the Twenty-four Priests. Some of these portraits still retain their bright color and minute detail. Since Saint Macarius maintained that throughout his life he was sustained by the divine power of the cherubim, in the northeast corner of the sanctuary the ancient artist depicted the cherubim supporting the dome. Dating from the seventh century, it is possibly the oldest known painting of the cherubim with all the characteristic details cited in the books of Ezekiel, Isaiah, and the Revelation of Saint John. The figure is surrounded by the four evangelical emblems of the lion on the left, the bull on the right, the eagle on top, and the human face at the bottom, while the wings are full of eyes.

The sanctuary of Saint John the Baptist was so named because it was said to contain the body of that saint, together with that of the prophet Elijah, which had been transported from Palestine to Alexandria in the fourth century during the patriarchate of Athanasius I. In the tenth century John's body was removed to the monastery, where the remains and those of some bishops and patriarchs were discovered in April 1976 while the church building was being restored. Hitherto known as the Sanctuary of Saint Mark on account of the presumption that the head of the evangelist was buried there, it since has been alternately identified as the sanctuary of Saint Mark and of Saint John the Baptist.

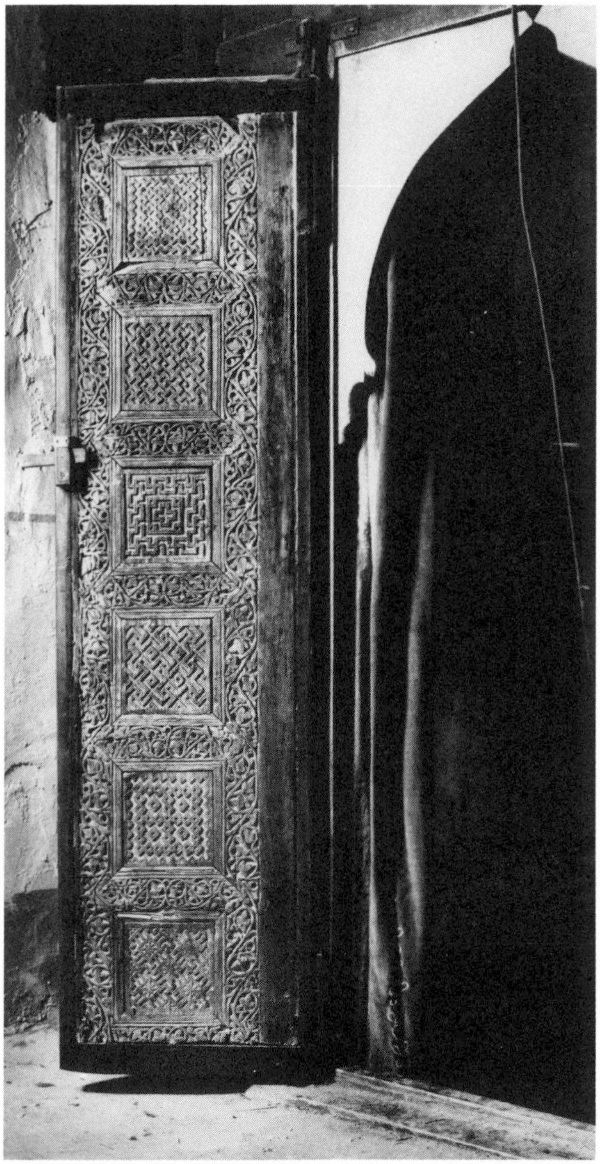

Sanctuary of Benjamin, Dayr Anbā Maqār. Detail of door. *Courtesy French Institute of Oriental Archaeology, Cairo.*

Sanctuary of Benjamin, Dayr Anbā Maqār. Intrados (interior) of the entrance arch. Painting depicting Nicodemus and Joseph of Arimathea carrying the body of Christ. *Courtesy French Institute of Oriental Archaeology, Cairo.*

Facing its altar was another, smaller one, apparently imposed by technical requirements, though according to ritual in the days of Saint ATHANASIUS a smaller altar was placed in the neighborhood of the main altar for keeping the holy bread before its introduction for sanctification. This smaller altar has been called in the Coptic rites the place of the eucharistic bread. Habitually this is to be found on the south side, never before the main altar, and was designated as the seating position where bishops and deacons received the remainders of the Precious Body and Blood, after the performance of Holy Communion for the monastic community.

The third sanctuary, known in the ancient manuscripts as that of the Three Youths, has been restored on the basis of an older one with its traditional three steps facing east. It is decorated with lively colored designs that represent the Eucharist and Baptism and date from the tenth century. It has a dome similar to that built by Saint Benjamin.

The Church of the Martyr Abiskharūn is dedicated to Abiskharūn al-Qallīnī al-Muqtadir. The surname is derived from Qallīn, a town in the Delta 22 miles (35 km) east of Damanhūr.

Renovations have cleared away the surrounding cells and rubble to reveal more fully the beauty of the building, which consists of a nave, a *khūrus* (room between naos and sanctuary), and three sanctuaries. As part of the renovations this building was given a traditional facade to blend with the classical style of the rest of the monastery. A remarkable dome surmounts the nave, which has been threatened by severe cracks. However, it was strengthened, and when a modern wall separating the nave from the *khūrus* was replaced by a light

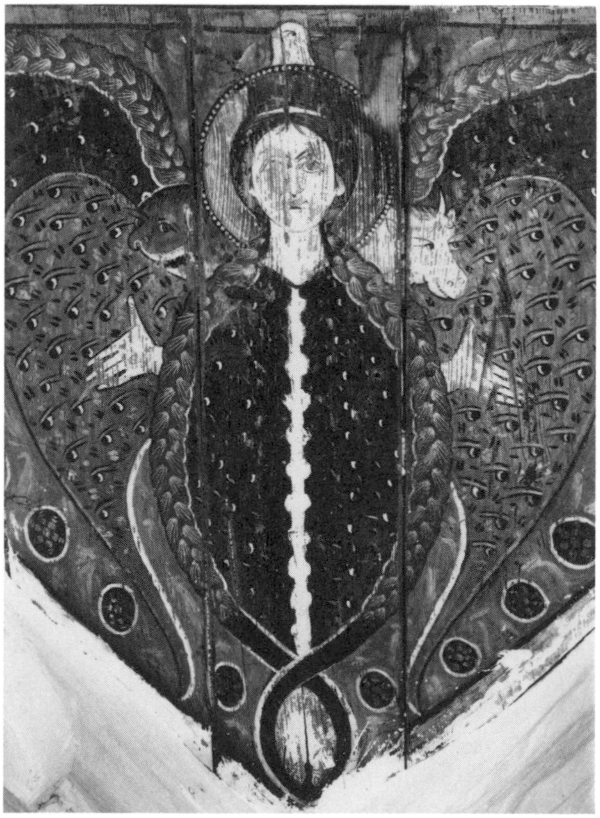

Sanctuary of Benjamin, Dayr Anbā Maqār. *Haykal.* Painting depicting cherubim supporting the dome. Seventh century. *Courtesy French Institute of Oriental Archaeology, Cairo.*

partition, the full splendor of this low quadrilateral dome (27 by 20 feet, or 8.3 by 6 m) was uncovered. It is built of thin baked brick bound with a rather thick layer of mortar and lime; it has been left unplastered, as the builder intended it. On the south side of the dome are two transverse vaults of more ancient origin. This dome has been dated to either the tenth or the thirteenth century.

The *khūrus* has a beautiful door in the north wall with regularly joined rows of red brick on either side, which cleverly bring out the horizontal lines of the door. A star-shaped geometric pattern is engraved in the brick above the door with an overlay of white stucco surrounded by a frieze with an Arabic inscription.

In the central sanctuary, restoration has uncovered basic architectural elements that may help facilitate further research and dating. Of note is its wooden screen, dating from 1866. In the southern sanctuary, which houses the relics of Saint JOHN COLOBOS (the Short), the most prominent feature is a circular white marble basin, intended to contain the sacramental oil for anointing the sick, an ancient Coptic tradition.

The Church of the Forty-nine Martyrs was built to commemorate the forty-nine monks who deliberately chose martyrdom during the third Berber sack of the monastery in 444. A platform in the nave marks the spot where they are thought to be buried.

Architectural features, such as the manner of lighting the interior, and the fact that the Jesuit Claude Sicard, who visited the monastery in 1712, made no mention of the church imply that this edifice was built at the beginning of modern times. This supposition is confirmed by a passage in the biography of the Coptic archon IBRAHĪM AL-JAWHARĪ, who is credited with its construction. However, some sections must date from an earlier period, such as those parts erected on the thick walls that are thought to be the remains of one of the old forts built during the ninth century.

Church of the Forty-nine Martyrs, Dayr Anbā Maqār. *Courtesy Father Martin, College of the Holy Family, Cairo.*

The keep (tower), Dayr Anbā Maqār. Door to one of the chapels. *Courtesy French Institute of Oriental Archaeology, Cairo.*

Constructed in the translateral style, it has an entrance to the southwest, a nave, a *khūrus* facing it, and one sanctuary only. A small belfry is connected with the southeast corner of the church.

The keep contains four small chapels, one on the first floor, dedicated to the Virgin, and three on the second floor, the Chapel of the Hermits, the Chapel of Anbā Anṭūniyūs (Saint ANTONY), and the Chapel of the Archangel Michael. There are excellent mural paintings in these last three, all being the work of a venerable Abyssinian monk, Thekla al-Ḥabashī. Dating from around the year 1517, these frescoes are notable for their bright reds and yellows and for

The keep, Dayr Anbā Maqār. Mural paintings of saints. *Courtesy French Institute of Oriental Archaeology, Cairo.*

their larger than life-size portraits of important personalities in the history of the church.

Of these four chapels, that of the archangel Michael appears to be the oldest. On the basis of the inlaid wooden screen, H. G. Evelyn-White (1926–1933) dated it to the fourteenth century. Situated at the end of the corridor on the north side, it once contained a magnificent wooden screen inlaid with ivory and ebony. This was, however, severely damaged, and what remained has been incorporated in the screens of the Church of Saint Macarius. The portraits in this chapel represent six warrior saints and the archangel Michael.

Situated south of the Chapel of the Archangel Michael is the Chapel of Anbā Anṭūniyūs, which is notable for three portraits by Thekla al-Habashī. These represent the earliest founders of Coptic monasticism, Anbā Anṭūniyūs, Anbā Būlā (PAUL OF THEBES), and Saint PACHOMIUS OF TABENNĒSĒ. The screen of the chapel is made of cheap wood dating from a late period.

The third chapel on the second floor, resembling that of Anbā Anṭūniyūs, is that of the Hermits. Like the other two, it is characterized by certain portraits of another class of saintly hermits, nine in number. Each of them appears in a tunic and a mantle, with arms resting on his chest and his hands clasping either a cross, a book, or a T-shaped monastic staff (the staff of Saint Macarius). The screen is a simple one belonging to the Ottoman period. These last two chapels were consecrated under the ninety-fourth patriarch JOHN XIII. This event is commemorated in a manuscript preserved in the monastery library from the year 1517.

The Chapel of the Virgin occupies the east side of the corridor on the first floor. The screens of the sanctuary, of delicate workmanship and belonging to different periods, are its most remarkable features. Also notable is the frame of the door in the central screen that is engraved with a continuous pattern of undulating foliage. Surmounting the door is a most exquisite carving of a peacock pecking a grape, symbolic in Byzantine and Coptic art of immortality and renewal of life. Evelyn-White (1926–1933) tended to set the date of this chapel between Greville's visit in 1875 and Alfred Butler's in 1884.

Because of the severely dilapidated condition of the keep, there has been much recent restoration. The wooden roof has been replaced by concrete;

Door in *hijāb* of the central *haykal*. Church of al-'Adhra', *Courtesy The Metropolitan Museum of Art, New York.*

Detail: left half of *hijāb* of south *haykal,* Church of al-ʿAdhrā', Dayr Anba Maqār. *Courtesy The Metropolitan Museum of Art, New York.*

the churches of the second floor have been made uniform in style; and the antique pieces of marble and wood have been transferred to a museum specially created in the monastery, where they remain safe and available to scholars for study and evaluation.

The revival of the Monastery of Saint Macarius began with the arrival of twelve monks on 12 May 1969 from Wādī al-Rayyān, a desolate spot in the Western Desert where they had lived in solitude for ten years without the shelter of a monastery or financial resources. They met with the head of the monastery, Anbā Mīkhā'īl, archbishop of Asyūṭ, and soon afterward, inspired by this meeting, one of the monks made a pencil sketch for a new monastery. This simple sketch became the guide for the extensive renovations to follow. The entire monastery was planned to be self-sufficient, with the monks' quarters separate, together with the places of service, in such a way as to allow the monks complete privacy. Through diligence, devotion, and self-denial, they erected the building at nearly half the estimated cost.

The monks' cells have emerged on three floors that line the contour of the monastery behind its extended new wall. Each cell space comprises a bedroom with a wooden floor to allow the monk to sleep on the ground, should he choose to do so; an office or study; a bathroom; and a kitchenette. Each cell is completely secluded to offer uninterrupted meditation, but adheres to modern health standards. A total of 140 cells of that description have been completed. Forty of them are devoted to novices.

In a modern refectory the monks convene once a day for their communal meal, with the abbot at the head of the table, the senior brother at his right, and the junior monk at his left. Appended to the refectory is a modern kitchen space equipped with up-to-date utensils and refrigeration capable of providing for 150 monks.

A library or modern scriptorium has been included in the planning, as a continuation of the literary tradition of this monastery. Apart from the remaining manuscripts from the monastery's vast original collection, efforts have been made to build up the present collection with an accumulation of theological and historical works of reference, together with microfilms of rare papyri and manuscripts from distant sources. There are plans for the publication of a catalogue raisonné of the manuscripts and an edition of the monastery's own manuscripts.

Figures of saints. Church of St. Michael, Dayr Anbā Maqār. Central figure holding the Gospels is identified by Coptic script as "Apa Makār"; incomplete figure on the right is identified as "Apa Apollo." *Courtesy The Metropolitan Museum of Art, New York.*

A monk. Dayr Anbā Maqār. *Courtesy Father Martin, College of the Holy Family, Cairo.*

A modern and elaborate printing press within the monastery has facilitated the task of publication of massive works by specialized monastic printers. Appended to the press is a computer and word processor capable of reproducing Arabic, Coptic, Greek, and Latin typefaces. So far the monks have produced more than thirty volumes, of which some are massive tomes, such as the *Life of Saint Athanasius* in eight hundred pages, as well as a monthly review, *Murqus* (Mark), in Arabic, English, Coptic, and Greek, full of illustrations and colored plates.

A museum has also been established to house all objects of antiquity discovered in the process of renovating the ancient structure. Marble capitals, pottery, woodwork, icons, and other objects of ecclesiastical significance continue to be assembled in this museum.

A hostelry for visitors and pilgrims was constructed in an area within the walls but far enough from the monastic cells to avoid any disturbance of the monks.

A hospital and an elaborate pharmacy were also developed for the care of the sick brothers and even for the secular workers recruited for the assistance of the monastic community. Here qualified physicians, surgeons, dentists, and pharmacists from among the monks attend to the needs of these establishments.

Outside the walls of the monastery, the monks not only seek the extension of their agricultural activity to ensure self-sufficiency and independence from the outside world but work hard to create an experimental station for the conquest of the desert on a scientific basis for the benefit of the whole country. So successful was the monks' venture that President Anwar el-Sadat gave them a thousand acres around the monastery for the extension of the work. They have been able to transform 400 acres of sand into agricultural soil that yields fruit, vegetables, and fodder for their cattle. This has necessitated the creation of workshops under qualified monastic engineers, a farmhouse for the toilers in the desert, and all sorts of establishments to meet the exigencies of modern growth. In a word, there has emerged a community of brothers devoted to the Pachomian rule of both manual and intellectual labor, while retaining the religious character of their daily travail.

BIBLIOGRAPHY

Amélineau, E. C. *Etude sur le christianisme en Egypte au septième siècle*. Paris, 1887.

Besse, J.-M. *Les Moines d'Orient antérieurs au Concile de Chalcedoine (451)*. Paris, 1900.

Curzon-Zouche, R. *Monasteries of the Levant*. London, 1897.

Evelyn-White, H. G. *The Monasteries of Wādī 'n Natrūn*, ed. Walter Hauser et al. 3 vols. New York, 1926–1933; cf. extensive bibliography in each volume.

Gayet, A. J. *Coins d'Egypte ignorés*, 2nd ed. Paris, 1905.

Hatch, W. H. P. "A Visit to the Coptic Convents in Nitria." *American Schools of Oriental Research* 6 (1924–1925):93–107.

Lewis, A. S. "A Visit to the Coptic Monasteries of Egypt." *Proceedings of the Cambridge Antiquarian Society* 10 (1898–1900):210–15.

Mackean, W. H. *Christian Monasticism in Egypt to the Close of the Fourth Century*. London and New York, 1920.

Russell, D. *Medieval Cairo and the Monasteries of the Wādī Natrun*. New York, 1962.

Walters, C. C. *Monastic Archaeology in Egypt*. Warminster, 1974.

Zotenberg, H. "Memoire sur la chronique de Jean, Evêque de Nikou." *Journal Asiatique*, ser. 7, 10 (1877):451–517; 12 (1878):245–347; and 13 (1879):291–366.

MATTĀ AL-MISKĪN

DAYR ANBĀ MATIYAS. *See* Dayr al-Fakhūrī.

DAYR ANBĀ PALAEMON. On the right bank of the Nile, to the north of the river, which at this point from Qenā as far as Nag Hammadi flows from east to west, to the east of the town of Al-Qasr wa-al-Ṣayyāḍ, is said to be the site of the ancient Sheneset (the Coptic name) or Chenoboskion (the Greek name). This was the site of Dayr Anbā Palaemon, the third monastery of Pachomius (on its pharaonic antiquity and the state of the place in the time of Pachomius, see Gauthier, 1904; Gauthier, 1912; and Lefort, 1939).

Dayr Anbā Palaemon was first mentioned by the Capuchin priests Protais and François in 1668 (see Sauneron, 1974, p.95; J. VANSLEB in 1677 followed their account, since he could not go beyond Jirjā, 1677, p. 413; English ed., 1678, p. 247). Sicard without doubt did not see it, since he does not speak of it. At the beginning of the twentieth century, it was mentioned by M. JULLIEN (1901, pp. 240–43), and O. Meinardus also describes it (1965, pp. 303–304; 1977, pp. 416–17). The Church of Saint Palaemon is now destroyed and rebuilt on a grander scale. It contains a good collection of liturgical manuscripts. The church called Sitt Dimyānah is without doubt the oldest, for it is 1.5 meters below the general level. A third church is consecrated to Saint MERCURIUS, and sometimes gives its name to the monastery (Dayr Abū al-Sayfayn).

An annual pilgrimage brings the Christians of the neighborhood together on 30 Ṭūbah and 25 Abīb, the days of the saint's feast and of the dedication of the church of Saint Mercurius.

BIBLIOGRAPHY

Abd al-Masīḥ Ṣalib al-Masū'dī al-Baramūsī'. *Kitāb Tuḥfat al-Sa'ilīn fī Dhikr Adyirat Ruhbān al-Miṣriyyīn.* Cairo, 1932.

Clarke, *Christian Antiquities in the Nile Valley.* Oxford, 1912.

Gauthier, H. "Notes géographiques sur le nome panopolite." *Bulletin de l'Institut français d'Archéologie orientale* 4 (1904):39–101.

______. "Nouvelles notes géographiques sur le nome panopolite." *Bulletin de l'Institut français d'Archéologie orientale* 10 (1912):89–130.

Jullien, M. "A la recherche de Tabenne." *Etudes* 89 (1901):238–58.

Lefort, L. T. "Les Premiers monastères pachomiens. Exploration géographique." *Le Muséon* 52 (1939):379–407.

Meinardus, O. *Christian Egypt, Ancient and Modern.* Cairo, 1965; 2nd ed., Cairo, 1977.

Muyser, J., and G. Viaud. *Les Pèlerinages coptes en Egypte.* Bibliothèque d'études coptes 15. Cairo, 1979.

Sauneron, S. *Villes et légendes d'Egypte,* 1st ed. Cairo, 1974.

Vansleb, J. M. *Nouvelle relation en forme de journal d'un voyage fait en Egypte en 1672 et 1673.* Paris, 1677. Translated as *The Present State of Egypt.* London, 1978.

RENÉ-GEORGES COQUIN
MAURICE MARTIN, S. J.

DAYR ANBĀ PISENTIUS. In 1926 W. E. CRUM left unanswered the question of the location of the monastery of Tsenti (al-Qassās in Arabic), where PISENTIUS, bishop of Qifṭ at the beginning of the seventh century, habitually lived and where it seems he died.

'ABD AL-MASĪH ṢALĪB AL-MASŪ'DĪ al-Baramūsī (1932, p. 184), however, mentions "in the mountain of al-Asas which extends to the west of Naqādah, the dayr of St. Anbā Bisantāwus, bishop of Qifṭ, to the south of Dayr Mār Jirjis, also called Dayr al-Majma'." He specified that formerly only the tomb of the saint was there, but that "around the year 1904 the dayr was built, that is to say a church and round it a wall enclosing about two *feddans.*"

The map of the Survey of Egypt (1943, 1954) marks at the edge of the desert to the west of the village of al-Baḥrī Qamūlāh, the Dayr Anbā Pisentius, about 430 yards (400 meters) south of DAYR AL-MAJMA', still called Dayr Mār Jirjis.

It seems then that the Dayr al-Majma' is indeed the monastery of Tsenti, of which the life of Pisentius speaks and near which Pisentius himself was buried. ABŪ ṢĀLIḤ THE ARMENIAN (1895, pp. 233–34) speaks of a monastery of Saint Pisentius, to the west of Qūṣ (no doubt the Dayr al-Majma'), outside of which was the tomb of the saint.

This monastery and tomb are not mentioned by O. Meinardus.

BIBLIOGRAPHY

Abd al-Masīḥ Ṣalīb al-Masū'dī al-Baramūsī. *Kitāb Tuḥfat al-Sā'ilīn fī Dhikr Adyirat Ruhbān al-Miṣriyyīn.* Cairo, 1932.

Winlock, H. E., and W. E. Crum. *The Monastery of Epiphanius at Thebes,* Pt. 1: *The Archeological Material.* New York, 1926.

RENÉ-GEORGES COQUIN
MAURICE MARTIN, S. J.

DAYR ANBĀ RUWAYS. *See* Dayr al-Khandaq.

DAYR ANBĀ ṢAMŪ'ĪL (Naqādah). *See* Dayr al-Sanad.

DAYR ANBĀ ṢAMŪ'ĪL OF QALAMŪN. [*The first part of this entry discusses the location and history of Dayr Anbā Ṣamū'īl of Qalamūn. Its present state and the previous architecture are described in the second part.*]

History

The monastery is situated in the southwest of the Fayyūm, in the northern part of the Wādī al-Muwaylih. One may reach it either from the valley, starting from al-Maghāghah, or from the south of the Fayyūm from Gharaq al-Sulṭānī. Because access is extremely difficult, it is still the most isolated monastery in Egypt.

The name Qalamūn comes from the Greek *kalamōn* (reed-bed, a place planted with reeds), a name no doubt due to the salt marshes described by ABŪ ṢĀLIḤ THE ARMENIAN and al-MAQRĪZĪ. The ancient texts most often specify "Kalamōn of the Arsinoite," to distinguish it from other places of the same name in Egypt. We know, for example, from John Moschus that fifteen miles (about 24 km) from Alexandria there was a LAURA of Kalamōn (PG 87, col. 3029) and from John CASSIAN that there was at SCETIS a place called Calamus (Evelyn-White, 1932, p. 155, n. 5). At present a village in the oasis of Dakhlah is called al-Qalamūn.

If we are to accord any historical value to the life of Saints PANINE AND PANEU, the valley of Kalamōn was already inhabited by hermits at the time of Diocletian's persecution during the years 284–305 (Orlandi, 1978, pp. 106–107). The alphabetical Greek series of the APOPHTHEGMATA PATRUM speaks of an Abbā Sisoes who lived at Kalamōn of the Arsinoite nome, and of Melitian monks who inhabited the same mountain (PG 65, cols. 401, 405). The patriarch CYRIL I (d. 444), in a letter addressed to Calosiris, bishop of Arsinoë, warns the monks of the desolate mountain of Kalamōn against ANTHROPOMORPHISM (Letter 83; PG 76, cols. 1066–77). We do not know if these monks lived in isolation or were grouped in a *koinobion* (monastery), but evidence indicates that Samuel, who lived during the seventh century, was not the initiator of monasticism in this mountain.

The Life of Ṣamū'īl of Qalamūn, preserved in Coptic, provides some information about the history of the monastery. After being driven from Scetis, where he was a monk, by the envoy of the Chalcedonian patriarch Cyrus after 631, Samuel took refuge first at Naqlūn (DAYR AL-NAQLŪN), from which he was again driven out, then at TAKINASH, near the valley of Qalamūn. From there he withdrew to a small church that appears to have been located in the valley; the church was encroached upon by the sands, which indicates that the monks had abandoned it. Ṣamū'īl came back to the church and restored it as well as the cells that surrounded it. Disciples came to join him from Takināsh and from Naqlūn, and eventually he built a great church that he dedicated to the Virgin. He died about the year 700, at the age of ninety-eight.

An apocalypse under his name adds some further details (Ziadeh, 1915–1917). It was composed probably at the end of the eighth century and has been translated from Coptic into Arabic. Stories of miracles of the Virgin at Qalamūn preserved in Arabic and in Ethiopic are dated in the Ethiopic version, the only one published, of A.M. 388/A.D. 671–672 and attributed to the abbot Isaac, possibly the same author who wrote the Life of Ṣamū'īl (Cerulli, 1943, pp. 158–78).

The monastery was plundered by the bedouins at a period difficult to specify *(Fourth Miracle of Saint Ptolemy,* PO 5, pp. 699 and 784–86). Another plundering (or perhaps the same) is mentioned in the Life of the patriarch SHENUTE I (858–880).

The monastery possessed a scriptorium, for the library discovered in 1910 at al-Ḥamūlī contained two codices, dating from the ninth century, which had been copied at the monastery of Qalamūn (Lantschoot, 1929, nos. 3 and 4, fasc. 2, pp. 11–12).

In the work attributed to Abū Ṣāliḥ, the report about al-Qalamūn is borrowed from a document dated A.M. 894/A.D. 1178. At this period the monastery was flourishing, occupied by 130 monks and with property in the valley at its disposal, not to mention the revenues from the salt-pits and palm groves.

The monastery is also mentioned by Yāqūt (Wüstenfeld, 1867, Vol. 2, p. 687), by Ibn Duqmāq (1893, Vol. 5, p. 4), and by al-Nābulsī (ed. Salmon, 1901, p. 72).

In 1353 the relic of Saint Ishkirūn, which had been in the monastery of al-Qalamūn, was transferred to the Monastery of Saint MACARIUS (DAYR ANBĀ

MAQĀR) in the Wādī al-Naṭrūn, without any reason being given, although the translation might have resulted from the decline of the monastery (Burmester, 1937).

In 1409 a monk from the monastery of Ṣamū'īl of Qalamūn became patriarch: GABRIEL V (1409–1427), who was to be renowned for his liturgical reforms.

The fairly long notice devoted to Dayr al-Qalamūn by al-Maqrīzī (1853, Vol. 2, p. 505) shows that the monastery was still inhabited in the fifteenth century, but had lost something of its past splendor, since it had only two towers instead of four as during the period described in Abū Ṣāliḥ.

The *Book of the Hidden Pearls,* about sixteenth century, still mentions it (Daressy, 1917, p. 204).

Thereafter it is European travelers who mention the monastery, sometimes perhaps from hearsay, for it was abandoned (Vansleb, 1671, p. 205: "monte Kelmon"; Sicard, 1982, Vol. 1, pt. 3, pp. 171, 189). In the 1722 map (drawn by order of C. Sicard) it is marked in the south of the Fayyūm, under the name of Saint PAPHNUTIUS; Belzoni (1820, pp. 432–33) is the first to describe the ruins of the abandoned monastery. Prisse d'Avennes (1848, p. 190) notes two churches at the site with frescoes of apostles and of several saints, as well as Coptic inscriptions. Whitehouse (1885–1886, p. 205) saw there in 1880 a painting of Saint George.

In 1898–1899 some monks who came from DAYR AL-BARAMŪS reoccupied it and reconstructed a small monastery dedicated to Saint Samuel.

The monastery today occupies only a small part of the ancient monastery, remains of whose encircling wall are still visible on the north and northwest. The limits are given by an extensive *kom* (mound). The monastery now has three churches: the subterranean one of Saint Samuel in an old *qaṣr* or tower, at about 10 yards (some 8 meters) below ground level, no doubt indicating the original level; and two recent churches, one dedicated to Saint Samuel, the other to the Virgin. From the ancient monastery there survive, in addition to the subterranean church, two Coptic inscriptions and the remains of fine carved decorations (friezes and capitals).

[*See also:* Abū al-Makārim; Ṣamū'īl of Qalamūn.]

BIBLIOGRAPHY

Abbott, N. *The Monasteries of the Fayyūm.* Studies in Ancient Oriental Civilization 16. Chicago, 1937.

Beadnell, H. J. L. *The Topography and Geology of the Fayum Province of Egypt.* Cairo, 1905.

Belzoni, G. B. *Narrative of the Operations and Recent Discoveries . . . in Egypt and Nubia.* London, 1820.

Burmester, O. H. E. "The Date of the Translation of Saint Iskhirun." *Le Muséon* 50 (1937):53–60.

Cauwenbergh, P. van. *Etude sur les moines d'Egypte depuis le concile de Chalcédoine (451) jusqu'à l'invasion arabe (640).* Paris and Louvain, 1914.

Cerulli, E. *Il Libro etiopico dei Miracoli di Maria.* Univ. di Roma, Studi Orientali 1. Rome, 1943.

Daressy, G. "Indicateur topographique du "Livre des perles enfouies et du mystère précieux.'" *Bulletin de l'Institut français d'Archéologie orientale* 13 (1917):175–230.

Evelyn-White, H. G. *The Monasteries of the Wadi'n Natrūn,* Pt. 2, *The History of the Monasteries of Nitria and Scetis.* New York, 1932.

Fakhry, A. "The Monastery of Kalamoun." *Annales du Service des antiquités de l'Egypte* 46 (1947): 63–83.

Ibn Duqmāq. *Kitāb al-Intiṣār,* ed. C. Vollers. Cairo, 1893.

Johann George, Duke of Saxony. *Neue Streifzüge durch die Kirchen und Klöster Ägyptens.* Leipzig and Berlin, 1930.

Lantschoot, A. van. *Recueil des colophons des manuscrits chrétiens d'Egypte,* Vol. 1: *Les Colophons coptes des manuscrits sahidiques.* Louvain, 1929.

Meinardus, O. *Christian Egypt, Ancient and Modern.* Cairo, 1965; 2nd ed., Cairo, 1977.

Munier, H. "Notes historiques sur le Ouady Mouellah." *Bulletin de la Société khédiviale de géographie* 18 (1932):47–51.

Orlandi, T. *Il Dossier copto del martire Psote.* Testi e Documenti per lo Studio dell'Antichità 61. Milan, 1978.

Prisse d'Avennes, Emile. *L'Egypte moderne.* Paris, 1848.

Salmon, G. "Répertoire géographique de la province du Fayyoum d'après le Kitâb Târîkh al-Fayyoûm d'an-Naboulsī." *Bulletin de l'Institut français d'Archéologie orientale* 1 (1901):29–77.

Sicard, C. *Oeuvres,* ed. M. Martin. Bibliothèque d'etudes 83–85. Cairo, 1982.

Simon, J. "St. Samuel de Kalamon et son monastère dans la littérature éthiopienne." *Aethiopica* 2 (1933):36–40.

______. "Le monastère copte de Samuel de Kalamon." *Orientalia Christiana Periodica* 1 (1935): 46–52.

Smolenski, T. "Le Couvent copte de St. Samuel à Galamun." *Annales du Service des antiquités de l'Egypte* 9 (1908):204–207.

Vansleb, J. M. *Relazione dello stato presente dell'Egitto.* Paris, 1671.

Whitehouse, C. "Researches in the Moeris Bassin." *Society of Biblical Archaeology, Proceedings* 8 (1885–1886):201–210.

Wüstenfeld, F. *Yāqūt's Geographisches Wörterbuch.* Leipzig, 1867.
Ziadeh, J. "L'Apocalypse de Samuel supérieur de Deir-el-Qalamoun." *Revue de l'Orient chrétien* 20 (1915–1917):374–404.

RENÉ-GEORGES COQUIN
MAURICE MARTIN, S.J.

Architecture

Because of the reoccupation of the monastery by monks from Dayr al-Baramūs at the end of the nineteenth century, a great part of the historical buildings has been lost. These buildings were destroyed to make room for new buildings. Johann Georg could still see remains of the old church, once richly painted (Johann Georg, 1931, p. 15). According to the description of G. Belzoni (1820, p. 433), "some of the paintings on the wall are very finely preserved, particularly the figures of the twelve apostles on the top of a niche, over an altar; the gold is still to be seen in several parts, and their faces are well preserved." Presumably this is the great church built by Ṣamū'īl and dedicated before 700 by Bishop Joseph of Arsinoë (see Cauwenbergh, 1914, p. 116). Today there is on the same spot an insignificant little modern chapel. The fine Corinthian limestone capitals of the old church lie in the north part of the monastery and adorn the entrance porches of the buildings in this area. They are older than Samuel's church and therefore were already used by him as *spolia* (capitals reused from older buildings). In style they are similar to the pieces from Oxyrhynchus, and may well have come from workshops there.

The only thing partly preserved is the old *jawsaq* (keep) of the monastery, which, together with its vault, is built in a good ashlar technique (Grossmann, 1980, p. 302). As usual, it is entered by a drawbridge at the second story. The staircase lies immediately to the right beside the entrance. The individual rooms in the still intact lower parts are accessible in a ring system. In the course of the reoccupation of the monastery, a small chapel, still in use today, was fitted up on the ground floor by removing the intermediate floor, carried on wooden beams. A small outlet, now walled up, in the north wall of the ground floor presumably led to a source of water lying outside the keep. The *jawsaq* may belong to the sixth century.

The high wall of the monastery shows numerous repairs, so that altogether it can scarcely be of very great age. According to Abū al-Makārim (ed. Evetts, fol. 71b), the monastery had four keeps, presumably displayed on all corners, and thus once it had an appearance not unlike that of the DAYR ANBĀ HADRĀ at Aswan. The present main entrance lies on the east side. Remains of some badly damaged mud brick buildings—perhaps hermitages of monks living outside the walls—can be seen in the north of the monastery.

BIBLIOGRAPHY

Belzoni, G. *Narrative of the Operations and Recent Discoveries in Egypt and Nubia,* p. 433. London, 1820.
Cauwenbergh, P. van. *Etude sur les moines d'Egypte depuis le concile de Chalcédoine,* pp. 39–50. Paris, 1914.
Fakhry, A. "The monastery of Kalamoun." *Annales du Service des antiquités de l'Egypte* 46 (1947): 63–83.
Grossmann, P. "Untersuchungen im Dair al-Qalamūn." *Archiv für Orientforschung* 27 (1980):301–302.
Johann Georg, Duke of Saxony. *Neueste Streifzüge durch die Kirchen und Klöster Ägyptens,* pp. 12–15. Leipzig, 1931.
Meinardus, O. *Christian Egypt, Ancient and Modern,* pp. 337–40. Cairo, 1965.
Wilkinson, G. *Modern Egypt and Thebes,* Vol. 2. London, 1843.

PETER GROSSMANN

DAYR ANBĀ SĀWĪRUS (Asyūṭ). The most ancient attestation of this monastery appears to be the colophon of a manuscript written there between 10 November 1002 and 29 August 1003, which then passed into the library of the White Monastery (DAYR ANBĀ SHINŪDAH) before ending up in the National Library, Paris (Copte 129:14, fol. 95; Crum, 1915, p. 47; Lantschoot, 1929 no. 70, fasc. 2, pp. 47–48). The text reads: "in the church and the monastery of the patriarch Severus which is in the ḥājir [edge of the desert] of Eribe to the south of the town of Asyūṭ." There is no patriarch of Alexandria of this name, and this is probably the patriarch of Antioch exiled in Egypt from 518 to 538. The SYNAXARION of the Copts perpetuates his memory on 2 Bābah and 14 Amshīr (the day of his death). This sojourn in Egypt by the champion of monophysitism is well known (Crum, 1922–1933; O'Leary, 1952).

At the beginning of the twelfth century, the bishop of Miṣr, Sanhūt, was obliged to flee from his see before the patriarch MICHAEL IV, who wished to establish his residence at Miṣr. He took refuge in the monastery of Saint Severus in the mountain of Asyūṭ.

Yāqūt (d. 1229) knew a monastery of Saint Severus near Asyūṭ, still inhabited (1870–1873, Vol. 2, p. 641). ABŪ ṢĀLIḤ THE ARMENIAN (beginning of thirteenth century) devoted a fairly long notice to it (1895, pp. 250–51). He notes that the monastery was flourishing up to the arrival of the Ghuzz and the Kurds (1161), but they heavily taxed the monastery. An old and pious monk of this monastery predicted to Talā'ī ibn Ruzzayj that he would become a minister, which came to pass. In recognition he made a gift to the monastery of a parcel of fertile land.

Al-MAQRĪZĪ (d. 1441) also gave a fairly long notice about the monastery (1853, Vol. 2, p. 506). It was situated on the border of the mountain of Durunkah. When Severus came into Upper Egypt, he made a prophecy to the monks. At his death a section of the mountain would fall upon the church without destroying it. When this came to pass, the monks were sure that the patriarch was dead, and from that day the monastery, which had been dedicated to the Holy Virgin, was named for Saint Severus.

In 1673 J. VANSLEB saw the ruins of the monastery of Severus from a distance, and the bishop of Asyūṭ related to him that formerly the monks occupied themselves with the search for the philosopher's stone (1677, p. 380; English ed., 1677, p. 229). In 1887 F. L. Griffith made some soundings and discovered two inscriptions, one of them dated 1091. The other, discovered at DAYR RIFAH, mentions Severus, archbishop of the city of Antioch (1889, p. 11, pl. 17).

Until 1965 one could see the two white domes of its church. They have disappeared since the construction of the military road that serves the quarries of the region.

BIBLIOGRAPHY

Crum, W. E. *Der Papyruskodex saec. VI–VII der Phillipsbibliothek in Cheltenham.* Schriften der Wissenschaftlichen Gesellschaft in Strasburg 18. Strasbourg, 1915.

______. "Sévère d'Antioche en Egypte." *Revue de l'Orient chrétien* 23 (1922–1923): 92–104.

Griffith, F. L. *The Inscriptions of Siut and Dēr Rifeh.* London, 1889.

Lantschoot, A. van. *Recueil des colophons des manuscrits chrétiens d'Egypte,* Vol. 1. Louvain, 1929.

O'Leary, De L. "Severus of Antioch in Egypt." *Aegyptus* 32 (1952):426–36.

Vansleb, J. M. *Nouvelle relation en forme de journal d'un voyage fait en Egypte en 1672 et 1673.* Paris, 1677. Translated as *The Present State of Egypt.* London, 1678.

Yāqūt ibn 'Abd Allāh al-Ḥamawī. *Geographisches Wörterbuch,* Vol. 2, ed. F. Wüstenfeld. Leipzig, 1870–1873.

RENÉ-GEORGES COQUIN
MAURICE MARTIN, S.J.

DAYR ANBĀ SHINŪDAH. *See* Dayr al-Ṣalīb.

DAYR ANBĀ SHINŪDAH (Fayyūm). *See* Monasteries of the Fayyūm.

DAYR ANBĀ SHINŪDAH (Qūṣ). *See* Monasteries of the Upper Ṣa'īd.

DAYR ANBĀ SHINŪDAH or al-Dayr al-Abyaḍ (White Monastery) (Suhāj). [*Dayr Anbā Shinūdah is described in this entry from the standpoint of its long and significant history, the architectural layout, and its architectural sculpture.*]

History

The church of this famous monastery still exists at the edge of the Libyan desert, on the left bank of the Nile, about 6 miles (10 km) from the town of Suhāj, often mentioned for its medieval paintings.

The name of the site is known from mummy labels, which give the Egyptian name "Atripe" (Arabic, Adrībah) and the Hellenized name "Triphiou," both of which come from the pharaonic Egyptian Ḥwt-Rpyt (house of [the goddess] Triphis; see Černý, 1976, p. 343). The place has often been confused with Atrīb in the Delta and also with Athlibis, which seems to have been close to it without being identified with it (as by Timm, 1984, Vol. 2, p. 602).

Very early, perhaps before the beginning of the fourth century, the mountain of Adrībah was frequented by Christian hermits. The Coptic fragments of the life of the martyr-monks PANINE AND PANEU do not speak of it, but it is mentioned in the long notice of the recension of the SYNAXARION from Upper Egypt. This speaks of their sojourn in the region and names the town of Idfā (not to be confused with the town of Idfū) and Adrībah. According to the Coptic tradition of the *Synaxarion* (7 Kiyahk), the beginnings of Christianity in this region date from long before SHENUTE. For later periods, we must have recourse to the information preserved for us by the Life of Shenute (in Arabic, Shinūdah), written by his disciple and successor BESA.

At the age of seven, Shenute was entrusted to his uncle Anbā PJOL, who gave him the monastic habit. He lived for some time with his uncle, who was a hermit in the mountain of Adrībah, and also with Abshāy (in Coptic, Pshoi), the titular head of a monastery near that of Shinūdah. He thus in the beginning followed the life of a hermit, and it is related in his Life, especially in the Arabic Life, that he often went off alone far into the desert and gave orders that he was not to be disturbed under any pretext. We have no documents to fix the chronology of the events in the life of Shenute. We know only that he took part with Patriarch CYRIL I in the Council of EPHESUS in 431, that he struggled violently against all the manifestations of paganism still alive at Plewit (the present Banāwīṭ) and at Akhmīm, and that he died in 466 (Bethune-Baker, 1908, pp. 601–605).

His immediate successor was his disciple and biographer Besa, who died after 474 (see Kuhn, 1954, pp. 36–48; 174–87; 1955, vol. 6, pp. 35, 48). After him ZENOBIOS, who had been Shenute's secretary, was archimandrite. It is known that he died on 6 Amshīr, for he was celebrated on that day according to the *Typika* (calendar). The Sahidic recension of the Synaxarion devotes a notice to him at the same day, and says that he founded a monastery of women opposite al-Marā'igh, near Akhmīm, a locality still in existence (Ramzī, 1953–1963, Vol. 2, pt. 4, p. 124). A leaf of parchment in East Berlin (Staatsbibliothek, Oct. 1609r., tenth to eleventh centuries) preserves a list of the archimandrites to be commemorated at the time of the eucharistic liturgy. It mentions, after PACHOMIUS, Shenute and Besa (curiously, Zenobios is not named), Aaron, John, Menas, David, and Andrew.

We must have recourse to the evidence of the papyri to find some names of abbots between the fifth and eighth centuries. We know a Peter, priest and archimandrite in A.D. 567 "of the monastery of Saint Shenute . . . situated in the mountain of Triphiou in the Panopolite nome." In another papyrus of the sixth century (Zeretelli and Jernstedt, 1925–1935, Vol. 3, no. 48) there is mention of a *pronoetes* (administrator) of the holy monastery, named Koursios, son of Joseph(ius). In another papyrus of 709 (Bell, 1910, Vol. 4, no. 1460) the monastery is called "of Saint Shenute," with others in the nome of Panopolis (Akhmīm) and that of Aphrodito (Kom Ishqāw). In a papyrus of the eighth century (no. 1471) it is mentioned again. The festal letter (in Greek) from the Patriarch ALEXANDER II (705–730) is probably addressed to Gennadius, abbot of the monastery (ed. Schmidt and Schubart, 1907, Vol. 6, pp. 55–109; Leclercq, 1937, cols. 1370–1520; Schubart, 1911, pl. 50). The HISTORY OF THE PATRIARCHS, in the notice on the patriarch Alexander II, names the holy and remarkable men and places among them "Apa Seth, archimandrite of the monastery of Saint Shinūdah, on the mountain of Adribah." We have thus the period (eighth century) of this saint, indicated in the *Typika* of the monastery of Shenute and the Sahidic recension of the Synaxarion at 29 Ṭobe (Coquin, 1978, p. 361).

The *History of the Patriarchs* also relates in the time of KHĀ'ĪL I, the forty-sixth patriarch (744–767), an event that happened to the governor al-Qāsim ibn ʿUbayd Allāh. He came to the monastery and wanted to enter the church on horseback with his troops and his favorite concubine. The superior, whose name is not given but who is said to have been aged, wished to forbid the woman to enter the church, but the governor pressed on. Then their horses fell and the concubine died. The governor understood, and gave the monastery 400 dinars as an offering. He wanted to carry off a wooden chest, the property of the monastery, but thirty men could not move it. In the face of this miracle, he made a gift to the monastery of a further 300 dinars.

In the same notice of the patriarch Khā'īl I there is mention of Paul, bishop of Akhmīm and "second superior of the monastery of Saint Shinūdah." The formula is obscure. It could indicate a bishop who had been *deuterarios* (prior, i. e., the second in rank after the abbot) before becoming bishop. This is not impossible. It could also refer to a bishop who was also superior of the monastery. It is well to note that the text uses the imperfect "was," or better "had been," and that the oldest manuscript (Hamburg Orient. 26) does not have the adjective *al-thānī*, "second" (see Seybold, 1912, p. 204, ll. 1ff.).

The fratricidal war waged between al-Muʿtazz and al-Mustaʿīn (about 866) affected many places, among them, according to the *History of the Patriarchs*, "the monastery of Abū Shinūdah," without specifying the site. It is no doubt the monastery of Saint Shinūdah, the best known of those dedicated to this saint.

In the eighth or ninth century, according to the Synaxarion (Sahidic recension) at 23 Kiyahk, Qafri, nephew through his father of a king of Nubia, after spending three years in a Pachomian monastery, obtained permission to visit a friend at the monastery of Shinūdah (probably that of Adrībah). This story also appears in a collection of forty stories of monks, of which those concerning this Qafri have been edited and translated by Crum (1932; Graf dates these stories to the seventh or eighth century; 1944, Vol. 1, p. 385).

For the period from the tenth to the thirteenth century, we have valuable information in the colophons of the manuscripts written for the library of this monastery or deposited in it. These codices have been divided up and dispersed among the libraries of the world, but the colophons have been patiently reunited, though without translation, but with numerous notes by A. van Lantschoot (1929). The most ancient of these codices, written "for the monastery of Shenute at Atripe," mentions Chael (Michael) as archimandrite; the manuscript is dated to 927–928 (van Lantschoot, 1929, p. 82). Another manuscript also names this archimandrite in 939–940 (van Lantschoot, 1929, pp. 84–86). The colophon of another manuscript, dated toward 1000, names the donor as Kolthe (Colluthus), superior of a monastery of Shenute, but although the leaf that contains the colophon comes from the library of the White Monastery, it no doubt refers to a monastery of the same name established at Rifah, near Asyūṭ (van Lantschoot, 1929, pp. 112–13). In another colophon, which the author dates from about the eleventh century, we cannot know who was the donor because of a lacuna, although the scribes were of the monastery of Karfūnah (an imitation of the Greek *graphon* or scribe) near Asyūṭ; the leaf was found in the library of the White Monastery. The name of the donor has been scratched out (van Lantschoot, 1929, pp. 114–15). The same fate befell a colophon in van Lantschoot's collection (pp. 116–17). First written for the monastery of Severus at Rīfah, it later passed, for an unknown reason, into the library of the monastery of Adrībah. A manuscript dated about 920–950 was written by Basil, steward of the White Monastery, for his monastery. The same thing is noted for the following manuscript (van Lantschoot, 1929, pp. 126–27). The manuscript next cataloged was copied by a monk of the White Monastery with a view to being given to the Monastery of the Virgin "in the desert of Apa Shenute, at Atripe." Van Lantschoot thinks (fasc. 2, p. 51) that it refers to a *topos* (church or monastery) situated not far from the White Monastery. The same colophon contains a prayer for the patriarch CYRIL II (1078–1092), which allows us to know the relative date of the manuscript, and also for the bishop of Akhmīm and the superior at the time, Klaute (Claudius; the manuscript is dated 1091). The colophon cataloged under the number LXXIX (van Lantschoot, pp. 132–33) also comes from the library of the White Monastery, to which it was given, but it supplies no further information. The following number (LXXX, pp. 133–37) is more loquacious. It indicates as contemporaries the patriarch MACARIUS II (1102–1128), the bishop of Akhmīm, John (the name is partly erased), the archimandrite Paul, known from other sources, and the *deuterarios* Pecosh. It is dated 1112. The colophon numbered LXXXI by van Lantschoot (pp. 137–39) mentions a church dedicated to Saint Seth (probably, for the proper name is in a lacuna), to the south of the White Monastery. This topographical indication is interesting; this manuscript, a lectionary, is dated 1118. The colophon of the manuscript numbered LXXXV by van Lantschoot (pp. 145–47) indicates the donor of the codex, the White Monastery, and the name of the superior of the time, Victor. The manuscript is dated 985.

Colophon number LXXXVII is notable, for it indicates that it was written for the house of the stewards of the White Monastery, and that this was in the eighth year of Apa Seth's rule as superior. We thus learn the date of the beginning of his rule. Van Lantschoot dates this manuscript to the tenth century, but we know that Apa Seth, unless it is another man of the same name, lived under the patriarch Alexander II. The codex whose colophon is numbered XCII by van Lantschoot (pp. 155–56) was made for the Church of the Virgin in the Desert of Apa Shenute (such was the true primitive title of the church; Shenute could not give his church any other titular). The manuscript whose colophon is cataloged by van Lantschoot under the number XCIII (pp. 157–58) was given to the church of the Monastery of Saint Shenute at Atrīpe. The colophon cataloged under the number XCI (pp. 153–55) indicates the archimandrite then in office, Apa Ioustos, "having power over the holy synagogue [community]." This codex would be of the tenth century. The manuscript with colophon number XCVI (pp. 161–

62) was given to the monastery of Apa Shenute, at Atrīpe. Colophons CI and CII are particularly interesting for the history of the monastery of Shenute and for that of all Egypt. They note, in fact, that the two codices of which they formed part were carried off as booty by the Ghuzz troops who under the leadership of Shirkūh made an incursion into Egypt in 1167, pillaging the monasteries. The manuscript of colophon CII is a Coptic Life of Saint Pachomius.

In the notice devoted to the patriarch Cyril II, the *History of the Patriarchs* gives a list of relics preserved in Egypt, and notes that the monastery of Anbā Shinūdah near Akhmīm preserves the relics of two apostles, Bartholomew and Simon the Zealot.

ABŪ ṢĀLIḤ THE ARMENIAN (beginning of the thirteenth century) devotes a long notice to the monastery. He mentions the relics of the two apostles and those of the founder Shenute, which are said to have been carried off at the time of Shirkūh's invasion, hence in 1167. Then he mentions the episode of al-Qāsim ibn 'Ubayd Allāh, indicating as his source the *History of the Patriarchs*. Later he reports the story of Bahrām, the Armenian minister who ended his days at the White Monastery. Abū Ṣāliḥ's evidence is precious here, for the Muslim historians use the plural "the white monasteries" for Bahrām's final residence. One might thus have some doubt that by this expression they meant the monastery of Anbā Shenute.

Thanks to the inscriptions from the church that have been published by Crum (1904, pp. 552–69) we learn some interesting dates. The apse fresco representing a *maiestas Domini* is accompanied by a bilingual notice in Coptic and Armenian saying that this fresco was executed in the time of the archimandrite Paul, Ezekiel being the *deuterarios* in 1124. Another speaks of the patriarchate of CYRIL III IBN LAQLAQ (1235–1243), the name of the archimandrite appearing to be John. He seems to be named in another inscription, dated this time 1258. The badly damaged painting of Saint Michael to the left of the left apse indicates the name of the archimandrite, Phoibammon, but unfortunately is not dated. In a passage that gives access to the south lateral apse, a table indicating the movable feasts associated with Easter for the years 1095 to 1219 was discovered in 1973, and another text mentions the rebuilding of the cupolas in 1259, as well as a history of the Coptic church in Coptic, beginning with Benjamin, unfortunately with many lacunae. The inscriptions in Armenian testify to the influence of the Armenian community in Egypt thanks to the power of Bahrām, who has already been mentioned. Three Armenian inscriptions on the fresco of the central apse bear witness to this influence (Strzygowski, 1918, pp. 731–32, 781; Clédat, 1910, Vol. 2, cols. 209ff.). An inscription, regrettably undated, mentions the painter Mercurius, no doubt the same who left a graffito dated 1301 in the neighboring Dayr Anbā Bishoi. He was a monk at Adrībah, and left inscriptions at ISNĀ (see Coquin, 1975, pp. 275ff.) and at Aswan (see Clédat, 1910, p. 51). That of Isnā is dated 1315–1316, that of Aswan 1317–1318.

The story of Bahrām, which is reported in summary form by Abū Ṣāliḥ, has been studied in detail by M. Canard in two articles (1954, pp. 84–113, and 1955, pp. 143–57). His power lasted from 1135 to 1137, and during this time the influence of the Armenians became very important in Egypt. The *History of the Patriarchs* also makes reference to Bahrām (Vol. 3, pt. 1, p. 31 [text], p. 50 [trans.]). Canard considers that we must follow Abū Ṣāliḥ and hence that Bahrām became a monk at the White Monastery and not in another monastery of the same name near Aswan. He thinks that the plural indicates the two neighboring monasteries, that of Shenute and that of Pshoi, the popular name of the one being applied for convenience to the second. Canard also presents a discussion of the date of the fresco of the central apse.

Al-MAQRĪZĪ (d. 1441) gives a fairly long notice in his roll of the monasteries of Egypt (1853, Vol. 2, p. 507). He knows the "Coptic" name "monastery of Saint Sinuthius," but he also knows the popular name, "also called the White Monastery." He situates it correctly "to the west of the province of Suhāj." He knows that it is ruined and that nothing remains but the church, which is built of dressed stone. He reports a rumor that the monastery possessed 4¾ *feddans* (about 7.5 acres). Finally he notes its antiquity. It will be gathered from this description that already in his time (fifteenth century) nothing remained but the famous church. We cannot say when and how the monastery disappeared. We may remark in passing that the name "White Monastery" was already known to Yāqūt (d. 1229), who gives it in his geographical dictionary (Yāqūt, 1866–1873, Vol. 2, p. 641), but we do not know the source of Yāqūt's information.

We must link with the sixteenth century an Ethiopian inscription that was in a square chapel before it was demolished at the time of the restorations in 1907, in the nave of the church and sheltering the pulpit (Lefebvre, 1916, Vol. 4, col. 493). It has been studied by Conti Rossini (1923, pp. 461–62), who dates it to 1563 and thinks that it was made by a member of a caravan of pilgrims visiting the holy places. V. de Bock at the beginning of this century wrongly dated it to 1730 (1901, p. 64). Conti Rossini thinks that a small Ethiopian community lived, at least for some time, at the monastery of Shenute, which would not be surprising since the Ethiopians had staging-posts at DAYR AL-MUḤARRAQ, in the Wādī al-Naṭrūn, and in Cairo on the road to Jerusalem.

A manuscript was written in 1587 for the monastery of Shenute on the mountain of Adribah (Crum, 1905, no. 866).

We have a final witness in an undated act of *waqf* (legacy); the writing of the codex is of the seventeenth century (National Library, Paris, Arabe 4761; Troupeau, 1972–1974, Vol. 2, p. 18). With the same century we must link the *Miracles of Ptolemy* (this is at least the date [1606] of the sole published manuscript), which mentions a monastery of women near that of Shinūdah at Atripe (*PO* 5, fasc. 5, p. 791).

Thereafter we have the reports of European travelers. The first among them to press his investigations so far into Upper Egypt appears to have been J. VANSLEB, describing the "monastery of Saint Sennode the archimandrite, called the White [Monastery]"; he was to note at the entrance of the choir two very fine columns of granite, and on the one on the left an epitaph to a certain Heliodorus. Though neither G. Lefebvre nor U. Monneret de Villard was able to find it and declared it vanished, it was indeed visible in April 1973. This is the more astonishing in that Lefebvre was to find at Akhmīm a similar column bearing the same epitaph with the same engraving. It is without doubt a case of a pair of columns from a pagan temple. It is astonishing that Lefebvre did not make the connection and note this reuse (Vansleb, 1677, pp. 372–74; English ed. 1678, pp. 223–25). He remarks that the church is demolished and that only the sanctuary is intact, which is still the present state.

We may also draw attention to the observations of other travelers. C. SICARD in 1722–1723 named it "monastery of Saint Sennodius," but did not linger there (1982, Vol. 2, pp. 225, 270). R. POCOCKE also mentioned it in *A Description of the East* (Vol. 1, pp. 79–80), as did Granger (1745, pp. 92–96) and F. L. Norden (1795–1798, Vol. 2, pp. 69–70 and pl. 89). Jean Baptiste Bourguignon d'Anville noted it in his map of Egypt. Finally V. Denon accompanied Napoleon there (1802, Vol. 1, pp. 157ff.).

For the nineteenth century, it is appropriate to mention G. Wilkinson (1843, Vol. 2, pp. 19, 98–102) and R. Curzon (1857, pp. 121–26). Butler described it in his *Ancient Coptic Churches of Egypt* (Vol. 1, pp. 351–57). For the beginning of the twentieth century we must cite the works of de Bock (1901, pp. 39–60, 68–70, 80–84), C. R. Peers (1904, pp. 131–53), W. M. F. Petrie (1908, pp. 13–5), and S. CLARKE (1912, pp. 145–61).

The *Comité de conservation des monuments de l'art arabe* gave all its care to this jewel of Coptic art, as its *Bulletin* proves. Thus one may consult the numbers of 1898 (pp. 67–72, "Notice sur les monuments coptes de la vallée du Nil," by de Bock), 1901 and 1903 (watercolors by Clédat of the frescoes of the Dayr al-Abyaḍ; reproduced in Simaykah, 1932, in Arabic, Vol. 2, p. 129), 1904 (p. 28, projects of restoration), 1906 (pp. 68, discovery of manuscripts), 1907 (pp. 26 and 36, discovery of gold dinars and of manuscripts), 1908 (p. 59, Herz's report), 1910 (p. 39; photos available), and 1912 (pp. 191–98, Simaykah's report). These projects were to be made use of by Monneret de Villard in his two volumes, *Les couvents près de Sohag,* a study at once historical and architectural. This was followed by A. L. Schmitz, "Das weisse und das rote Kloster" (1927).

The monastery is a popular place of pilgrimage, especially on 7 Abīb, the feast of Saint Shinūdah (1979, Viaud, pp. 55–56).

[*See also* Abū al-Makārim.]

BIBLIOGRAPHY

Amélineau, E. *Monuments pour servir à l'histoire de l'Egypte chrétienne aux IVe, Ve, VIe, et VIIe siècles.* Mémoires de la Mission archéologique française du Caire 4. Paris, 1886–1888.

Anville, J. B. B. d'. *Carte de l'Egypte, nommée dans le pays Missir.* Paris, 1765.

Bell, H. I. *Greek Papyri in the British Museum,* Vol. 4. London, 1910.

Bethune-Baker, J. F. "The Date of the Death of Nestorius: Schenute, Zacharias, Evagrius." *Journal of Theological Studies* 9 (1908):601–605.

Bock, V. de. *Matériaux pour servir à l'archéologie de l'Egypte chrétienne.* St. Petersburg, 1901.

Butler, A. J. *The Ancient Coptic Churches of Egypt,* 2 vols. Oxford, 1884.

Canard, M. "Un vizir chrétien à l'époque fatimide, l'arménien Bahram." *Annales de l'Institut d'etudes orientales de la Faculté des lettres d'Alger* 12 (1954):84–113.

______. "Notes sur les Arméniens à l'époque fatimide." *Annales de l'Institut d'études orientales de la Faculté des lettres d'Alger* 13 (1955):143–57.

Černý, J. *Coptic Etymological Dictionary*. Cambridge, 1976.
Clarke, S. *Christian Antiquities in the Nile Valley*. Oxford, 1912.
Clédat, J. "Baouit." In *Dictionnaire d'archéologie chrétienne et de liturgie*, Vol. 2, cols. 203–51. Paris, 1910.
———. "Les inscriptions de Saint Siméon." *Recueil de Travaux* 37 (1915):41–57.
Coquin, R.-G. "Les inscriptions pariétales des monastères d'Esna: Dayr al-Sûhadā', Dayr al-Fahūrī." *Bulletin de l'Institut français d'Archéologie orientale* 75 (1975):241–84.
———. "Le Synaxaire des Coptes: Un nouveau témoin de la recension de Haute Egypte." *Analecta Bollandiana* 96 (1978):351–65.
Crum, W. E. "Inscriptions from Shenoute's Monastery." *Journal of Theological Studies* 5 (1904): 552–69.
———. *Catalogue of the Coptic Manuscripts in the British Museum*. London, 1905.
———. "A Nubian Prince in an Egyptian Monastery." In *Studies presented to F. Ll. Griffith*, pp. 137–48. London, 1932.
Curzon, R. *Visits to the Monasteries in the Levant*. London, 1857.
Denon, V. *Voyages dans la Haute et Basse Egypte . . .*, 2 vols. Paris, 1802.
Granger, Sieur. *Relation du voyage fait en Egypte en l'année 1730*. Paris, 1745.
Kuhn, K. H. "A Fifth Century Egyptian Abbot." *Journal of Theological Studies*, n. s., 5 (1954):36–48; 174–87; 6 (1955):35–48.
Lantschoot, A. van. *Recueil des colophons des manuscrits chrétiens d'Egypte*, 2 fascs. Louvain, 1929.
Leclercq, H. "Papyrus." In *Dictionnaire d'archéologie chrétienne et de liturgie*, Vol. 13, pt. 1, cols. 1370–1520. Paris, 1937.
Lefebvre, G. "Dair al-Abiad." In *Dictionnaire d'archéologie chrétienne et de liturgie*, Vol. 4, cols. 459–502. Paris, 1910.
Leroy, L., ed. *Les miracles de saint Ptolémée. PO* 5, fasc. 5, pp. 779–806. Paris, 1910.
Maspéro, J. *Papyrus grecs d'époque byzantine*. Catalogue géneral du Musée du Caire, 3 vols. Cairo, 1910–1916.
Monneret de Villard, U. *Les Couvents près de Sohag*, 2 vols. Milan, 1925–1927.
Norden, F. L. *Voyage d'Egypte et de Nubie*, 3 vols., ed. L. Langlès. Paris 1795–1798.
Peers, C. R. "The White Monastery near Sohag in Upper Egypt." *Archaeological Journal*, ser. 3, 11 (1904):131–53.
Petrie, W. M. F. *Athribis*. London, 1908.
Pococke, R. *A Description of the East*. London, 1743.
Ramzī, M. *Al-Qāmūs al-Jughrāfī lil-Bilād al Miṣrīyyah*, 3 vols. Cairo, 1953–1968.
Rossini, C. Conti. "Aethiopica III." *Rivista di Studi Orientale* 9 (1923):461–62.
Schmidt, C., and W. Schubart. *Altchristliche Texte*. Berlin, 1910.
Schmitz, A. L. "Das weisse und das rote Kloster." *Antike* 3 (1927):326–50.
Schubart, W. *Papyri Graecae Berolinenses*. Bonn and Oxford, 1911.
Seybold, C. F. *Alexandrinische Patriarchengeschichte*. Hamburg, 1912.
Sicard, C. *Oeuvres*, 3 vols., ed. M. Martin and S. Sauneron. Bibliothèque d'étude 83–85. Cairo, 1982.
Simaykah, M. *Dalīl al-Mathaf al-Qibṭī*, 2 vols. Cairo, 1932.
Strzygowski, J. *Die Baukunst der Armenier und Europa*, 2 vols. Vienna, 1918.
Timm, S. *Das christlich-koptische Ägypten in arabischer Zeit*, Vol. 2. Wiesbaden, 1984.
Troupeau, G. *Catalogue de manuscrits arabes. Première partie, manuscrits chrétiens*, 2 vols. Paris, 1972–1974.
Vansleb, J. M. *Nouvelle relation en forme de journal d'un voyage fait en Egypte en 1672 et 1673*. Paris, 1677. Translated as *The Present State of Egypt*. London, 1678.
Viaud, G. *Les Pèlerinages coptes en Egypte*. From the notes of Jacob Muyser. Cairo, 1979.
Walters, C. C. *Monastic Archaeology in Egypt*. Warminster, 1974.
Wilkinson, G. *Modern Egypt and Thebes*, 2 vols. London, 1843.
Yāqūt ibn ʿAbd Allāh al-Ḥamawī. *Geographisches Wörterbuch*, 6 vols., ed. F. Wüstenfeld. Leipzig, 1866–1873.
Zeretelli, G., and P. Jernstedt. *Papyri russischer und georgischer Sammlungen*, 5 vols. Tiflis, 1925–1935.

RENÉ-GEORGES COQUIN
MAURICE MARTIN, S.J.

Architecture

Little is as yet known of the layout of the monastery. Through digging in 1908 south of the church, Flinders Petrie was able to identify a large building complex surrounded by a mud brick wall, which he rightly recognized as part of the former monastery. The ground plan of the area corresponds roughly to a triangle, in which the west walls once continued farther to the north beyond the end now visible.

Facing page: General plan of Dayr Anbā Shinūdah. *Courtesy Peter Grossmann.*

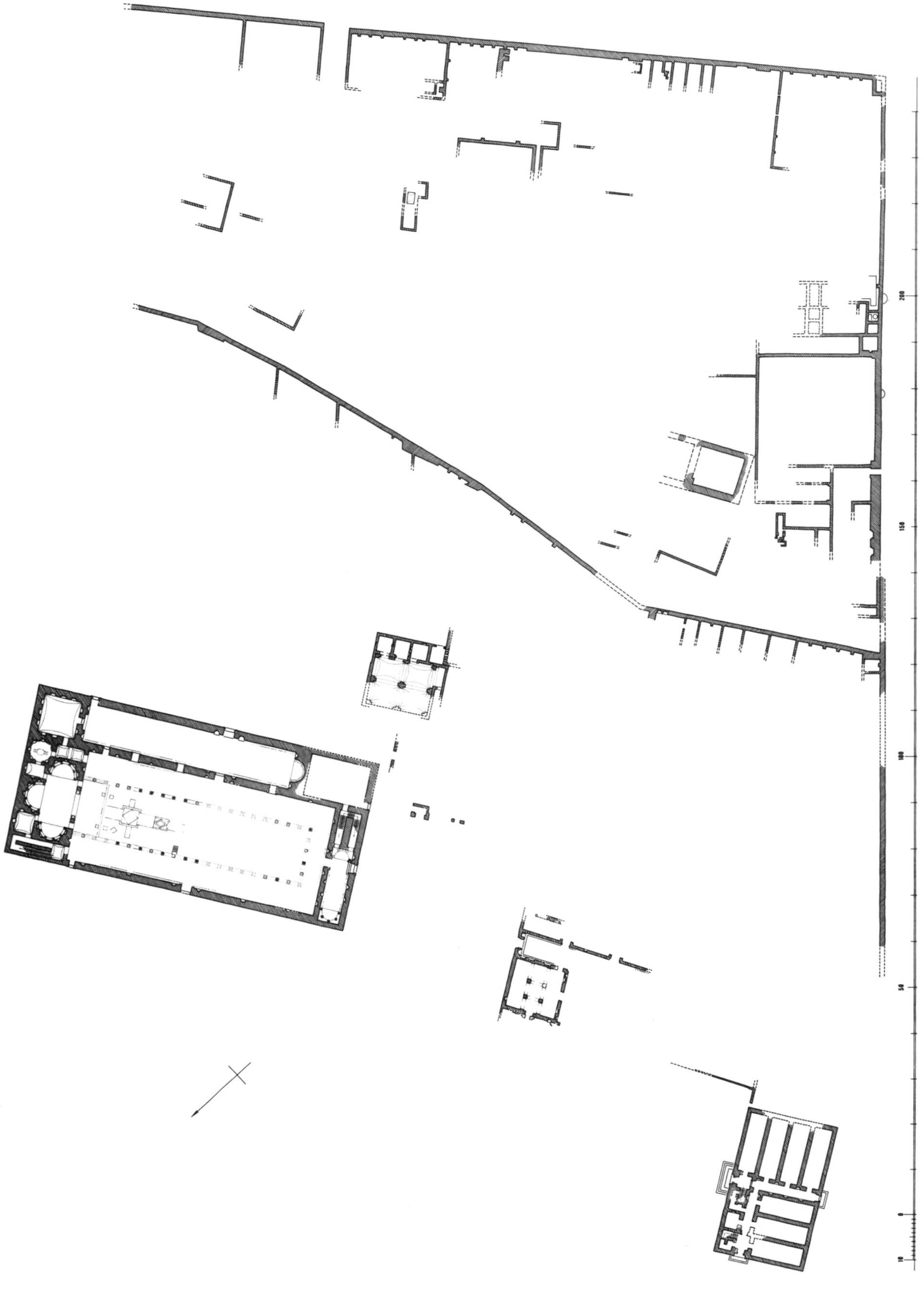
200
150
100
50
0
10

The present north wall, which in its main section follows an obliquely curving course, appears to have been merely an internal part wall to separate one section. The final extension to the north cannot be determined. In the same way, the boundary on the side toward the wheat fields has not survived. A large gate was identified on the south side, while on the west there is a smaller one.

In the 1980s the Egyptian Antiquities Organization started to conduct some excavations in the area of the ancient monastery. One of the major buildings is a rather well-preserved lodging house situated about 656 feet (200 m) to the west of the church at the western side of a large central square. Originally it comprised several floors, each with a number of long halls of equal size for the accommodation of the monks, for storage rooms, and for two staircases. All outer doors are nicely decorated with framing pilasters. At the eastern side of the same square, and thus closer to the church, stands a four-pillar building, in which a refectory can be recognized. The ruins to the north of it point to the existence of a large kitchen. Traces of buildings that might be identified as latrines are visible in the southern area.

Among the constructions outside the walls of the monastery are a quarry northwest, from which the majority of the material for the church probably came. On the upper desert plateau there is a small chapel completely buried with sand, which can be reached after a walk of about two and one-half hours.

The Church

The church of the monastery consists of an immense blocklike structure, widely visible, which recalls the form of a pharaonic temple (Deichmann, 1938, p. 34). Inside, it comprises several large spatial units, of which the area belonging to the church proper is on the north side. It may be divided into the western narthex, the naos, developed as a three-aisle basilica with a western return aisle and galleries, and in the east the group of rooms forming the sanctuary. In the autumn of 1984 the naos was cleared of its modern civilian structures by the Egyptian Antiquities Organization, and it again presents some impression of its original greatness. The sanctuary of the church is developed as a triconch, the walls of which are adorned with niches and applied columns. The altar must have stood in the center of the triconch. The slightly elevated presbytery extends for a small distance beyond the triumphal arch into the nave. At its western border two

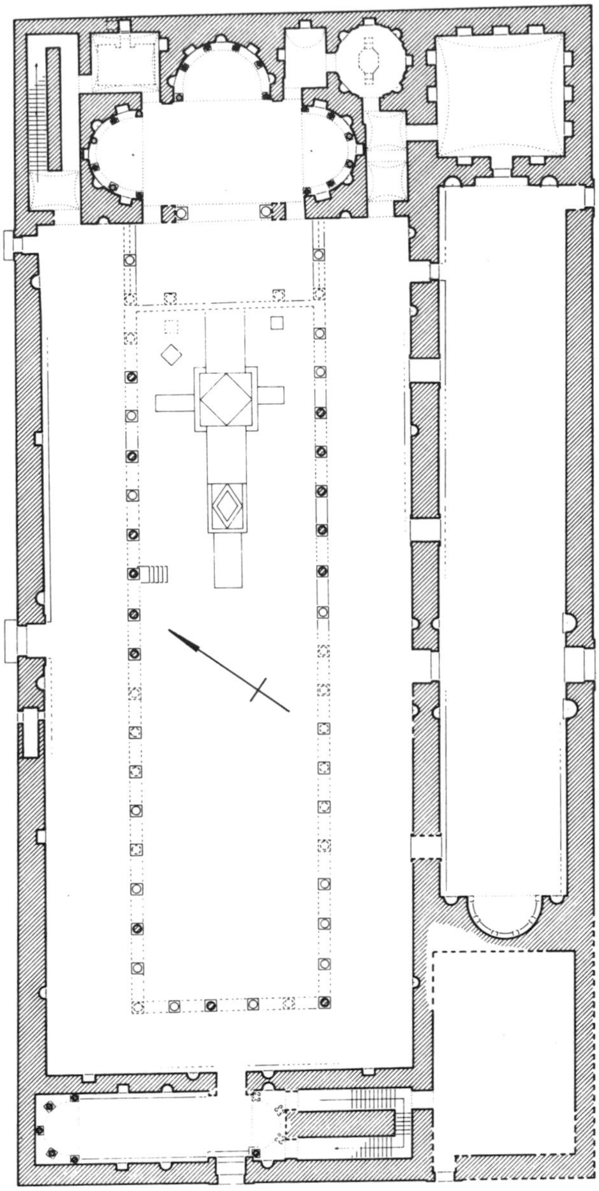

Plan of the church at Dayr Anbā Shinūdah. *Courtesy Peter Grossmann.*

columns were once standing, belonging, as in the church of Dayr Anbā Bishoi, to a second triumphal arch. The remaining rooms of the sanctuary fulfill subsidiary functions. On the north side is a staircase; in the octagonal southeast side room were the remains of a baptismal font. The significance of the rooms lying on the south side of the church is not clear. The eastern domed room with its many large niches could have been a library, while the long so-called south narthex with its large west apse was perhaps a chapter house.

There is scarcely any doubt that Shenute was the founder of this church. It is accordingly to be dated before the middle of the fifth century. At a date not exactly fixed, perhaps on the occasion of the Persian conquest of Egypt in 619, the church suffered severe damage by fire, after which the parts that had collapsed were rebuilt in ordinary fired bricks, but in exact conformity with the original plan. Even the lost granite pillars in the nave were built up again in bricks. Somewhere about the ninth century—corresponding to the usage of the time—a three-part *khūrus* (room between naos and sanctuary) with a high central opening was placed in front of the sanctuary. The domed vaulting over the center of the sanctuary derives from the middle of the thirteenth century (Grossmann, 1982, p. 120, n. 501). The domed vaulting over the *khūrus* is even later.

On the basis of its construction this church is beyond doubt the most important monument of early Christian architecture in Upper Egypt. It had a high architectural influence on church building in this region.

BIBLIOGRAPHY

Bock, V. de. *Matériaux pour servir à l'archéologie de l'Egypte chrétienne*, pp. 39–60. St. Petersburg, 1901.

Clarke, S. *Christian Antiquities in the Nile Valley*, pp. 145–61. Oxford, 1912.

Deichmann, F. W. "Zum Altägyptischen in der koptischen Baukunst." *Mitteilungen des Deutschen Archäologischen Instituts—Abteilung Kairo* 8 (1938):34–37.

Evers, H. G., and R. Romero. "Rotes und Weisses Kloster bei Sohag, Probleme der Rekonstruktion." In *Christentum am Nil*, ed. K. Wessel, pp. 175–94. Recklinghausen, 1964.

Grossmann, P. "Sohāg." *Archiv für Orientforschung* 25 (1974–1977):323–25.

______. *Mittelalterliche Langhauskuppelkirchen und verwandte Typen in Oberägypten*. Glückstadt, 1982.

______. "New Observations in the Church and Sanctuary of Dayr Anbā Sinūda." *Annales du Service des antiquités de l'Egypte* 70 (1984):69–73.

Monneret de Villard, U. *Les couvents près de Sohag*, Vols. 1 and 2. Milan, 1925–1926.

Petrie, W. M. F. "Athribis." *British School of Archeology in Egypt* 14 (1908):13–15.

PETER GROSSMANN

Architectural Sculpture

The architectural sculpture of the Church of Saint Shenute is one of the most important complexes of early Christian art in Egypt. Since this sculpture is unusually manifold in terms of materials, composition, and artistic impression, it has often had a confusing effect, has been variously assessed, and down to modern times has repeatedly been incorrectly dated (e. g., Akermann, 1976, pp. 7–9, following Drioton, 1942, pp. 10–11).

The complete wallwork of square limestone blocks seems to consist of reused, newly dressed material. The decorated pieces of work are to be divided into four groups: (1) older pieces that have been reused unchanged; (2) older pieces that have been worked over extensively or in part; (3) pieces made specially for the building itself; and (4) pieces later inserted into the remains of the original ensemble as a result of repairs (these include pieces deriving from the building and foreign material from other buildings). As a rule, the pieces in granite belong to the first two groups, those in marble to groups 1 and 4, those in limestone to groups 3 and 4.

In the entrances, older unchanged pieces in granite and newly cut pieces have been combined with isolated newly wrought decorative pieces in limestone (pilaster capitals) to form a new *shole* (foundation) (for details, see Deichmann, 1975, pp. 56–57). The granite columns and imperial granite capitals on the ground floor of the nave were taken over unchanged, as were the granite half-columns of the wall niches of the south narthex. On a granite slab in the floor of the nave, traces of hieroglyphs are still visible on the upper surface. Since they could have been chipped away, or the slab let in upside down, the ideological intention can be clearly grasped: to profane signs formerly regarded as sacred and to provide conspicuous proof of the Christian victory over paganism. In addition to these elements of granite architecture, marble pieces (e.g., capitals for the gallery story and column shafts) were reused in the church.

Alongside these reused pieces, which at least in part were quite clearly put on display as spoils or trophies of Christian victory, the church had an extensive amount of architectural sculpture in limestone made for this building. The reuse of older pieces was not simply a question of economy, utilitarian considerations, or lack of ability. Some of this rich decoration, wrought about the middle of the fifth century, is found in situ, for example, in the west narthex, wall niches and northern pillar setting; in the south narthex, niches and pilasters of the east façade and impost moldings; in the nave, wall niches and impost moldings; in the baptistery, the entire decoration, and further pilaster capitals at individual entrances.

The architectural sculpture in the sanctuary of the triconch was particularly splendid: columns with entablatures and cornices on two levels in front of the wall, and behind them an alternating system of wall niches (barrel-vaulted rectangular niches flanked by pilasters interchanging with hemispherical-vaulted semicircular niches flanked by half-columns, each crowned by a "broken" gable). This decoration was, however, severely damaged as a result of a partial collapse, and little remains in place other than some wall niches. The composition of the columns with entablatures and columns is the result of extensive repairs and contains the wreckage of the original decoration put together in makeshift fashion and complemented by the insertion of foreign material, including marble pieces. The original decoration of the triconch must in any case have been a homogeneous ensemble of contemporary local limestone sculpture (without the use of spolia). One can form a rough estimate of its effect by comparison with the well-preserved but much more modest decoration in the triconch of the church of DAYR ANBĀ BISHOI.

The architectural sculpture in the church of the monastery of Shenute is thus a unique, self-assured mixture of old pieces triumphantly pressed into the service of the Christian cult and of monumental contemporary decoration. The remains of the original decoration in limestone are an addition of considerable significance, since they provide a fixed point for many categories of architectural sculpture.

BIBLIOGRAPHY

Akermann, P. *Le décor sculpté du Couvent blanc. Niches et frises.* Bibliothèque d'études coptes 14. Cairo, 1977.

Deichmann, F. W. *Die Spolien in der spätantiken Architektur,* pp. 54–60. Munich, 1975.

Drioton, Etienne. *Les Sculptures coptes du nilomètre de Rodah.* Cairo, 1942.

Monneret de Villard, U. *Les Couvents près de Sohag,* Vols. 1 and 2, pp. 121ff. Milan, 1925–1926.

HANS GEORG SEVERIN

DAYR ANDARAWUS. *See* Dayr Abū al-Līf.

DAYR APA AGENIOS. *See* Monasteries of the Upper Ṣaʿīd.

DAYR APA ANŪB (Nūb), small monastery near Wādī al-Naṭrūn whose precise date of establishment is not known. Evelyn-White (1932, p. 369) remarked that MAWHŪB IBN MANṢŪR IBN MUFARRIJ, in his list of the relics venerated in Egypt in the *History of the Patriarchs* (written in 1088; Vol. 2, pt. 3, 1970), did not speak of this monastery. Hence, Evelyn-White concluded that the monastery could have been founded at the end of the eleventh century or the beginning of the twelfth. However, he emphasized that this monastery may have been no more than a cell dependent on the nearby Monastery of Saint John Colobos.

This monastery must not be confused with the monastery of the same name near al-Ashmūnayn, an error committed by the editors of this part of the *History of the Patriarchs* (Vol. 2, pt. 3, p. 361). Mawhūb cited the latter Monastery of Apa Anūb, noting (1895, p. 252 [trans.]) that the relics of more than sixty martyr monks were preserved there (Abū Ṣāliḥ spoke of sixty-three), so it therefore cannot be confused with the monastery of the same name in Wādī al-Naṭrūn.

It is not known when this small monastery ceased to function. The reports of consecrations of *myron* (consecrated oil), which traditionally took place at the Monastery of Saint Macarius (DAYR ANBĀ MAQĀR), do not speak of it, although such reports are available for the years 1342, 1346, 1377, and 1401. However, in the description of Wādī al-Naṭrūn in his historico-geographical work *Kitāb al-Khiṭaṭ,* the fifteenth-century Muslim writer al-Maqrīzī pointed out this Monastery of Apa Anūb, near that of John Colobos, and stated that Apa Anūb was a native of Samannūd and that his body was preserved there (this, then, is the martyr celebrated on 25 Abīb) but that this monastery was destroyed. Thus, it must have ceased to exist before the fifteenth century.

BIBLIOGRAPHY

Evelyn-White, H. G. *The Monasteries of the Wadi'n Natrūn,* Pt. 2, *The History of the Monasteries of Nitria and Scetis.* New York, 1932.

RENÉ-GEORGES COQUIN

DAYR APA HOR (Sawādah). At the foot of the great Christian necropolis of MINYĀ on the right bank of the Nile, about 2.5 miles (4 km) southeast of the town and just over half a mile (1 km) east of the village of Sawādah, are the remains of a monastery with a rock-cut church fitted up inside a tomb.

The site is described by E. F. Jomard (1821, Vol. 4, pp. 365–67). At this period the church had a peristyle in front, open to the sky; since then a cupola has been added.

Al-MAQRĪZĪ (1853, p. 504; ed. Wüstenfeld, 1845, p. 39 [text], p. 97 [translation]) explains that the name Sawādah comes from the name of an Arab tribe settled in the neighborhood, and that the Arabs destroyed the monastery. ʿAlī Mubārak (1886/87–1888/89, Vol. 12, p. 63) also mentions the monastery.

It is difficult to establish to which of the many saints who bore the name of Hor this monastery was dedicated. W. E. Crum drew up a list of the saints of this name (1913, p. 164, n. 1). It was completed by J. Muyser (1943, pp. 186–190). Among the eight anchorites of this name whom he counts, Muyser proposes to identify Apa Hor of Preht (Abrahat), the biographer of Apa Harmīn, with the namesake of the monastery of Sawādah, for he is often called "Apa Hor the monk," as in al-Maqrīzī's notice. Also, he was a native of Preht situated near Antinoë (Muyser, 1943, pp. 191–92, 209, n.5). Muḥammad Ramzī (1963, p. 66) identifies Preht/Abrahat with DAYR AL-BARSHAH, to the south of DAYR ABŪ ḤINNIS. However, some Coptic fragments indicate that this Apa Hor lived "in the mountain of Pisoben," which H. G. Evelyn-White identifies with Psoun (Bāṣūnah), to the north of Akhmīm (1926, p. 170).

About 1.25 miles (2 km) farther south, above the village of Zāwiyat al-Amwāt (or al-Mayyitīn) in the quarries northwest of the village, there is the choir of a church cut in the cliff. A small monastic funerary stela was found in the nearby cemetery. H. Munier, who published it (1917, p. 163) proposes to locate Hage at that place. J. F. Champollion had suggested putting it near Apollinopolis Parva (Kom Isfaḥt, see Amélineau, 1893, p. 191). A miracle story about Saint Colluthus indicates that the village of Hage was in the nome of Shmun. W. E. Crum's note (1922, p. 180, n.1) makes Munier's hypothesis plausible (see also M. Drew-Bear, 1979, pp. 55–56).

BIBLIOGRAPHY

ʿAlī Mubārak. *Al-Khiṭaṭ al-Tawfīqiyyah al-Jadīdah.* Cairo, 1886–1889.

Amélineau, E. *La Géographie de l'Egypte à l'époque copte.* Paris, 1893.

Crum, W. E. *Theological Texts from Coptic Papyri.* Oxford, 1913.

Crum, W. E., and H. I. Bell. *Wādī Sarjah.* Coptica 3. Copenhagen, 1922.

Drew-Bear, M. "Le nome hermopolite: Toponymes et sites." *American Studies in Papyrology* 21 (1979).

Evelyn-White, H. G. *New Coptic Texts from the Monastery of St. Macarius.* New York, 1926.

Jomard, E. F., ed. "Hypogée d'architecture dorique et carrières anciennes à Saouadeh." In *Description de l'Egypte,* Vol. 4: *Antiquités,* chaps. 16 and 13, pp. 361–67. Paris, 1821.

Munier, H. "Note sur le village de Hagé." *Annales du service des antiquités de l'Égypte* 17 (1917):163.

Muyser, J. "Ermite pérégrinant et pèlerin infatigable (Fragment arabe de la vie inédite d'Anbā Harmīn racontée par son compagnon de voyage, Apa Hor de Preht)." *Bulletin de la société d'archéologie copte* 9 (1943):159–236.

Ramzī, M. *Al Qāmūs al Jughrāfī lil al-Bilād al-Misriyyah,* Vol. 2, pt. 4. Cairo, 1963.

RENÉ-GEORGES COQUIN

DAYR APA HOR (Siryāqūs). This monastery, probably situated near the town of Siryāqūs, in the province of al-Qalyūbīyyah, about 12 miles (20 km) north of Cairo, is described by al-Shābushtī (end of tenth or beginning of eleventh century) as populated by numerous monks. Its festivals attracted a great number of people. The author relates the medicinal practice employed in this monastery for the cure of scrofula. When an invalid presented himself, the superior brought a pig that licked the affected parts without touching the healthy, then spread over these affected areas the ashes of a pig previously used for a similar operation, and also oil from the church lamp. The invalid was thus healed. The pig that had devoured the scrofula was killed and burned, and its ashes preserved for the treatment of another invalid. This legend cannot be earlier than the Arab period. The words "pigs" and "scrofula" are the same in Arabic.

This notice is reproduced more or less literally by the medieval authors Yāqūt, al-Qazwīnī, and al-ʿUmarī (see the references given by Atiya, 1939, pp. 8–9). It may be noted that al-ʿUmarī (d. 1348) adds "that is so until now" (Atiya, 1939, p. 22, n. 6). Al-Maqrīzī also reproduced this passage from al-Shābushtī, but speaks of it in the past tense: "The monastery of Siryāqūs, this monastery was also called that of Abū Ḥūr . . ."; the final phrase of al-ʿUmarī ("there is at this monastery a great flow of those who suffer from this illness") becomes "there was . . . of those who suffered." This seems to indicate that in his time (fifteenth century) the monastery had already disappeared.

It is not certain to which saint this monastery was dedicated, though it was probably the martyr Hor, a native of Siryāqūs who was executed at Antinoë and whose feast day is 12 Abīb (see also Graf, 1944, Vol. 1, p. 534).

[*See also:* Pilgrimages.]

BIBLIOGRAPHY

Atiya, A. S. "Some Egyptian Monasteries According to the Unpublished Ms. of al-Shābushtī's 'Kitab al-diyārāt.'" *Société d'archéologie copte, Cairo. Bulletin* (1939):1–28.

Viaud, G. *Magie et coutumes populaires chez les coptes d'Egypte,* pp. 59, 92. Sisteron, 1978.

René-Georges Coquin

DAYR APA ISḤĀQ (Isnā). A little to the north of the present DAYR AL-SHUHADĀ' (Monastery of the Martyrs) at Isnā are some ruins that the inhabitants call the Monastery of Apa Isḥāq (Isaac). In the "new" church, which according to the inscriptions dates at least from the end of the twelfth century, an inscription commemorates the *nanasia* (church?) of Apa Isḥāq the anchorite (Coquin, 1975, pp. 247–51).

We propose the following hypothesis about this inscription: When Apa Isḥāq's hermitage fell into ruin, a church was built adjacent to the north of the Church of the Martyrs dedicated to Apa Isḥāq, whose hermitage, a place of pilgrimage, was in ruins. Some distorted Greek word is hidden behind this word *nanasia,* perhaps simply the Greco-Coptic word *ecclesia.* However that may be, we may suppose that the hermitage of this holy personage survived in the form of a second church added to the first one "of the martyrs."

It is more difficult to know to what period this foundation of Dayr Apa Isḥāq goes back. This hermitage is mentioned in the panegyric of John (Khater, 1981, pp. 17 [text] and 23 [trans.]). We prefer this name to that of Paul, for it is attested in the oldest manuscripts. This text is preserved by several manuscripts of which the oldest dates from 1520 (Khater, 1981, p. 6), but some authors write that this author could be of the thirteenth century (Sbath, 1938–1940, p. 74, no. 606). It follows that the Dayr Apa Isḥāq could be older than that period.

We must also mention the panegyric attributed to a bishop of Isnā called Dorotheus and preserved in an Arabic version in two manuscripts (unpublished). This author would be of the fourth century, but he does not speak at all of a hermitage of Apa Isḥāq nor of a pilgrimage to this sanctuary. One must conclude that this small monastery did not exist when Dorotheus delivered his sermon in honor of Ammonius, his predecessor in the see of Isnā.

We must add that the recension of the SYNAXARION from Upper Egypt, in its notice concerning Saint Ammonius and the martyrs of Isnā on 13 Kiyahk, also mentions Dayr Apa Isḥāq, but one cannot date this recension with any precision (perhaps twelfth to thirteenth century), and we do not know what sources the author used.

One may conclude from this evidence that Dayr Apa Isḥāq was founded and frequented after the fourth century, but had fallen into ruin after the twelfth. A photo of these ruins is given by L. T. Lefort (1939, pl. 14).

BIBLIOGRAPHY

Coquin, R.-G. "Les Inscriptions pariétales des monastères d'Esna: Dayr al-Suhadā'–Dayr al-Fakhūrī." *Bulletin de l'Institut français d'Archéologie orientale* 75 (1975):241–84, with 10 plates.

Khater, A. "Martyre des citoyens d'Esna." *Studia orientalia christiana* 18. Cairo and Jerusalem, 1981.

Lefort, L. "Les premiers monastères pachômiens, exploration topographique." *Le Muséon* 52 (1939):379–407.

Sbath, P. *Al-Fihris, Catalogue de manuscrits arabes.* Cairo, 1938–1940.

René-Georges Coquin
Maurice Martin, S.J.

DAYR APA JEREMIAH (Damietta). *See* Monasteries of the Daqahliyyah Province.

DAYR APA JEREMIAH (Jirjā). *See* Monasteries of the Upper Ṣa'īd.

DAYR APA JEREMIAH (Saqqara). [*This entry consists of four articles:* History, Archaeology, Sculpture, *and* Paintings.]

History

We do not know if Jeremiah was the founder of the monastery that bears his name, or if he succeeded someone else. According to JOHN OF NIKIOU (*Chronicle*, chap. 89, pp. 4–14), Anastasius, the future emperor of Byzantium (491–518), visited Saint Jeremiah in his lifetime, when he himself was exiled in Egypt by his predecessor ZENO (474–491).

In the first half of the sixth century the monk Theodosius in his *Itinerary* mentioned this monastery (Quibell, 1912, p. 3).

Two Arabic authors, Safī al-Dīn ʿAbd al Mu'min (739) and Ibn ʿAbd al-Ḥakam (870–871), mention the Dayr Harmīs (Quibell, pp. 3–4). The name Abū Harmīs is mentioned by ABŪ ṢĀLIḤ THE ARMENIAN at the beginning of the thirteenth century. The last author to speak of it is al-MAQRĪZĪ in the fifteenth century.

The excavations carried out at the site have shown that the monastery disappeared in the middle of the tenth century (Cauwenbergh, 1914, p. 131).

The name of Jeremiah was venerated not only at this site, as the inscriptions prove, but is also among the saints invoked in the litanies of BĀWĪṬ and the monasteries depending on it (Sauneron et al., 1972, Vol. 4, p. 60).

An important number of papyri have been found, and were published by E. Revillout (1876, p. 1–111); publication was completed by J. Krall (pp. 63–79).

BIBLIOGRAPHY

Cauwenbergh, P. van. *Etude sur les moines d'Egypte*. Paris, 1914.

Chronicle of John, bishop of Nikiou, The, trans. R. H. Charles, Text and Translation Society 3. London, 1916.

Krall, J. "Neue koptische und griechische Papyrus." *Recueil des Travaux* 6 (1885):63–79.

Maspero, G. "Note sur les objets recueillis sous la pyramide de Ounas." *Annales du Service des Antiquités* 3 (1902):185–90.

Quibell, J. E. *Excavations at Saqqara (1905–1910)*, 4 vols. Cairo, 1907–1913.

Revillout, E. *Actes et contrats des musées égyptiens de Boulaq et du Louvre*, pp. 1–111. Paris, 1876.

Sauneron, S., and J. Jacquet. *Les Ermitages chrétiens du désert d'Esna*. 4 vols. Fouilles de l'Institut français d'Archéologie orientale 29, pt. 4. Cairo, 1972.

RENÉ-GEORGES COQUIN
MAURICE MARTIN, S.J.

Archaeology

Dayr Apa Jeremiah is situated at the western edge of the site of the ruins of Saqqara, the old necropolis of Memphis, which continued to serve as a burial ground to the inhabitants of Memphis into the late Roman period. The northern confines of the monastery lie approximately at the causeway of the pyramid of Unas. From there it stretches about 325 yards (300 meters) to the south. The eastern boundary may be discerned in the hill of the temple of Nesitahuti. The extension of the monastery to the west has so far not been established. The monastery was not exclusively a male monastery; inscriptions, pictorial representations (Rassart-Debergh, 1981, pp. 214–18), and burials show that it existed in close contact with a convent for nuns.

Since the monastery was already in existence at the time of the exile of the later emperor Anastasius (491–518), the foundation of the monastery has conventionally been set at around 470 (Quibell, 1908–1912, 3. iii).

Archaeologically, however, none of the extant remains have been shown to be older than the middle of the sixth century. Also John of Nikiou's report (*Chronicle* 89.15) concerning the foundation of a large church by Anastasius has not been confirmed. The earliest members of the monastery presumably established themselves in the still intact, but otherwise disused mausoleums of the necropolis of Saqqara, and the decision to set up new buildings was made only later. The old church, which doubtless belonged to the first of these buildings, is scarcely to be dated before the middle of the sixth century.

A change took place with the reconstruction of the church in the seventh century. Only at this time

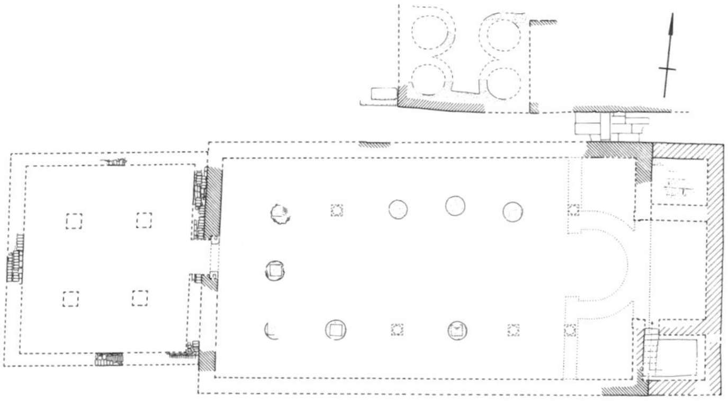

Plan of the main church at the center of Dayr Apa Jeremiah. *Courtesy Peter Grossmann.*

did the monastery appear to have developed fully and a rich building activity sprang up. Most of the edifices date from the late seventh and eighth centuries. The monastery was certainly in full operation until the middle of the eighth century. The great majority of the dated tombstones belong to the second half of the eighth century. A decline seems, nevertheless, to have set in toward the end of the eighth century. The floor of the southern porch of the main church was repaired with tombstones dating from the middle of the eighth century. After 750 all coins disappeared as well. Evidently the repercussions of the revolts of the Copts against Arab supremacy in the eighth and ninth centuries did not pass the monastery by without leaving traces.

To the last building activity belongs the addition of large buttresses onto the most important structures in the area surrounding the church. Quibell dates these to the time of Mūsā ibn ʿIsā (c. 791). Inside the church itself an attempt was made to save the roof of the nave from falling in by propping it up with a few very crudely raised pillars. Evidence of this kind shows clearly that the monastery was coming to its end. It was abandoned probably around the middle of the ninth century.

The monastery of Apa Jeremiah is so far one of the few archaeologically available examples of a monastery of cenobitic monks. They did not live, as in the KELLIA, as hermits, alone or with only very few disciples in independent habitations separated by wide distances, but were densely drawn together in large communal buildings. Each monk possessed in these buildings only one cell, which was entered from a common antechamber. No one prepared his own meals; these were taken in the common dining halls, the refectories. In accordance with the requirements of a large community, the monastery was provided with all kinds of economic establishments, a bread bakery, an oil press, and the accompanying storerooms. In several places small cisterns were dug. To the southwest a couple of workshops—for example, a laundry—may also be discerned; doubtless a joiner's shop and a dyer's establishment were also to be found. To protect against attacks, the monastery was encircled by a wall. The remains of such a wall, as well as of a gate, have been ascertained to the south, near the southern building. The existence of a western gate is known from an inscription.

The main church today is still situated in the center of the monastery, and is doubtless the most important building of the establishment. The recent excavations identified two main building phases. The evolution taking place during the first phase clearly reflects the gradual growth of the monastery. Originally the church stood as a quite small and simple chapel built of sun-dried mud bricks on a square plan and probably possessing only a simple niche in the east wall. As the building was enlarged, this chapel was integrated into the first church as a vestibule (narthex). This first church was already constructed as a columned basilica, and should be dated to the second half of the sixth century. It possessed five pairs of columns, as well as a fully developed sanctuary with a central apse flanked by rectangular lateral chambers on each side.

As far as its method of construction is concerned, the church was already provided with an outer facing socket of stone, consisting of reused but in no way reworked ashlars. An ashlar building in the real sense, with horizontal joints adjusted permanently during the process of building, came into being only when the church was extended by a further pair of columns toward the east, and a new sanctuary was added here at the same time. In this new building the lateral chamber south of the apse was constructed, peculiarly, as a basement room. For the construction of the stairs a fine pottery vessel was used, datable around 600. Consequently, this extension took place about a quarter century later.

During the change in the political situation in Egypt caused by the Arab invasion in 639–641, the number of monks seems to have increased considerably. The existing church was then no longer sufficient, and thus the main church that can be seen today came into being. It is substantially larger than its predecessor, and possesses a typically Egyptian basilican plan, with narthex, return aisle, and a sanctuary divided into a central apse and two rectangular side chambers. In front of the sanctuary there is a rather narrow space out of which the *khūrus*, an important feature of early medieval monastic church architecture in Egypt, was developed. A peculiarity of the side chambers of the sanctuary is that they are on a lower floor level. The sole access to them is by short stairs from inside the apse. On the southern side of the church in front of the south portal there once was a small protruding terrace reached by stairs to overcome the difference in level. This terrace was subsequently replaced by an external portico with an Ĺ-shaped plan.

The building materials of the church, including

the majority of its columns, derive exclusively from demolished late Roman—presumably in some cases still pagan—mausoleums, which explains the variety of types and the fact that they often occur in pairs. The original owners of those mausoleums were the rich landowners of Memphis, who left the country after the Arab invasion (Ibn ʿAbd al-Ḥakam, 1924, p. 231).

Building 1823, designated "tomb church" by Quibell, has emerged from the recent excavations as a nonecclesiastical edifice. The similarity with a three-aisled church, including the accentuation of its eastern termination by a triumphal arch, is purely external. It is, moreover, sunk halfway into the ground. Its furnishings suggest that it is the upper structure of presumably a still pagan hypogeum (underground chamber) of the late fourth or early fifth century. The shaft descending to the underground burial chambers was located along the southern row of columns. Nothing remains, however, from its original use. The tombs built into the upper chamber that can be seen today are at least two centuries later, and caused all kinds of damage to the building. The floor likewise belongs to this later use of the building. The original floor was presumably removed along with the remnants of its original use.

The Southern Building, discovered at the southern edge of the monastery, is not a church either. The arrangement of the columns brings to mind rather an atrium with a roofless center. The column rows were only subsequently made closer through the insertion of intermediate columns. To the same complex belongs a two-aisled hall that branches northward at the end of the north wall. The other buildings are mud-brick structures that were in part added subsequently, having in some instances a quite irregular character. Of more recent date is the external portico on the south side of the southern building. The entire arrangement suggests that this was a less important section of the monastery. Perhaps the guest quarters were situated here, an interpretation suggested at least by the proximity to the monastery's south wall and the south gate discovered there.

The original refectory, belonging to the predecessor of the main church, was discovered in 1979. It was probably a two-aisled mud brick building north of the church. In the interior the remains of circular benches set against the side walls may be discerned.

The new refectory constructed after the enlargement of the monastery was recognized by Quibell as the three-aisled hall situated in a north–south orientation about 95 feet (30 m) north of the main church. The nave is unaccentuated. It was evidently intended that all the aisles should offer the same amount of space. However, the circular benches found elsewhere in the refectories of Egyptian monasteries, and also in the old refectory of this monastery, are absent. Instead the room is furnished with benches that run continuously along the walls. A large kitchen establishment adjoins the northeast

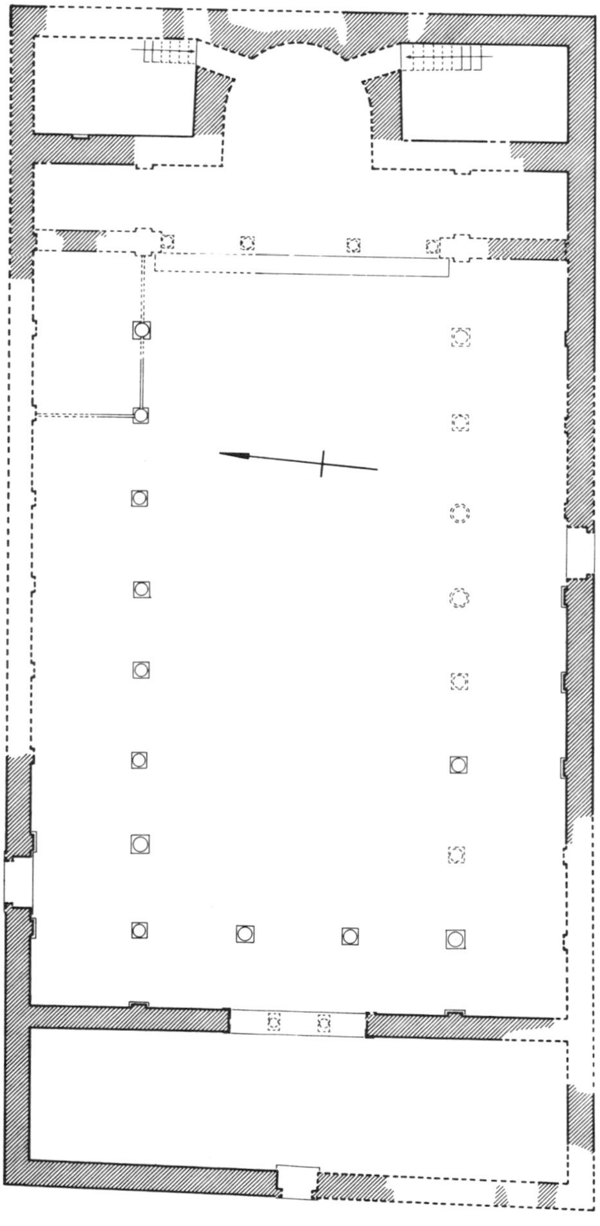

Plan of the church built at Dayr Apa Jeremiah following the Arab invasion. *Courtesy Peter Grossmann.*

corner of the hall, and this fits in with the interpretation of the hall as a refectory.

At the south end of the east wall, the hall opens into a small lateral chapel designed as a four-columned structure, the refectory chapel. It is provided with a complete sanctuary with three rooms and is thus fully functional for liturgical use.

Further to the northeast is a two-aisled hall (Room 726), which Quibell gave the provisional designation of infirmary. This building is probably a refectory as well, the more so since a monastery of this size could certainly have use for two refectories. In the present case, the fact should also be taken into account that the monastery included a section for nuns, who doubtless took their meals in a separate refectory. An infirmary, however, probably did not form part of the ancient convents. The sick stayed in their cells and were attended to by those in charge of the sick.

BIBLIOGRAPHY

Grossmann, P. "Reinigungsarbeiten im Jeremiaskloster von Saqqāra," I–III. *Mitteilungen des Deutschen Archäologischen Instituts, Abteilung Kairo* 27 (1971):173–80; 28 (1972):145–52; 36 (1980):193–202.

Grossmann, P., and H.-G. Severin. "Reinigungsarbeiten im Jeremiaskloster von Saqqāra," IV. *Mitteilungen des Deutschen Archäologischen Instituts, Abteilung Kairo* 38 (1982):155–93.

Ibn ʿAbd al-Ḥakam. *Futūḥ Miṣr*, trans. O. Toussoun. *Bulletin de la Société archéologique d'Alexandrie* 5 (1924):231.

Quibell, J. E. *Excavations at Saqqara*, Vols. 2–4. Cairo, 1908–1912.

Rassart-Debergh, M. "Quelques remarques iconographiques sur la peinture chrétienne à Saqqara." *Acta ad archaeologiam et artium historiam pertinentia* 9 (1981):207–220.

PETER GROSSMANN

Sculpture

The rich finds of sculpture from the area of Dayr Apa Jeremiah, almost exclusively architectural sculpture and tomb reliefs, are now for the most part in the Coptic Museum, Cairo, and at the place of excavation. There is a small collection in the British Museum, London. Since the excavations by J. E. Quibell, the sculptures have been considered as original elements of the monastery architecture and are dated to the sixth century, corresponding to the supposed period when the monastery was in full flower. Only since 1978–1979 have new investigations of the whole stock laid the basis for a different and more discriminating judgment (Severin, 1982, pp. 170ff.).

The only building from late antiquity with original sculpture in the area of the later monastery may be the great mausoleum lying to the west (Building 1823, called a tomb-church by Quibell), probably the family tomb of rich citizens from Memphis. Of its architectural decoration, capitals of columns and pilasters and bases of pilasters of various orders have in particular survived (catalog by Severin 1982, pp. 171–79). They convey the impression of an architectural decoration full of character, well executed, and with a strong local stamp; on the one hand, the decoration carries on traditions of a variegated decorative profusion, but on the other it shows considerable reduction in motifs and is unable to conceal irregularities in the detailed execution, particularly in the capitals. The building and its homogeneous decoration are to be dated to the fifth century.

In all the other buildings with sculpture in the area of the monastery, and above all in the great church of the seventh century, the building material and almost the entire architectural decoration may have been reused. The dating of the sculptures already points to this (chiefly fifth century and first half of the sixth). But reemployment can be demonstrated in technical matters also. There are only a few decorated pieces, such as stands for water-basins, which are relatively late (end of the sixth century to the beginning of the seventh century) and were probably made for buildings of the monastery.

In contrast all the remaining architectural sculptures from Saqqara South were scarcely produced

Capital from Dayr Apa Jeremiah. *Courtesy Coptic Museum, Cairo.*

for church or monastic architecture. More likely products of local workshops were employed in the necropolis architecture of late antiquity in Saqqara South, the sculptures of a pretentious private funerary architecture. In addition, peculiarities of certain sculpture groups point a priori to this type of architecture, for example, standardized pieces with a couple of corner pilaster capitals and bases and the small quantity both in decoration and in dimensions of homogeneous column capitals.

Through their reuse in the monastery, the original wholes were destroyed, so that we can now assess them only as isolated individual pieces. From the surviving stock, a continuous production in these workshops can be reconstructed, which, with its center of gravity in the fifth century, extended as far as about the middle of the sixth. Scarcely any architectural sculpture from the third and fourth centuries is known from Saqqara South. Probably the necropolises of that period lay in other territory and have not yet been discovered. A notable peculiarity is that contemporary creations of the Constantinople workshops were also known and imitated, in particular impost capitals in the form of basket-shaped capitals or impost capitals of fold-type from the second quarter of the sixth century. Further, Saqqara South offers the only example known to me in Egypt of a column capital with windblown acanthus in a local reproduction that, however, comes closer to the original than the nearest provincial imitation, in the church of the Monastery of Saint Catherine in Sinai.

In terms of date, motif, and technique, there are noteworthy agreements with the architectural sculpture of BĀWĪṬ; these two complexes stand apart from the architectural decoration of Bahnasā (OXYRHYNCHUS).

BIBLIOGRAPHY

Quibell, J. E. *Excavations at Saqqara, 1907–1908.* Cairo, 1909.

______. *Excavations at Saqqara 1908–9, 1909–10.* Cairo, 1912.

Severin, H. G. "Zur spätantiken Bauskulptur im Jeremiaskloster." *Mitteilungen des deutschen archäologischen Instituts—Abteilung Kairo* 38 (1982): 170–93.

H. G. SEVERIN

Paintings

The central element of the group around which the cells of Dayr Apa Jeremiah were assembled was the "Main Church," a building of three naves with an inscribed apse on the east, a narthex on the west, and a gallery on the south. Since J. E. Quibell's excavations, it has lost the painted decor that, according to this archaeologist, adorned the walls. The columns—as photographs of the period show —also served to support scenes with figures: personages on foot surmount medallions enclosing ducks, all above draperies. Quibell identified two other halls as being churches: Room 1952 (numbering according to Quibell's system), called the "Southern Church," which possessed a painted decoration, entirely lost at present, and the "Tomb Church," whose walls were covered with marble slabs, a rare occurrence.

Like every monastery, Dayr Apa Jeremiah contained all the halls used for holy services plus a refectory, kitchens, storage rooms, wine press, hospital, et cetera. However, most of the rooms served as living quarters for the monks. Most often these cells were square or slightly rectangular, with an entrance on the south. In many cases, a semicircular apse was hollowed out in the center of the eastern wall, vaulted in a *cul de four* (quarter of a sphere) resting on a table of marble or other less precious stone. Such an arrangement, added to the fact that these niches contained the cell's principal decoration, led Quibell to refer to them as altar tables. Two rectangular cavities on each side of the niche held the monk's personal effects, liturgical objects, and lamp.

Much has disappeared from the cells since the work of Quibell. Some paintings were removed and placed in the Coptic Museum, Cairo, among which were several niches. The rough brick walls were covered with one or several superimposed layers of stucco upon which the paintings were displayed. When there was only one thick layer of stucco, it is assumed that it crumbled at the touch and that the colored pigments fell away or faded in the air and light; this would explain the high percentage of decoration and scenes that could not be saved from destruction.

All the walls doubtlessly had paintings covering their entire height; but being less well protected by the sand, the upper part has disappeared, or only meager traces thereof remain. At times there was a monochrome background of Pompeian red, but in general the decoration was more elaborate, consisting of geometric or floral patterns. These patterns were frequently lozenges or Us decorated with leaves that covered entire wall-panels like draperies, or they were arranged in a simple uniform row that separated the upper and lower decorations.

These rows may have comprised a succession of geometric panels, whose design and arrangement evoked marble slabs. Lines of local saints no doubt surmounted these panels as they also did in some cells and in the Court of Octagons.

The central niche of the eastern wall was completely decorated, on the inside with Christological themes, and on the outside with an architectonic frame where painting and sculpture were combined. In some places, the small columns, their capitals, and the vault were sculpted in stone (Cell 728); elsewhere, the ensemble was worked in brick, stuccoed, and then covered with paintings in imitation of marble, prophyry, or other precious stones (this is the case for most of the niches). The two techniques may be used simultaneously, as in Cell A, where columns and capitals, whose relief is simply suggested by painting, support the sculpted archivolt.

It is logical to suppose that here as at Bāwīṭ the paintings could have surmounted the niche, again as in Cell A, where there are still traces of feet and lower parts of clothing above the principal niche.

Too few of the paintings uncovered at the time of excavations have survived to permit a true stylistic study. At the most, only a detailed description of some scenes can be given along with a determination of the scale of colors used. Further, given the state of present knowledge and in the absence of detailed research on the techniques of the preserved paintings, it is impossible to attempt to establish a precise dating. In general, they may be placed between the sixth and eighth centuries. On the other hand, the themes employed can easily be listed.

The niche of the eastern wall is decorated with a Christ Enthroned and with Mary holding Jesus on her lap, framed by archangels, Jeremiah, and Enoch. Sometimes one theme or the other is depicted separately; sometimes they appear together. Christ, seated upon a jeweled throne, gives a benediction with one hand and holds the Holy Book in the other; a mandorla, which is supported by a tetramorph, forms a casket around him. This *maiestas Domini* adorns the conch of the niche, while on the walls the Virgin is portrayed seated and holding the Child, who is worshiped by the archangels Michael and Gabriel and saints. Sometimes Christ in majesty, giving a benediction, and the archangels surrounding Him fill the entire niche. The *maiestas Domini* is sometimes the only motif. Other niches are decorated only with Mary and Joseph surrounded by the archangels, as well as Enoch and Jeremiah. Sometimes the Virgin is simply the THEOTOKOS; elsewhere, in a theme particularly loved by the Copts, she offers her bare breast to the hungry mouth of the Child.

The archangels are always associated with the theme of Christ in glory or with the Virgin and Child, as are Jeremiah and Enoch, the patrons and protectors of the monastery. These are the only personages to adorn the eastern niche with the exception of Cell F, where, on the left of the Virgin, an archangel is pictured as a *silentiarius* (an official in Byzantine court), along with Peter the monk, Enoch, and another monk (doubtless Paniseu). The right section, which has not been identified either by Quibell or later scholars, shows in succession an archangel, a bearded man, a woman, and a second bearded man.

Little is known about the holy personages. Among the monks depicted at Saqqara, there is a certain Peter holding a codex; he is said to be "from the Southern House," which presupposes the existence of a monastery dependent upon the main one. Another monk, Panesneu, is pictured praying, or holding a book. Two other saints or monks depicted in the niche of Cell F also appear to clasp a book to their hearts. A woman, clothed like the monks in a long tunic and cloak, her head covered with a *maphorion* (shawl edged with fringe) and carrying a codex, is pictured among the saints in the eastern niche of Cell F, and upon a column of the Main Church as well as in two other cells. However, there is no inscription to identify her. Little more is known about the cavalier saints mentioned several times by Quibell since he left neither description nor photograph.

Several saints are depicted seated or standing in the Refectory and Court of Octagons; but again there is no inscription and no special item in the traits, clothing, or attributes to identify them precisely. However, an exception to this rule exists for the saints of the northern wall of Cell A, where there are inscriptions naming Apollo and Macarius; a third saint on the left of Macarius may very probably be Onophrius; at his feet there was a sixth person (mentioned but not photographed by Quibell) who can be tentatively identified as Paphnutius, the disciple of Onophrius; at Apollo's side, Phib, his companion, may be recognized. The identity of the personages crouching at their feet remains an open question.

Biblical themes do not seem to be as numerous here as at Bāwīṭ and in the paintings of the necropolises. The sacrifice of Isaac appears in the center of a group decorating the north wall of the Refectory; the other scenes have not been identified, and the paintings have disappeared. In cell F, on the eastern wall to the right of the central niche, the Three Children in the Furnace, protected by the angel of God, are standing in the midst of the flames. In this same cell there may have been another painting of this biblical theme, but it was neither conserved nor even photographed at the time of the excavation.

The cross appears either as an ornament or it takes on a religious function. In Cell 709 it plays a particularly important role, since it is repeated three times, studded with gems, adorned with garlands, and resting upon a platform. Here it is associated with allegorical pictures of the virtues—half-angels, half-women—holding a disk in their hands.

There are also some scenes of daily life depicted on the walls: boats and monks standing watch, a man holding a crocodile, waving a cane, and cutting palms. However, the majority of these merit no more than a brief mention.

This painting—richer and more varied than the extant works would lead one to believe—illustrates, by its very repetition of similar motifs in similar location, the existence of definite iconographical programs, all of which constitutes a major contribution to Coptic studies.

BIBLIOGRAPHY

Moorsel, P. van, and M. Huybers. "Repertory of the Preserved Wallpaintings from the Monastery of Apa Jeremias." *Miscellanea Coptica/Acta ad archaeologiam et artium historiam pertinentia* 9 (1981):125–86.

Quibell, J.E. *Excavations at Saqqara, 1906–1907.* Cairo, 1908.

______. *Excavations at Saqqara, 1907–1908.* Cairo, 1909.

______. *Excavations at Saqqara, 1908–1909.* Cairo, 1912.

Rassart-Debergh, M. M. "La Décoration picturale du monastère de Saqqara. Essai de reconstitution." *Miscellanea Coptica/Acta ad archaeologiam et artium historiam pertinentia* 9 (1981):9–124.

______. "Quelques remarques iconographiques sur la peinture chrétienne à Saqqara." *Miscellanea Coptica/Acta ad archaeologiam et artium historiam pertinentia* 9 (1981):207–220.

Rassart-Debergh, M. M., and Debergh, J. "A propos de trois peintures de Saqqara." *Miscellanea Coptica/Acta ad Archaeologiam et artium historiam pertinentia* 9 (1981):187–205.

MARGUERITE RASSART-DEBERGH

DAYR APA MACARIUS. *See* Monasteries of the Upper Ṣa'īd.

DAYR APA NOB. *See* Monasteries of the Upper Ṣa'īd.

DAYR APA PHOIBAMMON. [*This article is composed of two parts—a section on the history of Dayr Apa Phoibammon and one describing the relationship of the buildings of the* dayr *with the temple of Queen Hatshepsut.*]

History

The monastery of Phoibammon is situated between MADĪNAT HĀBŪ and Armant, at the end of a narrow wadi ending in a circular cliff about 80 feet (25 m) high. It was excavated in 1947 and 1948 by Charles Bachatly, secretary-general of the SOCIETY OF COPTIC ARCHAEOLOGY. Graffiti on the cliff face confirm that the monastery was dedicated to Saint Phoibammon, though to which of the four known saints of that name is uncertain. It is probably the soldier saint commemorated on 1 Ba'ūnah, concerning whom there exists a homily in Arabic. Over 200 graffiti in Greek and Coptic were found on the site but no manuscripts and few ostraca.

One of the monks of this monastery, Abraham, became (about 590) bishop of Hermonthis. Because of the remote position of the monastery and the wish of Patriarch DAMIAN, he left this monastery and founded another monastery of Phoibammon near the town of Djeme in the former Temple of Hatshepsut (Dayr al-Bahri). The existence of this monastery was known from documents found at different sites of the Theban mountain, in particular at Dayr al-Bahri and DAYR AL-BAKHĪT, where manuscripts and ostraca originating from the monastery of Phoibammon were found.

The monastery excavated by Bachatly was probably voluntarily abandoned in the eighth century, presumably because it was feared that the whole cliff against which the monastery was built might crumble. In a cave on the rocky terrace above the monastery, fifteen inscriptions were found, three of which bear the name of Apa Pisenthius.

BIBLIOGRAPHY

Bachatly, C. *Le Monastère de Phoebammon dans la Thébaïde.* Cairo, 1982.

Ghali, M. *Note sur la découverte du monastère de Phoebammon dans la montagne thébaine.* Cairo, 1948.
Khater, A. and O. H. E. Burmester. *L'Archéologie du site.* Cairo, 1981.
Krause, M. "Zwei Phoibammon-Kloster in Theben-West." *Mitteilungen des deutschen archäologischen Instituts. Abteilung Kairo* 37 (1981):261–66.
______. "Die Beziehungen zwischen den beiden Phoibammon-Klöstern auf dem thebanischen Westufer." *Bulletin de la Société d'archéologie copte* 27 (1985).
Rémondon, R.; Y. 'Abd al-Masīh; W. C. Tilland; and O. H. E. Burmester. *Le monastère de Phoebammon dans la Thébaïde,* Vol. 2, *Graffiti, inscriptions et ostraca.* Cairo, 1965.
Tackholm, V.; E. A. M. Greiss; A. K. el-Duweini; and Z. Iskander. *Identifications botaniques, zoologiques et chimiques.* Cairo, 1961.

MIRRIT BOUTROS GHALI

Buildings

Dayr Apa Phoibammon in Dayr al-Bahri was erected on the uppermost platform of the Temple of Queen Hatshepsut and over the northwestern part of the middle platform, which during the Coptic period was buried under debris and sand as high as the level of pavement of the upper portico. The whole monastic building was disassembled by A. Mariette and E. Naville in the second half of the nineteenth century in an effort to uncover the temple, and all monastic relics were removed without documentation. Today, to regain information on the site of the monastery, we have to consult archival descriptions from travelers in the eighteenth and nineteenth centuries. Of extreme value are the sketches, plans, and surveys in the British Library made by R. Hay during his travels to Egypt (1824–1838). Very important also are Coptic graffiti and drawings preserved on the walls of the temple.

Dayr Apa Phoibammon, one of the largest monastic complexes in Upper Egypt, made partial use of the pharaonic buildings situated on the upper platform of the temple. These were from the south vestibule of the royal chapels of Hatshepsut and Tothmoses, the little southwestern room, the main sanctuary (except for the Ptolomaic chapel), and the northwestern chapel of Amon-Re. Obviously the central court was also used, and relics of a few separate buildings were discovered there. The 26-foot tower, located in the southeastern corner of the court, was best preserved. The northern part of the eastern portico on the third platform and northwestern section of the second platform were occupied by a huge brick construction, preserved up to the second floor until the middle of the nineteenth century. The premises of Dayr Apa Phoibammon extended as well throughout the embankment covering the court with the sun altar in the northern part of the upper platform where a building with a central dome was recorded by R. Hay (B. L. Mss, no 135), R. Lepsius, and the French Expedition. On the southeastern part of the middle platform, a building separated from the monastic complex was also recorded by Hays.

Little can be told about the functional use of particular monastic premises. Undoubtedly, the Hatshepsut chapel functioned as the monastic church. Very likely in the earlier days of the monastery the main sanctuary of the temple served a similar function, with buildings on the middle platform being used most probably as cells by monks. The function of the buildings on the upper platform is unclear except for the tower. The building over the court with the sun altar was used most probably as a monastic archive, and E. Naville found there a few hundred Coptic ostraca. The vestibule of the royal chapels in the last years of the monastery's existence was used as a cemetery, and E. Naville uncovered there several Coptic mummies.

The ostraca uncovered during the excavations of the Egypt Exploration Fund led by Naville at Dayr al-Bahri on Hatshepsut Temple and at Mentuhotep Temple (1894–1895) are now in the British Museum and in the Egyptian Museum, Cairo. They were partly published by W. E. Crum (1902) and R. H. Hall (1905). Similar documents were found by H. E. Winlock (1926, Vol. 1, p. 20) during the excavations of the Metropolitan Museum of Art Expedition, and can now be found in the Egyptian Museum in Cairo and in the collection of Columbia University, New York. Most probably the wooden box containing Coptic papyri connected with Dayr Apa Phoibammon (testaments of abbots, deeds, and legal documents) accidentally uncovered during the winter of 1854–1855 was also found in the ruins of the monastic building at Dayr al-Bahri. All these documents, including the group of the so-called Djeme papyri, edited by Crum and G. Steindorff (1912, Vol. 1 [text and indexes]; repr. Leipzig, 1971), were kept in the archives of Dayr Apa Phoibammon. It is very likely that another Djeme papyrus, concerning private affairs, had been deposited in the monastery.

The testament of Apa Jakob, abbot of the monastery (late seventh century), gives evidence that at this post he was preceded by bishop Abraham, priest Victor, and priest Petros. Therefore, bishop Abraham (590–620) was apparently the first abbot and founder of Dayr Apa Phoibammon at Dayr al-Bahri. The foundation of the monastery is recorded as well in *Koptische Rechtsurkunden des achten Jahrhunderts aus Djeme* 105 (Steinwenter, 1935, pp. 380–85) dated to the end of the sixth century. In this document the whole village (most probably Djeme) is granted the title of ownership of the estate (most probably at Dayr al-Bahri) to Dayr Apa Phoibammon on which the monastic building could be erected. The same fact is reported also in Coptic Ostraca Ad. 59 (Crum, 1902).

Dayr Apa Phoibammon flourished during the seventh and first half of the eighth centuries. The last documents connected with this monastery belong to the end of the eighth century. At that time, during the revolt in Upper Egypt against Abbasid power, the monastery undoubtedly was deserted. Dayr al-Bahri was visited by several people, including bishops, during the tenth and eleventh centuries, as we know from Coptic graffiti preserved inside the Hatshepsut chapel.

BIBLIOGRAPHY

Crum, W. E. *Coptic Ostraca.* London, 1902.

Crum, W. E., and G. Steindorff. *Koptische Rechtsurkunden des Achten Jahrhunderts aus Djeme (Theben).* Leipzig, 1912.

Godlewski, W. "Remarques sur la création du monastère de St. Phoebammon à Deir el Bahari." *Africana Bulletin* 31 (1982):107–113.

———. "The Late Roman Necropolis in Deir el Bahari." *Graeco-Coptica* 48 (1984):111–19.

———. *Deir el Bahari V. Le monastère de St. Phoebammon.* Warsaw, 1986.

Hall, R. H. *Coptic and Greek Texts of the Christian Period.* London, 1905.

Krause, M. "Apa Abraham von Hermonthis. Ein oberägyptischer Bischof um 600." Ph.D. diss. Berlin, 1956.

———. "Die Testamente der Äbte des Phoibammon-Kloster in Theben." *Mitteilungen des deutschen archäologischen Instituts—Abteilung Kairo* 37 (1981):261–66.

———. "Die ägyptischen Klöster. Bemerkungen zu den Phoibammon Klöstern in Theben-West und den Apollon-Klöstern." *Proceedings of the Third International Coptic Congress in Warsaw, 20–25 August, 1984.* Warsaw, 1984.

Naville, E. "The Excavations at Deir el Bahari During the Winter, 1894–5." *Archaeological Report* (1894–1895):33–37.

Steinwenter, A. "Zur Edition der koptischen Rechtsurkunden aus Djeme." *Orientalia* n.s. 4 (1935):377–85.

Till, W. C. *Datierung und Prosopographie der koptischen Urkunden aus Theben.* Vienna, 1962.

———. *Die koptischen Rechtsurkunden aus Theben.* Vienna, 1964.

Winlock, H. E., and W. E. Crum. *The Monastery of Epiphanius at Thebes,* 2 vols. New York, 1926.

W. GODLEWSKI

DAYR APA PSOTE. *See* monasteries of the Upper Ṣaʿīd.

DAYR APA SERGIUS. *See* Monasteries of the Upper Ṣaʿīd.

DAYR APA THOMAS, monastery near the town of Fāwjilay, which is about 5 miles (8 km) north of Akhmīm. A small church survives from a monastery commemorating the holy hermit Thomas of Shinshif. The name of this mountain (Shinshif) is retained in that of a village near the church, called Najʿ al-Shinshifī.

There is a reference to this Thomas in the Life of SHENUTE, and his feast was celebrated at the Dayr al-Abyad, as is shown by the *Typika* (calendar) of this monastery. The presence of this church allows us to locate exactly this Coptic placename Shinshif, which Amélineau (1893, pp. 453ff.) was not able to do. S. Clarke identifies a church of Saint Thomas at al-Sawamʿah (1972, p. 213, no. 18).

Some reproductions of paintings from this church are given by Nabīl al-Manqabadī (1984, pp. 94–99). The monastery is briefly mentioned by J. Muyser and G. Viaud (1979, p. 57).

BIBLIOGRAPHY

Amélineau, E. *La Géographie de l'Egypte à l'époque copte.* Paris, 1893.

Clarke, S. *Christian Antiquities in the Nile Valley.* London, 1912.

Muyser, J., and G. Viaud. *Les pèlerinages coptes en Egypte.* Bibliothèque d'études coptes 15. Cairo, 1979.

[Nabil al-Manqabadi.] *Coptic Egypt.* Cairo, 1984.

RENÉ-GEORGES COQUIN
MAURICE MARTIN, S.J.

DAYR AL-ARBAʿĪN SHAHID (or Dayr Theophilus). *See* Monasteries of the Upper Saʿīd.

DAYR AL-ARMAN. The fifteenth-century Muslim historian al-Maqrīzī said that at the time the conqueror ʿAmr ibn al-ʿĀṣ arrived in Egypt in 641, there were a hundred monasteries in Wādī al-Naṭrūn. He named some that were destroyed in his time, among them the Monastery of the Armenians, or Dayr al-Arman. For his part, MAWHŪB IBN MANṢŪR IBN MUFARRIJ, who continued the HISTORY OF THE PATRIARCHS, named only seven monasteries in Wādī Habīb, the name then given to Wādī al-Natrūn. He did not speak of a Monastery of the Armenians. The existence of a Monastery of the Armenians, the patron saint being unknown, must have been toward the end of the Fatimid period when the influence of the Armenians was very strong.

H. G. Evelyn-White (1932) placed its establishment after 1088 and before 1136, which is the date of the loss of the Armenians' political power. It was, in his opinion, a symbol of the views shared by Copts and Armenians regarding the orthodox faith, for the Armenians, too, were anti-Chalcedonians. A man of Armenian origin, Badr al-Jamālī, became first minister at the end of the eleventh century and was succeeded by his son, and an Armenian Christian, Bahram, was proclaimed vizier by the troops in 1134, but two years later he had to abdicate, which marked the end of Armenian power in Egypt.

Proof of the presence of the Armenians in Wādī al-Naṭrūn is found in two multilingual manuscripts of the twelfth century deriving from Scetis. They are written in Armenian, Coptic, Arabic, Syriac, and Ethiopic. (This polyglot Bible is in the Ambrosian Library at Milan.)

There is no document that allows one to give a precise date for the disappearance of this monastery. One may remark only that the Armenians, more than any others, suffered from the invasion of Shīrkūh and his army (Lane-Poole, 1925, pp. 179–85). Perhaps Dayr al-Arman disappeared at the time of the third invasion of Shīrkūh (1168–1169).

BIBLIOGRAPHY

Evelyn-White, H. G. *The Monasteries of the Wadi 'n Naṭrūn*, Pt. 2, *History of the Monasteries of Nitria and Scetis*, New York, 1932; repr. 1973.

Lane-Poole, S. *A History of Egypt in the Middle Ages.* History of Egypt 6. London, 1925.

RENÉ-GEORGES COQUIN

DAYR AL-ʿASAL (Minyat Banī Khaṣīb). This monastery, which ancient authors spoke of, seems to have disappeared. Yāqūt (1866–1873, Vol. 2, p. 681) described it as very well situated and populated by numerous monks. Ibn Duqmāq (1893, p. 16) mentioned it with Abyūhah 9 miles (15 km) to the south of Minyā.

ABŪ ṢALIḤ THE ARMENIAN (1895, pp. 248–49), who wrote in the early thirteenth century, indicated that it is near Munyat Banī Khaṣīb and that the principal church is dedicated to Saint George. He also notes that there were two keeps and fourteen churches, and that it possessed a garden, a mill, and an oil press.

The HISTORY OF THE PATRIARCHS (1959, Vol. 2, pt. 3, pp. 226 [text], 357 [trans.]) gave an account of the miracles wrought by Saint George in his church. "L'Etat des provinces" (A.H. 777/A.D. 1375) also mentioned it (al-Latif, 1810, p. 693).

G. DARESSY (1917, p. 199) said that it is still in existence, but he must have been mistaken, for travelers have not spoken of it. Perhaps he confused it with the church of Saint George at MINYĀ. Ramzī (1953–1968, Vol. 1, p. 258; Vol. 2, pt. 3, pp. 200–201) remarked that an agrarian inventory of the year A.H. 911 (A.D. 1505–1506) mentioned Dayr al-ʿAsal as being Dayr al-Ṣafṭ al-Khammār, at the same time as the nearby villages were called Banī Aḥmad and Tahnashā. It is probable that the Dayr al-ʿAsal survives as a village with the name of DAYR ʿAṬIYYAH.

BIBLIOGRAPHY

ʿAbd al-Laṭīf. *Relation de l'Egypte de ʿAbd al-Latif*, trans. and ed. A. I. de Sacy. Paris, 1810. "L'Etat des provinces" is translated in an appendix.

Daressy, G. "Indicateur topographique du 'Livre des perles enfouies et du mystère précieux.'" *Bulletin de l'Institut français d'Archéologie orientale* 13 (1917):175–230.

Ibn Duqmāq. *Kitāb al-Intisār.* Cairo, 1893.

Ramzī, M. *Al-Qāmūs al-Jughrāfī lil-Bilād al-Miṣriyyah*, 3 vols. Cairo, 1953–1968.

Yāqūt ibn ʿAbd Allāh al-Ḥamawī. *Geographisches Wörterbuch aus den Handschriften*, 6 vols., ed. F. Wüstenfeld. Leipzig, 1866–1873. Repr. Beirut (4 vols.), 1955–1957; Tehran, 1965.

RENÉ-GEORGES COQUIN
MAURICE MARTIN, S.J.

DAYR ASFAL AL-ARḌ. The most detailed description of this convent near Alexandria is given by

Abū al-Makārim (1984, pp. 161, 168). He indicates that this monastery was situated east of the town and bore the name of Saint Mark. It was extensive, surrounded by gardens and cultivated land, and had no fewer than four keeps. In its underground church there were two altars where Saint Mark was commemorated. Many relics were preserved there, including those of Saint Sophia and her three daughters. After the Council of Chalcedon in 451, the church returned to the Melchites with Saint Mark's body, while the saint's head was assigned to the Copts with Saint Mark's church, called al-Qamḥah, also situated outside the town. The geographical situation of this Dayr Asfal-al-Arḍ is again specified by Abū al-Makārim: "it is related that it used to be the house of the oxen, where Saint Mark was martyred and from which he was dragged, attached by the feet, through the whole town." This monastery must therefore be near, if not in the same place as, the martyrium of Saint Mark, which was situated near the sea and which was burned by ʿAmr ibn al-ʿĀṣ on the second capitulation of the town in 646 (Butler, 1978, p. 475). The recension of the SYNAXARION from Lower Egypt, in the account of Benjamin on 8 Ṭūbah, adds an interesting detail to the text of the HISTORY OF THE PATRIARCHS: "ʿAmr ibn al-ʿĀṣ burned many churches, among others that of Saint Mark at the sea side, known today under the name of the lowland church" (Kanīsat Asfal al-Arḍ). This formula "known today under the name of the lowland church," added by the author of the Synaxarion, confirms Abū al-Makārim's note on the topographical situation of the convent that bears the same name.

It is very probable that it refers to the same monastery as the one described by Bernard the Wise toward 870 (see MONASTERIES IN AND AROUND ALEXANDRIA). The church of al-Qamḥah, for its part, after being rebuilt either by Patriarch AGATHON or by John of Samannūd (Chaîne, 1924), was destroyed in 1218, when the Crusaders, led by Jean de Brienne, threatened Alexandria. The Ayyubid sultan al-ʿAdil Ayyūb ibn Abū Bakr had it demolished for fear that the Franks would use it as a fortress (al-Qalqashandī, 1922–1923, p. 134). It is not known where this Church of Saint Mark al-Qamḥah was located—perhaps it is the same as the one placed by the Synaxarion (4 Abīb) to the south of the town. But the edition of the Synaxarion from Lower Egypt, which is certainly later than 1218, shows from its text that the two sites must be distinguished. The Church of Saint Mark called al-Qamḥah was destroyed by 1218, and the Church of Saint Mark called Asfal al-Arḍ, with the neighboring convent of the same name, was still in existence at the time when the editor of the Synaxarion was writing.

BIBLIOGRAPHY

Abū al-Makārim. *Tārikh al-Kanā' is wa al-Adyirah,* ed. Ṣamū'īl al-Suryānī. Dayr al-Suryān, 1984.

Butler, A. J. *The Arab Conquest of Egypt,* 2nd ed. P. M. Fraser. Oxford, 1978.

Chaîne, M. "L'Eglise de Saint-Marc à Alexandrie construite par le patriarche Jean de Samanoud." *Revue de l'Orient chrétien* 24 (1924):372–86.

Qalqashandī, al-. "La liste des Patriarches d'Alexandrie dans . . .," trans. E. Tisserant and G. Wiet. *Revue de l'Orient chrétien* 23 (1922–1923):123–43.

RENÉ-GEORGES COQUIN
MAURICE MARTIN, S.J.

DAYR AL-ʿASKAR. This monastery is one of a group of four briefly described by al-MAQRĪZĪ (A.D. 1442), in the neighborhood of Bilqās, to the northeast of the province of Gharbiyyah. He placed it at one day's march from the Dayr al-Mighṭās and near the salt marsh from which the so-called Rashīd (Rosetta) salt comes. He added that it was dedicated to the apostles and that no more than one monk lived there (1845, pp. 45 [text], 109 [trans.]; 1853, Vol. 2, p. 508).

Ramzī (1953–1963, Vol. 1, p. 84) notes that al-ʿAskar was a village placed by Yāqūt (A.D. 1229) in his *Kitāb Muʿjam al-Buldān* near Damīrah. In the later documents and up to 1809, this locality was associated with al-Maymah (see DAYR AL-MAYMAH) in the district of Danjawāy, and their linking might have been the origin of the town of Bilqās in the *markaz* (district) of Ṭalkhā.

The name ʿAskar was doubtless given to this place by reason of the presence of a military camp (Maspero and Wiet, 1919, p. 127), and the monastery mentioned by al-Maqrīzī no doubt took the name of the neighboring small town. It is not to be concluded from this notation by al-Maqrīzī that this monastery was still in existence in the fifteenth century, for this author compiled many chronicles and other, earlier works.

BIBLIOGRAPHY

Maspero, J., and G. Wiet. *Matériaux pour servir à la géographie de l'Egypte.* Mémoires de l'Institut français d'Archéologie orientale 36. Cairo, 1919.

Ramzī, M. *Al-Qāmūs al-Jughrāfī lil-Bilād al Misriyyah,* 3 vols. Cairo, 1953–1968.

Yāqūt ibn ʿAbd Allāh al-Ḥamawī. *Kitāb Muʿjam al-Buldān,* 10 vols. Cairo, 1956–1957.
______. *Jacūt's Geographisches Wörterbuch.* 6 vols., ed F. Wüstenfeld. Leipzig, 1866–1873. Repr. Tehran, 1965; Beirut, 4 vols., 1955–1957.

RENÉ-GEORGES COQUIN
MAURICE MARTIN, S.J.

DAYR ʿATIYYAH. This place-name, which may preserve the name of a vanished monastery, still exists today in the district of al-Ashmūnayn.

Ramzī (1953–1968, Vol. 2, pt. 3, p. 200) notes that in a document of A.M. 911/A.D. 1505–1506, this *dayr* bears the name of Dayr Ṣafṭ al-Khammār. Today it is situated in the *markaz* (district) of Minyā; it is mentioned in the *State of Provinces* in 1375 (p. 689) under the name of Dayr ʿAtiyyah.

Ramzī (Vol. 1, p. 258) seems to identify this place with DAYR AL-AʿSAL.

BIBLIOGRAPHY

ʿAbd el-Latīf. *Relation de l'Egypte de ʿAbd el-Latif,* trans. and ed. A. I. S. de Sacy. Paris, 1810.
Ramzī, M. *Al-Qāmūs al-Jughrāfī lil-Bilād al Miṣrīyyah,* 3 vols. Cairo, 1953–1968.

RENÉ-GEORGES COQUIN
MAURICE MARTIN, S.J.

DAYR AL-ʿAWANAH (Asyūṭ). The village of al-ʿAwanah is situated on the right bank of the Nile to the southeast of Asyūṭ, about 11 miles (18 km) to the north of the basin of al-Badārī and about 7 miles (12 km) to the south of DAYR AL-BIṢRAH. The monastery of al-ʿAwanah is today a Christian quarter with a church that is to the south of the village.

V. de Bock (1878, pp. 67–72) drew attention to it as worthy of interest and called it Deir Awana Cherbana. The atlas of the *Description de l'Egypte* (1821–1829, fol. 12) also registers it in its place.

The ancient part of the church is formed by a choir with three altars under deep, perforated domes and, in front of them, a bay of joists roofed by three similar domes. This is Type C in S. Clarke's classification (1912, p. 109). The back of the church has a ceiling opposite the dome.

The church is dedicated to Saint George. Perhaps it is the same as the one called Dayr Mār Jirjis of Khammās (or Ḥammās) by al-Maqrīzī (1853, Vol. 2, p. 503). But the name of this town does not appear to be attested elsewhere.

BIBLIOGRAPHY

Bock, V. de. "Notice sur les monuments coptes de la vallée du Nil." *Comité de conservation des monuments de l'art arabe* 15 (1878):67–72.
Clarke, S. *The Christian Antiquities in the Nile Valley.* London, 1912.
Description de l'Egypte. Paris, 1821–1829.

RENÉ-GEORGES COQUIN
MAURICE MARTIN, S.J.

DAYR AL-ʿAYN. *See* Dayr al-Malāk Mīkhāʾīl (Qamūlah).

DAYR AL-ʿAZAB (Fayyūm). [*This entry consists of two articles: the history of this monastery, and its architecture.*]

History

The monastery of Dayr al-ʿAzab does not seem to have been mentioned, at least under this name, by any author before the traveler J. M. Vansleb in 1672, who placed it halfway between Madīnat al-Fayyūm and the DAYR AL-NAQLŪN (1677, p. 274; 1678, p. 166). In fact, it is about 4 miles (6 km) to the south of the capital of the Fayyūm.

M. Ramzī (1953–1968, Vol. 1, p. 253; Vol. 2, pt. 3, p. 95) thought that this was the same monastery as the Dayr Dimūshyah mentioned by al-Nābulsī (Salmon, 1901, p. 64) to the south of the small town called Dimūshiyah. However, this town is situated about 3 miles to the west of that called al-ʿAzab.

Descriptions were given by Johann Georg (1930, p. 19 and figs. 38–40, under the name al-Azrab) and O. Meinardus (1965, p. 332; 1977, p. 447). S. Clarke (1912, p. 205, no. 17) mentioned a church of the Virgin at al-ʿAzab, in the district of Iṭsā. Al-Baramūsī (1932, p. 157) indicated two churches in this monastery, one of the Virgin, the other of Saint Mercurius (ABŪ AL-SAYFAYN), and called the monastery Dayr al-ʿAdhrāʾ (Monastery of the Virgin).

A new and very large church and other buildings have recently been constructed, because of pilgrimage to the tomb of the very popular Anbā ABRAAM, monk of DAYR AL-MUḤARRAQ and then bishop of the Fayyūm, who died in 1914.

BIBLIOGRAPHY

ʿAbd al-Masīḥ Ṣalīb al-Masūʿdi al-Baramūsī. *Tuḥfat al-Sāʾilīn fī Dhikr Adyirat Ruhbān al-Misriyyīn.* Cairo, 1932.

Clarke, S. *Christian Antiquities in the Nile Valley.* Oxford, 1912.
Johann Georg, Duke of Saxony. *Neue Streifzüge durch die Kirchen und Klöster Ägyptens.* Leipzig and Berlin, 1930.
Meinardus, O. *Christian Egypt, Ancient and Modern.* Cairo, 1965; 2nd ed., 1977.
Ramzī, M. *Al-Qāmūs al-Jughrāfī lil-Bilād al Miṣriyyah,* 3 vols. Cairo, 1953–1968.
Salmon, G. "Répertoire géographique de la province du Fayyoum d'après le Kitāb Tarikh al-Fayyoum d'an-Nāboulsī." *Bulletin de l'Institut français d'Archéologie orientale* 1 (1901):29–77.
Vansleb, J. M. *Nouvelle Relation en forme de journal d'un voyage fait en Egypte en 1672 et 1673.* Paris, 1677. Translated as *The Present State of Egypt.* London, 1678.

RENÉ-GEORGES COQUIN
MAURICE MARTIN, S.J.

Architecture

Dayr al-ʿAzab lies in the Fayyūm, close to the road from Madīnat al-Fayyūm to Banī Suef, and is still a very obscure complex to assign (Abbott, 1937, pp. 62f.) Today at that place there is an extensive modern cemetery with a large late-nineteenth-century church. The church to the northeast of this, hidden behind several neighboring buildings, seems still to include different components of an earlier basilican building. The semicircular main *haykal* (sanctuary) with five very deep niches, and several wall sections of the two immediately adjoining secondary *haykals,* including the southern outer wall, might even go directly back to a previous three-nave building. The two secondary *haykals* would have to be considered as remodeled side rooms for the apse. Everything else was added in building activities of a much more recent date. The two cupolas over the central nave date from the Ottoman period. There is no *khūrus.*

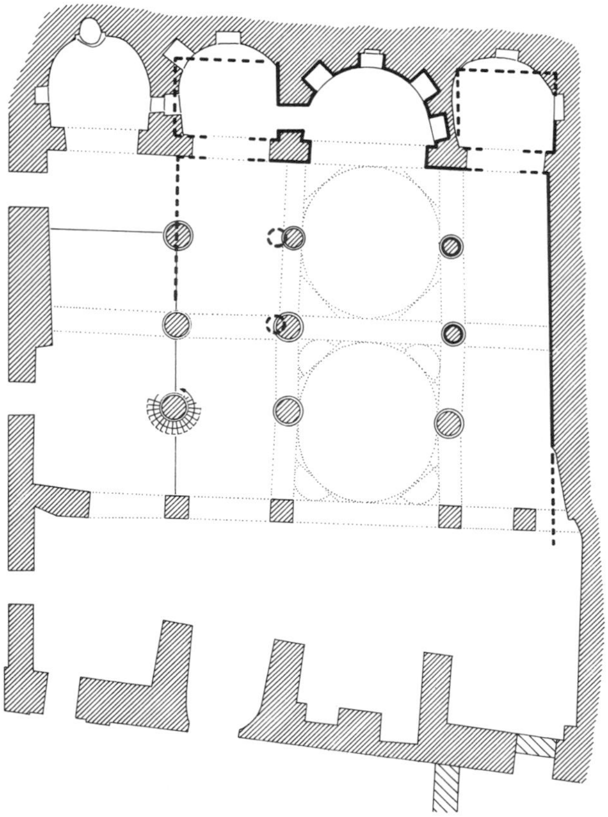

Plan of the church at Dayr al-ʿAzab. *Courtesy Peter Grossmann.*

BIBLIOGRAPHY

Abbott, N. *The Monasteries of the Fayyūm.* Chicago, 1937.
Grossmann, P. *Mittelalterliche Langhauskuppelkirchen und verwandte Typen in Oberägypten,* pp. 36ff. Glückstadt, 1982.

PETER GROSSMANN

DAYR AZILUN. *See* Monasteries of the Middle Ṣaʿīd.

DAYR BABLŪN AL-DARAJ. *See* Babylon.

DAYR AL-BAGHL. *See* Dayr al-Quṣayr (Ṭūrāh).

DAYR AL-BAHRI. *See* Dayr Apa Phoibammon.

DAYR AL-BAKARAH. *See* Dayr al-ʿAdhrāʾ (Jabal al-Tayr).

DAYR AL-BAKHĪT (Luxor). [*This entry consists of two parts: the history of this monastery, and its architecture.*]

History

The name of this monastery could only be the Arabic transcription of a Coptic word meaning "of the north," in contrast to Dayr al-Qiblī (Monastery of the South), the name given to the temple of Hadrian to the south of Madīnat Hābū. This appellation could be older than the typically Arabic name Dayr al-Bahri, identical in terms of sense, given to the DAYR APA PHOIBAMMON established in the temple of Hatshepsut (Winlock and Crum, 1926, Vol. 1, p. 116, n. 1). This name would indicate its more ancient origin, when Coptic was a spoken language and before Arabic became preponderant. These two monasteries bearing the same name, the one Coptic, the other Arabic, are close to one another on the left bank of the Nile, opposite Luxor.

The ruins of the Dayr al-Bakhīt were still clearly visible at the beginning of the century. The best description was given by Winlock and Crum (Vol. 1, pp. 21–22). Despite its being termed a DAYR, it was, it seems, much more a center combining the services of a community of hermits living in caves rather than a true monastery. Mention of it will be found in Lepsius (1852, p. 267).

BIBLIOGRAPHY

Lepsius, R. *Letters from Egypt . . . 1844–45.* London, 1852.

Winlock, H. E., and W. E. Crum. *The Monastery of Epiphanius at Thebes,* 2 vols. New York, 1926.

RENÉ-GEORGES COQUIN
MAURICE MARTIN, S.J.

Architecture

Considerable remains of the small monastery complex were still standing on the plateau of Dirā' Abū al-Najā, east of Qurnah, in the nineteenth century. Travelers reported several residential buildings, the doors of which had pointed arches. Today most of it has collapsed, but still standing are numerous traces of walls of buildings, sometimes of several stories, with large and small rooms. The construction shows mud brickwork on a high socle of masonry. The location of the church cannot be determined without excavation. Also there are no traces to show the course of the surrounding wall. The area of the monastery yielded several chance finds of ostraca and papyri from the sixth to seventh century (so far unpublished). It is not yet clear with what ancient site the monastery is to be identified.

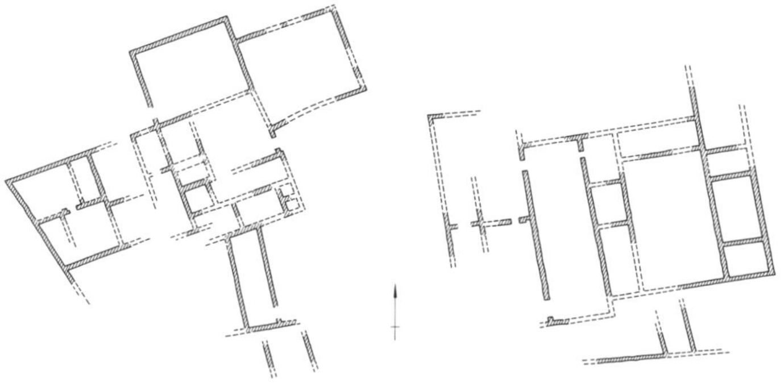

Plan of the traces of residential buildings found at Dayr al-Bakhīt. *Courtesy Peter Grossmann.*

BIBLIOGRAPHY

Timm, S. *Das christlich-koptische Ägypten in arabischer Zeit,* Vol. 2, pp. 682–84. Wiesbaden, 1984.

Winlock, H. E., and W. E. Crum. *The Monastery of Epiphanius at Thebes,* Vol. 1, pp. 21–22. New York, 1926.

PETER GROSSMANN

DAYR AL-BALAʿYZAH. [*This entry consists of two parts: the history of this monastery, and its architecture.*]

History

This monastery, of which nothing but vast ruins remain, was situated on the left bank of the Nile, about 11 miles (18 km) to the south of ASYŪṬ. About 2.5 miles (4 km) from the DAYR AL-ZĀWIYAH, on the cliff that carries the desert plateau, some ancient quarries were first fitted out as dwellings; then down the slope, a whole series of buildings was constructed in tiers the length of the slope, the whole surrounded by an encircling wall that certainly exceeds a mile in length. The base of the wall is thick and made of large stones bound together with clay, while the wall itself is constructed of unbaked bricks. At the bottom, where the wall includes a large, deep tomb well (only traces of it remain), one can see in the southeast corner the remains of a small construction outside the wall. This was, then, a fortified monastery.

It was excavated in 1907 by W. M. F. Petrie, who was in search of papyri, but a plan was not drawn up (1907, Vol. 1, p. 9, pls. 38, 39; 1909, Vol. 1, p. 29, pls. 53, 54; see also *Archaeological Report,* 1906–1907, pp. 29, 75). According to P.E. KAHLE (1954), it was ruined about 750 and abandoned thereafter, but the presence of a strong encircling wall would argue for a date of abandonment later than 750.

BIBLIOGRAPHY

Archaeological Report, 1906–1907, ed. F. L. Griffith. Egypt Exploration Society.

Kahle, P. E. *Balā'izah,* 2 vols. London, 1954.

Petrie, W. M. F. *Gīzeh and Rīfeh.* London, 1907.

______. *Memphis,* Vol. 1. London, 1909.

RENÉ-GEORGES COQUIN
MAURICE MARTIN, S.J.

Architecture

The *dayr* consists of an extended, rectangular walled area, inside which still stand the remains of many buildings, some rising to a considerable height. Remains of the site of a gate have been found in the side on the lower parallel slope. Because of the uniformity of the surrounding wall, there is no doubt that this monastery is not a laura but a cenobium, inhabited by a large community of monks. The buildings are basically constructed of mud bricks and in places show evidence of several stories. On the upper slope, buildings are more numerous, disclosing also at the upper edge a row of large pharaonic quarry caves, used also for monastic purposes, as can be understood from the many representations of crosses preserved on their rock walls. Below, on the valley side, fewer buildings are preserved. Obviously, what remained has been more vigorously plundered.

Remains of a small church have been found in the lower southwest corner of the *dayr.* It has a naos that, in spite of its slight width of 26 feet (8.6 m), was very probably planned with three aisles, for the thin side walls (2 feet or 60 cm) are far too weak to bear ceiling beams of a span of almost 30 feet (9 m). The sanctuary adjoining the east end has a relatively deep apse, of which the inner curve shows a row of recesses. It is very likely that these once held a surrounding circle of columns. The passages to the rectangular side rooms lay in the forward area of the apse. Beyond that, on the northern exterior, is a stair projecting over the whole frontage, an uncommon feature. From a later time dates a narthex on the west side of the church, with a second stair to the south.

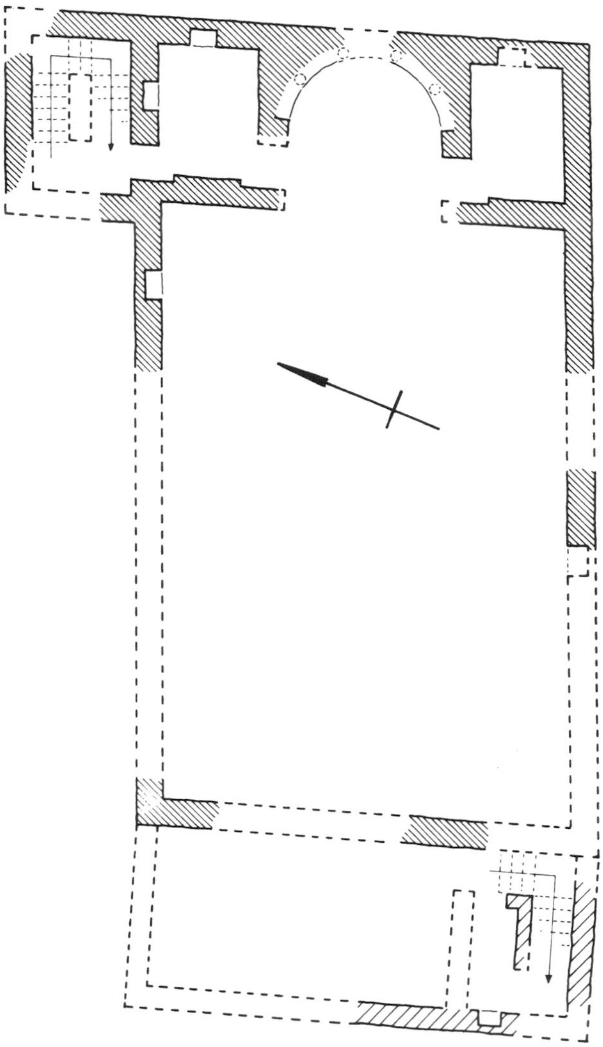

Plan of the church at Dayr al-Bala'yzah. *Courtesy Peter Grossmann.*

BIBLIOGRAPHY

Grossmann, P. "Die Unterkunftsbauten des Koinobitenklosters 'Dair al-Balāyza' im Vergleich mit den Eremitagen der Mönche von Kellia." In *Le site monastique copte des Kellia, Actes du Colloque de Genève 13 au 15 août 1984,* pp. 33–40, fig. 2. Geneva, 1986.

Kahle, P. E. *Balā'izah,* 2 vols. London, 1954.

Meinardus, O. *Christian Egypt, Ancient and Modern,* pp. 286–87. Cairo, 1965.

Petrie, W. M. F. *Gīzeh and Rīfeh,* p. 30, no. 83, pl. 37B–38B. London, 1907.

PETER GROSSMANN

DAYR AL-BALLĀṢ (Qifṭ). This monastery-village is situated on the left bank of the Nile to the north of the town of al-Ballāṣ, which has given its name to the large jars in which water is carried. There is neither archaeological nor ancient literary evidence, only the name of the hamlet, al-Dayr, to show that a monastery existed there, and the church that survives indicates that it was dedicated to Saint George (Mār Jirjis).

"The State of the Provinces" (al-Laṭīf, 1810, p. 703), drawn up in A.H. 777/A.D. 1375–1376, mentions it under the title of Dayr al-Kahmas. A fifteenth-century manuscript published under the title *Book of the Hidden Pearls* (Daressy, 1917, p. 200) also mentions it.

At the beginning of the twentieth century, the ruins of a monastery could still be seen (Weigall, 1913, p. 83). It is mentioned in reference to the Church of Saint George by S. Clarke (1912, p. 216, no. 2; it is attached to the bishopric of Isnā).

ʿAbd al-Masīḥ (1924, p. 181) cited it as a monastery dedicated to Mār Jirjis. Quibell noted remains of hermitages to the west of the present hamlet of al-Dayr (1896, p. 1).

BIBLIOGRAPHY

ʿAbd al-Laṭīf. *Relation de l'Egypte de ʿAbd al-Latīf*, trans. and ed. A. I. S. de Sacy. Paris, 1810. "L'Etat des provinces" is translated in an appendix.

ʿAbd al-Masīḥ Ṣalīb al-Masūʿdi al-Baramūsī. *Kitāb Ṭuhfat al Sāiʾlīn fī Dhikr Adyirat Ruhbān al-Miṣriyyīn*. Cairo, 1924.

Daressy, G. "Indicateur topographique du 'Livre des perles enfouies et du mystère précieux.'" *Bulletin de l'Institut français d'Archéologie orientale* 13 (1917):175–230.

Quibell, J. E. *Ballas*. London, 1896.

Weigall, A. E. P. *A Guide to the Antiquities of Upper Egypt from Abydos to the Sudan Frontier*. London, 1913.

RENÉ-GEORGES COQUIN
MAURICE MARTIN, S.J.

DAYR BĀLŪJAH.

DAYR BĀLŪJAH. Al-MAQRĪZĪ mentions in his list of monasteries a convent that he places at about two hours' walk opposite Daljah (southwest of Mallawī), near al-Manhā, that is to say, the Baḥr Yūsuf. He describes it as having been one of the largest monasteries in Egypt, but destroyed in his period (fifteenth century) and inhabited by only one or two monks. It should be noted that in ancient times Daljah was on the right bank of the Baḥr Yūsuf and not on the left as today. It has been suggested that this monastery of Bālūjah should be identified with that of BĀWĪṬ, at present about 6 miles (10 km) south of Daljah, because the SYNAXARION for 25 Bābah places the monastery of Apollo at Ablūj. However, the two names are too different to be explained by a copyist's error, and Bāwīṭ does not correspond to al-Maqrīzī's description.

For his part ABŪ ṢĀLIḤ THE ARMENIAN mentions a church in the district of Bālūjā, dedicated to the apostles, which he places, as it seems, on the east bank and near to Iṭfīḥ, which does not correspond with the details given by al-Maqrīzī.

There appears to be no village of this name in this region of Middle Egypt. G. Maspero has noted a place called Dayr al-Jarādāwī, which is located almost at the site indicated by al-Maqrīzī for Bālūjah (1892, p. 201). See also E.-F. Jomard in *Description de l'Egypte* (Vol. 4, p. 314).

BIBLIOGRAPHY

Jomard, E. F., in *Description de l'Egypte*, Vol. 4. Paris, 1821.

Maspero, G. "Notes au jour le jour." *Proceedings of the Society of Biblical Archeology* 14 (1892):170–204, 305–327.

RENÉ-GEORGES COQUIN
MAURICE MARTIN, S.J.

DAYR AL-BANĀT (Cairo). *See* Babylon.

DAYR AL-BANĀT, a women's convent in the Fayyūm. This is a small complex of ruins in a valley on the southern edge of the Fayyūm not far from DAYR AL-NAQLŪN. The ruins, which can still be seen, lie within an extensive cemetery and point to the presence of an earlier monastic settlement in this place. Up to now it has not been possible to determine to which of the monasteries of the Fayyūm this site belonged. S. Timm (1984, pp. 762–65) connected all known names of the Dayr al-Naqlūn to originally independent complexes. N. Abbott (1937, p. 46) knows of another monastery situated nearby with the name of Dayr al-Shallah.

The dominant building of Dayr al-Banāt is the church, which has been almost completely reduced to a few remnants. It was built with fired bricks and had a western narthex, as well as a nearly square and presumably three-aisled naos, to which was added a series of rooms on the north and perhaps also on the south side. The sanctuary had no great depth, but extended over the whole width of the building so that it assumed almost the character of a transept. No genuine apse can be made out. Presumably it was represented by a somewhat larger

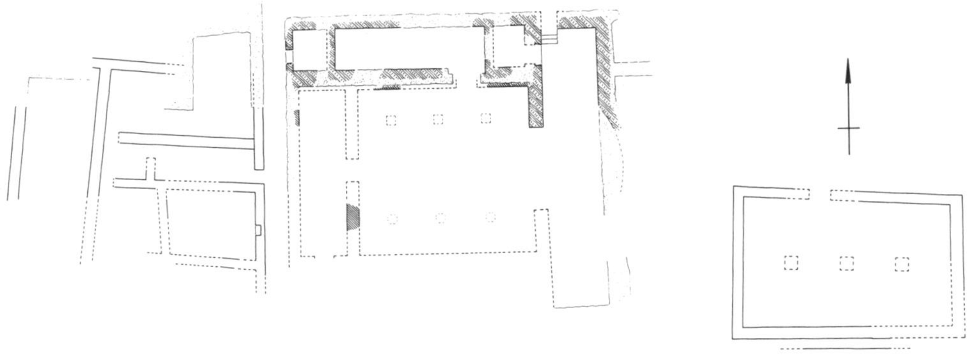

Plan of Dayr al-Banāt showing, from west to east, living quarters, church, and refectory. *Courtesy Peter Grossmann.*

wall niche that did not reach down to the floor, and is now lost.

The other buildings are made of mud bricks and therefore are in slightly better condition. The building to the west of the church appears to have been the living quarters. It was rebuilt on a number of occasions and contained a central corridor and several rooms arranged irregularly on both sides. East of the church lies what was probably once a two-aisled hall, which may be identified as the refectory of the monastery. The nature of the buildings that are distinguishable, especially the refectory where the meals could be taken together by the community, indicates that the inhabitants of the monastery lived in the cenobitic manner. There are no remainders of a surrounding wall in evidence.

BIBLIOGRAPHY

Abbott, N. *The Monasteries of the Fayyūm.* Chicago, 1937.

Khorshid, M. F. A. *Churches and Monasteries in the Province of al-Fayyūm* (in Arabic). Ph.D. diss., Asyūṭ, 1982.

Timm, S. *Das christlich-koptische Ägypten in arabischer Zeit,* Vol. 2, pp. 691–92. Wiesbaden, 1984.

PETER GROSSMANN

DAYR BANŪB. *See* Dayr Abū Nūb.

DAYR AL-BARAMŪS. [*This entry consists of three articles:* History, Architecture, *and* Church Paintings.]

History

This monastery is farthest to the northwest in the monastic colony of Wādī al-Naṭrūn (ancient Scetis). The topographic allusions in ancient literature lend some credence to the statement by the author of the Coptic Life of Saint Macarius (probably of the eighth century; cf. Guillaumont, 1968–1969, pp. 182–83) that Dayr al-Baramūs evolved from the earliest monastic settlement in Scetis. If so, the original settlement was formed at, or near, the site of the present monastery between 330 and 340 by admirers gathering around MACARIUS THE EGYPTIAN, although his name has remained associated with another monastery, DAYR ANBĀ MAQĀR. The latter monastery grew from a second settlement of admirers of Macarius near the place toward the eastern end of Scetis to which he moved later in his life.

The monastery's name, al-Baramūs, is an Arabized form of the Coptic *paromeos,* which can mean either "the one of the Roman" or "the one of the Romans." It is conceivable that around the middle of the fifth century the monastery was called Paromeos from association with one eminent Roman, ARSENIUS, who had been tutor of the two sons of the emperor Theodosius I, the future emperors Arcadius and Honorius. This can be true only if Arsenius, who went to Scetis around 394 and left around 434, is the Romaeus of the APOPHTHEGMATA PATRUM, who lived for many years near al-Baramūs. However, in the Coptic Life of Maximus and Domitius, which was composed as the monastery's foundation legend, probably in the late fifth century or the early sixth century, the Romans are not one but

View from the northwest. *Courtesy The Metropolitan Museum of Art, New York.*

two. In the Coptic legend, MAXIMUS AND DOMITIUS are presented as sons of the Roman emperor of the West, Valentinian I, both of whom went to Scetis in the days of Macarius the Egyptian, lived there in a monastic cell, died, and were buried nearby. After their deaths, Macarius, according to the legend, had the church built that became the center of the monastic settlement and that, at Macarius' own bidding, was to be called the "Cell of the Romans" in their memory.

Although Valentinian had no known sons, and he certainly had no legitimate sons, Maximus and Domitius may have been historical persons, but of a somewhat later period. In the Coptic Life, they seem to have been identified with the two unidentified foreigners in Macarius' time. The story of the life and death of these foreigners in Scetis is found in the *Apophthegmata Patrum* (Macarius, sec. 33) and is essentially similar to that of Maximus and Domitius in the later Coptic legend, except for the absence of any mention of a church built or a place named in their memory. The Coptic Life of Maximus and Domitius shows an etiological concern with providing a reason for the monastery's being called Paromeos. This may reflect a vague historical memory of the monastery's association with a Roman (Arsenius) and of his close association earlier with two Roman princes. If so, confusion of the two Roman princes in vaguely remembered stories about Arsenius with the two foreigners in Scetis in Macarius' time is the product of imaginative speculation, and their further confusion with Maximus and Domitius is, then, historically inaccurate. In any case, the Coptic legend agrees with the Coptic Life of Saint Macarius in making Macarius himself the central figure in the origin of the settlement from which Dayr al-Baramūs evolved.

Interior. General view from southwest enclosure, looking northeast. *Courtesy The Metropolitan Museum of Art, New York.*

The history of Dayr al-Baramūs through the centuries is almost entirely undocumented in historical records, but the known details of the general history of Scetis are certainly valid for the history of Dayr al-Baramūs. Like the other monastic establishments in Scetis, it suffered times of destruction by barbarians, followed sooner or later by periods of reconstruction. In the Christological controversy that divided the Egyptian Monophysites into a party adhering to the views of SEVERUS OF ANTIOCH, led by the patriarch THEODOSIUS I, and a party adhering to the views of JULIAN OF HALICARNASSUS, led by GAIANUS, Dayr al-Baramūs, like other monasteries of the valley, came under the control of the Gaianite faction among the monks. The Severan followers of Theodosius, who had to leave their monastery sometime between 535 and 580, proceeded to establish a monastery dedicated to the Virgin as a counterpart to their original monastery.

Although the monastery is mentioned in the occasional itineraries of Wādī al-Naṭrūn (known in the Middle Ages as Wādī Habīb) that have come down from the medieval and early modern periods, little is said of its condition, and nothing is said of events in its history. With its twenty monks in 1088 it was, except for the somewhat elusive "Cave of Moses," the smallest of the autonomous communities enumerated in a list of the monasteries of Wādī al-Naṭrūn drawn up that year. Both the original monastery and its counterpart, the Monastery of the Virgin of Baramūs, founded by the dispossessed Theodosians in the sixth century, existed when al-MAQRĪZĪ wrote his *History of the Copts* around 1440, but the question rises whether the monastery that has survived to the present day is the original monastery or its counterpart.

While the once great Dayr Anbā Maqār suffered particularly in the general eclipse of the ancient monasteries of Scetis after the first half of the fourteenth century, Dayr al-Baramūs maintained its numbers better than did some of the other three monasteries that ultimately survived. When Jean de Thévenot visited in 1657, he found that Dayr al-Baramūs had more monks than the other monasteries, and he attributed that to the monastery's better revenues. Robert Huntington found a superior and twenty-five monks there in 1678 or 1679, and Claude Sicard in 1712 found between twelve and fifteen monks there and in Dayr al-Suryān, but only three or four in each of the other two monasteries. In the case of Dayr al-Baramūs, that number seems to have been maintained as an average, despite rises and falls, through the eighteenth and nineteenth centuries. In the last two decades of the nineteenth century, the monastery became better known among the Coptic faithful through the popular theological and apologetical publications of the Syrian Afrām ʿAdad, who had become a monk there and who regularly signed his published works with the pseudonym "The Monk of Baramūs." From Dayr al-Baramūs have come the Coptic patriarchs CHRISTODOULUS, MATTHEW III, MATTHEW IV, CYRIL V, JOHN XIX, and CYRIL VI.

In 1976 there were thirty-five monks at Dayr al-Baramūs, of whom twenty lived in the monastery itself and fifteen were at its dependent estate in the Nile Delta or elsewhere in the service of the church. In recent years the monastery has been known for the quality of the calligraphy and manuscript copying done by some of its monks.

Interior. Gate house from the southeast. *Courtesy The Metropolitan Museum of Art, New York. Photography by Egyptian Expedition.*

BIBLIOGRAPHY

Amélineau, E. *Histoire des monastères de la Basse-Egypte*, pp. 46–117 (life of Macarius), 262–315 (lives of Maximus and Domitius). Annales du Musée Guimet 25. Paris, 1894.

Evelyn-White, H. G. *The Monasteries of the Wadi'n Natrūn*, pt. 2, *The History of the Monasteries of Nitria and of Scetis*. New York, 1932.

Guillaumont, A. *Annuaire de l'Ecole pratique des Hautes Etudes, Section de Sciences religieuses* 76 (1968–1969):182–83.

Meinardus, O. *Monks and Monasteries of the Egyptian Deserts*, pp. 150–56 (for the recent period not covered by Evelyn-White). Cairo, 1961.

______. "Zur monastischen Erneuerung in der koptischen Kirche." *Oriens Christianus* 61 (1977):59–70.

AELRED CODY, O.S.B.

Architecture

Like the other Egyptian monasteries, the monastery of Baramūs is surrounded by a high wall that prescribes a rectangle stretching out in a east–west direction. The wall has also preserved the upper ambulatory. The main entrance lies on the north side, although the monastery today is normally entered through a small side door on the west side. In contrast to the other monasteries in Egypt, its inner area is hardly spoiled by new building and has, as a consequence, best preserved its earlier character. Courtyards and gardens are in evidence. The visitor is welcomed in a friendly guesthouse. The cells of the monks are distributed in a number of rows along the walls and courtyards. The main church, dedicated to the Virgin Mary, the oldest preserved church in Wādī al-Naṭrūn, is located in the eastern half of the monastery. A second, modern church is situated next to the west entrance. Between the al-ʿAdhrāʾ church and the northern main gate is the keep (*jawsaq*) to the southwest of the church, the oil press, and the two refectories, neither of which is in use today.

The al-ʿAdhrāʾ Church, the chief church of the monastery, today heavily built up, goes back in its origins presumably to the seventh century and is thus the oldest remaining church in Wadī al-

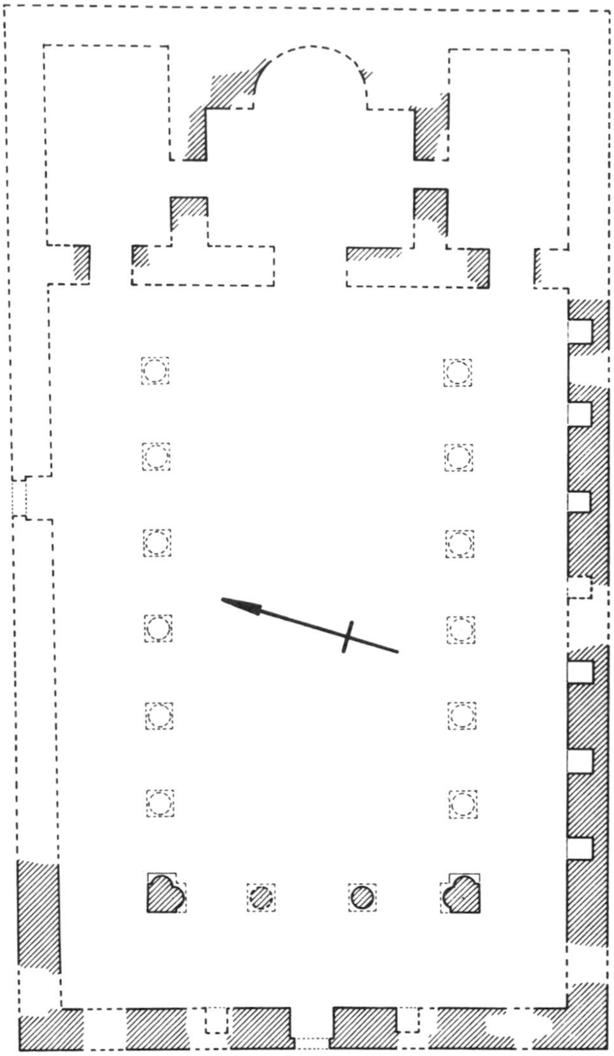

Plan of the original basilica at Dayr al-Baramūs. *Courtesy Peter Grossmann.*

Naṭrūn. In the course of the excavations, which were carried out in March 1979, the ground plan of the first basilica could be determined more precisely. It consisted of a three-room sanctuary the central main room of which extended east beyond the rest of the rooms. In the eighth or early ninth century, in accordance with the practice at that time, the church was provided with a *khūrus* (room between the naos and the sanctuary). The reconstruction of the sanctuary was carried out, to judge from the forms of the cupolas, in the late twelfth century. Finally, at an even later period, the width of the originally wood-covered nave was reduced, in order to accommodate a barrel vault over it. The original single columns were replaced by a series of oblong pillars given the form of double columns.

The Church of Saint John the Baptist was first built at the end of the nineteenth century, being a simple structure with four pillars, in line with the appearance of most church buildings from this period. As usual, the church contains three altars. At the west end it has an epiphany tank, the only one in Wādī al-Naṭrūn.

As is customary, the tower may be entered from the south over a retractable drawbridge on the first upper floor. Passing through its entire length is a corridor on both sides of which, right up to the stairs in the front southwest corner, a number of similar rooms are attached. Deserving of notice is the subterranean spring—found to the west outside the tower—that enabled the monks to withstand a long siege. It is difficult to make a decision on the date of the tower. At all events, it is older than the other towers still standing in Wādī al-Naṭrūn, although it is later than the very simple towers in KELLIA.

Contemporary visitors are told that a very long room on the south side of the al-ʿAdhrāʾ Church is the old refectory of the monastery. The room is

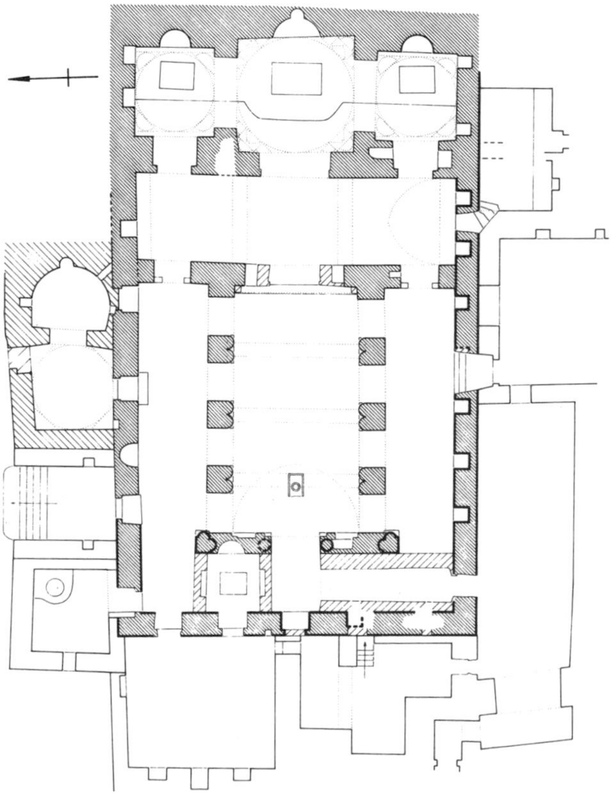

Plan of the basilica at Dayr al-Baramūs as it appears today. *Courtesy Peter Grossmann.*

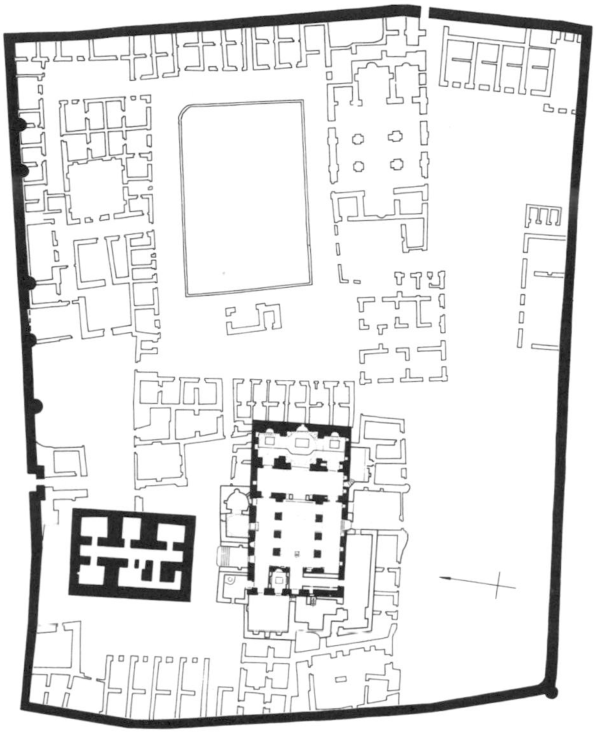

General plan of Dayr al-Baramūs. *Courtesy Peter Grossmann.*

divided up into three domed bays by two pointed transverse arches. A brick table about 3 feet (90 cm) high occupied the entire length of the room. Parallel to it on both sides are likewise brick benches. At the east end of the room there is a lectern also built of brick.

A second, appreciably older refectory is found on the west wall of the monastery and is used today as a storeroom. It consists of a square room with a central oblong pillar from which arches spring on all four sides and divide the room up into four domed bays approximately the same in size. The monks sat in this refectory on benches arranged in a circle, a practice that seems to have been common up to the end of the Fatimid period.

BIBLIOGRAPHY

Grossmann, P. *Mittelalterliche Langhauskuppelkirchen*, pp. 122–23, fig. 51. Glückstadt, 1982.

PETER GROSSMANN

Church Paintings

In 1986 by chance huge fragments of wall paintings in the al-ʿAdhra' Church were discovered by the monks of Dayr al-Baramūs. In 1988 a French-Netherlands Mission started to work on these paintings, and this work was resumed in 1989.

Three layers of paint have been discovered, the oldest of which has been best preserved and seems, furthermore, of the best quality. The decoration of the central apse, however, dates from a second master, for whom we unfortunately have no date. This apse gives the usual double theme: below is an enthroned Virgin between two archangels and above is an enthroned Christ between fragments of the four living creatures and other angels.

At both sides of this apse we see huge fragments of apostles, obviously painted by the first master and belonging to an earlier apse composition of the same type as described above. Above the three apostles at the northern side, fragments of a sacrifice of Isaac were found, while at the southern side an impressive scene showing Melchizedek giving a spoon from his chalice to Abraham had been dis-

Abraham and Melchizedek. Work of the first Master. *Courtesy Hans Hondelink.*

covered. No other traces of paint have been discovered in this central sanctuary.

In the southern sanctuary, two rows of male saints have been uncovered: on the east wall, from left to right, Saint Paul the Hermit, Saint Antony the Great, covered by a great veil, Saint Macarius the Great, accompanied by a cherub, a certain Saint John, Saint Maximus, and Saint Domitius. Inscriptions give their names.

On the southern wall we see, from left to right, the lower parts of Saint Pachomius, a monk with a dark skin (Moses the Black?), Saint Barsūm the Syrian, Saint Paphnutius (?), and Saint Onophrius; for some we have their names in inscriptions. From the first master (perhaps assisted by a second painter) we find huge parts of a Christological cycle in the central nave. On the southern wall of the nave, we see from left (east) to right (west): the annunciation by Gabriel to the Holy Virgin, the Holy Virgin embracing Elizabeth, fragments of both a Nativity scene and a wedding of Cana (?), and a great composition of Christ's entry into Jerusalem. The discoveries on the northern wall are very poor, except for important fragments of a scene of Pentecost at the right side. From that we may conclude that in fact once a complete cycle must have been painted here.

In one of the intercolumnia at the southern part of this nave a huge Archangel Michael can be made out and, not far from there, a huge cross, painted on different layers.

For the first master we have no other date than a *post quem*, given by the supposed reconstruction of the sanctuaries around 1300. The work of the third painter, on the upper layer, is of much less importance. In the murals of the first master, Dayr al-Baramūs has given us work of great quality, while the presence of huge parts of a Christological cycle has to be considered as rather exceptional for medieval Egypt.

Barsūm the Syrian (detail). Work of the first Master. *Courtesy Hans Hondelink.*

Saint Mary embracing Elizabeth (detail). Work of the first Master. *Courtesy Hans Hondelink.*

PAUL VAN MOORSEL

DAYR BARJANŪS. *See* Dayr Anbā Bākhūm (Barjanūs-Minyā).

DAYR AL-BARSHAH and DAYR AL-NAKHLAH. [*The first name is that of a village south of* DAYR ABŪ ḤINNIS. *It is a modern village, inhabited by Copts on the site of an old monastery, of which—apart from the old church—no parts worth mentioning have survived. The second is that of a village near the first, around which tomb hermitages are numerous. The first part of this entry reviews the history of these two villages. The second part discusses the architecture of both places.*]

History

The church of Dayr al-Barshah is dedicated to Anbā Bishoi. According to tradition, Anbā Bishoi, monk of SCETIS, fled before the Maziques, who devastated Scetis in 407, along with JOHN COLOBOS, who took refuge at Clysma (al-Qulzum). Anbā Bishoi, for his part, fled into the mountain of Antinoopolis where he died in 417. His body is said to have been transferred in the ninth century to Wādī al-Naṭrūn. Dayr al-Barshah is supposed to have been founded by him (Evelyn-White, 1932, pp. 158ff.). The same story is mentioned in the SYNAXARION at 8 Abīb. A description was given by J. M. VANSLEB (1677, p. 397; 1678, p. 237). E. F. Jomard also gave an account of it (Vol. 4, pp. 324–25). S. Clarke mentioned it (1912, p. 181), as did M. Jullien (Munier, 1940, p. 157).

Ramzī (1953–1963, Vol. 2, pt. 4, p. 66) thought that the Dayr al-Barshah was the Roman military post called Preht in the Coptic texts and Abrahat in the Arabic texts.

Dayr al-Nakhlah is today a village, but was formerly a monastery dedicated, according to M. Jullien (1894, p. 157), to Saint Isaiah the Solitary. Near the monastery a wadi a kilometer in length bears the name Wādī al-Nakhlah. It contains numerous caves or tombs that were inhabited by anchorites. Vansleb was the first European to notice it (1677, p. 396; 1678, p. 237). The caves are mentioned by Wilkinson (1843, Vol. 2, p. 62), and Jullien (1894, p. 494) also described them. Excavations have been carried out on the site, and the results will be found in Newberry (1873, Vol. 2, pp. 57–64) and Aḥmad Kamāl (1901, pp. 221–22). The graffiti and inscriptions were published by A. H. Sayce (1881–1882, p. 181; 1886–1887, p. 196) and by J. Clédat (1901, p. 102; 1902, pp. 66–67). The Greek texts were published by G. Lefebvre (1907, p. 43).

The site was described by Johann Georg (1930, p. 22) and O. Meinardus (1965, pp. 267–68; 1977, p. 375). It is not known whether the tombs were occupied by several hermits or by a more organized colony of anchorites.

BIBLIOGRAPHY

Aḥmad Kamāl. "Rapport sur les fouilles exécutées à Deir el-Bersche." *Annales du Service des antiquités de l'Égypte* 2 (1901):206–222.

Clarke, S. *Christian Antiquities in the Nile Valley.* Oxford, 1912.

Clédat, J. "Notes sur la nécropole de Bersheh." *Bulletin de l'Institut français d'Archéologie orientale* 1 (1901):101–102.

______. "Notes archéologiques et philologiques." *Bulletin de l'Institut français d'Archéologie orientale* 2 (1902):41–70.

Evelyn-White, H. G. *The History of the Monasteries of Nitria and of Scetis,* Pt. 2, *The Monasteries of the Wādi 'n Natrūn.* New York, 1932.

Johann Georg, Duke of Saxony. *Neue Streifzüge durch die Kirchen und Klöster Ägyptens.* Leipzig and Berlin, 1930.

Jomard, E. F. *Description de l'Egypte,* Vol. 4. Paris, 1822–1826.

Jullien, M. *Les Grottes de la Basse Thebaïde.* Lyons, 1894.

Lefebvre, G. *Recueil des inscriptions chrétiennes d'Egypte.* Cairo, 1907.

Meinardus, Otto. *Christian Egypt, Ancient and Modern.* Cairo, 1965; 2nd ed., 1977.

Muḥammad Ramzī. *Al-Qāmūs al-jughrāfī lil-bilād al Miṣriyyah,* 3 vols. Cairo, 1953–1968.

Munier, H. "Les Monuments coptes d'après les explorations du père Michel Jullien." *Bulletin de la Société d'Archéologie copte* 6 (1940):141–68.

Newberry, P. E. *Ed Bershek,* 2 vols. Archeological survey of Egypt, ed. F. Griffith. With appendix, plans and measurement of tombs by G. Willoughby Frazer. London, 1873.

Sayce, A. H. "Coptic and Early Christian Inscriptions in Upper Egypt." *Proceedings of the Society of Biblical Archaeology* 4 (1881–1882):117–23.

______. "Dated Inscriptions of Amenophis III." *Proceedings of the Society of Biblical Archaeology* 9 (1886–1887):195–97.

Vansleb, J. M. *Nouvelle Relation en forme de journal d'un voyage fait en Egypte en 1672 et 1673.* Paris, 1677. Translated as *The Present State of Egypt.* London, 1678.

Wilkinson, G. *Modern Egypt and Thebes,* Vol. 2. London, 1843.

RENÉ-GEORGES COQUIN
MAURICE MARTIN, S.J.

Architecture

Several neglected monks' dwellings with crosses and inscriptions in the pharaonic quarries and graves of the adjacent Wādī al-Nakhlah point to the former existence of a monastic settlement in this place (Newberry, 1873, 57.62ff.).

The Church of Anbā Bishoi in Dayr al-Barshah is essentially a modern building, but at least some parts go back to an older foundation, which can perhaps be dated from the twelfth or thirteenth century. The northern section especially, with the apse, the *khūrus* (room between the naos and the sanctuary), and both the middle pillars in the naos,

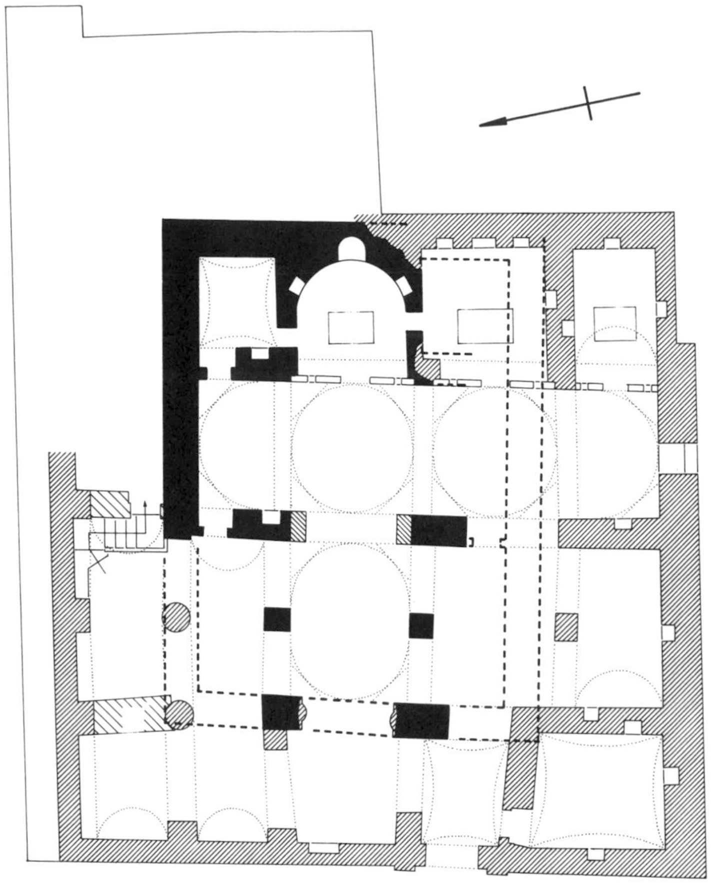

Plan of the church of Anbā Bishoi, Dayr al-Barshah. *Courtesy Peter Grossmann.*

might be original. The area to the left next to the apse has kept its old form, a simple side room of the apse, and is reached through an ordinary door, but it is now furnished as a loge (MAQṢŪRAH) with many paintings. The side opening that connects the room with the apse serves as an area for women to receive communion. By a stair in the outer northern aisle at about the height of the *khūrus* partition wall, the so-called upper church is reached, a *parekklesion* from a later time.

BIBLIOGRAPHY

Grossmann, P. *Mittelalterliche Langhauskuppelkirchen,* pp. 39ff. Glückstadt, 1982.

Meinardus, O. *Christian Egypt, Ancient and Modern,* pp. 267ff. Cairo, 1965.

PETER GROSSMANN

DAYR BARSŪM AL-IRYAN. *See* Pilgrimages.

DAYR BAWLOS. *See* Monasteries of the Upper Ṣa'īd.

DAYR BI'L-HABASH (Monastery in the Quarter of the Ethiopians). The first foundation of the Muslims on the site known as al-Fusṭāṭ—that is, modern-day Old Cairo—included to the south a pool that was called the Pool of the Ethiopians (it is not known where the name comes from). This appellation is ancient, for it is given by al-Shābushtī (1939, pp. 13 [text], 25 [trans.]), who died at the end of the tenth century or beginning of the eleventh. This pool (now dried up) gave the name "of the Ethiopians" to the surrounding neighborhood; consequently people came to speak of "the Monastery [in the quarter] of the Ethiopians." Several monasteries may have borne this title, because they were more or less adjacent to the pool. This was the case with the DAYR AL-NASṬŪR, the DAYR AL-ṬĪN, and the Dayr of Saint Victor, although the latter place-name is mentioned as a *dayr* only in a single witness, a manuscript in Paris (National Library, Arabe 181; cf. Troupeau, 1972, Vol. 1, p. 156, [Ms 181] I). Everywhere else it is mentioned as being a church. It therefore remains doubtful that it was a genuine *dayr.*

BIBLIOGRAPHY

Shābushtī, al-. "Some Egyptian Monasteries According to the Unpublished MS of al-Shābushtī's 'Kitāb al-Diyarāt,'" trans. and ed. A. S. Atiya. *Bulletin de la Société d'Archéologie copte* 5 (1939):1–28.

Troupeau, G. *Catalogue des manuscrits arabes,* Vol. 1, *Manuscrits chrétiens.* Paris, 1972.

RENÉ-GEORGES COQUIN

DAYR AL-BIṢRAH (Buṣrah) (Asyūṭ). [*This entry consists of two parts: the history of this monastery, and its architecture.*]

History

Dayr al-Biṣrah is a small Coptic village on the right bank of the Nile, south of the extremity of the basin of Abnūb, at the place where the mountains are very close to the Nile, opposite Shuṭb, the homeland of the father of Saint THEODORUS "the General" (*stratelates*) according to the Coptic texts.

The oldest documents mentioning this site are

Coptic texts relating to Saint Theodorus. Whether they are in Sahidic or Bohairic, they mention "the port of Paphor of Shot." E. QUATREMÈRE wished to identify the latter with Dayr Biṣrah (1812, p. 33). ABŪ ṢĀLIḤ THE ARMENIAN (1895, p. 247), at the beginning of the thirteenth century, knew two places dedicated to Saint Theodorus. One stood on the left bank at Shuṭb and contained the relics of the saint—Dayr Abū al-Sarī. He seems here to have copied the HISTORY OF THE PATRIARCHS OF THE EGYPTIAN CHURCH (Vol. 2, pt. 3, pp. 227 [text], 360 [trans.]), which contains a list of the relics of saints in Egypt and mentions those of Theodorus "in the Monastery of Abū al-Sarī at Shuṭb." The second monastery noted by Abū Ṣāliḥ was Abū al-Ṣādir (or Theodorus), which he placed on the right bank. Al-Maqrīzī, before 1441, did indeed know the Monastery of Abū al-Sarī and placed it on the right bank, a little to the north of al-Maʿsarah, but he said that it was dedicated to Saint GEORGE. He placed the second monastery on the left bank below that of Saint SEVERUS (1853, Vol. 2, pp. 503, 506).

J. VANSLEB mentioned on the east bank "the church of Saint Theodore, martyr, son of John at Bossra" (1677, p. 361; 1678, p. 217). Quatremère knew only Vansleb's Boṣra and suggested identifying it with the Paphor of the Coptic texts (1812, p. 33). S. Clarke, in his list of the churches, cited at Boṣra that of Theodore the General (1912, p. 210, no. 14).

An ancient stela has been published that derives from the cemetery adjacent to this church (Lefebvre, 1915, Vol. 15, pp. 125–26). Beaugé described the village and the church (1923, pp. 196–201), not without some fantasies, for there is no painting.

BIBLIOGRAPHY

Beaugé, C. *A travers la Haute-Egypte*. Alençon, 1923.

Clarke, S. *Christian Antiquities in the Nile Valley*. Oxford, 1912.

Lefebvre, G. "Nouvelle Série d'inscriptions coptes et grecques." *Annales du Service des antiquités de l'Egypte* 15 (1915):112–39.

Quatremère, E. *Observations sur quelques points de la géographie de l'Egypte pour servir de supplement aux Mémoires historiques et géographiques sur l'Egypte et sur quelques contrées voisines*. Paris, 1812.

Vansleb, J. M. *Nouvelle Relation en forme de journal d'un voyage fait en Egypte*. Paris, 1677. Translated as *The Present State of Egypt*. London, 1678.

RENÉ-GEORGES COQUIN
MAURICE MARTIN, S.J.

Architecture

The church at Dayr al-Biṣrah is dedicated to Theodorus the General, who, according to local tradition, here suffered martyrdom and was buried. From the architectural point of view, it is a modern four-columned building with the usual three sanctuaries. However, it presumably stands on the site of an older church (Vansleb, 1677, p. 361). Early Christian spolia have been built into many houses in Dayr al-Biṣrah, and these may derive from this older building. The church itself contains some old icons. Also, a few inscriptions from this place are known (Lefebvre, 1915, pp. 125–26).

BIBLIOGRAPHY

Lefebvre, G. "Nouvelle Série d'inscriptions coptes et grecques." *Annales du Service des antiquités de l'Egypte* 15 (1915):112–39.

Timm, S. *Das christlich-koptische Ägypten in arabischer Zeit*, Vol. 2, pp. 696–98. Wiesbaden, 1984.

Vansleb, J. M. *Nouvelle Relation en forme de journal d'un voyage fait en Egypte*. Paris, 1677. Translated as *The Present State of Egypt*. London, 1678.

PETER GROSSMANN

DAYR BU MAGHAM. *See* Dayr Abū Bifām (Ṭimā).

DAYR BUQṬUR OF SHŪ. This monastery, of which nothing remains but the church rebuilt in the sixteenth century, is situated on the right bank of the Nile about 3 miles (5 km) north of Abnūb, in the direction of DAYR AL-JABRĀWĪ. It is dedicated to Saint VICTOR (Buqṭur), a soldier in the fort of Shū who was martyred at Mūshā on the left bank, where he was thrown into a bathhouse furnace.

The church of Buqṭur of Shū is to the east at the edge of the village called Dayr Shū (Ramzī, 1953–1963, Vol. 2, pt. 4, p. 6, mentions the village but not the church). The SYNAXARION at 5 Kiyahk refers to the fort of Shū where Victor was a soldier and to Mūshā where he was martyred, and where a church was erected. It is perhaps this monastery which ABŪ ṢĀLIḤ cites; he also mentions its relics. Al-MAQRĪZĪ (d. 1441) mentions the monastery but adds that it is already abandoned (1853, Vol. 2, p. 503). He also notes the church at Mūshā, and writes that it is constructed over a bath (pp. 518–19).

It was in the monastery of Saint Victor that in January 1597 Patriarch GABRIEL VIII signed the Act of Union of the Coptic church with the Roman church, which was presented to Pope Clement VIII by a delegation of Coptic priests (cf. Buri, 1931, and Rabbat, 1905); but it is not clear whether this refers to Dayr Buqṭur of Shū or to Dayr al-Jabrāwī.

J. Vansleb in 1673 saw only the church at "Musie," but curiously adds that it is that of Victor of "Sciu which was near Abnūb and today ruined" (1677, p. 366; Eng. trans., 1678, p. 210). S. Clarke mentions the church, but in his list in English the titles of the churches of Dayr Buqṭur of Shū and Dayr al-Jabrāwī must be inverted (1912, p. 210, nos. 24–25). O. Meinardus describes the present state of this church (1965, pp. 278–79; 1977, pp. 387–88).

BIBLIOGRAPHY

Buri, V. *L'unione de la chiesa copta con Roma sotto Clemente VIII.* Orientalia Christiana 23, pt. 2. Rome, 1931.

Clarke, S. *Christian Antiquities in the Nile Valley.* London, 1912.

Meinardus, O. *Christian Egypt, Ancient and Modern.* Cairo, 1965; 2nd ed., Cairo, 1977.

Rabbat, A. *Documents inédits pour servir à l'histoire du christianisme en Orient,* Vol. 1, pp. 194–314. Beirut, 1905.

Ramzī, M. *Al-Qāmūs al-Jughrāfī lil-Bilād al Miṣrīyyah,* 3 vols. Cairo, 1953–1968.

Vansleb, J. M. *Nouvelle relation en forme de journal d'un voyage fait en Egypte en 1672 et 1673.* Paris, 1677. Translated as *The Present State of Egypt.* London, 1678.

RENÉ-GEORGES COQUIN
MAURICE MARTIN, S.J.

DAYR BUṬRUS WA BŪLUS. *See* Dayr al-Qaṣriyyah.

DAYR COLLUTHUS. *See* Monasteries of the Upper Ṣa'īd.

DAYR DHAT AL-SAFĀ. *See* Monasteries of the Fayyūm.

DAYR AL-DĪK. [*This monastery, now in ruins, is situated on the right bank of the Nile, a good hour's walk to the north of* ANTINOOPOLIS. *There were also on the edge of the river some cells fitted up with a church in caves in the cliffs that overhang the river.*]

History

The monastery of Dayr al-Dīk is cited, but without any name, in the atlas of the *Description de l'Egypte* (1821–1829, pl. 14; Wilkinson, 1843, Vol. 2, p. 57; Maspero, 1891, p. 521).

On the other hand, the excavations by GAYET in 1898–1899 in "the cemetery of Deir al-Dyk" were made farther to the south, in the necropolis placed at the foot of the DAYR AL-NAṢĀRĀ, the confusion between the two place-names having already been made by Wilkinson (1843, Vol. 2, pp. 60–61; see the descriptions of Lefebvre, 1910, pp. 260–70; Leclercq, 1907–1939, Vol. 4, cols. 2501ff.)

The rock church of the laura was described by J. CLÉDAT (1902, pp. 68–69). Some inscriptions were collected and published by S. Donadoni (1959, pp. 479–87). The whole was described by O. Meinardus (1977, p. 369) and above all by M. Martin (1971); C. E. Walters (1974, p. 108) proposed to see in the series of the great quarries, which no doubt sheltered the communal services of the laura, a simple hermitage similar to those of ISNĀ or KELLIA. But the much greater dimensions and the complexity of the whole are against this.

The laura may date from the sixth century, but the monastery is without doubt later. Neither ABŪ ṢĀLIḤ THE ARMENIAN nor al-MAQRĪZĪ seems to have known it. Probably it had already been destroyed or abandoned well before the thirteenth century with the decline of Antinoopolis.

BIBLIOGRAPHY

Clédat, J. "Notes archéologiques et philologiques." *Bulletin de l'Institut français d'Archéologie orientale* 1 (1901):87–97; 2 (1902):41–70.

Description de l'Egypte. Paris, 1821–1829.

Donadoni, S. "Epigrafia minore di Antinoë." In *Studi in onore di Calderini e Paribeni,* Vol. 2, pp. 479–87. Milan, 1959.

Gayet, A. *Le Costume en Egypte du IIIe au XIIIe siècle.* Paris, 1900.

Leclerq, H. "Egypte." In *Dictionnaire d'archéologie chrétienne et de liturgie,* Vol. 4, pt. 2, ed. F. Cabrol. Paris, 1907–1939.

Lefebvre, G. "Egypte chrétienne." *Annales du Service des antiquités de l'Egypte* 10 (1910):260–84.

Martin, M. *La Laure de Der al Dik à Antinoé.* Bibliothèque des études coptes 8. Cairo, 1971.

Maspero, G. "Notes au jour le jour." *Proceedings of the Society of Biblical Archaeology* 13 (1891): 298–315, 407–37, 496–525.

Meinardus, O. *Christian Egypt, Ancient and Modern,* 2nd ed. Cairo, 1977.

Walters, C. C. *Monastic Archaeology in Egypt.* Warminster, 1974.
Wilkinson, G. *Egypt and Thebes,* Vols. 1–2. London, 1843.

RENÉ-GEORGES COQUIN
MAURICE MARTIN, S.J.

Architecture

A late Roman military camp is situated close to the river; extensive sections of its surrounding wall, with its rounded corners, as well as parts of the buildings inside, have been preserved. It would appear that after the ARAB CONQUEST OF EGYPT the complex was converted into a monastery. From the first period, remainders of the living quarters on the north wall and a cruciform apsidal structure with four square rooms in the corners have survived. From the monastery period comes a single-aisle hall, which still remains standing and which is subdivided into a number of bays by transverse walls projecting from both sides. Some 110 yards (100 m) east of the camp on the upper mountain slope are numerous quarry caves that in the early Christian period were converted by monks into living quarters and small chapels. There can be no doubt that these monks were connected with the later inhabitants of Dayr al-Dīk or settled there themselves after the departure of the troops.

BIBLIOGRAPHY

Grossmann, P. "Neue frühchristliche Funde aus Ägypten." *Actes du XIe congrès international d'archèologie chrètienne, Lyon, 21–28 septembre 1986,* Vol. 2, p. 1870, fig. 11. Paris, 1989.
Martin, M. *La Laure de Dêr al Dîk à Antinoé.* Bibliothèque des études coptes 8. Cairo, 1971.

PETER GROSSMANN

DAYR DIMŪSHIYYAH. *See* Monasteries of the Fayyūm.

DAYR DISYĀ. *See* Monasteries of the Fayyūm.

DAYR DURUNKAH, today the church of the Holy Virgin near the village called Dayr Durunkah, to distinguish it from the more important village called Durunkah. It is situated about 6 miles (10 km) southwest of ASYŪṬ on the edge of the mountain in the quarries and tombs.

ABŪ ṢALIḤ THE ARMENIAN (beginning of the thirteenth century) mentions a church in the region of Durunkah and three monasteries (pp. 250–51) dedicated to the Holy Virgin: that of Qarfūnah, near the Monastery of Saint Severus, it seems, and those of Azilūn and Abū Harīth.

Al-MAQRĪZĪ (d. 1441) devotes a fairly long notice to the monasteries of the region of Durunkah, and mentions three that bore the name of the Holy Virgin: Qarfūnah, Saint Severus, and Isaac (1853, Vol. 2, p. 506). The one where the church is still standing perhaps corresponds to the monastery that Abū Ṣāliḥ and al-Maqrīzī call Qarfūnah. Al-Maqrīzī explains that the name comes from the Greek *grafōn* and means "scribe" because this monastery had a famous scriptorium for the copying of manuscripts. In fact, there exists a manuscript from the library of Dayr al-Abyad that was written there, as its colophon shows (van Lantschoot, 1929, no. 69, fasc. 2, p. 47). A very archaic funerary stela probably comes from this monastery. In fact, it carries the very name, "monastery of the scribes" (Elanskaya, 1975–1976, pp. 221–22). This would indicate that the monastery is very old.

The inscriptions and graffiti have been published by the following authors: F. L. Griffith (1889, pl. 19); Aḥmad Kamāl (1916); A. J. Gayet (1900, pp. 53ff.; Gayet speaks of the textiles found in the cemetery); and G. Maspero (1893, p. 208). The travelers J. VANSLEB (1677, pp. 364, 394–95; Eng. ed., 1678, pp. 218, 227) and M. JULLIEN (1901, p. 213) have described the site. The present state is given by O. Meinardus (1965, p. 384; 1977, pp. 394–95).

Today, Dayr Durunkah is a place of pilgrimage, the *mawlid* (birthday) of which is held from 1 to 16 Misrā (Muyser, 1979, pp. 52–53). The church was reconstructed in 1955. A good description of the ancient state is given by S. Clarke (1912, p. 175).

BIBLIOGRAPHY

Aḥmad Kamāl. "Fouilles à Deir Dronka et à Assuit." *Annales du Service des antiquites de l'Egypte* 16 (1916):64–66.
Clarke, S. *The Christian Antiquities in the Nile Valley.* London, 1912.
Elanskaya, A. J. "Quelques stèles coptes des musées de Leningrad et de Moscou." *Orientalis Lovaniensia Periodica* 6/7 (1975–1976):215–22.
Gayet, A. J. *Le Costume en Egypte du IIIe au XIIIe siècle.* Paris, 1900.

Griffith, F. L. *The Inscriptions of Siūt and Dēr Rīfeh.* London, 1889.
Jullien, M. "A travers les ruines de la Haute Egypte à la recherche de la grotte de l'abbé Jean." *Etudes* 88 (1901):205–217.
Lantschoot, A. van. *Recueil des colophons des manuscrits chrétiens d'Egypte.* Bibliothèque du Muséon 1. Louvain, 1929.
Maspero, G. *Etudes de mythologie et d'archéologie égyptienne,* Vol. 1. Paris, 1893.
Meinardus, O. *Christian Egypt, Ancient and Modern.* Cairo, 1965; 2nd ed., Cairo, 1977.
Vansleb, J. M. *Nouvelle relation en forme de journal d'un voyage fait en Egypte en 1672 et 1673.* Paris, 1677. Translated as *The Present State of Egypt.* London, 1678.

RENÉ-GEORGES COQUIN
MAURICE MARTIN, S.J.

DAYR EBIFANIA. The SYNAXARION of the Copts, in its recension from Lower Egypt, indicates that the patriarch PETER IV, thirty-fourth patriarch of Alexandria, lived in this Monastery of the Epiphany after his election because of political and religious circumstances. The monastery, it is said, was situated to the south of that of ENATON, in the Mareotis region. Unfortunately the copyists mistranslated the Greek name, and in the manuscripts used by R. Basset and J. Forget it became in Arabic transcription the Monastery of al-Fāniyah or Anbāniyah. Only the Cairo edition of ʿAbd al-Masīḥ Mīkhā'īl and Armāniyūs Ḥabashī Shaṭā al-Birmāwī (1935–1937; repr., 1972, Vol. 2, p. 376), preserves the true reading, which was that of the manuscripts used. Likewise, the most ancient manuscript, dating from 1470 (*Mingana Arab. Christ.* 152 [Add. 267], fol. 275, 25 Ba'ūnah), gives *abifania.*

Furthermore, Abū al-Makārim, an author at the end of the twelfth century and beginning of the thirteenth, mentions a monastery "of his epiphany" in the Mareotis area (1984, p. 174). A list of the churches and monasteries of Egypt had already been given after Abū al-Makārim's text by Philūthāwūs ʿAwad in Simaykah (1930–1932, Vol. 2, p. 240), which carries the same text.

BIBLIOGRAPHY

ʿAbd al-Masīḥ, Mīkhā'īl, and Armāniyūs Ḥabashī Shaṭā al-Birmāwī, eds. *Al-Sinaksār,* 2 vols. Cairo, 1935–1937.
Abū al-Makārim. *Tārīkh al-Kanā'is wa al-Adyirah fī al-Qarn al-Ṯhānī ʿAshar al-Mīlādī li-Abī al-Makārim,* ed. Samū'īl al-Suryānī. Cairo, 1984.
Simaykah, M. *Dalīl al-Mat̩ḥaf al Qibṭī,* 2 vols. Cairo, 1930–1932.

RENÉ-GEORGES COQUIN
MAURICE MARTIN, S.J.

DAYR EPIPHANIUS, a small semi-anchoritic community that existed around 580–640 on the "Holy Hill of Djeme" (Madīnat Hābū) in Western Thebes in Upper Egypt. The hermits who dwelled there had, like those in Kellia, Nitria, and Scetis, formed a laura around the cell of a Monophysite Coptic anchorite. In this case, it was Epiphanius who had taken up residence in the Eleventh Dynasty tomb of the vizier Daga. The site, first identified in 1820 by Yanni Athanasi, was thoroughly excavated by the staff of New York's Metropolitan Museum of Art in 1912 and 1914. The most important of the artifacts discovered are today found in the Metropolitan Museum of Art and the Cairo Museum.

As indicated by the terms of a seventh-century will in which a certain Jacob and Elias bequeathed the *topos* (site) of the monastery to another monk named Stephen, the boundaries of the whole community encompassed about 47 acres. This tract was on the southwestern slopes of what is today known as Shaykh ʿAbd al-Qurnah Hill, near the modern villages of Qurnah and Baʿarāt. It provided the hermits with a good view of the Nile River, the neighboring site of the Monastery of Cyriacus, and the major track to Dayr al-Baḥarī. The mouth of the Valley of the Kings near the Nile lay approximately a mile to the northeast.

Found within the boundaries of the Monastery of Epiphanius were "dwelling places" located in the entrances to, and interiors of, six dynastic tombs, as well as some twenty separate rooms with walls of brick and/or stone. During the life of the community, two towers, or keeps, were built to provide places of vigil and refuge. The first, on which Epiphanius himself had worked, was 33 feet (10 m) square at the base and some 50 feet (16 m) high. The second was not as tall. Evidence uncovered indicates that some monks dwelled in cells within these keeps. Interestingly, no traces of a church or a common eating place have been uncovered. The entire complex was surrounded by a brick wall some 2.75 feet (70 cm) thick, to which there was later added an eastern extension. The wall had two entrances, one on the east side and the other on the north. Lying beyond these entrances were three cells that were probably occupied by members of the monastic community. Also outside the boundary wall, on the northwest side of the monastery, was a small cemetery that contained a maximum of eleven graves. Because the total population of the community seems to have been larger (some fifty-five different names are found in texts recovered), it is probable that only prominent members of the monastery were buried there, and the rest, elsewhere.

As is true of most of the anchorite settlements in Upper Egypt, a precise date for the founding of the community of Epiphanius cannot be established. Its general historical development, however, can be reconstructed. Analysis of surviving literary remains led Winlock and Crum (1926, Pt. 1, pp. xxvi, 220) to conclude that Epiphanius himself arrived at the Hill of Djeme around, or just prior to, the beginning of the sixth century. At that time, as indicated in several ostraca, his contemporaries and perhaps predecessors would have been other anchorites: Apa Moses, Apa John, Enoch, Apa Victor. Epiphanius himself may have gone there from a cenobitic monastic community in Upper Egypt that had been formed on the Pachomian model. If so, he may have been seeking a more solitary life, emulating Christ's own retreat to do battle with temptation in the wilderness.

Epiphanius probably supported himself by various humble crafts, such as spinning, weaving, making ropes and mats, and doing leather work. Over time, his reputation for piety, wise counsel, and perhaps miracles of healing grew. Other hermits were attracted to him. Lay persons and fellow monks engaged him in a growing correspondence, seeking his help and prayerful intercession regarding such issues as sickness, bereavement, imprisonment, hunger, poverty, and salvation itself. Civic officials in nearby Djeme, bishops such as PISENTIUS of Coptos, and fellow monks increasingly addressed him as one revered and venerated, as one who had the power to benefit them. Though he is never addressed with the title of any formal office, it is clear that Epiphanius exercised some type of headship over the monastic community. His correspondents referred to him with such appellations as "holy father," he "that truly beareth Christ" and *pneumatoforos*, "perfect in all virtues," "the new psalmist," and "the prophet." In turn, these correspondents often referred to themselves as his "humblest servants" who venerate the dust of his feet and even his footprints. Following his death, pilgrims to the tomb of Daga left graffiti on the walls that invoke the help of Epiphanius in seeking God's favor.

There is also evidence, however, that the revered anchorite was not left isolated from important events in the larger world beyond Western Thebes. Three letters allude to "Persians" arriving, occupying, and then being evacuated from the Theban area. When read in light of other writings found in the monastery ruins—writings from DAMIAN (patriarch at Alexandria in 569–605), Pisentius of Coptos, and Apa Abraham (bishop of Ermont and head of the Monastery of Saint Phoibammon at Dayr al-Baḥarī in the early seventh century)—these allusions clearly refer to the Persian occupation of Egypt under Chosroes II in 616–628. During that period, according to his extant biography, Pisentius of Coptos fled southward to Djeme. There he probably took refuge with his revered friend Epiphanius prior to hiding out in a rock tomb in the desert, possibly in the Valley of the Kings. Many letters addressed to the bishop were preserved by Epiphanius, who appears to have acted as a go-between and thus seems to have engaged in a form of passive resistance to the Persians.

Since the will left by Apa Jacob and Apa Elias in the first half of the seventh century speaks of both Epiphanius and his disciple and successor Apa Psan as now deceased, it is possible that Epiphanius died before the end of the Persian occupation. Complete silence about the Arabs in literary remnants from the monastery seems to indicate that after the death of Epiphanius, the community declined and the site became virtually deserted either prior to or shortly after the ARAB CONQUEST OF EGYPT.

The provision of separate dwellings for single hermits and groups, the lack of a central church or communal dining facility, and the following of individual "polity" instead of rules and canons like those of PACHOMIUS or ATHANASIUS all underscore the loose, semi-anchoritic organization of the Monastery of Epiphanius. Its informal life is further indicated by the lack of evidence for such things as a training period for monks prior to their admission to the community, preliminary tonsure, or oblates.

Resident monks seem in the main to have been Egyptians. The presence of graffiti and practice alphabets written in Syriac, however, suggest that a few Syrian monks lived there. Such would not be unnatural, given the close relations between the Egyptian and Syrian branches of the Monophysite church in the sixth and seventh centuries.

Food consumed was typical of that found among Pachomian monks of southern Egypt. The staples were bread (made from wheat), salt, vinegar, water. Letters recovered also indicate receipt of occasional gifts of green vegetables. More rarely mentioned in recovered literary remains are lentils, beans, fruit (especially figs), honey, pickles, milk, eggs. Oil was provided for invalids. Numerous amphorae indicate the use of wine, at least on special occasions and feast days.

Texts painted on the vestibules of monk cells, as well as remnants of theological books and tracts they read, provide reliable evidence of theological views. Long extracts have been found from the works of SEVERUS OF ANTIOCH, Cyria, Athanasius, DIOSCURUS, TIMOTHY II AELURUS, and Peter the Iberian. The Monophysite doctrine of Damian, patriarch of Alexandria, was dominant at the time of Epiphanius. Though preoccupation with doctrinal subtleties is not evidenced, there was interest in ascetic ideals commonly associated with the monastic life.

In addition to meditation and prayer, the hermits of the Monastery of Epiphanius engaged in several types of income-producing work: rope, mat, and basket-making; weaving and tailoring of linen; the preparation of flax and some wool for weaving; leatherwork (including bookbinding); pottery making; and baking. Both for themselves and for occasional suppliants, the monks would offer home remedies and prayers for the sick, as well as special blessings and "eulogies" to convey the blessings, such as a piece of blessed bread. They would also observe certain fasts, especially Lent, maintain vigils prior to key festivals, write letters of introduction, appeal for the poor, intervene to secure the release of prisoners, and commemorate the dead.

Literary remnants of the community include texts written in Sahidic Coptic (displaying significant subakhmimic influences), Greek, and Syriac. The largest group comprises letters, mostly on ostraca, many probably being informal communiqués between monks possibly committed to vows of silence. Also found are texts that are biblical (mainly from the Old Testament), liturgical (mostly prayers), homiletic (moralizing compositions), legal (wills, deeds), epistolary (intended for circulation), patristic, and dogmatic. Accounts (records of payments) and lists appear also, as do graffiti, school pieces, and some frescoed texts from the tomb of Daga. Materials used include parchment, wood, papyrus, and ostraca. Such a hoard of literary evidence has proven vitally important in interpretation of the other archaeological remains.

BIBLIOGRAPHY

Bouriant, U. "L'Eglise copte du tombeau de Déga." *Mémoires publiés par les membres de la Mission archéologique française au Caire I*, 1 (1881–1884):33–50.

Johann Georg, Duke of Saxony. *Neue Streifzüge durch die Kirchen und Kloster Ägyptens*. Berlin, 1931.

Winlock, H. E., and W. E. Crum. *The Monastery of Epiphanius at Thebes*. 2 vols. New York, 1926–1933.

MALCOLM L. PEEL

DAYR AL-FAKHŪRĪ. [*This entry consists of two parts: the history of this monastery, and its architecture.*]

History

The "Monastery of the Potter" (it is not known whence this appellation comes) is situated on the edge of the desert, about 6 miles (9 km) north of Isnā, near the ancient Asphynis (present-day Aṣfūn al-Maṭā'nah). The monastery also bears the name of "Matthew the Poor." This personage, whose Life survives (or rather Coptic fragments of it), appears to have lived at the end of the Byzantine period. According to his Coptic Life, he founded a monastery in the name of Saint PACHOMIUS, near Isnā and no doubt at Aṣfūn, but he had a cell in the desert. The HISTORY OF THE PATRIARCHS OF THE COPTIC CHURCH speaks in the notice of the patriarch ALEXANDER II (705–730) of the personages celebrated in his time and mentions a native of Iṣfant (no doubt a copyist's error for Aṣfūn), a monk—also called a fisherman or hunter, for the Arabic word is ambiguous—who founded a monastery in the nome of Isnā and was famous for his miracles. It relates the miracle of the woman pregnant from two brothers, which we also read in the Coptic Life of Matthew. It must be noted that the Hamburg manuscript speaks not of Matthew, but of one Timothy (Seyboldt, 1912, p. 147).

The SYNAXARION from Lower Egypt, as a result of a confusion in writing, speaks not of Aṣfūn but of Aswān, and ABŪ ṢALĪḤ THE ARMENIAN at the beginning of the thirteenth century seems indeed to have placed this monastery at Antinoë, or ANTINOOPOLIS (confusion between Anṣinā and Isnā). He also quoted the *History of the Patriarchs*, a proof that he knew that text, but still made the same error (p. 230). The monastery was known by al-MAQRĪZĪ in the fifteenth century as a large monastery formerly well populated but in his time destroyed and abandoned.

However, from the seventeenth century on, European travelers mention it. The first seem to have been the fathers Protais and François (Sauneron, 1983, pp. 79ff.). J. M. VANSLEB copied their text (1677, p. 406; 1678, p. 243). C. Sicard mentioned it in passing, while he dwelt at length on the temple, now disappeared, of the fish-god Latus (1982, Vol. 3, pp. 7–9). In the nineteenth century, W. de Bock took note of it (1901, pp. 72–73). Other noteworthy authors are M. Jullien (1903, pp. 250–52, 283), S. Clarke (1912, p. 216, no. 8), Johann Georg (1914, pp. 56–59), and L. T. Lefort (1939, pp. 404–407). O. Meinardus gives a fairly detailed description of it (1965, pp. 323–25; 1977, pp. 438–41). Published simultaneously were J. Leroy (1975) and R.-G. Coquin (1975, pp. 240–84). Walters (1974) studied it for various subjects. One may note that Saint Pachomius founded a monastery at Phnoum, in the nome (not, as Lefort incorrectly translates, mountain) of Isnā, of which he was a native. But we do not know where this Phnoum was situated (Halkin, 1932, sec. 83; Lefort, 1939, pp. 404–406, and 1943, p. 120).

BIBLIOGRAPHY

Bock, V. de. *Matériaux pour l'archéologie chrétienne d'Egypte*. St. Petersburg, 1901.

Clarke, S. *Christian Antiquities in the Nile Valley*. Oxford, 1912.

Coquin, R.-G. "Les Inscriptions pariétales des monastères d'Esna: Dayr al-Shuhadā', Dayr al-Fakhūrī." *Bulletin de l'Institut français d'Archéologie orientale* 75 (1975):240–84.

Halkin, F. *Sancti Pachomii vitae graecae*. Subsidia Hagiographica 19. Brussels, 1932.

Johann, Georg, Duke of Saxony. *Streifzüge durch die Kirchen und Klöster Ägyptens*. Leipzig and Berlin, 1914.

Jullien, M. "Quelques anciens couvents de l'Egypte." *Missions catholiques* 35 (1903):188–90, 198–202, 212–14, 237–40, 250–52, 257–58, 274–76, 283–84.

Lefort, L. T. "Les Premiers monastères pachomiens, exploration topographique." *Le Muséon* 52 (1939):379–407.

______. *Les Vies coptes de saint Pachôme*. Bibliothèque Muséon 16. Louvain, 1943.

Leroy, J. *Les Peintures des couvents du désert d'Esna*, Vol. 1: *La Peinture murale chex les Coptes*. Mémoires de l'Institut français d'Archéologie orientale 94. Cairo, 1975.

Meinardus, O. *Christian Egypt, Ancient and Modern*. Cairo, 1965; 2nd ed., 1977.

Sauneron, S. *Villes et légendes d'Egypte*. Bibliothèque d'étude 90. Cairo, 1983.

Seyboldt, C. *Severus ibn al-Muqaffa': Alexandrinische Patriarchen Geschichte*. Hamburg, 1912.

Sicard, C. *Oeuvres*, ed. S. Sauneron and M. Martin. Bibliothèque d'étude 83–85. Cairo, 1982.

Vansleb, J. M. *Relation en forme de journal d'un voyage fait en Egypte en 1672 et 1673*. Paris, 1677. Translated as *The Present State of Egypt*. London, 1678.

Walters, C. C. *Monastic Archaeology in Egypt*. Warminster, 1974.

RENÉ-GEORGES COQUIN
MAURICE MARTIN, S.J.

Architecture

The monastery is a vast complex of unbaked brick surrounded by an enclosing wall. Only the eastern part of this wall is still partially visible, with an entrance gate and two or perhaps three semicircular towers on the outside, the staircases of which

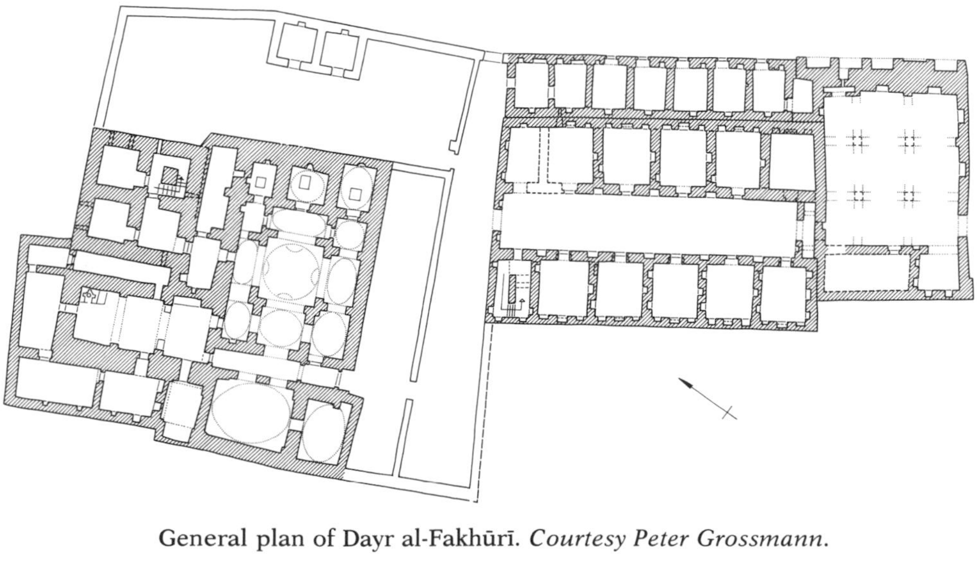

General plan of Dayr al-Fakhūrī. *Courtesy Peter Grossmann.*

are backed to the right-hand side of the interior. Of the south part of the wall, traces of a rectangular tower can be seen. The interior structures of the monastery consist of two groups of buildings of different orientation, separated by a large circulation area: to the north are the church, the keep (*jawsaq*), and their annexes; to the south are the monks' dwellings and the refectory.

The northern complex is served by a single entrance located on its south side. The church is situated to the east of this entrance. In the center, it includes a square hall covered by a dome. This hall is surrounded by the narthex, the aisles, and the *khūrus*, which thus form a sort of ambulatory. To the east, three sanctuaries open on the *khūrus*. To the west of the entrance, two domed chambers serve for the secondary functions of the church. In the north aisle of the church, a door allows access to the keep. The antechamber before this door contains the tomb of a saintly person.

The keep has three stories. It is built on a square plan, and each story is subdivided into four rooms. The staircase occupies the chambers in the southeast corner. In ancient times the entrance to the keep was on the second story, on the south face of the staircase well. The exterior wall is crowned by a cavetto of pharaonic type. Auxiliary halls are found in the northwest corner of the complex. These form a suite of three vaulted halls (with thick walls) surrounded by secondary rooms.

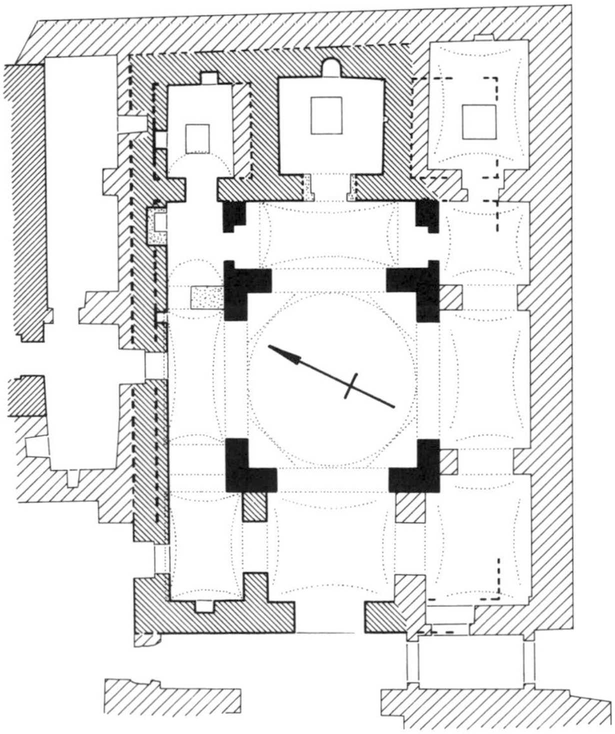

Church in the northern complex of Dayr al-Fakhūrī. *Courtesy Peter Grossmann.*

The southern complex is comprised of three buildings. The principal block of cells is to the west. It consists of a wide vaulted corridor flanked by cells, and its principal entrance is situated to the north, in the axis of the corridor. To the west of this entrance a staircase allowed access to the cells on the upper floor. Each cell contains a series of niches. The central niche, located in the exterior wall, is equipped with a shaft for ventilation; the others served the needs of the monks. The number of these niches provides information about the number of monks for each cell. To the south of the corridor a door gave access to the refectory, which occupied the whole of the southern part of the complex. This door was equipped with a shaft for ventilation and for light.

The refectory is a square hall with four pillars. Arcades springing from the pillars and the surrounding walls subdivided the whole area into nine bays, all square and covered by domes. To the west of the refectory, some halls now in ruins served as annexes (perhaps kitchens). The outer face of the east wall of the refectory is unusual: five arcades in baked brick form a series of buttresses in the interior of the wall. To the east, a row of secondary cells is built against the principal block. These cells open onto the exterior of the complex.

Remains of paintings are extant in the central hall of the church. They represent Saint John, apostle and evangelist; Saint Matthew, priest and anchorite; Christ and the twelve apostles; and Christ himself. Prophets portrayed include Moses, Ezekiel, Habakkuk, Joel, Jeremiah, Aaron, Joshua, Malachi, Isaiah, and Daniel. Saint Ardellittes the ascetic, Saint John of the Golden Gospel, Saint John the Baptist, and Apa Psate are also portrayed.

Some paintings bear names and dates. The name of the painter is effaced near the painting of the cherubim in the north arch, but it is dated A.M. 1148, or A.D. 1431–1432.

Named painters include Mercurius of DAYR ANBĀ SHINŪDAH (Suhāj), A.D. 1315–1316; Isaac of Panopolis, graffiti dated A.D. 1272–1273; and Pakire, monk of the Mountain of the Blessings (a site north of Isnā), graffiti dated A.D. 1368–1369.

The oldest parts of the church are the central hall, built of baked brick, the side walls of the *khūrus*, and the north exterior wall, all belonging to the first quarter of the eighth century. The restorations roughly around the end of the twelfth century affected the principal sanctuary, the northern sanctuary, and the northwest part of the church.

BIBLIOGRAPHY

Coquin, R.-G. "Les Inscriptions pariétales des monastères d'Esne: Dayr al-Shuhadā' et Dayr al-Fakhūrī." *Bulletin de l'Institut français d'Archéologie orientale* 75 (1975):261–84.

Grossmann, P. *Mittelalterliche Langhauskuppelkirchen und verwandte Typen in Oberägypten,* pp. 31–36. Glückstadt, 1982.

Johann George, Duke of Saxony. *Streifzüge durch die Kirchen und Klöster Ägyptens,* pp. 58–60. Leipzig and Berlin, 1914.

Leroy, J. *Les Peintures des couvents du désert d'Esna.* Mémoires de l'Institut français d'Archéologie orientale 94. Cairo, 1972.

Sauneron, S. "Les Neuvième et Dixième Campagnes archéologiques à Esna." *Bulletin de l'Institut français d'Archéologie orientale* 67 (1969):101–110.

GEORGES CASTEL
PETER GROSSMANN

DAYR AL-GHANĀYIM. The ruins of this monastery occupy a position similar to 'AYN 'AMŪR, on the eastern edge of the depression of the oasis of Khargah, but near the caravan track linking the oasis to Jirjā, in the valley of the Nile. Situated 1.25 miles (2 km) to the north of Jabal Umm al-Ghanāyim and 17 miles (26 km) to the southeast of the necropolis of al-BAGAWĀT, they are probably the remains of a Roman fortress that was later occupied by Christian hermits, as the numerous graffiti bear witness (de Bock, 1898, pp. 67–68; Legrain, 1897, pp. 207–208; Vercoutter, 1977, p. 280). Meinardus presents the site in his *Christian Egypt* (1965; pp. 345–66; 1977, pp. 487–88).

BIBLIOGRAPHY

Bock, V. de. "Notice sur les monuments coptes de la vallée du Nil." *Bulletin du Comité de conservation des monuments de l'art arabe (1898):67–68.*

Legrain, G. "Etude sur les Aquabas." *Bulletin de l'Institut d'Egypte,* ser. 3, 8 (1897):207–208.

Meinardus, O. *Christian Egypt, Ancient and Modern.* Cairo, 1965; 2nd ed. 1977.

Vercoutter, J. "Travaux de l'IFAO en 1976–7." *Bulletin de l'Institut français d'Archéologie orientale* 77 (1977):280.

RENÉ-GEORGES COQUIN
MAURICE MARTIN, S.J.

DAYR GHUBRIYĀL. In the notice concerning Anbā Yūnā (perhaps Jonas) for 2 Ṭūbah, the Sahidic recension of the SYNAXARION of the Copts mentions the Dayr Ghubriyāl as one of the residences of the saint. It adds that the monastery was in the desert. According to the context, one must suppose that this desert was near the town of Armant, of which the saint was a native. Unfortunately no written document and no excavation allow us to identify the site with any probability.

S. Timm (1984, no. 41/2, p. 717) remarks that the name of Gabriel is no doubt that of a superior or founder, for if the monastery were named after the Archangel Gabriel it would be called Dayr al-Malāk Ghubriyāl.

BIBLIOGRAPHY

Timm, S. *Das christlich-koptische Ägypten in arabischer Zeit.* Wiesbaden, 1984.

RENÉ-GEORGES COQUIN
MAURICE MARTIN, S.J.

DAYR AL-ḤADĪD. The name of this monastery, no longer in existence, is today preserved by the locality 'Izbat Dayr al-Ḥadīd, situated on the right bank of the Nile opposite al-Fashn. The village sits on a mountainside in the upper reaches of which are large caves (Daressy, 1917, pp. 202, 227; 1918, p. 18). Daressy identified it with Ahrīt, known from Coptic and Arabic texts as the site of a monastery, that of Saint ONOPHRIUS, and also from the *Futūḥ al-Bahnasā* (Galtier, 1909, p. 131), which speaks of Ahrīt and of Sharūnah (about 12 miles, or 20 km, to the south of 'Izbat Dayr al-Ḥadīd). Ramzī (1953–1963, Vol. 1, pp. 133–34) thought that Ahrīt was the present-day village of al-Shaykh Faḍl, opposite Banī Mazār, 8 miles (12 km) south of Sharūnah. Drew-Bear (1979, p. 101) placed Ahrīt in the nome of Hermopolis.

BIBLIOGRAPHY

Daressy, G. "Indicateur topographique du 'Livre des perles enfouies et du mystère précieux'." *Bulletin de l'Institut français d'Archéologie orientale* 13 (1917):175–230; 14 (1918):1–32.

Drew-Bear, M. *Le Nome Hermopolite: Toponymes et sites.* American Studies in Papyrology 21. Missoula, Mont., 1979.

Galtier, E., ed. *Foutouh al-Bahnasa.* Memoires publiés par les membres de l'Institut français d'Archéologie orientale 22. Cairo, 1909.

Ramzī, M. *Al-Qāmūs al-Jughrāfī lil-Bilād al Miṣrīyyah,* 3 vols. Cairo, 1953–1968.

RENÉ-GEORGES COQUIN
MAURICE MARTIN, S.J.

DAYR AL-ḤAJAR (Monastery of Stone). Six miles (10 km) to the north of the oasis of Dakhlah, which is about 130 miles (200 km) from Khargah, are the ruins of a temple of the Ptolemaic period that the inhabitants call Dayr al-Ḥajar, although there is no evidence that Christian hermits or monks were once there. The first to have pointed it out appears to have been G. Rohlfs (1875, pp. 339–40). It was also mentioned by H. King (1925). O. Meinardus described it briefly (1965, pp. 346–47; 1977, pp. 448–49).

BIBLIOGRAPHY

King, H. *Mysteries of the Libyan Desert.* London, 1925.
Meinardus, O. *Christian Egypt, Ancient and Modern.* Cairo, 1965; 2nd ed. 1977.
Rohlfs, G. *Drei Monate in der libyschen Wüste.* Cassel, 1875.

RENÉ-GEORGES COQUIN

DAYR AL-HAMAMAH. *See* Dayr Abū Sayfayn (Qūṣ).

DAYR HAMAS. *See* Dayr al-ʿAwanah.

DAYR AL-ḤAMMĀM (Dayr Abū Isḥāq). [*This entry consists of two parts, one discussing the history of Dayr al-Hammām, and the other describing the architecture, particularly of the old church that still remains standing.*]

History

This monastery is situated in the south of the Fayyūm, on the desert rim of the Nile Valley, 5 miles (8 km) north of al-Lāhūn. It derives its two names from the proximity of the village of al-Ḥammām and from the martyr Isaac, no doubt Isaac al-Difrāwī (province of Gharbiyyah), celebrated on 6 Bashans, to whom a small church was dedicated. The identification of the two names is suggested by the *Book of the Hidden Pearls,* which says: "Dayr Abū Isḥāq: climb to the monastery starting from al-Ḥammām" (Daressy, 1917, p. 198). N. Abbott did not see that the two names indicated a single monastery (1937, pp. 57, 63–64).

The monastery seems very old, because traces of the original construction remain, but the buildings have been reconstructed. A collection of papyri was found by Flinders Petrie in 1889 and published by W. E. CRUM (1893, pp. 5–6). The documents recovered can be dated from the beginning of the eighth to the eleventh century. The existence of this monastery was attested by ABŪ ṢĀLIḤ THE ARMENIAN (fols. 73[a–b]; *The Churches . . .* 1895, p. 210). Al-MAQRĪZĪ did not mention it, which may indicate the decline of the monastery by the fifteenth century.

Abū Ṣāliḥ described the principal church dedicated to the Virgin as large and similar to that of DAYR ANBĀ ṢAMŪʾĪL OF QALAMŪN and surrounded by a triple wall of stone. M. Jullien (1903, p. 257) depicted the church "with two apses which face one another as at Saint Simeon" in Aswan, noting columns and capitals. That church disappeared, and a new one was built at the beginning of the twentieth century (Teilhard de Chardin, 1907; Giamberardini, 1956). However, Johann Georg (1930, pp. 19–20) noted a door ornament and some capitals that he dated back to the sixth century. The present state is described by O. Meinardus (1965, pp. 233–34; 1977, pp. 457–58). OMAR TOUSSOUN mentioned a Dayr Afitam (1925, Vol. 1, p. 156) in the region of al-Ḥammām, which may be located here.

BIBLIOGRAPHY

Abbott, N. *The Monasteries of the Fayyūm.* Studies in Ancient Oriental Civilization 16. Chicago, 1937.
Crum, W. E. *The Coptic Manuscripts Brought from the Fayyum by W. M. Flinders Petrie.* London, 1893.
Daressy, G. "Indicateur topographique du 'Livre des perles enfouies et du mystère précieux.'" *Bulletin de l'Institut français d'Archéologie orientale* 13 (1917):175–230.
Giamberardini, G. "Itinerari e abitazioni di S. Antonio Abate—al-Fayyum." *La voce del Nilo* 15 (1956):25–46.
Johann Georg, Duke of Saxony. *Neue Streifzüge durch die Kirchen und Klöster Ägyptens.* Leipzig and Berlin, 1930.
Jullien, M. "Quelques anciens couvents de l'Egypte." *Missions catholiques* 35 (1903):257–58.
Meinardus, O. *Christian Egypt, Ancient and Modern.* Cairo, 1965; 2nd ed., 1977.
ʿOmar Toussoun. *Mémoire sur l'histoire du Nil,* 3 vols. Mémoires de l'Institut d'Égypte 8–10. Cairo, 1925.
Salmon, G. "Répertoire géographique de la province du Fayyoûm d'après le Kitâb Târîkh al-Fay-

youm d'an-Nâboulsî." *Bulletin de l'Institut français d'Archéologie orientale* 1 (1909):29–77.

Teilhard de Chardin, P. "Huit jours au Fayoum." *Relations d'Orient* Dec. (1907):279.

Zeki, A. "Une Description arabe du Fayyoum au VIIe s. H." *Bulletin de la Société khédiviale de géographie* 5 (1899):253–95.

RENÉ-GEORGES COQUIN
MAURICE MARTIN, S.J.

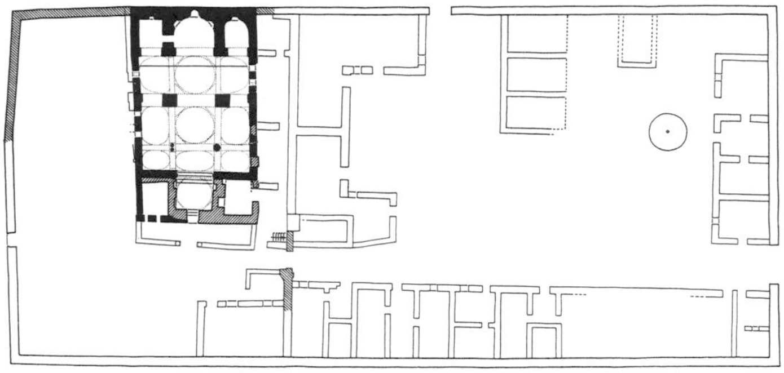

General plan of Dayr al-Hammām. *Courtesy Peter Grossmann.*

Architecture

Although only the church now remains standing, an enormous mound of debris, with much pottery and fragments of brick, spreading over an extensive area, points to an earlier settlement of notable size. Today isolated remains of cemetery enclosures rise above the ground. The present-day *dayr* harbors within its outer wall, probably of quite recent vintage, a few empty shelters for pilgrims. The church situated in the northeast sector is still in use and may, in its present form, reach back to the Mamluk period. Remains of an older building are visible on the north side. That the history of the church began much earlier is shown by several decorative pieces that have been built over at various places.

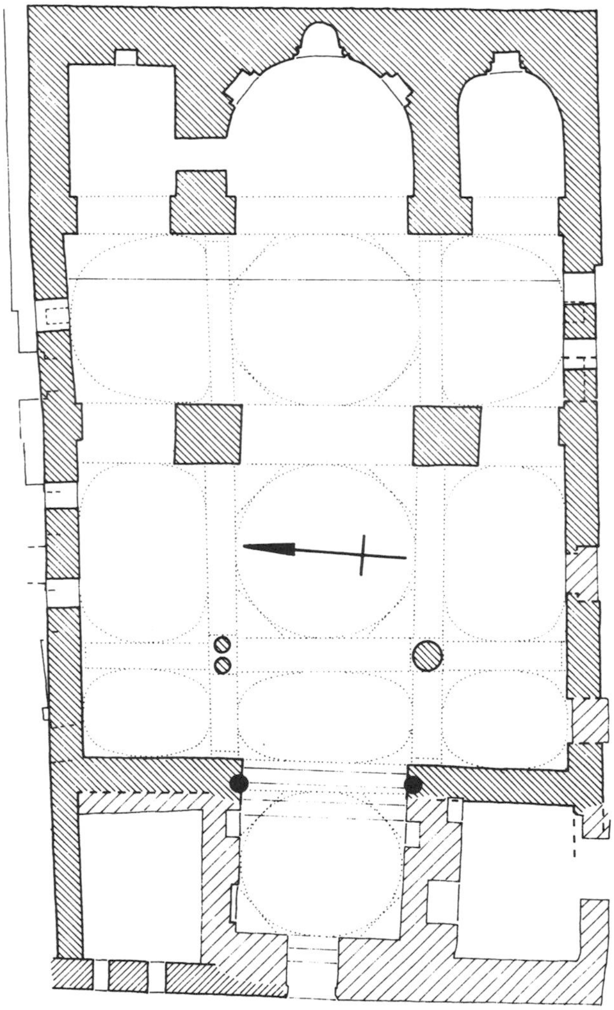

Plan of the church still in use at Dayr al-Hammām. *Courtesy Peter Grossmann.*

The church still contains a *khūrus* (the room between the naos and the sanctuary) deriving from the Fatimid period. As a result of the great breaches in the wall into the naos, however, it has largely been deprived of its spatial independence. It is connected with the central apse in the form of a triconch. The side rooms of the apse appear to have acquired their present function as subsidiary sanctuaries only in recent times.

The naos of the church is arranged on the plan of a cross-in-square building with four pillars, but this plan has been reduced to a single pair of pillars. In addition, the two sides are very differently formed, with a double pillar on the north and a massive single pillar on the south. West of the naos there was a later narthex, which evidently originally corresponded with the whole width of the church. Through the separating-off in modern times of two outer wing rooms, only a small central room remains. By means of several steps, this provides access between the outer level and the lower level inside the church.

BIBLIOGRAPHY

Adli, S. "Several Churches in Upper Egypt." *Mitteilungen des Deutschen Archäologischen Instituts* 36 (1980):4ff.

Meinardus, O. *Christian Egypt, Ancient and Modern, pp. 333–34.* Cairo, 1965; 2nd ed., 1977.

PETER GROSSMANN

DAYR AL-HANADAH. *See* Monasteries of the Middle Ṣaʿid.

DAYR HARMĪNĀ (Asyūṭ), monastery in the desert at the foot of the mountain that contains the underground construction of the ancient Qaw, about a mile (1.5 km) northwest of the village of ʿIzbat al-Aqbāṭ (farm of the Copts).

The Life of Saint Harmīnā is given in summary form by the recension from Upper Egypt of the SYNAXARION of the Copts for 2 Kiyahk. The Life is known in greater detail from several Arabic manuscripts (e.g., National Library, Paris, Arabe 148; Troupeau, 1972, Vol. 1, p. 114). One of them, in the Coptic Museum, Cairo (Arabic, History 475), has been edited and translated by Muyser (1943, pp. 199–236). The monastery is not further attested before the fifteenth century.

The Churches and Monasteries of Egypt makes mention only of a church in Harmīnā's name near al-Bahnasā, his birthplace. Evetts, the editor, wrongly translates the name as "Armenius" (p. 211). The fifteenth-century historian al-MAQRĪZĪ mentions a Dayr Harmīnā to the north of Qaw al-Kharāb, which corresponds to the present Dayr al-Naṣārā. The church of the neighboring village called ʿIzbat al-Aqbāṭ is dedicated to Anbā Harmīnā (Clarke, 1912, p. 211, no. 22).

An enclosure wall of unbaked bricks about 130 by 195 feet (about 40 by 60 m) surrounds the ruins, where one can distinguish a modern tomb, a chapel to the south, and a deep well that is mentioned in the saint's Life. The church is of Somers CLARKE's "type c" (1912). It presents an ancient part to the south and a more recent addition on the north. The first part includes the sanctuary with three altars and two parallel bays of joists. They are roofed by twelve deep and perforated cupolas. The iconostasis is made of black and red bricks, alternating with white stones. To the right of the entrance is a tomb under an arch.

A little to the south of the monastery on the site of the ancient Qaw, excavations have yielded some monastic stelae, on which are invoked the traditional saints of Bāwīṭ, Shenute, Moses, et cetera (Brunton, 1930, Vol. 3, pp. 30, 33, 34; Vol. 1, pls. 1, 7; the maps will be found useful for locating the site).

BIBLIOGRAPHY

Brunton, G. *Qau and Badari,* Vol. 3. London, 1930.

Clarke, S. *Christian Antiquities in the Nile Valley.* London, 1912.

Muyser, J. "Ermite pérégrinant et pèlerin infatigable." *Bulletin de la Société d'archéologie copte* 9 (1943):159–236.

Troupeau, G. *Catalogue des manuscrits arabes,* Vol. 1. Paris, 1972.

RENÉ-GEORGES COQUIN
MAURICE MARTIN, S. J.

DAYR AL-HAWA. *See* Dayr al-Naṣārā (Antinoopolis).

DAYR HELIAS. *See* Scetis.

DAYR IBSIDIYYAH. *See* Monasteries of the Middle Ṣaʿīd.

DAYR AL-IKHWAH. The "Monastery of the Brothers" was located in the western part of the Fayyūm, to the south of the town of Saylah. Its existence was attested by ABŪ ṢĀLIḤ THE ARMENIAN (fol. 73a; p. 209). He stated that it had a church dedicated to Saint Menas (ABŪ MĪNĀ) and that the patriarch JOHN III (681–689) was living there as a monk-priest when he was elected to the See of Alexandria. The HISTORY OF THE PATRIARCHS (PO 5, p. 8) says that John was first a monk in the Monastery of Saint Macarius (DAYR ANBĀ MAQĀR) at SCETIS and that he then went off to live in a monastery in the Fayyūm. John was there when the patriarch AGATHON sent for John to come to Alexandria.

Al-Nābulsī (Salmon, 1901, p. 45) indicated only a single monastery to the south of the town of Saylah, without specifying its name, but Abū Ṣāliḥ mentioned a second dedicated to the Virgin (DAYR AL-ʿADHRĀʾ).

BIBLIOGRAPHY

Abbott, N. *The Monasteries of the Fayyūm,* pp. 29–77. Studies in Ancient Oriental Civilization 16. Chicago, 1937.

Salmon, G. "Répertoire géographique de la province du Fayyoûm d'après le Kitâb Târikh al-Fayyoûm d'an-Nâboulsî." *Bulletin de l'Institut français d'Archéologie orientale* 1 (1901):29–77.

RENÉ-GEORGES COQUIN
MAURICE MARTIN, S.J.

DAYR ISIDORUS. *See* Dayr al-Madīnah.

DAYR AL-ʿIẒĀM (Asyūṭ). [*This entry consists of two parts: the history of this monastery, and its architecture.*]

History

The "Monastery of the Bones" is bounded on three sides by a cemetery (whence, no doubt, its name), today in disorder. It is situated on the desert plateau that dominates the necropolis of ASYŪṬ, about 2 miles (3 km) southwest of the mausoleum of Shaykh Abū Ṭūq.

A jar found in situ bears a Coptic inscription dated 1156 and naming the site "Apa John of the Desert" (Maspero, 1900; Crum, 1902, no. 8104, pl. 1; Wiet, Vol. 2, cols. 1053–54). The same expression is found in a number of the Coptic texts (Kahle, 1954, Vol. 1, pp. 22ff.; van Lantschoot, 1929, Vol. 1, pt. 2, p. 33; Crum, 1902, Vol. 2, no. 84). This is certainly what was transcribed into Arabic by ABŪ ṢĀLIḤ THE ARMENIAN at the beginning of thirteenth century: "the Monastery of Abū Yuḥannis, called Ibshāy" (this last word being the transcription of the Coptic *pdjaie,* the desert).

One thinks naturally of JOHN OF LYCOPOLIS, of whom the HISTORIA MONACHORUM IN AEGYPTO (Chapt. 1, pp. 9–35) and the *Historia lausiaca* of PALLADIUS (Vol. 2, chap. XXXV) speak. The first speaks of 5 miles between Asyūṭ and the hermitage of John; the second, of 3 miles only. John being a recluse, it is understandable that he should have chosen a site so remote in the desert; it is the only example in the region. It is possible that this is the "Monastery of Seven Mountains" mentioned by al-MAQRĪZĪ (1853, p. 506), although he placed it under the name of JOHN COLOBOS, a confusion frequent in al-Maqrīzī and the Coptic authors. He added that it was destroyed in A.H. 821/A.D. 1418.

Modern descriptions of the site are given by Jollois and Devilliers (1820–1826, Vols. 4, pp. 154–56, and 15, p. 201, n. 1), M. Jullien (1901, p. 208), S. Clarke (1912, pp. 178–79), and O. Meinardus (1965, p. 283; 1977, pp. 392–93).

BIBLIOGRAPHY

Bock, V. de. *Matériaux pour l'archéologie chrétienne de l'Egypte.* St. Petersburg, 1901.

Clarke, S. *Christian Antiquities in the Nile Valley.* Oxford, 1912.

Crum, W. E. *Coptic Monuments.* Cairo, 1902.

Jollois, J. B. P., and R. E. du Terrage Devilliers, in *Description d'Egypte,* Vols. 4 and 15. Paris, 1821–1829.

Jullien, M. "A travers les ruines de la Haute Egypte." *Etudes* 88 (1901):204–217.

Kahle, P. *Bala'izah,* 2 vols. London, 1954.

Lantschoot, A. van. *Recueil des colophons des manuscrits chrétiens d'Egypte.* Bibliothèque du Muséon 1. Louvain, 1929.

Maspéro, G. "Les Fouilles du Deir al-Aizam." *Annales du Service des antiquités de l'Egypte* 1 (1900):109–119, with plan.

Meinardus, O. *Christian Egypt, Ancient and Modern.* Cairo, 1965; 2nd ed., 1977.

Wiet, G. "Kibt." In *l'Encyclopédie de l'Islam,* Vol. 2, pp. 1048–61. Leiden, 1927.

Winlock, H. E., and W. E. Crum. *The Monastery of Epiphanius at Thebes,* 2 vols. New York, 1926.

RENÉ-GEORGES COQUIN

MAURICE MARTIN, S.J.

Architecture

The monastery was destroyed in the late 1960s by units of the Egyptian army stationed in the immedi-

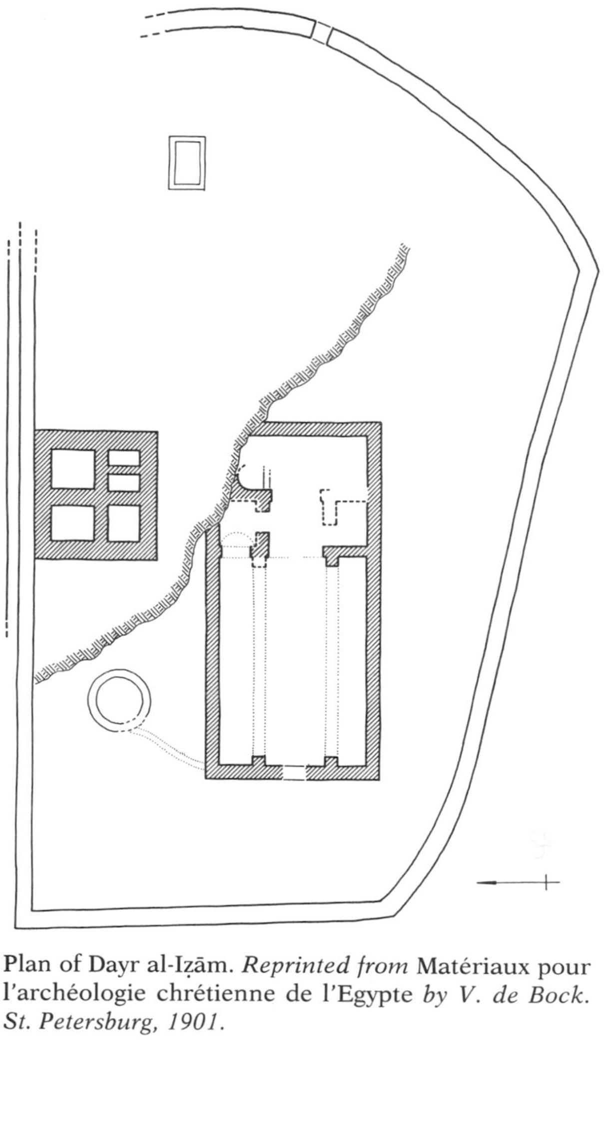

Plan of Dayr al-Iẓām. *Reprinted from* Matériaux pour l'archéologie chrétienne de l'Egypte *by V. de Bock. St. Petersburg, 1901.*

ate area. According to an old survey plan of 1901 (de Bock, 1901, pp. 88–90, fig. 100), it was surrounded by an irregular wall, inside which were a church and a keep (*jawsaq*), in addition to the remains of a few insignificant residential buildings for the monks.

The church was a long building and, according to the plan, appears to have been set out as a basilica with three aisles. Between the naos and the actual sanctuary a *khūrus* (room between the naos and the sanctuary) was added, as has been the custom since the eighth century, particularly in the churches of monasteries. An apse was no longer recognized even at this time. Worthy of note is the curve in a northerly direction in the sanctuary area.

The keep, located on a raised terrace on the north wall, had a square ground plan and was divided into four chambers, with the stair in the southeast. The entrance, therefore, lay either on the south or on the east side. Typologically this keep still belongs to the older examples.

BIBLIOGRAPHY

Bock, V. de. *Matériaux pour servir à l'archéologie chrétienne de l'Egypte, pp. 18–20.* St. Petersburg, 1901.

Clarke, S. *Christian Antiquities in the Nile Valley,* p. 178. Oxford, 1912.

Crum, W. E. *Coptic Monuments.* Cairo, 1902.

Grossmann, P. *Mittelalterliche Langhauskuppelkirchen und verwandte Typen in Oberägypten,* p. 109, fig. 43. Glückstadt, 1982.

PETER GROSSMANN

DAYR AL-ʿIẒĀM (Monastery of the Bones), a former Coptic monastery, lying about halfway between al-Fusṭāṭ (Old Cairo) and al-Maṭariyyah, on the site of the later mosque of al-Aqmar. The name refers to the bones of deceased monks who once belonged to it, preserved in the monastery—probably in special charnel houses—as is usual in other monasteries (for example, in the monastery of Saint Catherine on Mount Sinai). This name thus cannot be the right one, but only a description of the monastery that was usual in common parlance. When Cairo was founded in 969 by the Fatimid commander Jawhar al-Rūmī, the monastery was pulled down because it stood in the way of the planned caliph's palace. Only the monastery well remained, and it was still known in the fifteenth century by the designation Bīr al-ʿAẓāmah, a corruption of Bīr al-ʿIẓām (Ravaisse, 1887, p. 478). In compensation, a new monastery was built at the instance of Jawhar in the region of al-Khandaq, north of the Bāb al-Naṣr, to which the bones of the monks were also transferred. The latter is perhaps to be identified with the monastery of Mār Jirjis at al-Khandaq mentioned by Abū al-Makārim (*The Churches,* 1895, fol. 98b).

[*See also:* Dayr al-Khandaq.]

BIBLIOGRAPHY

Ravaisse, P. "Essai sur l'histoire et sur la topographie du Caire." In *Mémoires publiés par les membres de la mission archéologique française au Caire,* Vol. 1, pt. 3. Cairo, 1887.

PETER GROSSMANN

DAYR AL-JABRĀWĪ (Asyūṭ). [*This entry covers two aspects of Dayr al-Jabrāwī, site and history, and the architectural elements of the ruins.*]

History

This monastery, according to al-MAQRĪZĪ (1853, p. 503), was situated 5 miles (8 km) northwest of Abnūb, hence on the right bank of the Nile, opposite Manfalūṭ, on the edge of the desert in the *ḥajir* (stony area) at the foot of the mountain. The site included the Monastery of Saint VICTOR, son of Romanos, and a LAURA in the neighboring hypogea. The Monastery of Saint Victor has been replaced by a Christian village. The present church is recent (Meinardus, 1965, p. 277; 1977, pp. 386–87), but the ancient church was described in 1716 by C. Sicard (1982, pp. 13–15) and a century later by G. Wilkinson (1843, Vol. 2, p. 82).

The monastery or the church is mentioned in the Coptic texts relating to Saint Victor under the name Camp (castrum) of Hierakion (Budge, 1914, pp. 1–45; Constantine of Asyūṭ, 1970, p. 529, n. 3; Drescher, 1942, p. 77, n. 2, and 1944, p. 65). This name is taken up under the form Hierakon in the *Itinerarium* of Antoninus Placentinus (1899), and Sicard noticed, inserted into the ICONOSTASIS, a Latin inscription that allowed him to locate this Hierakon of the *Itinerarium* or the *hierakion* of the Coptic at Dayr al-Jabrāwī, which in Arabic had become Qasr al-Bāriqūn, to be read al-Yāriqūn (Amélineau, 1888, Vol. 2, p. 15; cf. Von Lemm, 1900, pp. 63–64). In the Arabic texts the place is called al-Khuṣūṣ.

In 1597 the patriarch GABRIEL VIII signed the Act of Union with Pope CLEMENT VIII at the Monastery of Saint Victor (Buri, 1931, p. 182; Graf, 1951, Vol. 4, pp. 120–22), but it is not clear whether this refers to DAYR AL-JABRĀWĪ or to DAYR BUQṬUR OF SHŪ. J. M. VANSLEB also made mentions of it in *Nouvelle Relation* (1677, p. 361; 1678, p. 217).

Round about the castrum, one notices an ancient Christian necropolis (Lefebvre, 1910, pt. 2, p. 272).

The laura lies between the hypogea on the mountain and the *ḥājir* extending from the foot of the mountain to the village. Also at the foot of the mountain in the old Roman castrum of Hierakon, a church of Saint Barbara and some cells are to be found.

Hermits lived in the hypogea, as is attested by the Coptic inscriptions (Newberry, 1892–1893, p. 13, quotations from the church fathers and from Scripture; Davies, 1902; the Davies inscriptions are collected by Crum, Vol. 2, pp. 45–46, pl. 29; the founders of Bāwīṭ are mentioned: APOLLO, ANUB, and Phīb, Ammonius of Thone, Psoi of Jeremias, etc.).

BIBLIOGRAPHY

Amélineau, E. *Contes et romans de l'Egypte chrétienne,* 2 vols. Paris, 1888.

______. *La Géographie de l'Egypte à l'époque copte.* Paris, 1893.

Antoninus Placentinus. *Itinerarium,* ed. P. Geyer. Corpus Scriptorum Ecclesiasticorum Latinorum 39. Vienna, 1898.

Budge, E. A. T. W. *Coptic Martyrdoms.* London, 1914.

Buri, U. *L'unione della chiesa copta con Roma sotto Clemente VIII.* Orientalia Christiana 62. Rome, 1931.

Constantine of Asyūṭ. *Panégyrique de St. Claude,* ed. G. Godron. PO 35. Turnhout, 1970.

Crum, E. W. "The Coptic Texts." Appendix 1 in *The Rock Tombs of Deir el Gebrawi,* ed. N. de Garis Davies. Egyptian Exploration Society. Archeological Survey, 11th and 12th Memoirs. London and Boston, 1902.

Davies, N. de G. *The Rock Tombs of Deir el-Gebrāwi,* 2 vols. London, 1902.

Drescher, J. "Apa Claudius and the Thieves." *Bulletin de la Société d'archéologie copte* 10 (1942):63–87.

______. "Encomium Attributed to Severus of Antioch." *Bulletin de la Société d'archéologie copte* 10 (1944):43–68.

Lefebvre, G. *L'Egypte chrétienne,* pt. 2. Annales du Service des antiquités de l'Egypte 10 (1910):50–65; 260–84.

Lemm, O. von. "Kleine koptische Studien 6." *Bulletin de l'Académie de Léningrad* 10 (1899):412–14; 12 (1900):1–163.

Meinardus, O. *Christian Egypt, Ancient and Modern.* Cairo, 1965; 2nd ed., 1977.

Newberry, P. E. "Progress of Egyptology." In *Archaeological Report,* ed. E. L. Griffith. Egypt Exploration Fund, 1892–1893.

Sicard, C. *Oeuvres,* 3 vols., ed. S. Sauneron and M. Martin. Cairo and Paris, 1982.

Vansleb, J. *Nouvelle Relation en forme de journal d'un voyage fait en Egypte en 1672 et 1673.* Paris 1677. Translated as *The Present State of Egypt.* London, 1678.

Wilkinson, G. *Egypt and Thebes,* Vols. 1–2. London, 1843.

RENÉ-GEORGES COQUIN
MAURICE MARTIN, S.J.

Architecture

Remains of a long, brick, columned basilica are in a field on the northeast edge of the modern village identified with the site of Dayr al-Jabrāwī, of which, however, only parts of the two rows of columns have survived, often wrongly understood as the remains of a former church. The columns were entirely built of baked bricks, but only their bases have remained standing. In some places there are still the connections for the *cancelli.* A layer of bricks at the east end of both rows of columns is probably the steps at the entrance to the sanctuary. Nothing of the outer walls has survived above ground.

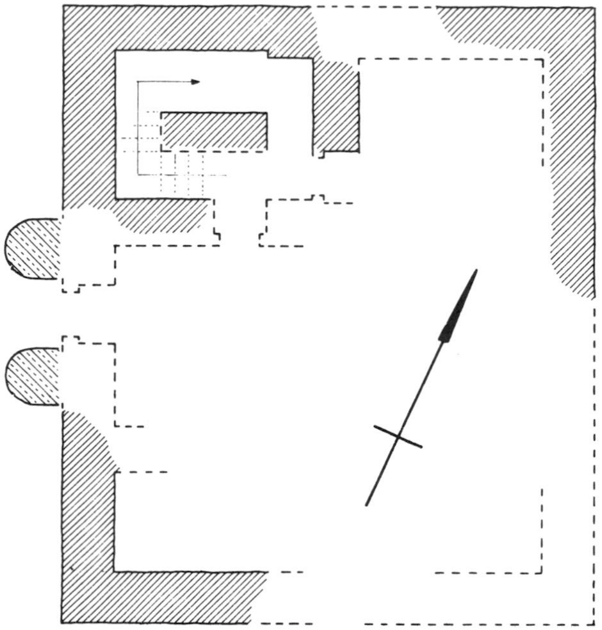

Plan of the towerlike building at Dayr al-Jabrāwī. *Courtesy Peter Grossmann.*

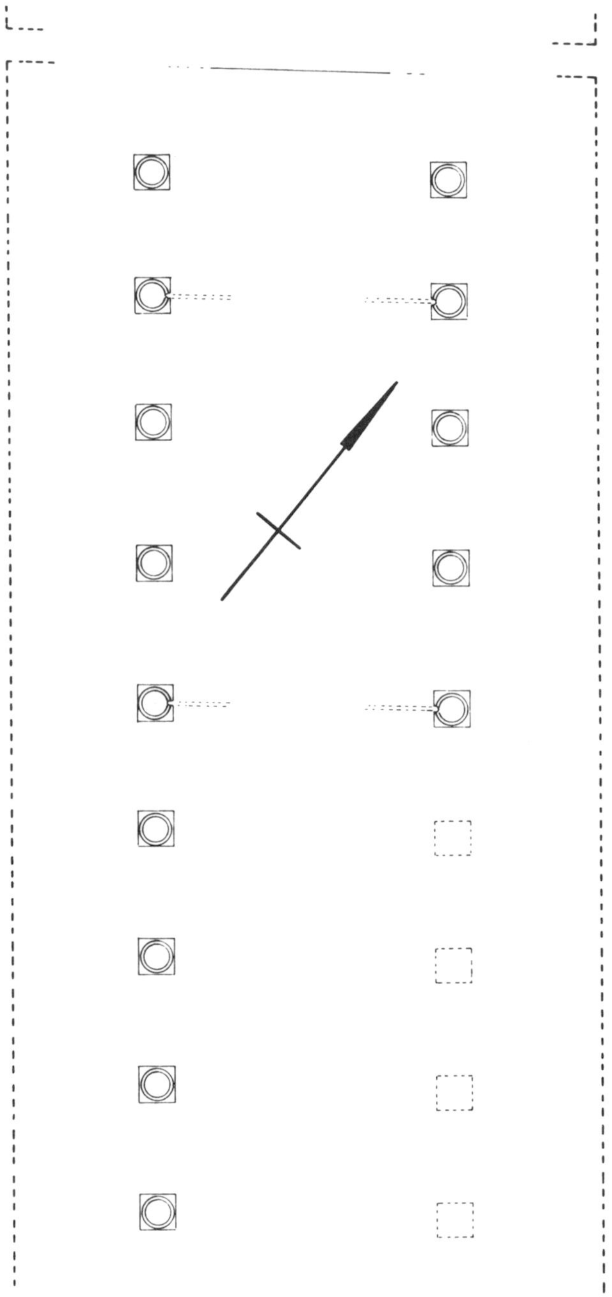

Plan of the long, columned basilica at Dayr al-Jabrāwī. *Courtesy Peter Grossmann.*

Apparently the two colonnades originally formed the lateral porticoes of the forum within the castrum of the "cohors I Augusta praetoriana Lusitanorum," known until now only by some ancient inscriptions from the area. After the departure of the soldiers the castrum probably was occupied by monks who turned the old forum into a church.

Individual buildings of a LAURA that presumably dates from early Christian times are on the plain northwest of the modern village. They consist of single houses of varying sizes lying scattered about, always in rectangular enclosures. They are not unlike the monks' dwellings in the great laura of KELLIA. In several of these buildings, walls with painted plaster surfaces stick up out of the earth. The detailed inner arrangement of the rooms has not yet been investigated. So far there is a survey only of a later addition, a towerlike building with thick, half-round projections on both sides of the entrance and a stair in the northwest corner. How the other rooms were arranged cannot be determined.

Ruins of a Saint Barbara's Chapel lie on the upper side of that plain at the southwestern slope of the desert, partly built into the rock. The interior consists of a square naos, once covered with a sailing vault, joined at the east end to a semicircular apse with several irregularly distributed niches, and a rectangular side room to the south. A northern side room does not exist, for here the rock blocks the space. Only above this is the outer wall continued directly, but here it serves to underpin a cornice led along the edge of the roof. The chapel may belong to the seventh or eighth century.

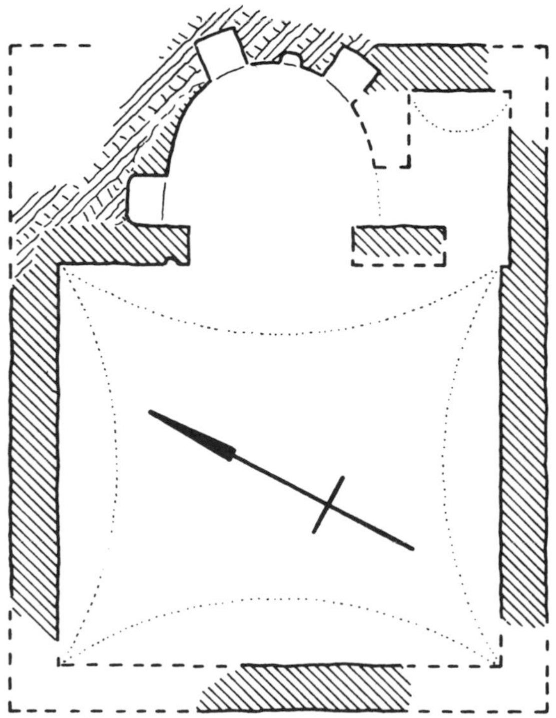

Plan of Saint Barbara's Chapel at Dayr al-Jabrāwī. *Courtesy Peter Grossmann.*

BIBLIOGRAPHY

Kurth, D., and U. Rössler-Köhler. *Zur Archäologie des 12. oberägyptischen Gaues.* Wiesbaden, 1987.

PETER GROSSMANN

DAYR AL-JANADLA. *See* Dayr Abū Maqrūfah.

DAYR AL-JARNŪS (Maghāgha). This monastery—today a Christian village—is situated on the Nile's left bank, but to the east of Bahr Yūsuf, some 5 miles (8 km) to the north of al-Bahnasā. It is one of the places where the Holy Family in its flight from Herod is said to have made a halt on the way to al-ASHMŪNAYN. In some texts this monastery is called Pei-Isus (Coptic) or Bayt Isūs or Dayr Bisūs (Arabic)—that is to say, "House of Jesus." Other texts give al-Jarnūs (the modern name) or Arganūs (the ancient name). The origin of this place-name is obscure, but it is clear that these are all the same place, for the localization is the same: near al-Bahnasā or near Ishnīn al-Naṣārā, and the date of its feast is identical, 25 Bashans. The well, an ancient NILOMETER, with its rite for predicting the height of the river's inundation, was mentioned by several authors in relation to either Dayr al-Jarnūs or Dayr Isūs.

The oldest testimony is beyond doubt the homily of Cyriacus, bishop of al-Bahnasā, the Arabic version of which has come down to us (Graf, 1944, Vol. 1, p. 232). This text is certainly earlier than the Muslim conquest.

At the beginning of the thirteenth century, ABŪ ṢALĪḤ THE ARMENIAN also mentioned the monastery of Bisūs and its well.

The Ethiopian SYNAXARION (translated around 1397 on the basis of the Arabic Synaxarion) mentions Baysūs at 24 Genbōt/24 Bashans in the itinerary of the FLIGHT INTO EGYPT before al-Ashmūnayn, and mentions the Nilometer-well, but the Arabic Synaxarion at 24 Bashans does not speak of it (Budge, 1928, Vol. 3, p. 924).

The HISTORY OF THE PATRIARCHS of the Egyptian church (Vol. 2, pt. 3, pp. 227 [text], 361 [trans.], under the patriarch CYRIL II) speaks of the monastery of Bisūs as a stage in the flight of the Holy Family before al-Ashmūnayn.

Butrus ibn al-Rahīb, at the end of the thirteenth century, also mentioned this monastery in his calendar of the Coptic feasts (Sidarus, 1975, pl. 7, 25 Bashans). A century later al-Qalqashandi cited it under the name of Isūs (Coquin, 1975–1976, p. 402).

In 1442 al-MAQRĪZĪ (1853, Vol. 2, p. 505) devoted a notice to Dayr Isūs and indicated the significance of the name Jesus and that this is the Dayr Arjanūs, the feast of which is on 25 Bashans; he also noted the rite of the well, which takes place on the night of that day. Ibn Iyās (d. 1524; 1955, Vol. 1, p. 187) also mentioned this monastery in almost the same terms as the preceding authors.

The monastery is also mentioned by travelers: J. M. VANSLEB (1677, pp. 69–71; 1678, pp. 42–43); B. de Maillet (1735, p. 63); C. Sicard (1982, Vol. 1, p. 46), who also wrote of the monastery of Jarnūs and its well; and M. Jomard (1826, Vol. 18, pt. 1, p. 625), who described the village of al-Jarnūs and the rite of the well, no doubt as it was at the time of Napoleon's expedition.

The *hegumenos* 'ABD AL-MASĪḤ ṢALĪB AL-MASŪ'DĪ (1924, p. 190) spoke of the water of the well, which is miraculous, and gave the date of 24 (instead of 25) Bashans as that of the feast.

The Church of the Virgin at al-Jarnūs is still in existence (Clarke, 1912, p. 206, no. 17; Meinardus, 1962, pp. 3–34).

BIBLIOGRAPHY

'Abd al-Masīḥ Ṣalīb al-Masū'di al-Bāramūsī. *Kitāb Tuḥfat al-Sā'ilīn fī Dhikr Adyirat Ruhbān al-Miṣriyyin.* Cairo, 1924.

Budge, E. A. W. *The Book of the Saints of the Ethiopian Church,* Vol. 3. Oxford, 1928.

Clarke, S. *Christian Antiquities in the Nile Valley.* London, 1912.

Coquin, R.-G. "Le Calendrier copte des fêtes de saints chez al-Qalqasandi." *Parole de l'Orient* 6–7 (1975–1976):387–411.

Ibn Iyās. *Journal d'un bourgeois du Caire,* Vol. 1, trans. G. Wiet. Paris, 1955.

Jomard, M. "Memoire sur la vallée du Nil et la nilomètre de l'ile de Roudah." In *Description de l'Egypte,* Vol. 18, pt. 1, pp. 556–643. Paris, 1826.

Maillet, B. de. *Description de l'Egypte,* ed. Abbé Le Mascrier. Paris, 1735.

Meinardus, O. "The Itinerary of the Holy Family in Egypt." *Studia Orientalia Christiana Collectanea* 7 (1962):3–34.

Sicard, C. *Oeuvres,* Vol. 1, ed. S. Sauneron and M. Martin. Bibliothèque d'étude 83. Cairo and Paris, 1982.

Sidarus, A. Y. *Ibn ar-Rahibs, Leben und Werk.* Islamkundliche Untersuchungen 36. Freiburg, 1975.

Vansleb, J. *Nouvelle relation en forme de journal d'un voyage fait en Egypte en 1672 et 1673.* Paris, 1677. Translated as *The Present State of Egypt.* London, 1678.

RENÉ-GEORGES COQUIN
MAURICE MARTIN, S.J.

DAYR AL-JAWLĪ. The village of al-Jawlī is to the south of Manfalūṭ. To the south of the village, then called al-Jāwiliyyah, al-MAQRĪZĪ (1853, Vol. 2, p. 506) situated a monastery dedicated to Saint Mercurius. J. VANSLEB also knew it but reduced it to a church (1677, p. 361; 1678, p. 217). S. Clarke noted under the name al-Jawlī a church dedicated to Saint Mercurius, whose nickname was Abū al-Sayfayn (1912, p. 209, no. 8). O. Meinardus described the present state of this Dayr Abū al-Sayfayn (1965, p. 276; 1977, p. 385). The church, which is all that survives, has been reconstructed on the plan of the old one. The monastery was also mentioned by the *hegumenos* 'ABD AL-MASĪḤ ṢALĪB AL-MASŪ'DĪ (1924, p. 167).

BIBLIOGRAPHY

'Abd al-Masīḥ Ṣalīb al-Masū'dī al-Baramūsī. *Kitāb Tuḥfat al-Sā'ilīn fī Dhikr Adyirat Ruhbān al Miṣriyyīn.* Cairo, 1924.
Clarke, S. *Christian Antiquities in the Nile Valley.* London, 1912.
Meinardus, O. *Christian Egypt, Ancient and Modern.* Cairo, 1965; 2nd ed., 1977.
Vansleb, J. M. *Nouvelle relation en forme de journal d'un voyage fait en Egypte en 1672 et 1673.* Paris, 1677. Translated as *The Present State of Egypt.* London, 1678.

RENÉ-GEORGES COQUIN
MAURICE MARTIN, S.J.

DAYR AL-JAZIRAH. *See* Dayr al-Rūmāniyyah.

DAYR AL-JŪ'. This place-name was mentioned by Ibn Duqmāq (1893, p. 8), who indicated its location and revenues. It is also cited in the *State of the Provinces* ('Abd al-Laṭīf, 1810, p. 689) in A.H. 777/A.D. 1375. It seems to have disappeared.

These two documents situate it in the province of al-Bahnasā on the left bank of the Nile, near AQFAHṢ. Perhaps it is the same as the one placed by al-MAQRĪZĪ (1853, Vol. 2, p. 505) at the boundary of the district of Manharah. It was a place of evil reputation, he wrote, because the monks refused to give any food to passing travelers; indeed, the name Dayr al-Jū' means Monastery of Hunger.

BIBLIOGRAPHY

'Abd al-Laṭīf. *Relation de l'Egypte de 'Abd al-Latif,* trans. and ed. A. I. S. de Sacy. Paris, 1810. *L'Etat des provinces* is translated in an appendix.
Ibn Duqmāq. *Kitāb al-Intiṣār,* ed. C. Vollers. Cairo, 1893.

RENÉ-GEORGES COQUIN
MAURICE MARTIN, S.J.

DAYR AL-KHĀDIM. Ibn Duqmāq (1893, p. 8) and al-MAQRĪZĪ (1853, Vol. 2, p. 505) mentioned a Dayr al-Khādim that was near Baḥr Yūsuf (al-Manhā) in the province of Bahnasā and was dedicated to the angel GABRIEL.

The *State of the Provinces* in 1375 indicates the same ('Abd al-Laṭīf, 1810, p. 689). Ramzī (1953–1968, Vol. 2, pt. 3, p. 217) thought that this was the same as the DAYR AL-SANQŪRIYYAH, but the latter is consecrated to Saint Theodorus.

'ABD AL-MASĪḤ ṢALĪB AL-MASŪ'DĪ (1924, pp. 163, 179) distinguished the two monasteries very clearly, the first having disappeared but the second still being in existence, at least its church.

ABŪ ṢĀLIḤ THE ARMENIAN (1895, p. 245) placed Dayr al-Khādim at Antinoë (ANTINOOPOLIS).

BIBLIOGRAPHY

'Abd al-Laṭīf. *Relation de l'Egypte de 'Abd al-Latif,* trans. and ed. A. I. S. de Sacy. Paris, 1810. *L'Etat des provinces* is translated in an appendix.
Abd al-Masīḥ Salīb al-Masū'dī al-Baramūsī. *Kitāb Tuḥfat al-Sā'ilīn fī Dhikr Adyirat Ruhbān al-Miṣriyyīn.* Cairo, 1924.
Ibn Duqmāq. *Kitāb al-Intiṣār,* ed. C. Vollers. Cairo, 1893.
Ramzī, M. *Al-Qāmūs al-Jughrāfī lil-Bilād al Miṣrīyyah,* 3 vols. Cairo, 1953–1968.

RENÉ-GEORGES COQUIN
MAURICE MARTIN, S.J.

DAYR AL-KHANDAQ. This monastery was founded around 970 on a large tract of land to the north of Cairo. It also included a cemetery and replaced another monastery-cemetery situated on what is now the site of al-Aqmar Mosque, which dates from the Fatimid period. Near this tract was the moat (*khandaq*) that General Jawhar al-Siqillī had dug against the Carmathians (al-Maqrīzī, 1853, Vol. 2, p. 507; cf. Casanova, 1901, p. 167).

At that time, Dayr al-Khandaq included five churches dedicated to the Virgin: the churches of Mār Jirjis, Theodorus, Mercurius, Abū Maqār, and Apollo, son of Justus (Abū al-Makārim, 1984, pp. 18f.). There was also a dayr al-Malāk Ghubrīyāl alongside Dayr al-Malāk Mīkhā'īl ('Abd al-Masīh Ṣalīb al-Masū'di al-Baramūsī, 1924, p. 153).

The Coptic patriarch CYRIL II gave the Church of Saint Macarius to the Armenians; they gave it the patronage of Saint George. At the same period, the Church of Saint Apollo, son of Justus, was given to the Syrians (HISTORY OF THE PATRIARCHS 1959, Vol. 2, pt. 3, pp. 225 [text], 355–56 [trans.]).

Al-MAQRĪZĪ (1853, p. 511) wrote that the Church of Mār Jirjis was transformed into the church of Anbā Ruways, a church that still exists. The tomb of the saint, who died in 1404, survives (Graf, 1947, Vol. 2, p. 475; Troupeau, 1972, Vol. 1, pp. 252–53). The patriarch MATTHEW I and his three successors were buried in the Church of Anbā Ruways (Meinardus, 1965, p. 216; 1977, p. 309).

Two Arabic manuscripts were written for Dayr al-Malāk al-Baḥarī in 1660 and for Anbā Ruways in 1740 (Simaykah and Yassa 'Abd al-Masīḥ, 1942, Vol. 2, 1, nos. 787 and 1072), showing that the dayr still existed at that time.

Those churches actually surviving are the Church of Anbā Ruways, near the new Cathedral of Saint Mark, and the Church of Saint Michael al-Baḥarī, near the Dimirdāsh railway station. The Church of Saint Apollo has disappeared. For an account of the present situation, see Burmester (1955, pp. 87, 89).

[*See also:* Dayr al-'Iẓām (Cairo).]

BIBLIOGRAPHY

'Abd al-Masīḥ Ṣalīb al-Masū'dī al-Bāramūsī. *Kitāb Tuḥfat al-Sā'ilīn fī Dhikr Adyirat Ruhbān al-Miṣriyyīn.* Cairo, 1924.

Abū al-Makārim. *Tārīkh al-Kanā'is wa-al-Adyirah,* ed. Ṣamū'īl al-Suriyānī. Cairo, 1984.

Burmester, O. *A Guide of the Ancient Coptic Churches of Cairo.* Cairo, 1955.

Casanova, P. "Les Noms coptes du Caire." *Bulletin de l'Institut français d'archéologie orientale* 1 (1901):139–224.

Meinardus, O. *Christian Egypt, Ancient and Modern.* Cairo, 1965; 2nd ed., 1977.

Troupeau, G. *Catalogue des manuscrits arabes,* Vol. 1. Paris, 1972.

RENÉ-GEORGES COQUIN
MAURICE MARTIN, S.J.

DAYR KHARFŪNAH. *See* Dayr al-Muṭṭin.

DAYR AL-KHASHAB. *See* Dayr al-Naqlūn.

DAYR AL-KUBĀNIYYAH. [*This article is composed of two brief parts: the history and the architecture of Dayr al-Kubāniyyah.*]

History

About 6 miles (10 km) from the town of Aswan on the left bank of the Nile are the ruins of a Coptic monastery of the sixth or seventh century, excavated by the Vienna Academy of Sciences. It was named after the neighboring village of al-Kubāniyyah (the Mountain of Isis). It is also called Dayr al-Shaykah, but the primitive name of this monastery is not known. The seven Coptic inscriptions were published by the archaeologists H. Junker and H. Demel (1922). One may consult with profit the reviews of De L. O'Leary (1923; 1924). The site was briefly described by O. Meinardus (1965, p. 327; 1977, p. 443).

BIBLIOGRAPHY

Junker, H., and H. Demel. *Das Kloster am Isisberg.* Akademie der Wissenschaften. Vienna, 1922.

Meinardus, O. *Christian Egypt, Ancient and Modern.* Cairo, 1965; 2nd ed., 1977.

O'Leary, De L. Review of Junker and Demel work above. *Journal of Egyptian Archaeology* 9 (1923): 233.

———. Review of Junker and Demel work above. *Journal of the Royal Asiatic Society* 56 (1924): 309–310.

RENÉ-GEORGES COQUIN
MAURICE MARTIN, S.J.

Architecture

Since being uncovered in the winter of 1910–1911 by H. Junker, the site has again been completely covered by sand. Particularly important is the church, which is an octagon-domed building of a type otherwise known only in Greece. A brick dome with a span of 23 feet (7 m) is carried by a substructure consisting of eight supports linked by a continuous circle of arches. An ambulatory surrounds this central structure on three sides, in the manner of side aisles. On the east side are the

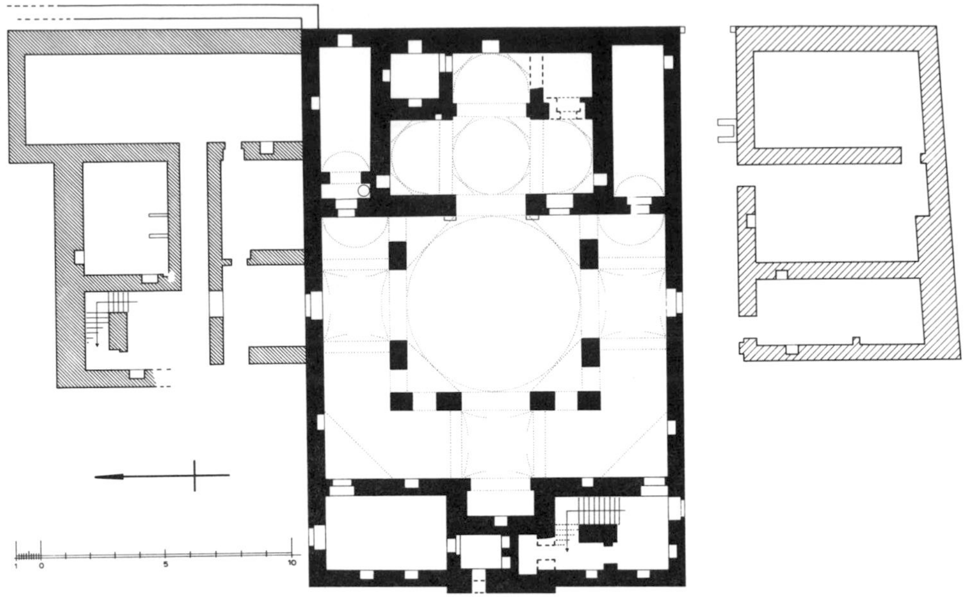

Plan of the octagon-domed church at Dayr al-Kubāniyyah. *Courtesy Peter Grossmann.*

khūrus (room between the naos and the sanctuary); the three-part sanctuary, with a rectangular altar chamber and two rectangular side chambers in the middle; and two further longitudinal rooms at the sides. On the west a projecting structure accommodates several side rooms and a staircase leading upward. The remaining subsidiary buildings, which were probably shelter for the monks, are unimportant. An outer wall was not identified, although there certainly must have been one. In the same way, there is no indication of the location of the ancillary buildings.

BIBLIOGRAPHY

Grossmann, P. *Mittelalterliche Langhauskuppelkirchen und verwandte Typen in Oberägypten,* pp. 34ff. Glückstadt, 1982.

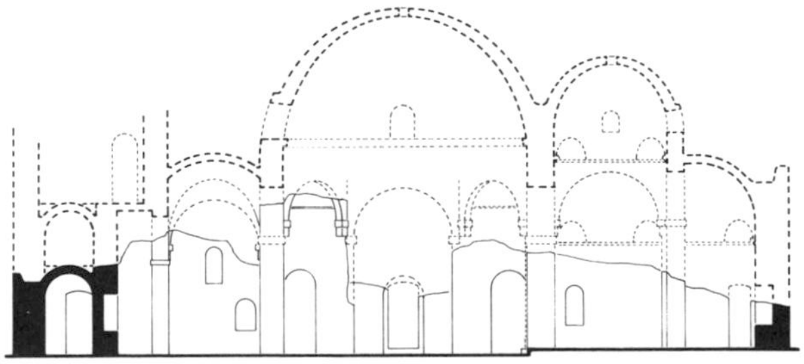

Elevation of the octagon-domed church at Dayr al-Kubāniyyah. *Courtesy Peter Grossmann.*

Junker, H., and H. Demel. *Das Kloster am Isisberg.* Akademie der Wissenschaften. Vienna, 1922.

Monneret de Villard, U. *Il monastero di S. Simeone presso Aswân,* Vol. 1, pp. 45ff. Milan, 1927.

PETER GROSSMANN

DAYR AL-KULAH. *See* Dayr Mār Buqṭur (Qamūlah).

DAYR KYRIAKUS. *See* Dayr Epiphanius.

DAYR AL-MADĪNAH. [*This entry encompasses two aspects of Dayr al-Madīnah. The history is known through expeditions and published reports of visitors. A description of remaining signs of the art and architecture of the site comprises the second part.*]

History

This small monastery is situated on the left bank of the Nile, opposite Luxor. The area around the *dayr* is known as West Thebes. The monastery was installed in the ruins of a small temple of the Ptolemaic period dedicated to the goddess Hathor. It was given its name, Monastery of the Town, no doubt because of its proximity to the town of Jeme, established in the Coptic era in the temple of Ramses III at MADĪNAT HĀBŪ. Because of the change in religion, the temple was used in other ways. This is the explanation given by Winlock and Crum (1926, Vol. 1, p. 8).

When the monastery was installed in the temple of Hathor, the temple was transformed into a church and received the name of the martyr Isidorus, as is shown by several inscriptions (Winlock and Crum, 1926, pt. 1, p. 8; Munier, 1918, p. 99, n. 3). In a small cemetery to the north of the monastery eleven tombs have been counted. Several things indicate that this monastery was flourishing at the same period as the DAYR EPIPHANIUS (that is, in the seventh century). Its monks, or at least some of them, must have been weavers or tailors, for on the facade of the ancient temple are engraved instructions for the dimensions of various garments (Winlock and Crum, 1926, pt. 1, p. 9). These inscriptions have been published by E. Lepsius (1897–1913, Vol. 2, p. 102) and Sayce (1881–1882, pp. 117–23). On the state of the monastery at the beginning of the twentieth century, one may read the description of M. Jullien (1902, pp. 247–48) and G. Maspero (1911, pp. 145–51). On the excavations on this site, see E. Baraize (1914, pp. 19–42) and B. Bruyère in the *Rapport sur les fouilles de Deir el-Médinah (1939–40)*, in particular that of January–March 1939. For a recent description, one may read Johann Georg (1930, p. 21) and O. Meinardus (1965, p. 314; 1977, p. 427).

[*See also:* Memnonia.]

BIBLIOGRAPHY

Baraize, E. "Compte-rendu des travaux exécutés à Deir el-Médineh." *Annales du Service des antiquités de l'Egypte* 13 (1914):19–42.

Bruyère, B. *Rapport sur les fouilles de Deir el-Médineh (janvier-mars 1939)*. Fouilles de l'Institut français d'Archéologie orientale 20. Cairo, 1948–1952.

———. "Fouilles de Deir el-Médineh." *Chronique d'Egypte* 28 (1939):271–76.

Johann Georg, Duke of Saxony. *Neue Streifzüge durch die Kirchen und Klöster Ägyptens*. Leipzig and Berlin, 1930.

Jullien, M. "*Le Culte chrétien dans les temples de l'antique Egypte*." Etudes 92 (1902):237–53.

Lepsius, E. *Denkmäler aus Ägypten und Äthiopien . . .*, 5 vols. Leipzig, 1897–1913; repr. Osnabrück, 1970–1971.

Maspéro, G. "Notes de voyage." *Annales du Service des antiquités de l'Egypte* 10 (1910):5–13, 11 (1911):145–61.

[Mu]nier, H. "Les Actes du martyre de saint Isidore." *Bulletin de l'Institut français d'Archéologie orientale* 14 (1918):97–190.

Sayce, A. H. "The Coptic Inscriptions of Beni-Hassan and Deir el-Medineh." *Proceedings of the Society of Biblical Archaeology* 4 (1881–1882):117–23.

Winlock, H. E., and W. E. Crum. *The Monastery of Epiphanius at Thebes*, 2 vols. New York, 1926.

RENÉ-GEORGES COQUIN
MAURICE MARTIN, S.J.

Art and Architecture

The monastery of Dayr al-Madīnah is mixed up with the Ptolemaic temple at the site and the space included between it and the encircling wall of unbaked brick of the same period. That wall surrounds it at the foot of the north slope of the valley, in which farther to the west is located the village of the laborers of the pharaonic period. In this space on the north side of the temple, tombs of monks have been found, one of the characteristics of which is the enveloping of the bodies in a leather apron.

The entrance contrived in the thickness of the encircling wall on the east side allows one to see in the same line, 165 feet (50 m) away, the entrance to the temple itself. On the left of this entrance a seated personage has been copper-engraved full-face on a flat stone revetment. The figure is clothed in a pallium with oblique folds on the shoulders, over a tunic with wavy horizontal folds that fall to his feet. The right foot, covered with a sandal, is turned toward the right; the left is bare, with the toes clearly traced vertically. He is haloed, and a long stick with a knob rests upon his shoulder and projects above his head. The stick is drawn obliquely and rests in front of the length of his right foot. The right arm rests on his right knee and rises to the height of his head, perhaps in a gesture of benediction. The left arm rests on the knee of the same side, holding an object that could be a vase. The features of the face cannot be identified. But under this figure, in a register of the same stone revetment, an inscription of the priest Paul mentions that he served the Church of Apa Isidorus the Martyr. Without doubt, this is the one to whom the monastery was dedicated.

The presence of monks on this site is attested by an important number of Coptic inscriptions that follow one another in fairly regular lines from register to register on the facade, sometimes covering two or three stones of it. These are for the most part funerary inscriptions, one of them even forming a chronological list of names of monks, with indication of the day and month of their death.

Other isolated inscriptions are found on the outer face of the north wall, and another group is situated on the roof, composed of incised forms of feet, which, however, are isolated, and in which is also incised a name. One monk's name is found incised on a plane surface under a Ptolemaic scene decorating the exterior face of the south wall of the temple.

Crosses, some elaborate and others very simple, as well as incised designs of birds or quadrupeds, very rough, stand out on the outer face of the north wall of the temple and on the interior face of the east part of the encircling wall.

It is remarkable—and this cannot be emphasized too much—that the Coptic monks never made any attempts to deface the Ptolemaic representations or inscriptions of this temple. For their own works and inscriptions, they used only the spaces left untouched by the previous occupants. This example of the respect they showed the past disproves allegations of vandalism leveled against the monks.

BIBLIOGRAPHY

Baraizc, E. "Comptc-rcndu dcs travaux cxécutés à Deir el-Médineh." *Annales du Service des antiquités de l'Egypte* 13 (1914):19–42.

PIERRE DU BOURGUET, S.J.

DAYR AL-MADWID. *See* Dayr al-Sab'at Jibāl.

DAYR AL-MAGHṬIS or Dabra Metmāq. AL-MAQRĪZĪ indicated that this monastery stood "beside the saline marshes, near the Lake of al-Burullus . . . and in the neighborhood is the salt-marsh from which the Rashidic [Rosetta] salt is obtained" (1845, pp. 44–45 [text], 108–109 [trans.]; 1853, Vol. 2, p. 508). He later indicated that DAYR AL-'ASKAR is one day's march from Dayr al-Maghṭis, but al-'Askar was quite near present-day Bilqās, in the northeast of the province of Gharbiyyah. This would locate Dayr al-Maghṭis to the north of Bilqās in the neighborhood of Abū Māḍī, on the shores of the Lake of al-Burullus.

This monastery played an important part in the medieval period of the Coptic church. The Ethiopian SYNAXARION, in its second recension at the end of the sixteenth or the beginning of the seventeenth century, for the 24 Genbot/24 Bashans account of the Holy Family's FLIGHT INTO EGYPT, identifies the place where Jesus left his footprint on a stone (Bi Khā Īsūs, or Jesus' heel, in the Coptic Synaxarion) with Dabra Meṭmāq—that is, the Monastery of the Pool, or Dayr al-Maghṭis in Arabic (Budge, 1928, Vol. 3, p. 923). In the Synaxarion account of the flight into Egypt, the episode of Jesus' heel is placed after the crossing of the Damietta branch of the Nile at Samannūd. This indication from the Ethiopian Synaxarion thus agrees with al-Maqrīzī's statement.

In ABŪ AL-MAKĀRIM's work at the beginning of the thirteenth century, the same identification is given, although the name Dayr al-Maghṭis is not specifically mentioned. However, according to the author, a miracle happened at Minyat Ṭānah on the day of the Epiphany. It occurred in a pool inside a church of an unnamed monastery where the miraculous stone bearing the footprint of Jesus was kept until it disappeared at the time of the Arab conquest (Abū al-Makārim, 1984, pp. 70–71). The article on CYRIL II in the HISTORY OF THE PATRIARCHS places Minyat Ṭānah, the place where the Synaxarion mentions Bi Khā Īsūs (Bisūs), after Basṭah in the list of stages of the flight into Egypt (HISTORY OF THE PATRIARCHS, 1959, Vol. 2, pt. 3, pp. 227 [text], 361 [trans.]). The identification of Dayr Minyat Ṭānah, Bi Khā Īsūs, and Dayr al-Maghṭis with one another is evident.

Philūthāwus 'Awaḍ (Simaykah, 1932, Vol. 2, p. 224) thought that this monastery was near DAYR SITT DIMYĀNAH and that it disappeared under the rising water level of the Lake of al-Burullus. M. Ramzī (1954, Vol. 1, p. 309) thought that Minyat Ṭānah was at the site of the farm of Dayr Sitt Dimyānah, about 6 miles (10 km) to the north of Bilqās. Neither writer took account of the statements of al-Maqrīzī.

Noted above was the tradition linking Dayr al-Maghṭis and the flight into Egypt. At some unknown point in the Middle Ages, this monastery became a very important pilgrimage center, as the *Book of Mary's Miracles* in its Ethiopian recension recounts. A résumé of this work dealing with Dayr al-Maghṭis is inserted in the Ethiopian Synaxarion for 21 Genbot/21 Bashans (Budge, 1928, Vol. 3, pp. 917–18). The *Book of Mary's Miracles* is a compilation of accounts concerning Dabra Meṭmāq and, in particular, the Virgin's appearances on a luminous boat on 21 Genbot/21 Bashans. This is clearly translated from the Arabic, but unfortunately the Arabic original has been lost. Al-Maqrīzī recorded that people went there on pilgrimage from all over Egypt as much as to the Church of the Resurrection at Jerusalem and that the feast of the appearance of the Virgin is in the month of Bashans. He adds that this monastery was destroyed in Ramadan of A.H. 841/A.D. 1438, a date that corresponds exactly with the data of the Ethiopian *Book of the Miracles of Mary* (Cerulli, 1943, pp. 143–44), which attributes this destruction by fire to the Mamluk sultan Barsbay al-Malik al-Ashraf Sayf al-Dīn. In 1441 the patriarch JOHN XI sent an embassy led by Michael, the bishop of Ṣandafā (near al-Maḥallah al-Kubrā), on whom Dayr al-Maghṭis then depended, to Ethiopia to warn the negus Zarʿa Yaʿqob (1434–1468). This bishop and this embassy are unknown elsewhere (Munier, 1943; Wiet, 1938).

Several similarities will be noted between these appearances of the Virgin and saints at Dayr al-Maghṭis and those of Dayr Sitt Dimyānah: they take place at the same time of the year, in the month of Bashans; the monasteries are not far from one another, being in the same region of the Delta; and, although here and there the Virgin appears even more than at Sitt Dimyānah, the duration of the appearances is similar: five days at Dayr al-Maghṭis, three days at Dayr Sitt Dimyānah. Appearances of the same type were taking place in other churches of the Delta at the beginning of the thirteenth century, according to the *History of the Patriarchs* (1974, Vol. 4, pt. 1, pp. 23 [text], 48–49 [trans.]). One might propound the hypothesis that after the fire at Dayr al-Maghṭis in 1438, the pilgrimage of the month of Bashans was moved to Dayr Jimyānah (which had become Dayr Sitt Dimyānah), which would explain the spread of the cult of Saint Jimyānah (or Dimyānah, according to the two well-attested spellings).

BIBLIOGRAPHY

Abū al-Makārim. *Tārīkh al-Kanā'is wa-al-Adyirah,* ed. Ṣamū'īl al-Suryānī. Cairo, 1984.

Amélineau, E. *La Géographie de l'Egypte à l'époque copte,* p. 259. Paris, 1893. (This cites Minyat Ṭānah, but places it too far south.)

Budge, E. A. W. *The Book of the Saints of the Ethiopian Church,* 4 vols. Cambridge, 1928.

Cerulli, E. *Il libro etiopico dei miracoli di Maria.* Studi orientali pubblicati a cura della Scuola Orientale 1. Rome, 1943.

Munier, H. *Recueil des listes épiscopales de l'église copte.* Cairo, 1943.

Muyser, J., and G. Viaud. *Les Pèlerinages coptes en Egypte,* pp. 10–11. Bibliothèque d'études coptes 15. Cairo, 1979.

Ramzī, M. *Al-Qāmūs al-Jughrāfī lil-Bilād al Miṣrīyyah,* 3 vols. Cairo, 1953–1968.

Simaykah, M. *Dalīl al-Mathaf al-Qibṭī,* Vol. 2. Cairo, 1932.

Wiet, G. "Les Relations égypto-abyssines sous les sultans mamlouks." *Bulletin de la Société d'archéologie copte* 4 (1938):115–40.

RENÉ-GEORGES COQUIN

DAYR AL-MAJMAʿ. [*This entry consists of two parts:* History *and* Architecture. *The first deals with written accounts concerning the dayr, and the second discusses what remains of the four churches that were in the confines of the monastery.*]

History

This monastery, now also called Dayr Mār Jirjis, is situated to the west of the village called al-Baḥrī Qamūlah, southwest of NAQĀDAH, at the foot of the Libyan massif on the edge of the desert named Jabal al-Aṣāṣ, between DAYR ABŪ LĪFAH to the north and Dayr Mār Buqtur to the south. The term *al-majmaʿ* was understood in the sense of *synod* by C. SICARD (1982, Vol. 2, pp. 66, 227), but Winlock and Crum (1926, p. 115) remarked that it is the Arabic equivalent of the Greek *koinobion,* and underlined the fact that in the Sahidic Life of Pisentius the Monastery of Tsenti (in Arabic, al-Aṣāṣ), which was his *episkopeion* (episcopal dwelling) and where his body was laid before being buried "in the mountain," bears this name (Budge, 1913, pp. 120, 126). Now DAYR ANBĀ PISENTIUS, where his tomb is still found today, is only a quarter mile (400 m) distant.

Yūḥannā ibn Saʿīd ibn Yaḥyā ibn Minyā ibn al-Qulzumī, in his notice about the patriarch CYRIL II, mentioned in "a monastery to the west of Qūṣ [the body] of Abba Pisentius and to the west of the monastery a spring of water" (HISTORY OF THE PATRIARCHS 1959, Vol. 2, pt. 3, pp. 228 [text], 362 [trans.]).

ABŪ ṢĀLIḤ THE ARMENIAN (fol. 81^{b}; 1895, pp. 233–34) seems indeed to have referred to this monastery, although he placed it under the name of PISENTIUS, bishop of Qifṭ (Coptos) at the beginning of the seventh century: "This monastery stands to the west of Quṣ; and it contains the tomb of saint Pisentius. Outside the monastery and to the west of it, there is a well of water which was visited by our Lady and the Lord Christ with the righteous old man Joseph." But the Evetts translation could be corrected thus: "There is the tomb of saint Pisentius outside [the monastery], and to the west of it. . . ."

In 1668, Fathers François and Protais spoke of the monastery "el-Migmir [Majmaʿ] where Bishop Abifentaous, who died with a reputation for sanctity, is buried" (Sauneron, 1969, p. 137), an easy confusion between Dayr al-Majmaʿ and the nearby tomb of Saint Pisentius.

It is at this time that Abū Ṣāliḥ—or at least the single manuscript that has come down under his name—still placed the tomb of Saint Pisentius in the Monastery of Saint Michael (Dayr al-Malāk Mīkhāʾīl) at Qamūlah (fol. 104[b]; *The Churches . . .*, 1895, pp. 283–84), which he also names Dayr al-ʿAyn, because of a famous well of water.

This is the largest of the monasteries of this region between Naqādah and Qamūlah. It is described by S. CLARKE (1912, pp. 130–40) as having cells and four churches, of which the oldest, dedicated to Saint George, is laid out on a basilica plan and contains remains of paintings, with a *maiestas Domini* (majesty of the Lord) in the conch of the apse. Abū Ṣāliḥ indicated that the church is consecrated to the Virgin, and there is still a small church of the Virgin, although badly damaged, in the Dayr al-Majmaʿ.

[*See also:* Dayr Abū al-Līfah; Dayr Anbā Pisentius; Dayr al-Malāk Mīkhāʾīl (Qamūlah); Pisentius (bishop of Qifṭ).]

BIBLIOGRAPHY

Budge, E. A. W. *Coptic Apocrypha in the Dialect of Upper Egypt*. London, 1913.

Clarke, S. *Christian Antiquities in the Nile Valley*, pp. 130–40. Oxford, 1912.

Doresse, J. "Monastères coptes-thébains." *Revue des conférences françaises en Orient* Nov. 1949: 1–16.

Johann Georg, Duke of Saxony. *Streifzüge durch die Kirchen und Klöster Ägyptens*. Leipzig, 1914.

______. *Neue Streifzüge durch die Kirchen und Klöster Ägyptens*. Leipzig and Berlin, 1930.

Monneret de Villard, U. *Il monastero di S. Simeone presso Aswan*. Milan, 1927.

Sauneron, S. "Villes et légendes d'Egypte, XXVIII, La Thébaïde en 1668." *Bulletin de l'Institut français d'Archéologie orientale* 67 (1969):121–42.

Sicard, C. *Oeuvres*, Vol. 2, *Relations et mémoires imprimés*, ed. M. Martin. *Bibliothèque d'études* 84. Cairo, 1982.

Vansleb, J. M. *Nouvelle relation en forme de journal d'un voyage fait en Egypte en 1672 et 1673*. Paris, 1677. Translated as *The Present State of Egypt*. London, 1678.

Walters, C. C. *Monastic Archaeology in Egypt*. Warminster, 1974.

Winlock, H. E., and W. E. Crum. *The Monastery of Epiphanius at Thebes*, Vol. 1. New York, 1926.

RENÉ-GEORGES COQUIN
MAURICE MARTIN, S. J.

Architecture

Of the four churches that were once part of this monastery in the early and high Middle Ages, only the Church of Saint John remains standing as a ruin. The small al-ʿAdhrāʾ Church (Church of the Virgin) is at present blocked up, and the two most important churches, those of Malāk Mīkhāʾīl (Saint Michael) and Mār Jirjis (Saint George), were leveled to the ground in the 1920s and replaced by insignificant modern structures.

The Church of Mār Jirjis appears to be the oldest. The building is divided up very clearly. It had the form of a columned basilica with a series of sturdy

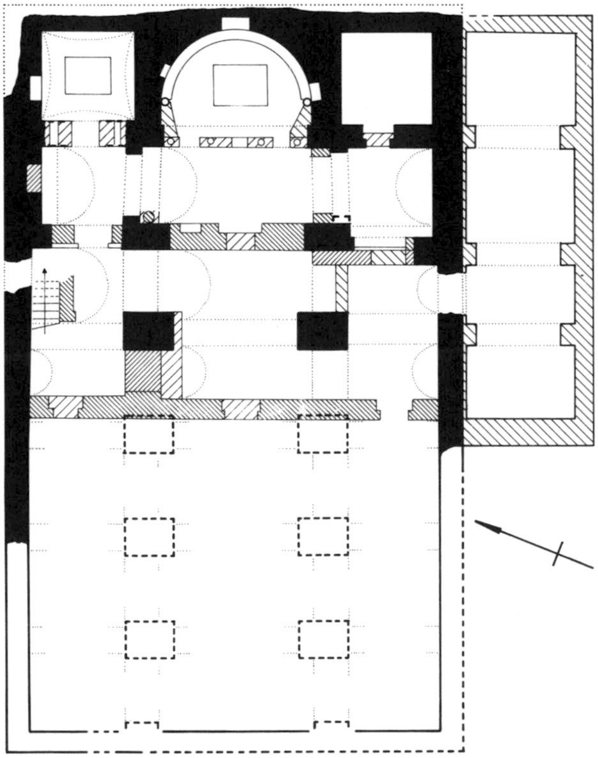

Plan of the Church of Mār Jirjis at Dayr al-Majmaʿ. *Courtesy Peter Grossmann.*

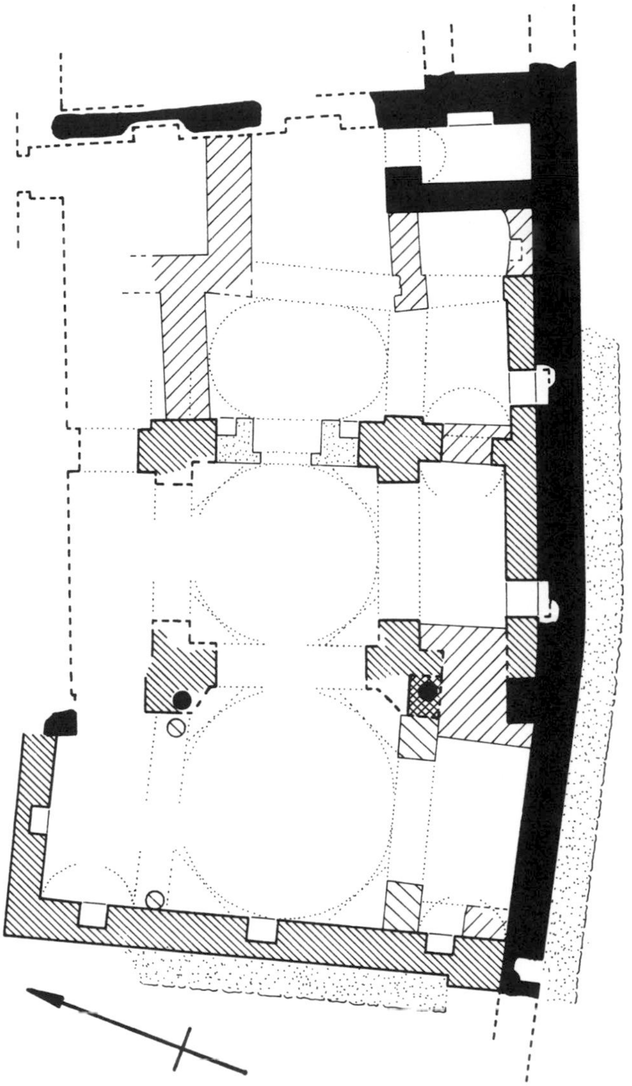

Plan of the Church of Saint John at Dayr al-Majmaʿ. *Courtesy Peter Grossmann.*

transverse arches between which was erected a roof construction in the shape of a transverse barrel vault. Technically this kind of roof covering may be compared with the transverse system of arches used in churches in the Haurān (Butler, 1929, pp. 17–24, 178–79). The Church of Saint George in Dayr al-Majmaʿ has been the only known example of this kind in Egypt, and its loss is therefore all the more regrettable. The sanctuary followed the normal plan, with an apse in the center and two rectangular side rooms. The church dated from the eleventh century.

To the north and immediately adjoining the Church of Saint George, the Church of Saint Michael was so poorly rebuilt by the time S. Clarke discovered it that the original structure could no longer be recognized. In the condition reported by Clarke, it was similar to the churches of the sixteenth and seventeenth centuries from the Akhmīm area.

In its present condition the Church of Saint John represents at least three distinct phases of building. Of these, the middle phase, which has the form of a domed basilica consisting of two domed rooms one behind the other, was the most important. The previous structure, considerable sections of which are preserved on the south and east sides, appears to have been primarily a building with columns. What it looked like originally can be ascertained only by excavation.

Last, the al-ʿAdhrā' Church was a small, insignificant chapel. Despite its narrowness, the naos was subdivided into three aisles that had once been barrel-vaulted. Attached to the *khūrus* (room between the naos and sanctuary) in the east, it was separated by a thick wall with a single opening in the middle. The actual sanctuary had a central apse and two side rooms.

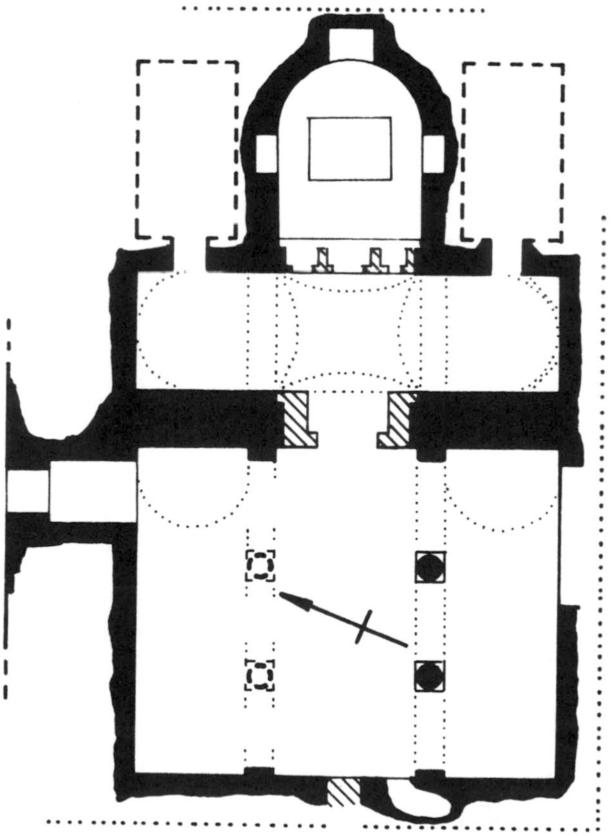

Plan of the al-ʿAdhrā' Church at Dayr al-Majmaʿ. *Courtesy Peter Grossmann.*

BIBLIOGRAPHY

Butler, H. C. *Early Churches in Syria.* Princeton, 1929; repr. Amsterdam, 1969.

Clarke, S. *Christian Antiquities in the Nile Valley,* pp. 130–40. Oxford, 1912.

Grossmann, P. *Mittelalterliche Langhauskuppelkirchen und verwandte Typen in Oberägypten,* pp. 22–25, 109, 137–39. Glückstadt, 1982.

Meinardus, O. *Christian Egypt, Ancient and Modern,* p. 311. Cairo, 1965.

Monneret de Villard, U. *Deyr el-Muḥarraqah,* p. 14. Milan, 1928.

PETER GROSSMANN

DAYR AL-MALĀK (Dākhlah Oasis), a badly decayed mud brick ruin of a monastery, lying in the middle of an inundation area about 11 miles (7 km) northeast of Mūt. The interior of the church is divided by four cruciform pillars into nine equal bays. In the east there are three apses lying side by side, each of which probably once contained an altar. Remains of two further apses were identified in the middle of the south and west sides, and very probably there was also an apse on the north side. These apses give an architectural emphasis to the two main axes, so that the church itself is to be evaluated typologically as a cross-shaped building, even if that does not find expression in the dimension of the different spatial areas. The bays were all covered with domes. The central dome may have been raised above the other domes, and was probably constructed on squinches. Chronologically, the building is a relatively late foundation and resembles the churches of the sixteenth century in the area of Akhmīm. A small later chapel adjoins on the south side.

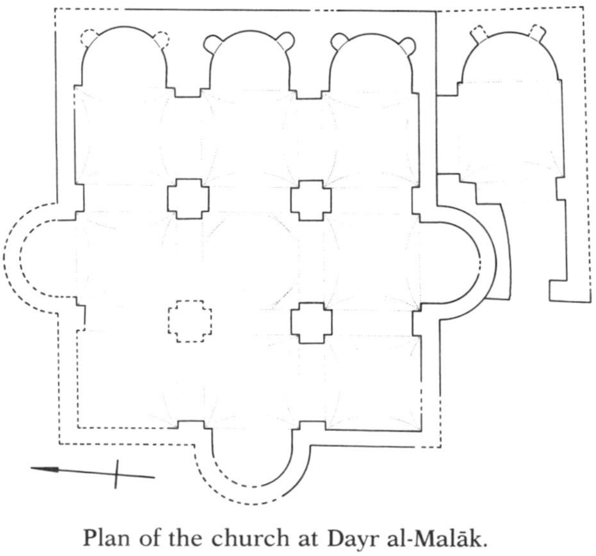

Plan of the church at Dayr al-Malāk.

BIBLIOGRAPHY

Grossmann, P. "Bibliographie." *Byzantinische Zeitschrift* 75 (1982):503.

Mills, A. J. "The Dakhlah Oasis Project." *Journal of the Society for the Study of Egyptian Antiquities* 11 (1981):184–185.

PETER GROSSMANN

DAYR AL-MALĀK. This small monastery is situated on the right bank of the Nile in the part between Qinā and Nag Hammadi where the river flows not from south to north but from east to west. The monastery is thus to the north of the Nile. It is 1 km west of DAYR ANBĀ PALAEMON and near the east side of the town of al-Dābbah.

For want of archaeological investigation, the date of the monastery's foundation cannot be fixed, and no ancient testimony about the monastery exists. It was briefly mentioned by L. T. LEFORT (1939, pp. 386–87). Doresse (1958, p. 148; 1960, p. 131) mentioned it, setting alongside it some tombs where the so-called NAG HAMMADI LIBRARY of Gnostic papyri is said to have been found. O. Meinardus (1965, p. 305; 1977, p. 417) described it briefly.

At present the monastery serves as a church for the Christians of the neighboring town of al-Dābbah and is inhabited by the clergy of the town.

BIBLIOGRAPHY

Doresse, J. *Les Livres secrets des gnostiques d'Egypte.* Paris, 1958. Translated as *The Secret Books of the Egyptian Gnostics.* London, 1960.

Lefort, L. T. "Les Premiers monastères pachômiens: Exploration topographique." *Le Muséon* 52 (1939):379–407.

Meinardus, O. *Christian Egypt, Ancient and Modern.* Cairo, 1965; 2nd ed., 1977.

RENÉ-GEORGES COQUIN
MAURICE MARTIN, S.J.

DAYR AL-MALĀK AL-BAHRI (Cairo). *See* Dayr al-Khandaq.

DAYR AL-MALĀK GHUBRIYĀL. *See* Dayr al-Naqlūn.

DAYR AL-MALĀK MĪKHĀ'ĪL (Akhmīm). [*This article discusses two aspects of Dayr al-Malāk Mīkhā'īl—the history and the architecture.*]

History

This small monastery, of which nothing remains but the church surrounded by an enclosure, is near the village of al-Salāmūnī on the edge of the desert, 1.25 miles (2 km) north of al-Hawāwīsh, on the right bank of the Nile, almost 4 miles (6 km) from Akhmīm.

It seems to have been described by al-MAQRĪZĪ (1853, Vol. 2, p. 504). He called it Dayr Ṣabrā from the name of the Arab tribe that had established itself there. He also noted that it was dedicated to Saint Michael and that it had only a single monk.

O. Meinardus depicted its modern state and gave information about reaching it (1965, pp. 295–96; 1977, pp. 406–407). A pilgrimage unites the Christians of the region each year on the great feasts of Saint Michael: 12 Hātūr and 12 Ba'ūnah (cf. Muyser and Viaud, 1979, pp. 57–58).

BIBLIOGRAPHY

Meinardus, O. *Christian Egypt, Ancient and Modern.* Cairo, 1965; 2nd ed., 1977.

Muyser, J., and G. Viaud. "Les Pèlerinages coptes en Egypte." Bibliothèque d'études coptes 15. Cairo, 1979.

RENÉ-GEORGES COQUIN
MAURICE MARTIN, S.J.

Architecture

The plans of the churches in this and nearby DAYR AL-'ADHRĀ' are similar. Both represent a local form of the medieval hall church with columns (Grossmann, 1982), having originally three sanctuaries and two corner rooms at the east and two rows of five bays divided by columns at the west. Later, another sanctuary and adjacent rooms were added on the north side. The original sanctuaries have the local peculiarity of being deep, with straight sides leading up to curved ends. Another local characteristic is the presence of a vaulted corridor behind the sanctuaries. This church is unique among those of the region in that, although built mainly of brick, it has stone voussoirs in the arches. These appear to be spoils. Several are carved, and one in the door

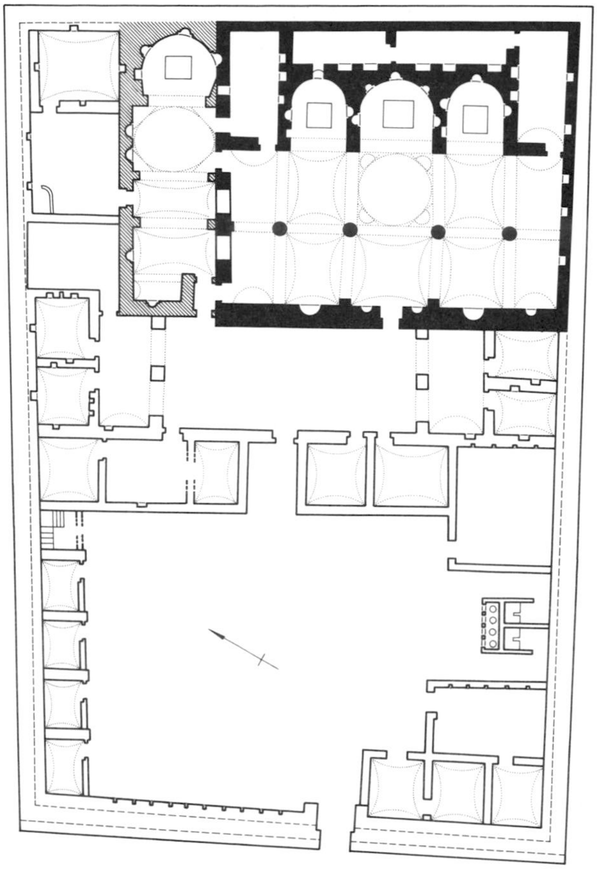

Plan of Dayr al-Malāk Mīkhā'īl near Akhmīm. *Courtesy Peter Grossmann.*

from the northern addition bears a fragmentary Greek inscription. Rooms of a later date have been added along the north side. O. Meinardus recorded a tradition that this monastery was built in the thirteenth century. The spoils suggest an earlier foundation in the area, although other signs point to DAYR AL-SHUHADĀ' at Akhmīm as the earliest of three neighboring structures. The church is at the east of a large courtyard with numerous remains of other monastery buildings: rooms for animals and baking, a fountain house for water, and so on. A separate structure nearby is said to have been built for guests.

BIBLIOGRAPHY

Grossmann, P. *Mittelalterliche Langhauskuppelkirchen und verwandte Typen in Oberägypten.* Glückstadt, 1982.

Meinardus, O. *Christian Egypt, Ancient and Modern.* Cairo, 1965; 2nd ed., 1977.

SHELA MCNALLY

DAYR AL-MALĀK MĪKHĀ'ĪL (Fayyūm). The ruins of this monastery are still visible in the district of Ibshāwāy, in the west of the Fayyūm, in the desert some distance from the village of al-Hamūlī (Meinardus, 1965, pp. 335–36; 1977, pp. 462–63).

In the manuscripts deriving from this monastery, its position is given in terms that differ according to the period, the neighboring village having no doubt changed its name. In the oldest, the monastery is placed "on the border of the desert of the Monē [way station, halting place] of Alli or of Perkethaut," but in the most recent, from the end of the ninth century, "on the border of the desert of Sôpehes" (van Lantschoot, 1929, pp. 7–8).

The existence of this monastery was revealed by a chance discovery in the autumn of 1910, dug up by fellahin in search of *sibākh* (fertilizer deriving from the decomposition of organic matter in a *kom*). Details of the precise circumstances are unfortunately lacking. As often happens in such cases, the finders divided their discovery of writings from an important Coptic library into small lots, breaking up several manuscripts in the hope of securing a larger profit. Hence, it is not known exactly how many codices were found intact in the hiding place: fifty-eight according to Tisserant (1950, p. 219), but sixty according to Hyvernat (1919, p. xiii). A large number of volumes were reassembled by an antique dealer and sent to Paris, where they were bought by an American patron, J. Pierpont Morgan, in 1911. Other manuscripts, more or less complete, were bought by him later. They are now deposited in the Pierpont Morgan Library in New York. However, five manuscripts and some isolated leaves remained in Egypt and are now preserved in the Coptic Museum in Cairo.

Unfortunately, systematic excavation could not be carried out at the site. The only information available about this monastery is given by the colophons, the notes added by the copyists or by readers at the end of the manuscripts: they were published by van Lantschoot (1929, nos. 1–50). Twenty manuscripts are dated between A.D. 823 and 914, but none of the undated codices is later than 914. This indicates at least that the monastery was flourishing during this period. In a Bohairic manuscript from DAYR ANBĀ MAQĀR in Wādī al-Naṭrūn at the Vatican (Coptic 68, fol. 162v), a reader has added a note dated 25 Misrā 730 of Diocletian (i.e., 18 August A.D. 1014). The deacon Joseph, a native of Tuṭūn in the Fayyūm, related that he went to DAYR ANBĀ MAQĀR (Monastery of Saint Macarius) at the time when the churches and monasteries in the Fayyūm were destroyed in the early eleventh century during the reign of al-Ḥākim (Hebbelynck and Van Lantschoot, 1937, Vol. 1, pp. 510–11; Evelyn-White, 1932, pp. 343–45). In fact, no dated Coptic manuscript written in the Fayyūm after A.D. 1007 survives. It therefore seems that the Monastery of Saint Michael at Sôpehes was destroyed at the time of this persecution and that before taking flight, the monks hid their library just where the fellahin found it in 1910.

In addition to the names of the copyists, many of them natives of Tuṭūn, these colophons make known five archimandrites of the monastery: Damien in 822–823; Cosmas and Khael (Michael), two PROESTOS, curiously named together, in 854–855; John in 889 and again no doubt shortly before 901; and Elias at the beginning of the tenth century.

Two other monasteries in the Fayyūm are mentioned, the existence of which would not otherwise be known: that of Saint George at Narmoute (MADĪNAT MĀḌĪ), in the south of the Fayyūm, and that of Saint Epima of Pshante, also at Narmoute, with its archimandrite Papios in 871–872. Also mentioned is the deacon Apa Ioulei, monk of this monastery and master of the school. This provides indirect evidence for a school in this monastery (van Lantschoot, 1929, nos. 13, 26, 44, 49).

BIBLIOGRAPHY

Evelyn-White, H. G. *The Monasteries of the Wadi'n Natrūn*, Pt. 2, *The History of the Monasteries of Nitria and Scetis*. New York, 1932.

Gaselee, S. "Christian Egypt." In *Archaeological Report*, ed. F. L. Griffith, p. 19. 1909–1910.

Hebbelynck, A., and A. van Lantschoot. *Codices Coptici*, Vol. 1, *Codices Coptici Vaticani*. Vatican City, 1937.

Hyvernat, H. "The J. P. Morgan Collection of Coptic Manuscripts." *Journal of Biblical Literature* 31 (1912):54–57.

______. "Coptic Literature: The Morgan Collection." In *The Catholic Encyclopedia*, Vol. 16, pp. 27–29. New York, 1914.

______. *A Check List of Coptic Manuscripts in the Pierpont Morgan Library*. New York, 1919.

Lantschoot, A. van. *Recueil des colophons des manuscrits chrétiens d'Égypte*, Vol. 1, *Les Colophons coptes des manuscrits sahidiques*. Bibliothèque du Muséon 1. Louvain, 1929.

Meinardus, O. *Christian Egypt, Ancient and Modern*. Cairo, 1965; 2nd ed., 1977.

Petersen, T. "The Paragraph Mark in Coptic Illuminated Ornament." In *Studies in Art and Literature for Belle da Costa Greene*, pp. 295–330 (for the Morgan Library, pp. 310–24). Princeton, 1954.

Tisserant, E. "Notes sur la restauration à la Bibliothèque Vaticane des manuscrits coptes de la Pierpont Morgan Library." In *Coptic Studies in Honor of Walter Ewing Crum,* pp. 219–27. Boston, 1950.

RENÉ-GEORGES COQUIN
MAURICE MARTIN, S.J.

DAYR AL-MALĀK MĪKHĀ'ĪL or Dayr Bakhūm (Idfū). This monastery, still in existence, is situated on the left bank of the Nile, almost 4 miles (7 km) west of the town of Idfū, on the slope of a hill in the stony area (*ḥājir* in Arabic) at the foot of the Libyan Mountains. It bears the names of the archangel MICHAEL and of PACHOMIUS in S. CLARKE (1912, pp. 111–13), the first in the body of this work, when Clarke gives its plan, and the second at the end of the book in the Coptic patriarchate's list of the churches (p. 216, no. 12). Daressy (1917, p. 204) thinks that the Dayr Manṣūr (Victor [?]) cited by the *Book of the Hidden Pearls* is identical with this monastery. The atlas of the *Description d'Egypte* (fol. 3; 1821–1829) names it Maḥallet Mangourah (perhaps Marqurah, Mercurius). An English traveler at the beginning of the twentieth century called it the Monastery of Saint George (Weigall, 1910, p. 397). The present monastery was built on the ruins of an ancient monastery, according to Fakhry (1947, p. 47). It is briefly described by Meinardus (1st ed., p. 326; 2nd ed., p. 441). About 1975, monastic life was restored there by a monk who came from DAYR ANBĀ MAQĀR in Wādī al-Naṭrūn.

It should be noted here that the British Library in 1913 and 1923 acquired twenty-two manuscripts, the majority on parchment, dating from the tenth and eleventh centuries, which derive from a Monastery of Saint Mercurius at Idfū (O'Leary, 1923, p. 234; Hyvernat, Vol. 16, pp. 29–30; de Rustafjaell, 1909, passim). If one believes the colophons, these manuscripts come from several monasteries at Idfū: *topos* (church or monastery) of Saint Michael, *topos* of Apa Aaron, the Monastery of Saint Mercurius. This shows that there were formerly several monastic sites at Idfū and that the present Monastery of Saint Bakhūm was not unique in this region.

This monastery was also mentioned by 'ABD AL-MASIḤ ṢALĪB AL-MASŪ'DI AL-BĀRAMŪSĪ (1924, p. 181), who called it Bakhūm.

BIBLIOGRAPHY

'Abd al-Masīḥ Ṣalīb al-Masū'dī al-Bāramūsī. *Kitāb Tuḥfat al-Sā'ilīn fī Dhikr Adyirat Ruhbān al-Miṣriyyin.* Cairo, 1924.

Clarke, S. *Christian Antiquities in the Nile Valley.* Oxford, 1912.

Daressy, G. "Renseignements sur la provenance des stèles coptes du Musée du Cairo." *Annales du Service des antiquités de l'Egypte* 13 (1914):266–71.

______. "Indicateur topographique du 'Livre des perles enfouies et du mystère précieux.'" *Bulletin de l'Institut français d'Archéologie orientale* 13 (1917):175–230, and 14 (1918):1–32.

Description de l'Egypte. Paris, 1821–1829.

Fakhry, A. "A Report of the Inspectorate of Upper Egypt." *Annales du Service des antiquités de l'Egypte* 44 (1947):25–54.

Hyvernat, H. "Coptic Literature." In *The Catholic Encyclopaedia,* Vol. 16, pp. 27–30. New York, 1914.

Meinardus, O. *Christian Egypt, Ancient and Modern.* Cairo, 1965; 2nd ed., 1977.

O'Leary, De L. "Christian Egypt." *Journal of Egyptian Archaeology* 9 (1923):8–26.

Rustafjaell, R. D. de. *The Light of Egypt.* London, 1909.

Weigall, A. E. P. B. *A Guide to the Antiquities of Upper Egypt.* London, 1910.

RENÉ-GEORGES COQUIN
MAURICE MARTIN, S.J.

DAYR AL-MALĀK MĪKHĀ'ĪL (Jirjā). This small monastery, today reduced to its church, was situated on the right bank of the Nile near the village called Naj' al-Dayr (village of the monastery), facing the town of Jirjā on the opposite bank. Since 1910 this site has been celebrated among archaeologists, because the discoveries made there have shed light on the region's prehistory. In fact, the monastery is near prehistoric cemeteries from ancient empires, and the one that adjoins the church still serves for the burial of the Christians of Jirjā.

The first mention of the monastery appears to be that of C. SICARD (1982, Vol. 2, p. 72), who visited it in 1714. He spoke of the place of worship of the Christians of Jirjā, but called it a church, not a monastery. R. Pococke (1743–1745, p. 82) also noted that it was the church of the Christians of Jirjā, who therefore had to cross the Nile. F. L. Norden also noted it (1795–1798, Vol. 2, p. 76). At the beginning of the twentieth century, S. Clarke gave the plan of the *dayr,* and it seems that despite the statements of S. Timm, who confused it with the church of the same name near Akhmīm (1984–1986, Vol. 2, p. 734), Clarke also placed it in his list in the appendix, putting it to the east of Jirjā (1912, pp. 140–41, 214, no. 29). Finally, O. Meinardus described it (1965, pp. 300–301; 1977, pp. 412–13).

In the small ancient necropolis in the cliff that overhangs the monastery, a chapel (perhaps) and a quarry were occupied by a hermit who has left his name: Samuel Koui (the Small). The Greek and Coptic graffiti were collected by A. H. Sayce (1885–1886, pp. 175–77; 1890, pp. 62–65). One of these inscriptions was discussed again by G. Lefebvre (1907, p. 68).

In the sixteenth century Jean Léon l'Africain related that a Monastery of Saint George situated 6 miles (10 km) south of Munsia (al-Minshāh) was in his time one of the largest and richest in Egypt. More than two hundred monks lived there, but it had been depopulated a century earlier by the plague and the bedouin had installed themselves on "the vast cultivated lands and the meadows" of the monastery, which was said to have been the origin of the town of Jirjā. One remains a little skeptical about this story: it seems an etymological fantasy, for it is known that Jirjā is very ancient and owes its name not to Saint George but to a pharaonic word (*djerdjé or kerkè;* establishment or hunting land). For the rest, no monastery or church of Saint George is known near Jirjā, and that of Saint Michael is the only one that is close to Jirjā. But none of its five altars is dedicated to Saint George, which could have been a vestige of an ancient entitlement of the monastery (Léon l'Africain, 1956, Vol. 2, p. 536).

BIBLIOGRAPHY

Clarke, S. *Christian Antiquities in the Nile Valley.* Oxford, 1912.
Jean Léon l'Africain. *La Description de l'Afrique,* ed. A. Epaullard. Paris, 1956.
Lefevbre, G. *Recueil des inscriptions grecques-chrétiennes d'Egypte.* Cairo, 1907.
Meinardus, O. *Christian Egypt, Ancient and Modern.* Cairo, 1965; 2nd ed., 1977.
Norden, F. L. *Voyage d'Egypte et de Nubie,* 3 vols. Paris, 1795–1798.
Pococke, R. *A Description of the East and Some Other Countries.* London, 1743–1745.
Sayce, A. H. "Coptic and Early Christian Inscriptions in Upper Egypt." *Proceedings of the Society of Biblical Archaeology* 8 (1885–1886):175–91.
______. "Gleanings from the Land of Egypt." *Recueil de Travaux* 13 (1890):62–67, 20 (1898): 111–112, 169–76.
Sicard, C. *Oeuvres,* ed. S. Sauneron and M. Martin, 3 vols. Bibliothèque d'étude 83–85. Cairo, 1982.
Timm, S. *Das christlich-koptische Ägypten in arabischer Zeit.* Wiesbaden, 1984–1986.

RENÉ-GEORGES COQUIN
MAURICE MARTIN, S.J.

DAYR AL-MALĀK MĪKHĀ'ĪL (Marāghah). ABŪ ṢĀLIḤ THE ARMENIAN (1895, p. 257) mentioned a monastery dedicated to the archangel MICHAEL near the town of al-Marāghah. Al-Idrisī (Vol. 1, p. 124) knew a town of this name near Antinoë (ANTINOOPOLIS), but the *State of the Provinces* in A.H. 777/A.D. 1375 placed it as it is now, in the district of Suhāj. It was then called al-Marāghāt (cf. Ramzī, 1953–1968, Vol. 2, pt. 4, p. 24). The name appears to be Arabic, not Egyptian (Gauthier, 1905, pp. 75–76). Al-Maqrīzī (1853, Vol. 2, p. 519) noted a church there, but did not say to which saint it was dedicated.

BIBLIOGRAPHY

'Abd al-Laṭīf. *Relation de l'Egypte de 'Abd al-Latif,* trans. and ed. A. I. S. de Sacy, Paris, 1810. *L'Etat des provinces* is translated in an appendix.
Gauthier, H. "Notes géographiques sur le nome Panopolite." *Bulletin de l'Institut français d'Archéologie orientale* 4 (1905):39–101.
Idrīsī al-Sarīf, al-. *Kitāb Nuzhat al-Mushtāq* (Book of the pleasures of the eager—dissertation of geography). French trans. P. A. Jaubert in 2 vols. Recueil de Voyages et de mémoires publiés par la Société de Géographie 5–6. Paris, 1836–1840. Repr. 1975.
Ramzī, M. *Al-Qāmūs al-Jughrāfī lil-Bilād al Miṣrīyyah,* 3 vols. Cairo, 1953–1968.

RENÉ-GEORGES COQUIN
MAURICE MARTIN, S.J.

DAYR AL-MALĀK MĪKHĀ'ĪL (Naj' al-Dayr), monastery slightly to the east of the village of Naj' al-Dayr, which is about 22 miles (35 km) south of Akhmīm. There are a church, a cemetery, and a few houses nearby but no other remaining monastery buildings. The church may originally have been a typical hall church with columns (see Grossmann, 1982, pp. 196ff.; he assigns this to his second group). The oldest part consists of three nearly rectangular sanctuaries flanked by rectangular corner rooms. The middle sanctuary is larger than the others. All three have an eastern niche covered by a fine, shell-decorated half-dome. West of these five original rooms are two rows of bays, subdivided by three columns and one pier. The three additional bays at the southwest and two asymmetrical entrances may represent later alterations. Other changes include the reshaping of the southeastern corner room and the addition of a sixth room at the northeast, with a bay west of it. Perhaps at the same time a separate building, containing a large LAQQĀN (mandatum tank) and a well, was added north of the church. It is difficult to establish a date for this church. Since a monastery at this place is mentioned in the early sixteenth century, it may belong to this period.

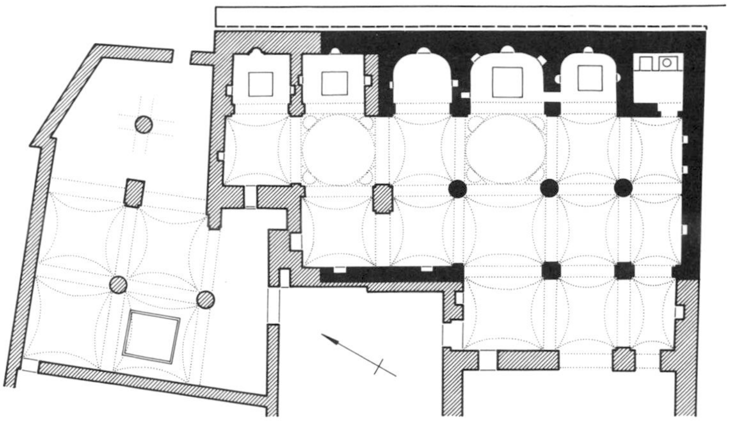

Plan of the church at Dayr al-Malak Mīkhā'īl near Najʿ al-Dayr. *Courtesy Peter Grossmann.*

BIBLIOGRAPHY

Clarke, S. *Christian Antiquities in the Nile Valley,* pp. 140ff., pl. 41, 2. Oxford, 1912.

Grossmann, P. *Mittelalterliche Langhauskuppelkirchen und verwandte Typen in Oberägypten,* p. 211. Glückstadt, 1982.

Meinardus, O. *Christian Egypt: Ancient and Modern,* pp. 300–301. Cairo, 1965.

Timm, S. *Das christlich-koptische Ägypten in arabischer Zeit,* Vol. 2, pp. 733–34. Wiesbaden, 1984.

SHELA MCNALLY

DAYR AL-MALĀK MĪKHĀ'ĪL (Naqādah). The strip of stony ground (*ḥājir* in Arabic) that separates the cultivated land from the Libyan Mountains on the left bank and extends from Naqādah to Qamūlah was called Jabal al-Aṣāṣ and was known to the Copts as the Mountain of Tsenti. This strip of about 6 miles (10 km) includes no fewer than eight monasteries, of which six were on the edge of the desert and two are cut into the rock.

The first of these monasteries is that of Saint Michael. It is 5 miles (8 km) southwest of Naqādah. It is situated within an ancient cemetery that extends some distance to the north. It contains two churches, of which the one situated to the southwest of the enclosure is completely ruined. Its church was mentioned by S. Clarke (1912, p. 215, n. 9). A good description was given by O. Meinardus (1965, pp. 311–12; 1977, p. 426).

BIBLIOGRAPHY

Clarke, S. *Christian Antiquities in the Nile Valley.* Oxford, 1912.

Meinardus, O. *Christian Egypt, Ancient and Modern.* Cairo, 1965; 2nd ed., 1977.

RENÉ-GEORGES COQUIN
MAURICE MARTIN, S.J.

DAYR AL-MALĀK MĪKHĀ'ĪL (Qamūlah). [*The first section of this entry discusses the location and history of this monastery. The second section addresses what little is known concerning the architecture.*]

History

This monastery, the most southerly of those on the left bank of the Nile between Naqādah and Qamūlah, is situated on the edge of the desert, less than a mile (1 km) from the cultivated lands and about 2 miles (3 km) from the town of Qiblī Qamūlah. A map published in 1943 and 1954 calls it Dayr Qamūlah al-Qiblī, no doubt in contrast to DAYR MĀR BUQṬUR, which it designates as Dayr Buqṭur al-Baḥarī (of the north).

It does indeed seem that this is the one named by ABŪ ṢĀLIḤ THE ARMENIAN (1895, pp. 283–84) at the beginning of the thirteenth century. According to this author, it is also called Dayr al-ʿAyn because of a neighboring well, the water of which was renowned.

Fathers Protais and François in 1668 spoke of five monasteries on the left bank at Naqādah, but named only three (Sauneron, 1974, p. 93). J. Vansleb, who was unable to go beyond Jirjā, copied their text and naturally named only three monasteries (1677, p. 411; 1678, p. 246). C. Sicard did not speak of it. In his list of the Coptic churches, S. Clarke named it as a church dependent on Qamūlah (1912, p. 216, no. 5); likewise, ʿABD AL-MASĪḤ ṢALĪB pointed out the monastery and remarked that its church was served by the clergy of Qamūlah

(1924, p. 180). O. Meinardus (1965, pp. 309–310; 1977, p. 423) described its modern state, mentioning two churches, one to the north and the other to the south of the monastery. Clarke (pp. 121–23) gave the plan of the more ancient church, that of the north, and A. J. Butler reproduced the plan drawn by Sir Arthur Gordon (1884, Vol. 1, p. 360).

BIBLIOGRAPHY

'Abd al-Masīḥ Ṣalīb al-Masū'dī al-Baramūsī. *Kitāb Tuḥfat al-Sā'ilīn fī Dhikr Adyirat Ruhbān al-Miṣriyyin.* Cairo, 1924.

Butler, A. J. *The Ancient Coptic Churches of Egypt,* 2 vols. Oxford, 1895.

Clarke, S. *Christian Antiquities in the Nile Valley.* Oxford, 1912.

Meinardus, O. *Christian Egypt, Ancient and Modern.* Cairo, 1965; 2nd ed., 1977.

Sauneron, S. *Villes et légendes d'Egypte.* Cairo, 1974.

Vansleb, J. M. *Nouvelle relation en forme de journal d'un voyage fait en Egypte en 1672 et 1673.* Paris, 1677. Translated as *The Present State of Egypt.* London, 1678.

RENÉ-GEORGES COQUIN
MAURICE MARTIN, S.J.

Architecture

The old church of the monastery belongs typologically to the last phase of development in Egyptian church building, in which the area of the naos is divided into nine equal-sized domed chambers (bays). It is distinguished from the very late churches of this type, deriving only from modern times, through the presence of a *khūrus* (room between the naos and the sanctuary), which was later abandoned. The only noteworthy feature in this building is the semicircular terminations on the narrow sides of the *khūrus.* In conjunction with the eastern apse, they unite into the architectural form of a triconch, which enjoyed particular favor in the early Christian architecture of Egypt, but is here no more than a late reminiscence. In later times, altars were installed in the apse side rooms, while the side doors of the *khūrus* were walled up. The monastery is mentioned by Abū Ṣalīḥ, 1895, fol. 104a; not to be confused with the second Monastery of Saint Michael, mentioned in fol. 104b and otherwise known as DAYR AL-MAJMA'). The present church, however, did not yet exist in his time, but may have been erected in the fourteenth century at the earliest. The small chapel on the north side belongs to modern times. It now lies in ruins.

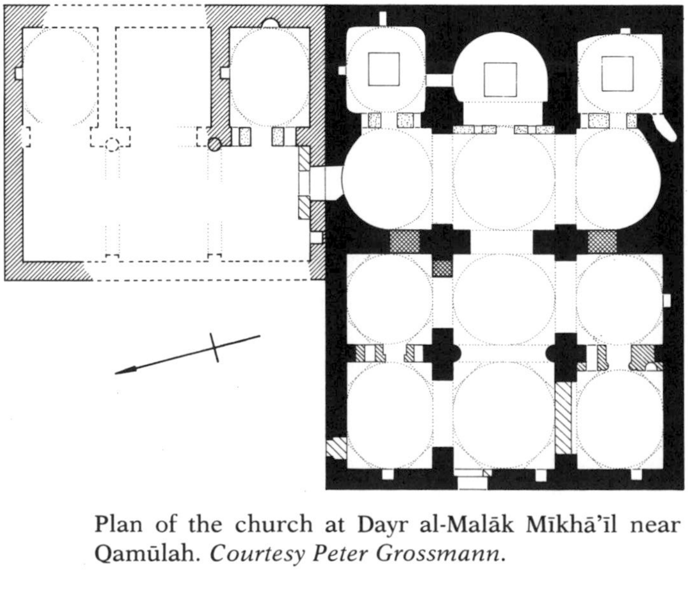

Plan of the church at Dayr al-Malāk Mīkhā'īl near Qamūlah. *Courtesy Peter Grossmann.*

BIBLIOGRAPHY

Clarke, S. *Christian Antiquities in the Nile Valley,* pp. 121–23. Oxford, 1912.

Grossmann, P. *Mittelalterliche Langhauskuppelkirchen und verwandte Typen in Oberägypten,* pp. 200–202. Glückstadt, 1982.

Monneret de Villard, U. *Dayr al-Muḥarraqah,* p. 13. Milan, 1928.

Timm, S. *Das christlich-koptische Ägypten in arabischer Zeit,* Vol. 2, pp. 734–37. Wiesbaden, 1984.

PETER GROSSMANN

DAYR AL-MALĀK MĪKHĀ'ĪL (Qinā). *See* Monasteries of the Upper Ṣa'īd.

DAYR AL-MALĀK MĪKHĀ'ĪL (Quṣ). *See* Monasteries of the Upper Ṣa'īd.

DAYR AL-MALĀK MĪKHĀ'ĪL (al-Rayramūn). This monastery is no doubt the same as the one mentioned by al-MAQRĪZĪ (1853, Vol. 2, p. 506) as being at al-Rayramūn, although he says it is dedicated to Saint Gabriel. In 1714 the Jesuit C. SICARD (1982, Vol. 2, p. 100) visited it. Nothing remained but a church, the monastery having been transformed into a village. F. L. Norden (1795–1798, Vol. 2, p. 46) also mentioned it. In the *Description de l'Egypte* (Jomard, 1820–1826, Vol. 4, p. 321), Jomard also called it Dayr al-'Aysh, and he referred to the village near al-Rayramūn as Dayr Reiramun. The church of al-Rayramūn was called Dayr al-Malāk Mīkhā'īl by S. CLARKE (1912, p. 208, no. 30).

BIBLIOGRAPHY

Clarke, S. *Christian Antiquities in the Nile Valley.* London, 1912.

Description de l'Egypte, Vol. 4. Paris, 1821–1829.

Norden, F. L. *Voyage d'Egypte et de Nubie,* ed. L. Langlès, 3 vols. Paris, 1795–1798.

Sicard, C. *Oeuvres,* Vol. 2, ed. S. Sauneron and M. Martin. Bibliothèque d'étude 84. Cairo and Paris, 1982.

RENÉ-GEORGES COQUIN
MAURICE MARTIN, S.J.

DAYR MANĀWUS. *See* Dayr al-Shuhadā' (Isnā).

DAYR MĀR BUQṬUR (Jeme). *See* Monasteries of the Upper Ṣa'īd.

DAYR MĀR BUQṬUR (Naqādah). *See* Dayr al-Malāk Mīkhā'īl (Qamūlah).

DAYR MĀR BUQṬUR (Qamūlah). [*This entry consists of two articles:* History *and* Architecture.]

History

This famous monastery is situated on the left bank of the Nile to the west of Qamūlah. It is without doubt the one mentioned in the thirteenth-century *Churches and Monasteries of Egypt.*

It is known above all because of one of its monks, Athanasius, who became bishop of Qūṣ in the fourteenth century. He was present at Dayr Mār Buqṭur and signed the record of the proceedings as a witness at the enthronement of Timothy, bishop of Qaṣr Ibrīm.

The monastery is named by the seventeenth-century Fathers Protais and François (see Sauneron, 1974, p. 93). J. Vansleb followed their text, being unable to pass beyond Jirjā (1677, p. 411; English ed., 1678, p. 246). In 1718 C. Sicard visited it and wrote his account (1982, Vol. 2, p. 227).

It had only a single church, noted by S. Clarke (1912, pp. 123–26). It escaped total destruction in 1917.

BIBLIOGRAPHY

Clarke, S. *Christian Antiquities in the Nile Valley.* Oxford, 1912.

Coquin, R.-G. "A propos des rouleaux coptes-arabes de l'évêque Timothée." *Bibliotheca Orient.* 34 (1977):142–47.

Mallon, A. "Une Ecole de savants égyptiens au Moyen-Age." *Mélanges de la Faculté orientale de Beyrouth* 1 (1906):109–131; 2 (1907):213–64.

Meinardus, O. *Christian Egypt, Ancient and Modern.* Cairo, 1965; 2nd ed., 1977.

Plumley, J. M. *The Scrolls of Bishop Timotheos.* Texts from Excavation, First Memoir. London, 1975.

Sauneron, S. *Villes et légendes d'Egypte.* Cairo, 1974.

Sicard, C. *Oeuvres,* 3 vols. Bibliothèque d'études 82–85, ed. S. Sauneron and M. Martin. Cairo, 1982.

Vansleb, J. M. *Nouvelle relation en forme de journal d'un voyage fait en Egypte en 1672 et 1673.* Paris, 1677. Translated as *The Present State of Egypt.* London, 1678.

RENÉ-GEORGES COQUIN
MAURICE MARTIN, S.J.

Architecture

Dayr Mār Buqṭur is now an uninhabited monastic complex surrounded by a wall. Only the old church merits some attention. In this building several phases can be detected. The oldest building to be erected in this spot was a basilica built of mud bricks. Only the outer walls of its naos have been preserved, however. On the basis of the shape of the niches contained in these walls, the church may be dated to the eighth or ninth century. Toward the end of the twelfth century, the church was transformed into a domed oblong church, of which the naos was covered by two domes, with a larger dome above the anterior bay of the nave and a smaller dome over the rear. To the east of the nave was a *khūrus* (room between the naos and the sanctuary) subdivided by transverse arches into three bays of equal size, each covered by a sail vault. In the same way, the three rooms of the eastern sanctuary were originally of approximately the same size. The rooms found there today came into being in modern times, when the church was enlarged toward the north. North of the church is an external portico dating perhaps from the Mamluk period. The bays of this portico were covered originally with genuine pendentive domes that have all fallen down. Examples of this type of dome are rare in

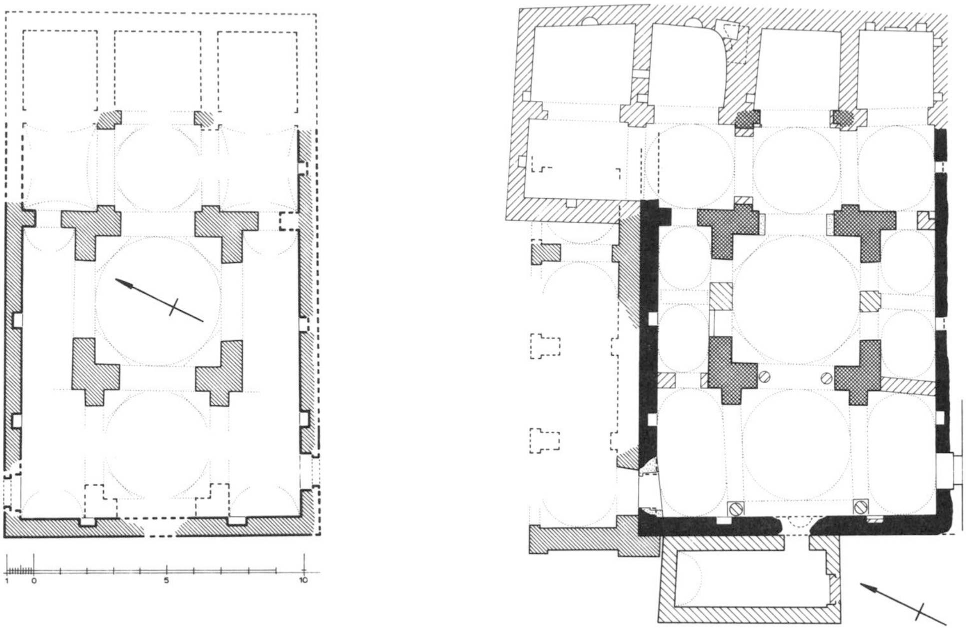

Plans of the old church at Dayr Mār Buqṭur showing successive stages of construction. *Courtesy Peter Grossmann.*

Egypt. At the southwest edge of the monastery are a couple of derelict mausoleums from the Ottoman period.

BIBLIOGRAPHY

Butler, A. J. *The Ancient Coptic Churches of Egypt*, Vol. 1, pp. 359–61. Oxford, 1884; repr., 1920.

Clarke, S. *Christian Antiquities in the Nile Valley*, pp. 123–26. Oxford, 1912.

Grossmann, P. *Mittelalterliche Langhauskuppelkirchen in Oberägypten*, pp. 26–31. Glückstadt, 1982.

Monneret de Villard, U. *Dayr el-Muḥaraqah*, p. 3. Milan, 1928.

Patricolo, A. "Couvents coptes de Nagada." *Bulletin du Comité de conservation des monuments de l'art arabe* 32 (1915–1919):703–705.

Vansleb, J. M. *Nouvelle relation en forme de journal d'un voyage fait en Egypte en 1672 et 1673*. Paris, 1977.

PETER GROSSMANN

DAYR MĀR BUQṬUR (Qifṭ). *See* Monasteries of the Upper Ṣaʿīd.

DAYR MĀR BUQṬUR (Qūṣ). *See* Dayr Abū Sayfayn (Qūṣ).

DAYR MĀR HANNĀ. *See* Dayr al-Ṭīn.

DAYR MĀR JIRJIS (Babylon). *See* Babylon.

DAYR MĀR JIRJIS (Dimiqrāṭ), monastery dedicated to Saint George on the left bank of the Nile, halfway between Luxor and Isnā on the edge of the desert, 2½ miles (4 km) to the west of the village of Naj' al-Dimiqriyyah, which occupies the site of the ancient al-Dimiqrāt.

The name al-Dimiqrāt is attested by a colophon of 960, in the form "Tmikra, in the nome of Armant" (Lantschoot, 1929, Vol. 1, p. 204), which Winlock and Crum (1926, Vol. 1, p. 122) proposes to identify with the bishopric of the same name, which is mentioned in certain geographical lists (Munier, 1939, p. 216).

The name is also attested to in a miracle that benefited a monk of this monastery, dating after the thirteenth century; the neighboring village is called al-Dimiqrāt (Crum, 1926, p. 205). It is mentioned again in connection with a bishop of Armant who is named in the council held at Cairo in 1086 under the patriarchate of CYRIL II (1078–1092). The village is also known as the birthplace of the Patriarch BENJAMIN II (1327–1339).

Since the beginning of the nineteenth century, the village has been called Najʻ al-Dimiqriyyah. It is also mentioned under the name of al-Dimiqrāt by ABŪ AL-MAKĀRIM at the end of the twelfth century.

This monastery is still a place of pilgrimage much frequented from 1 to 7 Hatūr, ending with the feast of Saint George the martyr of Alexandria.

BIBLIOGRAPHY

Lantschoot, A. van. *Recueil des colophons des manuscrits chrétiens,* Vol. 1: *Les Colophons coptes des manuscrits sahidiques.* Bibliothèque du Muséon 1. Louvain, 1929.

Munier, H. *Bulletin de la Société d'archéologie copte* 5 (1939):201–43.

Muyser, J., and G. Viaud. *Les Pèlerinages coptes en Egypte.* Bibliothèque d'études coptes 15. Cairo, 1979.

Winlock, H. E., and W. E. Crum. *The Monastery of Epiphanius at Thebes,* 2 vols. New York, 1926.

RENÉ-GEORGES COQUIN
MAURICE MARTIN, S.J.

DAYR MĀR JIRJIS (Naqādah) *See* Dayr al-Majmaʻ.

DAYR MĀR JIRJIS (Qifṭ). *See* Monasteries of the Upper Ṣaʻīd.

DAYR MĀR JIRJIS (Sadamant-Fayyūm), monastery dedicated to Saint George about 15 miles (25 km) south of Madīnat al-Fayyūm, northeast of the village called Sidmant al-Jabal, on the left bank of the Baḥr Yūsuf. It lies on the eastern edge of the Jabal al-Naqlūn, on the rim of the Nile Valley.

There is no evidence of its existence before the thirteenth century. A Coptic theologian, BUṬRUS AL-SIDMANTĪ (or al-Sadamantī), author of several famous works, one of them dated to 1260, lived in this monastery.

The encyclopedist Abū al-Barakāt IBN KABAR (fourteenth century) cites the peculiar ordo of the monks of Dayr Mār Jirjis at Sadamant, according to which they recited the entire Psalter every day (Villecourt, 1924, p. 232).

Al-MAQRĪZĪ (d. 1441) devotes some lines to this monastery, but remarks that it had lost much of its past prosperity, and that its inhabitants were few in number.

An Arabic manuscript in the Coptic Patriarchate, Cairo (Theology 13), was copied in 1849 by Isḥāq, officiating priest of Dayr Mār Jirjis at Sidmant.

The church and the neighboring cells were built in 1914. However, some ancient capitals at the entrance to the church and marble debris in the precincts bear witness to the antiquity of the site.

Every year toward Ascension, the feast of Saint George is celebrated at the monastery, an event that draws a great crowd (Muyser-Viaud, 1979, pp. 43–44).

BIBLIOGRAPHY

Abbot, N. *The Monasteries of the Fayyūm.* Studies in Ancient Oriental Civilization 16. Chicago, 1937.

Amélineau, E. *La Géographie de l'Egypte à l'époque copte.* Paris, 1893.

Muyser, J., and G. Viaud. *Les Pèlerinages coptes en Egypte.* Bibliothèque d'études coptes 15. Cairo, 1979.

Salmon, G. "Répertoire géographique de la province du Fayyoûm d'après le Kitâb Târîkh al-Fayyoûm d'an-Nâboulsī." *Bulletin de l'Institut français d'archéologie orientale* 1 (1901):29–77.

Van den Acker, P. *Buṭrus as-Sadamentī. Introduction sur l'herméneutique.* Recherches, n.s., fasc. B1. Beirut, 1972.

Vansleb, J. M. *Histoire de l'église d'Alexandrie.* Paris, 1677.

Villecourt, L. "Les observances liturgiques et la discipline du jeûne dans l'église copte." *Le Muséon* 37 (1924):201–280.

RENÉ-GEORGES COQUIN
MAURICE MARTIN, S.J.

DAYR MĀR JIRJIS AL-HADĪDĪ. [*This entry consists of two articles:* History *and* Architecture.]

History

This monastery, which like many others has become a Christian village inhabited by Coptic priests and their families, is situated near the right bank of the Nile about 5 miles (8 km) south of Akhmīm. We cannot say at what date it was founded, but it was established in honor of two Syrians martyred at the same place, probably Eulogius and Arsenius. The cult of these martyrs appears to be old, for one reads their names on several objects, such as a lamp found at Karnak and an ostracon in the collection of the Egypt Exploration Fund (Crum, 1902, p. 5, no. 26). Their feast (16 Kiyahk) is the same in both the SYNAXARION of the Copts from Upper Egypt and the *typica* of the White Monastery (DAYR ANBĀ SHINŪDAH). There is also a mention of their feast in a manuscript in the British Library (Crum, 1905, p. 154).

The present buildings were restored in 1870. G. Steindorff (in Baedeker, 2nd ed., 1902, p. 220) thought that the true name was Dayr Mār Jirjis al-Ḥadīthi (Mar Jirjis the younger), and S. Timm has recently believed that he was right (1984–1986, Vol. 2, pp. 713–14); but the titular saint of this monastery cannot be Saint George the younger, for two reasons.

First, the adjective *ḥadīdī* (of iron) refers to the word *dayr*, an allusion to the iron-covered entrance gate, and not to the saint. Besides, this saint did not receive the adjective *al-ḥadīthi* but *al-jadīd* (the new), more familiar to Egyptian Arabic.

Second, the dates of the *mawlids* (pilgrimages) are 7 Hatūr and 23 Baramūdah, which are the dates of the feast and of the consecration of the church of the great Saint George (of Cappadocia). The feast of the tenth-century Egyptian martyr George is on 19 Ba'ūnah.

Among the European travelers who mention the monastery are R. Pococke (1743–1745, p. 81), M. Jullien (1903, p. 275), and H. Munier (1940, pp. 157–58). S. Clarke set out the plan of the church and noted it in his list of the churches, reproduced from a list of the Coptic Patriarchate, Cairo (1912, pp. 142–44, 213, no. 13, and pl. 42, 1). Meinardus gives a good description (1965, pp. 298–99; 1977, pp. 410–11). Recently it has been the object, both from an architectural and from a sociological point of view, of the work of the architect Nessim Henry Henein (see the notes of Sauneron, 1972, pp. 209–210).

This monastery is still a place of pilgrimage for the feasts of Saint George (Muyser and Viaud, 1979, pp. 58–59).

BIBLIOGRAPHY

Clarke, S. *Christian Antiquities in the Nile Valley*, p. 142. Oxford, 1912.

Crum, W. E. *Coptic Ostraca from the Collections of the Egypt Exploration Fund.* London, 1902.

______. *Catalogue of the Coptic Manuscripts in the British Museum.* London, 1905.

Jullien, M. "Quelques anciens couvents de l'Egypte." *Missions Catholiques* 35 (1903):188–90, 198–202, 212–14, 237–40, 250–52, 257–58, 274–76, and 283–84.

Meinardus, O. *Christian Egypt, Ancient and Modern.* Cairo, 1965; 2nd ed., 1977.

Munier, H. "Les Monuments coptes d'après l'explorations de Père Michel Jullien." *Bulletin de la Société d'archéologie copte* 6 (1940):141–68.

Muyser, J., and G. Viaud. *Les Pèlerinages coptes en Egypte.* Bibliothèque d'études coptes, 15. Cairo, 1979.

Pococke, R. *A Description of the East and Some Other Countries.* London, 1743–1745.

Sauneron, S. "Travaux de l'Institut français d'archéologie orientale 1971–1972." *Bulletin de l'Institut français d'Archéologie orientale* 71 (1972):189–230.

Steindorff, G. In *Ägypten und der Sudan*, 2nd ed., ed. Baedeker. Leipzig, 1902.

Timm, S. *Das christlich-koptische Ägypten in arabischer Zeit*, Vol. 2, pp. 713–14. Wiesbaden, 1984.

RENÉ-GEORGES COQUIN
MAURICE MARTIN, S.J.

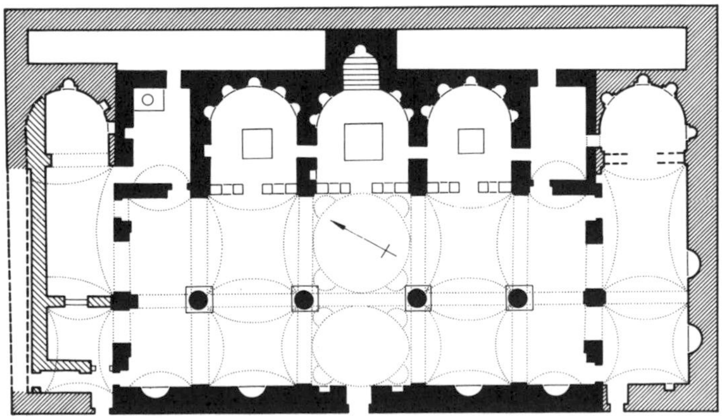

Plan of the church at Dayr Mār Jirjis al-Ḥadīdī. *Courtesy Peter Grossmann.*

Architecture

Within an enclosure wall stand several houses, an inner partition wall setting off the priest's house, and at the east the church, which has a central door and two side doors. The central doorway is decorated with lozenge-shaped bricks set in star patterns. The oldest part of the church is five units wide and three deep, a typical hall church with columns of the medieval period (see Grossmann, 1982, p. 196). There are three sanctuaries flanked by rectangular corner rooms. The sanctuaries are of a local type with straight walls leading to semicircles articulated by niches. Behind the altar in the central sanctuary is a bishop's throne. Domes on squinches cover the two bays in front of the central sanctuary; domes on pendentives, the bays in front of the side sanctuaries. The outer bays are barrel-vaulted. During a second building phase, two bays and a sanctuary were added to both the north and the south sides, making a wide, shallow, seven-by-three-unit interior. Perhaps at this time two corridors were added along the east end, divided by the space containing the bishop's throne (for such corridors in local churches, see DAYR AL-'ADHRĀ' near Akhmīm). In front of the central sanctuary stands a finely inlaid wooden iconostasis. The two original side sanctuaries are closed off by brick walls with cross-shaped openings at the top, central doors, and side windows. Header-stretcher construction in fired brick is apparently employed throughout the whole building, at present whitewashed. Hollow tubes admitting sunlight are set into all the domes and vaults, as at Saint Thomas near Akhmīm. Several spolia are to be found: a column forms the threshold of the doorway into the immediate forecourt of the church, and stone slabs are used for thresholds in the interior.

BIBLIOGRAPHY

Grossmann, P. *Langhauskuppelkirchen und verwandte Typen in Oberägypten.* Glückstadt, 1982.

Meinardus, O. *Christian Egypt, Ancient and Modern,* pp. 298–99. Cairo, 1965.

Munier, H. "Une Lampe chrétienne de Karnak." *Annales du Service des Antiquités de l'Egypte* 17 (1917):160–62.

Timm, S. *Das christlich-koptische Ägypten in arabischer Zeit,* Vol. 2, pp. 713–14. Wiesbaden, 1984.

SHELA MCNALLY

DAYR MĀR KYRIAKOS. *See* Monasteries of the Upper Ṣa'īd.

DAYR MĀR MĪNĀ (Gharbiyyah). The mention of a hermitage of recluses at Ibyār in the Gharbiyyah Province appears for the first time in A.D. 1118 when Mercurius, a recluse located there, was proposed for election to the bishopric of Miṣr (Old Cairo). In 1216, after the death of the Patriarch JOHN VI, an unnamed recluse from Ibyār was proposed as his successor. In 1221, the sultan al-Malik al-Kāmil ibn 'Ādil was cured by a recluse from Ibyār and therefore wanted to have him elected patriarch; the recluse refused. In 1223, during a long vacancy of the patriarchal seat, a recluse (possibly the same) from Ibyār was again proposed for election.

Abū al-Makārim (1177–1204) places Ibyār in the Jazīrat Banī Naṣr, which at that time was a province to the southwest of the Delta, bounded in the west by the Rosetta branch of the Nile and in the east by the canal called al-Bājūriyyah. Ibyār was its principal town (Maspero and Wiet, 1919, p. 3). Abū al-Makārim identifies it with old Niqyūs, which is inaccurate (Guest, 1912, p. 959 and map), since Niqyūs is situated by the historians in the south of the province of Jazīrat Banī Naṣr, while Ibyār was in the north. Abū al-Makārim estimates that there were several churches in the town, and locates in the northern part of its district a church dedicated to Saint Menas, including a hermitage of recluses, surrounded by a wall.

In the eighteenth century, C. Sicard mentioned "the monastery of Saint Mennas" outside the town which he sites "two short leagues north east of Cafre Zaiat on the Nile" (1982, Vol. 3, p. 110).

The monastery still exists under the name of Dayr Mār Mīnā al-Ḥabīs (Monastery of Saint Menas the Recluse). This designation may perpetuate the name of a recluse called Menas, or it may confuse Ibyār with Niqyūs, the birthplace of the great martyr according to the *Encomium* of the Patriarch JOHN III (Drescher, 1946, p. 131) and the SYNAXARION for 15 Hatūr. The church is still famous for an annual pilgrimage on 15 Ba'ūnah, the date of the discovery of the relics of Saint Menas at Maryūt, which might indicate that the saint traditionally venerated at Ibyār is not a local saint, but the martyr of Maryūt (Muyser and Viaud, 1982, pp. 29–30).

BIBLIOGRAPHY

Drescher, J. *Apa Mena (textes et documents).* Cairo, 1946.

Guest, R. "The Delta in the Middle Ages." *Journal of the Royal and Asiatic Society* (1912):941–80.

Maspero, J., and G. Wiet. *Matériaux pour servir à la géographie de l'Egypte.* Mémoires de l'Institut français d'archéologie orientale, 36. Cairo, 1919.

Muyser, J., and G. Viaud. *Les Pèlerinages coptes en Egypte.* Bibliothèque d'études coptes 15. Cairo, 1979.

Sicard, C. *Oeuvres,* 3 vols., ed. M. Martin. Bibliothèque d'Etudes 85. Cairo, 1982.

RENÉ-GEORGES COQUIN
MAURICE MARTIN, S.J.

DAYR MĀR MĪNĀ (Hiw/Nag Hammadi), monastery-village just south of the town of Hiw on the Left Bank of the Nile, at the edge of the desert but still in the cultivated area. It is today inhabited by secular priests and their families. It appears that it was already in existence in the fifteenth century, for we are informed of its church by al-MAQRĪZĪ (d. 1441).

In 1668 this monastery was mentioned by the Capuchins Protais and François (see Sauneron, 1973, p. 95). This church is also cited as being in the district of Nag Hammadi by S. Clarke (1912, p. 216, no. 1). Meinardus gives a good description of it (1965, pp. 302–3; 1977, pp. 415–16); the earliest date he noticed was 1729, carved in the enclosure of the sanctuary.

BIBLIOGRAPHY

Clarke, S. *Christian Antiquities in the Nile Valley.* Oxford, 1912.

Meinardus, O. *Christian Egypt, Ancient and Modern.* Cairo, 1965. 2nd ed., 1977.

Sauneron, S. *Villes et légendes d'Egypte.* Cairo, 1974.

RENÉ-GEORGES COQUIN
MAURICE MARTIN, S.J.

DAYR MĀR MĪNĀ (Jabal Abū Fūdah), monastery famous for its picturesque character. It hangs on a cliff on the south of the Jabal Abū Fūdah opposite Manfalūṭ. Its situation in caves high up and the method of approaching it by means of a chain and walks hollowed into the rock have led to several travelers' calling it Dayr al-Bakarah (monastery of the pulley). This creates some confusion with the Dayr al-Ṭayr near Minyā, which is also called Dayr al-Bakarah.

The most ancient author who speaks of this monastery seems to be al-MAQRĪZĪ (d. 1441). He calls it "monastery of the cave of Shaqalqīl." This is the name of an island and of a village near it. He notes its situation and its mode of access. He also writes that it is dedicated to Saint Menas and indicates the day of his feast. Since there is no village nearby that could serve as a geographical landmark, al-Maqrīzī gives it the name "the cave of Shaqalqīl" because near the monastery there was a cave famous for the heaps of mummified fish of which he speaks elsewhere (some references on this subject will be found in Maspero and Wiet, 1919, p. 114).

This monastery is mentioned by some travelers. The first European who passed this way appears to have been J. Vansleb, who noted "the monastery of Saint Menas surnamed the thaumaturge at . . ." The placename is left blank by the author, who did not know al-Maqrīzī's geographical landmark. C. Sicard spoke of it several times. He knew the lofty situation of the monastery and its unusual mode of entry. He called it now the monastery of Saint Menas, now that of Pithirion, no doubt the one of which the HISTORIA MONACHORUM IN AEGYPTO speaks. R. Pococke described it without giving it a name (1743–1745, p. 75). F. L. Norden called it "monastery of the pulley" (1795–1798, Vol. 2, p. 51), as did G. Wilkinson (1843, Vol. 2, p. 75). G. Legrain (1900, p. 5) and J. Maspero (1910, p. 19) also often call it "monastery of the pulley." S. Clarke described it in passing (1912, p. 178).

The monastery is a center of pilgrimage, much frequented especially on the day of the feast of Saint Menas, 18 Ba'ūnah (Muyser and Viaud, 1979, pp. 50–51).

BIBLIOGRAPHY

Clarke, S. *Christian Antiquities in the Nile Valley.* London, 1912.

Doresse, J. "Monastères coptes de moyenne Egypte." *Bulletin de la Societé française d'Egyptologie* 59 (1970):7–29.

Legrain, G. "Notes archéologiques prises au gebel Abū Fuda." *Annales du Service des Antiquites de l'Egypte* 1 (1900):3–14.

Maspero, G. *Ruines et paysages d'Egypte.* Paris, 1910.

Maspero, J., and G. Wiet. *Matériaux pour servir à la géographie de l'Egypte.* Cairo, 1919.

Muyser, J., and G. Viaud. *Les Pèlerinages coptes.* Bibliothèque d'études coptes 15. Cairo, 1979.

Norden, F. L. *Voyage d'Egypte et de Nubie,* Vols. 1 and 2. Paris, 1795–1798.

Pococke, R. *A Description of the East and Some Other Countries.* London, 1743–1745.

Sicard, C. *Oeuvres,* ed. M. Martin. Bibliothèque d'étude 83. Cairo, 1982.

Vansleb, J. M. *Nouvelle relation en forme de journal d'un voyage fait en Egypte en 1672 et 1673.* Paris, 1677. Translated as *The Present State of Egypt.* London, 1678.

Wilkinson, G. *Modern Egypt and Thebes,* Vols. 1 and 2. London, 1843.

RENÉ-GEORGES COQUIN
MAURICE MARTIN, S.J.

DAYR MĀR MĪNĀ and the church of Mār Minā. *See* Babylon.

DAYR MĀR MURQUS AL-RASULI. *See* Qurnat Mar'i.

DAYR MARQŪRAH. *See* Monasteries of the Middle Ṣa'īd.

DAYR MARQŪRYUS. *See* Dayr Abū Sayfayn (Cairo); Dayr al-Malāk Mīkhā'īl (Idfū).

DAYR MĀR STEFANOS. *See* Monasteries of the Upper Ṣa'īd.

DAYR MART MARYAM, monastery near Bilbeis. The HISTORY OF THE PATRIARCHS records the following episode, before the election of the forty-sixth patriarch, KHĀ'ĪL I (744–767). Toward the end of al-Qāsim ibn 'Ubaydallāh's governorship of Egypt (therefore before 743), a bedouin tribe comprising more than 30,000 horsemen was encamped in the Eastern Desert between Bilbays and al-Qulzum. Their tents were erected as far as the vicinity of the monastery of the Virgin Mary, Dayr al-Sayyidah Mart Maryam, in the neighborhood of Bilbeis. The general of these bedouin troops and his two brothers plundered and pillaged the monastery and the church, the superior of which was Epimachus of Arwāṭ. The author of the life of the patriarch Khā'īl I tells us that Epimachus had come from the Monastery of Saint Macarius at the Wādī Habīb (Wādī al-Naṭrūn), and that he afterward became a bishop of Pelusium. This Epimachus was one of the disciples of John, the superior of SCETIS (c. 585–675). Menas, who became bishop of Memphis, was also a monk there. This monastery was, therefore, closely linked with that of Saint Macarius in the Wādī al-Naṭrūn (Evelyn-White, 1932, pp. 277, 284).

The editor of ABŪ AL-MAKĀRIM, Samū'īl (1984, p. 39, n. 1), proposes the identification of this convent with the village called Kafr al-Dayr, in the district (*markaz*) of Minyā al-Qamḥ (Sharqiyyah), or else with the one named al-Dayr in the *markaz* of Ṭūkh (see MONASTERIES OF THE PROVINCE QALYŪBIYYAH), but both these sites are too far from Bilbeis.

BIBLIOGRAPHY

Evelyn-White, H. G. *The Monasteries of the Wadi'n Natrūn*, pt. 2; *The History of the Monasteries of Nitria and Scetis*. New York, 1932.

Seybold, C. F. *Severus ibn al-Muqaffa' Alexandrinische Patriarchengeschichte*. Hamburg, 1912.

RENÉ-GEORGES COQUIN

DAYR MĀR TUMĀS. This Church of Saint Thomas lies at the edge of the desert cliffs about 8 miles (13 km) northeast of Akhmīm. It is entered from a courtyard that contains no other buildings, and no trace of other monastery buildings survives. The church was built of baked brick in two building phases. The original structure is a centralized, domed building with three apses forming a triconch, a scheme typical for the medieval period from at least the eleventh century (see Grossmann, 1978, pp. 142–43). It is three units wide and three deep. At the east is an apse with three niches flanked by rectangular corner rooms. The southern

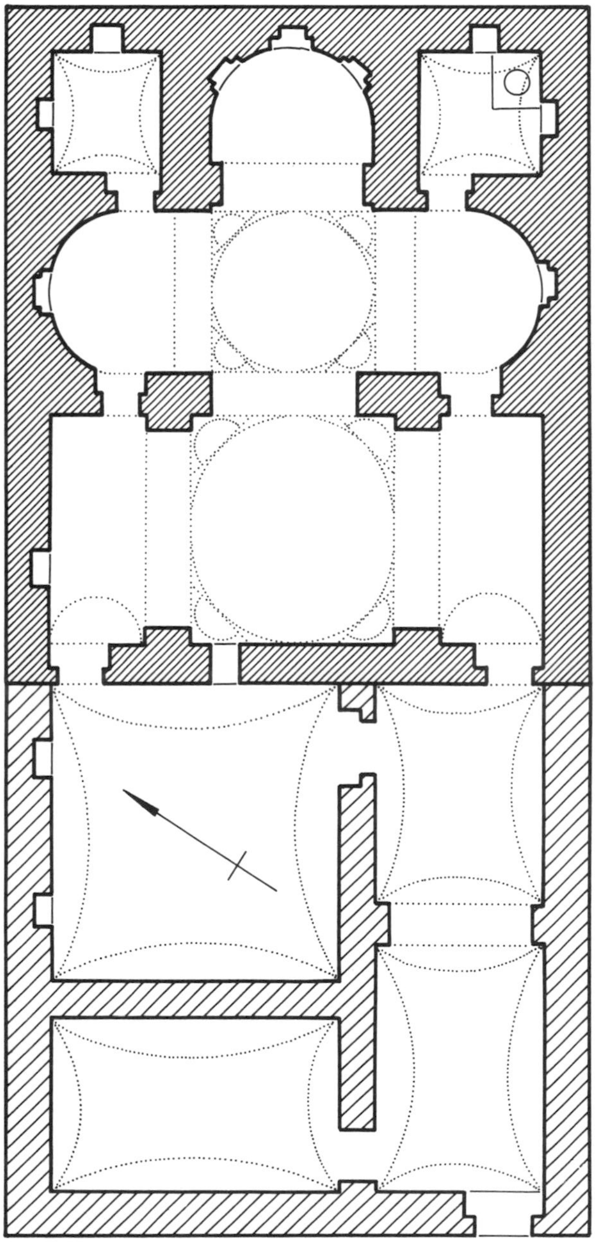

Plan of the Church of Saint Thomas, the only surviving building at the site of Dayr Mār Tumās. *Courtesy Peter Grossmann.*

room contains a grave attributed to Saint Thomas. In front of these corner rooms, apses with one niche each face north and south. A central bay separates the apses, and there is a row of three bays along the west. The units are divided by arches running from piers to pilasters on the west wall and on the eastern spur walls. A mud-brick screen (between the piers) and narrow doorways (between piers and walls) divide this choir bay and apses from the western bays. The two central bays are covered by domes on squinches, the south and northwest bays by barrel vaults, the apses by semidomes, and the south and northeast rooms by domes on pendentives. The two central domes are pierced by circular tubes that allow light into the interior. The bricks are painted red and black, as in many churches of the area (see DAYR AL-'ADHRĀ' near Akhmīm), but the brickwork itself appears earlier than in the similarly painted ones. Four rooms have been added to the west, connected with the original church only by two small doors and a window. Their roofs are also pierced by circular tubes admitting light. Concerning the date of the church, it might belong, as similar structures do, to the sixteenth century.

SHELA MCNALLY

BIBLIOGRAPHY

Grossmann, P. "Der christlicher Baukunst in Ägypten." *Enchoria* 8 (1978):142–43.

DAYR AL-MAṬMAR.

DAYR AL-MAṬMAR. [*This article consists of two parts—history and architecture, ruins of the church being all that remain today.*]

History

About 6 miles (9 km) west of Armant, on the stony desert (*ḥājir* in Arabic) but at the edge of the cultivated land, is situated a *kom* (mound) covered with the debris of pottery, fragments of brick, and the like and thus given this name Dayr al-Maṭmar (the Buried Monastery). It is also called Dayr al-Abyaḍ (the White Monastery) and DAYR ANBĀ SHINŪDAH, although the reason for this appellation is not known. There is no possibility of attaching this site to any name attested in the literary sources, but one may suppose that its foundation goes back to the Byzantine period. It is briefly described by J. Doresse (1949, esp. p. 346) and by O. Meinardus (1977, p. 435). The exact geographical situation is found in the plan given by R. Mond and O. H. Myers (1937, Vol. 1, no. 2).

BIBLIOGRAPHY

Doresse, J. "Monastères coptes aux environs d'Armant en Thébaïde." *Analecta Bollandiana* 67 (1949):327–49.

Meinardus, O. *Christian Egypt, Ancient and Modern,* 2nd ed. Cairo, 1977.

Mond, R., and O. H. Myers. *Cemeteries of Armant,* 2 vols. Egypt Exploration Society Memoirs 42. London, 1937.

RENÉ-GEORGES COQUIN
MAURICE MARTIN, S.J.

Architecture

Dayr al-Maṭmar is a hilly field of debris covering several hectares to the west of Armant. The only ruin that still projects to some extent above the general rubble is the church, built of mud bricks.

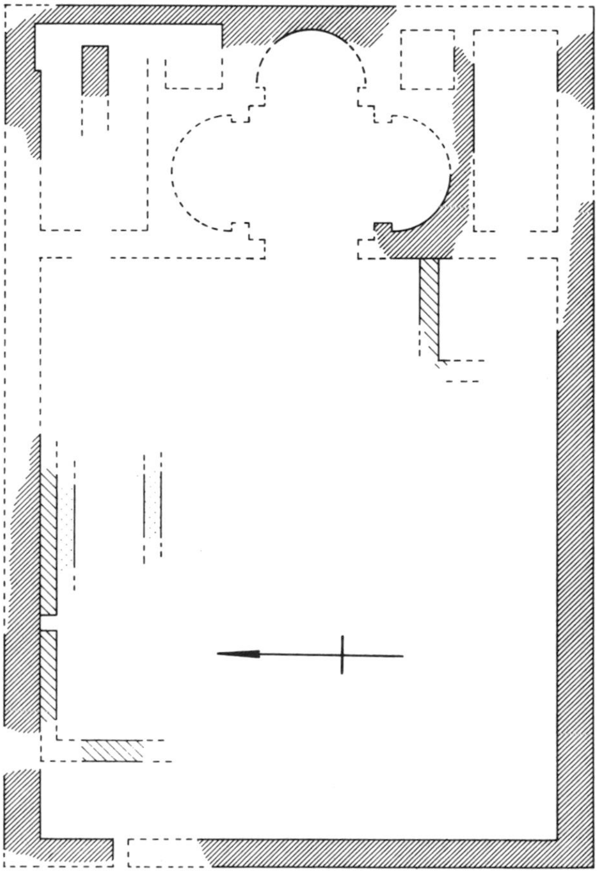

Plan of the church at Dayr al-Maṭmar. *Courtesy Peter Grossmann.*

However, most of this, too, is covered up. What can still be recognized is the course of the outer walls, as well as part of the internal arrangement of the sanctuary. In the latter, one can see in shadowy form the spatial plan of a triconch. On the two sides of the triconch are two large side chambers, the northern one of which evidently held the staircase. The naos seems to have been a three-aisled one. How and where the rows of columns ran cannot, however, be determined. In the same way, there are no indications of the front triumphal arch, which appears in all other triconch churches. Of the later interior structures, the wall sections in the southeast corner of the naos could belong to a *khūrus* (room between naos and sanctuary), which was in use in monastery churches from the early eighth century. The church of Dayr al-Maṭmar is probably to be assigned to the sixth century.

BIBLIOGRAPHY

Doresse, J. "Monastères coptes aux environs d'Armant en Thébaïde." *Analecta Bollandiana* 67 (1949):346.

Grossmann, P. "Neue frühehristliche Funde aus Ägypten." *Actes du XIe congrès international d'archéologie chrétienne, Lyon, 21–28 septembre 1986*, vol. 2, p. 1892, fig. 22. Paris, 1989.

Timm, S. *Das christlich-koptische Ägypten in arabischer Zeit*, Vol. 2, p. 740. Wiesbaden, 1984.

PETER GROSSMANN

DAYR MAṬRĀ.

When the patriarch BENJAMIN I returned to Alexandria in 644 from his exile in Upper Egypt, he chose as the episcopal residence the monastery of Maṭrā, because it was the only one in the region of Alexandria whose monks had resisted the pressure of the emperor Heraclius to accept the dogma of CHALCEDON (451). ABŪ AL-MAKĀRIM, who gives the same information (1984, p. 158) but writes Baṭrā instead of Maṭrā, adds that the patriarch ISAAC (689–692 A.D.) renewed its building. Unfortunately, neither of these two witnesses gives us an indication of the geographical situation of the monastery. However, there still exists a place called al-Maṭrās near Wardiyan on the shores of Lake Maryūt to the west of Alexandria, in which the name of this monastery is perhaps perpetuated (Breccia, 1919, pp. 180–81).

The question is whether this monastery was connected with Saint Metras, a martyr at Alexandria under Decius (8 Bābah and 10 Misrā). Several texts mention his martyrium on the outskirts, to the east of the town, near the so-called Sun Gate (Calderini, 1935, Vol. 1, p. 175; "Life of John the Almoner," PG 93, col. 1647; "Nicephorus Callistus," *Historia ecclesiastica* 5, 30, PG 145, col. 1124; "Miracles of Saints John and Cyrus," PG 87, col. 3464). It will be noted that in the SYNAXARION, the saint's name is written in the same way as in the *History of the Patriarchs* and in Abū al-Makārim. The latter seems to indicate in his book that after the burning down of his church, the saint's head was left there, which may mean that the monastery did indeed bear this martyr's name and that it was distinct from the martyrium.

BIBLIOGRAPHY

Abū al-Makārim. *Tārīkh al-Kanā'is wa-al-Adyirah*, ed. Ṣamū'īl al-Suryānī. Cairo, 1984.

Breccia, E. "Ancora un epitaffio di monaco alessandrino." *Bulletin de la Société royale d'archéologie d'Alexandrie* 17 (1919):179–81.

Calderini, A. *Dizionario dei nomi geografici e topografici dell'Egitto greco e romano*. Cairo, 1935.

RENÉ-GEORGES COQUIN
MAURICE MARTIN, S. J.

DAYR MAWAS.

See Monasteries of the Middle Ṣa'īd.

DAYR AL-MAYMAH

(Gharbiyyah). This monastery is part of a group of four that, according to the indications of al-MAQRĪZĪ, may be situated "in the region of the salt-marshes near Lake al-Burullus" (1845, pp. 45 [text], 109 [trans.]; 1853, Vol. 2, p. 508, correcting *al-Maymanah* to *al-Maymah*) in the neighborhood of Bilqās, in northeast Gharbiyyah. Al-Maqrīzī (d. 1441) indicated that the Dayr al-Maymah was near the DAYR AL-'ASKAR, and he added that formerly there was not in the delta a monastery inhabited by a greater number of monks. He also said that its prosperity had vanished, the monastery had been destroyed, the army (reading *al-jaysh*, not *al-ḥabash* or Ethiopian) camped there, and the area had been built up.

It is noteworthy that ABŪ AL-MAKĀRIM, who was writing at the beginning of the thirteenth century, did not speak of Dayr al-Maymah, no doubt because the ruin of which al-Maqrīzī spoke was already in that state. Al-Maqrīzī was doubtless quoting an older author, as was his custom.

M. Ramzī (1953–1968, Vol. 2, p. 2, p. 27) showed that in several medieval documents the areas called al-Maymah and al-ʿAskar were situated near one another and then were gradually joined to form the town of Bilqās, in the present *markaz* (district) of Bilqās. Until A.H. 1244/A.D. 1809, al-Maymah was associated with al-ʿAskar in the area of Danjawāy, which confirms the information of al-Maqrīzī, who placed the two similarly named monasteries near one another. It is very probable that both these monasteries had received the names of the neighboring villages.

In the life of Sitt Dimyānah (or Jimyānah, according to the writing in all the manuscripts; Sidawi, 1917, p. 83), JOHN, bishop of Parallos (al-Burullus), told of having heard the tradition concerning this saint from a monk of Dayr al-Maymah (which, according to al-Maqrīzī, had the largest community). According to this special tradition, the saint, when only one year old, had been offered by her father to the church of Dayr al-Maymah (see DAYR SITT DIMYĀNAH). Unfortunately, there is no information to fix the period when John lived. Some manuscripts give him the surname Niʿmatallāh (Graf, 1944–1953, Vol. 1, pp. 468, 532).

BIBLIOGRAPHY

Ramzī, M. *Al-Qāmūs al-Jughrāfī lil-Bilād al Miṣriyyah,* 3 vols. Cairo, 1953–1968.

Sidawi, E. "Sitt Dimiana, sa légende, son mouled." *Bulletin de la Société sultanieh de géographie* n.s. 8 (1917):79–99.

RENÉ-GEORGES COQUIN

DAYR AL-MAYMŪN.

[*Dayr al-Maymūn is discussed in this entry from two perspectives, history and architecture.*]

History

It is known that Saint ANTONY at first lived near the Nile before going into isolation near the Red Sea. This place near the Nile was called Pispir or Tilodj (Palladius, 1898–1904, chap. 25). Thus, one finds: "When I arrived at his monastery which is near the river, at the place named Pispir . . . I waited for him five days" (Rufinus, PL 21, II, 8; Lefort, 1943, p. 267, n. 2).

There is sometimes hesitation about thinking that Dayr al-Maymūn perpetuates the ancient Pispir. It may be thought that the latter has gradually been moved closer to the river.

According to tradition, two monasteries preserve the memory of Saint Antony, the one near the Red Sea and the other near the Nile. The oldest testimony appears to be that of Postumianus: "Duo beati Antonii monasteria adii, quae hodieque ab eius discipulis incoluntur" (I came to two monasteries of the Blessed Antony, which even today are inhabited by his disciples).

ABŪ ṢĀLIḤ THE ARMENIAN (1895, p. 163), at the beginning of the thirteenth century, called it Dayr al-Jummayzah and mentioned thirty monks. AL-MAQRĪZĪ (d. 1441; 1853, Vol. 2, p. 502) placed it opposite al-Maymūn and also called it Dayr al-Jūd.

A marginal note in the manuscript of Saint Antony (Theol. 209), reproduced by Kāmil Ṣāliḥ Nakhlah (1954, pp. 74, 75), explains that DAYR ANBĀ ANṬŪNIYŪS was called Dayr al-Jummayzah, where Antony lived. This note was added after the patriarch GABRIEL VII died in this church in 1568 (Coquin and Laferrière, 1978, pp. 276–77).

It was mentioned by sixteenth-century travelers such as O. d'Anglure (1878, p. 68) and J. Coppin (1971, p. 204), and in the seventeenth century by J. VANSLEB (1677, p. 294; 1678, p. 178). The eighteenth century produced the testimony of C. SICARD (1982, Vol. 1, p. 75), who spoke of "the little Saint Antony on the Nile"; R. POCOCKE (1743, p. 70); and F. L. Norden (1795–1798, Vol. 2, p. 31, pl. 69).

The *Book of the Hidden Pearls* (Daressy, 1917, pp. 199, 201, 203) calls it Dayr al-Badla (Monastery of the Exchange), for one exchanged the Nile boat for a desert mount when one went to Saint Antony. The site is certainly very old; the great church dedicated to Saint Antony is built on rock.

[*See also* Abū al-Makārim.]

BIBLIOGRAPHY

Anglure, O. d'. *Le Saint voyage de Jherusalem,* ed. F. Bonnardot and A. Longnon. Paris, 1878.

Coppin, J. *Les Voyages en Egypte.* Cairo, 1971.

Coquin, R.-G., and P.-H. Laferrière. "Les Inscriptions pariétales de l'ancienne église du monastère de St. Antoine dans le désert oriental." *Bulletin de l'Institut français d'Archéologie orientale* 78 (1978):266–321.

Daressy, G. "Indicateur topographique du 'Livre des perles enfouies et du mystère précieux.'" *Bulletin de l'Institut français d'Archéologie orientale* 13 (1917):175–230.

Lefort, L. T. *Les Vies coptes de St. Pachôme.* Bibliothèque du Muséon 16. Louvain, 1943.

Nakhlah, Kāmil Ṣāliḥ. *Silsilat Tārīkh al-Batārikah,* Pt. 4, Dayr al-Suryan in Wādī-al-Naṭrūn, 1954.

Norden, F. L. *Voyage d'Egypte et de Nubie,* ed. L. Langlès, 3 vols. Paris, 1795–1798.

Pocoke, R. *A Description of the East and Some Other Countries,* Vol. 1. London, 1743.
Sicard, C. *Oeuvres,* Vol. 1, ed. S. Sauneron and M. Martin. Bibliothèque d'étude 83–85. Cairo and Paris, 1982.
Vansleb, J. *Nouvelle relation en forme de journal d'un voyage fait en Egypte en 1672 et 1673.* Paris, 1677. Translated as *The Present State of Egypt.* London, 1678.

RENÉ-GEORGES COQUIN
MAURICE MARTIN, S.J.

Architecture

Dayr al-Maymūn has its origin, according to the probably reliable local tradition, in the former supply station of the hermitage of Saint Antony on the Red Sea (Abū al-Makārim, fol. 55b; al-Maqrīzī, trans. Wüstenfeld, 87, no. 6, Dayr al-Jummayzah). From here camel caravans set out at regular intervals to supply the needs of the saint, his disciples, and his guests, and here, too, every visit to the monastery down to modern times had its starting point. Today there is a modern village on the site of the monastery, and the old monastery buildings have disappeared. Only two churches situated close beside one another recall the old tradition. The older is dedicated to Saint Mercurius. Its nave consists of a domed two-column building (rather a reduced four-column building), which a three-part sanctuary adjoins on the east. There is no *khūrus* (room between the naos and sanctuary). The larger and slightly later church of Saint Antony has been spoiled by later additions. In the nineteenth century it still possessed a dome supported by granite columns with Corinthian capitals, the supporting arches of which had lower vaults in the shape of semidomes attached on all four sides (Chester, 1873, pp. 111f.). Originally this building seems also to have been of basilican structure, as is suggested by various reused marble pillars and all kinds of capitals lying about in the area. Of the sanctuary, only the small south room has retained its original form, that of an apse side room. The two northern rooms are side *haykals* (sanctuaries) with an amorphous rotunda appearance. Both churches in their present form probably derive only from the Ottoman period.

BIBLIOGRAPHY

Chester, G. J. "Notes on the Coptic Dayrs." *Archeology Journal* 30 (1873):111ff.

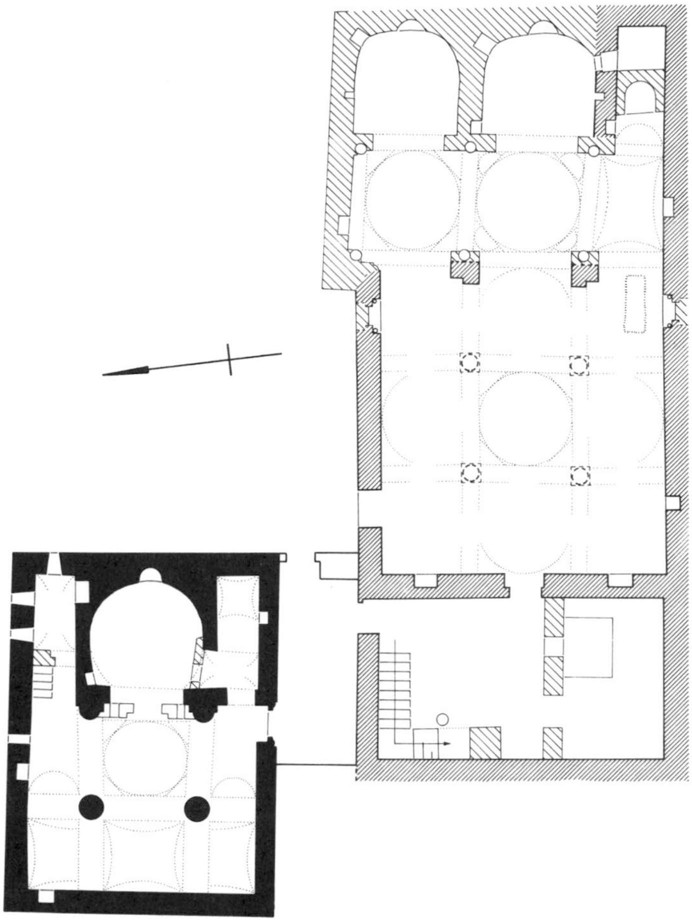

Plan of the church dedicated to Saint Mercurius and the church dedicated to Saint Anthony, Dayr al-Maymūn. *Courtesy Peter Grossmann.*

Grossmann, P. *Mittelalterliche Langhauskuppelkirchen und verwandte Typen in Oberägypten,* pp. 178–80. Glückstadt, 1982.
Meinardus, O. *Monks and Monasteries of the Egyptian Desert,* pp. 21–23. Cairo, 1961.
Timm, S. *Das christlich-koptische Ägypten in arabischer Zeit,* Vol. 2, pp. 742–749. Wiesbaden, 1984.

PETER GROSSMANN

DAYR MINYAT ṬĀNAH. *See* Dayr al-Maghṭis.

DAYR AL-MISAYKRAH. Northwest of Armant is a small cluster of ruins situated on a promontory on the slope of the desert plateau, wrongly described by Doresse (1949, p. 327) and by Timm (1984, p. 767) as DAYR AL-NAṢĀRĀ. Two structures may be distinguished, the larger of which probably

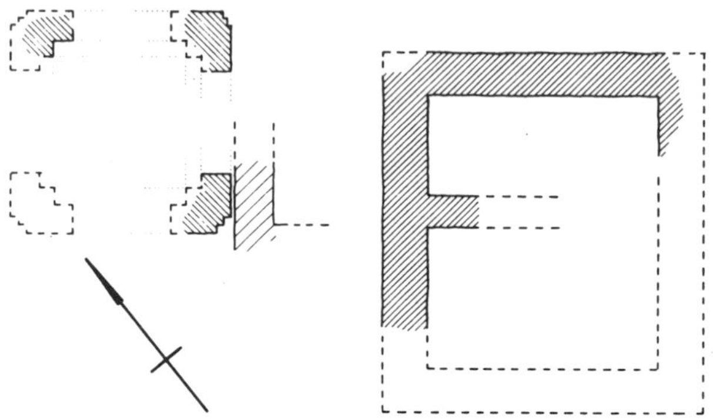

Plan of the ruins at Dayr al-Misaykrah.

comprises the ruins of a residential building. The second structure, standing to the east and immediately next to it, is a tomb in the shape of a tetrapylon made out of mud bricks. The tomb makes it likely that this site is to be identified with DAYR ANBĀ DARYŪS, mentioned in the SYNAXARION at 2 Ṭūbah, the festal date of Apa Victor and Apa Jonas.

BIBLIOGRAPHY

Doresse, J. "Monastères coptes aux environs d'Armant en Thébaïde." *Analecta Bollandiana* 67 (1949):327–49.

Timm, S. *Das christlich-koptische Ägypten in arabischer Zeit,* Vol. 2, pp. 663–64, 767. Wiesbaden, 1984.

PETER GROSSMANN

DAYR AL-MUHARIB. *See* Dayr al-Amīr Tadrūs (Luxor).

DAYR AL-MUḤARRAQ. Nothing is known for certain about the date of the foundation of this monastery. A sermon attributed to the patriarch THEOPHILUS OF ALEXANDRIA (384–412) credits him with a vision of the Holy Virgin in which she revealed to him that the principal church of the monastery in the place where Mary and her son sojourned during their flight from Herod was consecrated by Jesus himself, assisted by his disciples. Guidi (1917) has published the Oriental versions. The Arabic text is also given in a work entitled *Al-La'ālī'* (1966, pp. 56–70). A reworking of this sermon is attributed to Zechariah, bishop of Sakhā at the beginning of the eighth century (pp. 40–55).

The monastery is said to have been founded by Saint PACHOMIUS (Simaykah, 1932, Vol. 2, p. 121), but the Lives of Pachomius, both Greek and Coptic, do not speak of it. The most ancient source appears to be the HISTORY OF THE PATRIARCHS of the Egyptian church, which in its list of the places where the Holy Virgin stayed with Jesus in Egypt names Qūsqām, but not Dayr al-Muḥarraq.

The clearest source is without doubt ABŪ ṢĀLIḤ THE ARMENIAN from the beginning of the thirteenth century (1895, pp. 224–27). He knew the legend of the Holy Family's FLIGHT INTO EGYPT and of the consecration of this church, but he never spoke of a monastery. The SYNAXARION recalls these events at 6 Hātūr. The recension of the Synaxarion from Upper Egypt names the Dayr al-Muḥarraq in the notice of the martyr Elias, bishop of this monastery and of al-Qūṣiyyah (20 Kiyahk). The Ethiopian Synaxarion also mentions the monastery at Qusqām at 24 Bashans (Feast of the Coming of Jesus into Egypt), which the Arabic Synaxarion of the Copts does not do (Budge, 1928, Vol. 3, p. 926). A manuscript of the Synaxarion deriving from the library of the Dayr al-Muḥarraq indicates the feast of the *qūmmūṣ* ʿAbd al-Malāk on 18 Bābah. This saint built or restored the Church of Saint George. He lived in the Arab period, prior to the date of the manuscript (1867, according to Troupeau, 1974, Vol. 2, p. 30).

In 1305 Marqus, bishop of Qusqām, was present at the preparation of the chrism (Munier, 1943, p. 37), and in another manuscript about the same event, Marqus is called bishop of al-Qūsiyyah. Since the monastery is only a little over 4 miles (7 km) from this town, he was probably bishop of these two places (Muyser, 1945, p. 158).

In the fourteenth and fifteenth centuries, several monks of Dayr al-Muḥarraq became patriarchs of Alexandria: in 1370 GABRIEL, in 1378 MATTHEW I, in 1452 MATTHEW II, and in 1484 JOHN XIII.

In 1396 a miracle of the Holy Virgin took place in the monastery, recounted by the Ethiopic *Book of the Miracles of Mary* (Cerulli, 1943, p. 209). In addition, this text shows that there were fairly close relations at this period between the monks of Saint Antony and those of al-Mūḥarraq.

Before 1441, al-MAQRĪZĪ mentioned Dayr al-Muḥarraq (1853, Vol. 2, p. 506). He was familiar with the legend of the Holy Family's sojourn, and noted that this was a place of pilgrimage twice a year, on Palm Sunday and at the feast of Pentecost.

In 1597, the *qummuṣ* Gabriel was one of the envoys of the patriarch GABRIEL VIII to Pope Clement VIII to seal the union of the Coptic church with the Roman church (Buri, 1931; Graf, 1951, Vol. 4, p. 122). In 1668 two Capuchins, Protais and François, said that the monastery was inhabited by the Abyssinians and spoke of the Holy Family's sojourn (Sauneron, 1969, p. 141). The Dominican J. VANSLEB noted on the west bank of the Nile the monasteries of Muḥarraq and of the Abyssinians nearby. Jomard, in the *Description d'Egypte* (Vol. 4, p. 301), noted that there were twenty religious and two hundred inhabitants.

In the nineteenth century, the number of monks having decreased, a secular priest from al-Qūṣiyyah came to the monastery to perform the offices. Gradually prosperity returned. A description of the modern state of the site was given by O. Meinardus.

The presence of the Ethiopian monks is attested from the thirteenth century (and perhaps earlier) by the Ethiopic manuscripts deriving from it. Among them, one should note in the *Catalogue of the Bibliothèque Nationale* (Paris), by Zotenberg, nos. 32, 35, 42, and 52. It does, indeed, seem from these manuscripts that the community of Qusqām formed a single unit with that of HĀRIT ZUWAYLAH and that of Jerusalem. The monastery served as a staging post for the Ethiopian monks on pilgrimage to Jerusalem. It is not known what bond united this community with the other groups of Ethiopian monks established in Egypt, in particular at SCETIS and at Saint Antony (DAYR ANBĀ ANṬŪNIYŪS).

The Capuchins Protais and François wrote simply in 1668 that the Dayr al-Muḥarraq was inhabited by the Abyssinians (Sauneron, 1969, p. 141). Vansleb noted their presence in 1673 alongside Dayr al-Muḥarraq (1677, p. 361; 1678, p. 217). He also called it the Monastery of Saints Peter and Paul (Quatremère, 1812, p. 15). In the Ethiopic manuscripts this monastery of the Ethiopians is called the Monastery of the Apostles. In 1716 the Jesuit C. Sicard spoke of it as being in ruins (1982, Vol. 1, pp. 10–11). The monastery of the Abyssinians has disappeared, but around 1950, several Ethiopian monks were still living at the Dayr al-Muḥarraq.

On the links between the Dayr al-Muḥarraq and the Ethiopian church, reference may be made to Crawford (1958, pp. 121ff.).

BIBLIOGRAPHY

Budge, E. A. W. *The Book of the Saints of the Ethiopian Church,* 4 vols. Oxford, 1928.

Buri, V. *L'unione della chiesa copta con Roma sotto Clemente VIII.* Orientalia Christiana 23. Rome, 1931.

Cerulli, E. *Il Libro etiopico dei Miracoli di Maria e le sue fonti nelle letterature del medio evo latino.* Rome, 1943.

Crawford, O. G. S. *Ethiopian Itineraries circa 1400–1524.* Cambridge, 1958.

Gregorios, Bishop. *Al-Dayr al-Muḥarraq.* Cairo, n.d.

Guidi, M. "La omelia di Teofilo di Alessandria sul monte Coscam nelle letterature orientali." *Rendiconti della R. Academia dei Lincei,* 5th ser. Classe di Scienze Storiche 26 (1917):381–91.

Jomard, E. F. "Deir al-Moharrag ou el-Maharraq." In *Description de l'Egypte,* Vol. 4, pp. 301–302, ed. C. F. L. Pancoucke. Paris, 1821.

Monneret de Villard, U. *Deyr al-Muharraqeh: Note archeologiche.* Milan, 1928.

Munier, H. *Recueil des listes épiscopales de l'église copte.* Cairo, 1943.

Muyser, F. "Contribution à l'étude des listes épiscopales de l'église copte." *Bulletin de la Société d'archéologie copte* 10 (1944):115–76.

Quatremère, E. M. *Observations sur quelques points de la géographie de l'Egypte.* Paris, 1812.

Sicard, C. *Oeuvres,* Vol. 1, ed. M. Martin. Bibliothèque d'étude 83–85. Cairo and Paris, 1982.

Simaykah, M. *Guide to the Coptic Museum, Cairo,* Vol. 2. Cairo, 1932 (in Arabic).

Troupeau, G., ed. *Catalogue des manuscrits arabes,* Vol. 2, *Manuscrits chrétiens.* Paris, 1974.

Vansleb, J. M. *Nouvelle relation en forme de journal d'un voyage fait en Egypte en 1672 et 1673,* p. 361. Paris, 1677. Translated as *The Present State of Egypt.* London, 1678, p. 217.

Zotenberg, H. *Catalogue des manuscrits éthiopiens de la Bibliothèque nationale.* Paris, 1877.

RENÉ-GEORGES COQUIN
MAURICE MARTIN, S.J.

DAYR AL-MUḤARRAQAH. ABŪ ṢĀLIḤ THE ARMENIAN, who wrote in the early thirteenth century, is the only ancient author who mentions Dayr al-Muḥarraqah. He situated it in Giza near Bunumrus, also known as Abū al-Numrus (Ramzī, 1953–1968, Vol. 2, pt. 3, p. 3 and p. 39). There is still a village of this name to the south of the pyramid of Licht.

It is clear that the tradition at a very early date fixed the FLIGHT INTO EGYPT at al-Ashmūnayn: "We have seen also another holy man of the name of Apollo, in the borders of Hermopolis in the Thebaid, where the Saviour went with Mary and Joseph . . . we have seen there the temple where, when the Saviour entered the town, all the idols fell down with their faces to the ground" (Festugière, 1971, p. 47). The fifth-century Greek historian Sozomen, in his *Ecclesiastical History* (5, 21), also spoke of Hermopolis in the Thebaid and of the miracle of the idols.

The Coptic story of the martyrdom of Saints PAESE AND TECLA makes Mary say, "I stayed in the town of Shmūn, I and my small child sucking my breast." (The manuscript in the Pierpont Morgan Library in New York, deriving from al-Hamūlī in the Fayyūm, dates from 861; cf. Reymond and Barns, 1973, pp. 57 [text], 167 [trans.].)

Other more recent texts report the same tradition: the apocryphal Gospel of Pseudo-Matthew, chapter 25; the Arabic Gospel of the Infancy, chapters 24–25; and sermons attributed to THEOPHILUS OF ALEXANDRIA by ZACHARIAS, bishop of Sakhā.

In the HISTORY OF THE PATRIARCHS OF THE EGYPTIAN CHURCH the author Yuḥannā ibn Saʿīd ibn Yaḥyā ibn Mīnā, with the surname Ibn al-Qulzumī, who compiled the notices of the patriarchs CYRIL II, MICHAEL IV, and MACARIUS II, provided a list of the places sanctified by the presence of the Holy Family. It is remarkable that he names Qusqām and al-Muḥarraqah. Hence these two places are different from one another. According to the author, the departure of the Holy Family for Palestine began from al-Muḥarraqah and took them through Cairo.

The Coptic SYNAXARION mentions the return from al-Ashmūnayn via al-Muḥarraqah and Miṣr. The Ethiopian Synaxarion follows the Coptic but adds the mention of Dabra Qusqām (Budge, 1928, Vol. 3, p. 925).

It is probable that Dayr al-Muḥarraqah perpetuates, in the province of Giza, the memory of the passage of the Holy Family.

BIBLIOGRAPHY

Budge, E. A. W. *The Book of the Saints of the Ethiopian Church,* Vol. 3. Oxford, 1928.

Ramzī, M. *Al-Qāmūs al-Jughrāfī lil-Bilād al Miṣrīyyah,* 3 vols. Cairo, 1953–1968.

Reymond, E. A. E., and J. W. B. Barns. *Four Martyrdoms from the Pierpont Morgan Coptic Codices.* Oxford, 1973.

RENÉ-GEORGES COQUIN
MAURICE MARTIN, S.J.

DAYR MUṢṬAFĀ KĀSHIF.

To the northwest of the capital of the oasis of Khargah, about 1.25 miles (2 km) northwest of the necropolis of al-Bagawāt on the summit of a hill where the tombs rise in tiers (Jabal al-Ṭayr), are some ruins that some interpret as those of a monastery (de Bock; Meinardus). Others describe them as those of a Roman fort later utilized as a dwelling by Christian hermits (Fakhry). Whatever its original purpose, its last inhabitants have left numerous graffiti (de Bock, 1901, p. 35ff.). It was excavated by the German Institute (Müller-Wiener, 1963, pp. 121–40).

The inscriptions have been copied several times: first by the archaeologist Fakhry, who published them in 1951 (pp. 401–434). G. Roquet has copied but not yet published them (see Leclant, 1977, p. 269). Roquet has remarked that some have been written by the same personages as at al-Bagawāt, for they bear the same titles.

BIBLIOGRAPHY

Bock, V. de. *Matériaux pour servir à l'archéologie de l'Egypte chrétienne.* St. Petersburg, 1901.

Fakhry, A. "The Rock-Inscriptions of Gabal el-Teir at Kharga Oasis." *Annales du Service des antiquités de l'Egypte* 51 (1951):401–434.

Leclant, J. "Fouilles et travaux en Egypte et au Soudan, 1975–1976." *Orientalia* 46 (1977):233–99.

Meinardus, O. F. A. *Christian Egypt, Ancient and Modern.* Cairo, 1965; 2nd ed., Cairo, 1977.

Müller-Wiener, W. "Christliche Monumente im Gebiet von Hibis (el Kharga)." *Mitteilungen des Deutschen Archäologischen Instituts* 19 (1963):121–40.

RENÉ-GEORGES COQUIN
MAURICE MARTIN, S.J.

DAYR AL-MUṬṬIN.

This is the name now given to a cluster of ruins situated at the edge of the western desert at ASYŪṬ, about a mile from the town, beside the ancient necropolis at the mausoleum of Shaykh Abū Ṭūq.

ABŪ ṢĀLIḤ THE ARMENIAN, at the beginning of thirteenth century, knew four monasteries to the west of Asyūṭ: the one called Karfūnah, dedicated to the Holy Virgin; that of Saint Severus; and two monasteries of the Holy Virgin, called Dayr Azīlūn and Abū al-Ḥārith. Unfortunately, it is difficult to determine to what the monasteries he lists actually correspond, except for that of Saint Severus.

Al-MAQRĪZI (d. 1441) in his *al-Kitāb al-Khiṭāṭ* (1853) indicated some monasteries on the west bank of the Nile; these are the Monastery of Seven Mountains or of John Colobos (today called DAYR AL-ʿIẒĀM); and DAYR AL MUṬṬIN, or rather, according to the spelling proposed by S. Timm (1984, Vol. 2, p. 758), Dayr al-Maẓall, a difference that in Arabic requires only the change of a diacritical point.

Al-Maqrīzī added that the monasteries of this region were numerous, but that many were at that time destroyed. He later named those of the region of Durūnkah, to the south of Asyūṭ. It seems that the ruins today called Dayr al-Muṭṭin correspond to what al-Maqrīzī called Dayr al-Mazall.

Down to the beginning of the twentieth century, one could find there the remains of buildings of unbaked brick described by Napoleon's engineers and by V. de Bock. They also found in the pharaonic tombs some "chapels" (tombs fitted out as cells), below and to the east of the tomb of Shaykh Abū Ṭūq. The inscriptions have been published by G. Lefèbvre (1910, Vol. 2, pp. 50–58) and J. Clédat (1908, pp. 216–22). One may also consult A. Kamāl (1916, pp. 97–99). Unfortunately they disappeared when archaeologists wished to restore the pharaonic tombs (Chassinat and Palanque, 1911).

On the present state, one may consult O. Meinardus (1965, pp. 282–83; 1977, pp. 391–92).

Some ancient tombs of the necropolis preserve without doubt traces of a very ancient monastic occupation, naming the three founders of BĀWĪṬ: Apollo, Anub, and Phib (Palanque, 1903, pp. 126–28).

BIBLIOGRAPHY

Bock, V. de. *Matériaux pour servir à l'archéologie chrétienne d'Egypte.* St. Petersburg, 1901 (in Russian and French).

Chassinat, E., and C. Palanque. *Une Campagne des fouilles dans la nécropole d'Assiut.* Mémoires de l'Institut français d'Archéologie orientale 24. Cairo, 1911.

Clédat, J. "Notes d'archéologie copte." *Annales du Service des antiquités de l'Egypte* 9 (1908):213–30.

Jollois, J. B. P., and E. Devilliers, in *Description de l'Egypte,* Vol. 4. Paris, 1821–1829.

Kamāl, A. "Fouilles à Deir Drūnka et à Assiut." *Annales du Service des antiquités de l'Egypte* 16 (1916):65–114.

Lefèbvre, G. "Egypte chrétienne." *Annales du Service des antiquités de l'Egypte* 10 (1910):50–58.

Meinardus, O. *Christian Egypt, Ancient and Modern.* Cairo, 1965; 2nd ed., 1977.

Palanque, E. "Notes de fouilles dans la nécropole d'Assiut." *Bulletin de l'Institut français d'Archéologie orientale* 3 (1903):119–28.

Timm, S. *Das christlich-koptische Ägypten in arabischer Zeit,* 2 vols. Wiesbaden, 1984.

RENÉ-GEORGES COQUIN
MAURICE MARTIN, S.J.

DAYR NAHYĀ (Giza), monastery that enjoyed an extraordinary renown even among the Muslims. It was situated near the village of the same name (Nahyā), to the northwest of Giza at the foot of the Jabal Abū Rūwāsh.

According to *The Churches and Monasteries of Egypt,* it was founded by a merchant who came from the west before DIOCLETIAN.

In the seventh century some monks from Scetis, fleeing from the persecution of the Melchite patriarch Cyrus (631–644), took refuge at Nahyā (Evelyn-White, 1932, pp. 255–56; Cauwenbergh, 1914, p. 132) and in the tenth century one could still see the cells in which they lived (p. 185, n. 3). The HISTORY OF THE PATRIARCHS, under the Patriarch KHĀ'ĪL (744–767), mentions the monastery as the residence of Moses, bishop of Wasīm. The Caliph al-Mu'izz (972–975) is said to have camped with his troops before the walls of the monastery. The monastery is described by al-Shābushtī (end of the tenth or beginning of the eleventh century; 1939, pp. 17 and 26). The Caliph al-Ḥakim (996–1021) set fire to the monastery and afterward reconstructed it.

The imam al-Amīr bi-Aḥkām Allāh (1101–1130) visited the monastery and gave 1000 dirhams to the monks; he also gave about thirty *feddans* (acres) for cultivation, which remained the property of the monks until the arrival of the Ghuzz and the Kurds. Another biographer (1100–1130) in the *History of the Patriarchs* had as informants John, abbot of the monastery of Nahyā, as well as his brother.

In 1330 the patriarch BENJAMIN II, returning from the monastery of Saint Macarius, where he had gone for the consecration of the CHRISM, stopped on the way at the monastery of Nahyā (Evelyn-White, 1932, p. 396).

The historian al-MAQRĪZĪ (d. 1441) contented himself with copying al-Shābushtī, and laconically added that the monastery was destroyed in 1354–1355 at the same time as that of other churches in Cairo.

This monastery must have been very rich and possessed a good library. Biblical manuscripts from this library are today preserved in the Freer Collection, Washington (Sanders, 1909, pp. 130–41).

The site was excavated at the beginning of the twentieth century by the Institut français d'Archéologie orientale (Palanque, 1902, pp. 163–70; see also Crum, 1890–1909, p. 15; Daressy, 1917, pp. 274–76). According to some authors, the name "monastery of the vine-dresser" (Dayr al-Karrām) is another name for the monastery of Nahyā (Daressy, 1917, pp. 203–204).

BIBLIOGRAPHY

Cauwenbergh, P. van. *Etude sur les moines d'Egypte*. Paris, 1914.

Crum, W. E. *Christian Egypt (Archaeological Report 1890–1909)*. London, 1908–1909.

Daressy, G. "Indicateur topographique du 'Livre des Perles Enfouies et du mystère précieux.'" *Bulletin de l'Institut français d'Archéologie orientale* 13 (1917):175–230.

______. "Le Couvent de Nahyeh." *Annales du Service des Antiquités de l'Egypte* 17 (1917):274–76.

Evelyn-White, H. G. *The Monasteries of the Wādi 'n Natrūn*, pt. 2, *The History of the Monasteries of Nitria and of Scetis*. New York, 1932.

Palanque, C. "Rapport sur les fouilles d'el-Deir, 1902." *Bulletin de l'Institut français d'Archéologie orientale* 2 (1902):163–70.

Sanders, H. A. "Age and Ancient Home of the Biblical Manuscripts in the Freer Collection." *American Journal of Archeology* 13 (1909):130–41.

Shābushtī, al-. "Some Egyptian Monasteries," ed. A. Atiya. *Bulletin de la Société d'archéologie copte* 5 (1939):1–28.

RENÉ-GEORGES COQUIN
MAURICE MARTIN, S.J.

DAYR AL-NAKHLAH. *See* Dayr al-Barshah.

DAYR AL-NĀMŪS (Armant). [*This is a two-part article, including history and architecture.*]

History

About 6 miles (9 km) northwest of Armant in the stony desert, one comes upon a fairly wide field of ruins designated as Dayr al-Nāmūs by the people of the region. The term *dayr* makes one think of an establishment of monks, but on the spot one can see only "the remains of several series of large buildings, some of which had more than one story" (Doresse, 1949, p. 343). From the neighboring cemetery come numerous Coptic funerary stelae, which in the museums are marked as deriving from Armant (according to Daressy, 1914, p. 270).

The ancient name of the site is not known. One may deduce from the Coptic stelae, which testify to ancient Coptic art, that the site was founded in the Byzantine era.

The atlas of the *Description de l'Egypte* names it Kharāb al-Nāmūs (Jomard, 1821, fol. 5). The exact geographical situation was given by R. Mond and O. H. Myers (1937, Vol. 1, pl. 2). O. Meinardus described the site briefly (1977, p. 435).

BIBLIOGRAPHY

Daressy, G. "Renseignements sur la provenance des stèles coptes du Musée du Caire." *Annales du Service des antiquités de l'Egypte* 13 (1914):266–71.

Description de l'Egypte. Paris, 1821–1829.

Doresse, J. "Monastères coptes aux environs d'Armant en Thébaïde." *Analecta Bollandiana* 67 (1949):327–49.

Meinardus, O. *Christian Egypt, Ancient and Modern*, 2nd ed. Cairo, 1977.

Mond, R., and O. H. Myers. *Cemeteries of Armant*, 2 vols. Egypt Exploration Society Memoirs 42. London, 1937.

RENÉ-GEORGES COQUIN
MAURICE MARTIN, S.J.

Architecture

Dayr al-Nāmūs is a complex of ruins situated on the edge of the desert northwest of Armant, also called simply Dayr Nāmūs by the local population. A considerable number of Coptic stelae (Daressy, 1914) came from the vicinity of this site and are now preserved in the Coptic Museum in Cairo. A number of generally one-room buildings that are laid out close together at right angles can be identified. They have a fairly regular arrangement of windows and niches on both sides. In the northeast, a larger building stands that consists of several rooms of this sort. One can hardly fail to recognize these structures as living quarters for the monks of a cenobite monastery. A few outcrops of a wall situated on the outskirts also indicate that the area was originally walled in. However, no remains of a building that may be regarded as a church have been recognized.

BIBLIOGRAPHY

Daressy, G. "Renseignements sur la provenance des stèles coptes du Musée du Caire." *Annales du Service des antiquités de l'Egypte* 13 (1914):266–71.

Doresse, J. "Monastères coptes aux environs d'Armant en Thébaïde." *Analecta Bollandiana* 67 (1949):344–45.

PETER GROSSMANN

DAYR AL-NAQLŪN or Dayr al-Malāk Ghubriyāl. [*This entry consists of two parts—the history and the architecture of Dayr al-Naqlūn, which is situated in the Fayyūm.*]

History

By the middle of the third century, Christianity was well established in the oasis of the Fayyūm. EUSEBIUS mentioned Bishop Nepos of the Fayyūm, who in the first half of the third century was known for his millennial interpretation of the Scriptures. During the Diocletian persecution, Theophilus, Patricia, Bartholomew and his wife, and Abbā Kāw, together with five hundred to eight hundred Christians, suffered martyrdom in the Fayyūm. Saint ANTONY is reported to have visited the region, where he made many monks, "confirming them in the Law of God." By the fourth century, monasticism was as much developed in the Fayyūm as in the Nile Valley. The foundation of the LAURA of al-Naqlūn, southeast of the Fayyūm, is related to the Coptic legend of Aūr, the illegitimate son of the queen's daughter and Abrāshit the magician. Throughout this story the angel GABRIEL appears as the guardian of Aūr, who was led to the Mountain of al-Naqlūn, where he built a Church of Saint Gabriel. Later, Aūr was ordained priest and consecrated bishop. From the fourth to the sixth centuries, the Monastery of Saint Gabriel (Dayr al-Malāk Ghubriyāl) of al-Naqlūn was the leading monastic center in the Fayyūm.

With the emergence of the Monastery of al-Qalamūn under Saint SAMUEL, the al-Naqlūn monastery was gradually pushed into the background, and by the seventh century al-Qalamūn surpassed al-Naqlūn in importance. In the middle of the tenth century only one monk inhabited the Monastery of Saint Gabriel.

A renaissance occurred in the twelfth century, for ABŪ ṢALĪḤ THE ARMENIAN referred to two churches, those of Saint Michael and Saint Gabriel. According to medieval tradition, the Old Testament patriarch Jacob enjoyed the shade here, and by the twelfth century the relics of Abbā Kāw were venerated at this monastery. The fifteenth century saw the decline of the Monastery of al-Naqlūn.

When J. M. VANSLEB visited the Fayyūm in 1672, he found the Monastery of al-Naqlūn almost completely ruined, though the Church of Saint Gabriel was still adorned with wall paintings depicting scenes from the Holy Scriptures. The church was rebuilt at the beginning of the twentieth century by Bishop Abraam, the first bishop of the Fayyūm oasis. Ever since, the church has served as a place for occasional services. For the annual *mawlid* (festival) of Saint Gabriel pilgrims from the Fayyūm and the region around Banī Suef gather in large numbers in and around the monastery.

Noteworthy are the numerous Corinthian capitals used in the construction of the church. The icons have been ascribed to the eighteenth and nineteenth centuries. There is also a well-preserved Jerusalem *proskynitarion* (a hagiographical-topological painting of the Holy City). Southeast of the Monastery of al-Naqlūn, on the slopes of the Naqlūn mountain range, are numerous one- and two-room caves, which at one time were inhabited by hermits and belonged to the laura of al-Naqlūn. The laura of al-Naqlūn is mentioned in the story of Aūr: "This mountain shall prosper, and shall become as crowded as a dovecote by reason of the immense multitudes of people who shall come to visit it from all countries of the earth, and their prayers shall mount up to God."

BIBLIOGRAPHY

Abbott, N. *The Monasteries of the Fayyūm,* pp. 22–66. Chicago, 1937.

Amélineau, E. *Les Actes des martyrs de l'église Copte,* pp. 69–71. Paris, 1890.

Budge, E. A. W. *The Book of the Saints of the Ethiopian Church,* Vol. 1, p. 263. Cambridge, 1928.

______. *Egyptian Tales and Romances,* pp. 12, 29, 247–63. London, 1931.

Johann Georg, Duke of Saxony. *Neue Streifzüge durch die Kirchen und Klöster Ägyptens,* p. 19. Berlin, 1930.

Meinardus, O. "The Laura of Naqlūn." *Bulletin de la Société de géographie d'Egypte* 40 (1967):173–85.

OTTO MEINARDUS

Architecture

Of the old monastery buildings of al-Naqlūn, only parts of the walls and the church today remain standing. The hermits' cells in the rock caves of the surrounding Naqlūn mountains are abandoned. There is now a necropolis in the area of the monastery. The church itself has been much altered, but is still in use, and now serves in particular for pilgrims attending the annual festival of Saint Gabriel.

The church's architectural form suggests that it

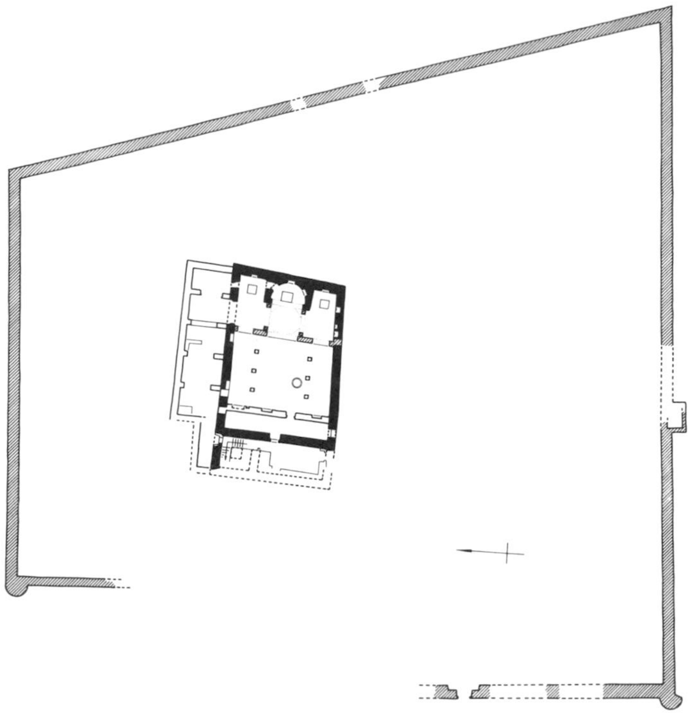

Plan of the monastery area, Dayr al-Naqlūn. *Courtesy Peter Grossmann.*

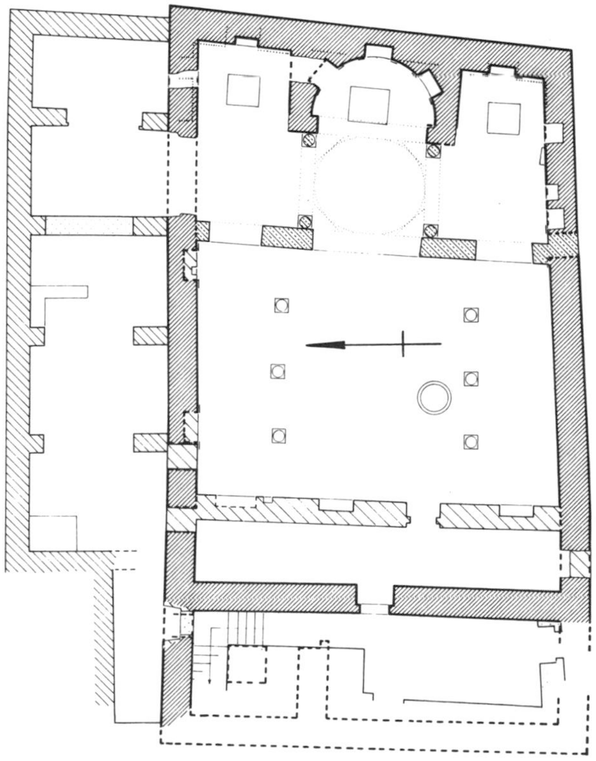

Plan of the church at Dayr al-Naqlūn. *Courtesy Peter Grossmann.*

dates from the seventh or eighth century. It is built of burnt brick and arranged on the plan of a basilica with three aisles. The ground plan, however, has come out rather askew. The apse and the outer walls on the north and south are certainly original. At the north end of the original narthex, there was a stairway to the gallery and the rooms above the sanctuary. The columns—all of them spolia (plundered from earlier monuments) with limestone Corinthian capitals—probably no longer stand in their original places. The western row of columns is walled up by a later part or wall. Also uncertain is the original form of the side rooms to the apse. Various factors suggest that there was once a broad forechoir in front of the apse. The side chambers of the apse would then have had the form of a gamma.

A long hall divided by several transverse arches was built against the northern side of the church, probably in the Fatimid period, and in more recent times the sanctuary was provided with a *khūrus* (room between the naos and the sanctuary). The ground plan looks like a refectory. Later its eastern bay was linked with the interior of the church and rebuilt into a baptistery. However, it is also possible that here is the second church of the monastery mentioned by Abū Ṣaliḥ (ed. Evetts, pp. 205–206) and Vansleb (pp. 275–276).

During excavations in the 1980s in the area of the monastery that were carried out by a mission of the Polish Archaeological Center in Cairo, some new buildings were unearthed. One is described as a towerlike structure with very thick walls and with an apse originally projecting on the eastern side. Later in this same building a small basilica-shaped church was installed, with three aisles and an eastern *khūrus* in front of the apse.

The clearing of some of the caves in the mountains produced a number of typical hermitages. They contain several irregularly shaped chambers with cooking places and store rooms in the entrance hall.

BIBLIOGRAPHY

Abbott, N. *The Monasteries of the Fayyūm*, pp. 46ff. Chicago, 1937.

Adli, S. "Several Churches in Upper Egypt." *Mitteilungen des Deutschen Archäologischen Instituts, Abteilung Kairo* 36 (1980):2f., fig. 1.

Grossmann, P. *Mittelalterliche Langhauskuppelkirchen und verwandte Typen in Oberägypten*, p. 121, fig. 49. Glückstadt, 1982.

Vansleb, J. M. *Nouvelle Relation en forme de journal d'un voyage fait en Egypte en 1672 et 1673.*

Paris, 1677. Translated as *The Present State of Egypt*. London, 1678.

PETER GROSSMANN

DAYR AL-NAṢĀRĀ (Antinoopolis). [*This entry consists of two brief parts—the location and condition of the* dayr *as reported by those who actually saw the place, and a few facts about the architecture.*]

History

This complex of ruins is on a rocky spur almost 4 miles (about 7 km) northeast of the ruins of ANTINOOPOLIS, in the angle of the amphitheater formed by the Arabian chain where it rises perpendicularly above the Nile. The town of Antinoë occupies approximately the center. It was seen by M. Jomard (*Description d'Egypte*, 1822–1828, Vol. 4, pl. 541), who gave a good description at a time when it was in a better state than it is today.

G. Wilkinson (1843, Vol. 2, pp. 60–61) also saw it, although he named it Dayr al-Dīk and noted on the lower level a cave with an engraved cross. This is no doubt the same one published with greater care by S. Donadoni (1950, Vol. 2, pp. 481–82). It appears that the excavations by Albert GAYET were carried out at the necropolis of Dayr al-Naṣārā, and not, as he wrote, at the site of Dayr al-Dīk (cf. Martin, 1971, p. 9, n. 1).

BIBLIOGRAPHY

Clédat, J. "Notes archéologiques et philologiques." *Bulletin de l'Institut oriental* 2 (1902):42–70.
Donadoni, S. *Epigrafia minore di Antinoe: Studi in onore di A. Calderini e R. Paribeni*. Milan, 1950.
Jomard, M. *Description d'Egypte*, Vol. 4. Paris, 1822–1828.
Martin, M. *La Laure de Deir al-Dik à Antinoé*. Bibliothèque d'études coptes 8. Cairo, 1971.
Mi'sā'il Baḥr. *Ta'rikh al Qiddīs al-Anbā Yuḥannis al-Qaṣīrwa-Mantiqat Anṣinā*. Alexandria, 1957.
Wilkinson, G. *Modern Egypt and Thebes*, Vols. 1–2. London, 1843.

RENÉ-GEORGES COQUIN
MAURICE MARTIN, S.J.

Architecture

The layout of the courtyard is adapted to the contours of the terrain and is surrounded on all sides by rooms, single and in series. What remains of an entrance may be discerned in the northeast corner. The badly ruined little church, which, to judge by the capitals strewn about, was designed as a basilica, is on the east side of the courtyard. All that is left visible are bits of the apse, the forechoir, and a few side rooms. More accommodation for monks is found in the neighboring caves.

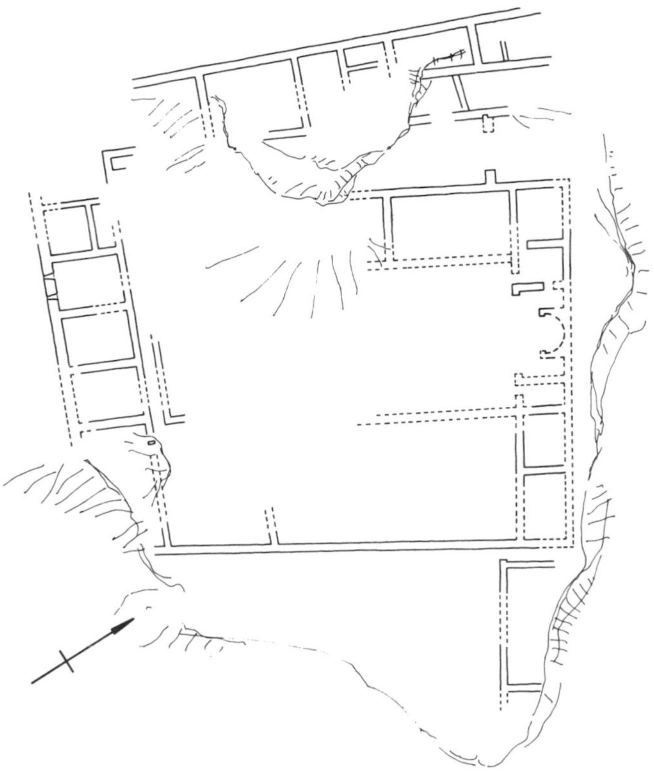

Plan of the ruins of Dayr al-Naṣārā near Antinoopolis.

BIBLIOGRAPHY

Martin, M. *La Laure de Dêr al Dîk à Antinoé*. Bibliothèque d'études coptes 8. Cairo, 1971.

PETER GROSSMANN

DAYR AL-NAṢĀRĀ (Armant), modern name for a rock cave situated deep in the desert north of Armant, adapted by early Christian monks for living quarters. Today one can see no more than a large square tower rising from the ruins of buildings. They are in the stony area at the foot of the mountain. One cannot say if it is the ruins of a real monastery, a cenobium, or a rest house for the hermitages that were numerous in the mountains between them and the cultivated lands. This monastery cannot be identified with any site attested by the texts. G. Daressy (1914, pp. 266–271) believed, without offering any proof, that it was Dayr Anbā Daryūs, of which the Sahidic recension of the Coptic SYNAXARION speaks at 2 Ṭūbah. J. Doresse has briefly described it (1949, p. 345).

BIBLIOGRAPHY

Daressy, G. "Renseignements sur la provenance des stèles coptes du Musée du Caire." *Annales du Service des antiquités de l'Egypte* 13 (1914):266–71.

Doresse, J. "Monastères coptes aux environs d'Armant en Thébaïde." *Analecta Bollandiana* 67 (1949):327–49.

Meinardus, O. *Christian Egypt, Ancient and Modern.* Cairo, 1965; 2nd ed., 1977.

Mond, R., and O. H. Myers. *Cemeteries of Armant,* 2 vols. Egypt Exploration Society Memoirs 42. London, 1937.

Timm, S. *Das christlich-koptische Ägypten in arabischer Zeit,* Vol. 2, pp. 767–68. Wiesbaden, 1984.

RENÉ-GEORGES COQUIN
MAURICE MARTIN, S.J.

DAYR AL-NAṢĀRĀ (Asyūṭ), monastery southeast of Asyūṭ. It should not be confused with the monastery of the same name to the northwest of Armant. It is a walled ecclesiastical complex on the edge of the desert. The unpretentious small church is restored and contains a number of extensions on both sides. In its oldest part, it is related to the Akhmimic churches of the sixteenth and seventeenth centuries and may also go back to the same period. It contains a central apse and, separate from it, two rectangular side altars. The walled ICONOSTASIS is modern. However, the *khūrus* (room between naos and sanctuary) is original. It is connected to the lay area by a central main door and a smaller side door on the south side, and so still follows the early medieval plan. The actual lay area has the depth of a single bay.

PETER GROSSMANN

DAYR AL-NASṬŪR. According to ABŪ ṢĀLIḤ THE ARMENIAN (1895, pp. 134–36) in the thirteenth century, this monastery was to the south of Old Cairo, on the edge of Lake al-Ḥabash. It was a monastery of the Nestorian rite, dedicated to Saint George. In 1102–1130, under the caliphate of al-Amīr, Shaykh Abū al-Faḍā'il, a Nestorian, restored this monastery at his own expense. But the caliph, displeased at this restoration undertaken without his permission, had a mosque built within the monastery grounds.

According to the same historian, the monastery passed into the hands of Copts under the twelfth-century patriarch MARK III ibn Zar'ah, who consecrated the church to Saint Philotheus of Antioch in 1183. The costs of the restoration were assumed by Shaykh Abū al-Manṣūr ibn Būlus and his son. At the time of Abū Ṣāliḥ, the monastery was prosperous and visited by the pilgrims from Upper Egypt.

Several Coptic patriarchs and bishops of Miṣr were buried in the adjoining cemetery: Zechariah, ATHANASIUS III, JOHN VII, THEODOSIUS II, and JOHN IX.

Two manuscripts derive from this monastery. The first (National Library, Paris, Arabe, 167; Troupeau, 1972, Vol. 1, p. 141) was completed at the Monastery of Saint Philotheus in 1227 and collated with the aid of Anbā Dāwūd, the future patriarch CYRIL III IBN LAQLAQ. The second (National Library, Paris, Arabe, 181; Troupeau, 1972, p. 156) was sold in 1315 to the priest of the Church of Saint Philotheus, who sold it again to the superior of the Monastery of Saint Victor.

The future patriarch Cyril ibn Laqlaq resided in this monastery before becoming patriarch. Al-MAQRĪZĪ did not speak of it, nor any author after him; however, a manuscript was copied for Dayr al-Nasṭūr, known under the name of Dayr Phīlūthawus, in 1735 (Simaykah, 1942, Vol. 2, pt. 1, no. 652).

J. B. Fiey (1972–1973, pp. 335–36) thought that there was a second Dayr al-Nasṭūr farther to the south, near Adawiyyah, but he assumed that the first was to the north of Lake al-Ḥabash, which was not the case, as is shown by the map established by Casanova (1901).

BIBLIOGRAPHY

Cahen, C. "La 'Chronique des Ayyoubides' d'al-Makīn b. al-'Amīd." *Bulletin d'études orientales* 15 (1955–1957):109–184.

Casanova, P. "Les Noms coptes du Caire et localités voisines." *Bulletin de l'Institut français d'Archéologie orientale* 1 (1901):139–224.

Fiey, J. B. "Coptes et Syriaques, contacts et échanges." *Collectanea* 15 (1972–1973):297–365.

Troupeau, G. *Catalogue de manuscrits arabes,* Vol. 1. Paris, 1972.

RENÉ-GEORGES COQUIN
MAURICE MARTIN, S.J.

DAYR NUJTUHUR. *See* Monasteries in the Province of Qalyubiyyah.

DAYR ONOPHRIOS. *See* Monasteries of the Middle Ṣa'īd.

DAYR PAMPANE. *See* Monasteries of the Middle Ṣa'īd.

DAYR PAPNUTE. *See* Monasteries of the Upper Ṣa'īd.

DAYR PATERMUTHIUS. *See* Monasteries of the Upper Ṣa'īd.

DAYR PHILEMON. *See* Monasteries of the Middle Ṣa'īd.

DAYR PISENTIUS (Luxor). *See* Monasteries of Upper Egypt.

DAYR PISENTIUS (Naqādah). *See* Dayr al-Malāk Mīkhā'īl (Naqādah).

DAYR POSIDONIOS, place, which disappeared no doubt at the Arab conquest, situated "in the mountain of Armant" and known through a graffito found near the DAYR AL-BAKHĪT (Petrie, 1909, pl. 47), two ostraca (unpublished) from QURNAT MAR'Ī, and some inscriptions in the caves of the mountain of Armant. J. Doresse has given this site its present name (1949, p. 345), based on the remains of painting and graffiti with the names of Pisentius and Posidonios. Posidonios was without doubt the founder and donor or the superior. He appears to be different from the monk living in Palestine of whom PALLADIUS speaks in his *Lausiac History.* In the ostraca from Qurnat Mar'ī it is called a *topos;* this suggests not a true monastery but a gathering place where the hermits living in the neighborhood met on Saturday and Sunday every week. The monastery is also mentioned, in passing, by Meinardus (1965, p. 321; 1977, p. 435).

BIBLIOGRAPHY

Doresse, J. "Monastères coptes aux environs d'Armant, en Thébaïde." *Analecta Bollandiana* 67 (1949):327–49.

Meinardus, O. *Christian Egypt, Ancient and Modern.* Cairo, 1965; 2d ed., 1977.

Petrie, W. M. F., and J. H. Walker. *Qurneh.* British School of Archaeology in Egypt 16. London, 1909.

RENÉ-GEORGES COQUIN
MAURICE MARTIN, S.J.

DAYR QAMŪLAH AL-QIBLĪ. *See* Dayr al-Malāk Mīkhā'īl (Qamūlah).

DAYR AL-QAṢRIYYAH. [*This small entry consists of two parts—the history and the architecture of Dayr al-Qaṣriyyah.*]

History

According to al-MAQRĪZĪ (1853, Vol. 2, pp. 501–502), this monastery was situated less than a mile south of Aṭfīḥ and was known as Dayr al-Qaṣriyyah even though it was dedicated to the apostles Peter and Paul, whose feast was commemorated on 5 Abīb.

Aṭfīḥ was a bishopric down to the seventeenth century (Vansleb, 1677, pp. 26–27). The present church of the village is dedicated to the apostles (Clarke, 1912, p. 205, no. 15); it is of ancient reused materials, and the level is very much below ground. Around it is a Christian hamlet, which has taken the place of the monastery and its cemetery.

An official document of the seventeenth century mentions Dayr al-Aṭfīḥiyyah (Slane, 1883–1895, no. 319).

BIBLIOGRAPHY

Clarke, S. *Christian Antiquities in the Nile Valley.* London, 1912.

Slane, W. MacGuckin, Baron de. *Catalogue des manuscrits arabes de la Bibliothèque nationale.* Paris, 1883–1895.

Vansleb, J. *Histoire de l'église d'Alexandrie.* Paris, 1677.

RENÉ-GEORGES COQUIN
MAURICE MARTIN, S.J.

Architecture

A four-columned building, the small church is of familiar pattern, with remarkably stout square pillars and three sanctuaries. The middle part is slightly emphasized in its width. There is no *khūrus* (room between naos and sanctuary). All the bays are roofed with domes of the same kind on squinches, the three middle domes being furnished with a ring of windows. The date of the church follows from the date on the *hijāb* (screen) of the main sanctuary, A.M. 1246/A.D. 1530.

BIBLIOGRAPHY

Timm, S. *Das christliche-koptische Ägypten in arabischer Zeit,* Vol. 1, pp. 251–56. Wiesbaden, 1984.

PETER GROSSMANN

DAYR QIBRIYŪS, monastery near Alexandria. The HISTORY OF THE PATRIARCHS records that the future patriarch BENJAMIN I (622–661) took refuge, a year before the death of his predecessor the patriarch ANDRONICUS, in a monastery situated "to the northeast of the town," close to a holy old man named Theonas. The monastery had not been destroyed by the Persians in 619, because the army was defending it. Unfortunately the name of the monastery has been distorted by the copyists: it is sometimes written without diacritical points, twice Qīr[i]nūs, three times Qībriyūs, and in the oldest manuscript Niqiyūs (PO 1, pt. 1, p. 487; ed. Seybold, 1912, p. 96). In the SYNAXARION for 8 Ṭūbah we read: "in a monastery to the west of Alexandria," which the 1935 Cairo edition makes specific: "in the monastery of Saint Qibriyūs" (ʿAbd al-Masīḥ Mīkhaʾīl, 1935, p. 276). Abū al-Makārim obviously copied the *History of the Patriarchs,* but called the monastery "the monastery of Niqiyūs" and thus followed a manuscript containing the same reading as the Hamburg manuscript edited by C. F. Seybold. J. Maspero (1916, pp. 43–46) corrected the manuscripts to read "Canopus," which seems plausible, given the orientation "to the northeast of the town."

The major objection to this identification (Qibriyūs/Qirinūs/Niqiyūs or Canopus) was advanced by W. E. Crum (1924, p. 429): in the century preceding Benjamin's stay, the monastery of Canopus (the METANOIA) appears to have been inhabited by Chalcedonian monks, for the religious policy of JUSTINIAN (527–565) had driven the anti-Chalcedonians out of the monasteries of the Pachomian congregation. But it is possible that there was to the northeast of the town only a single monastery, that of the Metanoia, at Canopus.

BIBLIOGRAPHY

Crum, W. E. Review of "L'Histoire des patriarches d'Alexandrie depuis la mort de l'empéreur Anastase jusqu'à la réconciliation des églises jacobites" by Jean Maspero. *Journal of Theological Studies* 25 (1924):425–32.
Maspero, J. "Graeco-arabica." *Bulletin de l'Institut français d'Archéologie orientale* 12 (1916):43–51.
Seybold, C. F., ed. *Alexandrinische Patriarchengeschichte von S. Marcus bis Michael I.* Hamburg, 1912.

RENÉ-GEORGES COQUIN
MAURICE MARTIN, S.J.

DAYR AL-QIDDIS YUHANNIS. *See* Dayr al-Sāqiyah.

DAYR QUBBAT AL-HAWĀ. [*This entry consists of two parts: the history of Dayr Qubbat al-Hawā, and monuments of the* dayr.]

History

This Coptic monastery, today in ruins, took its name from the hill where a *shaykh* is buried, on the flanks of which are the tombs of the governors of Aswan during the New Kingdom, in particular those of Koui (Khui) and Kounes (Khune). These tombs seem to have been inhabited by one or more hermits and to have been the nucleus from which developed a monastery or hermitage, the ruins of which can be seen above the tombs. It has sometimes, but without proof, been given the name of Saint George or of Saint Laurentius. C. Sicard calls it "of the Saviour" (Vol. 3, pp. 167, 196), as does J. B. d'Anville (p. 215). Denon calls it that of Saint Laurentius (Vol. 2, p. 52). R. Pococke conjectures, because he saw a fresco of Saint George, that it had the patronage of this saint (Vol. 1, p. 118). The 1821–1829 *Description de l'Egypte,* in the atlas (1828, fol. 1), also names it that of Saint Laurentius.

There are descriptions written when it was less ruined than today. Jomard, for instance, describes it in *Description de l'Egypte* ("Description de

Syene," Antiquités, Vol. 1, p. 143). Others who wrote on it are F. L. Norden (Vol. 3, pp. 97–99), H. Light (p. 51 [engraving]), G. B. Belzoni (pp. 59–60), and V. de Bock (p. 87). E. A. Wallis Budge wrote on the excavations carried out on the site (pp. 39–40).

The present state is described by O. Meinardus (1965, p. 328; 1977, p. 443).

BIBLIOGRAPHY

Anville, J. B. d'. *Mémoires sur l'Egypte, ancienne et moderne*. Paris, 1766.

Belzoni, G. B. *Narrative of the Operations and Recent Discoveries Within the Pyramids, Temples, Tombs and Excavations in Egypt and Nubia*. London, 1820.

Bock, V. de. *Matériaux pour l'archéologie chrétienne d'Egypte*. St. Petersburg, 1901.

Budge, E. A. W. "Excavations Made at Aswān by Major-General Sir F. Grenfell, During the Years 1885 and 1886." *Proceedings of the Society of Biblical Archaeology* 10 (1887–1888):4–40.

Denon, V. *Voyage dans la Haute et la Basse Egypte pendant les campagnes du général Bonaparte*, 2 vols. and atlas. Paris, 1802.

Description de l'Egypte, 24 vols. of text and 12 vols. of plates, including atlas. Vol. 1. Pancoucke edition. Paris, 1821–1829.

Light, H. *Travels in Egypt, Nubia, Holy Land, Mount Lebanon and Cyprus in the Year 1814*. London, 1818.

Meinardus, O. *Christian Egypt, Ancient and Modern*. Cairo, 1965; 2nd ed., Cairo, 1977.

Norden, F. L. *Voyage d'Egypte et de Nubie*, 3 vols. Langlès edition. Paris, 1795–1798.

Pococke, R. *A Description of the East and Some Other Countries*, 2 vols. in 3. London, 1743–1745.

Sicard, C. *Oeuvres*, 3 vols., ed. S. Sauneron and M. Martin. Bibliothèque 83–85. Cairo, 1982.

RENÉ-GEORGES COQUIN
MAURICE MARTIN, S. J.

Monuments

The monastery at Qubbat al-Hawā is a second monastery on the west bank at Aswan, and presumably a dependent of DAYR ANBĀ HADRĀ. It might be identified with a monastery of Antonius mentioned by ABŪ AL-MAKĀRIM (ed. Evetts, p. 277). According to E. Edel, the site lent itself to the establishment of a monastery, particularly because of the large number of tombs of the nobles of the New Kingdom, which had already been adapted by the monks for use as dwelling places in the early Christian period. The church was at first accommodated in the tomb of Khune *(Kounes)*, constructed as a three-aisle pillared hall in which the rooms necessary for the sanctuary were located at the east end. Some traces of walls from this building are still clearly visible, as are the beginning of vaults of a central hanging dome over the altar chamber. In the other tombs, various systems of basins and new floors were introduced, in addition to numerous dividing walls.

The golden age of the monastery, like that of Dayr Anbā Hadrā, was in the Fatimid period. At that time a large residential building of several stories was erected above the line of tombs, with a central corridor and sleeping rooms arranged on either side (sketch in Monneret de Villard, pp. 16ff., ill. 2). A fairly large building to the southeast of the residential building may have been the refectory. In front of the entrance to the tomb of Khune a new church was erected; it is noteworthy in that it follows the plan of an octagon-domed structure, such as is found in the two other Aswan monasteries, Dayr Anbā Hadrā and Dayr al-Shaykhah. The ground plan, however, has been distorted to form a parallelogram. Despite the considerable mounds of debris, the supports for the domed area, the ambu-

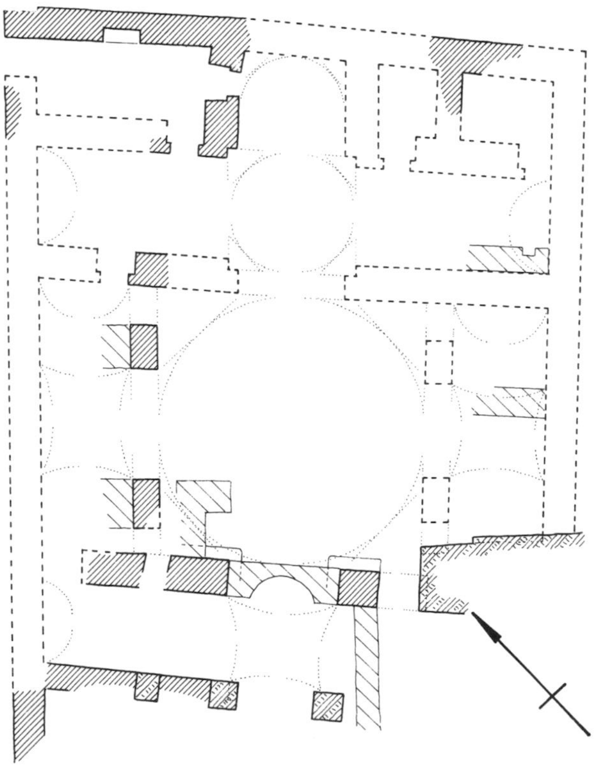

Plan of the church in the tomb of Khune at Dayr Qubbat al-Hawā. *Courtesy Peter Grossmann.*

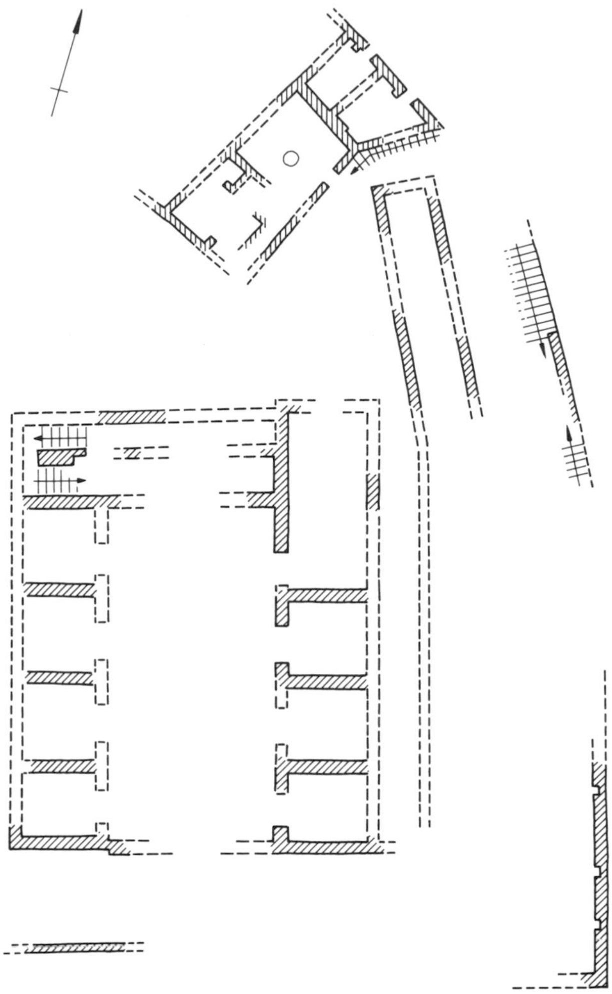

Plan of the residential building at Dayr Qubbat al-Hawā. *Courtesy Peter Grossmann.*

latory, and parts of the sanctuary, including the *khūrus,* can be recognized with certainty. Additional domed and vaulted buildings, which are indirectly connected with the church, can be seen northwest of it. The church was connected with the residential buildings on the upper terrace by an outside staircase cut in the rock.

BIBLIOGRAPHY

Edel, E. *Die Felsgräber der Qubbet el Hawa bei Assuan.* Wiesbaden, 1967–1975.

______. "Qubbat al-Hawā." *Lexikon der Ägyptologie,* Vol. 5, pp. 54–68. Wiesbaden, 1984.

Grossmann, P. "Ein neuer Achtstützenbau im Raum von Aswān in Oberägypten." In *Mélange Gamal Mokhtar,* pp. 332–48. Bibliothèque d'études coptes 92. Cairo, 1985.

Monneret de Villard, U. *Il monastero di S. Simeone presso Aswân,* pp. 16ff. Milan, 1927.

Morgan, J. de. *Catalogue des monuments et inscriptions de l'Egypte antique,* Vol. 1, p. 158 (tomb of Khui/Koui), pp. 162ff. (tomb of Khune). Vienna, 1894.

Timm, S. *Das christlich-koptische Ägypten in arabischer Zeit,* Vol. 1, p. 234, n. 53. Wiesbaden, 1984.

PETER GROSSMANN

DAYR QURNAT MAR'Ī. *See* Qurnat Mar'ī.

DAYR AL-QURQĀṢ. The first and only ancient author who pointed out this monastery was al-MAQRĪZĪ (d. 1441), in his list of the monasteries (1853, Vol. 2, p. 504). He indicated that this monastery was perched on the mountain behind DAYR AL SAB'AT JIBĀL (Monastery of Seven Mountains) and that one could reach it only by paths hollowed into the rock. It is three hours' walk between the site and Dayr al-Sab'at Jibāl at AKHMĪM—that is, Dayr al-Madwid at the entrance of Bīr al-'Ayn, east of Akhmīm. He noted that a well of fresh water was situated below the monastery, surrounded by "ban" trees (a kind of willow).

In 1820, Belzoni (1820, p. 32) heard tell of it. J. A. St. John (1834, p. 277) asked for information about this monastery, but could obtain no confirmation. The most precise information was given by M. JULLIEN. He reported information supplied to him by the inhabitants of Akhmīm. Mounting the plateau, one finds a road that goes to the southeast. Following it for three hours' walk, one comes to the remains of a monastery, Dayr Ascaros and Siclavios (Dioscorus and Aesculapius, two martyrs of Akhmīm, whose memory is preserved at 1 Ṭūbah in the Coptic recension of the SYNAXARION from Upper Egypt (Basset, PO 18, p. 510; Forget, CSCO 49, p. 362 [text]; 78, p. 295 [trans.]). The Synaxarion speaks of a pool to the east of the town; Jullien also spoke of a pool near the monastery (Martin, 1972, pp. 126–27).

Unfortunately, there is no description of this monastery or of what may survive of it.

BIBLIOGRAPHY

Belzoni, G. *Narrative of the Operations . . . in Egypt and Nubia.* London, 1820.

St. John, J. A. *Egypt and Mohamed Aly, or Travels in the Valley of the Nile.* 2 vols. London, 1834.
Martin, M. "Notes inédites du père Jullien sur trois monastères chrétiens d'Egypte: Deir Abū Fana; le couvent 'des sept montagnes'; Deir anbā Bisāda." *Bulletin de l'Institut français d'Archéologie orientale* 71 (1972):79–127.

RENÉ-GEORGES COQUIN
MAURICE MARTIN, S.J.

DAYR AL-QUṢAYR. From this village and as far as the one called DAYR AL-JABRĀWĪ, the Arabian or eastern mountains between the Nile and Red Sea form a massif called Jabal Abū Fūdah, which borders the Nile very closely for some 9 miles (15 km). There are two monasteries there, dedicated to Saint Theodorus and Saint Menas, the first almost at the middle of the massif and the second to the south, but other places also preserve Christian memorials. Near the tomb of Shaykh Mabarī is a Christian cemetery; some quarries famous for the first drawing before the carving of a capital of the goddess Hathor, where some Coptic graffiti can be seen; and finally a Christian necropolis around the tomb of Shaykh Abū Mishāl. A description of the site and a collection of the inscriptions will be found in G. Legrain (1900, pp. 3–14), J. Clédat (1900, pp. 81–87), and A. Kamal (1913, p. 165).

Dayr al-Quṣayr is a large village on the right bank of the Nile, on the latitude of al-Qūsiyyah. No church now exists there; only the name and the presence of a cemetery indicate an ancient monastery. Neither ABŪ ṢĀLIḤ THE ARMENIAN nor al-MAQRĪZĪ speaks of it. M. Jomard (1822–1826, Vol. 4, pp. 302–303) said that this village had two names, Dayr al-Qeisar and Dayr Bosrah. J. VANSLEB (1677, p. 360; 1678, p. 217), in naming the churches and monasteries of Jabal Abū Fūdah, starting from the north, pointed out first the church "of St. Theodore, son of John at Bossra." One may raise two questions: (1) Is Vansleb not thus designating the monastery of Saint Theodorus? (2) Has Jomard not confused Dayr al-Quṣayr and Dayr Bosra?

Jomard also notes a wadi with brick ruins and some potsherds and, above it, some quarries and hypogea with Greek inscriptions. The site was seen by F. L. Norden (1795–1798, Vol. 2, p. 49), G. Wilkinson (1843, Vol. 2, p. 78), G. Maspero (1892, p. 189), and G. Legrain (1900, p. 71). Excavations have recently brought to light a Coptic cemetery (Leclant, 1968, p. 109; 1969, p. 260).

About 4 miles (6 km) from Dayr al-Quṣayr and a little beyond the village of al-Qūsiyyah is the rock church called Mazār al-Sayyidah al-ʿAdhrā'. It is still the place of the pilgrimage and thus linked to the little town of Umm al-Quṣūr.

[*See also:* Abū al-Makārim.]

BIBLIOGRAPHY

Clédat, J. "Notes archéologiques et philologiques." *Bulletin de l'Institut français d'Archéologie orientale* 1 (1900):91–97.
Jomard, E. F. in *Description de l'Egypte,* Vol. 4. Paris, 1821–1829.
Kamāl, A. "Rapport sur les fouilles de Saʿid bey Khachaba au Deir al-Gebrawi." *Annales du Service des antiquités de l'Egypte* 13 (1913):161–78.
Leclant, J. "Fouilles et travaux en Egypte et au Soudan." *Orientalia* 37 (1968):94–136; 38 (1969):240–307.
Legrain, G. "Notes archéologiques prises au gebal Abū Fūda." *Annales du Service des antiquités de l'Egypte* 1 (1900):3–14.
Maspéro, G. "Notes au jour le jour." *Proceedings of the Society of Biblical Archaeology* 14 (1892):170–204, 305–327.
Norden, F. L. *Voyage d'Egypte et de Nubie,* 2 vols. Paris, 1795–1798.
Vansleb, J. *Nouvelle relation en forme de journal d'un voyage fait en Egypte en 1672 et 1673.* Paris, 1677. Translated as *The Present State of Egypt.* London, 1678.
Wilkinson, G. *Modern Egypt and Thebes,* Vols. 1–2. London, 1843.

RENÉ-GEORGES COQUIN
MAURICE MARTIN, S.J.

DAYR AL-QUṢAYR (Ṭurah). [*This article is made up of two parts, history and architecture. More information has accumulated about Dayr al-Quṣayr than about many other monasteries.*]

History

This ruined monastery in the Middle Ages was called Dayr al-Baghl (Monastery of the Mule); Dayr al-Yunān; Dayr al-Haraqal (Monastery of Heraclius); and Dayr Arsāniyūs, for according to the tradition, it was to a cavern in the region of Ṭurah (Troa) that Saint Arsenius retired after spending forty years at SCETIS, ten at Ṭurah "to the south of Babylon and opposite Memphis," three at Canopus, and then two more years at Ṭurah (Evelyn-White, 1932), where he died (*Apophthegmata Patrum,* PG 65, col. 197;

for the dates of the life of Arsenius, see Evelyn-White, 1932, p. 162).

According to a tradition reported by Eutychius (Sa'id ibn al-Batriq, 1863, Vol. 1, p. 537; PG 111, col. 1028) and taken up by ABŪ ṢĀLIḤ THE ARMENIAN (1895, p. 145) and al-MAQRĪZĪ (1853, Vol. 2, p. 503), the monastery is said to have been built over the tomb of Arsenius by Arcadius, whose tutor Arsenius had been.

Eustathius, who was a monk at this monastery and Melchite patriarch of Alexandria in 813–817, was at that time superior of this monastery and built the church of the apostles Peter and Paul and a hermitage for the bishops (Abū Ṣāliḥ, 1895, pp. 146–47).

At the end of the tenth century or beginning of the eleventh, al-Shābushtī (1939, pp. 10, 24) mentioned the *dayr* and was echoed by al-MAQRĪZĪ (1853, Vol. 2, p. 502). The monastery and this church were destroyed in 1010 by order of al-ḤĀKIM. Some time afterward they were restored.

Murqus ibn Qanbar, a Coptic dissident, took refuge at the monastery and died there in 1208. Under the patriarch CYRIL III IBN LAQLAQ, the Melchite monks of al-Quṣayr obtained from the Sultan al-Malik al-Kāmil a reduction of taxes.

In 1320 the Dominican F. Pepin (1859, p. 412) visited the monastery. He found there some Greek monks and, in the cells in the vicinity, some Jacobite hermits. The following year, in the course of popular riots, fourteen monks of the monastery were burned, and the monastery itself was abandoned (al-Maqrīzī, 1853, Vol. 2, pp. 512–17). In the time of al-Maqrīzī, there was only a single guardian in the monastery.

In 1518, a Russian merchant, Basil Posniakoff, visited the monastery, which was then deserted (Volkoff, 1972, p. 19).

B. de Maillet (1735, p. 320) visited the monastery at the beginning of the eighteenth century. In the same period C. SICARD (1982, Vol. 2, pp. 157–58) called attention to the ruins of the Monastery of Saint Arsenius on Mount Tora or Troyen.

In 1941, soldiers of the British army, while clearing out a cavern, discovered nearly two thousand pages of papyrus belonging to eight codices, the greater part of which consisted of works of ORIGEN and DIDYMUS THE BLIND. These papyri must have been hidden at the time of Origenist controversy. Various scholars have published on the subject (Koenen, 1968).

Abū Ṣāliḥ (1895, p. 147) mentioned that between Ṭurah and the Nile, half a day's walk from Dayr al-Quṣayr, was another monastery, Dayr al-Quṣayr al-Ḥaqqānī, at that time already deserted.

BIBLIOGRAPHY

Beaugé, C. "Un Réformateur copte au XIIe siècle." *Revue des Questions historiques* 106 (1927):5–34.

Evelyn-White, H. G. *The Monasteries of the Wadi'n Natrūn,* Pt. 2, *The History of the Monasteries of Nitria and Scetis.* New York, 1932.

Graf, G. *Ein Reformversuch innerhalb der koptischen Kirche im zwölften Jahrhundert.* Collectanea Hierosolymitana 2. Paderborn, 1923.

Koenen, L., and W. Müller-Wiener. "Zu den Papyri aus dem Arsenios-Kloster bei Tura." *Zeitschrift für Papyrologie und Epigraphie* 2 (1968):53–63.

Maillet, B. de. *Description de l'Egypte,* ed. Abbé Le Mascrier. Paris, 1735.

Pepin, F. *Dritte Wanderung nach Palästina,* ed. Tobler. Gotha, 1859.

Sa'id ibn al-Batrīq. *Annales.* PG 111. Paris, 1863.

Shābushtī, al-. "Some Egyptian Monasteries," ed. A. S. Atiya. *Bulletin de la Société d'archéologie copte* 5 (1939):1–28.

Sicard, C. *Oeuvres,* Vol. 2, ed. M. Martin. Cairo and Paris, 1982.

Volkoff, O. *Voyageurs russes en Egypte.* Cairo, 1972.

RENÉ-GEORGES COQUIN
MAURICE MARTIN, S.J.

Architecture

The remains of the medieval monastery are situated in a forbidden military zone and consequently can be visited at present only by special authorization. A fleeting visit in 1963 (Müller-Wiener, 1968, p. 58) determined that the main building was a complex approximately square in shape, which spread out on both sides of a ridge of rock that had been partially hollowed out and left behind by quarry workmen in ancient times. Furthermore, the two parts were connected with each other by a kind of cave passage. The domestic facilities appear to have been situated in the northern area. The entrance gate stood on this side, and presumably, here too were the cisterns, which were replenished by carrier donkeys that worked in relays to transport water from the river to the monastery. The southern area contained the living quarters of the monks. Further accommodation of this kind may be recognized in a large building, at one time multistoried, situated in the southeast corner. Other single rooms extend along the south wall. No remains of a *jawsaq* (keep), which is a necessary part of all other Egyptian monasteries, have been located, on account of the high level of rubble.

The church is in the extreme southeast corner of the main building mentioned above. It has a narthex-like anteroom and an almost square naos, the walls of which are strengthened on all four sides by buttresses that protrude on the inside. Similar wall supports are also found in the Greek octagon-domed churches and appear again in the church of DAYR ANBĀ HADRĀ at Aswan. Consequently, the building is likewise supplied with a large dome constructed on squinches. There are sufficient reasons, therefore, for identifying it with the Sabas church founded before 1125 and described by Abū Ṣāliḥ: "Over the midst of the church there is one large cupola of conspicuous size" (ed. Evetts, p. 150). The sanctuary of the church followed convention and consisted of three sections, but no details of the layout of the rooms have survived. A crypt was discovered beneath the church.

Of the rest of the numerous churches of the monastery that at one time existed, at least one with a large apse can be recognized in a quarry cave to the east of the walled area of the monastery. For the most part, the rest of the churches consist of the same kind of rock-hewn chapels. Finally, attention may be drawn to a tomb construction situated

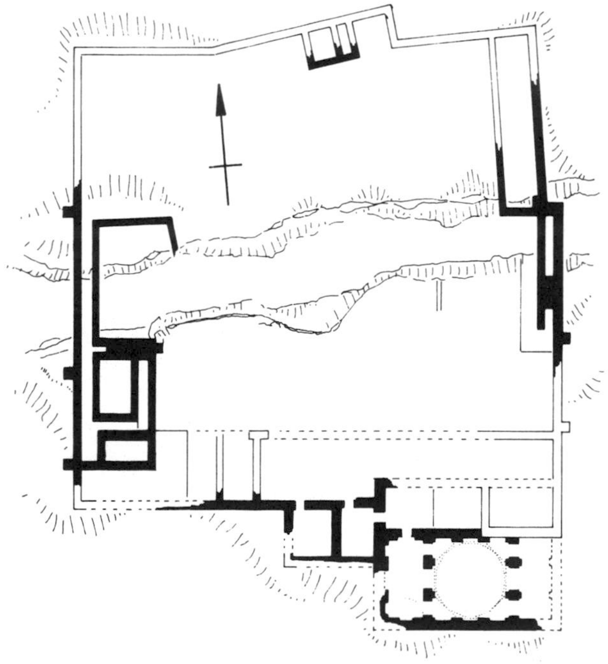

General plan of Dayr al-Quṣayr. *Courtesy Peter Grossmann.*

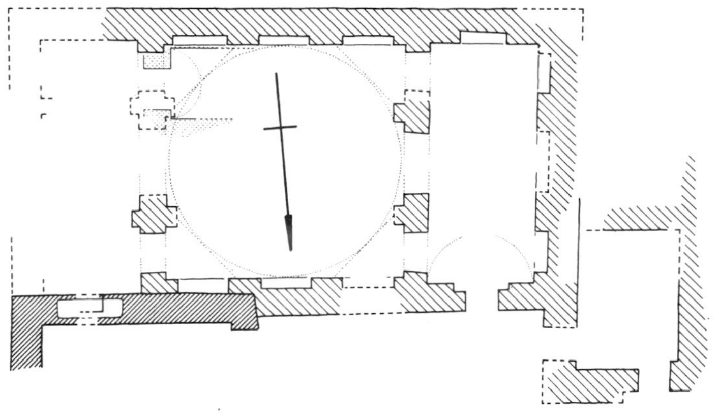

Plan of the church at Dayr al-Quṣayr. *Courtesy Peter Grossmann.*

a small distance south of the church that could be that of Abū al-Faḍā'il, mentioned by ABŪ ṢĀLIḤ (p. 151).

None of the recognizable churches are older than the Middle Ages and, in all probability, they date back only to the period after the destruction under al-Ḥākim in 1010. Remains of the early Christian settlement—which, according to textual sources, was a group of anchorite dwellings—may be recognized in the earlier quarry caves that extend less than a mile to the south of the monastery and contain remains of small building extensions over a wide area.

BIBLIOGRAPHY

Meinardus, O. *Christian Egypt, Ancient and Modern,* pp. 248–50. Cairo, 1965.

Müller-Wiener, W. "Zur Baugeschichte des Arsenios-Klosters." *Zeitscrift für Papyrologie und Epigraphik* 2 (1968):53–63.

Novello, A. A. *Grecia Bizantina,* pp. 52–60. Milan, 1969.

Stikas, E. *L'Eglise byzantine de Christianou,* pp. 35–47. Paris, 1951.

Timm, S. *Das christlich-koptische Ägypten in arabischer Zeit,* Vol. 2, pp. 779–90. Wiesbaden, 1984.

PETER GROSSMANN

DAYR RĪFAH (Asyūṭ), village situated on the edge of the desert plateau about 3 miles (5 km) from DAYR DURUNKAH. This was not a monastery in the ordinary sense of the word but the use of pharaonic tombs by the hermits. A church was fitted up there, making use of a larger tomb that forms the west part of the church. It is still dedicated to the Virgin Mary.

The Churches and Monasteries of Egypt (beginning of the thirteenth century) indicates to the south of Asyūṭ three churches or monasteries consecrated to the Virgin Mary. The one situated at Rīfah and Durunkah is probably the church of Dayr Durunkah. The other two named are those of Azilūn and Abū Harīth. We do not know where they were. One of these *dayrs* could be Dayr Rīfah.

The historian al-MAQRĪZĪ (d. 1441) does not seem to cite this *dayr* but places more to the south of the monastery of Severus that of Saint Theodore, the slayer of dragons. There is in this *dayr,* in addition to the principal church of the Virgin Mary, a secondary church dedicated to Saint Theodorus.

A description of the places may be read in M. Jullien (1901, pp. 210–12). A plan of the whole and a tomb plan will be found in M. Pillet (1912, pp. 62, 72). S. Clarke has given a plan of the church of the Virgin Mary (1912, pp. 176–77), but not of the Church of Saint Theodorus (tomb no. 3 in Pillet's plan).

Some lintels of the doors deriving from other Christian buildings have been reused, among others, and one of them still mentions the name of the neighboring monastery of Severus (Griffith, 1889, pl. 17–18); Petrie (1909, Vol. 1, pl. 52) has also published a wooden lintel with names of a scribe in Coptic. A fine lintel of sculptured stone from the entrance door of the church of the Virgin Mary is reproduced in part by Martin (1966, pl. 10). A Greek graffito in front of the church of Saint Theodorus is unfortunately unpublished.

BIBLIOGRAPHY

Clarke, S. *The Christian Antiquities in the Nile Valley.* London, 1912.

Griffith, F. L. *The Inscriptions of Siūt and Dēr Rifeh.* London, 1889.

Jullien, M. "A travers les ruines de la Haute Egypte à la recherche de la grotte de l'abbé Jean." *Etudes* 88 (1901):205–217.

Martin, M. "Laures et ermitages du désert d'Egypte." *Mélanges de l'Université de St. Joseph* 42 (1966):183–98.

Petrie, W. M. Flinders. *Memphis I.* London, 1909.

Pillet, M. *Structure et décoration architectonique de la nécropole antique de Deir Rifeh.* Mélanges Maspero 1. Mémoires de l'Institut français d'Archéologie orientale 66. Cairo, 1912.

RENÉ-GEORGES COQUIN
MAURICE MARTIN, S.J.

DAYR AL-RŪMĀNIYYAH. On the right bank of the Nile, about 2 miles (3 km) north of the town of Isnā, is situated the village of al-Dayr (the Monastery), the name of which suggests a monastic origin. Near this village are the ruins that the inhabitants call DAYR AL-RŪMĀNIYYAH (the Greek Monastery).

This is without doubt the one that F. L. Norden (1795–98, Vol. 2, p. 138) called Deir Omali. In fact, Ramzī (1953–1968, Vol. 2, pt. 4, p. 154) wrote that the ancient name was Jazīrat al-Dayr (Island of the Monastery) or Dayr al-Jazīrah (Monastery of the Island), which seems to indicate that the monastery was at first on an island. *The State of the Provinces* (al-Latif, 1810), dating from A.H. 777/A.D. 1375–1376, calls it Jazīrat al-Dayr wa Umm ʿAli (Island of the Monastery and of Umm ʿAli), which explains the name transcribed by Norden.

These ruins were excavated by A. H. Sayce (1905, p. 159). Meinardus (1965, p. 324; 1977, p. 439) mentioned them, although he was mistaken in his reference, sending the reader to Palanque's article, but the latter concerns a village of the same name situated near the ancient Monastery of Nahyā, not that placed to the north of Isnā.

BIBLIOGRAPHY

ʿAbd al-Laṭīf. *Relation de l'Egypte de ʿAbd al-Latif,* trans. and ed. Antoine Isaac Silvestre de Sacy. Paris, 1810. *L'Etat des provinces* is translated in an appendix.

Meinardus, O. *Christian Egypt, Ancient and Modern.* Cairo, 1965; 2nd ed., 1977.

Norden, F. L. *Voyage d'Egypte et de Nubie,* ed. L. Langlès. Paris, 1795–1798.

Ramzī, M. *Al-Qāmūs al-Jughrāfī lil-Bilād al-Miṣrīyyah,* 3 vols. Cairo, 1953–1968.

Sayce, A. H. "Excavations at el-Deir." *Annales du Service des antiquités de l'Egypte* 6 (1905):159–167.

RENÉ-GEORGES COQUIN
MAURICE MARTIN, S.J.

DAYR AL-RŪMĪ. [*This entry consists of two sections: history and architecture.*]

History

On a rocky spur at the mouth of the Valley of the Queens, less than a mile west of the ancient town of Jeme (present-day MADĪNAT HĀBŪ), a tomb cut into the rock forms the kernel of this so-called *dayr.* It is the inhabitants of the region who gave it the name Dayr al-Rūmī (the Monastery of the Greeks). One can only regret that excavations have not taken place at the site, for they would without doubt have revealed its true name. It seems that this was not a true cenobium but rather a center fitted up near the place of residence of a celebrated hermit with a church to serve as a meeting place for hermits who lived in the vicinity.

The oldest mention appears to be that of Bononi (Newberry, 1906, p. 82, no. 45). It was also noted by E. Schiaparelli, an Italian archaeologist who worked at DAYR AL-MADĪNAH (1924, Vol. 1, p. 126, n. 1). Grossmann (1974, pp. 25–30) gave a brief description. One may, like H. E. Winlock and W. E. Crum (1926, Vol. 1, pp. 7–8), date this site to the second half of the sixth century or the beginning of the seventh, for the buildings are similar to those of DAYR EPIPHANIUS or the *dayr* in QURNAT MAR'Ī and the surface pottery is identical. According to Baraize, use was made of blocks that came from DAYR AL-BAHRI and Dayr al-Madīnah (cf. Winlock and Crum, 1926, Vol. 1, p. 8, n. 1). The site was briefly noted by O. Meinardus (1965, p. 313; 1977, p. 427).

BIBLIOGRAPHY

Grossmann, P. "Untersuchungen im Dair ar-Rumi bei Qurna in Oberägypten." *Mitteilungen des deutschen archäologischen Instituts Abteilung Kairo* 30 (1974):25–30.

Meinardus, O. *Christian Egypt, Ancient and Modern.* Cairo, 1965; 2nd ed., 1977.

Newberry, P. E. "Topographical Notes on Western Thebes Collected in 1838 by Bononi." *Annales du Service des antiquités de l'Egypte* 7 (1906):78–86.

Schiaparelli, E. *Relazioni sui lavori della Missione archeologica italiana in Egitto,* Vol. 1. Turin, 1924.

Winlock, H. E., and W. E. Crum. *The Monastery of Ephiphanius at Thebes,* 2 vols. New York, 1926.

RENÉ-GEORGES COQUIN
MAURICE MARTIN, S.J.

Architecture

Like many other *dayrs,* Dayr al-Rūmī relates clearly to an older rock tomb. This rock tomb also had a projecting structure built as an open-domed tetrapylon, which was later transformed into a church by the monks who settled there. In the process, a small apse flanked by columns was built into the eastern opening in the wall. The residential quarters of the monks, which are in part several stories high, attach directly to the church on the south and fill a small hollow bounded on the south by a huge rock fragment. Inside is a wide corridor running east and west, from which the sleeping chambers of the monks branch off on the south. It also contains on the north a covered entrance corridor, the actual access to the church, as well as a small refectory. The ancillary buildings lie southeast of the church. The date of the monastery's founding is not clear, but it can scarcely predate the seventh century. Evidently the monastic community that lived here was very small.

BIBLIOGRAPHY

Grossmann, P. "Untersuchungen in Dair ar-Rūmī bei Qurna in Oberägypten." *Mitteilungen des Deutschen Archäologischen Instituts, Abteilung Kairo* 30(1974):25–30.

Winlock, H. E., and W. E. Crum. *The Monastery of Epiphanius at Thebes,* Vol. 1, pp. 7ff. New York, 1926.

PETER GROSSMANN

DAYR AL-RUSUL. *See* Monasteries of the Middle Ṣa'īd.

DAYR AL-SAB'AT JIBĀL. [*In two parts this entry discusses the history and description, as well as the architecture of Dayr al-Sab'at Jibāl.*]

History

This monastery is in Wādī bīr al-'Ayn, southwest of AKHMĪM. It is without doubt the one called Dayr Abū Ḥalbānah by ABŪ ṢĀLIḤ THE ARMENIAN (1895, p. 243), for this author placed the latter to the east of Akhmīm near a spring that flows in the mountain not far from a cistern, which corresponds very well to the present position of Dayr al-Madwid.

Al-MAQRĪZĪ (d. 1441; 1853, Vol. 2, p. 504) called it Dayr al-Sab'at Jibāl (Monastery of Seven Mountains) because of its situation among lofty mountains. The sun, he said, gives light there only two hours after sunrise, and similarly night falls two hours before sunset. Near the spring grew a willow that, according to al-Maqrīzī, gave its name to the monastery (Dayr al-Ṣafṣāfah). The wadi in which this monastery is situated is called Wādī al-Mulūk by reason of the plant, *al-mulūkah,* according to al-Maqrīzī.

This monastery has been described by travelers: P. Lucas (1719, Vol. 2, p. 362); R. Pococke (1743–1745, Vol. 1, p. 78); and G. MASPERO (1886, pp. 213–14), who cited the preceding authors and described the state of the monastery around 1880. Others were A. Gayet (1905, pp. 26–50); M. Jullien (Martin, 1972, pp. 125–27); G. Daressy (1917, p. 13); and O. Meinardus (1965, p. 298; 1977, p. 410), who described it in its present state.

The Coptic and Greek inscriptions have been collected by U. Bouriant (1888, pp. 131–59) and G. Lefebvre (1907, p. 66, nos. 351, 352).

Some have wished to locate here the last place of exile of Nestorius because his name appears ten or twelve times (cf. Gayet's article, which was criticized in *Archaeological Report;* Griffith, 1904–1905, p. 82).

The description of the site invites consideration of it not as a monastery in the proper sense but as a small LAURA. The hermits were no doubt attracted there by the frequenting of the spring to which the people attached superstition, since this is desert country; and perhaps by its proximity to the road from Akhmīm to the Red Sea (cf. Nassiri Khosrau, 1881, p. 175).

BIBLIOGRAPHY

Bouriant, U. "Notes de voyage," sec. 3, "Le Rocher de la vallée d'Akhmim." *Recueil des travaux relatifs à la phililogie et à l'archéologie égyptiennes* 11 (1888):131–59.

Daressy, G. "Indicateur topographique du Livre des perles enfouies et du mystère précieux." *Bulletin de l'Institut français d'Archéologie orientale* 13 (1917):175–230.

Gayet, A. *Coins ignorés d'Egypte.* Paris, 1905.

Griffith, F. Ll., ed. *Archeological Report.* Egypt Exploration Fund. London, 1904–1905.

Lefebvre, G. *Recueil des inscriptions grecques-chrétiennes d'Egypte.* Cairo, 1907.

Lucas, P. *Troisième voyage du sieur Paul Lucas fait en 1714.* Rouen, 1719.

Martin, M. "Notes inédites du père Jullien sur trois monastères chrètiens d'Egypte: Dayr Abū Fana; le couvent de 'sept montagnes'; dayr anbā Bisāda." *Bulletin de l'Institut français d'Archéologie orientale* 71 (1972):119–129.

Maspéro, G. "Sur les fouilles et travaux exécutés en Egypte, pendant l'hiver de 1885–1886." *Bulletin de l'Institut égyptien* (1886):196–271.

Meinardus, O. *Christian Egypt, Ancient and Modern.* Cairo, 1965; 2nd ed., 1977.

Nāsir I. Khosrau. *Sefer Nameh,* ed. C. Schefer. Paris, 1881.

Pococke, R. *A Description of the East and Some Other Countries,* 2 vols. London, 1743–1745.

RENÉ-GEORGES COQUIN
MAURICE MARTIN, S.J.

Architecture

This frequently mentioned but rarely visited monastery is distinguished not so much by its actual significance as by its almost mythical fame, in part attributable to its remoteness. It is found in the vicinity of a small watering place, reached after a walk of about an hour and a half from the entrance to the valley, and offers a modest horticultural living for the few people who have their residence there. Consequently, the colony of monks that resided there could not at any time have been large. In fact, besides a few Greek and Coptic graffiti, the remains of the monks' accommodations can be recognized only in an almost inaccessible position against the rock wall. The small building with a semicircular buttress projecting from one of the walls in the bottom of the valley was regarded by Christians as a church (among others, Munier, 1940, p. 156; Meinardus, 1965, p. 298) and by Muslims as a mosque, but it is, in fact, a cistern dating from the early medieval period. The water of this spring was already attracting visitors in pharaonic times and is still regarded by the population as possessing healing powers. However, it is wrong to think that caravans used to traverse this valley, since a few hundred meters beyond the spring the terrain is impassable.

BIBLIOGRAPHY

Kuhlmann, K. P. *Materialien zur Archäologie und Geschichte des Raumes von Achmīm,* pp. 7–9. Mainz, 1983.

Meinardus, O. *Christian Egypt, Ancient and Modern.* Cairo, 1965.

Munier, J. "Les Monuments coptes d'après les explorations du Père Jullien." *Bulletin de la Société d'archéologie copte* 6 (1940):141–168.

Timm, S. *Der christlich-koptische Ägypten in arabischer Zeit,* Vol. 2, pp. 793–94. Wiesbaden, 1984.

PETER GROSSMANN

DAYR AL-ṢALĪB. [*This entry about a small monastery consists of two parts. The first tells the history;*

the second the architecture, but chiefly of the church.]

History

This small monastery is situated on the edge of the desert in the village called Ḥajar Danfīq on the left bank of the Nile. The site is ancient, for it is named in the Arabic Life of Pisentius (O'Leary, PO22) and in that of Saint Andrew, superior of Dayr al-Ṣalīb (Winlock and Crum, 1926, Vol. 1, pp. 114–15).

It was not until 1668 that it was cited by European travelers, the Capuchin fathers Protais and François (Sauneron, 1974, p. 93). They were to be copied by J. VANSLEB (1677, p. 411; 1678, p. 246). At the beginning of the eighteenth century C. SICARD (1982, Vol. 2, p. 227) knew this monastery. S. CLARKE (1912, pp. 126–30) described its church and drew up a plan of it. U. Monneret de Villard (1926, Vol. 2, p. 62, fig. 97) corrected this plan.

Unfortunately this ancient building fell into ruin and was demolished in 1917 (Clarke, 1919, p. 527). It was to be replaced by a modern structure. The present state of the site was described by O. Meinardus (1965, pp. 311–12; 1977, p. 425).

This monastery is also sometimes called that of Shenute ('Abd al-Masīḥ Ṣalīb, 1924, p. 176). It is perhaps the one noticed by ABŪ ṢĀLIḤ THE ARMENIAN (1895, p. 280) at the beginning of the thirteenth century. It rather seems that it took the name of a neighboring monastery, since fallen to ruin (Winlock and Crum, 1926, Vol. 1, p. 112, n. 12).

BIBLIOGRAPHY

'Abd al-Masīḥ Ṣalīb al-Masū'dī al-Baramūsī. *Kitāb Tuḥfat al Sā'ilin fi Dhikr Adyirat Ruhbān al-Miṣrīyyīn.* Cairo, 1924.

Clarke, S. *Christian Antiquities in the Nile Valley.* Oxford, 1912.

Comité de conservation de l'art arabe. Procès-Verbaux des séances 32. Cairo, 1919.

Meinardus, O. *Christian Egypt, Ancient and Modern.* Cairo, 1965; 2nd ed., 1977.

Monneret de Villard, U. *Les Couvents près de Sohāg,* Vol. 2. Milan, 1926.

O'Leary, De L., ed. *The Arabic Life of St. Pisentius.* PO 22, pt. 3. Paris, 1930.

Sauneron, S. *Villes et légendes d'Egypte.* Cairo, 1974.

Sicard, C. *Oeuvres,* Vol. 2, ed. M. Martin. Bibliothèque d'étude 84. Cairo, 1982.

Vansleb, J. M. *Nouvelle relation en forme de journal d'un voyage fait en Egypte en 1672 et 1673.* Paris, 1677. Translated as *The Present State of Egypt.* London, 1678.

Winlock, H. E., and W. E. Crum. *The Monastery of Epiphanius at Thebes,* Vol. 1. New York, 1926.

RENÉ-GEORGES COQUIN
MAURICE MARTIN, S.J.

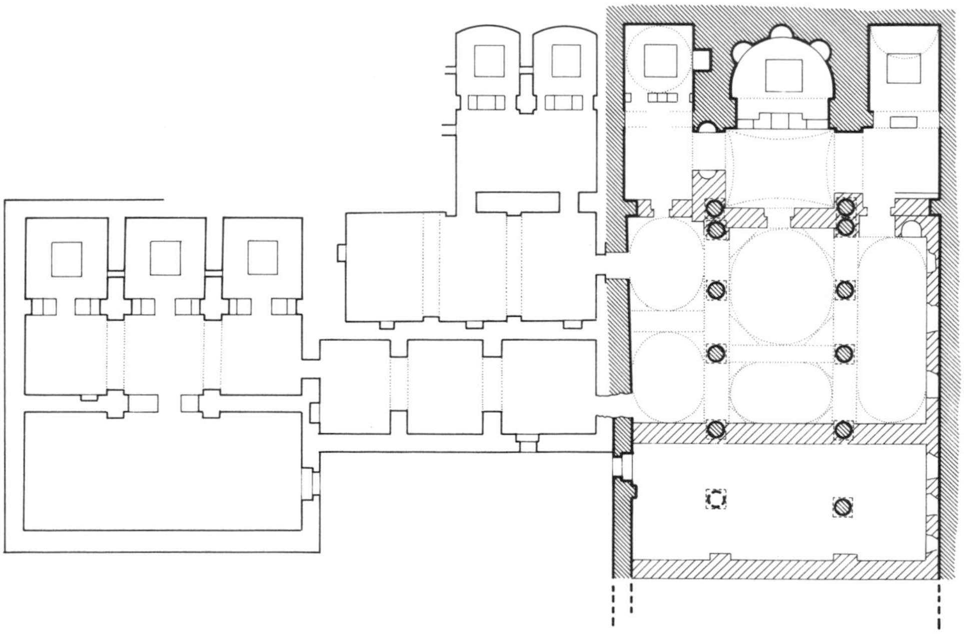

Plan of Dayr al-Ṣalīb.

Architecture

Dayr al-Ṣalīb (Monastery of the Holy Cross) is an unimportant and today uninhabited monastery. Down to the second decade of the twentieth century it contained an old church arranged as a three-aisle basilica (Clarke, 1912, pp. 126ff.). Still standing were the sanctuary, the remains of the *khūrus* (room between naos and sanctuary), several pillars (taken from pharaonic buildings), and the outer walls on the long sides. In the twelfth or thirteenth century—probably after the loss of the original wooden roof—it was converted to a vaulted structure. Further, in the course of several building operations the separation between the *khūrus* and the naos became more and more strongly marked. The church is an example of the way in which, with the increased frequency of masses in the Mamluk period, the original side rooms of the apse were converted into additional altar areas by pulling down the former entrance walls. The remaining churches of the monastery are modern, as is the not very high surrounding wall.

BIBLIOGRAPHY

Clarke, S. *Christian Antiquities in the Nile Valley,* pp. 126–30. Oxford, 1912.

Grossmann, P. *Mittelalterliche Langhauskuppelkirchen und verwandte Typen in Oberägypten,* pp. 42–45. Glückstadt, 1982.

Monneret de Villard, U. *Les Couvents près de Sohâg,* Vol. 1, p. 62. Milan, 1925.

______. *Deyr el-Muḥaraqah,* p. 13. Milan, 1928.

PETER GROSSMANN

DAYR AL-SANAD (Naqādah). This monastery is built into the mountain, an hour and a half's walk to the west of Naqādah, on the left bank of the Nile. It is attested very early by a Coptic contract (Crum, 1921, no. 340), by the SYNAXARION in the recension from Upper Egypt at 21 Kiyahk, and by the Arabic life of Pisentius (O'Leary, PO 22, pp. 454, 462). In the Arabic texts it is called Dayr al-Sanad, a word that recurs in the place-names of the region but the meaning of which remains a debated question. It would have been inhabited from the sixth century to the fourteenth.

It was mentioned by 'ABD AL-MASĪḤ al-Masū'dī (1924, p. 183). He noted that its ruined state precludes its use for worship. It is also called the Monastery of Samuel and Dayr al-Jizāz. This is at least an identification proposed by J. Doresse, who excavated and described it (1949, pp. 508–510; 1951–1952, pp. 70–71).

It is not known whether this was a real monastery or rather a center for communal services where the hermits of the vicinity gathered together on Saturdays and Sundays.

BIBLIOGRAPHY

'Abd al-Masīḥ Salīb al-Masū'dī al-Baramūsī. *Kitāb Tuḥfat al-Sā'ilīn fī Dhikr Adyirat Ruhban al-Miṣriyyīn.* Cairo, 1924.

Crum, W. E. *Short Texts from Coptic Ostraca and Papryi.* London, 1921.

Di Bitonto Kasser, A. "Ostraca scolastici copti a Deir Gizāz." *Aegyptus* (Milan) 68 (1988):167–75.

Doresse, J. "Monastères coptes thébains." *Revue des Conférences françaises en Orient* (1949):3–16.

______. "Recherches d'archéologie copte: le couvent de Samuel près de Negada." *Bulletin de l'Institut d'Egypte* 34 (1952):470–71.

O'Leary, De L. *The Arabic Life of Saint Pisentius.* PO22, pp. 313–488.

Winlock, H., and W. E. Crum. *The Monastery of Epiphanius at Thebes,* 2 vols. New York, 1926.

RENÉ-GEORGES COQUIN
MAURICE MARTIN, S.J.

DAYR SANNURIS. *See* Monasteries of the Fayyūm.

DAYR AL-SANQŪRIYYAH. Of this ancient monastery, which has now disappeared, there remains no more than the name and the church dedicated to Saint Theodorus. The latter was perhaps named by ABŪ ṢĀLIḤ THE ARMENIAN (1895, p. 212), who situated it at Kufūr.

Al-MAQRĪZĪ did not speak of it, but the church was noted by C. SICARD (1982, Vol. 2, p. 271), who placed it outside the town and near the cemetery. A modern description was supplied by O. Meinardus (1965, p. 257; 1977, pp. 361–62).

M. Ramzī (1953–1968, Vol. 2, pt. 3, p. 217) thinks that this is the DAYR AL-KHADĪM, but the latter, according to al-Maqrīzī, was dedicated to the angel GABRIEL. 'ABD AL-MASĪḤ al-Masū'dī (1924, pp. 163, 191) cited al-Sanqūriyyah as the first among the monasteries existing in the province of Banī Suef, and Dayr al-Khādim among those that have disappeared.

[*See also:* Abū al-Makārim.]

BIBLIOGRAPHY

ʻAbd al-Masīh Ṣalīb al-Masūʻdi al-Baramūsī. *Tuḥfat al Sāʼilīn fī Dhikr Adyirat Ruhbān al-Miṣriyyīn.* Cairo, 1924.

Meinardus, O. *Christian Egypt, Ancient and Modern.* Cairo, 1965; 2nd ed., 1977.

Ramzī, M. *Al-Qāmūs al-Jughrāfī lil-Bilād al Miṣrīyyah,* 3 vols. Cairo, 1953–1968.

Sicard, C. *Oeuvres,* Vol. 2, ed. M. Martin. Bibliothèque d'étude 85. Cairo, 1982.

RENÉ-GEORGES COQUIN
MAURICE MARTIN, S.J.

DAYR AL-SĀQIYAH. This monastery, today in ruins, was situated on the left bank of the Nile 2.5 miles (4 km) north of the DAYR AL-NAṢĀRĀ, at the bottom of a large wadi that opened on the stony desert at the foot of the mountain. At the foot of a high cliff is a rectangular enclosure 200 by 264 feet (60 by 80 m), a deep hole that marks the position of a well, and another excavation occupied by an enormous antique capital. The remains of brick structures are distinct. At the foot of the cliffs are two caves and, in front of them, a church, marked by the remains of columns and capitals. Coins of the fifth century have been found there (Mond and Myers, 1937, Vol. 1, pp. 77–79; 1940, Vol. 1, pp. 146–50). Drawings and graffiti from the site will be found reproduced in Winkler (1938–1939, Vol. 1, p. 17 and pl. I.3). Like DAYR EPIPHANIUS and other *dayrs,* this one seems to have been a religious center for hermits living in the adjoining caves. This may be the Monastery of Ezekiel of which the Upper Egypt recension of the SYNAXARION speaks at 14 Kiyahk and 2 Ṭūbah, with reference to Anbā Ezekiel and Anbā Victor and his nephew Anbā Yūnā (perhaps Jonas).

The archaeologists R. Mond and O. H. Myers, who excavated the site, gave it the name Monastery of Saint John. Several documents deriving from Thebes mention a topos (church or monastery) of Saint John; some add "in the desert" (cf. Crum, 1902, no. 310; Winlock and Crum, 1926, Vol. 1, p. 114, and Vol. 2, nos. 84 and 397; Revillout, 1900, pp. 143–44; Crum, 1921, no. 139). This is perhaps a case of different sites with the same name, but the specification "in the desert" seems to be added to distinguish this *dayr* from the others and fits well with the situation of the site.

BIBLIOGRAPHY

Crum, W. E. *Coptic Ostraca from the Collections of the Egypt Exploration Fund, the Cairo Museum and Others.* London, 1902.

______. *Short Texts from Coptic Ostraca and Papyri.* London, 1921.

Doresse, J. "Monastères coptes aux environs d'Armant en Thebaïde." *Analecta Bollandiana* 67 (1949):327–49.

Mond, R., and O. H. Myers. *Cemeteries of Armant,* 2 vols. London, 1937.

______. *Temples of Armant,* 2 vols. London, 1940.

Revillout, E. "Textes coptes, extraits de la correspondance de St. Pesunthius, évêque de Coptis et de plusiers documents analogues (juridiques ou économiques)." *Revue d'égyptologie* 9 (1900):133–77; 10 (1902):34–47; and 14 (1914):22–32.

Winkler, H. A. *Rock-Drawings of Southern Upper Egypt,* 2 vols. Egypt Exploration Society, Archaeological Survey 26–27. London, 1938–1939.

Winlock, H. E., and W. E. Crum. *The Monastery of Epiphanius at Thebes,* 2 vols. New York, 1926.

RENÉ-GEORGES COQUIN
MAURICE MARTIN, S.J.

DAYR SAWĀDAH. *See* Dayr Apa Hor (Minyā).

DAYR SAYLAH. *See* Dayr al-ʻAdhrāʼ (Fayyūm); Dayr al-Ḥammām.

DAYR AL-SHAHĪD PHĪLŪTHĀWAUS (Jirjā). On the map of the *Survey of Egypt* (1928), Nag Hammadi section, one notes a Najʻ al-Dayr (Village of the Monastery) on the right bank of the Nile. In the village is a small monastery dedicated to the martyr Saint PHILOTHEUS. It is not known to which Saint Philotheus this monastery is consecrated, the martyr of Antioch or the more recent martyr of A.M. 1097/A.D. 1380, a native of Durunkah. Since this town is near ASYŪṬ and hence somewhat distant from the present monastery, the martyr of Antioch seems the more likely dedicatee.

The first mention of the monastery appears to be that of S. Clarke (1912), in his appendix, which gives a list of churches and monasteries that is the official one of the Coptic patriarchate. He placed it to the east of al-Khiyām in the *mudiriyyah* (province) of Jirjā, which corresponds to its actual situation, between al-Khiyām and al-Naghāmīsh (p. 214, no. 41). 'ABD AL-MASĪḤ al-Masū'dī assigned it the same geographical position and indicated that Saint Philotheus is commemorated on 16 Ṭūbah; it would then be the Philotheus of Antioch who is the titular saint (1924, p. 176). This would be the only church dedicated to this martyr still in use in Egypt, although ABŪ ṢĀLIḤ THE ARMENIAN (1895, pp. 134–35) said that the church of the DAYR AL-NASṬŪR was dedicated to Saint Philotheus when the monastery became the property of the Copts. The veneration of this martyr was important in Egypt, as is shown by the number of the manuscripts of his Passion and his miracles (cf. Orlandi, 1978, pp. 117–20).

Unfortunately there has been no archaeological study of this *dayr* to determine exactly the date of the present buildings.

BIBLIOGRAPHY

'Abd al-Masīḥ Ṣalīb al-Masū'dī al-Baramūsī. *Kitāb Tuḥfat al-Sā'ilīn fī Dhikr Adyirat Ruhbān al-Miṣriyyīn.* Cairo, 1924.

Clarke, S. *Christian Antiquities in the Nile Valley.* Oxford, 1912.

Orlandi, T. "Il 'dossier copto' di san Filoteo d'Antiochia." *Analecta Bollandiana* 96 (1978):117–20.

Survey of Egypt. Cairo, 1928.

RENÉ-GEORGES COQUIN
MAURICE MARTIN, S.J.

DAYR AL-SHAHĪD TADRUS (Qamūlah). *See* Monasteries of the Upper Ṣa'īd.

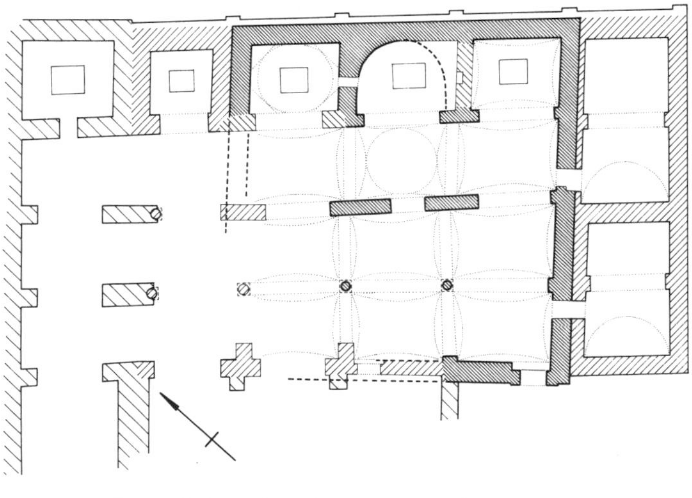

Plan of the church at Dayr al-Shahīd Tadrus al-Muḥārib. *Courtesy Peter Grossmann.*

DAYR AL-SHAHĪD TADRUS (Qifṭ). *See* Monasteries of the Upper Ṣa'īd.

DAYR AL-SHAHĪD TADRUS AL-MUḤĀRIB, unoccupied monastery southwest of MADĪNAT HĀBŪ, the great Temple of the Dead of Ramses III. Also located in the vicinity is a Coptic cemetery that is still in use today. The church of this monastery has five altars arranged side by side, of which, however, only the three southern ones have a primitive origin. They belong to a hall church with three aisles, whose naos was subdivided into nine large domed bays of approximately the same size and of slightly accentuated breadth. The precinct of the *khūrus,* (room between naos and sanctuary), separated from the lay area only by two stretches of wall standing in the middle of the room, is thus already clearly seen to be in the process of changing. The center bay of the *khūrus* supports a more lavishly shaped and more elevated dome. This first building may have been erected in the advanced Mamluk period.

BIBLIOGRAPHY

Clarke, S. *Christian Antiquities in the Nile Valley,* pp. 116–18. Oxford, 1912.

Grossmann, P. *Mittelalterliche Langhauskuppelkirchen,* pp. 203–205. Glückstadt, 1982.

Timm, S. *Das christlich-koptische Ägypten in arabischer Zeit,* Vol. 2, p. 796. Wiesbaden, 1984.

PETER GROSSMANN

DAYR SHAHRĀN, monastery south of Cairo that was restored and dedicated under the Patriarch ZACHARIAS (1004–1032) by the monk Poemen, who had embraced Islam and then returned to the Christian faith and became its abbot.

In this monastery BARSŪM THE NAKED lived for seventeen years (1300–1317), and here he was buried. Toward 1320 Abū al-Barakāt IBN KABAR described the procession of the Palms (referring to Palm Sunday) to the monastery in his encyclopedia, *Misbaḥ al-Ẓulmah* (Villecourt, 1925, p. 271).

Two Coptic patriarchs were buried in the monastery of Shahrān, JOHN VIII (1300–1320) and BENJAMIN II (1327–1339).

Al-MAQRĪZĪ (d. 1441) described the monastery, which he says was well populated in the fourteenth century. According to him, Shahrān was an educated Christian or a king. In the seventeenth century J. Vansleb mentioned the monastery under the name of Barsūm the Naked (1677, p. 294; English ed., p. 178).

Several manuscripts were written at or for the monastery (Simaykah, 1942, Vol. 2, pt. 1, nos. 5, 149, 10, 709, 81, 865; Troupeau, 1972, Vol. 1, nos. 113, 278). The four most ancient manuscripts mention the monastery under the name of Mercurius at Shahrān; the two latest from the eighteenth century under that of Barsūm the Naked.

The patriarch CYRIL V (1854–1861) built a tower and later opened the church for parochial service. [*See also:* Barsūm the Naked.]

BIBLIOGRAPHY

Troupeau, G. *Catalogue des manuscrits arabes,* Vol. 1. Paris, 1972.

Vansleb, J. *Nouvelle relation en forme de journal d'un voyage fait en Egypte en 1672 et 1673.* Paris, 1677. Translated as *The Present State of Egypt.* London, 1678.

Villecourt, L. "Les Observances liturgiques et la discipline du jeûne dans l'église copte." *Le Muséon* 36 (1923):249–92; 37 (1924):201–80; 38 (1925): 261–320.

RENÉ-GEORGES COQUIN
MAURICE MARTIN, S.J.

DAYR SHALLA.

See Monasteries of the Fayyūm.

DAYR AL-SHALWĪT.

About 6 miles (10 km) northwest of Armant is a small temple erected by the Roman emperors Hadrian and Antonius Pius in honor of the goddess Isis that is described by the local inhabitants under the name Dayr al-Shalwīt. It was occupied by a Christian community, as is shown by numerous graffiti traced on the roof, but no one can say which community, Pachomians or semihermits. A Coptic contract of the seventh or eighth century makes mention of the *castrum* (camp) of Shlout as the place of residence of one of the signatories, while the others are of the nome of Armant (Hall, 1905, pl. 74, no. 21293/2; Till, 1956, no. 19/2). It is probable that this gives this site its Coptic name. The present Arabic name takes up the Coptic name, playing on the fact that the Coptic name has a parallel in Arabic: *shalwīt* (distant). It is curiously called Dayr Katreh in the *Description de l'Egypte* (Jomard, 1821, Vol. 2, p. 141), but the name Dayr al-Shalwīt was attested in 1830 by Bononi (Newberry, 1906, pp. 78–86). It was described by J. Doresse (1949, p. 343) and by O. Meinardus (1965, p. 320; 1977, p. 434–35).

BIBLIOGRAPHY

Description de l'Egypte. Paris, 1821–1829.

Doresse, J. "Monastères coptes aux environs d'Armant en Thebaïde." *Analecta Bollandiana* 67 (1949):327–49.

Hall, H. R. *Coptic and Greek Texts.* London, 1905.

Meinardus, O. *Christian Egypt, Ancient and Modern.* Cairo, 1965; 2nd ed. 1977.

Newberry, P. E. "Topographical Notes on Western Thebes Collected in 1830 by J. Bononi." *Annales du Service des antiquités de l'Egypte* 7 (1906):78–86.

Till, W. "Die koptischen Arbeitsverträge." *Eos* 481 (1956):273–329.

RENÉ-GEORGES COQUIN
MAURICE MARTIN, S.J.

DAYR AL-SHAMʻ.

The most ancient testimony is that given at the beginning of the thirteenth century by ABŪ ṢĀLIḤ THE ARMENIAN (1895, pp. 194–95), who saw an inscription dating a reconstruction of the monastery from the year 951.

Abū Ṣāliḥ explained the nickname Dayr al-Shayāṭīn (Monastery of the Demons) by saying that the monks had abandoned it because of mysterious apparitions. It was repopulated by PAPHNUTIUS, who came from SCETIS. This Paphnutius would have been the one who was present at the death of ONOPHRIUS and buried him. The body of Paphnutius, on Abū Ṣāliḥ's report, rested in this monastery.

According to the HISTORY OF THE PATRIARCHS OF THE EGYPTIAN CHURCH (1959, Vol. 2, pt. 3, pp. 241 [text], 384 [trans.]), the patriarch MICHAEL IV placed the monastery under the jurisdiction of the bishop of Giza. The patriarch GABRIEL II restored the monastery (Vol. 3, pt. 1, pp. 34 [text], 55 [trans.]; Abū Ṣāliḥ, 1895, p. 195). In the time of the patriarch MICHAEL V Ibn Nafrā was consecrated bishop in this monastery (Vol. 3, pt. 1, pp. 59 [text], 63 [trans.]).

The list of relics drawn up by the *History of the Patriarchs* includes the body of the martyr Paphnutius, preserved in the Dayr al-Shamʻ. This text appears to contradict Abū Ṣāliḥ, who does not speak of a martyr.

Abū Ṣāliḥ (1895, pp. 192, 194, 195) situated the monastery at Minyat al-Shammās and said that in his time the church had three altars, one dedicated

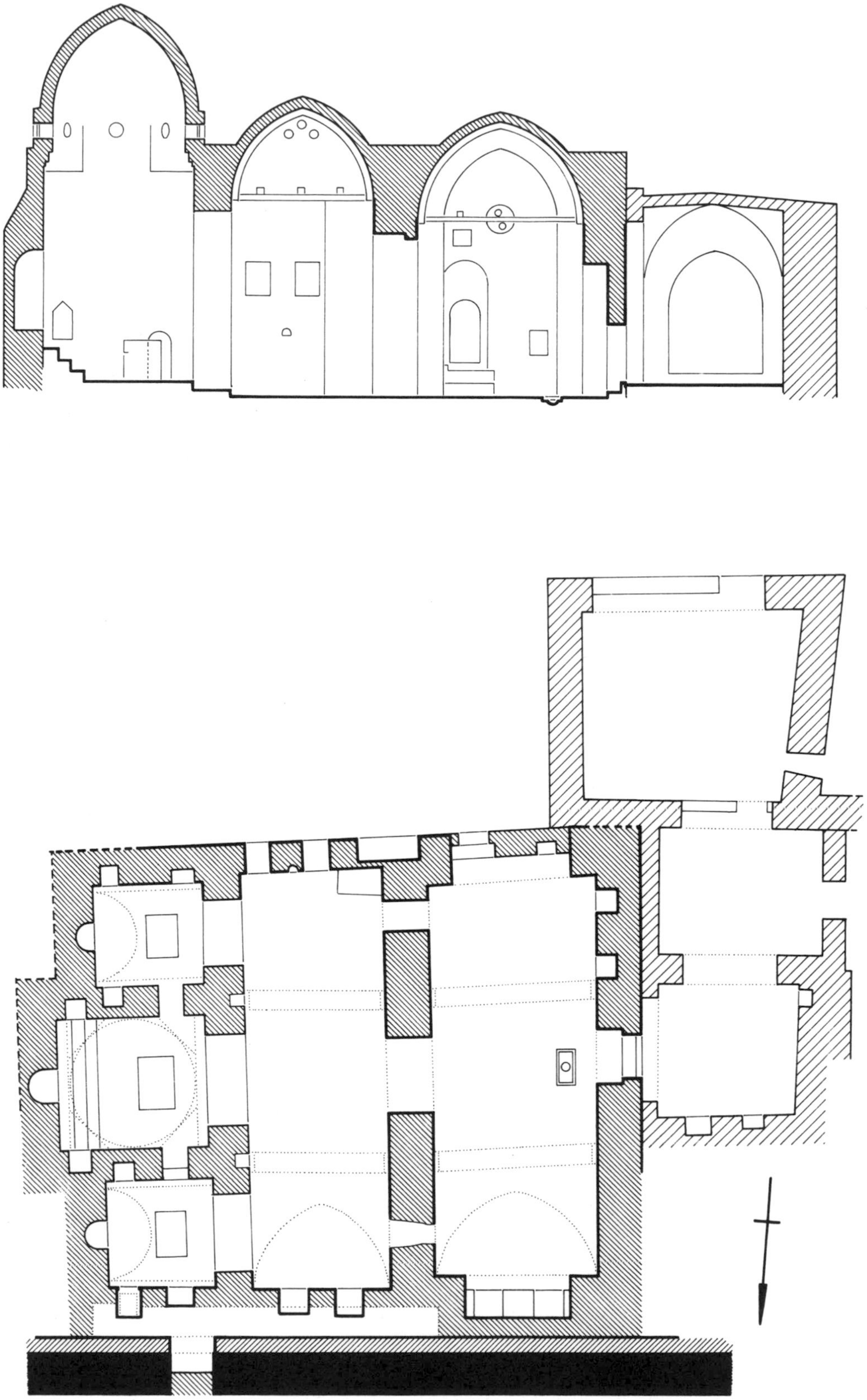

Elevation and plan of the Roman temple known as Dayr al-Shalwīt. *Courtesy Peter Grossmann.*

to ANTONY, the second to SHENUTE, and the third to Paphnutius, and that it had many monks.

In the middle of the thirteenth century the monastery depended on the patriarch, for CYRIL III IBN LAQLAQ died and was buried there.

In the thirteenth century Yāqūt (1870–1873, Vol. 2, p. 673) also knew this monastery; he pointed out that it served as residence for the patriarch when the latter came to Cairo and that the monastery was three *parasangs* distant from al-Fusṭāṭ (Old Cairo), passing by the Nile. The monastery was still mentioned in 1375 in the *State of the Provinces* (ʿAbd al-Laṭīf, 1810; Abū Ṣāliḥ, 1895, p. 192, n. 2). The *Livre des perles enfouies* (Daressy, 1917, p. 201) also cites it, although placing it at Asyūṭ. Al-MAQRĪZĪ (d. 1441) knew nothing of this monastery, which seems to have disappeared before his time.

Modern authors place it at Mīt Shammās, less than a mile southwest of Ṭamwayh, in the *markaz* (district) of Giza (Ramzī, 1953–1963, Vol. 2, pt. 3, p. 22). JIRJIS PHĪLŪTHĀWUS ʿAWAḌ also placed it at Mīt Shammās (cf. Simaykah, 1930, Vol. 2, pp. 243–45).

BIBLIOGRAPHY

ʿAbd al-Laṭīf. *Relation de l'Egypte de ʿAbd al-Latif*, ed. and trans. A. I. S. de Sacy. Paris, 1810. *L'Etat des provinces* is translated in an appendix.

Daressy, G. "Indicateur topographique du 'Livre des perles enfouies et du mystère précieux.'" *Bulletin de l'Institut français d'Archéologie orientale* 13 (1917):175–230.

Ramzī, M. *Al-Qāmūs al-Jughrāfī lil-Bilād al-Miṣrīyyah*, 3 vols. Cairo, 1953–1968.

Simaykah, M. *Guide to the Coptic Museum*, Vol. 2. Cairo, 1932 (in Arabic).

Yāqūt. *Geographisches Wörterbuch*, 6 vols., ed. F. Wüstenfeld. Leipzig, 1870–1873.

RENÉ-GEORGES COQUIN
MAURICE MARTIN, S.J.

DAYR AL-SHAYKHAH. *See* Dayr al-Kubāniyyah.

DAYR SHUBRA KALSA. *See* Monasteries in the Province of Gharbiyyah.

DAYR AL-SHUHADĀ' (Akhmīm). [*This entry is made up of two parts. The first gives the location and information about recorded history. The second part describes some of the findings there and what can be determined about the architecture.*]

History

The Monastery of the Martyrs is situated on a slight elevation in the desert, about half a mile north of al-Hawāwīsh, which is itself about 4 miles (6 km) east of Akhmīm. It is neighbor to two other monasteries, DAYR AL-MALĀK MĪKHĀ'ĪL and DAYR AL-ʿADHRĀ' (Monastery of the Virgin).

Several travelers mentioned it (Pococke; Granger). The fifteenth-century historian AL-MAQRĪZĪ made it very clear that the so-called Church of the Savior now bearing the name of the Martyrs is in the interior of Akhmīm. This cannot therefore be the Monastery of the Martyrs.

BIBLIOGRAPHY

Granger, N. *Relation du voyage fait en Egypte en l'année 1730*. Paris, 1745.

Meinardus, O. *Christian Egypt, Ancient and Modern*. Cairo, 1965; 2nd ed., 1977.

Pococke, R. *A Description of the East and Some Other Countries*. London, 1745.

Saint-Genis, A. B. "Notice sur les restes de l'ancienne ville de Chemnis ou Panopolis, aujourd'hui Akhmym, et ses environs." In *Description de l'Egypte, Antiquités*, Vol. 4, ed. E. F. Jomard. Paris, 1821.

RENÉ-GEORGES COQUIN
MAURICE MARTIN, S.J.

Architecture

This monastery is also known as Dayr al-Wusṭānī. A church with this dedication is mentioned by al-Maqrīzī in the fifteenth century. Its connection with the martyrs, its position near an early Coptic cemetery, and the large amounts of late Roman pottery found by its walls suggest that this building may be on the site of an early monastery of which there are now no visible remains. There is a large courtyard containing many tombs, a chamber with two small courts south of the entrance, a small room for water jugs, and several small rooms south of the church. The first phase of the church building has been assigned by P. Grossmann (1982, pp. 202–203) to his first group of hall churches. It was a square structure. On the east was a central curved sanctuary with five niches, and two rectangular rooms on

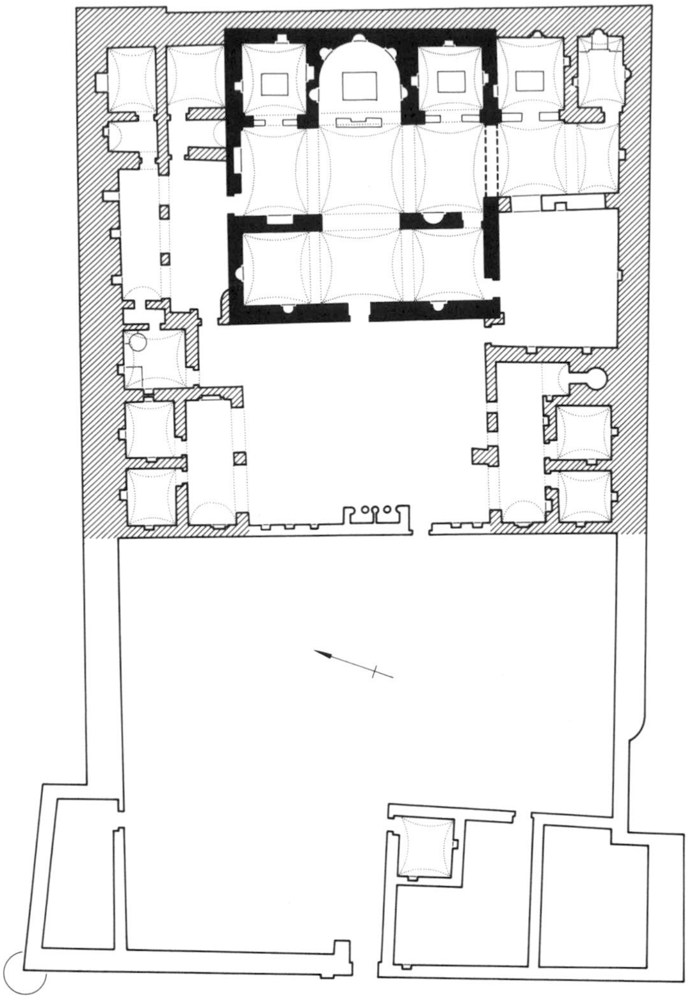

Plan of the church at Dayr al-Shuhadā'. *Courtesy Peter Grossmann.*

either side. West of them were two rows of two bays each, divided by side walls. Additional units were later added at the north and south to create a broad, shallow structure similar to the neighboring monasteries. The interior brickwork may have been painted in red and black patterns with white divisions, sometimes covering the mortar joins, at that time.

BIBLIOGRAPHY

Grossmann, P. *Mittelalterliche Langhauskuppelkirchen und verwandte Typen in Oberägypten,* pp. 202–203. Glückstadt, 1982.

Meinardus, O. *Christian Egypt, Ancient and Modern.* Cairo, 1965.

Timm, S. *Das christlich-koptische Ägypten in arabischer Zeit,* Vol. 2, pp. 808–810. Wiesbaden, 1984.

SHELA MCNALLY

DAYR AL-SHUHADĀ' (Isnā). [*This entry considers three aspects of Dayr al-Shuhadā'. The first section describes the setting and traditional history, as well as the information left by travelers in the nineteenth and early twentieth centuries—and that determined by more recent archaeological excavations. Part two discusses those remnants of artistic decoration that have been identified and described by experts. Part three reconstructs the architectural layout of the* dayr *and describes the two churches that are found in the complex.*]

History

This monastery is situated in the stony area (*ḥājir* in Egyptian Arabic) between the cultivated land and the mountain, about 3 miles (5 km) to the southwest of the town of ISNĀ (Sent in ancient Egyptian, Latopolis in the Hellenistic period). Its site is called Mountain of the Good (*agathon* in Greek) in the story of the martyrs of Isnā, composed on the basis of now-lost Coptic texts and in the panegyric on these saints pronounced by Dorotheus, bishop of Isnā in the fourth century (unpublished). It is surrounded by an enclosure wall and is thus a true cenobium. It is also called Dayr Manāwus (Ammonius); it is Ammonius to whom tradition attributes the foundation of the monastery, but no text or inscription accords to him this honor. It is only said that being bishop of Isnā, ordained by the martyr patriarch PETER I, he was martyred and buried at Antinoë (ANTINOOPOLIS), where his body remained. According to the panegyric on the martyrs of Isnā by John, bishop of Asyūṭ, Abū Tīj, and Manfalūṭ, the oldest manuscript of which is dated 1520 (but some authors say he lived in the thirteenth century; cf. Sbath, 1940, p. 71, no. 606), the monastery was erected on the very spot of the martyrdom of the saints of Isnā (Khater, 1981, pp. 55 [text], 66 [trans.]). Perhaps this author is the same one who attended at the preparation of the CHRISM in 1257 (Munier, 1943, p. 55). The fact that three episcopal sees were then united under the same titular head betrays a period when Christianity was in decline, which corresponds very well to the thirteenth century, although there is no other evidence that these three dioceses were united under a single name. If this personage was indeed of the thirteenth century, the monastery must have been established before that date.

However that may be, the oldest parts of the present buildings seem to date from the second half of

Dayr al-Shuhadā' (Isnā). *Courtesy Institut Français d'Archéologie Orientale, Cairo.*

the eleventh century. But the presence of numerous Greek funerary stelae in the neighboring cemetery proves that the site was venerated very early (Sauneron and Coquin, 1980, pp. 239–77 and pls. 39–44).

This monastery is well known, for it has been mentioned or described by European travelers from the seventeenth century on. The first appears to be that of the fathers Protais and François in 1668 (Sauneron, 1974, p. 79); J. VANSLEB (1677, p. 406; 1678, p. 243) copied their text, being unable to go beyond Jirjā. C. SICARD also mentioned it (1982, Vol. 2, p. 66; Vol. 3, p. 77: "la fameuse église des Martyrs à Assena").

In 1730–1732, the physician N. Granger (1745, p. 24) noted this monastery during his wanderings. It is fitting to note the descriptions of R. Lepsius (1842–1845: Griechisch [Vol. 4], pp. 172–75), C. E. Wilbour (1936), and R. POCOCKE (1743–1745, p. 112). Granger mentioned two monks at the monastery. In the *Description de l'Egypte* that resulted from Napoleon's expedition, P. Jollois and E. Devilliers, in a chapter entitled "Description des dégats d'Esna et de ses environs" (Vol. 1, pp. 397–98), attributed the devastation to the Mamluks. S. CLARKE (1912, p. 111) drew up the plan of the *dayr,* and V. de Bock (1901, p. 75) published Uspenskij's notes.

In the twentieth century the monastery was often visited: by M. JULLIEN (1903, pp. 250–52, 283), Johann Georg (1914, pp. 58–59), and L. T. LEFORT (1939, pp. 404–407). T. Smolenski (1910, pp. 27–34) was to study the inscriptions noted by Granger. Since 1967, DAYR AL-FAKHŪRĪ and Dayr al-Shuhadā' have been included in a vast program covering all the archaeological data about the region of Isnā; to date there have been published works by J. Leroy (1975, Vol. 1) and R.-G. Coquin (1975, pp. 241–61).

O. Meinardus gave a good description of Dayr al-Shuhadā' (1965, pp. 324–25; 1977, pp. 440–41). Walters (1974) frequently quoted him.

BIBLIOGRAPHY

Bock, V. de. *Matériaux pour servir à l'archéologie de l'Egypte chrétienne,* pp. 71–78. St. Petersburg, 1901.

Clarke, S. *Christian Antiquities in the Nile Valley.* Oxford, 1912.

Coquin, R.-G. "Les Inscriptions pariétales des monastères d'Esna." *Bulletin de l'Institut français d'Archéologie orientale* 75 (1975):241–284.

Granger, N. *Relation d'un voyage fait en Egypte en l'année 1730.* Paris, 1745.

Johann Georg, Duke of Saxony. *Streifzüge durch die Kirchen und Klöster Ägyptens.* Leipzig, 1914.

Jollois, P., and E. de Villiers. "Description d'Esna et de ses environs." In *Description de l'Egypte,* Vol. 1, pp. 397–98. Paris, 1821.

Jullien, M. "Quelques anciens couvents de l'Egypte." *Missions catholiques* 35 (1903):188–90, 198–202, 212–14, 237–40, 250–52, 257–58, 274–76, 283–84.

Khater, A. *Martyre des citoyens d'Esna.* Cairo and Jerusalem, 1981.

Lefort, L. T. "Les Premiers Monastères pachômiens, exploration topographique." *Le Muséon* 52 (1939):377–407.

Lepsius, R. *Denkmäler aus Ägypten und Äthiopien.* Leipzig, 1842–1845.

Leroy, J. *La Peinture murale chez les coptes,* Vol. 1. *Les Peintures murales des couvents du désert*

d'Esna. Mémoires de l'Institut français d'Archéologie orientale 94. Cairo, 1975.
Meinardus, O. *Christian Egypt, Ancient and Modern*. Cairo, 1965; 2nd ed., 1977.
Munier, H. *Recueil des listes épiscopales*. Cairo, 1943.
Pococke, R. *A Description of the East and Some Other Countries*. London, 1743–1745.
Sauneron, S. *Villes et légendes d'Egypte*. Cairo, 1974.
Sauneron, S., and R. G. Coquin. "Catalogue provisoire des stèles d'Esna." In *Livre du centenaire de l'I. F. A. O.*, pp. 239–77 and pls. 39–44. Mémoires de l'Institut français d'Archéologie orientale 104. Cairo, 1980.
Sbath, P. *Al-Fihris* (Catalogue of Arabic Manuscripts). Cairo, 1938–1940.
Sicard, C. *Oeuvres*, ed. S. Sauneron and M. Martin, 3 vols. Bibliothèque d'études 83–85. Cairo, 1982.
Smolenski, T. "Les Inscriptions grecques du sieur Granger." *Bulletin de la Société royale d'archéologie d'Alexandrie* 12 (1910):27–34.
Vansleb, J. M. *Nouvelle relation en forme de journal d'un voyage fait en Egypte en 1672 et 1673*. Paris, 1677. Translated as *The Present State of Egypt*. London, 1678.
Walters, C. C. *Monastic Archaeology in Egypt*. Warminster, 1974.
Wilbour, C. E. *Travels in Egypt, December 1880 to May 1891*. Brooklyn, N.Y., 1936.

RENÉ-GEORGES COQUIN
MAURICE MARTIN, S.J.

Art

The monastery called Dayr al-Shuhadā' (Monastery of the Martyrs) and sometimes Dayr Anbā Bakhūm (Pachomius) recalls the martyrs massacred in the town of Isnā, mentioned in the SYNAXARION at 7 and 13 Kiyahk (CSCO 49, pp. 321–323, 333–336 [Arabic text]; Vol. 78, pp. 189–192, 226–231 [Latin translation]). The use of the name Pachomius here derives from the fact that he was born and lived his early years near this town, where he also spent the night in prison at the time of his recruitment into the army of Constantine. The church of this monastery, which for a long time past has not given shelter to any monks, has been used for occasional services in recent decades.

The church is the juxtaposition of two different buildings. To the south there is a church of basilica form with three aisles and a transverse choir and the ordinary sanctuary complex placed between two side rooms, the one on the north no doubt serving as a baptistery, as the presence of a trough seems to indicate. Immediately to the north of this church is another one, with two aisles and a transept giving on to two conch-shaped apses set in the east wall. The pictorial decoration is distributed in the first on the walls of the sanctuary, and in the second, in the apses.

It appears very probable that the south church was built on the site of an older church (Clarke, 1912, p. 114). An inscription below the fresco decorating the right wall of the sanctuary was noted by V. de Bock and copied by him (1901, p. 76 and n. 77). It was not noted at all by J. Leroy, who reproduced de Bock's iconographic description, stopping just before this detail. It is dated to the year A.M. 502/A.D. 786. If one takes this date into account, one of the buildings would be largely anterior to that date.

Among the paintings that decorate the two churches, few have remained legible, but what remains of them reveals work of high quality. Of those who have noticed them, de Bock was the most explicit, but his work appeared posthumously, and its editors could only transcribe the statements that he left, many of his thoughts remaining unrecorded. Jules Leroy and his party, who visited the site more than seventy years later, were able to identify only some of the pictures that de Bock mentioned; these are discussed below.

In the south church, the right wall to the east above blind niches is occupied by a fresco showing Christ in majesty. He holds a square codex in his left hand and raises his right, with the palm forward. At his sides the archangels MICHAEL and GABRIEL bend toward him, their arms raised and their heads full-face. Their wings, which extend on the side under the arcosolium, shelter respectively Saint Basil (?) and the bishop Saint Gregory, near whom is a beardless young man whose probable counterpart at the side of Saint Basil has disappeared. All are portrayed full-face (Leroy, 1975, pl. 4).

Opposite this painting and above the door, de Bock noted an enthroned Virgin with Child, between two angels standing with bare feet, their hands joined in front (de Bock, 1901, p. 76). Leroy apparently did not find it again (Leroy, 1975, p. 4).

The north church is richer in surviving art. In the apse to the right of the entrance of the first chapel backing on the east wall, two frescoes are placed one above the other (de Bock, 1901, pp. 76–77: Leroy, 1975, pl. 12–13). In the higher of the two, Christ is seated on a bench without a back in front of a circular mandorla, beyond which extend the top of his nimbus, the end of his right hand, and his feet. His left hand holds by the top a square codex, the cover of which is spanned by a cross pattée between stars. His right hand is raised in blessing. The heads of the four evangelical symbols project from the middle and lower parts on each side of the mandorla. On the lower sides, an angel in profile, his head in three-quarter view, walks bending with his hands raised toward Christ, one of his wings being lowered, the other raised. Two busts, one of them in the orant posture, are placed in a small conical vault, each near to the feet of Christ.

Under this ensemble, to the measure of the diameter of the mandorla, is placed a rectangle filled by an enthroned Virgin with Child. Flanking this are the archangels Michael and Gabriel crowned, both standing full-face and holding a globe in the left hand in a flap of the upper garment; in the right hand Michael holds a long rod ending in a cross and Gabriel a sword hanging at his side.

On the intrados of this chapel stands Saint Peter, long-haired and bearded, holding in his left hand a bunch of two keys, to which he draws attention with his right, and under a cross with the fleur-de-lis, Saint Stephen, beardless, the second and third fingers of his right hand resting on a chalice that he holds with his left hand.

The north church presents another fresco of Christ in majesty (Leroy, 1975, pl. 29–38) in the second chapel situated to the north. The upper central part of the subject is illegible, but the lower part and the sides are relatively legible. The scene differs from the preceding one only in that Christ's feet are on a stool and the archangels Michael and Gabriel are on one knee on the ground, with arms stretched forward and the wings forming a right angle in the corner where the head of each is set.

In a chapel against the north wall there is an immense archangel (7.2 feet, or 2.20 m, in height), beyond doubt Gabriel, standing and haloed, with a globe decorated with a rosette in his left hand and resting on the flap of his *himation* (mantle); in his right hand he holds a rod ending in a cross. Near his right foot is traced the form of a building with three domes, probably a picture of the church, fulfilling a role analogous to that of similar detail near the mount of each saint on horseback portrayed in the entrance of the church of the Monastery of Saint ANTONY of the Desert, near the Red Sea.

Finally, one must note in the transept the representation of a saint on horseback on each of three walls. The only ones that can be identified are Saint Claudius (south wall) and THEODORUS (west wall); like the one on the north wall, whose name has disappeared, they are presented in rich colors.

The datings given by Leroy (1975, p. 33), although only suggestive, point toward the beginning of the twelfth century. He expressed complete admiration for the style and the grandeur of these paintings (ibid., p. 12).

BIBLIOGRAPHY

Amélineau, E. *La Géographie de l'Egypte à l'epoque copte.* Paris, 1893.

Bock, V. de. *Matériaux pour servir à archéologie de l'Egypte chrétienne.* St. Petersburg, 1901.

Clarke, S. *Christian Antiquities in the Nile Valley.* Oxford, 1912.

Leroy, J. *Les Peintures des couvents du désert d'Esna,* Vol. 1. *La peinture murale chez les coptes.* Mémoires de l'Institut français d'Archéologie orientale 94. Cairo, 1975.

PIERRE DU BOURGUET

Architecture

Dayr al-Shuhadā' is a rectangular complex closed in by a surrounding wall of unbaked bricks. Its present entrance is on the north. It contains on the east some ruined buildings arranged round a courtyard, and on the west a group of buildings separated by a narrow street. To the north of this street are the medieval church and its auxiliary buildings, and to the south, the modern church of Saint Ammonius and the Martyrs, built in 1901 on the ruins of the ancient cells of the monastery. In ancient times the entrance to the monastery was to the west, on the axis of the street. To the south of this entrance the remains of an ancient cell and a keep still survive.

The medieval church is dedicated to Ammonius and contains three aisles. The main aisle consists of two square areas roofed over by domes. The side aisles and the *khūrus* (room between naos and sanctuary) form a sort of ambulatory around the main aisle. On the east, the sanctuary and its two adjoining chambers open onto the *khūrus.* That on the north now serves as a baptistery; that on the south gives access to a new baptistery and its appurtenances built in 1901. In ancient times, the sanctuary communicated with the north chamber and was wide open to the *khūrus.* Later it was divided by a partition (*hijāb*) in the middle, the sanctuary being to the east and the western part becoming the *khūrus.*

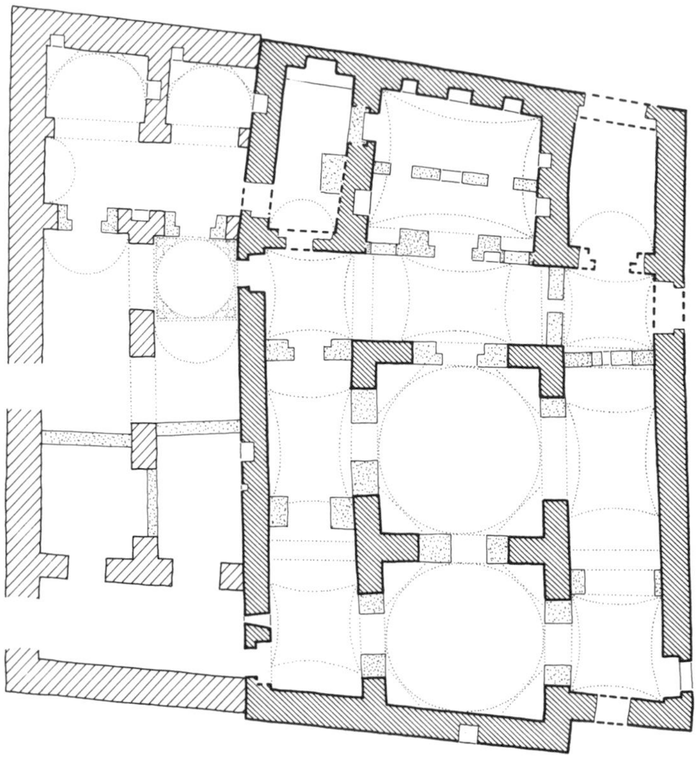

Plan of the medieval church and the adjoining secondary church at Dayr al-Shuhadā'. *Courtesy Peter Grossmann.*

A smaller church, dedicated to the martyrs of Isnā, was built between the medieval church of Ammonius and the north surrounding wall of the monastery. This church contains two aisles, a narthex, and two sanctuaries with *khūrus*. Each sanctuary is closed off by a recent partition. The north aisle contained some tombs. The door situated in the *khūrus* of the medieval church gave access into this secondary church; the hall in front of this door is roofed by a Fatimid cupola set on decorated squinches. Later the aisles of this church were divided again by a transverse wall and a new church, the Church of the Three Peasants, was fitted up in the western part. From this period date the two openings (today walled up) in the north surrounding wall that allowed pilgrims to enter directly into the churches from outside the monastery.

BIBLIOGRAPHY

Bock, V. de. *Matériaux pour servir à l'archéologie de l'Egypte chrétienne,* pp. 71–78. St. Petersburg, 1901.

Clarke, S. *Christian Antiquities in the Nile Valley,* pp. 113–16. Oxford, 1912.

Coquin, R.-G. "Les Inscriptions pariétales des monastères d'Esna." *Bulletin de l'Institut français d'Archéologie orientale* 75 (1975):241–42, 285.

Grossmann, P. *Mittelalterliche Langhauskuppelkirchen und verwandte Typen in Oberägypten,* pp. 3–7. Glückstadt, 1982.

Leroy, J. *Les Peintures des couvents du désert d'Esna,* Vol. 1. *La peinture murale chez les coptes.* Mémoires de l'Institut français d'Archéologie orientale 94. Cairo, 1975.

Monneret de Villard, U. *Il monastero di S. Simeone presso Aswan,* Vol. 1, p. 59. Milan, 1927.

Timm, S. *Das christlich-koptische Ägypten in arabischer Zeit,* Vol. 2, pp. 811–15. Wiesbaden, 1984.

G. CASTEL
PETER GROSSMANN

DAYR SIM'ĀN, an erroneous name, used mainly by Europeans for DAYR ANBĀ HADRĀ on the west bank at Aswan.

PETER GROSSMANN

DAYR SITT DIMYĀNAH, monastery near Bilqās. [*This entry consists of two articles:* History *and* Architecture.]

History

It is very probable that the Dayr Jimyānah (or Dimyānah) described by al-MAQRĪZĪ (d. 1441) and the present Dayr Sitt Dimyānah (to the north of Bilqās) are one and the same place, as suggested by 'ABD AL-MASĪḤ ṢALĪB AL-MAS'ŪDĪ (1924, p. 149). The orthography given by al-Maqrīzī, *Jimyānah,* is the same as that of the oldest manuscripts (sixteenth to eighteenth centuries) of the life of the saint (see the catalogs cited by G. Graf, Vol. 1, pp. 468 and 532) and of the European travelers of the seventeenth and eighteenth centuries. This orthography was still attested in 1903 by M. Jullien.

There is also confusion about the geographical situation. Al-Maqrīzī indicates, admittedly without orientation, that the Dayr Jimyānah is three hours away (on foot or on an ass) from the DAYR AL-'ASKAR, which was quite near the present Bilqās. The Dayr Sitt Dimyānah is today about 6 miles (10 km) north of Bilqās. Moreover, al-Maqrīzī indicates that the festival of the monastery is in the Coptic month of Bashans, after that of the DAYR AL-MAGHṬIS; the festival of the Dayr Sitt Dimyānah is on 12 Bashans. It might be argued that according to al-Maqrīzī this Dayr Jimyānah is dedicated to Saint George, but the dedications given by this author are not always exact.

The most ancient witness, as indicated, is al-Maqrīzī (d. 1441). The Dayr Jimyānah was part of a group of four monasteries, the only ones in the area of the salt marshes to the south of the lake of al-Burullus. Two of these, Dayr al-ʿAskar and DAYR AL-MAYMAH, were quite close to Bilqās; the other two, Dayr al-Maghṭis and Dayr Jimyānah, were farther to the north. The first was one day's distance from Dayr al-ʿAskar and the second, Dayr Jimyānah, three hours from this same Dayr al-ʿAskar.

ABŪ AL-MAKĀRIM, who wrote at the beginning of the thirteenth century, does not speak of it, and *The Churches and Monasteries of Egypt,* a little later, does not mention any monastery or church in Upper Egypt dedicated to Saint Jimyānah/Dimyānah.

O. Meinardus (1969, pp. 56, 68) rightly notes that the development of the cult of Saint Dimyānah is no earlier than the beginning of the seventeenth century. Her life does not figure in the most ancient manuscripts of the SYNAXARION. However, the dedication of her church is inserted at 12 Bashans in a manuscript of 1713 (Vatican Library, Arabic 63). In a marginal note only, hence by a reader later than the copyist, her feast is mentioned on 13 Ṭūbah in another manuscript of 1712 (Coptic Museum, Cairo, Liturgy 45a). It is remarkable that the Ethiopic Synaxarion, which was translated from Arabic at the beginning of the fifteenth century in the monastery of Saint Antony (DAYR ANBĀ ANṬŪNIYŪS), makes no mention of Saint Dimyānah.

It must, however, be noted that the author of the Life of Saint Jimyānah/Dimyānah (the name cannot be the feminine of Damian, as Meinardus affirms), John, bishop of Parallos, reports having found the story in the Dayr al-Maymah, to the south of al-Zaʿfarān. At the beginning of the Life it is related that the saint at the age of one year was offered by her father to the church of Dayr al-Maymah, located near Bilqās. Since this monastery was in ruins (probably before the thirteenth century), it is possible that the life of the saint was composed when Dayr al-Maymah was still flourishing, or before the thirteenth century. It is therefore well to distinguish clearly between the expansion of the cult of Saint Dimyānah and the origin of her life preserved only in Arabic. (A résumé of this life has been inserted into the Cairo edition of the Synaxarion at 13 Ṭūbah and at 12 Bashans).

On the other hand, it seems significant that the appearances of the Virgin that are related by the travelers to the Dayr Jimyānah in the seventeenth and eighteenth centuries strangely resemble those described by the Ethiopic sources at the Dayr al-Mighṭās, which was scarcely more than some 9 miles (15 km) distant. We may therefore ask whether, after the destruction of Dayr al-Mighṭās in 1438, the devotion of the faithful was not transferred to Dayr Jimyānah, which was the origin of the cult of the saint who was honored there.

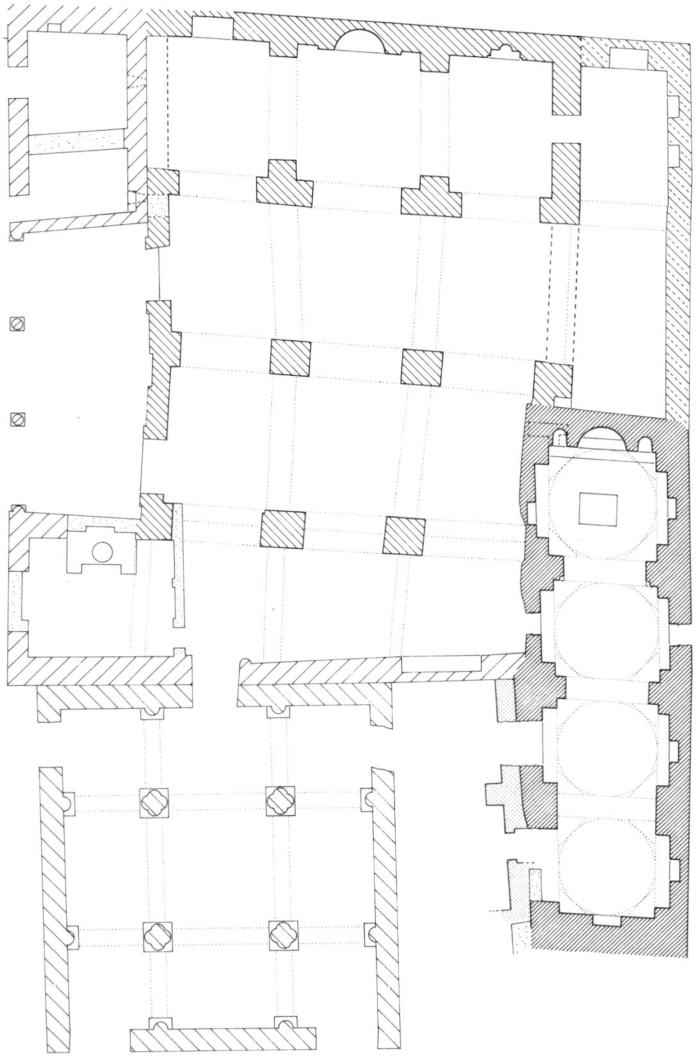
Plan of the churches at Dayr Sitt Dimyānah. *Courtesy Peter Grossmann.*

BIBLIOGRAPHY

Meinardus, O. "A Critical Study of the Cult of Sitt Dimiana and Her Forty Virgins." *Orientalia Suecana* 18 (1969):45–68.

Sicard, C. *Oeuvres,* 3 vols., ed. M. Martin. Bibliothèque d'études 83–85. Cairo, 1982.

Vansleb, J. M. *Nouvelle relation en forme de journal d'un voyage fait en Égypte en 1672 et 1673*. Paris, 1677. Translated as *The Present State of Egypt*. London, 1678.

RENÉ-GEORGES COQUIN
MAURICE MARTIN, S.J.

Architecture

Dayr Sitt Dimyānah contains several large churches, of which only the small Church of the Epiphany possesses some claim to antiquity. Lying in the southwest of the main complex and evidently deriving from the Ottoman period, it consists of four domed compartments (bays) ranged one after another. The eastern one serves as a sanctuary, with an altar of fired bricks, and traces of work at the entrance that indicate the existence of a wooden iconostasis. The east wall, in front of which is a synthronon, contains several niches. Northeast of this church lies an irregularly constructed modern hall church which Vansleb in 1672 saw under construction (1677, pp. 158ff). It is provided—as is usual today—with three sanctuaries. In more recent times it was enlarged on the south side by an additional aisle. On the north side there is an entrance hall, also added in modern times, the western side room of which was developed into a baptistery.

Entirely modern are the Church of Sitt Dimyānah lying to the west of the hall church, which was constructed as a four-pillar church with an ambulatory and quatrefoil-shaped pillars, and a large pilgrim church to the east.

The monastery has become a famous pilgrim center, which annually attracts thousands of pilgrims on 20 January and 21 May.

BIBLIOGRAPHY

Grossmann, P. *Mittelalterliche Langhauskuppelkirchen und verwandte Typen in Oberägypten*. Glückstadt, 1982.

Meinardus, O. *Monks and Monasteries of the Egyptian Deserts*, pp. 333ff. Cairo, 1961.

Munier, H. "Les monuments coptes d'après le père Michel Jullien." *Bulletin de la Société d'archéologie copte* 6 (1940):141–68.

Sidawi, E. "Une Excursion à Sitti Dimiana." *Bulletin de la Société de géographie* 8 (1917):84ff.

PETER GROSSMANN

DAYR AL-SULṬĀN, one of the most important Coptic monasteries in Jerusalem. It lies between the Coptic Patriarchate to the north and the Holy Sepulcher to the south. In the southwest corner of the monastery are two ancient churches. On the eastern side of the courtyard is the residence of the abbot and some rooms for the use of visiting Ethiopian monks. On the western side of the courtyard are two rooms used by the Ethiopians as a church.

G. Williams, who visited the monastery in 1842, records in his book *The Holy City* the legend that a sultan offered a generous reward to his Coptic clerk in return for his long service. The clerk asked instead for permission to renovate the devastated monastery and this was granted. In memory of this, it is said, the monastery was named after the sultan, and an iron chain was fastened in the wall by the gate as a sign that the monastery was under his protection.

The sultan's messengers and envoys used to reside at the monastery while in Jerusalem. One of these was Manṣūr al-Tīlbānī, who built a church in the monastery in the days of Patriarch CYRIL II (1078–1092). This is the most likely explanation for the name of the monastery.

When the Crusaders entered Jerusalem in 1099 they dismissed some of the clergy of the Oriental churches, among them the Copts, and confiscated their holy relics. However, it seems that they later allowed the Copts to stay in Jerusalem, since John of Wurzberg, who visited the city in 1165, and Theodoric, who was there in 1172, mention that Copts were among the Christian sects in the holy places at the time. When Saladin recaptured Jerusalem (1187), he restored to the Copts their churches and monasteries.

L. Cust, in *The Status Quo in the Holy Places* (1929), remarks that during the Crusades the monastery was occupied by Augustinian monks, but that the Copts regained it in the days of Anbā BASILIOS I, archbishop of Jerusalem from 1236 to 1260.

The connection between the Ethiopians and the monastery began when they were invited to stay there as they needed a shelter after they lost their monastery of Mār Ibrāhīm and some other holy places in Jerusalem in 1654, when they were unable to pay their taxes. In *Voyage nouveau de la Terre Sainte* (1679) M. Nau mentions "a church that was discovered a few years ago and is called the Church of the Apostles. This place belonged previously to the Ethiopians, but since they failed to pay the taxes to the Turks they had to withdraw and leave their possessions to the Greeks." This story is confirmed by other writers, including Chrysostomos Papadopoulos (1910) who states that "the Armenians . . . took over all the belongings of the Ethiopians in 1654." A decree issued by the court of Jerusalem and registered in its records for 1654 states that the Greeks received from the Armenians all that belonged to the Ethiopians by the order of the sultan.

The Copts have carefully maintained Dayr al-Sulṭān in their possession. An important document preserved in the Patriarchate in Jerusalem records renovations carried out by the Copts at the monastery in 1686, and refers to the monastery as the "monastery of the Coptic sect in the protectorate of Holy Jerusalem, known in the past as Al-Sulṭān monastery." An inventory compiled in 1820 indicates places that needed renovation, and a decree approving the work was issued in the same year. There are other records of renovations undertaken at the monastery.

Under Turkish rule, despite the Copts' generosity and hospitality toward them, the Ethiopians soon turned against their hosts and attempted to obtain rights in the monastery. These attempts were in vain, but in 1878 the keys of the church were stolen. Anbā BASILIOS II, archbishop of Jerusalem (1856–1899), complained to the Great Council of the city, which ordered that they should be returned to the Copts.

When it was decided to enlarge the gate of the monastery with the approval of the authorities, the Ethiopians attempted to prevent the work from taking place, but the authorities confirmed that "the monastery belongs to the Copts" and the work was completed.

The Ethiopians enlisted the help of Russia in their attempts to obtain rights in the monastery and they sent many delegations to the sultan in Istanbul, but in vain. The sultan's order was given in 1905 that "the demands of the Ethiopians cannot be accepted." A further decree issued by the governor of Jerusalem in 1907 reaffirmed the rights of the Copts in the monastery.

The government of the British mandate showed respect for the status quo in the holy places. Despite the repeated attempts of the Ethiopians at that time, they failed to obtain rights to the monastery and retained only the right of transient hospitality.

During Jordan's rule of the Holy City, the government conformed with and preserved the status quo in the holy places, including Dayr al-Sulṭān. However, things changed when diplomatic relations between Egypt and Jordan were broken off. In 1959 the Ethiopian bishop in Jerusalem took advantage of the political conflict and the fact that the see of Jerusalem was vacant following the death of Anbā Yacobos, and asked the government to restore what he called the rights of the Ethiopians. The Coptic patriarchate in Jerusalem, however, defended its right of ownership of the monastery, and the Jordanian committee that had been set up to examine the issue never met.

In 1960, when relations between Egypt and Jordan had deteriorated once more, the governor of Jerusalem attempted to reopen the subject of the monastery. The Coptic archbishop, Basilios IV, who was present at a meeting called by the governor, refused to discuss the subject on the grounds that there was no dispute over the ownership of the monastery. He notified the patriarchate in Cairo about the meeting, and CYRIL VI sent a cable to the Jordanian prime minister in which he pointed out that the status quo in the holy places was governed by international agreement and could not be revoked by any local authority.

Pope Cyril also asked the archbishop of Jerusalem not to attend any further meetings called by the governor of Jerusalem concerning the monastery, lest his presence be interpreted as approval of the eligibility of the Jordanian authorities to deal with the subject.

In 1961, the governor summoned the Coptic archbishop and produced a copy of a decree stipulating that Dayr al-Sulṭān should immediately be taken over by the Ethiopians. The archbishop rejected the decree and asked for time to consult higher authorities. The governor refused and threatened to take over the monastery by force. When the archbishop refused once more to surrender the monastery, the governor ordered the military commander of the area to break down the doors and occupy it. These orders were carried out, and a group of armed soldiers was placed inside the monastery.

The archbishop had a meeting with King Hussein to explain that the monastery had belonged to the Copts for centuries, and that the Ethiopians had no rights in the monastery except that of transient hospitality. The archbishop asked the king to revoke the decision and to restore the status quo in the monastery. The king promised to consider the matter. Evidence of the Copts' ownership of the monastery was presented to the authorities, and a document that listed all the possessions of the Copts was submitted. In this document Archbishop Basilios declared that the governor was responsible for any alterations to, tamperings with, or losses of any of these holy possessions that might result from the seizure of the monastery. The archbishop sent a copy of this declaration to the Jordanian prime minister and to the minister of the interior.

Archbishop Basilios, however, was unable to contact the patriarchate in Cairo, due to the political situation. He was compelled to send the steward of the Coptic monasteries in Jerusalem to Cairo, carrying a message from himself to the pope, in which he requested that the Egyptian government protest officially against the seizure of the monastery, cancel pilgrimages from Egypt, and call for an urgent meeting of the Holy Council.

In March 1961, a Coptic delegation arrived in Jerusalem with a message to the Jordanian king from Cyril VI. The delegation met the king and the prime minister and discussed the subject of the ownership of the monastery with them, pointing out that the government had acted illegally in taking over the monastery.

On 1 April, it was decreed that the status quo should be restored in the monastery, and it was handed back to the Copts on the same day. The governor of Jerusalem conveyed this decision to the Ethiopian bishop in Jerusalem, and a copy was sent to the Coptic archbishop.

After the June 1967 war and Israel's occupation of the Holy City, trouble arose from the favor shown by the Israeli authorities to the Ethiopians, with whom they maintained good relations. The Copts, on the other hand, considered themselves to be in a state of war with the Israelis. Although the Israeli prime minister announced to all the religious leaders that the Israeli government recognized the status quo in the holy places, the Israeli government soon began putting pressure on the Copts to give rights to the Ethiopians in Dayr al-Sulṭān. The Coptic archbishop steadfastly resisted this pressure and insisted upon the preservation of the status quo in the monastery.

On Easter Eve 1969, the Israeli government attempted to install large numbers of police inside the Coptic Patriarchate and Dayr al-Sulṭān, but the Copts prevented them. The Israeli police then attacked the Coptic priests and laymen, and several were injured. The archbishop presented a strong protest against the behavior of the authorities. Before Easter 1970, Archbishop Basilios, being worried lest the authorities should repeat their attack, wrote to various ministries asking them to respect the status quo in the holy places and to allow the performance of the religious rites in peace. However, on Easter Eve hundreds of police officers and armed guards occupied the Patriarchate and Dayr al-Sulṭān. They refused to leave when requested and changed the locks of the doors leading to the two Coptic churches in the monastery and to the road leading from the churches to the yard of the Holy Sepulcher. They seized the two churches and handed them over to the Ethiopians. When the Copts found out what had happened, some priests went to the monastery but were prevented from entering. They then informed the archbishop, who interrupted his prayers, and went to the monastery with large numbers of priests, Copts, and Christians of other sects. On arriving at the monastery, they were threatened by the soldiers. More armed police arrived, and the people were led at gunpoint through the streets to the Patriarchate. Some who refused to obey were beaten.

The same night the archbishop tried unsuccessfully to contact government officials. He therefore brought the case before the Israeli supreme court in Jerusalem, and on 16 March 1971 it decreed that what had happened was a flagrant violation of security and public order and asked the minister of police to restore the usurped places to the Copts.

Despite this, the Israeli government entered a temporary decision against the Copts, while setting up a committee to reexamine the issue and to submit its recommendations to the cabinet. This committee did nothing to resolve the situation, and the archbishop was compelled to go once more to the supreme court in 1977. Although the five judges were not unanimous in their findings, on 1 January they adopted a unified attitude critical of the government.

After the signing of the peace treaty between Egypt and Israel the archbishop wrote to the Israeli head of state, its prime minister, the minister of foreign affairs, the minister of the interior, the minister of police, and the minister of religions, asserting that the peace between the two countries conflicted with the pressure exerted by the authorities against the Copts. He once more requested that the temporary decision made by the government against the Copts in 1971 should be revoked and that the Coptic possessions should be returned to them. The question has still not been resolved satisfactorily.

BIBLIOGRAPHY

Basilios IV (Anbā). *The Unjust Aggression on the Coptic Holy Places.* Jerusalem, 1970.
Cerulli, E. *Etiopi in Palestina.* Rome, 1943.
Colbi, S. P. *Christianity in the Holy Land.* Tel Aviv, 1969.
Cust, L. G. A. *The Status Quo in the Holy Places.* Jerusalem, 1929.
Harvey, W. *Church of the Holy Sepulchre.* Oxford, 1935.
Jirjis Phīlūthā'us Awaḍ. *Coptic Possessions in Jerusalem.* Cairo, 1924. In Arabic.
Meinardus, O. F. A. *The Copts in Jerusalem.* Cairo, 1960.
Moore, E. A. *The Ancient Churches of Old Jerusalem.* Beirut, 1961.
Nau, M. *Voyage nouveau de la Terre Sainte.* Paris, 1679.
Timotheus (Anbā). *Collection of Documents and Deeds Proving the Coptic Ownership of Dayr al-Sultan and Other Places in Jerusalem.* Cairo, n.d. In Arabic.
Williams, G. *The Holy City: Historical, Topographical and Antiquarian Notices on Jerusalem,* 2 vols. London, 1949.
Zander, W. "On the Settlement of Disputes about the Christian Holy Places." *Israel Law Review* 8, no. 3 (July, 1973).

ARCHBISHOP BASILIOS

DAYR SUNBĀṬ, complex of ruins northeast of the ruins of ANTINOOPOLIS, in the angle of the amphitheater formed by the Arabian chain, of which the town of Antinoopolis occupies approximately the center.

The whole complex, established on the spur of the mountain that overhangs Antinoopolis, includes the monastery itself, two chapels, and several cells.

The monastery was built of unbaked bricks (see the schematic plan drawn up by Martin, 1971, p. 65). It consists chiefly of a massive building of about 26 by 13 feet (8 by 4 m) in the middle of a courtyard about 65 feet (20 m) on each side. The building is divided into two small halls, the vault of which has collapsed. Along the north and south walls of the courtyard, five small rooms 13 by 13 feet (4 by 4 m), all that remain, are disposed along each side. To the east of the *dayr* is a large quarry, which may have served as a storehouse. The area around the monastery is full of slighter structures.

Martin counts two chapels. To these he adds the hall numbered 4. Although it has an apse, it does

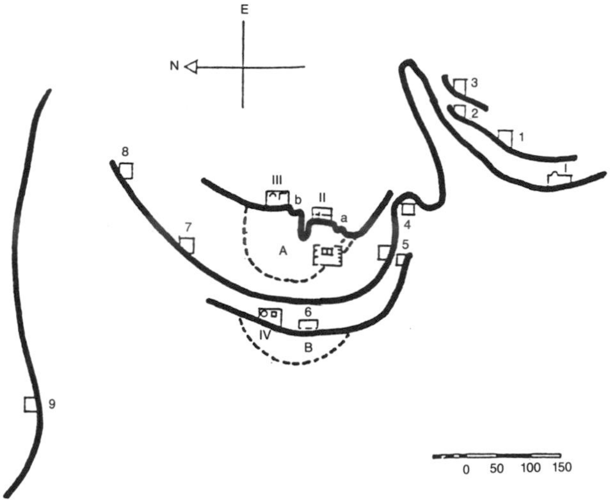

Map showing the location of Dayr Sunbāṭ in relation to other buildings in the area. I: church; II: storehouse; III: church; IV: room of undetermined religious purpose; 1–9: cells; A and B: two sites of potsherds and bricks. *Courtesy René-Georges Coquin.*

not seem that this was a chapel, for it was oriented north and south.

The site of the monastery must have included cells on either side of the large quarry, behind the monastery. Moreover, the quarries that served as cells almost all have in front of them an artificial terrace with a retaining wall.

The inscriptions are given in Martin (1971, pp. 81–86).

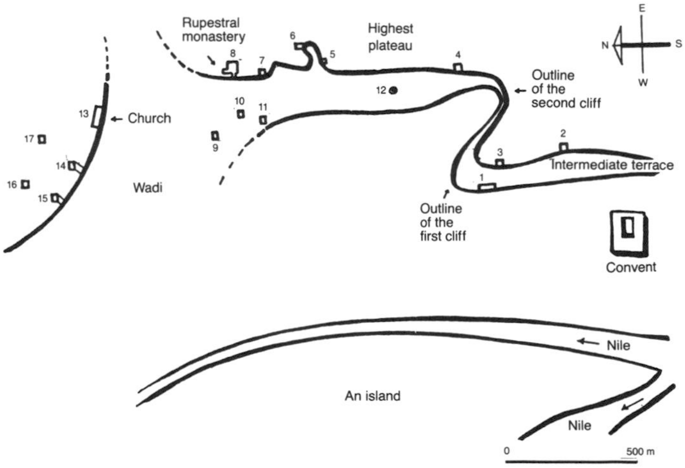

Map showing the general layout of the monastery. 1: church; 2–7: cells; 8: Rupestral monastery; 9–11: cells; 12: outline of a sculptured stele or cella; 13: church; 14–17: cells. *Courtesy René-Georges Coquin.*

Sometimes the south church and the cells that surround it, forming a complex, are called Dayr al-Hawā (cf. Mīṣā'īl Baḥr, 1957, p. 107).

BIBLIOGRAPHY

Clédat, J. "Notes archéologiques et philologiques." *Bulletin de l'Institut français d'Archéologie orientale* 2 (1902):41–70.

Jomard, E. F., in *Description de l'Egypte,* Vol. 4. Paris, 1821.

Martin, M. *La Laure de Der al Dik à Antinoè*. Bibliothèque des études coptes 8. Cairo, 1971.

Mīṣā'īl Baḥr. *Tarīkh al-Qiddīs al-Anbā Yuḥannis al-Qaṣīr wa Manṭiqat Anṣinā*. Alexandria, 1957.

RENÉ-GEORGES COQUIN
MAURICE MARTIN, S.J.

DAYR AL-SURYĀN. [*This article concerns a monastery that is still functioning. One section discusses the past and the more recent history of the* dayr, *the other the architecture at present and some of the changes that have taken place during the centuries.*]

History

This is one of the four monasteries still functioning in Wādī al-Naṭrūn (the ancient desert of SCETIS) southwest of the Nile Delta. In the earliest explicit references that have survived (in notes written into three Syriac manuscripts shortly after A.D. 851), it is called the Monastery "of the Mother of God of the Syrians [one note adds "of Abba Bishoī"] which is in the desert of Egypt [or "of Scetis"]." From its library, now mostly but not entirely in the British Library, the Vatican Library, the National Library in Paris, and elsewhere in Europe, have come many of the most important Syriac manuscripts extant.

The records of its early period seem to have perished in the general devastation of the monasteries in Wādī al-Naṭrūn by Arab marauders around 817. It is not one of the original monasteries of Scetis. It was established for those monks of the neighboring monastery of DAYR ANBĀ BISHOI who were doctrinal partisans of SEVERUS OF ANTIOCH. In the first decades after 518, the opposing party, which subscribed to the Christological views of JULIAN of Halicarnassus, had gained control of the four original monasteries. Each was then doubled by a new and separate monastery dedicated to the THEOTOKOS (mother of God), to which those members of the community who were doctrinal followers of Severus moved.

Eventually, perhaps after the reconciliation of the Gaianite (Julianist) party and the Theodosian (Severan) party in Egypt around 710, the *dayr* was bought from the Copts and converted into a Syrian monastery by a certain Marutha, a man of Takritan (i.e., East Syrian, but Monophysite) origin who had risen to high position in the government of Egypt. It was, at any rate, a Syrian monastery by 850 when the buildings, including the present principal church, were already taking form. The massive fortifying walls of the late ninth century still surround the monastery.

The monastery's most memorable abbot was Moses of Nisibis, whose reign spanned most of the first half of the tenth century, when the present *haykal* (sanctuary) screen and choir screen of the principal church, the mural decoration of its apse, and the Chapel of the Forty-Nine Martyrs were put in place. Abbot Moses was sent to Baghdad around 927 with a delegation seeking the exemption of bishops, monks, and infirm Christians from the capitation tax recently imposed in Egypt. He stayed on for some time after that goal was attained and collected a choice array of manuscripts in Mesopotamia and northern Syria, which he brought back to the monastery library in 931–932.

Church of Sitt Maryam. *Courtesy The Metropolitan Museum of Art, New York.*

Detail of door between nave and choir. Church of Sitt Maryam. *Courtesy The Metropolitan Museum of Art, New York.*

The sources of the monastery's income are unknown. It is unlikely that it possessed endowments or land in the fertile parts of Egypt in the Middle Ages. In 987 the Syrian patriarch of Antioch felt constrained to write to the Coptic patriarch to ask that the latter be attentive to the needs of the monks of Dayr al-Suryān and their nourishment. The monks continued to be recruited mainly from the Eastern (Takritan) dioceses of the Antiochene Syrian church until at least the early eleventh century, and throughout that period their recorded benefactors were for the most part Takritans of Mesopotamia or Egypt. In 1088, Dayr al-Suryān, with sixty monks, was the third largest of the seven monasteries then existing in Wādī al-Naṭrūn.

After 1100, the monks seem to have come rather from the western part of the Church of Antioch. The accession of new manuscripts continued, but their limited range of content (mostly biblical, liturgical, hagiographical, and ascetical) reflects a narrowing of the community's interests. The Black Death that struck Egypt in 1348–1349, the famine and pestilence twenty-five years later, and the ravages of Tamerlane (Timur) and his Mongols in Syria at the turn of the century help to explain why a visiting monk from Syria found a single monk in the monastery in 1412–1413. A revival, evident after 1484, continued into the early years of the next century, with some Takritans joined by several monks from Lebanon, including the administratively vigorous abbot Cyriac.

The community was gradually becoming more Coptic than Syrian. Of its forty-three monks in 1515–1516, only eighteen were Syrian, while the other twenty-five were Copts. The monks who left to repopulate the monasteries of Saint Antony (DAYR ANBĀ

Detail of panel, *haykal* screen. Church of al-ʿAdhrā'. *Courtesy The Metropolitan Museum of Art, New York.*

Haykal, central part, east niche. Church of al-ʿAdhrā'. *Courtesy The Metropolitan Museum of Art, New York.*

Frieze and panel of *haykal*, Church of al-ʿAdhrā'. *Courtesy The Metropolitan Museum of Art, New York.*

ANṬŪNIYŪS) and of Saint Paul (DAYR ANBĀ BŪLĀ) in the Eastern Desert later in the century were presumably Copts, but the monastery received aid from the Syrian patriarch Dāwūd-Shāh in the late sixteenth century. The steward in 1626–1627 was a Syrian, but the Coptic patriarchal synod installed a new abbot in 1636–1637. After that, Dayr al-Suryān can be considered a Coptic monastery, although a church in the compound was still said to be for

Church of al-ʿAdhrā'. Detail of a conch: Nativity Scene. Joseph in the foreground, right of center and the Three Magi at the far right. Inscriptions above are in Syriac. *Courtesy Institut Français d'Archéologie Orientale, Cairo.*

Church of al-ʿAdhrā'. Detail of a conch: Annunciation Scene. Inscriptions in Syriac and Coptic. *Courtesy Institut Français d'Archéologie Orientale, Cairo.*

Syrian use in 1657, and Robert Curzon, visiting the monastery in 1837, found a group of Ethiopian monks living in a part of the enclosure.

Today the monks of the monastery, who in 1976 numbered thirty in the monastery itself and ten active elsewhere in Egypt and in the Coptic establishments of Jerusalem, play an important role in the current Coptic monastic renaissance. Physical improvements reflecting the growth of the monastery since 1950 include a building for the museum and library, a small printing press, and provisions for running water. Pope Shenouda III, elected in 1971, was a monk of the community.

BIBLIOGRAPHY

For what can be known of the history of the community, its buildings, and its library down to the nineteenth century, the meticulously documented work of H. G. Evelyn-White, *The Monasteries of the Wadi'n Natrun,* Vol. 2, *The History of the Monasteries of Nitria and of Scetis,* pp. 232–35, 309–321, 337–38, 414–16, 439–57 (New York, 1932); Vol. 3, *Architecture and Archaeology,* pp. 167–220 (New York, 1933), is the source of almost all that has been published since.

A new document from the reign of Abbot Cyriac has been published by J. Leroy, "Un témoignage inédit sur l'état du monastère des Syriens au Wadi'n Natrūn au début du XVIe siècle," *Bulletin de l'Institut français d'Archéologie orientale* 65 (1967):1-23.

Brief notices on the Syrian presence in the monastery documented by Arabic sources, mainly of the late fifteenth and early sixteenth centuries but as late as 1632, mostly unknown to Evelyn-White, can be found in G. Graf, *Geschichte der christlichen arabischen Literatur,* Vol. 3 (Vatican City, 1949), p. 55, and Vol. 4 (Vatican City, 1951), pp. 8, 11, 23.

Still unavailable when Evelyn-White was doing his work on the churches was U. Monneret de Villard, *Les Eglises du monastère des Syriens au Wādī en-Naṭrūn* (Milan, 1928).

Accounts of modern visitors are of unequal value; one, in Arabic, is that of the Copt Zakī Tawadrūs in *Al-Karmah* 16 (1930):490-502.

The monastery's history and archaeology, with some data not gleaned by Evelyn-White, are included, with information on the monastery in recent years, in O. Meinardus, *Monks and Monasteries of the Egyptian Deserts* (Cairo, 1961). Subsequent developments are chronicled in O. Meinardus, "Recent Developments in Egyptian Monasticism 1960-1964," *Oriens christianus* 49 (1965):79-87, and his "Zur monastischen Erneuerung in der koptischen Kirche," *Oriens christianus* 61 (1977):59-70.

A brief historical and artistic sketch, based entirely on Evelyn-White's work, is given by O. H. E. Burmester, *A Guide to the Monasteries of the Wadi'n-Natrun* (Cairo, 1955), pp. 13-21.

AELRED CODY, O.S.B.

Architecture

The *dayr* is situated barely 110 yards (100 m) to the west of the Dayr Anbā Bishoi and is the smallest among the still inhabited monasteries of Wādī al-Naṭrūn. Only in the modern period have extensive gardens been joined to the monastery, on its east side.

The monastery proper, which is enclosed by a high wall, possesses an east–west orientation in its main extension and is about 165 yards (150 m) long. The main entrance lies at the west end of the northern girdle wall. It leads immediately into a small court that is bounded on the north by the cloister wall and on the west and south by the *jawsaq* (keep) and its outer stairs. Adjoining this court is a larger court that includes a garden. Along the south side it is bordered by the al-'Adhrā' Church and by several monastic cells. To the west of the church lies the refectory, no longer in use, and the kitchen belonging to it, as well as a small courtyard that also extends to an area west of the *jawsaq.*

The other buildings are also situated right next to the wall. The central area is thereby left clear for passages and modest gardens. The row of cells along the north wall is interrupted by the Church of Sitt Maryam. A third church, that of Saint John (Evelyn-White, 1973, pt. 3, pp. 217–20), is found at the far eastern end in the northeast corner of the monastery. This is a small single-aisled chapel that is no longer in use as such but instead now serves as a kitchen and storehouse. Along the south wall of the monastery several uniformly executed cells have been set up. A few steps to the east of the al-'Adhrā' Church a modern guesthouse has been constructed.

The al-'Adhrā' Church (Grossmann, 1982, pp. 113ff., fig. 47; Evelyn-White, 1973, pt. 3, pp. 180ff.) is the most important church edifice of Wādī al-Naṭrūn and, in its plan, almost completely preserved. Very probably this is the church built by Syrian monks in the former Theotokos monastery of Dayr Anbā Bishoi, which was sold into Syrian hands after 710. The church may thus be dated to the first quarter of the eighth century. Originally it stood unconnected on all sides. Only in recent

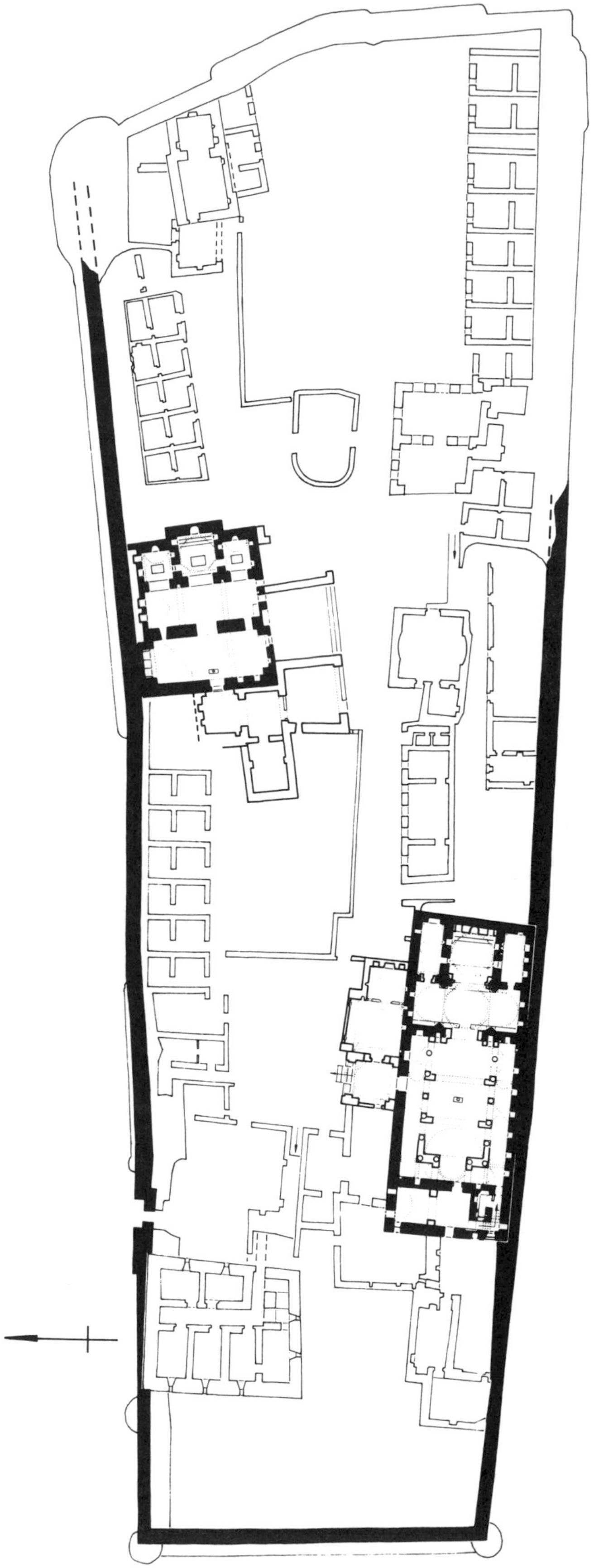

times was the south wall of the monastery erected along the south wall of the church.

In its constructional design, the church is a basilica. It was originally covered by a wooden roof and had a return aisle at the west end and a tripartite sanctuary with an original *khūrus*. The latter has been combined with the altar chamber into a triconch, whose center is emphasized by four half-columns. In the south wall of the naos the original sequence of niches has been preserved. The room to the west of the church that occupies the position normally held by the narthex is accessible only from within the church. In the southwest corner of this chamber are the stairs leading up to the roof. The area beneath the staircase was made accessible from the church only at a later stage when it was developed into a supplementary vestry.

The greatest change undergone by the building is the transformation in the tenth century of the *haykal* into a domed area provided with a rich stucco ornamentation. This is the earliest attested instance of the erection of a full dome over a *haykal*. The dome itself was restored again in the Fatimid period, as was the one over the intersection of the *khūrus*. To the external additions on the north side belong a portal building added in the Mamluk period and originally executed as a tetrapylon, and a building set up as early as the tenth century and once richly decorated with stuccoed wall niches. The original purpose and size of this edifice are unknown; in recent times it was transformed into the Chapel of the Forty-nine Martyrs.

The Church of Sitt Maryam (Grossmann, 1982, pp. 106ff.; Evelyn-White, 1973, pt. 3, pp. 212ff.) seems not to have been constructed before the eleventh century. Moreover, only the naos, designed as an undivided transverse room, and the *khūrus*, of similar shape but more shallow, date from this period. The two rooms were originally connected by a large central arch and a narrower passage on the southern side. The northern side passage was opened only subsequently. The sanctuary with its three *haykals*, the central one of which protrudes from the east wall, dates only from the fourteenth or fifteenth century. From a deep niche in the north wall of the north *haykal* lies the access to a cache (KHIZĀNAH) placed between the church and the outer wall of the monastery.

The *jawsaq* (Evelyn-White, 1932, pt. 3, pp. 175ff.) of the monastery is situated next to the entrance

Plan of Dayr al-Suryān. *Courtesy Peter Grossmann.*

gate, against the north wall, and still imparts an idea of the original strength of the walls, which elsewhere have been consistently fortified on the inside. Judging from its plan, it belongs to the less developed examples from the older period; it already possesses, however, a more complex arrangement of rooms. Like those other examples, it must be entered at the second floor by means of a drawbridge hinged at the external wall of the tower and leading from a separately erected staircase building situated to the east. This floor also contains quarters for the monks, whereas the rooms in the basement and on the first floor for the most part have no windows and were storerooms and archives. Only a larger broad room on the first floor containing a niche in the east wall with a small recess underneath it, such as it is often found in the oratories of the monastic cells of KELLIA, probably served originally as a common oratory. The furnishings on the third floor, with a library and a chapel, belong to the modern period. According to H. G. Evelyn-White (1973, pt. 3, p. 178), the latter dates to the fifteenth century, whereas the erection of the tower itself is dated by him to around 850.

BIBLIOGRAPHY

Evelyn-White, H. G. *The Monasteries of the Wâdi 'n Natrûn*, pt. 3, *The Architecture and Archeology*, pp. 167–220. New York, 1933.

Grossmann, P. *Mittelalterliche Langhauskuppelkirchen und verwandte Typen in Oberägypten*. Glückstadt, 1982.

Monneret de Villard, U. *Les Eglises du monastère des Syriens au Wādī en-Naṭrun*. Milan, 1928.

PETER GROSSMANN

DAYR TĀSĀ, today the name of a Coptic village on the right bank of the Nile on the edge of the desert, south of ABNŪB and opposite ABŪ TĪJ. The cemetery and ancient church have been preserved.

No ancient author mentions it. S. CLARKE in 1912 noted the church and its titular, the archangel Michael, in his list of the Coptic churches (1912, p. 217, no. 21). This church is an attractive modern four-column building probably of the late eighteenth century, with walled-up columns and stuccoed capitals.

A little farther to the north some quarries fitted up as cells and containing Coptic inscriptions and a prayer niche are noted by G. Lefebvre (1908, p. 161).

BIBLIOGRAPHY

Clarke, S. *Christian Antiquities in the Nile Valley*. London, 1912.

Lefebvre, G. "Note sur Khawaled." *Annales du Service des Antiquités de l'Egypte* 9 (1908):161.

RENÉ-GEORGES COQUIN
MAURICE MARTIN, S.J.

DAYR AL-ṬĪN. This monastery was mentioned for the first time by al-Shābushtī (Atiya, 1939, pp. 25, 26), who died at the end of the tenth century or the beginning of the eleventh. He called it Mār-Ḥannā and situated it on the edge of Lake al-Ḥabash, near the Nile. The HISTORY OF THE PATRIARCHS OF THE EGYPTIAN CHURCH (Vol. 3, pt. 1, pp. 34 [text], 55 [trans.]) mentions under the patriarch GABRIEL II a church dedicated to Saint George situated at Dayr al-Ṭīn.

At the beginning of the thirteenth century ABŪ ṢĀLIḤ THE ARMENIAN (1895, pp. 128–30) distinguished two monasteries, those of Saint John (Mār Yūḥannā) and of Saint John the Baptist, the first Coptic and the second Melchite, both south of Old Cairo between Lake al-Ḥabash and the Nile. Near this monastery, according to the same author (p. 131), was a Church of Saint George, belonging to the Copts, which has since been destroyed by the Nile. Before 1400, Ibn Duqmāq (1893, pp. 107–108) situated the two churches at Dayr al-Ṭīn. This author called the church of the Copts the Church of Abū Jirj. Al-MAQRĪZĪ (Vol. 2, p. 503) repeated al-Shābushtī and added that the monastery was then called Dayr al-Ṭīn.

The two monasteries and the Coptic church became Muslim under the caliphate of al-Ḥāfiẓ and the patriarch Gabriel II, according to Abū Ṣāliḥ (1895, pp. 127–30).

Several manuscripts were written for this monastery or this church: Simaykah (1942), Catalogue 2, no. 298, is undated and, according to Graf (1934, p. 136), dates from the fourteenth century. Another manuscript of the fourteenth century, National Library, Paris, Arabe 18, carries a copy of a letter dated 1591 and intended for Yūḥannā of the Church of Saint George at Dayr al-Ṭīn (Troupeau, 1972, Vol. 1, p. 21). Another manuscript, National Library, Paris, Arabe 181, contains a note of the sale of this manuscript to the superior of the Monastery of Saint Victor at Birkat al-Ḥabash in 1318 (Troupeau, p. 156).

The two manuscripts of the list of the Egyptian

churches mention "Apa Victor in al-Ḥabash." E. AMÉLINEAU (1893, p. 162) did not fully understand this text, which has been elucidated by P. Casanova (1901, p. 172).

Another manuscript dating from 1638 mentions a Monastery of Nuzhah. This is a certificate naming the steward of Dayr al-ʿAdawiyyah and of Dayr al-Nuzhah near Dayr al-Ṭīn. It is probable that this is another name of Dayr al-Ṭīn (Slane, 1883–1895, no. 319).

BIBLIOGRAPHY

Amélineau, E. *La Géographie de l'Egypte à l'époque copte*. Paris, 1893.
Atiya, A. S. "Some Egyptian Monasteries According to the Unpublished MS of al-Shābushtī's ʿKitāb al-Diyārāt.'" *Bulletin de la Société d'archéologie copte* 5 (1939):1–28.
Casanova, P. "Les Noms coptes du Caire et localités voisines." *Bulletin de l'Institut français d'Archéologie orientale* 1 (1901):139–224.
Ibn Duqmāq. *Kitāb al-Intiṣār*, ed. C. Vollers. Cairo, 1893.
Graf, G. *Catalogue de manuscrits arabes chrétiens conservés au Caire*. Studi e testi 63. Vatican City, 1934.
Slane, W. MacGuckin, Baron de. *Catalogue des manuscrits arabes de la Bibliothèque nationale*. Paris, 1883–1895.
Troupeau, G. *Catalogue de manuscrits arabes*, Vol. 1. Paris, 1972.

RENÉ-GEORGES COQUIN
MAURICE MARTIN, S.J.

DAYR TON ETHIOPON.

See Dayr al-Muḥarraq.

DAYR ṬŪRĀH.

See Dayr al-Quṣayr (Ṭūrāh).

DAYR AL-ṬURFAH.

This *dayr* has disappeared. M. Ramzī (1953–1968, Vol. 1, p. 260) situated it in the district of Samalūṭ. *The State of the Provinces* in A.H. 777/A.D. 1375 still mentions it. It is not known on which bank of the Nile it was, though Ramzī says that it was situated on the left bank.

BIBLIOGRAPHY

ʿAbd al-Laṭīf. *Relation de l'Egypte de ʿAbd al Laṭif*, trans. and ed. A. I. S. de Sacy. In *Relation de l'Egypte*. Paris, 1810. *L'Etat des provinces* is translated in an appendix.
Ramzī, M. *Al-Qāmūs al-Jughrāfī lil-Bilād al-Miṣrīyyah*, Vol. 1. Cairo, 1953.

RENÉ-GEORGES COQUIN
MAURICE MARTIN, S.J.

DAYR UMM ʿALI.

See Dayr al-Rūmāniyyah.

DAYR AL-WASTANI.

See Dayr al-Shuhadā' (Akhmīm).

DAYR YŪḤANNĀ

(Damanhūr Shubra), monastery, celebrated for pilgrimages to the body of Saint John that attracted many faithful, mentioned by al-Shābushtī at the end of the tenth or beginning of the eleventh century.

ABŪ AL-MAKARĪM (1177–1204) devotes a short passage to Damanhūr Shubra (1984, p. 25). According to this author, the body of Saint John of Sanhūt was preserved in the church of Saint Theodorus at Shubra. It was transferred to the Church of Our Lady in the same town.

Al-MAQRĪZĪ (d. 1441) devotes a chapter to the feast of Saint John, which was fixed at 8 Bashans (Vol. 1, pp. 68–80). This was a great feast, to which people came from every quarter. The feast was forbidden from 1303 to 1337, then authorized again, and finally prohibited in 1354. In that year the emir ʿAlā' al-Din ibn ʿAlī ibn al-Kūrānī, governor of Cairo, came to Shubra and destroyed the Christian churches and, taking away the saint's finger, had it burned in a public place and the ashes thrown into the Nile, that the Christians might not recover it. From that time to the present, adds al-Maqrīzī, the feast of the martyr has no longer been celebrated.

In an eighteenth-century list of churches, of which two manuscripts are extant (published by Amélineau, 1893, pp. 578, 580) the church of Saint John of Sanhūt is still mentioned at Damanhūr Shubra. We do not know at what period Dayr Yūḥannā actually disappeared.

BIBLIOGRAPHY

Amélineau, E. *La Géographie de l'Egypte à l'époque copte*. Paris, 1893.
Casanova, P. "Les Noms coptes du Caire et localités voisines." *Bulletin de l'Institut français d'Archéologie orientale* 1 (1901):139–224.

Maspero, J., and G. Wiet. *Matériaux pour servir à la géographie de l'Égypte.* Mémoires publiés par les membres de l'Institut français d'Archéologie orientale 36. Paris, 1919.

RENÉ-GEORGES COQUIN
MAURICE MARTIN, S.J.

DAYR YUḤANNIS (Al-Minshāh). On the right bank of the Nile, about 6 miles (10 km) south of DAYR ANBĀ BISĀDAH, and hence of the town of al-Minshāh (the ancient Psoi/Ptolemais Hermiou), are the ruins of a village, a necropolis, and a Coptic monastery named for Saint John. A little farther to the south, in the quarries at the foot of the Jabal Tūkh, some Coptic inscriptions indicate that hermits lived there. Some invoke among others an Apa Johannes; one may consult Morgan and Bouriant (1894, pp. 370–1) and Sayce (1908, p. 18). More recent excavations are described by Klemm (1979, pp. 103–40).

BIBLIOGRAPHY

Klemm, D. R. "Bericht über die erste Gelandekampagne im September/Oktober 1977." *Studien zur altägyptischen Kultur* 7 (1979):103–140.

Morgan, J. de, and U. Bouriant. "Note sur les carrières antiques de Ptolemaïs (Menshiyèh)." *Mémoires de l'Institut français d'archéologie orientale* 8 (1894):370–71.

Sayce, A. H. "Notes on Assyrian and Egyptian History." *Proceedings of the Society of Biblical Archaeology* 30 (1908):13–18.

RENÉ-GEORGES COQUIN
MAURICE MARTIN, S.J.

DAYR YUḤANNIS KAMA. Amid a vast field of ruins southeast of DAYR AL-SURYĀN and DAYR ANBĀ BISHOI stand the remains of Dayr Yuḥannis Kama in Wādī al-Naṭrūn (SCETIS) in the western desert of Egypt. This monastery was built in the ninth century (c. A.D. 840). Tradition has it that the founder himself, Abbā Yuḥannis, built the commanding towers and the strongly fortified walls in addition to the church that was dedicated to the Virgin Mary. Actually this church was called after the Holy THEOTOKOS as she appeared to Abbā Yuḥannis in a glorious vision. She then expressed her desire to have a holy community and a convent built on the site.

In the last decades of the tenth century the monastery was pillaged. The remains of the interior buildings, however, suggest that they were quadrilaterally structured, leaving the center open for plants.

Most prominent among these buildings was the *qaṣr,* an isolated triple-storied tower adjacent to the principal church reached from the first-floor level by a drawbridge. Its major function was to serve as a fortress enabling the monks to withstand prolonged sieges. For this reason it contained a corn mill, a well, a few cells, and a chapel on the top floor. Monastic possessions and rare manuscripts were kept there also.

It is believed that this monastery survived until about the second decade of the fifteenth century after which it was totally abandoned. It was still flourishing when Patriarch BENJAMIN II visited it in 1330. The fourteenth-century traveler Ludolf von Suchem visited it before the turn of the century. In 1430 its monks migrated to Dayr al-Suryān, transferring with them the relics of their patron saint.

BIBLIOGRAPHY

Burkitt, F. C. "The Monasteries of the Wadi'n-Natroun." *Journal of Theological Studies* 28 (1927):320–25; 34 (1933):188–92; 36 (1935):105–107.

Davis, M. H. "The Life of Abba John Khamé." Coptic text ed. and trans. from the Codex Vaticanus 60. *PO* 14, pp. 313–72. Paris, 1920.

Evelyn-White, H. G. *The Monasteries of the Wadi'n Natrūn,* Pt. 1, *New Coptic Texts from the Monastery of St. Macarius.* New York, 1926; Pt. 2, *The History of the Monasteries of Nitria and Scetis.* New York, 1932; Pt. 3, *The Architecture and Archeology.* New York, 1933.

Martin, C., "Les Monastères du Wadi Natroun." *Nouvelle Revue Théologique* 62 (1935):113–34, 238–52.

FAYEK ISHAK

DAYR YUḤANNIS AL-QAṢĪR (Asyūṭ). *See* Dayr al-ʿIẓām (Asyūṭ).

DAYR YUḤANNIS AL-QAṢĪR, monastery in Wādī al-Naṭrūn founded in the fourth century (c. A.D. 380) by Abba Yuḥannis according to the instructions of his father, Amoi. Tradition relates that the latter planted his staff in the sand and asked his son to water it regularly, although the closest well was 12 miles (19 km) away. It is said that the staff, known in the tenth century as the "tree of obedience," bloomed for more than six centuries.

This monastery is situated southeast of DAYR AL-SURYĀN and DAYR ANBĀ BISHOI and had dependent cells that formed units surrounded by a high wall. These swelling houses, as they were called, were in no way fortified at the beginning of their construction. Fortifications that included the nucleus or the central court and the surrounding buildings were introduced in the later decades of the ninth century.

In spite of these interior and exterior fortifications, this monastery, like many others in the Nitrian Valley, was sacked and rebuilt many times. It was crippled financially and was totally abandoned after the crushing blow of the Berber incursion in the middle of the fourteenth century. At present only small parts of the southern and western sides are somewhat better preserved than the enclosure walls, which had fallen into ruin. The materials of the collapsed walls and ruined enclosures seem to have been used by the monks of the adjacent Dayr al-Suryān and Dayr Anbā Bishoi for their cells and other monastic buildings.

BIBLIOGRAPHY

Kersting, A. E. "The Coptic Monasteries of Wadi Natrūn." *The Bulletin* (July 1949):9–15.

Walters, C. C. *Monastic Archaeology in Egypt.* Warminster, England, 1974.

FAYEK ISHAK

DAYR AL-ZĀWIYAH.

The village today called al-Zāwiyah is situated about 3 miles (5 km) from Rīfah and 9 miles (15 km) from ASYŪṬ on the edge of the desert. The monastery is south of the village. An ancient cemetery borders the village to the east in the desert, where one finds Roman pottery. W. M. F. Petrie (1907, p. 2) concluded that al-Zāwiyah must have been an ancient Roman fort. M. Ramzī (1953–1968, Vol. 2, pt. 4, p. 27) said that this village was formerly called Minshā'at al-Shaykh. ABŪ ṢALĪH THE ARMENIAN, at the beginning of the thirteenth century, did not seem to know it. Two centuries later al-MAQRĪZĪ (1853, Vol. 2, p. 506), speaking of the Monastery of the Apostles in the district of Durunkah, noted that this village built beside it was called Minshu'at al-Shaykh because a *shaykh* named Abū Bakr al-Shadhlī had founded the village and established a garden there.

The *dayr* itself is formed of a vast quadrilateral about 90 by 110 yards (80 by 100 m) bounded by an encircling wall with a very pronounced batter. The entrance is to the west, with stone uprights, a reused lintel, and a heavy door edged with iron. Inside, a village has replaced the monks. All that survives of the ancient *dayr* is the church, which is at a lower level. It contains a transverse vaulted narthex and a nave in which four massive columns (undoubtedly enclosing more slender columns, the capitals of which can be seen) support a high dome, while the aisles are simply ceiled. In the apse, the niches on the second register have a broken pediment, as at Dayr al-Aḥmar (DAYR ANBĀ BISHOI) in Suhāj. Four have conches, the fifth, which occupies the center, presents a sculpted column. In the first register, three arcades with semicircular arches and two arched doorways give access to chapels. The pediments, the arcades, and the bands that separate them are finely sculpted. Everything recalls the great churches of the monasteries of Suhāj, DAYR ANBĀ SHINŪDAH and Dayr Anbā Bishoi. One may reasonably conclude that this church of al-Zāwiyah dates from the same period as those of Suhāj.

J. VANSLEB said that this church was called Sauwie and was dedicated to Saint Athanasius but that it presented no trace of antiquity (1677, pp. 364, 378; 1678, pp. 219, 227). M. Jullien saw it in dilapidated condition (1901, pp. 214–15), which explains why neither V. de Bock nor S. Clarke showed any interest in it. O. Meinardus (1965, p. 286; 1977, p. 397) ignored the *dayr* and spoke only of the church of the village, dedicated to the healing saint Abū Tarbū. The church of the *dayr* merits an architectural study.

BIBLIOGRAPHY

Jullien, M. "A travers les ruines de la Haute Egypte à la recherche de la grotte de l'abbé Jean." *Etudes* 88 (1901):204–217.

Meinardus, O. *Christian Egypt, Ancient and Modern.* Cairo, 1965; 2nd ed., 1977.

Petrie, W. M. F. *Gīzeh and Rīfeh.* London, 1907.

Ramzī, M. *Al-Qāmūs al-Jughrāfī lil-Bilād al-Miṣrīyyah,* 3 vols. Cairo, 1953–1968.

Vansleb, J. M. *Nouvelle relation en forme de journal d'un voyage fait en Egypte en 1672 et 1673.* Paris, 1677. Translated as *The Present State of Egypt.* London, 1678.

RENÉ-GEORGES COQUIN
MAURICE MARTIN, S.J.

DAYR AL-ZAYTUN.

See Sharunah.

DAYR AL-ZUJAJ.

See Enaton.

DEACON, third and lowest rank in the threefold hierarchy of orders in the Coptic church, being subordinate to the presbyter and the bishop.

The term deacon, derived from the Greek *diakonos,* meaning "servant," signified one who performed menial tasks such as waiting at table. It occurs in the New Testament with wider and more comprehensive connotation, including daily ministration to the needy, the service of the Word, as well as serving at table (Acts 6:1, 2, 4). In Saint Paul's epistles, its usage covers both temporal and spiritual services.

At the beginning of the apostolic age, the apostles realized that the nascent Christian church needed their full attention. So they chose seven men of good reputation and filled with the Spirit to minister at tables, attend to the poor, and distribute alms to widows. These seven were Stephen, who was "full of faith and of the Holy Spirit," Philip, Prochorus, Nicanor, Timon, Parmenas, and Nicolaus of Antioch (Acts 6:5, 6). Thus the diaconate came into being as a recognized office in the church, to fulfill a secondary, albeit essential, task in the religious life of the community.

The apostles prayed and laid their hands upon them. Soon, some of these seven deacons distinguished themselves in the spiritual sphere. With remarkable evangelistic enthusiasm, Stephen used to reason with others in a spirit of inspired wisdom, performed great miracles, and was eventually destined to be the first Christian martyr (Acts 6 and 7). Philip was active in preaching the Word, proclaiming the Messiah, effecting cures, and accomplishing miracles among the people who listened eagerly to his preaching (Acts 8).

The First Epistle to Timothy (3:8–10) lists the qualities to be expected in candidates for the diaconate. To be admitted, they must be men of high principles, above reproach, not given to hypocrisy or double-talk, not indulging in excessive drinking or amassing of riches. Above all, they must command a firm hold on the basic truths of the Christian faith.

It is noteworthy that these qualities are almost identical with the prerequisites for the episcopate, a fact that reflects the high regard in which the diaconate was held. No less than bishops, deacons must be subjected to a close scrutiny as to their character, and if found faultless, they may be allowed to serve.

Similar to priests, deacons receive their ordination by the imposition of hands from a bishop. According to the *Apostolic Canons,* "Let a presbyter, deacon, and the rest of the clergy be ordained by one bishop" (*Apostolical Canons 2,* 1956, p. 594). Likewise, the *Apostolic Constitutions* stipulate, "Thou shalt ordain a deacon, O bishop, by laying thy hands upon him in the presence of the whole presbytery, and of the deacons, and shalt pray . . ." (*Constitutions of the Holy Apostles 8,* 1956, p. 492).

The minimum age of a deacon at ordination should be twenty-five years (*Canons of the Council of Trullo,* 1956, p. 372). Like the presbyter, a deacon is subject, after ordination, to the same rules regarding marriage, according to which digamy is denied to both.

Deacons are, first and foremost, subordinate assistants to priests and bishops, and are not entitled to perform any of the sacramental services that are the prerogatives of the presbytery and the episcopate. They perform essential duties both inside the sanctuary and outside it during the church services:

> As to the deacons . . . let some of them attend upon the oblation of the Eucharist, ministering to the Lord's body with fear. Let others of them watch the multitude, and keep them silent. But let that deacon who is at the high priest's hand say to the people, let no one have any quarrel against another; let no one come in hypocrisy . . . . Let the deacon pray for the whole church, for the whole world, and for the several parts of it, and the fruits of it, for the priests and the rulers, for the high priest and the king, and the peace of the universe . . . [*The Constitutions of the Holy Apostles* 7.57, 1951, pp. 421, 422].

Besides making responses to the officiating priest, the main duties of the deacon serving at the altar include the preparation and arrangement of the altar's vessels and utensils, bringing water for the hands of the celebrant and for washing the chalice, paten, spoon, and asterisk (see EUCHARISTIC VESSELS) after administering Holy Communion, looking after the censer, and using a fan (see LITURGICAL INSTRUMENTS) when necessary to drive insects away from the oblations.

Outside the sanctuary a deacon leads the congregation's responses during the liturgy. The various lections of the day are read by deacons, unless a priest chooses to read the Gospel. A deacon may also deliver the sermon, if he is particularly endowed with the gift of preaching, subject to permission from the priest or bishop.

A deacon may also be entrusted with the general discipline of the congregation and maintaining order during the service. "Let the deacon be the disposer of the places, that everyone of those that comes in may go to his proper place, and may not sit at the entrance. In like manner, let the deacon oversee the people, that nobody may whisper, nor slumber, nor laugh, nor nod; for all ought in the church to stand wisely, and soberly, and attentively, having their attention fixed upon the word of the Lord" (*Constitutions of the Holy Apostles* 7.57, 1951, p. 421).

In earlier centuries, the number of deacons was restricted to seven even in the largest metropolis, apparently to conform with the precept set by the apostles: "The deacons ought to be seven in number, according to the canon, even if the city be great. Of this you will be persuaded from the book of the Acts" (*Canons of the Holy and Blessed Fathers* 15, 1956, p. 86). Together with this limitation in number, they were entrusted with certain administrative and pastoral tasks, such as assisting the bishop and priests during the sessions of ecclesiastical courts, distribution of the funds belonging to widows and orphans, and visiting the sick and those in prison.

It seems, however, that at times some deacons misunderstood these responsibilities and arrogated to themselves powers and authorities beyond what they were entitled to. To stop such irregularities the first ecumenical Council of NICAEA (325) defined their privileges and obligations as follows:

> It has come to the knowledge of the holy and great Synod that, in some districts and cities, the deacons administer the Eucharist to the presbyters, whereas neither canon nor custom permits that they who have no right to offer should give the Body of Christ to them that do offer. And this also has been made known, that certain deacons now touch the Eucharist even before the bishops. Let all such practices be utterly done away, and let the deacons remain within their own bounds, knowing that they are the ministers of the bishop and the inferiors of the presbyters. Let them receive the Eucharist according to their order, after the presbyters, and let either the bishop or the presbyter administer to them. Furthermore, let not the deacons sit among the presbyters, for that is contrary to canon and order [*The Canons of the Holy Fathers* 18, 1956, p. 38].

Deacons who prove genuinely dedicated to the ecclesiastical service may be ordained priests, subject to the general approval of the church congregation.

BIBLIOGRAPHY

Habīb Jirjis. *Asrār al-Kanīsah al-Sab'ah,* 2nd ed., p. 220. Cairo, 1950.

Ibn al-'Assāl, al-Ṣafī. *Kitāb al-Qawānīn,* pp. 63–65. Repr. Cairo, 1927.

Mīkhā'īl Mīnā. *'Ilm Al-Lāhūt,* pp. 543–45. Cairo, 1936.

William Sulaymān Qilādah. *Kitāb al-Disqūliyah, Ta'ālīm al-Rusul,* pp. 178, 204–205, 836. Cairo, 1979.

ARCHBISHOP BASILIOS

DEACON AND ARCHDEACON, ORDINATION OF.

The ordination of a deacon or archdeacon usually takes place after the Prayer of Reconciliation. The candidate is presented to the bishop (or metropolitan or patriarch) who is celebrating the Divine Liturgy, and kneels before the steps of the sanctuary.

Deacon

When the bishop has ascertained from the clergy that the candidate is worthy of the diaconate, he offers incense and says the Prayer of Thanksgiving and the Prayer of Incense. He then turns toward the east and says this prayer:

> Lord, God of hosts, who hast brought us unto the lot of this ministry, Who searchest the hearts and veins, do hearken unto us according to the multitude of Thy tender mercies, and purify us from all the stains of body and of spirit. . . . Fill us with Thy Divine Power, the Grace of Thy only-begotten Son and the Gift of Thy Holy Spirit . . . , and accept the diaconate of Thy servant who is kneeling here in expectation of Thy heavenly gifts.

The deacons respond with the KYRIE ELEISON thrice and the archdeacon says:

> May the grace of our Lord Jesus Christ, which fills up our shortcomings, by the good will of God the Father and the Holy Spirit, descend upon [name], who approaches the holy altar in fear and trembling, lifting up the eyes of his heart unto Thee who dwellest in heaven, awaiting Thy heavenly gifts, in order that he may pass from the rank of subdiaconate to the order of the diaconate in the holy church of [name]. Pray that the gift of the Holy Spirit may come upon him.

The deacons respond with the *Kyrie eleison.* The bishop turns to the west, lays his right hand upon the candidate's head, and says the following prayer:

> Master, Lord God Almighty, who art truthful in Thy promises and generous to those who call upon Thee, hear us as we entreat Thee, show Thy countenance upon Thy servant [name], who hath

> been recommended for the diaconate through the judgment of those who have presented him. Fill him with the Holy Spirit, with wisdom and power as Thou filled Stephen, the first deacon and martyr. . . . Establish him as a servant for Thy holy altar so that by pleasing Thee in the service entrusted to him, without blame or sin, he may attain to a higher grade. It is not through the imposition of our hands that grace can be obtained, but through the visitation of Thy rich compassion to those who deserve it.

Facing the east, the bishop says:

> Yes, Lord, make him worthy of the call of the diaconate, that through Thy loving-kindness to man, he may become worthy of Thy holy name, to worship Thee, to serve Thy altar and find mercy before Thee, for mercy and tenderness are from Thee. . . . Look upon us, Lord, and upon our service, purify us of all uncleanness, and send down from heaven Thy grace upon Thy servant [name] that he may complete his diaconate without reproof.

The bishop turns to the west and crosses the candidate's forehead with his thumb, saying, "We consecrate thee, [name], deacon in the Holy Church of God." The archdeacon announces, "[name] is consecrated deacon in the Holy Catholic Apostolic Church of God." Here again the bishop makes the sign of the cross on his forehead, saying, "We ordain thee, [name], a deacon for the holy altar of the Orthodox Church of [name] in the name of the Father and the Son and the Holy Spirit." He makes three signs of the cross over the candidate's forehead in the name of the Holy Trinity, and turning to the east, he says:

> We give thanks to Thee, Master, Lord God Almighty, for everything and in every condition. We praise and glorify Thy Holy Name. . . . Take pleasure in the imposition of hands which hath taken place upon Thy servant [name] through the descent upon him of Thy Holy Spirit.

The bishop then turns to the candidate and places the orarion on his left shoulder and passes it underneath his right arm, saying, "Glory and honor to the Consubstantial Trinity, the Father, the Son and the Holy Spirit. Peace and edification unto the Church of God, the One Only, Universal, Apostolic, Holy Church, Amen."

The bishop then delivers this instruction to the new deacon:

> My son, thou hast been entrusted with a great service of ministration, which thou shouldst accomplish to the full, as thou art counted among the children of Stephen, the first deacon. It is thy duty to visit the people of the Lord, the widows and orphans, and all those who are in affliction, to help them as much as thou canst. Be a good example to them so that they see thy good deeds and glorify God. Be an assistant to thy bishop and thy priest, and take them to visit those who are afflicted. Honor the presbyters, who are senior to you in rank, and treat each of them as a father, that you may be worthy of the blessing of Christ who said, "If any man serve me, him will my Father honor," and also according to the apostle Paul, "For they that have used the office of a deacon well, purchase to themselves a good degree, and great boldness in the faith which is in Christ Jesus." Be appreciative of the honor accorded to thee, as you hold [the chalice of] the Real Blood, which gives salvation to the world. Glory be to Christ Jesus, our God. Amen.

Here the new deacon kneels before the sanctuary, kisses the cross in the bishop's hand, and kisses the altar. After communion, the bishop insufflates on his face, saying, "Receive ye the Holy Spirit," and lays his hand upon him saying *axios* [worthy] three times.

Archdeacon

When a deacon of proven aptitude has been recommended for the order of archdeacon, the bishop says this prayer:

> Master, Lord God, great in mercy and righteousness, who, through Thy only-begotten Son Jesus Christ, hast established the heavenly Jerusalem and given all the orders and canons of the Church, do Thou now, our King who lovest mankind, accept our supplications, and send the grace of Thy Holy Spirit upon Thy servant [name], who hath been called to the archdeaconate by the recommendation of those who have given account of him. Make him worthy to be archdeacon in Thy Holy Church, in the likeness of one of the seven ministrants set up by the pure apostles, namely Stephen, the first deacon and first martyr. Fill him with power and understanding like Stephen, the first archdeacon, in Thy Holy Church [to assist the priest] at the service of the bloodless sacrifices and hold the chalice of the Precious Blood of the Lamb without blemish, which is Thine only-begotten Son, that he may minister unto the orphans, help the widows, attend to worshipers, teach the unenlightened, censure the ill-bred, chide the insubordinate and bring back the stray. . . . May he become a good example to all ministrants and attain an elevated degree. It is not through the imposition of our hands that this grace is given, but by the visita-

tion of Thy rich compassion, O Lord. Now also, our Master, we pray and beseech Thee, Thou Good One and Lover of Man, on behalf of Thy servant [name], to make him worthy of the calling of the archdeaconate through the descent upon him of Thy Holy Spirit. Do Thou purify me, as well, of all sin and release me from my transgressions, through Thy only-begotten Son, our Lord and God and Savior, Jesus Christ. . . .

Here the newly ordained archdeacon kneels before the sanctuary, kisses the cross in the bishop's hand, and kisses the altar. After communion, the bishop gives him the blessing, as in the consecration of the deacon.

ARCHBISHOP BASILIOS

DEACONESS, woman in charge of the sick and the poor of her own sex. In the early church, deaconesses were recognized as a distinct order of women who were vowed to perpetual chastity. They were, nevertheless, allowed to perform only certain duties in the care of women, and no sacerdotal services in the church.

In the New Testament we have names of various women who dedicated their lives to the service of God during and following Christ's ministry on earth and His Resurrection, but they cannot be considered deaconesses in the strict sense of the term. The only woman whose name is mentioned explicitly in this capacity is Phoebe, on whose behalf Saint Paul writes: "I commend to you our sister Phoebe, a deaconess of the church at Cenchreae" (Rom. 16:1). The author of 1 Timothy speaks implicitly of deaconesses where, after listing the qualities required in candidates for the male diaconate, he speaks of women who must be "serious, no slanderers, but temperate, faithful in all things" (1 Tm. 3:11).

Most commentators are of the opinion that these words refer to deaconesses in particular. Hence Saint JOHN CHRYSOSTOM affirms: "Some have thought that this is said of women generally, but it is not so, for why should he introduce anything about women to interfere with his subject? He is speaking of those who held the rank of Deaconesses" (*Homilies on . . . Timothy* 11, 1956, p. 441).

According to the *Constitutions of the Holy Apostles,* "a deaconess must be a chaste virgin or else a widow who has been but once married, faithful, and well esteemed" (*Constitutions* 6.17, 1951, p. 457). Canon 12 of the Fourth Council of Carthage (398) lays down the duties of widows and dedicated women *(sanctimoniales)* who are chosen to assist at the baptism of women: "They should be so well instructed in their office as to be able to teach aptly and properly unskilled and rustic women how to answer at the time of their baptism to the questions put to them, and also how to live godly after they have been baptized."

Women were not admitted to this office in the early church unless they were over sixty years of age, in accordance with the testimonies of Tertullian (*On the Veiling of Virgins* 9, 1951), BASIL THE GREAT (*The Canons of Basil* 24, 1956), and others. Sozomen also informs us that the emperor Theodosius (379–395) "who was always zealous in promoting the glory of the church, issued a law, enacting that women should not be admitted to the diaconate, unless they were upwards of sixty years of age, according to the precept of the Apostle Paul" (1978, p. 387). Two centuries later devout women of forty were admitted by the Council of CHALCEDON (451). The female diaconate did not continue for long, and in the Western church had virtually disappeared by the tenth century, though in the Eastern church it lingered on until the end of the twelfth in the convents of Constantinople (Thomassin, 1679–1681, bk. 3).

That deaconesses were not to perform any of the duties ascribed to deacons was stipulated by the church in various apostolic constitutions, and in particular their duties during the administration of the sacrament of BAPTISM: "as to women's baptizing, we let you know that there is no small peril to those that undertake it . . . . For if the man be the head of the woman, and he be originally ordained for the priesthood, it is not just to abrogate the order of the creation, and leave the principal to come to the extreme part of the body. . . . For if baptism were to be administered by women, certainly our Lord would have been baptized by His own mother, and not by John; or when He sent us to baptize, He would have sent along with us women also for this purpose. But now He has nowhere, either by constitution or by writing, delivered to us any such thing. . . ." (*Constitutions of the Holy Apostles* 3.9, 1951, p. 429; see also *Apostolic Constitution* 2.26, p. 410, and 3.6, p. 427).

BIBLIOGRAPHY

Percival, H. R. "Excursus on the Deaconess of the Early Church." In *A Select Library of the Nicene and Post-Nicene Fathers of the Christian Church,* 2nd Ser., Vol. 14, ed. P. Schaff and H. Wace, pp. 41–42. Grand Rapids, Mich., 1971.

Robinson, C. *The Ministry of Deaconess.* London, 1898.

Thomassin, L. *Ancienne et nouvelle discipline de l'église.* Paris, 1679–1681.

Turner, C. H. "Ministries of Women in the Primitive Church: Widow, Deaconess and Virgin in the First Four Christian Centuries." *Constructive Quarterly* 7 (1919).

ARCHBISHOP BASILIOS

DEAD, PRAYER FOR THE. The Coptic church, which believes in one final, decisive day of judgment, does not recognize the concepts of purgatory or of a particular judgment to each individual soul at its separation from the body at the time of death. This attitude is supported by Christ's description of the second coming of the Son of Man, and also by the intrinsic significance of His parables of the kingdom of heaven. Thus, as the souls of the departed await the resurrection of the dead for judgment, prayers and intercessions may be offered on their behalf, both by individuals and by the church as a whole.

In the evening service of the raising of incense, the prayers for the dead, known as intercessions for the dormant, are recited by the priest, with response from the deacon and the congregation.

Similar intercessions are mentioned at the following significant points in the course of the celebration of Divine Liturgy: the offertory, the mystery of the Gospel, the diptych, the prayers preceding and following the fraction, in the prayer of absolution to the Father.

These prayers were prescribed among other practices of the early church. The APOSTOLIC CONSTITUTIONS, referring to cemeteries or burial places as "dormitories," laid down this command: ". . . assemble in the dormitories, reading the Holy Books, and singing for the martyrs which are fallen asleep, and for all the saints from the beginning of the world, and for your brethren that are asleep in the Lord, and offer the acceptable Eucharist . . . both in your churches and in the dormitories."

Tertullian (c. 160–c. 220), the earliest of the fathers who mentioned the prayers of the dead in their writings, describes their departure as the birthday into a new stage of life: "We offer sacrifices for the dead on their birthday anniversaries."

Reference to these prayers was also made by CYRIL OF JERUSALEM (c. 315–386), in his *Catechetical Lectures:* "After the spiritual sacrifice, the bloodless service is completed, over that sacrifice of propitiation we entreat God for the common peace of the Churches, . . . we commemorate also those who have fallen asleep before us; . . . and in a word of all who in past years have fallen asleep among us, believing that it will be a very great benefit to the souls, for whom the supplication is put up, while that holy and most awful sacrifice is set forth."

ARCHBISHOP BASILIOS

DECIUS, Roman emperor (full name, Gaius Messius Quintus Trajanus Decius) from the autumn of 249 to late June 251. Born about 200 at Sirmium in Pannonia, he became an important senator and married into the Roman noble house of the Herennii. In 248, when the Goths were exerting intense pressure on the Danube frontier provinces, Decius was charged by Emperor Philip the Arabian to take over the defenses of Pannonia and Moesia. The Goths were checked, and mutinies among the legions were quelled. Decius was proclaimed emperor by his troops, and after fruitless negotiations with Philip, he confronted the imperial forces near Verona in the late summer of 249. In the ensuing battle Philip was defeated and slain. Decius is recorded as emperor in Egypt by 27 November 249 (Oxyrhynchus Papyrus XII.1636).

EUSEBIUS OF CAESAREA says that Decius "on account of his enmity toward Philip raised a persecution against the churches" (*Historia ecclesiastica* VI.39.i). This is partially corroborated by the writer (c. A.D. 265) of XIII (Jewish) Sibylline (ll. 79–88). Decius' aim, however, may have been wider: a general restoration of the virtues associated with the republic and early empire. His revival of the office of censor and his assuming the name Trajanus, after the *optimus princeps* (Trajan), indicate this. This outlook also included religion. It would seem that to underline the necessity of renewed popular acknowledgment of the role of the Roman gods in restoring the empire, Decius ordered that the annual sacrifice and *vota* performed in honor of Jupiter on the Capitoline Hill in Rome (3 January 250) should be repeated throughout the cities of the empire. At least one Italian town, Ansedona (modern Cosa), hailed Decius as "the restorer of the sacred rites and liberty" *(restitutor sacrorum et libertatis).*

The counterpart of this policy was the immediate arrest of prominent Christians, including Pope Fabian, who was tried before the emperor and executed on 20 January 250 (*Libri pontificalis,* p. 27). Other prominent Christians were arrested, including Babylas, bishop of Antioch, and Alexander of Jerusalem. DIONYSIUS of Alexandria, the fourteenth patriarch, escaped through a lucky accident (Eusebius, *Historia ecclesiastica* VI.39.2), and Cyprian of Carthage went into hiding (Cyprian, *Letters* 8, written by Roman presbyters to him and included in his collection of letters).

Though there can be no certainty, it would seem that these measures directed against individuals and resulting in trials and executions were distinct from the general sacrifice that resulted from the repetition of the annual imperial *vota* on an empirewide scale. The requirement was for all Roman citizens, who since the Antonine Constitution of 212 included nearly all free inhabitants of the empire, to demonstrate their allegiance to the *dei publici.* They would do this by offering incense to the gods, pouring a libation, and eating sacrificial meat. The acts would be supervised by a commission drawn from the chief citizens of the district. In Egypt, forty-three certificates *(libelli)* given to individuals who had sacrificed have been discovered, mainly from Oxyrhynchus but also from Arsinoë and Alexander's Isle in the Fayyūm.

Two examples may be quoted:

> *1st Hand:* To the commission chosen to superintend the sacrifices at the village of Alexander's Isle. From Aurelius Diogenes, son of Satabous, of the village of Alexander's Isle, aged seventy-two years, with a scar on the right eyebrow. I have always sacrificed to the gods, and now in your presence, in accordance with the edict, I have made sacrifice, and poured a libation, and partaken of the sacred victims. I request you to certify this below. Farewell. I, Aurelius Diogenes, have presented this petition.
>
> *2nd Hand:* I, Aurelius Syrus, saw you and your son sacrificing.
>
> *3rd Hand:* . . . onos. . . .
>
> *1st Hand.* The year 1 of the Emperor Gaius Messius Quintus Trajanus Decius Pius Felix Augustus, Epiph 2 [26 June 250].
>
> To the commission chosen to superintend the sacrifices. From Aurelia Ammonous, daughter of Mustus, of the Moeris quarter, priestess of the god Petesouchos, the great, the mighty, the immortal, and priestess of the gods in the Moeris quarter. I have sacrificed to the gods all my life and now again, in accordance with the decree and in your presence, I have made sacrifice, and poured a libation and partaken of the sacred victims. I request you to certify this below.

Both *libelli* indicate the solemn character of the action, obligatory even to those who already held priesthoods in local cults.

As a demonstration of solidarity toward the empire and its rulers, Decius' measure was extremely successful. Given the alternatives of formally acknowledging the empire and its gods and standing ostentatiously aside from any outward show of loyalty, the great majority of Christians seem to have chosen the former. At Alexandria, Bishop Dionysius paints an awe-inspiring picture of the mixture of panic, confusion, and resigned acceptance of the imperial edict by the mass of the Christian population (in Eusebius, *Historia ecclesiastica* VI.41.10.14). At Smyrna, the see of the martyr-bishop Polycarp, Bishop Euctemon was among those who sacrificed to the gods (*Martyrdom of Pionius* 15.1), and the confessor Pionius won scant support for his defiance. Pity and ridicule were the principal emotions he aroused among the populace of Smyrna (*Martyrdom* 16). At Carthage, Cyprian admits that the great majority of his congregation lapsed (*Letters* 11.1), an assessment that was confirmed a year later when he wrote the *De lapsis.* Would-be sacrificers to Jupiter were turned away at the temple and asked to return on the morrow, so overwhelming was the response (*De lapsis* 8). In the country areas, whole congregations seem to have apostatized; one, that of Sutunurca, was led to the pagan altars by the bishop himself (*Letters* 59.10). In Alexandria, there was some resistance. Dionysius mentions seventeen martyrs, six significantly being recorded as "Libyans" (Eusebius, *Historia ecclesiastica* VI.41.14–42.4). He also describes vividly how in some cities and villages, pagans turned on the Christians and massacred them or forced them to flee into the desert, where death or slavery at the hands of Saracen tribes awaited them (Eusebius, *Historia ecclesiastica* VI.42.1–4). In general, resistance came from those who had little to lose and little standing in their communities. At Carthage, Lucianus, the leader of the confessors, is described as "little instructed in holy scripture"; and another, Aurelius, "did not know letters" (Cyprian, *Letters* 27.1).

Decius delivered a heavy blow to the church, the more effective because Christianity was still very largely an urban religion, whose adherents therefore were more easily identifiable. The mystique of the emperor and the empire was still a living factor in the lives of the provincials. Defiance, even at the orders of bishops, was only rarely acceptable.

No one can tell what would have happened if Decius had lived and his long duel with the Gothic king Kniva had not ended in his defeat and death in the marshes of Abrittus, near the delta of the Danube (June 251). Cyprian's return to Carthage in the spring of 251 and his ability to hold a council not long after Easter of that year, before Decius met his end, suggests that there would have been a slow recovery. The reign of Decius indicates, however, that in Egypt, as elsewhere in the empire, Christianity could be contained. There were still forces of loyalty and devotion to tradition that would safeguard the empire from disintegration in the twenty years of civil war and barbarian invasion that followed the death of the emperor.

BIBLIOGRAPHY

Alföldi, A. "The Crisis of the Empire (A.D. 249–270)." In *Cambridge Ancient History*, Vol. 12, pp. 165–230. Cambridge, 1939.

Clarke, G. W. "Some Observations on the Persecution of Decius." *Antichthon* 3 (1969):63–76.

Gross, K. "Decius." In *Reallexikon für Antike und Christentum*, Vol. 3, pp. 611–29. Stuttgart, 1957.

Knipfing, J. R. "The *Libelli* of the Decian Persecution." *Harvard Theological Review* 16 (1923):345–90.

Libri pontificalis, ed. T. Mommsen. Monumenta Germaniae Historica. Gestorum pontificum Romanorum 1. Berlin, 1898.

Martyrdom of Pionius the Presbyter and His Companions. In *Acts of the Christian Martyrs*, ed. H. Musurillo, pp. 136–67. London, 1972.

Olmstead, A. T. "The Mid-3rd Century of the Christian Era." *Classical Philology* 37 (1942):241–62, 398–420.

Oracula Sibyllina, ed. J. Geffcken. Leipzig, 1902.

Salisbury, F. S., and H. Mattingly. "The Reign of Trajan Decius." *Journal of Roman Studies* 14 (1924):1–23.

W. H. C. FREND

DEFENSOR ECCLESIAE, a layman, usually a lawyer, charged with the defense of the interests of the church in lawsuits and in any conflicts with secular authorities. Most of the evidence for the existence of *defensores ecclesiae* comes from North Africa, where they are mentioned by Possidius, bishop of Calama in 403 (*Vita Augustini* 12). They are also the subject of a law of Emperor Honorius (15 November 407), addressed to Porfyrius, proconsul of Africa, maintaining the inviolability of the privileges of the African clergy that had been requested by the North African bishops (*Codex Theodosianus* XVI.2.38: see also *The Canons of the 217 Blessed Fathers* . . . 1956, canon 97). The institution was found in other churches in the West, including Rome (Pope Zosimus, 1721, *Letters* 9.3), but no evidence has survived of its existence in Egypt.

BIBLIOGRAPHY

The Canons of the 217 Blessed Fathers who Assembled at Carthage. African Code XCVII. In *A Select Library of Nicene and Post-Nicene Fathers of the Christian Church*, 2nd ser., ed. Philip Schaff and Henry Wace. Grand Rapids, Mich., 1956.

Martroye, F. "Les defensores ecclesiae aux Ve. et VIe. siècles." *Revue historique de Droit français et étranger*, 4th ser., (1923):597–622.

W. H. C. FREND

DEFROCKING OF PRIESTS (Greek, apóklēros). According to the extant texts from the correspondence of bishops, especially that of bishop ABRAHAM of Hermonthis from the period around 600, the process of exclusion from the clergy is the same as that of excommunication. After the bishop has been informed of transgression by clergy, these offenses are placed on record and the bishop notifies the clergy of suspension. In addition, the superiors of these clergy are informed of the punishment of their subordinates, or it is communicated to all the clergy in circular letters. This exclusion is not final; it is in force until the person excluded comes to the bishop or fulfills a commission he has failed to complete, for which failure he has been excluded from the clergy. The following grounds are named for exclusion: disobedience toward the bishop, holding a communion service at the wrong time, incorrect ordering of divine service, offenses against the professional duties of the clergy, failure to keep night watches or to hold divine service, refusal to accept a church canon, and failure to appear before a court. In addition, stewards are punished if on Saturday and Sunday they have deserted their monasteries without previous inspection.

The bishop expressly threatens exclusion from the clergy in cases of disobedience of his instructions, for instance, if the cleric does not go to a particular person and give him communion or if he does not deliver a letter. Clergy who act as security for a man also are threatened with exclusion if they do not report the man's disobedience to the bishop.

MARTIN KRAUSE

DEIR. *See* Dayr.

DEMETRIUS I, twelfth patriarch of the See of Saint Mark (189–231). He succeeded JULIAN and was a contemporary of eight Roman emperors, from Commodus (180–192) to Alexander Severus (222–235), through the age of persecutions, which were particularly harsh in the reign of Septimius Severus (193–211).

Until the time of Demetrius, the church had been passing through a period of growing pains about which very little is known beyond the names and dates of the successive bishops. The HISTORY OF THE PATRIARCHS offers little information on the early bishops, who moved secretly in Egypt to strengthen the faithful and to appoint the priests who were entrusted with the surveillance of the spiritual welfare of their congregations. The *History of the Patriarchs* begins to discuss more events and details from Demetrius onward, although its statements often mingle historic events with legendary elements and miraculous episodes.

These begin with the election of Demetrius, an ordinary person from Coptic farmer stock, both illiterate and married. The *History of the Patriarchs* relates that his predecessor, Julian, had a dream in which the angel of the Lord appeared to him and told him that the man who would bring him a bunch of grapes in the morning would be patriarch after him. And so it was, when a peasant found some grapes, out of season, and took them to the patriarch on his deathbed. Julian at once told his companions about the celestial ordinance in his dream and died.

People took Demetrius, against his protests that he was married, tied him in chains, and had him consecrated as patriarch. In reality, he was married by his parents as a child to a cousin, also a child, who was living with them after her parents' death. The two children lived together like brother and sister. After their marriage, they continued to live together without a marital relationship. Nevertheless, some people began to raise questions. The angel of the Lord appeared to Demetrius in a dream and commanded him to reveal the truth about his conjugal life. Accordingly, the patriarch asked his archdeacon to solicit the congregation to remain after the liturgy, at which time Demetrius took the embers from some burning wood with his hand and placed them on his cloak, without burning it. His wife then had the embers placed in her headdress or pallium, which also did not burn. Then he told the spectators about the realities of his conjugal life, and all prayed and gave thanks to the Lord for their appeasement by this miracle.

Apart from these episodes, registered in detail in the *History of the Patriarchs,* and generally accepted by the pious Copts, it may seem strange to have a bishop who was illiterate. Demetrius must have memorized the liturgies, a phenomenon that was customary with the old school of Copts until recent times. However, Demetrius proved himself to be an extraordinary patriarch, both active and inflexible in the defense of his church against all heresies. Though illiterate, he took a great interest in the CATECHETICAL SCHOOL OF ALEXANDRIA, which peaked during his reign and became the center of religious scholarship and theology in the whole world.

Internally, Demetrius was indefatigable in moving throughout the country ordaining priests to meet the spiritual needs of the increasing Christian population. For the first time in the history of the church, he decided to consecrate three more bishops to relieve him from the growing pressures of an expanding community in the midst of relentless Roman persecutions. He appointed illustrious personalities as heads of the Catechetical School, such as CLEMENT OF ALEXANDRIA and ORIGEN, the greatest Coptic religious scholar, with whom he had a falling out later over matters of doctrine.

On the international scene, he dispatched PANTAENUS on a mission to South India in answer to a request from the Indian governor. We are not sure whether this was the second such mission to India, but it was recorded in the *Historia ecclesiastica* by EUSEBIUS OF CAESAREA (5.10). Demetrius also commissioned Origen to go to Arabia for the settlement of some of their theological problems. Throughout his patriarchate he issued epistles on a variety of subjects, including one to his peers, the bishops of Antioch, Caesarea, and Jerusalem, on the dating of Easter. The authority of the bishopric of Alexandria was universally recognized in combating heresies and heretics.

Throughout his episcopate of forty-three years, Demetrius led a precarious life amid waves of Roman persecutions. The *History of the Patriarchs* enumerates martyrs who perished in the persecutions of Emperor Septimius Severus. Among those cited are Origen's father, Leonidas (*Historia ecclesiastica* 6. 1); a woman called Herais; Basilides, who was a Roman legionary; a woman called Potamioena and her mother (*Historia ecclesiastica* 6. 5); a patrician by the name of Anatolius, described as "father of princes"; Eusebius; and Macarius, "uncle of Claudius, Justus, and Theodorus the Eastern," who were all martyred (see also *Historia ecclesiastica* 11. 41). Plutarch and Severus were buried alive. A virgin by the name of Thecla perished at the hands of the imperial executioner.

Apparently the later years of the life of Demetrius were consumed by his differences with Origen.

Though he was responsible for appointing Origen as head of the Catechetical School, Demetrius became disenchanted with Origen's writings, and it is unclear whether the patriarch was able to digest Origen's philosophy and theology. In the heat of their arguments, Origen journeyed to Palestine, where his profound learning was highly appreciated. He was made a priest by the bishops of Caesarea and Jerusalem (*Historia ecclesiastica* 6. 8), a step that infuriated the imperious Demetrius, who protested vehemently against the encroachment on his jurisdiction. The historian Eusebius devotes a number of chapters to Origen and his works (*Historia ecclesiastica* 6.2), which must have mystified a patriarch whose education was so restricted. The gnostic sections in Origen's religious philosophy were readily repudiated by the authoritarian head of the church. The *History of the Patriarchs* states that among his many blasphemies was "his doctrine that the Father created the Son, and the Son created the Holy Ghost; for he denied that the Father, Son, and Holy Ghost are not one God." The *History of the Patriarchs* paints a willful picture of Origen, who is said to have composed "unlawful books of magic," and that therefore Demetrius excommunicated him. The great mentor then emigrated to Caesarea, where he remained until his own pupil HERACLAS succeeded Demetrius after his death. In vain Heraclas attempted to persuade Origen to return after the death of Demetrius.

Sanctified in the Coptic church, Demetrius is commemorated in the Coptic SYNAXARION on 12 Hātūr.

BIBLIOGRAPHY

Altaner, B. *Patrology*, Eng. trans. Hilda Graef. London, 1958.

Bardenhewer, O. *Geschichte der altkirchlichen Literatur*, 3 vols. Freiburg, 1902–1912.

Duchesne, L. *Early History of the Christian Church*, Vol. 1, pp. 341ff. London, 1909.

Quasten, J. *Patrology*, 3 vols. Utrecht and Antwerp, 1975.

AZIZ S. ATIYA

DEMETRIUS II, 111th patriarch of the See of Saint Mark (1862–1870). Formerly abbot of DAYR ANBĀ MAQĀR, he was elected in 1862. In 1867, the year that saw the establishment of the first Protestant church by the missionaries in Asyūt, he made a tour of Upper Egypt to rally the Coptic flock round the Mother Church. In 1869 he attended the inauguration ceremony of the Suez Canal and had an audience with Sultan ʿAbd-al-ʿAzīz. The sultan donated some farmland to the Coptic church, the proceeds of which Demetrius used to finance Coptic schools and other charities. He died on the eve of the Epiphany of 1870, after occupying Saint Mark's throne for seven years, seven months, and seven days.

After his death, the patriarchate remained vacant for four years because of indecision in the Holy Synod about a worthy successor. During that period, the archbishop of Alexandria, Anbā Murqus, was nominated as vice-patriarch to run the church until a successor was elected in the person of CYRIL V.

MOUNIR SHOUCRI

DEMETRIUS OF ANTIOCH, a fictitious character created by the originators of a literary CYCLE during the late period in Coptic literature. Demetrius was a figure behind whom a later Coptic author (or authors) hid in order to lend an image of antiquity and authority to theological and moral arguments. A hagiographical thread was added by locating Demetrius in Antioch, making him bishop of that city, and the man who consecrated JOHN CHRYSOSTOM as a presbyter. The most "authoritative" text to affirm this story is an *Encomium in Victorem,* expressly attributed to John Chrysostom, in which the supposed author tells of "the time when I was at Antioch and stood with my father and teacher, Apa Demetrius, the archbishop" (Bouriant, 1893, pp. 234–35). The only possible forerunner to such a tale is the authentic manuscript of John Chrysostom's *Ad Demetrium (Clavis Patrum Graecorum* 4308; PG 47, pp. 319–86), for which a Coptic translation is extant (Orlandi, 1970). Since Flavian, who in fact consecrated Chrysostom, was not recognized by the see of Alexandria, the idea of replacing Flavian with a fictitious person might have occurred to the Copts.

In any event, Demetrius is supposed to have authored two hagiographical texts and two homilies. The hagiographical texts concern two martyrs of Antioch under DIOCLETIAN:

1. *Encomium in Philotheum, Miracula Philothei:* The manuscript (Vergote, 1935) has reached us only in two brief fragments, but we may deduce that the entire text described a series of miracles occurring at the Sanctuary of Philotheus in Antioch. These excerpts present a decisive literary parallel to the analogous *Miracula Coluthi,* and in fact both martyrs were especially venerated at Antinoë (ANTINOOPOLIS) as healers.

2. *Miracula Victoris:* The text has survived only in an Ethiopian translation, but it is very possible to postulate a Coptic text as the original.

The two homilies are:

1. *De Nativitate* (ed. Budge, 1915). This is a long work to be read at Christmas. First comes an account, based on well-known apocrypha, of the life of the Virgin from her birth to her betrothal. Then follows the sacred story of the Incarnation as told in the Gospels, that is, the Annunciation, Elizabeth's visit, the birth of Jesus, the visit of the Magi, the flight into Egypt, the Massacre of the Innocents, and the death of John the Baptist. Interpolated into this narration are interesting bits of an apocryphal nature, dealing with the story of Salome the midwife, and the dialogue between the Father and Son before the incarnation. Also, there is a polemic against NESTORIUS, and the conclusion includes an attack against certain theological ideas relating to Christology and the salvation of laymen.

2. *In Isaiam I:16–17* (ed. De Vis, 1929). This exegesis serves as an excuse for discussing many moral and social issues such as sin, wealth, poverty, the duty to correct one's neighbor, and the frailty of human nature. Unfortunately, the text is extremely mutilated in the principal manuscript that transmits this work (Vatican Library, Coptic 67, fols. 110–39), and upon which De Vis based his edition. Another manuscript at Turin (Rossi 1893–1894) is even more fragmentary.

BIBLIOGRAPHY

Bouriant, U. "L'éloge de l'apa Victor fils de Romanos." In *Mémoires de la Mission archeologique française au Caire* 8, pp. 145–266. Paris, 1893.

Budge, E. A. W. *Miscellaneous Coptic Texts*, pp. 74–110. London, 1915.

Orlandi, T. "Demetrio di Antiochia e Giovanni Crisostomo." *Acme* 23 (1970):175–78.

Rossi, F. "Di alcuni manoscritti copti che si conservano nella Biblioteca nationale di Torino." *Memorie dell'Accademie delle Scienze di Torino*, ser. 2, no. 43 (1893):223–340; 44 (1894):21–70.

Vergote, J. "Le Texte sous-jacent du palimpseste Berlin No. 9455." *Le Muséon* 48 (1935):245–96.

Vis, H. de. *Homélies coptes de la Vaticane*. Coptica 1, 5. Copenhagen, 1929.

TITO ORLANDI

DEMETRIUS' BOOK OF EPACT. *See* Book of Epact.

DEMONS. *See* Biblical Subjects in Coptic Art.

DENDERA. *See* Dandarah.

DEPOSIT. *See* Law, Coptic: Private Law.

DER. *See* Dayr.

DESERT FATHERS, expression describing the first anchorites. It was first used by one of the first "reporters" of these practitioners of the "flight to the desert," PALLADIUS himself. In fact, he twice, at least in explicit terms, used a form of this phrase to designate those who chose to live in the desert. The first time was to describe the companions of AMMONIUS of Kellia: "as the desert fathers attest concerning him." A less clear formula is used in the second instance: the sister of Pior, wishing to have news of her brother, who has gone to the desert, asks the bishop to write "to the fathers, those who are in the desert." In the same way, Cyril of Scythopolis (d. after 559) used the same expression with reference to a monk whose biography he wrote: in the *Life of Saint Sabas* he spoke of the "desert fathers" (Schwartz, 1939, p. 180).

This formula was popularized by the work of Arnaud d'Andilly entitled *Vies des saints pères des déserts*, which appeared at Paris in 1688. The expression was then taken up by a number of works in various languages.

Numbered among the desert fathers are the great founders of monasticism of the fourth and fifth centuries: ANTONY, PAUL OF THEBES, MACARIUS ALEXANDRINUS, MACARIUS THE EGYPTIAN, Ammonius, PACHOMIUS and his disciples THEODORUS and HORSIESOS, and EVAGRIUS. Other celebrated figures to be noted are ONOPHRIUS and PAPHNUTIUS. The works that relate their exploits or repeat their sayings include the APOPHTHEGMATA PATRUM, the HISTORIA MONACHORUM IN AEGYPTO, the *Historia lausiaca* of Palladius, and the LETTER OF AMMON. To these may be added, by reason of their role in Coptic Christianity, the later names of SHENUTE and his disciple BESA and of MOSES OF ABYDOS and his disciple MACROBIUS.

BIBLIOGRAPHY

Andilly, A. d'. *Vies des saints pères des déserts*. Paris, 1688.

Chitty, D. J. *The Desert a City*. London and Oxford, 1966.

Schwartz, E. *Kyrillos von Skythopolis*. Texte und Untersuchungen 49. Leipzig, 1939.

RENÉ-GEORGES COQUIN

DEUTERARIOS, a term of Greek origin (from *deuteros,* second), which in later Greek and in Coptic texts denotes the "deputy" of the superior of a monastic community. The term was used in Pachomian monasteries, where it denoted both the deputy of the superior and the deputy of the head of the house. Mention about them is found also in Pachomian Rules and Lives. The *deuterarios* did not have a specific range of activity; his role consisted in substituting for a given monastic dignitary. At the DAYR ANBĀ SHINŪDAH, a *deuterarios* who was the deputy of the superior has his presence confirmed for the Arabic period as well as in a liturgical text and a colophon of a manuscript dated 1112 (both texts published by Crum, 1905, nos. 154, 489).

Apart from the Pachomian monasteries, the occurrences of the term *deuterarios* are rare. The title was used in the monastery of DAYR APĀ JEREMIAH at Saqqara. It also appears in Wādī Sarjah. P. Cauwenbergh mentions the appearance of the title in inscriptions from a monastic center of Al-Mīnā (1914, p. 121). Finally, *deuterarios* occurs in a list, of unknown origin, of monastic officials dating from the sixth and seventh centuries (Crum, 1909, no. 224).

The small number of texts in which the term *deuterarios* or its Coptic counterpart appears should not incline us to the conclusion that the deputy of the superior was a rarity in monastic centers. Probably in the majority of such centers, the superior had formally recognized deputies who either went without titles or used others such as *pronoetes, dioiketes,* and so forth. In a document published in *Koptische Rechtsurkunden des achten Jahrhunderts aus Djeme* (Crum and Steindorff, 1912, no. 106), two officials bear the title *sygkathedros* together with the "great *proestos.*" In another text, the same functionaries are described as PROESTOS (Schiller, 1932, no. 4). It is not by coincidence that the majority of the evidence concerning the title *deuterarios* comes from monasteries with clearly defined rules in which the organizational structures were more distinctly regulated and "named." We can presume that the deputies of the superior were often stewards especially as regards everything connected with economic matters.

BIBLIOGRAPHY

Biondi, G. "Inscriptions Coptes." *Annales du Service des antiquités d'Egypte* 8 (1907):94, no. 26.

Cauwenbergh, P. *Etude sur les moines d'Egypte depuis le concile de Chalcédoine.* Paris, 1914.

Crum, W. E. *Catalogue of the Coptic Manuscripts in the British Museum.* London, 1905.

______. *Catalogue of the Coptic Manuscripts in the Collection of the J. Rylands Library.* Manchester, 1909.

Crum, W. E., and H. I. Bell, eds. *Wādī Sarjah Coptic and Greek Texts.* Huniae, 1922.

Crum, W. E., and G. Steindorff, eds. *Koptische Rechtsurkunden des achten Jahrhunderts aus Djeme.* Leipzig, 1912.

Leipoldt, J. *Schenute von Atripe,* p. 135. Leipzig, 1903.

Ruppert, F. *Das Pachomianische Mönchtum und die Anfänge des klösterlichen Gehorsams,* pp. 282–327. Münster-Schwarzbach, 1971.

Schiller, A. A. *Ten Coptic Legal Texts.* New York, 1932.

Steidle, B. "'Der Zweite' in Pachomius' Kloster." *Benediktische Monatsschrift* 24 (1948):97–104, 174–79.

Thompson, H. *The Coptic Inscriptions, Excavations at Saqqara 1908–1909, 1909–1910.* Annales du Service des antiquités d'Egypte 1907.

EWA WIPSZYCKA

DEVAUD, EUGENE VICTOR (1878–1929), Swiss Egyptologist. He was born in Fribourg, studied in Lyons and Berlin, and then was appointed lecturer at Fribourg University. He made important contributions to Coptic etymology in various journals. His manuscripts are now in the Griffith Institute, Oxford. His Coptic contributions include *Etudes d'étymologie copte* (Fribourg, 1922) and *Psalterii Versio Memphitica e Recognitione Pauli de Lagarde,* reedited with Coptic text and Coptic characters in collaboration with O. Burmester (Louvain, 1925). He published several short papers on Coptic lexicography and etymology in *Kêmi, Zeitschrift für ägyptische Sprache, Recueil de travaux relatifs à la philologie et à l'archéologie égyptiennes, Le Muséon,* and *Sphinx.*

BIBLIOGRAPHY

Dawson, W. R., and E. P. Uphill. *Who Was Who in Egyptology,* p. 85. London, 1972.

Kammerer, W., comp. *A Coptic Bibliography.* Ann Arbor, Mich., 1950; repr. New York, 1969.

Montet, P. "Eugène Dévaud." *Kêmi* 3 (1930):20–22.

AZIZ S. ATIYA

DHIMMIS. *See* Ahl al-Dhimmah.

DIACONIA, a term of Greek origin with multiple meanings. The original sense of *diaconia* in classical and Hellenistic Greek was "service." In later Greek, *diaconia* practically always denoted religious service of one kind or another, or bodies that had to do with such services.

In later Greek texts from Egypt and in Coptic texts, we are able to discern two trends in the development of the meaning of *diaconia.*

Diaconia can be a task to be fulfilled by a monk or a cleric, for example, "diaconia of the gate." A specific modification of this is the meaning "good deed," as in a text referring to Saint MACARIUS published by E. Amélineau (1894, p. 167), "God writes down everything that we do: whether this is a diaconia or an additional prayer."

In certain literary texts, *diaconia* means monastic service, hence monastic community or monastery (Kahle, 1954). The meaning "monastic community" appears in documents, for example, in a letter published by W. E. Crum (1932): "the whole diaconia from small to great," where the author adopted a typical formula used in letters written by monks, "we greet everyone from the small to the great." In Greek papyri that pertain to economic problems of the monasteries, the same meaning occurs (Maspero, 1913, Vol. 2, no. 67138; Vitelli, 1913, Vol. 3, no. 285).

The starting point for a second semantic development is a meaning that appears in the New Testament, "a service necessary for preparing a meal" (Luke 10:40). Deriving from this is the use of the word in the meaning of "alms," hence food or things used as alms.

It is easy to see how, from the previous meaning, the use of *diaconia* as a term meaning "place in the monastery where the food was stored and prepared" was derived. Even today the place where bread is stored in Coptic monasteries is known in Arabic as the *daqūniyyah.* In the specific conditions of Egyptian LAURAS that were located outside the zone of cultivated land and that were composed of loosely scattered cells and oratoria, the diaconia became a sui generis economic center, clearly separated from the rest. As a rule, it was composed of a building in the shape of a tower in which it was possible to safeguard food and raw materials against robbers. The *diaconia* also contained storerooms, bread ovens, a kitchen, and a refectory, although sometimes the brothers ate separately. This is why it was possible to rent out quarters in the *diaconia* from the monastic authorities. After a suitable reconstruction, they could have been used as a hospice for guests, as mentioned in a papyrus published by J. Maspero (1911, Vol. 1, no. 67096).

Moreover, *diaconia* was applied to separate services connected with economic activity in monastic communities: renting land; making arrangements about work; dividing tasks among the monks; and purchasing food, clothing, and raw materials for handicraft.

In churches the term *diaconia* was applied to a separate unit of the episcopal personnel that administered property belonging to the church. It can be surmised that the *diaconia* also took care of philanthropic work. We still do not know whether the term was used for analogous but obviously much more modest services in the lower ranking churches.

The organization and range of activity of the *diaconia* in monastic communities depended upon the type and size of community. In large monasteries the *diaconia* could have expanded into a sizable body that was active in various areas, especially in those instances when the monastery was burdened with collecting taxes (Gascou, 1976). The fiscal product could have been, but did not have to be, partially handed over to the monastery and then used for philanthropic work. This was the case of the *diaconia* in the Pachomian monastery of the METANOIA in Alexandria, where taxes were collected in the nome of Antaiopolis and from which grain was transported in its own ships to Alexandria, and perhaps even to Constantinople.

It is difficult to know what the principles were according to which monks were selected to manage the affairs of the *diaconia,* with the exception of Pachomian monasteries where they were clearly described. One wonders if the monks belonged to the *diaconia* on a permanent basis; if it could have incorporated laics and not only monks, or clerics in the case of churches. These questions remain unsolved. Some texts contain a special term used to describe people of the diaconia. We may suppose that the *diaconia* was headed by the steward, although we find no information about this in the sources.

J. Maspero proposed another meaning of *diaconia:* "all property belonging to the monastery or church," but it seems that this interpretation cannot be proven by sources. His thesis concerns the inscriptions on silver boxes for storing incense. The inscriptions proclaiming that the boxes belong to the *diaconia* of a church administered by a priest called Praipositos, according to Maspero, can be explained as referring to the *diaconia* in a meaning considered relating to separate services connected with economic activity.

BIBLIOGRAPHY

An analysis of the meanings of the term *diaconia* was given by P. Kahle in *Bala'izah. Coptic Texts from Deir el-Bala'izah in Upper Egypt,* pp. 35–40, Oxford, 1954. The church *diaconia* is discussed by E. Wipszycka in *Les Ressources et les activitiés économiques des églises en Egypte,* pp. 125–30, Brussels, 1972. On the fiscal functions of the *diakonia,* see J. Gascou and P. Fouad, "Les monastères pachômiens et l'état byzantin," *Bulletin de l'Institut français d'Archéologie orientale* 76 (1976):178–83. The thesis proposed by J. Maspero was presented in "Sur quelques objets coptes du Musée du Caire." *Annales du Service des antiquités d'Egypte* 10 (1910):173–74.

Crum, W. E. *The Monastery of Epiphanius at Thebes,* Vol. 2, no. 178. New York, 1932.

Maspero, J., ed. *Papyrus grecs d'époque byzantine,* 3 vols. Cairo, 1911–1913.

Vitelli, G., ed. *Papiri Fiorentini.* Milan, 1913.

EWA WIPSZYCKA

DIACONICON. *See* Architectural Elements of Churches.

DIALECT, IMMIGRANT. *See Appendix.*

DIALECT, SPORADIC. *See Appendix.*

DIALECT G (BASHMURIC, OR MANSURIC). *See Appendix.*

DIALECT H (HERMOPOLITAN OR ASHMUNIC). *See Appendix.*

DIALECT I (PROTO-LYCOPOLITAN). *See Appendix.*

DIALECT P (PROTO-SAHIDIC). *See Appendix.*

DIALECT V (SOUTH FAYYUMIC). *See Appendix: Dialects.*

DIALECTS, COPTIC. *See Appendix.*

DIALECTS, GROUPING OF. *See Appendix.*

DIALECTS, MORPHOLOGY OF. *See Appendix.*

DIALOGUE OF THE SAVIOR, a Gnostic Christian dialogue known only from the Coptic (Sahidic) text found at Nag Hammadi in 1945. The title is indicated both at the beginning and at the end of the text. The fifth tractate in Codex 3 of the NAG HAMMADI LIBRARY, the *Dialogue of the Savior* survives in fragmentary condition. Most of its pages are filled with lacunae; some are missing altogether.

Despite the gaps in the text, the genre and structure of the treatise are fairly clear. *Dialogue of the Savior* consists of a conversation in which the twelve disciples and Mary Magdalene interrogate the Savior (also called Lord, but never Jesus) about spiritual matters. Unlike similar Gnostic Christian dialogues *(The Letter of Peter to Philip, The Sophia of Jesus Christ, The Gospel of Mary, The Gospel of Thomas,* and *The Book of Thomas the Contender), Dialogue of the Savior* has no literary framework but begins abruptly with questions and answers. Interspersed between dialogue, however, dramatic episodes occur throughout the writing. At one point, Judas throws himself down in reverence before the Lord; later, the disciples as a group give expression to their feelings of amazement evoked by the teachings of the Savior. There are also visions.

Although *Dialogue of the Savior* acknowledges the twelve disciples, most of the questions are put forth by Matthew, Judas, and Mary Magdalene. These three followers of Christ figure prominently in numerous Gnostic Christian writings. Matthew is known from *Pistis Sophia, The First Book of Jeu, The Sophia of Jesus Christ, The Gospel of Thomas,* and *The Book of Thomas the Contender.* Judas is usually called Judas Thomas *(The Gospel of Thomas* and *The Book of Thomas the Contender)* or simply Thomas *(The Sophia of Jesus Christ* and *Pistis Sophia).* Mary Magdalene, also known as both Maria or Mariham, plays a central role in *The Gospel of Mary, The Sophia of Jesus Christ, The Gospel of Thomas,* and *The Gospel of Philip*—where she is referred to as the *koinonos,* or consort of Jesus (59.20).

E. Pagels and H. Koester (1978) have suggested that the document may have been used as a teaching tool for initiation into Gnostic mysteries. Perhaps it was a catechetical handbook for baptism, in which were explained the sayings of the Savior, sayings such as those set forth, for example, in *The*

Gospel of Thomas. In addition, Pagels and Koester have drawn attention to a twofold eschatology that runs through the text. According to the Savior's teaching, a limited form of salvation is attained in baptism, to be followed at some later time by a fully realized salvation through spiritualization.

M. Krause (1977) points to the mention of two sacraments in *Dialogue of the Savior:* baptism (134.6–7) and the bridal chamber (138.19–20). Perhaps each sacrament corresponds to one eschatological stage. According to *Exegesis on the Soul,* a related Gnostic Christian homily, in baptism the Father (i.e., God) prepares the soul for eventual liberation from the earthly realm; and the bridal chamber is the setting in which that liberation is finally realized. It is in this second sacrament that the union of the soul and the spirit takes place, after which the spiritualized soul returns to its heavenly home.

The knowledge gained in baptism will serve to guide and protect the soul on its final journey. The powers that oppose the soul rule by means of fear (122.14). True knowledge about the nature of the cosmos and the destiny of the soul—especially its origins in a transcendent and undying reality (133.15)—dispels fear and serves thus to empower the soul in its confrontation with the powers of darkness and death.

BIBLIOGRAPHY

Attridge, H. W., trans. "The Dialogue of the Savior (III,5)." In *The Nag Hammadi Library in English,* pp. 230–38. San Francisco, 1977.

_____"The Dialogue of the Savior," In *The Other Gospels: Non-Canonical Gospel Texts,* ed. Ron Cameron, pp. 38–48. Philadelphia, 1982.

Facsimile Edition of the Nag Hammadi Codices, 10 vols. Leiden, 1972–1977.

Krause, M. "Der *Dialog des Soter* in Codex III von Nag Hammadi," In *Gnosis and Gnosticism,* ed. M. Krause, pp. 13–34. Leiden, 1977.

Pagels, E., and H. Koester. "Report on the *Dialogue of the Savior* (CG III,5)," In *Nag Hammadi and Gnosis,* ed. R. McL. Wilson, pp. 66–74. Leiden, 1978.

BEVERLY MOON

DICTIONARIES, COPTIC. *See Appendix.*

DIDACHE, a work, also known as *The Teaching of the Apostles,* discovered in 1873 by the Metropolitan Bryennios in a Greek manuscript written in 1056 (now Codex 54 in the Library of the Greek Patriarch in Jerusalem), which also contains the *Epistle of Barnabas* and the *Epistles of Clement* of Rome. The Greek text is otherwise represented only by Oxyrhynchus Papyrus 1782, written at the end of the fourth century, which contains no more than sixty-four words. In addition, there have survived excerpts of a Coptic version and of an Ethiopic version. The value of the complete Georgian version as an ancient textual witness of the work has been questioned recently, and it is said that it is, in effect, a modern version that probably goes back only to the first half of the nineteenth century.

The *Didache* may be described as a church manual. It consists of two parts. The first six chapters contain a moral treatise based on an ancient Jewish work called "The Two Ways." It sets forth the way of righteousness and life, on the one hand, and the way of unrighteousness and death, on the other. There are obvious affinities with the teaching of the Wisdom literature, the Qumran writings, and rabbinical teaching. An ancient Latin translation *(Doctrina apostolorum)* of a Greek work no longer extant contains these six chapters without the Christian accretions (1.3b–2.1), thus confirming the existence of an earlier, pre-Christian work, which scholars had suspected. This part of the *Didache,* without Christian interpolation, appears in a number of ancient Christian writings, including the *Apostolic Church Order,* the *Epistle of Barnabas,* the *Shepherd of Hermas,* and the Arabic version of the *Life of Shenute,* while the whole work is used in the *Didascalia* and in the *Apostolic Constitutions.*

After the moral teaching of the first six chapters, there follow liturgical directions and regulations relating to the ministry of the church. Chapter 7 deals in some detail with the rite of BAPTISM. Preferably it should be administered in running water, but alternatively the use of any other water, cold or warm, is permitted, and even the pouring of water on the baptismal candidate's head is allowed. Chapter 8 enjoins fasting on Wednesday and Friday, not on Monday and Thursday when the hypocrites, that is, the Jews, fast, and orders the praying of the Lord's prayer three times daily. The original setting of the prayers in Chapters 9–10 has been much discussed, for it is not altogether clear whether they refer to the Christian *agape* or to the EUCHARIST. It has been suggested, with some cogency, that the prayers in 9.1–10.5 preceded and followed the *agape,* while 10.6 introduces the liturgy of the celebration of the Eucharist that followed. But it should be noted that this is only one of a number of possible interpretations.

At the end of Chapter 10, the Coptic version adds a sentence that is not attested in the Greek, and it is therefore convenient to introduce the Coptic version at this point a little more fully. The papyrus leaf that contains the excerpt of the *Didache* (10.3–12.2) belongs to the British Library (Oriental 9271). It is thought to have been written in the fifth century, and the Coptic dialect of the text has been described as Middle Egyptian with Fayyumic influence. There is no firm evidence to enable us to say whether this excerpt has been translated directly from the Greek, or whether it has had a history within the Coptic tradition and was therefore translated earlier. It has even been suggested that the Coptic version was translated directly from the Syriac. Of special interest is the passage in the Coptic version which has no parallel in the Greek. It is a prayer of thanksgiving for the "perfume," which has often been interpreted as the fragrant oil, the myron, with its possible baptismal associations. More recently it has been suggested that it is rather a prayer over incense that was burned at the communal meal. Not only is the interpretation of the prayer in doubt, but so also is its authenticity, for it appears only in the Coptic version and in the recension of the *Didache* contained in the *Apostolic Constitutions* (VII.27), where it might be secondary.

Chapters 11–13 contain regulations about teachers, itinerant apostles, and prophets, while Chapter 14 gives instructions about the observance of Sunday. The celebration of the Eucharist is to be preceded by the confession of sins. Chapter 15 deals with the appointment of bishops and deacons, and the concluding Chapter 16 contains eschatological exhortations to watchfulness.

The primitive conditions reflected in the *Didache* suggest that it was written at an early date, perhaps the first half of the second century, although earlier and later dates have been put forward. The place of writing is generally thought to be Syria, but Egypt has been considered a possible place of origin by some scholars.

BIBLIOGRAPHY

Adam, A. "Erwägungen zur Herkunft der Didache." *Zeitschrift für Kirchengeschichte* 68 (1957):1–47.

Altaner, B., and A. Stuiber. *Patrologie,* pp. 79–82. Freiburg, 1966.

Audet, J.-P. *La Didachè: Instructions des apôtres.* Paris, 1958.

Gero, S. "The So-called Ointment Prayer in the Coptic Version of the Didache: A Re-evaluation." *Harvard Theological Review* 70 (1977):67–84.

Kahle, P. E. *Bala'izah,* Vol. 1, pp. 224–27. London, 1954.

Lefort, L.-T. *Les Pères apostoliques en copte.* CSCO 135–36; Scriptores Coptici 17, 18. Louvain, 1952.

Rordorf, W., and A. Tuilier. *La Doctrine des douze apôtres (Didachè).* Sources chrétiennes 248. Paris, 1978.

K. H. KUHN

DIDASCALIA. The complete title of this third-century work is *Didascalia id est doctrina catholica duodecim apostolorum et discipulorum sanctorum Salvatoris nostri* (Instructions, That Is, Catholic Doctrine, of the Twelve Apostles and Holy Disciples of Our Savior). Although originally written in Greek, it is currently extant in a Syriac translation and extensive Latin fragments. Portions of the Greek text are found in the fourth-century APOSTOLIC CONSTITUTIONS, for the compiler of that work used the *Didascalia* extensively in the early part of his work. Connolly has observed that the *Didascalia* makes considerable use of the Old Testament, especially Psalms, Proverbs, Isaiah, Jeremiah, and Ezekiel. The Gospels were used as sources, including the episode of the woman taken in adultery, and allusions to apostolic sources are apparent, though there are no references to them as written sources. The *Didascalia* makes use of both Old and New Testament apocryphal works, in addition to such works as the *Sibylline Oracles* and the DIDACHE.

The work is usually classified among writings dealing with ecclesiastical offices and orders, and it purports to be a compilation of instructions made by the apostles immediately after the Jerusalem Council of Acts 15. Following a brief opening address to all Christians to give heed to the teaching of the document, the treatise turns to the duties of bishops, including bishops' courts for lawsuits between believers and the conduct of worship services. There follow instructions on how to deal with widows, how to assign deacons and deaconesses in their responsibilities, and what to do with orphans. Other subjects included in the *Didascalia* are martyrdom, fasting and the Easter season, heresies and judgments against heretics, and the relationship of the Old Testament rituals to the New Testament church. Practical advice is given relating to morality, decency in language, dietary freedom, and how to treat visitors. Reference is also made concerning the assignment of the apostles to various provinces, though specific locations are not given.

Because the *Didascalia* was composed in the east, probably in Syria, its effect on developing church orders and regulations in the churches of the region should not be surprising, and indeed, reference to it in a gloss to a Coptic version of a letter of Athanasius argues for its presence in Egypt. Later references to the *Didascalia* are surprisingly rare, however, with Epiphanius being perhaps the earliest author to cite the work in his own writings.

BIBLIOGRAPHY

Connolly, R. H. *Didascalia Apostolorum.* Oxford, 1929; repr. 1969.

Funk, F. X. *Die apostolischen Konstitutionen.* Rottenburg am Neckar 1891; repr. Frankfurt, 1970.

———, ed. *Didascalia et Constitutiones Apostolorum.* Paderborn, 1905; repr. Turin, 1970.

C. WILFRED GRIGGS

DIDYMUS THE BLIND (ca. 313–398), the last great head of the CATECHETICAL SCHOOL OF ALEXANDRIA and one of its eminent and most prolific theologians. Although he had lost his sight at the age of four, he was able to command the admiration of his contemporaries by his extraordinary erudition, the amazing mass of his religious writings, and his creative theological acumen. He managed to keep away from the prevailing heretical teachings of his day, and thus ATHANASIUS I did not hesitate to appoint him to the presidency of the greatest theological institution of his time. He included among his students such illustrious figures as GREGORY OF NAZIANZUS, JEROME, and the historian RUFINUS. He was described by them as their *magister*, a *propheta*, and *vir apostolicus*.

While leading a strictly ascetic life as a hermit, Didymus was visited by ANTONY THE GREAT, who established the monastic rule, and by PALLADIUS, who rendered homage to him in his poor residence. His tremendous output in the field of biblical exegesis and theological studies seems to have suffered at the hands of those who cast dark shadows of Origenist suspicions on his work at the Second Council of CONSTANTINOPLE in 553. His support of ORIGEN'S creed of the preexistence of the soul was condemned as unorthodox.

The discovery in 1941 of papyrus documents at Ṭurah, south of Cairo, revealed a considerable number of hitherto lost writings from his literary heritage. Now it can be certified that the works of Didymus include the following wide range: *On the Trinity* (three books), *On the Holy Spirit, Against the Manichaeans, Commentaries on Job, Zechariah, Genesis and Ecclesiastes,* and *A Commentary on Psalms XX–XLXI.* The work entitled *Discourse Against Arius and Sabellius* is also ascribed to him, though its authenticity has yet to be proved. Even this monumental theological production does not seem to cover the work of Didymus. Palladius states that "he interpreted the Old and New Testaments, word by word, and such attention did he pay to the doctrine, setting out his exposition of it subtly yet surely, that he surpassed all the ancients on knowledge." Even if we allow for the exaggeration of some of his admirers, Saint Jerome concludes the listing of the works of Didymus by saying, ". . . and many other things, to give an account of which would be a work of itself."

Although his tremendous exegetical output is bound to leave the door open for doubtful statements in minor details, the orthodoxy of Didymus is entirely above reproach. His theological and pastoral teaching is identical with the doctrines of Athanasius I, a fact that clears him from the taint of heterodoxy. Throughout his lifetime and even beyond, his works were freely circulated by his unquestioning admirers.

BIBLIOGRAPHY

Quasten, J. *Patrology,* Vol. 3, pp. 85–100. Westminster, Md., 1963.

Roey, A. van. "Didyme l'Aveugle." In *Dictionnaire d'Histoire et de Géographie ecclésiastiques,* Vol. 14, cols. 416–27. Paris, 1960.

Roncaglia, M. P. *Egypte. Histoire de l'église copte,* Vol. 2, *Le Didascalée: Les hommes et les doctrines,* 2nd rev. and enl. ed. Beirut, 1987.

M. P. RONCAGLIA

DIFNĀR, a collection of hymns for the whole year, commemorating the saints associated with each day of the month. One of these is sung in the service of the PSALMODIA that follows the office of COMPLINE, after the LOBSH of the THEOTOKIA of the day. But if it has already been sung in the same service of the *psalmodia* after the office of midnight prayer, and after the *Theotokia* and its *lobsh* and before the hymn (ṬARḤ) of the day, it is omitted.

There are usually two *difnār* hymns for the same saint, one with a shorter meter for use when the commemoration falls on an ADĀM day, the other with a longer meter when it falls on a WĀṬUS day. Occasionally, the saints are different, as on 3 Ba'ūnah when the *adām* hymn commemorates Saint Martha of Egypt, whereas the *wāṭus* hymn commemorates Saint Alladius the Bishop.

The actual date of the compilation of the *difnār* is not known, but reference to such a book occurs as early as the eighth century. Apparently its contents are based mainly on the Arabic text of the SYNAXARION, because many of the proper names included in the Coptic text of the *difnār* are, in fact, transliterations of the Arabic form, not the proper Coptic (cf. Crum, 1909, p. 213).

Copies of the *difnār* are very rare. The text of the manuscripts in the John Rylands Library, Manchester (Coptic 21 and 22) is dated 1799 and contains only a record of the first four months. The manuscripts of the Library of the Coptic Patriarchate (Lit. 268, 269, 270) are dated 1790 and contain a complete series for all the months of the year. The Vatican manuscripts (53, 54, 59, 60, 104, 106) also are of the eighteenth century, but claim to be copies of a codex of the fourteenth century.

BIBLIOGRAPHY

Crum, W. E. *Catalogue of Coptic Texts in the John Rylands Library*. Manchester, 1909.

O'Leary, De L. *The Daily Office and Theotokia of the Coptic Church*. London, 1911.

______. *The Difnār (Antiphonarium) of the Coptic Church*. London, 1926–1930. Coptic text only.

EMILE MAHER ISHAQ

DIGAMY, practice of remarriage after the death of one's spouse. In the event of the dissolution of a Christian marriage through the death of either spouse, the surviving partner may, if desired, be married again in the church. Nevertheless, it is not strongly recommended by the church, in harmony with the Apostle Paul's teaching.

The early church fathers expressed their qualified approval of digamy and maintained the superiority of widowhood over second marriage. Within this general framework, they had varying degrees of reservation. Tertullian (c. 160–220) addressed *An Exhortation to Chastity* to a friend who had been recently widowed, discouraging him from remarriage and explaining that, although second marriage was tolerated by the church, it was merely an objectionable expedient to safeguard the weak against temptation. Saint Cyril of Jerusalem (c. 315–386), however, shows more leniency towards digamists: "Those who are once married, let them not hold in contempt those who have accommodated themselves to a second marriage. Continence is a good and wonderful thing; but still, it is permissible to enter upon a second marriage." (*Catechetical Lectures* 4.26). Saint Ambrose of Milan (c. 339–397) strikes a note of reserve in his attitude towards digamy: "What we suggest by way of counsel we do not command as a precept. . . . We do not prohibit second marriages, but neither do we recommend them" (*The Widows* 11.68).

Digamy is thus considered to be less meritorious than the first marriage, as is reflected in the following features: (1) the seventh canon of the Council of Neocaesarea (315) prohibits priests from attending the marriage feast (see Cummings, 1957, p. 512); (2) the Coptic service of digamy omits the crowning of the spouse who has been married before, and includes a petition for forgiveness and absolution; (3) penance was imposed on a digamist in the early church; (4) a digamist cannot be ordained to any rank of the presbytery or diaconate. According to Canon 1 of the First Council of Valence (374): "None after this synod . . . be ordained to the clergy from among digamists, or the husbands of previously married women."

BIBLIOGRAPHY

Cummings, D. *The Rudder (Pedalion)*. Chicago, 1957.

Fulton, J. *Index Canonum*, pp. 29, 294. New York, 1982.

Ḥabīb Jirjis. *Asrār al-Kanīsah al-Sab'ah*, 2nd ed., p. 173. Cairo, 1950.

Ludlow, J. M. "Digamy." In *Dictionary of Christian Antiquity*, ed. W. Smith and S. Cheetham. London, 1908.

Persival, H. R. *Excursus on Second Marriages, called Digamy*. In *A Select Library of the Nicene and Post-Nicene Fathers of the Christian Church*, 2d ser., Vol. 14, ed. P. Schaff and H. Wace. Grand Rapids, Mich., 1971.

ARCHBISHOP BASILIOS

DIKAION, a term of Greek origin, encountered from the sixth century on in many Greek and Coptic documents connected with the economic activity of monasteries or, more rarely, churches and philanthropic institutions. It is to be found predominantly in introductory formulas that describe the addressee or the institution issuing the document, for example, "the dikaion of the holy monastery of the holy Apa Apollo through me, Apa Abraham, the priest and prior" (Kahle, 1954, p. 109).

It is not easy to determine the sense of the term dikaion. Scholars interpreted it at first as denoting the council of a monastery. However, they abandoned this interpretation, considering that the term was also used in connection with churches and philanthropic institutions that had no councils. Therefore, attempts were made to interpret it as a term denoting a legal person. The interpretation offered by A. Steinwenter appears to be the most precise and convincing. According to him, the key is to be found in a comparison of the Greek and Latin versions of the so-called Edict of Milan of the year 313. The expression "oikia kai chōria ha tou dikaiou tou tōn Christianōn etygkhanon onta" (Eusebius of Caesarea, *Historia ecclesiastica* 9, 10, 11) corresponds to the Latin "loca ad ius corporis eorum id est ecclesiarum pertinentia" (Lactantius, *De mortibus persecutorum* 48). To *dikaion* thus corresponds the *ius corporis.* Examples of an analogous usage are to be found in Justinian's *Novellae.*

In all those cases *dikaion* means the right of a certain institution to possess a legal subjectivity and hence the right to all sorts of activity, particularly of an economic nature. It cannot be said how this subtle legal term, which emerged in Roman law, found itself in the terminology of notaries preparing documents in Egypt, just as explanations are difficult of its being used only in the domain of religious institutions. In the Edict of Milan, it was applied also to the fiscus, or the state treasury. Probably those who used it were not aware of its exact significance; for them it had become a sanctified formula. A list of texts in which *dikaion* occurs was provided by C. Schmidt and later on by P. Kahle.

The term *dikaion* was used inconsistently. Among the documents issued by or addressed to the same monastery in a single year some contain it, others do not, as, for example, the papyri published by J. MASPERO (1913, nos. 67170, 67171). This did not change the meaning of the documents. It is also impossible to capture a connection between the type of a given monastic community and the occurrence of the term. P. Kahle was of the opinion that one could determine its topographic range. He indicated that the term was used predominantly in the environs of Aphrodito, Balayzah, and to a smaller extent in al-Ashmūnayn. His hypothesis, however, is not acceptable. New documents have increased the number of occurrences from the area of al-Ashmūnayn. There is also evidence that the term was used in the region of Memphis. Moreover, one must keep in mind that the majority of known papyri comes from those very regions mentioned by Kahle.

BIBLIOGRAPHY

Khale, P. *Bala'izah. Coptic Texts from Deir el-Balaizah in Upper Egypt,* vol. 1, pp. 31–32. London, 1954.

Maspero, J. *Papyrus grecs d'époque byzantine.* Cairo, 1913.

Schmidt, C. "Das Kloster des Apa Mena." *Zeitschrift für Ägyptische Sprache* 68 (1932):60.

Steinwenter, A. "Die Rechtsstellung der Kirchen und Klöster nach den Papyri." *Zeitschrift der Savigny Stiftung für Rechtsgeschichte, Kanonistische Abteilung* 50 (1930):31–34.

______. *Das Recht der koptischen Urkunden,* p. 18. Munich, 1955.

Till, W. C., ed. *Corpus Papyrorum Raineri* 4, no. 34. Vienna, 1958.

Vitelli, G., ed. *Publicazioni della Società Italiana per la ricerca dei papiri,* Vol. 4, no. 284. Florence, 1917.

EWA WIPSZYCKA

DIKHAYLAH, AL-. *See* Enaton.

DIMAYRAH, name of two villages located near one another in the middle of the Delta in the province of Gharbiyyah. There exists today a village called Dumerah (or Dimerah) about 4 miles (6.5 km) west of al-Baramūn and 5 miles (8 km) north of Talkhā. North of this site is a village called Kafr Dimayrah al-Iadīd (earlier Dimayrah al-Baḥriyyah) and to the southwest is a village known as Kafr Dimayrah al-Qadīm (earlier Dimayrah al-Qibliyyah). The two villages known as Dimayratayn were located somewhere in this same area.

The SYNAXARION for 14 Bashans relates that Saint Epimachus went from al-Faramā to al-Bakrug, where the Roman governor tortured and killed him. After his death, 1,750 inhabitants of the two villages named Dimayratayn consoled his parents and became Christians. The HISTORY OF THE PATRIARCHS states that the patriarch Cosmas II (851–858) fled to Dimayrah, which was completely Christian at the time, to avoid the attempts of the Muslim authorities in Alexandria to rob him of his wealth. In the Synaxarion for 19 Ba'ūnah is the story of the martyr Jirjis al-Muzāḥim whose mother was born in Dimayrah. Though his father was a Muslim, Jirjis adopted the Christian faith due to the strong influence of his mother. On account of his conversion he was beheaded near the Church of Saint Michael in Dimayrah al-Qibliyyah.

Dimayrah was the seat of a Coptic bishop at least as early as the eleventh century.

BIBLIOGRAPHY

Amélineau, E. *La Géographie de l'Egypte à l'époque copte,* pp. 118–19. Paris, 1893.

Timm, S. *Das christlich-koptische Ägypten in arabischer Zeit,* pt. 2, pp. 520–23. Wiesbaden, 1984.

RANDALL STEWART

DIMIQRĀT. *See* Dayr Mār Jirjis (Dimiqrāt); Pilgrimages.

DIMYĀNAH AND HER FORTY VIRGINS. Dimyānah, or Damiana, is one of the most highly revered and cherished female saints and martyrs of the Coptic church. She was martyred with forty virgin companions in the third century during the reign of Emperor DIOCLETIAN (284–305). Their story is detailed in the Arabic SYNAXARION under the date of 13 Ṭūbah, the date of their martyrdom for standing firm by their Christian faith against their persecutors. She was the sole daughter of Marcus, Roman governor of the districts of Parallus (al-Burullus), Zaʿfarān, and Wādī al-Saysabān in the northern Delta of the Valley of the Nile. She was born at an unknown date in the third century in a Christian family, and at the age of one year she was taken by her father to the monastery of al-Maymah to receive the blessings of the holy fathers. When she reached the age of fifteen, her father wanted her to get married, but she refused and informed him that she had already made a vow of becoming the bride of Jesus Christ, a decision that delighted her pious father. She asked him to build a special place for her retirement with her virgin companions, where they spent their days in reading the scriptures and in prayer.

Diocletian brought Marcus to Rome and requested him to offer incense and libation to his idols. After some hesitation, to save his life, Marcus decided to accept the imperial command by worshiping his idols, and thus was left free to return to his province. On hearing this, Dimyānah went to her father and chided him for abjuring the faith of the creator of all the world to idolatrous beliefs. She also told him that she would have rather seen him dead than apostatizing. Marcus was deeply moved by his daughter's protest and returned to Diocletian to declare the reality of his Christian faith. When the emperor failed to deflect him from Christianity to the idols of Rome, he ordered him decapitated.

Diocletian discovered that Marcus' affirmation of his Christian faith had been encouraged by his daughter. So he sent one of his generals with a batallion of a hundred soldiers to her residence in Egypt. These were armed with instruments of persecution, but they tried first, without avail, to win her to the state religion by means of persuasion. Ultimately, the general ordered four of his men to place her between two iron sheets equipped with pointed spikes and squeeze her between them until her blood ran. Her forty virgins watched this atrocity, crying. When she was confined to prison, the angel of the Lord appeared to her and remedied her wounds. Consequently her body was dipped in boiling oil and lard and her flesh was torn by instruments of torture, and every time the Lord returned her safe and sound. When in the end the general despaired from forcing her to apostatize, he ordered her and all her companions decapitated, and thus all of them won the crown of martyrdom.

Dimyānah's story is recited in the liturgies of the Coptic church on the day of her commemoration, and the traditional site of her residence, now a nunnery, is a pilgrimage area for throngs of Copts every year.

[*See also:* Pilgrimages.]

AZIZ S. ATIYA

DINŪSHAR, town located in the middle of the Delta about 3.5 miles (5.5 km) southwest of al-Maḥallah al-Kubrā in the Gharbiyyah province. The HISTORY OF THE PATRIARCHS speaks in two different places about the building of a church to the martyr Ptolemaus in Dinūshar. The account of the life of the patriarch COSMAS II (851–858) describes briefly the erection of the church and states that Cosmas was interred there. But the life of KHĀ'ĪL III (880–907) states that the patriarch Khā'īl dedicated a church to Saint Ptolemaus in Dinūshar. The SYNAXARION for 20 Baramhāt recounts a conflict surrounding the dedication of the church at the time of the patriarch Khā'īl. Though these accounts are somewhat disparate, it is clear that in the ninth century there were Christians and a church of the martyr Ptolemaus in Dinūshar.

The name Dinūshar appears in medieval Copto-Arabic scales, but in the absence of other evidence it is uncertain whether this means the city was at one time the seat of a Coptic bishop.

BIBLIOGRAPHY

Amélineau, E. *La Géographie de l'Egypte à l'époque copte,* p. 143. Paris, 1893.

Timm, S. *Das christlich-koptische Ägypten in arabischer Zeit,* pt. 2, pp. 870–71. Wiesbaden, 1984.

RANDALL STEWART

DIOCLETIAN, Roman emperor (full name, Valerius Diocletianus; also called Diocles) from 20 November 284 to May 305. He was born in 245 of humble parents in the province of Dalmatia. He enlisted in the army and gained administrative experience in minor posts in Gaul under Aurelian (270–275), and in 282 became governor of Moesia under Carus. The next year he was made commander of the emperor's bodyguard, and in that capacity accompanied Carus on his Persian campaign.

Carus died on the campaign (8 September 283), and on the return march of the Roman army from Persia in 284, Diocles began his rise to eminence. Carus's younger son, Numerian, died in suspicious circumstances in the autumn of 284. Diocles was appointed emperor by a council of officers and avenged his predecessor's death by killing the praetorian prefect, Aper, who was suspected of the murder (17 November 284). Three days later Diocles was formally proclaimed emperor at Nicomedia in Bithynia.

Meantime, Carus's elder son, Carinus, had proved himself incapable of governing the western provinces of the empire. Diocles met his army at Horrea Margus in Pannonia in March 285. In the ensuing battle Carinus prevailed, but Diocles was rescued from the consequences of defeat through the murder of Carinus by an officer whose wife he had seduced. The leaderless army then accepted Diocles as sole emperor.

At this moment there was no reason to believe that Diocletian, as he now styled himself, would last any longer than his militarily more able predecessors. He was, however, to rule for twenty-one years, to abdicate, and then live for almost a decade in retirement in the majestic miniature *praetorium* that he had built for himself at Spalato (Split) on the Adriatic coast.

The reasons for the success of Diocletian were his ability to delegate responsibilities to trusted subordinates; to anchor his administrative reforms firmly on principles of government that recalled the virtues, real or imagined, of the Roman past; and to give his system of government a traditional religious basis through acceptance of the Roman gods Jupiter and Hercules as its patrons. He was an able and respected, if not particularly beloved, figure, a *vir rei publicae necessarius,* as he was called by the writer (or writers) of the *Scriptores historiae Augustae*—a ruler required by the times.

Diocletian quickly followed the example of Carus by delegating his authority in the West. In March 286 he elevated an old comrade in arms, Maximian, to the rank of Augustus and dispatched him to Gaul to deal with an uprising of peasants (Bagaudae) against the Gallic landowners and imperial authority (Aurelius Victor, *Liber de Caesaribus* 39.17). Maximian was successful, as he was later in three campaigns against the more formidable Kabyles in North Africa (287–289). Meanwhile, Diocletian was victorious in a campaign against Saracen Arabs threatening Syria, and in 292 against rebels in Coptos and Busiris in Upper Egypt. The cause of the rebellion is not known. The only reverse suffered by the emperors in this first decade of their rule was the revolt of Carausius, Maximian's commander of the fleet in the English Channel, in 287. He proclaimed himself emperor, but throughout his rule of six years in Britain (he was murdered in 293) he sought in vain to win acceptance as a "third emperor" rather than attempt to overthrow his "colleagues."

Carausius' success in maintaining himself may have contributed to a further delegation of power by the two emperors. In March 293 each nominated a deputy or Caesar. Diocletian chose Galerius, and Maximian chose a proven administrator, Constantius. To cement mutual loyalties, marriage contracts bound members of the tetrarchy together, and the religious element was placed to the fore in Diocletian and Galerius' assuming the style "Iovii" while Maximian and Constantius were "Herculii" (Seston, p. 97), able lieutenants of their seniors in the hierarchy as Hercules was to Jupiter in the hierarchy of the gods. To the imperial biographers (or their sources) the emperors were "courageous and wise, benign and open-handed, concerned for the welfare of the state, respectful to the Senate, friends of the people, serious-minded and pious toward the gods" (*Scriptores historiae Augustae,* Carus and Carinus XVIII.4).

Measures to restore the defenses and administration of the empire evolved slowly, as if they were responses to situations rather than the product of overall plans. The army, amounting to thirty-six legions under the Severi (193–235), was slowly increased until about double the effectives were under arms. Diocletian's policy was defensive. The fifth-century historian Zosimus wrote, "By the foresight of Diocletian, the frontiers of the Roman Empire were everywhere studded with cities and forts and towers . . . and the whole army was stationed along them so that it was impossible for the barbarians to break through, as the attackers were everywhere withstood by an opposing force" (*Historia nova* II.34). There is plenty of archaeological evidence from Syria, North Africa, and Britain, to name three provinces, to demonstrate the truth of this. Diocletian's concern for frontier defense had one effect on Egypt: the Dodekaschoenos, the area attributed to the direct governance of the goddess Isis, south of Aswan, was given up and the frontier brought back to the First Cataract. Defense against the marauding Blemmyes (see BEJA TRIBES) was entrusted henceforth to the friendly kingdom of NOBATIA.

Provincial reorganization followed the slow, deliberate pattern that had applied to the army. In the previous thirty years too many provincial governors had sought supreme power in the empire. Gradually the numbers of provinces and their governors was increased from forty-three to over one hundred. The reorganization affected Egypt as it did other areas. The Thebaid was detached from the unitary province of Aegyptius before 302, and from Libya before 308. The remainder of Egypt was destined to be subdivided into two further provinces, Iovia and Herculia, in 313. New provinces entailed new provincial organization and a revised system of taxation and coinage. Throughout the empire taxation was now based on a mixture of a poll tax *(capitatio)*, at first probably applied only to the rural population and later including town dwellers (Lactantius *De mortibus* xxiii.7), and a tax on land, based on ideal and arbitary units called *iuga*, graded according to official assessments of productivity. In Egypt the assessment extended to boys aged twelve (Jones, p. 51) and the urban poll tax was in force by 301 (Jones, p. 63). The land tax continued to be levied on the traditional measure of acreage, the *aroura*, of arable vineyards and olive trees.

To match these fiscal changes, the coinage was drastically reformed. The massive inflation that had destroyed the value of the *antoninianus* had also destroyed the value of the local urban and provincial currencies that had been one of the sources of pride in the city-states, especially in the eastern Mediterranean. Even the Alexandrian tetradrachm had become reduced to a small disk of alloy of a circumference no greater than one centimeter. In 295–296, perhaps influenced by Carausius' currency reform in Britain, Diocletian instituted an empirewide currency with gold, silver, and silver-covered pieces, the last of these minted in the tens of thousands at mints from Alexandria to Lyons and bearing the same inscription on the reverse: *Genio Populi Romani* (to the genius of the Roman people). Jupiter was shown standing and holding a sacrificial dish in his hand. Roman religion was never far from the emperor's mind.

Religious tradition and uniformity were foremost among both the motives and the consequences of Diocletian's reorganization of the empire. Both are in evidence in the legal decisions of the period. Justinian's code and minor collections preserve about 1,300 constitutions of Diocletian that range from simple matters of private law to important enactments concerned with social customs and religion (Jones, 1964, p. 37). The spirit of the emperor's legislation can be understood from the horror that he expressed when made aware of the custom in Egypt of marriage between brother and sister. In his decree *De nuptiis* (c. 295) he declared this was contrary to "the discipline of our times," "barbarian savagery," and "displeasing to the immortal gods," who would favor the empire, if the people would perceive how "all under our sway were living lives of piety and religious observance in quietude and chastity" (*Codex Gregorianus* v, *Mosaicarum et Romanorum legum collectio* vi.4, ed. Riccobono, Vol. 2, pp. 558–60). Roman religious observances were to have universal application.

Another imperial rescript, addressed to Julianus, proconsul of Africa, on 31 March 297 (or 302), foreshadowed Diocletian's later edicts against the Christians. This time the enemy was the Manichaeans. Issued probably at the outset of the war with Persia, the edict combines anger at the proselytizing activities of what was considered a religion serving the interests of the enemy with resolve to defend the traditional religion of Rome. "The wickedness of attempting to undo past tradition" required the emperor to act with great zeal "to punish the obstinacy of the perverted mentality of these most evil men." The leaders of the sect and their books were to be burned. Other adherents were to be put to death by beheading (*Mosaicarum et Ro-*

manorum legum collectio v.4, Vol. 2, pp. 580–81). Other dissidents could expect small mercy.

The attempt to reassert past values may have influenced another of Diocletian's policies: the restoration of the cities with their public buildings, and not least their temples. All over the empire the era of the tetrarchy witnessed a great effort to breathe new life into the cities. Inscriptions preserve evidence for the restoration of temples in eight North African towns, and public works are attested in many others.

However retrograde and oppressive in their effects some of these measures were, there is no denying the idealism that inspired even the most futile. The Edict of Prices of 301 was prefaced by the provincial governor of Caria, Fulvius Asticus, with the statement "This is also a sign of the divine foresight [of the emperor], namely, that a fair and fixed price should be laid down for everything." The aim was a plentiful livelihood for all and the curtailing of the greed of a few (see Crawford and Reynolds, 1975). Similarly, the census of 297 that preceded the institution of the new order of taxation was justified by the prefect of Egypt, Aristius Optatus, on the ground that to date "some taxpayers are undercharged and others overburdened" (Boak and Youtie, 1960, no. 1; Seston, 1946, pp. 283–84).

Diocletian's measures of reform were, however, immensely costly. The buildings alone, not least the new imperial palaces, must have consumed vast resources in manpower and wealth to yield little productive value. Gradually, society was reduced to a siege economy in which people and organizations were rigidly stratified, and social mobility was reduced to a minimum. Apart from officials the most favored were "the honorable soldiers," for whom *annona* (taxation in kind) must be provided (*Oxyrhynchus Papyrus* 1543, dated to A.D. 299); the least considered were the peasants, who by now were practically bound to the soil. In between were the urban middle classes, once the backbone of the empire but now increasingly anxious to avoid their traditional responsibilities of governing the cities and ensuring that these met the quota of taxes imposed on them.

Though many benefited from the emperor's measures, there was also bitter criticism, especially from the Christians, of whom the writer Lactantius, who spent ten years (293–303) as professor of (Latin) rhetoric at Diocletian's court at Nicomedia, was the most articulate. In his pamphlet *On the Deaths of the Persecutors (De mortibus persecutorum)*, written about 315, after the victory of Constantine, practically every one of Diocletian's major reforms was attacked. The reduction in the number of provinces was "chopping the provinces into slices" (vii.4). The tightening of administrative control by diminishing the areas for which individual officials were responsible was criticized as producing more officials and more departments in each district, as was usual in cities (vii.4). Even more vitriolic was his denunciation of the census: "Only beggars from whom nothing could be exacted escaped the measures of this pious man [Diocletian]. Neither age nor infirmity was accepted as an excuse. Old men and the sick were forced to appear [and register]. The age of each was estimated, years being added to that of children and deducted from that of the aged" (xxiii.4). The number of official recipients exceeded that of those paying. The country folk were oppressed and impoverished in particular, and the extravagant building program added to the universal distress (xxiii.7).

Exaggeration, perhaps, but as Eutropius (*Breviarium* ix.23) pointed out, taxation was oppressive, and not least in Egypt, where a new revolt broke out in 296. This time the rebels proclaimed a rival emperor, Domitius Celsus, with an effective field commander, Aurelius Achilleus. Diocletian was compelled to retake Alexandria from the rebels through the winter and into the spring of 296/297. Henceforth he had little love for the Egyptians. This episode unintentionally led to the greatest crisis of his reign: the final effort to destroy organized Christianity in the Great Persecution of 303–312.

The revolt in Egypt gave the Persians the chance to expel the pro-Roman king of Armenia, Tiradates, and establish their own candidate on the throne, thus provoking a war with Rome. In the first campaign during 297, Galerius, Diocletian's Caesar, was defeated; but in the spring of 298, reinforced by legions from the Danube and stung by Diocletian's unconcealed displeasure, he won a decisive victory over the Persian king Narses. The latter was forced to surrender five small provinces north of the upper Tigris to the empire, amounting to a protectorate over Armenia, where he acknowledged Roman interests. Galerius returned in triumph (May 298). There is no reason to disbelieve the testimony of Lactantius and Eusebius of Caeserea that henceforth the situation gradually worsened for the Christians (Eusebius *Chronica* ad annum 302). Not only was Galerius strongly anti-Christian (Lactantius *De mortibus* 9), but the Christian church now stood out as the one great organization that was outside the uniform structure that Diocletian had imposed on the empire.

"Little by little persecution against us began," wrote Eusebius (*Chronica* ad annum 302). Diocletian moved cautiously. At first, only Christian soldiers were forced to resign from imperial service, but by 302 the crisis point was approaching. Counsel was held with Galerius and senior officials, prominent among whom was Sossianus Hierocles, governor of Bithynia. They advised action. A visit in the winter of that year to the oracle of Apollo at Didyma near Miletus brought a similar result, the oracle replying that "an enemy of the divine religion" (i.e., the Christians) prevented him from uttering (*De mortibus* xi.7). The die was now cast, Diocletian's restraint being confined to his insistence that no blood should be spilled.

The feast of Terminalia, 23 February, was selected as the day that would set the term for the Christian faith. On that day, soldiers set about destroying the cathedral of Nicomedia, which stood in full view of the imperial palace. Diocletian signed a decree ordering the Christian sacred books to be handed over for burning and the churches to be destroyed. Christians were to be dismissed from public office. In civil life Christians of the upper classes, the *honestiores,* were to lose their privileges; and Christians could no longer act as accusers in cases of personal injury, adultery, and theft. Only their lives were spared.

In Egypt the persecution caused consternation among the Christian leaders. Bishop Peter (300–311) fled Alexandria to Oxyrhynchus, and thence probably from Egypt. One of the leading intellectuals, the presbyter Pierius, whose fame as a theologian and ascetic had earned him the title "Origen the Younger," seems to have conformed. So far as the church of Alexandria was concerned, he thereby disgraced himself. Many Christians, however, sacrificed to the Roman gods with him. In the countryside, churches were destroyed or dismantled, but in general the persecution caused more inconvenience than suffering to Christians (*Oxyrhynchus Papyrus* 2673).

The second and third edicts of persecution, in the summer and autumn of 303, were aimed at enforcing the conformity of the clergy, and a great sense of triumph was felt when they succeeded. However, up to the time Diocletian celebrated his *vicennalia* at Rome on 20 November 303, only those who deliberately defied the authorities or otherwise rushed to a martyr's death had lost their lives (thus Eusebius, *Martyrs of Palestine* i.1, concerning Procopius of Gaza, executed on 7 June 303). In the winter of 303/304, however, Diocletian became ill from a lingering malady, perhaps malaria, and power passed to Galerius. Up to then the persecution had affected "only the presidents of the churches" (*Martyrs of Palestine* iii.1) or at least only prominent Christians, but the fourth edict that Galerius promulgated in the spring of 304 required all to sacrifice to the gods on pain of punishment, including death. One notable martyr, Phileas, bishop of Tmuis, was arrested probably at this time. Even so, Egypt does not seem to have suffered more heavily at this stage than other parts of the empire. One reads in the account of the origins of the Melitian schism (preserved in Epiphanius *Panarion* 68.1) of clergy and monks imprisoned but not executed. The effect was that all Coptic Christians now found themselves drawn into a situation of opposition to the imperial authorities. The many martyrdoms recorded in Eusebius belong, however, to the reign of Maximin (305–313).

Diocletian recovered sufficiently to resume authority for a short time in the spring of 305. But he had decided, perhaps while in Italy, to abdicate and had persuaded his colleague Maximian to follow his example. According to Aurelius Victor, writing half a century after the event, he may have been plagued with forebodings over the future of the empire, or he may have yielded to pressure by Galerius. In any event, on 1 May 305, before a great parade of troops at Nicomedia, Diocletian laid aside the purple and stepped down from the dais a private citizen, the only Roman emperor ever to retire.

Diocletian was one of the great conservative reformers of history—the more effective, perhaps, because his reforms were in the nature of responses to situations rather than the result of long-preconceived policies. His reign saw a flowering of a new but authentically Roman form of art, particularly the imperial portraiture on the coinage, and architecture such as the Arch of Galerius at Salonika, as well as the emphasis on traditional religious and ethical values. The onslaught against the Christians, though it surprised contemporaries who saw it as an "act of madness" (Eusebius *De vita Constantini* 1.13), can be understood in retrospect as an almost inevitable result of the emperor's drive for uniformity throughout the empire. The two serious revolts in Egypt during his reign indicate, however, a deep resentment against the tetrarchy and its rule. With Christianity becoming increasingly strong, the emperor's initiation of the policy of persecution, and the involvement by 304 of the whole Egyptian

Christian population, was enough to cause the Copts to brand him the supreme persecutor, and to date the ERA OF THE MARTYRS from his accession. It was not an altogether just stigma.

BIBLIOGRAPHY

No full-scale study of Diocletian exists because W. Seston did not write the projected second volume of *Dioclétien et la Tétrarchie* (Paris, 1946), but a full account of the reign will be found in the *Cambridge Ancient History,* Vol. 12, chaps. 9–11, 19 (Cambridge, 1939); in A. M. M. Jones, *The Later Roman Empire,* chap. 2 (Oxford, 1964); and in W. Ensslin, "Valerius Diocletianus," in *Pauly-Wissowa,* ser. 2, Vol. 2, cols. 2419–2495 (Stuttgart, 1948).

See also Timothy D. Barnes, *Constantine and Eusebius* (Cambridge, Mass., 1981), and his companion volume, *The New Empire of Diocletian and Constantine* (Cambridge, Mass., 1981).

W. H. C. Frend, *Martyrdom and Persecution in the Early Church* (Oxford, 1965; and 2nd ed., Grand Rapids, Mich., 1981), chap. 15, is useful on the emperor's religious policy; see also G. E. M. de Ste. Croix, "Aspects of the Great Persecution," *Harvard Theological Review* 47 (1954):75–131; and J. Moreau, ed., *Lactance. De la mort des persécuteurs,* 2 vols. Sources Chrétiennes 39 (Paris, 1954).

On Diocletian's abdication, see G. S. R. Thomas, "L'abdication de Dioclétien," *Byzantion* 43 (1973):220–24.

On the public works undertaken in Diocletian's reign, see C. R. van Sickle, "The Public Works in Africa in the Reign of Diocletian," *Classical Philology* 25 (1930):173–79.

On the Edict of Prices see M. H. Crawford and Joyce Reynolds, "The Publication of the Prices Edict, a New Inscription from Aezani," *Journal of Roman Studies* 65 (1975):160–64, and K. T. Erim and Joyce Reynolds, "The Aphrodisias Copy of Diocletian's Edict on Maximus Prices," *Journal of Roman Studies* 63 (1973):99–110.

For the martyrdom of Phileas, see H. Musurillo, ed., *The Acts of the Christian Martyrs,* pp. 328–353 (Oxford, 1972).

W. H. C. FREND

DIOLKOS (province of Gharbiyyah), place-name cited by the geographer Ptolemy in the expression "false mouth of Diolkos." J. Ball (1942, p. 127) thinks that this was not the mouth of a branch of the Nile but of a small stream, perhaps following the present course of the Baḥr Basandīlah, which is about 15 miles (25 km) to the west of Damietta. Ball situates Diolkos to the west of the ʿIzbat Ashtūm Jamasah (p. 127).

Many anchorites lived in this vicinity in the fourth century, and several monasteries of cenobites were built, as is witnessed by John CASSIAN (*Collationes* 18.1; *Institutiones* 5.36), the HISTORIA MONACHORUM IN AEGYPTO, and the APOPHTHEGMATA PATRUM. The Greek historians Sozomen (*Historia Ecclesiastica* 6.29) and Nicephorus Callistus (*Historia Ecclesiastica* 11.35) take over from the *Historia Monachorum in Aegypto* the stories concerning John and Piammônas of Diolkos. The HEGUMENOS of a cenobium of Diolkos is cited, in 482, as one of the monks who refused to recognize Peter Mongus (PETER III) as patriarch because he had signed the HENOTICON of the emperor Zeno (Liberatus *Breviarium* 18). After this mention we have no further attestation relative to this monastic site.

A fairly precise description is given by John Cassian (*Institutiones* 5.36). This "desert" of monks was hemmed in between the Mediterranean and a branch of the Nile, the only source of drinkable water, which was more than three miles away. Unfortunately, John Cassian does not tell to which branch he refers, the Sebennytic (today disappeared) or the Phatnitic (i.e., that of Damietta).

BIBLIOGRAPHY

Amélineau, E. *La Géographie de l'Egypte à l'époque copte.* Paris, 1893. The author wrongly places Diolkos near Panephysis.

Ball, J. *Egypt in the Classical Geographers.* Cairo, 1942.

Regnault, L. *Les Sentences des pères du désert. Nouveau Recueil.* Solesmes, France, 1977.

RENÉ-GEORGES COQUIN
MAURICE MARTIN, S.J.

DIONYSIUS THE AREOPAGITE. According to the Acts of the Apostles (17:34), Dionysius and a woman named Damaris were converted by Saint Paul. His namesake Dionysius, bishop of Corinth (c. A.D. 170), asserts that he became first bishop of Athens. Later literature tended to confuse him with another Dionysius, otherwise Saint Denis of Paris (c. A.D. 250), whose writings in mystical theology are often described as pseudo-Areopagite or pseudo-Dionysian. This literature aimed at a combination of Christian doctrine and Neoplatonist philosophy. By such synthesis the author arrived at the creation of Christian mysticism, which found its way to the Coptic religious discussions of the later medieval works of Abū al-Barakāt IBN KABAR and Abū Isḥāq ibn al-ʿAssāl in their search for support of their monophysite beliefs in ancient documentary evidence.

BIBLIOGRAPHY

Cross, F. L. *The Oxford Dictionary of the Christian Church.* London, 1957.

AZIZ S. ATIYA

DIONYSIUS THE GREAT, fourteenth patriarch of the See of Saint Mark (247–264), whose letters dealt with the major religious issues of the time. Dionysius was born at an unknown date, probably in the last decade of the second century. The son of a wealthy pagan family, he was converted to Christianity at a mature age through the reading of an epistle of Paul. The story of his conversion is detailed in the HISTORY OF THE PATRIARCHS (Vol. 1, Pt. 1, pp. 175ff.) under HERACLAS, who was then still at the head of the CATECHETICAL SCHOOL OF ALEXANDRIA. His repudiation of the old pagan gods led to a breach with his family and the loss of his parents' great wealth. After his acceptance of the gospel he went directly to Bishop DEMETRIUS I, who baptized him. Then he enrolled in the Catechetical School, where he completed his theological education under ORIGEN and Heraclas, whom he eventually replaced in the presidency of the school after the elavation of Heraclas to the throne of Saint Mark in 231. He became presbyter in 233, and, in his turn, was elected to the episcopate after the death of Heraclas (*Historia ecclesiastica* 6.35). At this time he appears to have been a man of some age. He remained as patriarch until his death in 264. His episcopate coincided with the reigns of emperors Philippus (244–249), DECIUS (249–251), Gallus (251–253), VALERIANUS (253–260), and Gallienus (260–268).

The years of his episcopate were full of troubles and persecutions, which are eloquently described in his letters and literary remains. In the year of his succession, riots broke out in Alexandria, during which the pagan population attacked the Christians and pillaged their homes. Soon after the riots were quieted, the relatively mild reign of Philippus was replaced by that of Decius, who inaugurated one of the most ferocious waves of Christian persecutions.

The prefect of Alexandria, Sabinus, at once set out to arrest the patriarch, whom he pursued everywhere except in his house, from which he did not stir. Finally, after four days, the patriarch decided to flee from the city together with a group of Christian companions. But they were arrested and brought back to Taposiris (*History of the Patriarchs,* Vol. 1, Pt. 1, p. 179).

In the meantime, Timotheus, the patriarch's pupil, managed to escape and came across a peasant on his way to a wedding party, to whom he recounted the story of the patriarch's arrest. The peasant and the wedding party then stormed the police quarters, making a lot of noise and shouting, whereupon the frightened soldiers took flight, and the group entered the place where the patriarch was resting in a linen shirt. He thought they were brigands and offered them his cloak, which was all that he possessed. They beckoned him to rise and follow them. At first he resisted and offered them his head if they meant to kill him. On the contrary, they meant to save him. So they carried him hand and foot, placed him on a bare-backed donkey, and went away with him to a peaceful spot in the Libyan Desert, where he stayed until the persecutions abated. This dramatic tale was told by Dionysius in his letters, and he named as witnesses Gaius, Faustus, Petrus, and Paulus (*Historia ecclesiastica* 6.40. 179–80).

In an epistle to Fabius, bishop of Antioch, Dionysius recounted specific incidents depicting the horrible tortures to which the faithful were subjected at Alexandria during the persecutions of Decius. An elderly person by the name of Metras, who refused to obey his captors and worship their idols, was beaten, and his face and eyes were poked with sharp styli. He was dragged outside the city and stoned to death. A Christian woman by the name of Quinta was taken to a temple and ordered to pay homage to an idol. When she refused, they dragged her on the cobbled streets of the metropolis, beat her body against millstones, flogged her, and took her to the same place as Metras outside the city, where they stoned her to death. The houses of the faithful were plundered and their precious contents were ruined and set ablaze. The streets were strewn with broken articles and looked like a battleground. A certain Paul of Alexandria was murdered and received the martyr's crown with joy. Others followed willingly. Only a few recanted to escape a fearful fate. An aged virgin by the name of Apollonia had her bones fractured, her teeth broken, and was threatened with burning in a blazing fire. She responded by praying, and then zealously jumped into the fire and was burned alive. A man by the name of Serapion was arrested and tortured, his bones broken, and he was finally thrown from the top of a high building into the street.

All those who refused to render homage to the idols were systematically dragged, tortured, and burned alive. All this went on incessantly, day and night, without respite. A certain Julianus, who was old, arthritic, and unable to stand on his feet or walk, was taken with two Christians for torture. One of the two men recanted to escape the agony of torture and was spared. The other, named Cronin, remained in the faith. He and Julianus, with much reviling and beating, were carried on two camels through the city. In the end both were thrown into the blazing fire outside Alexandria, within sight of the populace. A military bystander who chided the mob for their behavior was seized, tried, and decapitated. A Libyan by the name of Macarius was also burned alive. A certain Epimachus and Alexander, who remained long in chains, were tortured by severe flogging and had their skin scraped by a sharp implement before they were thrown into the fire. Four women, including a chaste virgin by the name of Ammonarium, were tried before the prefect and severely tortured. A very famous old woman by the name of Mercuria, and another called Dionysia, who was a mother of numerous children and who defied the prefect and refused to bow to the idols, were all put to the sword and died, along with others. A company of three men and a youngster by the name of Dioscorus were tried. The men were killed, while the prefect tried to lure the boy and set him free in anticipation of getting him to recant. The boy did not recant, but simply awaited his turn for torture. An old man by the name of Theophilus, who stood trembling before the court, was almost frightened into lapsing, just as a group of legionaries named Ammon, Zenon, Ptolemy, and Anginus stormed the court shouting that they were Christians. The prefect was taken by surprise and fled from what looked like imminent danger, while the captives in court were saved. Numerous Christians were cut to pieces by infuriated pagans in the cities and the villages. One such was Iskhiron, who worked for a pagan governor and refused to bow to the idols and was instantly killed by his master. Many Christians fled to the wilderness and either perished from hunger and thirst or were taken captive by the fierce nomads.

Finally the dawn of a new era of peace began to break, and those who had lapsed for fear of torture and death started returning to the fold of the faithful. Consequently, the church faced the problem of the returned apostates and their acceptance back in the fold. Some zealots in Carthage, Rome, and Antioch hardened toward their acceptance, but Dionysius took the lead in a position of clemency toward all who repented and wished to return to their mother church. To this effect, he enjoined all his bishops and presbyters to welcome them. Furthermore, he circulated epistles to all the other bishops outside Egypt including Rome, requesting "the reception of those who had apostatized during the persecution of Decius." In the end, his eloquent appeal prevailed over his brother bishops, and harmony reigned again in the church.

Contingent with the readmission of apostates was the problem of their rebaptism. Here again, Dionysius played a prominent role, in which he was supported by Stephen, bishop of Rome. In his epistles he professed moderation and self-restraint with all heretics and apostates; in other words he opposed the idea of rebaptism, and his views seem to have been accepted by other bishops in spite of the obscurity of the *History of the Patriarchs* on this matter.

As soon as these controversies were settled and the peace of the church was reestablished, the atmosphere again became clouded by a new edict of persecution issued by Valerianus. This time, Dionysius was summoned by the prefect Aemelian for trial. He came with a number of clergy, and though some of his ardent companions perished in that encounter, Dionysius himself was only banished to a pagan district called Kefro in the Libyan Desert, where he succeeded in gaining converts. Later he was removed from Kefro to Collouthion in the district of Mareotis near Alexandria, and ultimately he made his escape to the metropolis.

Throughout the period, which was beset with immense hardships, Dionysius managed to save himself from martyrdom. This was counted against him by a certain Bishop Germanus, and Dionysius was constrained to come to his own defense in an epistle where he recounted the details of his arrest, trial, and exile, ultimately leading to his liberation and return to Alexandria at a moment when Valerianus was distracted by a barbarian invasion of the empire.

With the accession of Gallienus to the imperial throne, the church regained a breathing space. Paradoxically, the peace was reinforced by an outbreak of the plague, during which the pagan population was distracted from harassing the Christians. In fact, the Christians rendered a positive service to their enemies by helping to bury their dead and by comforting the sick. Furthermore, Gallienus issued orders for the return of churches and ecclesiastical properties to the bishops, who were then left to worship their own God undisturbed. At this point, the patriarch was advancing in years, and his health was failing under the weight of unremitting hardships. His episcopate was drawing to an end. Nevertheless, he continued to handle church crises in writing by the issuance of his epistles, whereby he tried to solve all problems, both national and international. Perhaps the most difficult problem he had to face was the scandalous affair of Paul of Samosata, bishop of Antioch, whose shadowy life was coupled with serious theological errors. A council at Antioch was convened by some seventy bishops, including those of Caesarea, Neocaesarea, Jerusalem, Tarsus, Pontus, Iconium, and Bostra, to consider the situation. The convened bishops wrote, inviting the participation of Dionysius. But the bishop of Alexandria was too old and too weak to appear in person, and consequently he wrote to the council giving his views on the situation, which ended with Paul's deposition from the bishopric of Antioch.

Throughout his episcopate, Dionysius continued to sponsor the Catechetical School, where he had previously studied under Origen and over which he had presided after Heraclas. His successor as head of the school was Theognostus, who is known to have written a treatise entitled *Hypotyposeis* in seven books, a kind of dogmatic summa, with an elegant style and Origenist leanings. This work is unfortunately lost, except for a fragment of the second book discovered in the 1980s in a fourteenth-century manuscript at Venice. On the other hand, the most brilliant literary work surviving from that age belongs to Dionysius himself. In spite of his immense trials and heavy burdens, he was able to devote some of his time and energy to religious writing and theological controversies, mainly as part of his pastoral duties. This is revealed in a number of examples.

The spread of the heresy of SABELLIANISM in the Pentapolis, which he regarded as part of his diocese, called for his attention. Sabellius, a presbyter of Ptolemais, maintained that godhead was revealed in three functions and not three persons. Dionysius immediately wrote an epistle to refute this heretical teaching (*Historia ecclesiastica* 7.6). Another instance nearer home occurred under Nepos, bishop of Arsinoë, who wrote a book entitled *The Refutation of Allegorists* that gained tremendous popularity among the citizens and villagers of his see, who regarded it almost as a Gospel. The book maintained that the statements in the book of Revelation were not allegorical. Dionysius became uneasy about the movement, which began to assume the shape of a schismatic sect. Consequently, he decided to go to Arsinoë himself to discuss the text with the priests and their congregations in an attempt to rectify the situation. For three days and three nights, he continued the discussion and was able to win the faithful back to his side; even Korakion, the leader of the group called Millenarians, ended by repudiating these errors. Out of these encounters, Dionysius later registered his thoughts in a treatise entitled "On the Promises." This led him to discuss the authorship of Revelation, in which he maintained that the book was written by another John, not the evangelist.

The literary genius of Dionysius is best represented in his epistles sent to councils and the bishops of Christendom on important matters emerging in his lifetime. EUSEBIUS OF CAESAREA has enumerated and summarized most of them in the *Historia ecclesiastica*. These epistles are historical documents of great importance in the ecclesiastical history of the third century. There is hardly a major movement in that age that does not figure in their texts. From the refutation of heresies to such burning questions as the PASCHAL CONTROVERSY, all were treated with great authority and theological objectivity. There is hardly a contemporary bishop with whom Dionysius did not correspond. The epistles exchanged with the bishop of Rome reveal that he was writing to a peer and that Alexandria was not under the authority of Rome, nor did Rome assert any claims of superiority over Alexandria. His epistle to Fabius, bishop of Antioch, on the Alexandrian martyrs in the persecution of Decius is a masterpiece of historical recording.

Dionysius' vast knowledge of Greek philosophy is demonstrated in a letter "On Nature" addressed to a spiritual son by the name of Timothy. Here he sets out to prove the order of the creation by divine providence against the Epicurean materialistic explanation of the universe and the atomistic discussions of Democritus.

Another work ascribed to Dionysius by Eusebius is entitled *Refutation and Apology*. This was addressed to his namesake of Rome in four books, in which he dealt with the trinitarian doctrine. He sought to prove that the Son coexisted with the Father for all eternity just like the sun and the day, whose coexistence was also eternal and inseparable. Another work, *On Temptations*, addressed to a certain Euphranus, is known to have existed but is now lost. His *Letters*, most of which have been quoted by Eusebius, are considered masterly works of religious writing, and serve as basic historical documents of the age of persecutions. One letter was addressed to Novatian the antipope, trying to conciliate him and avoid schism. Another letter, addressed to Basilides, bishop of the Pentapolis, answers his questions about the duration of Lent and the physical conditions necessary for the reception of the Eucharist. The aforementioned epistle to Fabius, bishop of Antioch, pleaded for leniency on behalf of the apostates who were victims of torture during the persecutions. Dionysius is possibly the first bishop to issue pastoral epistles to all the churches exhorting the faithful to observe the Lenten and Easter dates carefully. His epistle to Glavius, Domitius, and Didymas set forth a canon based on a cycle of eight years, with the Paschal celebration occurring at any time other than after the vernal equinox. In this way, he assumed a leading role in the Christian world of his day.

Dionysius is most highly revered in the Coptic church, and he is annually commemorated in the Coptic SYNAXARION on 13 Baramūdah. He is recognized as one of the principal fathers of the whole church, and he is universally acclaimed as "Dionysius the Great."

BIBLIOGRAPHY

Fragments of his work were edited by Simon de Magistris, Rome, 1796; see also PG 10, pp. 1233ff., 1575ff. A modern critical edition was prepared by C. L. Feltoe, Cambridge, 1904; the English translation by Feltoe was published by the *Society for Promoting Christian Knowledge,* London, 1918. See also S. D. F. Salmond in *Ante-Nicene Christian Library* (Edinburgh), Vol. 20, and *Ante-Nicene Fathers* Series (Buffalo and New York), Vol. 6.

Altaner, B. *Patrologie,* p. 175. Freiburg, 1950.

Bardenhewer, O. *Geschichte der altkirchlichen Literatur,* Vol. 2, pp. 167–91. Freiburg, 1902–1912.

Buriel, J. *Denys d'Alexandrie: Sa vie, son temps, ses oeuvres.* Paris, 1910.

Dittrich, F. *Dionysius der Grosse und Alexandrien.* Freiburg, 1867.

Marize, P. *Denys d'Alexandrie.* Paris, 1881.

Miller, P. S. "Studies in Dionysius the Great of Alexandria," Ph. diss., Erlangen, 1933.

Quasten, J. *Patrology,* Vol. 2, pp. 101–109. Utrecht and Antwerp, 1975.

AZIZ S. ATIYA

DIONYSUS. *See* Mythological Subjects in Coptic Art.

DIOS, SAINT, or Abadyus, a soldier who was martyred commemorated by the Copts (feast day: 25 Ṭūbah). He is but unknown in other traditions. The text of his Passion has survived in only a single Sahidic manuscript (Rossi, 1893, pp. 86–90). In this the martyrdom is dated to the time of Emperor Maximinus (235–238) in Egypt, and a *praepositus,* Dioparipe, and *princeps,* Paer (officers of the Tenth Legion), are named.

The story of the Passion is as follows. When the edict ordering sacrifice to the pagan gods arrives, the soldiers are paraded. One of them, Dios of Pelcoi, steps forward, removing his military belt and refusing to offer sacrifice. When the *princeps* threatens him, Dios prophesies the death of the *princeps's* son and is thereupon tortured. He then foretells the death of the wife of the *praepositus* as well. Both prophecies are fulfilled.

The legion is disturbed by all this, and Dios is imprisoned. The emperor arrives, and there is a long discussion between him and Dios. Dios is then killed. His body is protected by God and is buried by a holy monk from the vicinity.

The text belongs to the type produced in epic style (see HAGIOGRAPHY), but its style and content indicate that it is not of the later fictitious type but dates back (probably in Greek) to the classical period of epic passions, in other words to about the fifth century.

BIBLIOGRAPHY

Baumeister, T. *Martyr Invictus: Der Märtyr als Sinnbild der Erlösung in der Legende und im Kult der frühen koptischen Kirche.* Münster, 1972.

Rossi, F., ed. *Un nuovo codice copto del museo Egizio di Torino,* pp. 3–136. Rome, 1893.

TITO ORLANDI

DIOSCORUS I, saint and twenty-fifth patriarch of the See of Saint Mark (444–458). He succeeded Saint CYRIL THE GREAT and must be regarded as one of the chief architects of Coptic Christianity and the Egyptian church. Little is known about his early life beyond the supposition that he was a native of Alexandria, born in that city possibly at the close of the fourth century or the dawn of the fifth. Owing to his devotion to the faith and to his sterling character in the defense of his high principles, he was chosen by Cyril I to be his close companion in his religious meetings. Cyril made him an archdeacon. Apparently Cyril became Dioscorus' chief mentor, and together they attended the famous ecumenical Council of Ephesus I of 431 where Cyril's Christological formulas were accepted as the orthodox definition of the nature of Jesus Christ. And here we must assume that the archdeacon Dioscorus, as a power behind the throne of Cyril, who presided over the council, could have contributed some share toward the formulation of those conciliar decisions. It was on such occasions that the personality of Dioscorus became recognized within his own church and throughout the Byzantine empire, a fact that explains the ease and unanimity with which he was elected by the Alexandrian presbytery to succeed his mentor in 444.

At that time, the Alexandrian see had reached great heights in the Christian world. Although it had been acknowledged as second only to Rome by the Council of Nicaea in 325, through the influence of Saint ATHANASIUS and Cyril, it was regarded as parallel to the Roman see, with which it had remained in amicable and mutual relationship until the accession of Pope Leo I. Dioscorus conveyed the news of his assumption to the throne of Saint Mark by dispatching to Rome a special messenger, Possidonius, with a brief addressed to Pope Leo, who answered by an epistle declaring the uniformity between the two sees in all matters of sacramental discipline, the ordination of the presbyters, and the handling of the liturgy. This seems to have been the high moment of ostensible unity between Rome and Alexandria. Nevertheless, behind that formal facade, the spirit of jealousy and suspicion must have been lurking at the Curia of Rome, as will be seen from papal behavior in subsequent events.

What led to convening the Council of Ephesus II were the circumstances associated with a formula devised by EUTYCHES, a pious monk and archimandrite of a large monastery at Constantinople, who was no theological scholar. In his keen opposition to Nestorianism, he declared that the nature of Jesus was only divine, and consequently deprived the Lord of His human nature. Thus in 448, Eutyches was accused by Eusebius, bishop of Dorylaeum, of going to the other extreme from Nestorius by confounding the two natures of Christ for the sake of His unity. In the meantime, Pope Leo sent Flavian, archbishop of Constantinople, his letter or tome known as the *Tomus Leonis*, attacking this Christological misconception. Dioscorus, whose friendly relations with Eutyches simply expressed his own misunderstanding of a confused situation, remained nonaligned. In the meantime, Flavian took courage and deposed the archimandrite Eutyches as a symbol of disapproval of his views. Thus to all appearances, the Christian world became divided into two camps, with Leo and Flavian on one side and Dioscorus on the other. But Eutyches happened to have strong influence at the Byzantine court of Emperor Theodosius II (408–450) through a highly placed eunuch named Chrysaphius. Theodosius was thus persuaded to call a general council to reconsider the case under the chairmanship of Dioscorus, a fact that must have further enflamed Leo's jealousy. The Egyptian bishops, together with the Antiochene and Greek bishops, converged on Ephesus in 449 with a small Roman delegation, which came armed with a new tome from Pope Leo that recorded his position. Eutyches was summoned by Dioscorus to speak for himself. Moving from his earlier position of incorporating the human entirely into the divine nature of Christ, he proclaimed in writing the safer approach of his adherence to the Nicene Creed and to the formula of Saint Cyril, which are both recognized as the orthodox doctrine. Thus he was acquitted by the council and returned to his former position unscathed. The result of this verdict was the deposition of Flavian from the See of Constantinople together with his supporters, who were abused by the imperial guard through the influence of Chrysaphius.

This proved to be a further step toward the assertion of Alexandrian supremacy in ecclesiastical matters vis-à-vis both Constantinople and Rome, a situation that could hardly be swallowed by Leo, whose Tome was not presented for consideration at the council. This was probably an unwise action by Dioscorus and an unnecessary provocation of the Roman pope. Dioscorus possessed a strong and rather impassioned personality, and he inherited the supreme heritage of Athanasius and Cyril, his predecessors, but he was their unequal in tact and ecclesiastical diplomacy. Pope Leo's wrath was precipitated by the ostensible neglect of his Tome at the Council, and he could no longer conceal his antagonism to the Alexandrian prelate, whom he described openly as a "new Pharaoh" in the Church. In a letter to the emperor, he described the second Council of Ephesus in the abusive term *Latrocinium* (robber synod).

Hitherto the unity of the Eastern and Western churches remained intact. Ephesus II tolled the death knell of this unity, and the rupture between Alexandria and Rome was sealed by Leo's letter to Emperor Theodosius II. But the wholesome attitude of Theodosius toward Alexandria was soon interrupted by his death in 450. He was succeeded by an old senator and general of the Roman army credited for the quelling of a rebellion in Upper Egypt, Marcian (450–457), who became emperor after marrying PULCHERIA, a sister of Theodosius. She was a former nun, a religious but impetuous woman, who harbored tremendous hatred for Alexandrian supremacy over Constantinople as well as for the occupant of the throne of Saint Mark. From his past experience, her husband, too, could not sustain much sympathy for the Alexandrian see or Egypt, where he had just fought to curb its turbulent people. The result of these unfortunate circumstances was the reversal of the lenient policy of Theodosius and its replacement by an atmosphere of hostility toward the Eutychian party in Constantinople and toward Dioscorus. This new situation superbly suited Leo and the Roman party, which could not bear the growing influence of Alexandria and Dioscorus.

While the second Ephesian Council marked the peak of glory and universal influence of the Alexandrian patriarch, the Roman legate Parchasinus, an inveterate adversary of both Dioscorus and Alexandria, on 17 October 451 declared the acts of that council to be null and void. Rome requested the issuance of a special decree forbidding even the mention of the Council of Ephesus II. Thus the stage was set for the next move in fighting Alexandrian monophysitism. Leo suggested the convening of a new council in Italy, away from Eastern pressures. In the end, Emperor Marcian, or rather his wife Pulcheria, decided on Chalcedon (within reach of the Byzantine capital) for that next meeting, and Rome approved. Consequently, Marcian issued the formal invitation to the bishops of the East and the West for the Chalcedon meeting to be inaugurated on 8 October 451.

When that invitation reached Alexandria, the advisers and the attendants of Dioscorus addressed the patriarch, as a man of God, saying that the letter would bring death, meaning that it implied the end of Cyrillian and Alexandrian orthodoxy. In Rome, Leo instructed his new legate, Bonifacius, whom he entrusted with another famous tome, to be firm in opposing the Alexandrian party. In fact, the Roman legate refused categorically to be seated with Dioscorus and even demanded his expulsion from the assembly before any verdict was reached. However, the bishops who were gathered to discuss "Eutychianism" were deflected by the Roman legate, in conjunction with the imperial commissioners, to a trial of Dioscorus. After numerous discussions, a compromise was reached to let the patriarch remain in the assembly but to take a place only with the rest of the bishops. After that, Eusebius of Dorylaeum declared his list of charges against Dioscorus, which were confirmed by Bishop Theodoret of Cyrrhus.

In self-defense, Dioscorus reiterated that the reason for Flavian's condemnation was his assertion of the two natures after the Incarnation. Quotations were made from the Fathers Athanasius, Gregory, and Cyril, to the effect that after the Incarnation there were not two natures, but the incarnate nature of the Logos. He said that if he were to be expelled, the Fathers would be expelled too. He claimed not to deviate from their doctrine, but to defend it. The extracts, he said, were not gathered carelessly but verified by himself. Though none contested him, the discussion of the two natures continued, and Dioscorus stopped further argument, because he divined their motives.

Dioscorus refrained from attending the third session that was convened essentially against him. The assembly decided to send a delegation to him with the purpose of obtaining his signature on the Tome of Leo in exchange for his rehabilitation and reinstatement to the patriarchal see of Alexandria. But Dioscorus was not a man of compromises. Though he was not against Leo's Christology, he was adamant against the minutest change in the terms or words of the Nicene Creed. He was summoned three times, according to canonical rules, to accept the Roman "innovations," and thrice he refused to conform to their summons. Consequently, Dioscorus was declared fallen. A verdict for his removal from the patriarchal see was followed by his banishment to the island of Gangra in Paphlagonia. Defiantly and with dignity, he accepted the verdict of the council rather than move from his stand.

The council was terminated in the usual solemn ceremony on 25 October 451 in its sixth and final session. The attending bishops departed after the signature of the creed offered in Leo's Tome and after ascertaining that in substance it was in conformity with the teachings of Athanasius and Cyril. Paradoxically, this implied uniformity with Dioscorus, the dethroned bishop.

Though formally deposed at Chalcedon, Dioscorus remained for the Coptic people their legal patriarch until his death in exile. Even if some of his clergy signed the Chalcedonian verdict of his removal under imperial and Roman pressures, the Coptic nation itself as a whole refused to accept this decision, and this congregation was never reconciled to the consideration of Chalcedon as an ecumenical council. For the two centuries preceding the Arab conquest of Egypt, the Egyptian nation deprecated Chalcedon as an infamous gathering of misguided bishops. To the Copts, the last ecumenical council was Ephesus II in 449. They utterly contested the nomination by Constantinople of a Melchite Greek patriarch of Alexandria and, after the death of Dioscorus, continued to elect their own Monophysite patriarch in opposition to any Melchite nominee, until the advent of Arab rule that had been precipitated in part by this disunity in the church ranks.

The date of the death of Dioscorus is stated in most sources as 454, that is, approximately four years after his exile. According to the HISTORY OF THE PATRIARCHS by Sāwīrus ibn al-Muqaffaʿ, his death occurred in the year 458, which was also the year of the election of his successor TIMOTHY II (458–480). Dioscorus was canonized by the Copts, and his name appears in the SYNAXARION containing the names of saints and martyrs recognized by the Coptic church.

BIBLIOGRAPHY

Amélineau, E. C. *Monuments pour servir à l'histoire de l'Egypte chrétienne aux IVe, Ve, VIe et VIIe siècles.* Mission Archéologique Française au Caire, Mémoire 4. Paris, 1888–1895.

Bardenhewer, O. *Geschichte der altchristlichen Literatur,* Vol. 4, Das fünfte Jahrhundert mit Einschluss der syrischen Literatur des vierten Jahrhunderts. Freiburg im Breisgau, 1924.

Camelot, P.-T. *Ephèse et Chalcédoine.* London, 1953.

Crum, W. E. "Coptic Texts relating to Dioscorus of Alexandria." *Proceedings of the Society of Biblical Archaeology* 25 (1903):267–76.

Dallmayr, H. *Die grossen vier Konzilien. Nicaea—Konstantinopel—Ephesus—Chalcedon,* 2nd ed. Munich, 1963.

Frend, W. H. C. *The Rise of the Monophysite Movement.* Cambridge, 1979.

Grillmeier, A., and H. Bacht. *Das Konzil von Chalkedon. Geschichte und Gegenwart,* 3 vols. Würzburg, 1951–1954.

Harnack, A. von. *Lehrbuch der Dogmengeschichte,* Vol. 2. Darmstadt, 1964.

Hefele, C. J., and H. Leclercq. *Histoire des conciles d'après les documents originaux,* Vol. 2/2, pp. 469–857. Paris, 1908.

Lebon, J. "Autour du cas de Dioscore d'Alexandrie." *Le Muséon* 59 (1946):515–28.

Maspero, J. *Histoire des Patriarches d'Alexandrie depuis la mort de l'empereur Anastase jusqu'à la réconciliation des églises jacobites (518–616).* Paris, 1923; repr. Providence, R.I. 1975.

Nau, F. N. "Histoire de Dioscore, patriarche d'Alexandrie, écrite par son disciple Théopiste." *Journal Asiatique,* ser. 10, no. 1 (1903):5–108, 241–310.

Roncaglia, M. P. "Quelques questions ecclésiastiques et d'ecclésiologie au IIIe siècle à Alexandrie." *Proche-Orient Chrétien* 20 (1970):20–30.

Sellers, R. V. *The Council of Chalcedon: A Historical and Doctrinal Survey.* London, 1953.

MARTINIANO P. RONCAGLIA

DIOSCORUS II, thirty-first patriarch of the See of Saint Mark (515–517). A nephew of TIMOTHY II Aelurus, Dioscorus II had a brief but dramatic reign. He was first installed under the auspices of the government authorities, but when this roused protests, he secured a more proper ecclesiastical enthronement. Nevertheless, riots followed in which the Prefect Theodosius was killed. This brought down imperial punishment on the city and a number of executions. Dioscorus went to Constantinople to intercede with Emperor Anastasius and obtained pardon for Alexandria. A visiting Westerner, Maximian, later bishop of Ravenna, praised him as a good shepherd who was ready to lay down his life for his flock. However, at Constantinople he was hooted at by supporters of the Chalcedonian party and had to leave the capital hastily. SEVERUS OF ANTIOCH had sent Dioscorus greetings and assurance of his prayers on his way to Constantinople, also urging him to join in the policy of securing a formal anathema on CHALCEDON and the Tome of LEO I THE GREAT from Melchite converts, especially bishops.

BIBLIOGRAPHY

Frend, W. H. C. *The Rise of the Monophysite Movement,* pp. 73, 229. Cambridge, 1972.

Hardy, E. R. *Christian Egypt,* p. 120. New York, 1952.

E. R. HARDY

DIOSCORUS (bishop of Damanhūr, c. 392–402). The date of birth of this person is not known. It is known only that he became a monk in NITRIA and then became a priest. This took place around 391, when the celebrated monk of Nitria, Benjamin, died a little after the arrival of PALLADIUS in KELLIA. At the urging of the patriarch THEOPHILUS, Dioscorus agreed to become bishop of Damanhūr, in whose see Nitria lay.

Theophilus, at first an admirer of the writings of ORIGEN and hence very favorable to the intellectuals of Nitria, who thrived on these books (it was from the desert of Nitria that he chose several of the bishops of Damanhūr), changed sides in 399. He proved himself a relentless opponent of Origenist tendencies. Dioscorus, before acceding to the episcopate between 390 and 394, was one of the Tall Brothers (see AMMONIUS OF KELLIA and THEOPHILUS OF ALEXANDRIA) at Nitria who were persecuted by Theophilus.

Dioscorus, although by then no longer at Nitria, was a target in the persecution by Theophilus and indeed appears to have been evicted by him from the administration of his diocese (Chitty, 1966, p. 58). It is said that driven from his see, Dioscorus rejoined the Tall Brothers in Constantinople, where they were welcomed in their exile by John Chrysostom. For this, Theophilus was never to forgive him.

It does not appear that Dioscorus recovered his see at Damanhūr, and he probably died in Constantinople.

BIBLIOGRAPHY

Chitty, D. J. *The Desert a City.* London and Oxford, 1966.

RENÉ-GEORGES COQUIN

DIOSCORUS OF APHRODITO

DIOSCORUS OF APHRODITO (c. 520–after 585), jurist and poet. Born to hellenized Coptic gentry in the Upper Egyptian town of Aphrodite (later spelled Aphrodito) in the Antaeopolite nome, Dioscorus received the classical education of his time and station plus training in the law and, presumably at Alexandria, in philosophy (most likely under John Philoponus). He followed his father Apollos as *protokometes* (headman) of Aphrodite, and eventually became administrator of the monastery Apollos had founded before his death in 546. In 551 Dioscorus traveled to Constantinople to defend Aphrodite's *autopragia* (self-responsibility) rights of tax collection, a journey recalled in his earliest preserved poem (Heitsch, 6; MacCoull, 1988, pp. 63–66). From 566 to 573 he resided at Antinoopolis, seat of the duke of the Thebaid and administrative center of Upper Egypt. He practiced law, from which activity many documents in his own hand, in both Greek and Coptic, are preserved, and composed numerous Greek encomiastic poems in honor of dukes of the Thebaid and local officials. After 573 he returned to Aphrodite and continued to write and administer his lands. He lived into the reign of Maurice (after 585).

The archive of Dioscorus is a rich source of information about the cultural and economic life of late antique Egypt. As a *ktetor* (landowner) he was involved in numerous transactions involving both lay and monastic property. As a bilingual man of letters, he composed a Greek–Coptic poetic glossary that is of great interest for both linguists and historians. His poetry is a rich blend of pagan and Christian imagery, especially in praise of the emperor, epithalamia (wedding songs), and descriptions of Egyptian scenery. As a poet he owes much to the *Periphrasis* of St. John of Nonnus and to the philosophical vocabulary of Philoponus. In language and in piety, Dioscorus was Cyrillian; in matters of taste and in his sense of the majesty of the law, he reflected his age's acute sensibility and love of splendor and display. From his work we gain our fullest picture of life in Coptic Egypt at the time of its highest cultural flowering.

BIBLIOGRAPHY

Heitsch, E. *Die griechischen Dichterfragmente der römischen Kaiserzeit,* 2 vols. Abhandlungen der Akademie der Wissenschaften in Göttingen, philologisch-historische Klasse 49. Göttingen, 1964.

Kramer, B., and D. Hagedorn. *Papyrologische Texte und Abhandlungen,* Vol. 31, pp. 185–86. Bonn, 1984.

MacCoull, L. S. B. *Dioscorus of Aphrodito: His Life, His Work, His World.* Berkeley, Calif., 1988.

———. "The Coptic Archive of Dioscorus of Aphrodito." *Chronique d'Egypte* 56 (1981):185–93.

L. S. B. MACCOULL

DISCOURSE ON THE EIGHTH AND NINTH

DISCOURSE ON THE EIGHTH AND NINTH, sixth tractate in Codex VI of the NAG HAMMADI LIBRARY. The name of the tractate is derived from its contents, since its ancient form has not been preserved at the opening or ending of the text, although titles for parts of the treatise may appear in 53, 24–26 ("The Discourse on the Eighth and the Ninth") and in 61, 21–22 ("The Eighth Reveals the Ninth"). The interest of the document rests on the soul's arrival in the divine realms that lie beyond the seven malevolent spheres surrounding the earth. It is through these latter that the departed soul must pass before coming to regions controlled by the God who gives life.

The Coptic text, doubtless a translation from a Greek original, constitutes a rite of initiation into the mysteries of HERMES TRISMEGISTUS and employs the technique of teaching through ritual. In a formal sense, the piece consists of a dialogue between a teacher or mystagogue, who represents Father Hermes, and a pupil who is termed a son, an exchange that leads the latter to an ecstatic experience of the divine. The liturgical character of the document appears in a number of features such as the avowed goal of divine rebirth; the titles "father" and "son," which are joined to other "brothers" and "citizens" in the ogdoad, or eighth realm; a ritual embrace (57, 26–27); the pattern of prayer (55, 23–57, 25, which may be a literary intrusion); and the final oath sworn by initiates to guard the secrets of Hermes.

The text exhibits several links to Egypt. Among them, the Egyptian god Thoth, whose functions included serving as scribe for the divine child Horus-Harpocrates, had become identified with Hermes as early as Herodotus. Thoth was associated with magic, medicine, writing, and various other technologies. For Greeks, Hermes was the guide for departed souls as well as scientist and interpreter of the mysteries. Second, the numbers eight and nine display ties to Egyptian theology, for pantheons typically were made up of eight or nine deities (*ogdoad* or *ennead*). The interest in preserving the text in hieroglyphic characters illustrates a third point of contact.

The tractate is plainly bonded to the larger religious literature derived from the veneration of Hermes. But it embodies a hitherto unknown liturgy that may stand independent of other Hermetic documents. In addition, the text exhibits affinities with dualistic ideas that may be gnostic, as well as with other mystery religions.

BIBLIOGRAPHY

Brashler, J.; P. A. Dirkse; and D. M. Parrott, eds. and trans. "The Discourse on the Eighth and Ninth" (VI,6). In *The Nag Hammadi Library*, pp. 292–97, ed. J. M. Robinson. New York, 1977.

Dirkse, P. A., et al. "The Discourse on the Eighth and Ninth." In *Nag Hammadi Codices V, 2–5 and VI with Papyrus Berolinensis 8502, 1 and 4*, pp. 341–73, ed. D. M. Parrott. Leiden, 1979.

Keizer, L. S. *The Eighth Reveals the Ninth: A New Hermetic Initiation Disclosure*. Seaside, Calif., 1974.

Mahé, J.-P. *Hermès en Haute-Egypte: Les Textes hermétiques de Nag Hammadi et leurs parallèles grecs et latins*, Vol. 1. Quebec, 1978.

S. KENT BROWN

DISSOLUTION OF MARRIAGE. *See* Personal Status Law.

DJEME. *See* Madīnat Hābū; Memnonia.

DJINKIM. *See Appendix.*

DOCETISM. The term "docetism" comes from the Greek word *dokeo* (I seem, I appear), and was first used by Serapion, bishop of Antioch (190–208), to refer to certain heretics of the early church. In its earliest expression, docetism apparently grew out of the difficulties of explaining how the Son of God could be subject to the vicissitudes of humanity, including suffering and death. The earliest Docetists would explain that Christ only seemed or appeared to suffer, for He only seemed to be mortal and fleshly as other humans. In reality, they would argue, He is God and, therefore, not truly subject to the problems of humanity. It is generally assumed that the emphasis on the reality of Christ's physical body in John 1:14, 1 John 1:1–4 and 4:1–3, and 2 John 7 is a refutation of this incipient heresy. During the second century, the positions of Docetists were multiplied and amplified into various gnostic systems, including some that denied the substantive reality of the incarnate Christ, and others that stated that the heavenly Christ descended upon the mortal Jesus at His baptism and departed when Jesus was before Pilate. The crucifixion scene described in the APOCALYPSE OF PETER is an example of the latter, portraying the spiritual Savior laughing above the cross while soldiers nail the mortal Jesus to the tree.

Among those especially charged with docetism were Cerinthus and Marcion. There is also a docetic portrayal of Jesus in some anti-Christian writings of the Mandaean Gnostics. Irenaeus and Tertullian, both writing in the late second century, attacked this heresy, and Tertullian claimed that some Valentinians were guilty of docetism. Photius (ninth century) charged CLEMENT OF ALEXANDRIA with docetism, but Clement rebuked the denial of Christ's flesh in his own writings.

BIBLIOGRAPHY

Lidzbarski, M. *Ginza. Der Schatz oder das grosse Buch der Mandäer*, pp. 181–204. Gottingen, 1925.

C. WILFRED GRIGGS

DOLPHIN. *See* Symbols in Coptic Art.

DOME. *See* Architectural Elements of Churches.

DOMINICANS IN EGYPT. In 1928–1932 the Dominican friars founded a convent in the Abbasiyyah district of Cairo, where they started to form a library around which, in 1953, they established the Dominican Institute of Oriental Studies. It was opened to both Coptic and Muslim scholars under the directorship of G. C. Anawati. Born into a Christian family in Egypt, Anawati distinguished himself as a specialist in Muslim thought and Arab culture and civilization. He participated with the Copts in the organization of the ecumenical movement. Numerous Dominicans of that convent such as de Beaurecueil and Ibrahim Khouzam have fought for the reinstatement of the Coptic rite in the liturgy offered to their followers.

JACQUES JOMIER

DOMITIUS. *See* Maximus and Domitius, Saints.

DONATION OF CHILDREN, custom of giving a child up to a monastery for one of two reasons: having the child become a monk or making the child a serf of the monastery.

Instances of donating children who were intended to become monks are known from literary and especially hagiographic sources. The absence of sources other than literary ones limits our information. We do not know whether the donations were accompanied by a formal act that defined the duties of the parties involved and the question of the private belongings of the future monk. This could have been quite possible, taking into consideration the customs of the period. It is not possible to tell what happened if, upon growing up, the child did not accept the decision made by his parents. The church must have had unfortunate experiences with donations of small children, since during the Council in Trullo (691) it introduced a prohibition of monastic vows taken by children less than ten years old (canon 40).

The presence of children in monasteries is well proven as regards Pachomian congregations; it is mentioned in "Rules and Lives." The education of children was the object of special concern on the part of the founders of the congregation, who were also disturbed by the eventual homosexuality among the brothers. We also come across children in the monastery of Shenute. The Coptic inscriptions in the DAYR APA JEREMIAH at Saqqara mention a certain "Victor, he that belongs to the cell of children." This cell could have been the living quarters of children or, as the editor suggests, a school room (Thompson, 1912, no. 314). Children were also present in other monasteries, although practically nothing is known about the circumstances in which they arrived. Perhaps there were among them orphans whom the monasteries were entrusted to rear, when there were no rightful guardians or when designated guardians were unable to fulfill their obligations. We also do not know whether those children who were to become serfs were separated in everyday life from those who were to become monks.

A group of documents from DAYR ANBĀ PHOIBAMMON, of which the oldest dates back to the beginning of the eighth century and the latest one is dated at 781–791, was published in *Koptische Rechtsurkunden des achten Jahrhunderts aus Djeme* (Crum and Steindorff, 1912, nos. 78–103). It shows the existence of donations of another nature. Parents donated their children—as a rule boys—so that they would serve the monasteries. The acts inform us in detail about the circumstances in which such decisions were made, most frequently during a serious illness of the child, when the parents turned to Saint Phoibammon for help. Only one text makes no mention of an illness. In some texts the donors give an additional motivation for their decision. They say that they want to make a *prosphora,* offering, for the sake of their souls. According to the customs of the period, one was morally obliged to make an offering to a church or monastery; after the donor's death, mass was said on certain days in his behalf. Some texts also mention punishment in the form of illnesses brought by the saint if the parents neglected to fulfill their duty. There is no reason to distrust the sincerity of those declarations, although the possibility exists of other economic and social motives on the part of the parents. The very poor could have wanted to ensure for their children a modest but, in their eyes, secure existence. They could also have hoped that the monastery would protect its own people against violence committed by officials. After all, throughout the eighth century the Saint Phoibammon monastery remained influential and prosperous.

The parents claimed that their children became slaves similar to "those purchased," but this was obviously inexact. Certain documents state that after attaining maturity they were able to decide whether they wanted to remain in the monastery or to work outside, and then pay a certain sum (see Crum and Steindorff, no. 96). In one instance, the parents even fixed the amount of this payment (no. 78). Evidently the children offered to the monastery became its serfs.

The age of the children differed. In one instance the child was three years old, but it is uncertain whether he was handed over to the monastery immediately. It is far more likely that this took place some years after, when he could be useful as a servant. In one case the boy grew up and confirmed his parents' decision.

The deeds of donations defined the nature of the work to be performed by the children. They were to keep the monastery clean, to carry water, take care of lamps in the church, administer bread for guests, and in general do everything that the *oikonomos* told them to. No mention is made of their tasks outside the monastery.

One question might be whether the offered children became monks in the community which they previously served. The sources offer no direct answer to this question. The unmarried state was not tantamount to taking monastic vows. There may have existed a separate category of lower-ranking brothers in monasteries of the Arabian period, who were recruited from among the serfs of the monastery. This is a possible explanation of a group from DAYR ANBĀ HADRĀ in Aswan whose members were known as "the Faithful" (Munier, 1938). Unfortunately, the modest source materials at our disposal are not easy to interpret.

Besides donations of children there are instances of self-donations of adult men to monasteries. Such a donation is attested by *Koptische Rechtsurkunden des achten Jahrhunderts aus Djeme*, no. 104, where the reason adduced is the recovery from a serious disease. Evidence of similar donations occurs in literary texts concerning the saints George and Claudius. Sinners, who had been punished by the saints, offered themselves as soon as they obtained forgiveness (Till, p. 105; Godron, pp. 655, 663).

A separate category about which there is practically no information is composed of the children donated to priests, or the bishops, to be brought up as clerics (Till, p. 66, mentions Moses, the future famous monk).

BIBLIOGRAPHY

Amélineau, E. "Vie arabe de Schnoudi." *Mémoires publiés par les membres de la mission archéologique française au Caire* 4 (1888):331.

Bacht, H. *Das Vermächtnis des Ursprungs,* p. 231. Würzburg, 1972.

Crum, W. E., and G. Steindorff, eds. *Koptische Rechtsurkunden des achten Jahrhunderts aus Djeme.* Leipzig, 1912.

Godron, G., ed. *Second panégyrique de St. Claude par Constantin, évêque d'Assiout.* PO/35, pp. 655, 663.

Munier, H. "Le christianisme à Philae," *Bulletin de la Société d'archéologie copte* 4 (1938):46.

Steinwenter, A. "Kinderschenkungen an Koptische Klöster." *Zeitschrift der Savigny-Stiftung für Rechtsgeschichte, Kanonistische Abteilung* 42 (1921):175–207.

Thompson, H., ed. *The Coptic Inscriptions. Excavations at Saqqara 1908–1909, 1909–1910,* no. 314. Annales du Service des antiquités d'Egypte. (1912).

Till, W. C. *Koptische Heiligen- und Märtyrerlegenden,* Vol. 2, Rome, 1936.

EWA WIPSZYCKA

DONATIONS. *See* Law, Coptic: Private Law.

DONATISM, a schism in the church in North Africa that grew out of the Great Persecution under DIOCLETIAN and in some ways resembled the Melitian movement in Egypt. While the more profound causes lay in the puritanical ethic of the North African church, its opposition to the secular world, and its enthusiasm for the cult of martyrs, the immediate cause arose from differing attitudes adopted by clergy during the Great Persecution. In contrast to the persecution in Egypt, the repression of Christianity in North Africa was short and sharp, lasting only until the abdication of Diocletian and Maximian in May 305. During that time, however, many members of the clergy had lapsed and handed copies of the Scriptures and other church objects to the authorities. These clergymen, dubbed *traditores* (traitors; from *tradere,* to hand over) by their more intransigent brethren, were regarded as apostates incapable of administering a valid sacrament and, hence, of retaining their clerical office.

The simmering conflict erupted in 311. In that year, Bishop Mensurius of Carthage was cited to appear before the (usurping) emperor Maxentius

(306–312) to answer a charge of concealing in his house a presbyter who had published a libelous tract against the emperor. Mensurius vindicated himself but died on the return journey from Italy. There was at once a dispute over his successor. Aside from the problems caused by personality conflicts, the church in Numidia had acquired the right during the previous forty years to consecrate each new bishop of Carthage, and there was an element of rivalry between Carthage and the bishops in Numidia. Before the latter's representatives could arrive in Carthage, Mensurius' archdeacon, Caecilian, had been consecrated bishop and accepted by at least part of the congregation at Carthage.

There were, however, strong objections against him. It was said that during the persecution Caecilian had forbidden food to be sent to the imprisoned confessors who had been arrested in the township of Abitina in western Tunisia. He also had offended a wealthy member of his congregation named Lucilla by forbidding her to kiss a bone, allegedly of a martyr, before receiving communion. There were additional rumors that one of his consecrators, Felix of Aptunga, had been a *traditor* during the persecution, thereby rendering Caecilian's consecration invalid.

The various factions united with the Numidians in opposing Caecilian. Angry that he had been denied participation in Caecilian's consecration, the Numidian primate, Secundus, bishop of Tigisis, appointed an *interventor* (interim administrator) for the see of Carthage pending settlement of Caecilian's position. On the murder of the *interventor*, Secundus summoned a council of seventy Numidian bishops that condemned Caecilian to deposition.

This situation confronted Constantine after his victory over Maxentius at the Milvian Bridge on 28 October 312. For reasons that are unclear, the new emperor of the West took Caecilian's part from the outset. Funds were placed at his disposal and his enemies threatened with judicial penalties (Eusebius *Historia ecclesiastica* 10.6). Subsequently, clergy loyal to Caecilian were released from obligations to undertake municipal duties and pay municipal levies. This stung the opposition into action, and in April 313 its members appealed to Constantine to set up a commission of Gallic judges to arbitrate. Gallic judges were sought because Gaul, they said, had not suffered from the persecution (see Augustine, *Letters* 88.7, for the text of the petition). In his role as chief magistrate of the Roman people, the emperor remitted the case to the bishop of Rome, who happened to be an African.

The hearing on 2–5 October 313 went against the opposition, now led by a Numidian bishop named Donatus, from Casae Nigrae (Black Huts), on the edge of the Sahara. His vigorous leadership lasted until his death in exile in 355 and gave the opposition their name, Donatists. However, a council of the western provinces of the empire, assembled at Arles on 1 August 314, also decided in favor of Caecilian; and after his consecrator, Felix of Aptunga, had been cleared of the accusation of being a *traditor* (February 315), the emperor himself pronounced judgment in his favor on 10 November 316.

Nevertheless, Donatus prevailed. His ruthlessness, his self-confidence, and the conviction with which he inspired his adherents bear some resemblance to Athanasius. According to Jerome (*De viris illustribus* 93), he "deceived nearly all Africa." Evidence of the success of his movement is that Donatus won the allegiance of 270 bishops who attended a council over which he presided about 336 (Augustine, *Letters* 93.43).

Donatism remained the major form of Christianity in North Africa throughout the fourth century. This was due not only to the personalities of Donatus as bishop of Carthage and of his successor, Parmenian (355–391) but also to the fact that the Donatists continued the North African ecclesiastical tradition developed by Cyprian, combined with renewed acceptance of the role of martyrs and martyrdom in the church. Integrity and purity were, they claimed, the hallmarks of a Christian in the exclusive body of the elect who formed the church. This church was continuously directed by the Holy Spirit, a conviction that involved complete separation from the secular world and denial of the authority of the emperor in the affairs of the church; thus, the rhetorical question of Donatus to emissaries of Emperor Constans about 346: "What has the emperor to do with the church?" (Optatus *On the Donatist Schism* III.4). In addition, the Donatists were practically supreme in the province of Numidia, especially in the rural areas (Optatus III.4; Frend, *Donatist Church*, chap. 12). In these areas an extreme form of Donatism known as the Circumcellion movement emerged. It combined devotion to the shrines of martyrs (hence their name, derived from *circum cellas*, "around shrines") with acts of revolution and terrorism directed against the wealthy, whom they regarded as representatives of the devil (Optatus, III.4; Augustine, *Letters* 185.4.15).

The Donatists, therefore, became a far more formidable movement of dissent than the Melitians, and were more successful in retaining the loyalty of native Christians. Their weakness lay in the fact that the rest of Christendom accepted Caecilian and his successors as true bishops of Carthage; consequently the Donatists were not recognized by the emperors. It was only when prominent Numidian Donatists supported the rebellion against Emperor Flavius Honorius by Count Gildo (397–398), and lost, that their Catholic opponents could destroy them. Between 399 and 412 Augustine of Hippo and his friend Aurelius, bishop of Carthage, led an intensive and successful campaign against the Donatists. Propaganda, imperial legislation, and persecution all played their part. In May 411 the Donatists were forced into a conference at Carthage with their opponents, and after three sessions of debate were condemned and proscribed under imperial legislation against heretics *(Codex Theodosianus* XVI.5.52 of 30 January 412). Donatism was severely weakened and showed little sign of activity during the Vandal occupation of North Africa (429–534). At the end of the sixth century, however, a series of letters by Pope Gregory I (590–604) allude to a strong revival of Donatism in the heartland of southern Numidia. The movement may not have died out until the arrival of the Arabs in the seventh century.

Like the MELITIAN SCHISM, the Donatist movement illustrates the strength of feeling among native Christians in the Mediterranean lands against collaboration with the authorities during the Great Persecution. With a strong provincial base in Numidia, the Donatists combined powerful leadership and adherence to a traditional biblical theology. For his part, Caecilian was no Athanasius, and in North Africa there was neither Antony nor Pachomius to swing native Christianity into conformity with the orthodoxy represented by the church in Carthage, which had remained in communion with the rest of Christendom. Unlike the Melitians, the Donatists had to be suppressed by coercion. Only the combination of imperial power and the astute policies of Augustine and Aurelius prevented Donatism from permanently becoming the authentic voice of Christianity in North Africa. Its destruction may have contributed to the downfall of Christianity itself there. In North Africa there was no native "Coptic church" to withstand the onset of Islam in the seventh century.

BIBLIOGRAPHY

Berthier, A.; M. Martin; and F. Logeart. *Les vestiges du christianisme antique dans la Numidie centrale.* Algiers, 1942.

Brisson, J. P. *Autonomisme et christianisme dans l'Afrique romaine de Septime Sévère à l'invasion vandale.* Paris, 1958.

Brown, P. R. L. "Religious Coercion in the Later Roman Empire: The Case of North Africa." *History* 48 (1963):283–305.

Diesner, H. J. *Kirche und Stadt im spätrömischen Reich,* pp. 78–90. Berlin, 1963.

Frend, W. H. C. *The Donatist Church: A Movement of Protest in Roman North Africa.* Oxford, 1971.

Lepelley, C., ed. *Les Lettres d'Augustine découvertes par J. Divjak.* Etudes Augustiniennes. pp. 251–65. Paris, 1982.

Monceaux, P. *Histoire littéraire de l'Afrique chrétienne,* Vols. 4–6. Paris, 1912–1921.

Tengstrom, E. *Donatisten und Katholiken: Soziale, wirtschaftliche und politische Aspekte eines nordafrikanischen Kirchenstreit.* Göteborg, 1964.

Willis, C. G. *Saint Augustine and the Donatist Controversy.* London, 1950.

W. H. C. FREND

DONGOLA, often referred to as "Dongola al-ʿAjūz," the capital city of the medieval Nubian kingdom of MAKOURIA. It was situated on the east bank of the Nile about halfway between the Third and Fourth Cataracts. The name is said to be derived from a Nubian word for a hill or high place, perhaps reflecting the fact that the town occupied the top of a bluff overlooking the river.

Nothing is known either of Dongola or of Makouria in pre-Christian times, and the excavations thus far carried out at Dongola have not uncovered any remains of pre-Christian date. Makouria is first mentioned in the ecclesiastical histories of John of Ephesus and John of Biclarum dating from the sixth century, but neither of these sources names the capital of the kingdom. Dongola is first mentioned by name in medieval Arab histories dealing with the attempted Muslim conquests of Nubia in 641–642 and in 651–652. On each of these occasions the newly established rulers of Egypt attempted to extend their dominion over Nubia, and both military expeditions culminated in a battle before Dongola. On the first occasion, the invaders were successfully repulsed; on the second, the battle ended in a negotiated truce, the BAQṬ. Under its terms the Nubians were left free from foreign domination for over 600 years. As a result, Dongola and other Christian communities in Nubia grew and prospered.

The Fatimid envoy IBN SALĪM AL-ASWĀNĪ has left a remarkably vivid account of his visit to Makouria in the tenth century, but unfortunately he gives no specific information about the capital city. However, the information in ABŪ ṢĀLIḤ's *Churches and Monasteries of Egypt and Some Neighbouring Countries* is probably derived largely from Ibn Salīm. Of Dongola he writes: "It is a large city on the banks of the blessed Nile, and contains many churches and large houses and wide streets. The king's house is lofty, with several domes built of red brick, and resembles the buildings in Al-Irak. . . ." From another Arab source we learn that the royal palace was the only building of red brick. The other houses were of mud, reeds, or straw.

There are many references to Dongola in later medieval documents, dealing mainly with the Mamluk military campaigns in Nubia, but no descriptive information about the town is given. Archaeology shows, however, that the place had a long history, with many episodes of rebuilding. Even the destruction of the kingdom of Makouria in the fourteenth century did not spell the final downfall of its capital, for Dongola became the seat of a local chieftain of the Bedayria tribe. However, the French visitor Poncet described the houses as ill-built and the streets as half deserted and filled with sand when he passed by in 1698. Tribal chieftains, locally known as *meks,* continued to rule at Dongola until their power was finally extinguished by the Egyptian annexation of the Sudan in 1821. The new rulers established an administrative center at al-Urdī, about 100 km downstream from Dongola, and this place later came to be called Dongola al-Urdī or New Dongola, and finally just as Dongola. After its establishment, the old city was finally abandoned. Its ruins, which are still very conspicuous when seen from the river, are today usually designated as Old Dongola or Dongola al-ʿAjūz, to distinguish them from the newer administrative town.

The most conspicuous surviving building at Dongola al-ʿAjūz today is a two-story brick structure whose upper floor has been fitted out as a mosque. A stone tablet set into one of the walls proclaims that the mosque was dedicated in 1317. Prior to that time, and perhaps subsequently also, the building is believed to have been the royal palace. Archaeological excavations by a Polish expedition have also uncovered two impressive churches, one having sixteen columns of Aswan granite arranged in four rows, and the other having a cruciform plan like some of the churches in Syria and Armenia. Up to the present there has been little excavation in the townsite remains at Old Dongola, although the excavations are continuing.

The name of Dongola lives on in the tribal name of the Danaglah (sing., Dungulāwī) Nubians—the most southerly group among whom the Nubian language still survives.

BIBLIOGRAPHY

Adams, W. Y. *Nubia, Corridor to Africa,* pp. 464, 526–30, 583–84. Princeton, N.J., 1977.

Jakobielski, S. "Polish Excavations at Old Dongola, 1969." In *Kunst und Geschichte Nubiens in christlicher Zeit,* ed. E. Dinkler. Recklinghausen, 1970.

Michalowski, K. "Les fouilles polonaises à Dongola." In *Kunst und Geschichte Nubiens in christlicher Zeit,* ed. E. Dinkler. Recklinghausen, 1970.

Vantini, G. *Christianity in the Sudan,* pp. 63–64, 137–38, 171–90. Bologna, 1981.

WILLIAM Y. ADAMS

DOORS. *See* Woodwork, Coptic.

DORMITION OF THE VIRGIN MARY, FEAST OF THE. *See* Theotokos, Feast of the.

DOTAWO, a small, late medieval kingdom, probably the last surviving Christian polity in Nubia. The name in Nubian means "below Do," a place usually identified with the Ḍaww of medieval Arabic manuscripts and the JABAL ʿADDĀ of modern times. It is not certain whether "below" is to be read literally (since Jabal ʿAddā was on an elevated hilltop) or figuratively, as being under its administration, but at all events Dotawo was evidently a principality centered on the lower Nubian settlement of Jabal ʿAddā.

A certain King Siti of Dotawo is mentioned in two documents, dated in the year 1331, found at the monastery of Idfū. Apart from these, all known references to the kingdom are in documents in the Old Nubian language found in NUBIA itself, at Jabal ʿAddā and at QAṢR IBRĪM. These are presumed to have been the only two major settlements within the kingdom, the former being perhaps the royal capital and the latter the religious center. The surviving documents, which number more than twenty, are mostly of a legal or administrative nature; among other things they contain long lists of civil and ecclesiastical functionaries. The lack of differentiation between the two suggests that church and state may have been more or less merged, with the king of Dotawo at the head of both in this twilight era of Christianity in Nubia.

Many of the Dotawo documents are dated, and

they range from 1155 to 1484. The earlier documents fall within the period when Lower Nubia was still clearly subject to the kingdom of MAKOURIA and therefore raise a question as to the relationship of the two kingdoms. Since ABŪ ṢĀLIḤ THE ARMENIAN states that the "great king" of Nubia had thirteen lesser kings under him, the usual assumption is that the king of Dotawo was one of these. It is clear, however, that Dotawo outlived the parent kingdom and became fully independent after the disintegration of Makouria in the fifteenth century.

A second problem concerns the relationship of the kings of Dotawo to the eparchs of NOBATIA (called "Lords of the Mountain"), the viceroys of Lower Nubia appointed by the king of Makouria. Both kings and eparchs had their main seats of power at Jabal ʿAddā and Qaṣr Ibrīm. MONNERET DE VILLARD suggested that the dynasty of Dotawo was founded when the eparchs declared their independence of Makouria and established a hereditary rule in Lower Nubia. In the earlier Dotawo texts, however, the king and the eparch are named more than once as separate individuals. It has been suggested that the kings of Dotawo and other feudatories were responsible for local administration, while the primary responsibility of the eparch was for the conduct of relations with the Muslims, both in Nubia and in Egypt.

Altogether the texts have yielded the names of eight kings of Dotawo, the last of whom was named Joel. His name appears in a number of documents, of which the latest, not yet published, bears the date 1484. After that time nothing more is heard of Dotawo, and we remain ignorant as to the circumstances of its fate. It seems already to have disappeared before the Ottomans took possession of Nubia in the sixteenth century.

BIBLIOGRAPHY

Adams, W. Y. "The Twilight of Nubian Christianity." In *Nubia, récentes recherches*, ed. K. Michalowski, pp. 11–17. Warsaw, 1975.

______. *Nubia, Corridor to Africa*, pp. 531–36. Princeton, N.J., 1977.

Monneret de Villard, U. *Storia della Nubia cristiana*, pp. 140–42. Orientalia Christiana Analecta 118. Rome, 1938.

Plumley, J. M. "The Christian Period at Qasr Ibrim, Some Notes in the MSS Finds." In *Nubia, récentes recherches*, ed. K. Michalowski. Warsaw, 1975.

______. "New Light on the Kingdom of Dotawo." *Etudes nubiennes, colloque de Chantilly, 2–6 juillet 1975*, pp. 231–41. Cairo, 1978.

Vantini, G. *Christianity in the Sudan*, pp. 194–200. Bologna, 1981.

WILLIAM Y. ADAMS

DOXOLOGY, an acclamation in which glory (Greek, *dóxa*) is attributed to a particular person or persons. The earliest Christian doxologies are addressed to the Father or to the Son, but with the development of trinitarian theology, they began to express glory to the Father through the Son and Holy Spirit, or through the Son in the Holy Spirit. The subordinationist sense which Arians gave to formulas expressing glory to the Father through the Son (and Holy Spirit) led, by way of reaction, to the use of formulas expressing trinitarian consubstantiality. The fourth-century Syrian formula "Glory to the Father and the Son and the Holy Spirit" was eventually adopted in the church generally. The formula "Glory to the Father with the Son and Holy Spirit," which appeared in fourth-century Egypt, may have in its background the Coptic use of "with" as the copula "and."

The following doxologies may be noted in particular:

1. The Great Doxology, the doxological hymn beginning "Glory to God in the highest," which in Coptic Egypt is called "The Hymn of the Angels." In the traditions of both the Copts and the West Syrians it is attributed to Saint Athanasius, but the antiquity of this attribution is not certain. One recension of this doxological hymn is found in Book 8 of the *Apostolic Constitutions*, and so it was surely composed before the last quarter of the fourth century. In its Egyptian form, as in the form used in many other churches (but not in that of the Western mass), it was expanded with a second part, beginning typically with the Greek *kataxíoson*, Coptic *arikataxioin*, whose various verses, differing somewhat in various recensions, are drawn mainly from the Psalter. In established Coptic usage, part 1 (the original doxological hymn) is used in the morning office, while part 2 is used in compline (and was formerly used in vespers). There is some evidence suggesting that in the Coptic morning office as it was in the Middle Ages, part 2 was still joined to part 1, as it is in Byzantine *orthros* today.

2. The Minor Doxology, "Glory to the Father and the Son and the Holy Spirit, now and forever, and unto the ages of ages." In Coptic, Syrian, and Byzantine usages its two parts are often separated, the first part ("Glory to the Father . . .") being inserted before the penultimate verse or stanza, the second part ("Now and forever . . .") before the final one, in a series of verses or stanzas.

3. *Doxologia* (Arabic, *tamjīd*), a species of Coptic ecclesiastical hymnic composition, in stanzas, usually addressed to the Virgin, to the angels, to individual saints, or to a particular category of saints. The daily use of such doxologies, found in the liturgical collection called the *Psalmodia,* is prescribed at a certain point in the evening and morning offices of incense and in the sung offices, drawn from the *Psalmodia,* which follow the midnight office and the morning office as they are in the horologion. Special doxologies are prescribed for use on the greater feasts, on Lenten weekdays, on the Saturdays and Sundays of Lent, and in the month of Kiyahk. While certain stanzas of Coptic *Theotokia* exist in Greek, no Greek or Syriac equivalent of a stanza of a Coptic *doxologia* has been identified. From this, one may infer that the doxologies are original Coptic compositions. Comparison of various collections, ancient and modern, reveals a few instances in which the same stanza or series of stanzas appears in a doxology in one place but as a stanza of a *Theotokion* (see THEOTOKIA) in another. This permits one to conclude that a Coptic doxology in this sense is definable not by its literary form but by its hymnic content and by the place of its use in the structures of the Coptic offices.

BIBLIOGRAPHY

Capelle, B. "Le Texte du 'Gloria in excelsis.'" *Revue d'histoire écclesiastique* 44 (1949):439–57.

Leclercq, H. "Doxologies." In *Dictionnaire d'archéologie chrétienne et de liturgie,* Vol. 4, pt. 2, cols. 1525–36. Paris, 1921.

Quecke, H. *Untersuchungen zum koptischen Stundengebet,* pp. 52–56, 80, 174–90, 274–99. Louvain, 1970.

Yassa 'Abd al-Masih. "Doxologies in the Coptic Church." *Bulletin de la Société d'archéologie copte* 4 (1938):97–113; 5 (1939):175–91; 6 (1940):19–76; 8 (1942):31–61.

AELRED CODY, O.S.B.

DRAGUET, RENE (1896–1980), Belgian theologian. He was ordained a priest in 1919, became professor of fundamental theology at Louvain in 1927, and succeeded J.-B. Chabot as editor of the Corpus Scriptorum Christianorum Orientalium series in 1948. During his thirty-two-year tenure as editor, more than three hundred volumes of the series appeared. In 1960 he was made vice-president of *Le Muséon,* and in 1975, president. His academic specialty was early monasticism, and he produced works on the *Vita Antonii, Historia lausiaca,* and *Asceticon* of Abba Isajas.

BIBLIOGRAPHY

Garitte, G. "Le Professeur René Draguet, Président du Muséon." *Le Muséon* 94 (1981):3–4.

MARTIN KRAUSE

DRESCHER, JAMES ANTHONY BEDE (1902–1985), frequent contributor to the *Bulletin de la Société d'archéologie copte.* He was also the editor and translator of *Three Coptic Legends: Hilaria, Archellites, The Seven Sleepers* (Cairo, 1947) and *The Coptic (Sahidic) Version of Kingdoms I, II (Samuel I, II),* CSCO 313–314 (Louvain, 1970).

MIRRIT BOUTROS GHALI

DRIOTON, (CHANOINE) ETIENNE MARIE FELIX (1889–1961), French Egyptologist. He studied Egyptian and Coptic in the Ecole libre des Langues orientales at the Catholic Institute of Paris. Ultimately, he taught Egyptian philology and Coptic at the same institute. He produced a *Cours de grammaire égyptienne* (Paris, 1919).

Drioton worked with Charles Boreux at the Louvre in 1926, and in 1929 he undertook the epigraphic survey at the Medamud excavations of the Institut français d'Egypte directed by G. Foucart. In 1936 he succeeded Pierre Lacau as Director of the Egyptian Antiquities Service and lectured at the new Institute of Egyptology of the University of Cairo. After his return to France, he was appointed director of the Centre national de la Recherche scientifique and professor at the Collège de France.

His works in the field of Egyptology are numerous, but he contributed also to Coptic studies in many journals and reviews. Most titles are listed in *A Coptic Bibliography* (Kammerer, 1950, 1969). The last was published a year before his death, *Boiserie copte de style pharaonique* (Paris, 1960).

BIBLIOGRAPHY

Dawson, W. R., and E. P. Uphill. *Who Was Who in Egyptology, pp. 88–90.* London, 1972.

Kammerer, W., comp. *A Coptic Bibliography.* Ann Arbor, Mich., 1950; repr. New York, 1969.

AZIZ S. ATIYA

DUCHESNE, LOUIS (1843–1922), church historian. He was ordained to the priesthood in 1887 and completed his theological studies at Rome. His interest in the history of the early church was intensified by his travels in Greece and Asia Minor. He became a professor of ecclesiastical history at the Institut catholique in Paris in 1885, though he was forced to resign from that position for some ten years on account of his outspoken lectures on the history of doctrine, which were contrary to the accepted views of the Catholic hierarchy. In 1895 he was nominated director of the French School at Rome, a position he held until his death. He was elected a member of the French Academy in 1910. His major works concentrate on early church history. *L'Histoire ancienne de l'eglise chrétienne* (3 vols., Paris, 1905–1910; translated as *Early History of the Christian Church,* New York, 1909–1924) is a classic, but was put on the Index for his critical views. He supplemented it with *L'Eglise du VIe siècle,* published posthumously under the editorship of H. Quentin (Paris, 1926). Other important works include *Liber Pontificalis* (2 vols., Paris, 1886–1891), *Origines du culte chrétien* (Paris, 1920; translated by M. L. McClure, London, 1923), and *Fastes épiscopaux de l'ancienne Gaule* (3 vols., Paris, 1894–1915).

BIBLIOGRAPHY

Cabrol, F. "Mgr. Louis Duchesne: Son oeuvre historique." *Journal of Theological Studies* 24 (1922–1923):253–82.

Dupont, E. *Mgr. Duchesne chez lui en Bretagne 1843–1922.* Rennes, 1923.

Habloville, C. d'. *Grandes Figures de l'eglise contemporaine.* Paris, 1925.

A. S. ATIYA

DULAURIER, JEAN PAUL LOUIS FRANÇOIS EDOUARD LEUGE (1807–1881), French Orientalist. He was born in Toulouse and studied under Silvestre de Sacy. He published descriptions of the stelae in the Toulouse Museum and various Coptic texts (1833–1835). He visited London in 1838 and copied the manuscript *Pistis Sophia,* with a view to complete publication of the text, but he issued only a general account of it in 1847. He also published an examination of the doctrines of J.-F. Champollion (1847). He was elected to the Académie des Inscriptions et Belles-Lettres (1864).

BIBLIOGRAPHY

d'Amat, P. In *Dictionnaire de biographie française 12,* pp. 71–72.

M. L. BIERBRIER

DUMBARTON OAKS. *See* Museums, Coptic Collections in.

DUMYĀṬ, city in the northeastern part of the Nile Delta just west of Lake al-Manzalah. Dumyāṭ was the seat of a bishop at least as early as 431 when Bishop Herakleides of Tamiathis/Dumyāṭ took part in the First Council of EPHESUS (Munier, 1943, p. 17). In 459 Bishop Elpidios of Tamiathis signed the judgment against Eutychius (Munier, 1943, p. 23), and in 553 Bishop Bassos represented the city at the Second Council of CONSTANTINOPLE (Le Quien, 1958, Vol. 2, p. 589).

The Coptic community in the city of Dumyāṭ seems to have remained intact during the Arabic conquest, for Bishop Piamot of Dumyāṭ provided great support for the Alexandrian patriarchate in the reign of ISAAC (686–689). Barely forty years later, however, the city was declared heretical. In the patriarchate of ALEXANDER II (705–730), Bishop John of Ṣā reunited the heretical churches of Dumyāṭ, Banā, Abūṣīr, Samannūd, and Rashīd with the main Coptic church. Under authorization from the Islamic authorities, John had informed the Christian inhabitants of these cities that they would have to pay a double poll tax if they remained separate from the main body of the church. The threat was certainly a motivating factor in their reunion.

There is no evidence to indicate that the Coptic inhabitants of Dumyāṭ suffered in the various attempts of the Byzantines to capture the city in the first half of the eighth century. But in the renewed attacks of the Greeks in the ninth century Copts as well as Muslims were subdued and captured. Then, in the persecutions of al-ḤĀKIM around 1010, the Church of the Virgin Mary in Dumyāṭ, generally considered one of the most beautiful churches in the world, was destroyed and a mosque was built on the site. The Crusaders also inflicted heavy damage on the city in the eleventh through thirteenth centuries, but shortly after their departure in 1221, Bishop Christodoulos of Dumyāṭ regathered the members of his church and led them to prosperity.

In 1249, the Crusader Louis IX, king of France, captured and destroyed Dumyāṭ. The new Dumyāṭ was later rebuilt to the south of its former location, and the city continued to be the seat of a bishop. Around 1300 Bishop Mark administered in the diocese of Ashmūn and Dumyāṭ. He was present at the selection of the patriarch JOHN VII (Muyser, 1944, p. 155). From at least 1320 until 1330 the metropolitan Gregory served as bishop of Dumyāṭ (Munier, pp. 38–39).

Dumyāṭ was known in ancient times as an important center for the production of quality textiles and the copying of manuscripts. Mīkhā'īl (end of the eleventh to the beginning of the twelfth century), one of the most famous bishops of the city, wrote and copied a number of manuscripts himself. Manuscripts were still being copied in Dumyāṭ as late as 1769 (Graf, 1918, p. 139).

Around 1450 al-MAQRĪZĪ reported that there were in Dumyāṭ churches of Saint George, Saint John the Baptist, the Virgin Mary, and Saint Michael. In the seventeenth century, J. M. Vansleb wrote that there were about two hundred Greek Orthodox families in Dumyāṭ, but only about eight Coptic families. He said that the Turks had confiscated the Copts' church because the Copts had not paid the taxes (1678, p. 68).

BIBLIOGRAPHY

Amélineau, E. *La Géographie de l'Egypte à l'époque copte,* pp. 116–17. Paris, 1893.

Graf, G. "Katalog christlich-arabischer Handschriften in Jerusalem." *Oriens Christianus,* n.s., 7–8 (1918):133–46.

Le Quien, M. *Oriens Christianus,* 3 vols. Graz, 1958. Reprint of the Paris edition, 1740.

Munier, H. *Recueil des listes épiscopales de l'église copte.* Cairo, 1943.

Muyser, J. "Contribution à l'étude des listes épiscopales de l'église copte." *Bulletin de la Société d'archéologie copte* 10 (1944):115–76.

Porcher, E., ed. *Vie d'Isaac, patriarche d'Alexandrie de 686 à 689.* PO 11, pt. 3. Paris, 1915.

Timm, S. *Christliche Stätten in Ägypten,* pp. 81–82. Wiesbaden, 1979.

______. *Das christlich-koptische Ägypten in arabischer Zeit,* pt, 2, pp. 530–38. Wiesbaden, 1984.

Vansleb, J. M. *The Present State of Egypt.* London, 1678.

RANDALL STEWART

DURR AL-THAMĪN, AL- (the Pearl of Great Value), the title of two works. The first is ascribed to MURQUS IBN QANBAR, and the second to SAWĪRUS IBN AL-MUQAFFA'.

G. Graf (1947, pp. 331–32) says that it is likely that a commentary with this name on the Pentateuch (covering the first three books) is the work of Murqus ibn Qanbar. It exists in parts in a number of manuscripts including an American Bible Society edition. The work includes the biblical texts with their explanations for Genesis divided into lessons for evening services for all working days of the forty days of Lent (that is, without Saturdays and Sundays). The Exodus commentary has a few lessons of the total nineteen for holy days, while the Leviticus commentary, with thirteen lessons, relates none to holy days. The whole is largely instruction on the origin, necessity, and form of the confession of sins and their penance.

Sāwīrus ibn al-Muqaffa' is suggested as the probable author of the next ordered series of dogmatic articles subtitled "Exposition of Faith in Religion." Graf (1947, pp. 313–15) says that by its content it sets forth a Monophysite theology and Christology based on texts from the Bible and patristic literature. Articles of faith are given a basis and explained in the fifteen chapters; the subject matter is the trinitarian dogma, the hypostatic union in Christ during his life from His birth to His ascension, and the Holy Spirit. Graf goes on to say that the sources are Coptic texts, some not trustworthy, collected by the author for his own purposes and translated into Arabic. ATHANASIUS I (326–373) and CYRIL I of Alexandria (412–444) appear frequently, and the latest authority referred to is the patriarch BENJAMIN (622–661).

VINCENT FREDERICK

DURUNKAH, city in middle Egypt located on the left bank of the Nile about 5 miles (8 km) south of Asyūṭ.

The area south of Asyūṭ in which Durunkah is situated has long been a center of Christianity. However, the attestations of Christianity in Durunkah itself do not begin until the medieval era. *The Churches and Monasteries of Egypt* lists a number of churches and monasteries found in the region. Though this account does not give specific locations, it is reasonable to assume that some of the sites were in or near Durunkah. The fifteenth-century historian al-MAQRĪZĪ called the area around Durunkah one of the most Christian districts of Upper Egypt and he said that the Christians living there were schooled in their religion and used Coptic as their spoken language. He reported further that there were many monasteries in the mountainous region just south of the city, though most of these were in ruins. Among those still standing in his day were Dayr Abū Jirj, Dayr Arḍ al-Ḥājiz, Dayr Mīkā'īl, Dayr Karfūnah (D. AL-MUṬṬIN), Dayr Bū Baghām, and Dayr Bū Sawīrus. He also said there was a church in Durunkah of the three youths cast into the fiery furnace. The church is still standing.

Colophons in Coptic and Arabic manuscripts acquaint us with two fourteenth-century scribes from Durunkah: Shenute (John Rylands Library, Manchester, Coptic manuscript 423) and Peter, who calls himself a calligrapher, monk, and presbyter (Crum, 1909, no. 423). It is likely that there was a school for scribes in the city.

Apparently there was considerable persecution of Christians in Durunkah by the Muslim civil administration. On 2 Bashans, the SYNAXARION commemorates Philotheos from Durunkah who was martyred in 1396 because of his Christian faith.

From the time of Philotheos until the sixteenth century attestations of Christianity in Durunkah are wanting. Then in a manuscript from DAYR ANBĀ MAQĀR that describes the renovation of the church and the dedication of the keep in 1517, we read that Bishop Anbā Yu'annis from Durunkah attended the proceedings (Leroy, 1971, p. 228).

From the end of the seventeenth century many European travelers journeyed to Durunkah and gave descriptions of the city's Christian buildings. In the last third of the seventeenth century J. M. Vansleb described the church of the three youths cast into the fire and a "Monastery of the Blessed Virgin" located on a hill behind the city (1678, p. 219). This monastery was probably Dayr al-'Adhrā', the ruins of which are still to be seen next to the recently constructed Church of the Virgin Mary in the mountainous region west of Durunkah (Meinardus, 1965, p. 284). Vansleb also saw the Monastery of the Virgin, which along with its church was cut in the rock, and he visited the ruins of DAYR ANBĀ SĀWĪRUS (1678, p. 228).

A little more than a century later S. CLARKE toured the area around Durunkah and described the Church of the Archangel (Michael). The church that exists today with its altars for Anbā Pshoi and the archangel Michael was built in the nineteenth century, but it rests on much older foundations. Clarke also gave a description of the church of the Monastery of the Virgin Mary located in the mountainous region west of Durunkah. This church, as opposed to the Church of the Archangel, was very old and was built on the foundations of an even older church (Clarke, 1912, pp. 175–76). In the years since Clarke's visit, the appearance of this area has changed considerably. Next to the church in the rock, the bishop of Asyūṭ has built himself a residence and many new buildings have been constructed for the people who come to the area for the annual festival (7–22 August) in commemoration of the visit of the Holy Family to Asyūṭ on their FLIGHT INTO EGYPT (Meinardus, 1965, p. 285).

BIBLIOGRAPHY

Clarke, S. *Christian Antiquities in the Nile Valley.* Oxford, 1912.

Crum, W. E. *Catalogue of the Coptic Manuscripts in the Collection of the John Rylands Library, Manchester.* Manchester, 1909.

Leroy, J. "Complément à l'histoire des couvents du Ouadi Natroun d'Evelyn White." *Bulletin de l'Institut français d'Archéologie orientale* 70 (1971):225–33.

Meinardus, O. F. A. *Christian Egypt, Ancient and Modern.* Cairo, 1965.

Timm, S. *Das christlich-koptische Ägypten in arabischer Zeit,* pt. 2, pp. 892–99. Wiesbaden, 1984.

Vansleb, J. M. *Nouvelle relation en forme de journal d'un voyage fait en Egypte en 1672 et 1673.* Paris, 1677. Translated as *The Present State of Egypt.* London, 1678.

RANDALL STEWART

DŪSH. In the extreme south of the oasis of Khargah, at Dūsh, the ancient Kysis, the papyrological dossier of the gravediggers reveals the existence in the second half of the third century (between 224 and 306) of one of the most ancient Christian communities of Egypt. This community, headed by the priest Apollo, was to receive the mummy of a certain Palitice, sent there for burial.

The Christian traces at Dūsh are insignificant. At the beginning of the nineteenth century, Cailliaud of Nantes could still see a church with some texts, but it has not been possible to identify this monument until now. The excavations of the Institut français d'Archéologie orientale in the hypostyle hall of the temple have brought to light a Christian imprecation that calls down the punishment of Christ on anyone who blasphemes against him. A deeply cut cross has been substituted for the uraeus that overhung the entrance gate of the sanctuary. The cemeteries excavated by the institute are pagan, and to date it is not known where the Christian cemetery was. The names on the Greek and Coptic ostraca from west of Dūsh testify to the presence of numerous Christians among the inhabitants and, more particularly, among the soldiers stationed at or in transit through Kysis in the fourth and at the beginning of the fifth century.

BIBLIOGRAPHY

Naldini, M. *Il Cristianesimo in Egitto,* no. 21, 131–135. Florence, 1968. Latest edition of the letter to the priest Apollo.

Sauneron, S., et al. "Douch, Rapports Préliminaires 1976." *Bulletin de l'Institut français d'Archéologie orientale* 78 (1978):1–33.

Wagner, G. "Les ostraca grecs de Doush." In *Proceedings of the XVI International Congress of Papyrology*. Chico, Calif., 1981.

Wagner, G., et al. "Douch, Rapports Préliminaires 1979." *Bulletin de l'Institut français d'Archéologie orientale* 80 (1980):287–345.

GUY WAGNER

DUWAYR, AL-, village south of ASYŪṬ and site of excavations in 1914 carried out by Claudius Labib that brought to light a necropolis of the Ptolemaic and Byzantine period. Several STELAE were found, two of which mention a list similar to those of Saqqara or Bāwīṭ, and name the famous triad of these monasteries: Apollo, Anub, and Phib (see Munier, 1922, pp. 49–59).

In a nearby valley two Greek inscriptions have been found on the walls of a cave and a tomb, which appear to reveal monastic occupation (Aḥmad Kamāl, 1902, pp. 32–35, and Lefebvre, 1907, p. 45, nos. 235, 236).

BIBLIOGRAPHY

Aḥmad Kamāl. "Exploration dans la province de Siūt." *Annales du Service des antiquites de l'Egypte* 3 (1902):32–35.

Lefebvre, G. *Recueil des inscriptions grecques chrétiennes d'Egypte*. Cairo, 1907.

Munier, H. "Les résultats épigraphiques des fouilles d'al-Qariah bil Dueir." *Annales du Service des antiquités de l'Egypte* 22 (1922):49–59.

RENÉ-GEORGES COQUIN
MAURICE MARTIN, S.J.

DYEING. *See* Textiles, Coptic: Manufacturing Techniques.

E

EAGLE. *See* Symbols in Coptic Art.

EASTER SUNDAY. *See* Feasts, Major.

EBIONITES, Judaizing Christians who developed into a separate sect by the last quarter of the second century and had some influence on the early history of the church in Egypt.

The term "Ebion" is probably derived from the Hebrew *ebyon* (the poor). It is an attribute of those who serve the Lord, in contrast with him who "would not make God his refuge but trusted in the abundance of his riches" (Psalm 52:7). The Covenanters of the Dead Sea regarded themselves as the "Congregation of the Poor" who would inherit the earth (*Commentary on Psalm 37* in Vermes, 1975, pp. 243–44). Among the Essenes—who, if not identical with the Covenanters, were closely allied to them and had settled near Alexandria (Eusebius *Historia ecclesiastica* 2.18)—equality in wealth and community of property were strictly adhered to. The description of Josephus (*Jewish War* II.8.3), "It is impossible to find anyone amongst them exceeding others in possessions . . . ," is that of an ideal that was to pass into Egyptian monasticism.

Jesus' ideal as recorded in the Gospels was close to that of the Essenes and Covenanters so far as it concerned possessions. "Take no thought for the morrow," "Blessed are the poor" (Luke 6:20), and the dispatch of the Twelve to teach the Kingdom and heal, "taking nothing for their journey, no staff, nor bag, nor bread, nor money" (Luke 9:3) are entirely in harmony with those who equated the Congregation of Israel with "the Poor." The ideal of poverty, however, was one of those that did not survive the Pauline revolution. Paul's hearers were not to be found among the rural poor but were recruited largely from the literate congregations of the Hellenistic synagogues in the larger towns of western and southern Asia Minor and Greece. It may well be that proponents of poverty in the sixth and seventh decades of the first century were to be found among Paul's opponents, the "Judaizers." That the two began to be equated is evident from a statement made by Ignatius of Antioch about 109 in his letter to the Philadelphians. Criticizing the Judaizers, he asserts, "such a man is poor of understanding as he is by name an Ebionite" (*Ad Philadelphenses* 6).

With the triumph of Paul's interpretation of the Gospel, the Ebionites gradually became reduced to the level of a sect. From the writings of Irenaeus, Tertullian, and Hippolytus, it would seem that by the end of the second century, they could be identified as those who insisted on strict Jewish ritual, including the observance of the Sabbath and circumcision for their members. They accepted one Gospel only, that of Matthew, and rejected the Pauline Epistles. They believed that Jesus was born a man by ordinary birth, but became exalted to a status greater than Moses and higher than the prophets through his outstanding virtues, because God's angel dwelt in him. They practiced strict asceticism in their lives. In the fourth century Epiphanius (*Panarion* XXX) describes the Ebionites as having their own Gospel, which seems to have been identical to that described by Origen (*Homiliae in Lucam* 1.1) as the "Gospel of the Twelve Apostles."

The Ebionites' link with Egypt apart from the Alexandrian Essenes continued but is not easy to follow. One may discern it through the numerous fragments of Matthew's Gospel found at Oxyrhynchus and the association of those with fragments of the *Gospel of Thomas* (see *Oxyrhynchus Papyri* 1 and 654). The latter's praise of abstinence, poverty, and the solitary life (cf. *Logia* 49, 69, 75) is in line with Ebionite teaching. If one accepts the Gospel of Thomas as one of the influences that contributed to Egyptian monasticism, then the Ebionites must be included among the movements that lay behind this feature of the Coptic church.

The monastic ancestry of the Coptic church extended back through Thomas to the Essenes and the ascetic movements within Judaism at the time of Jesus, and included the Ebionites among its formative influences.

BIBLIOGRAPHY

Drijvers, H. J. W. "Edessa und das jüdische Christentum." *Vigiliae Christianae* 24 (1970):4–33.

Schmidtke, A. "Zum Hebräerevangelium." *Zeitschrift für die neutestamentliche Wissenschaft und die Kunde der älteren Kirche* 35 (1936):24–44.

Schoeps, H. J. *Jewish Christianity: Factional Disputes in the Early Church,* trans. D. R. A. Hare. Philadelphia, 1969.

Vermes, G., ed. *The Dead Sea Scrolls in English,* 2nd ed. Harmondsworth, 1975.

Waitz, H. "Neue Untersuchungen über die sogenannten jüdenchristlichen Evangelien." *Zeitschrift für die neutestamentliche Wissenschaft und die Kunde der älteren Kirche* 36 (1937):60–81.

W. H. C. FREND

EÇÇAGĒ. The title and office of the *eçç̣agē* (high church dignitary) have been of national importance in Ethiopia for several centuries. Insofar as the ABUN was alien to the language and culture of the country, it was necessary for an Ethiopian dignitary to be appointed as chief administrator of the church. The Nebura'ed of Axum had filled the office until the thirteenth century, and the Aqqābē Sa'at of Hayq monastery in the fourteenth and fifteenth, followed by the *eçç̣agē* in the subsequent centuries.

The philological origin of the title *eçç̣agē* is obscure, and a few inconclusive opinions have been expressed about it. It was in any case used as the title of the abbot of Dabra Libānos, a famous monastery in Shewa at least since the sixteenth century. According to some church traditions, Saint Takla Hāymānot (1215–1313) was said to have been the first to bear the title; but the royal chronicles do not attest to this. The abbots of Dabra Libānos in the fourteenth and fifteenth centuries were referred to by such terms as *aba menēt* (head of the monastery), *abbā* (father), and *mamher* (master).

The dignitary seems to have gained special importance first through the crucial role of *eçç̣agē* Abraham during the reign of Emperor Susenyos in the late sixteenth and early seventeenth centuries. The *eçç̣agē* resided near the imperial court wherever it might be, and his residence was a sanctuary where criminal and political fugitives alike could take temporary refuge until he brought them to justice or permitted their escape to safety out of the region. The *eçç̣agē* was the highest church dignitary and as such he presided over church councils together with the sovereign and the *abun.* He also participated in other councils that dealt with matters of state.

He acted, besides, as the liaison officer between the imperial court and the clergy.

In the spiritual sphere, the *eçç̣agē's* authority did not exceed that of a priest. He was a monk chosen from the order of Dabra Libānos regardless of his origin, but perhaps on grounds of his learning, integrity, and wisdom. He could be dismissed from office at any time by order of the sovereign or at the demand of the society of monks in Dabra Libānos. He could by no means substitute for the *abun* as the spiritual head of the church, though traditions allege that Saint Takla Hāymānot had combined both functions. Abuna Sāwiros and Abun Bāslyos have certainly done so in the twentieth century.

BIBLIOGRAPHY

Cerulli, E. "Gli abbati di Dabra Libanos, capi del monachismo etiopico, secondo la 'lista rimata' (sec. XIV–VIII)." *Orientalia* n.s., 12 (1943):226–53; 13 (1944):137–82.

______. "Gli abbati di Dabra Libanos, capi del monachismo etiopico, secondo le liste recenti (sec. XVIII–XX)." *Orientalia* n.s., 14 (1945): 143–71.

Dastā Takla Wald. *'Addis Yāmāreññā Mazgaba Qālāt. Bakāhnātennā Bahagara Sab Qwānqwā Taṣāfa,* p. 916. Addis Ababa, 1962.

Guèbrè Sellasié. *Chronique du règne de Ménélik II, roi des rois d'Ethiopie,* ed. M. de Coppet, Vol. 1, pp. 279–82. Paris, 1930–1931.

Guidi, I. *Vocabolario amarico-italiano,* p. 511. Rome, 1901. Repr., 1953. Supplement, p. 148. Rome, 1940.

Heruy Walda Śellāsē. *Wāzēmā. Bamāgeśtu Ya'ityoṗeyān Nagaśtāt Yatārik Ba'āl lamākbar,* pp. 101–120. Addis Ababa, 1921.

Kidāna Wald Keflē. *Maṣḥafa Sawāsew Wagess*

Wamazgaba Qālāt Ḥaddis. Nebābu Bage'ez Feččew Bāmāreññā, p. 457. Addis Ababa, 1948.

Māhtama Śellāsē Walda Masqal. *Zekra Nagar*. Addis Ababa, 1942; 2nd ed., Addis Ababa, 1962.

BAIRU TAFLA

ECCLESIASTES. *See* Old Testament, Coptic Translations of the.

ECHOS. *See* Music, Coptic: Description; Music, Coptic: History.

ECTHESIS, "statement of the faith," a formula issued by Emperor Heraclius in 638 as a substitute for "energies" (the Greek *energiai*), which had been prohibited from use in relation to the person of Jesus. According to this formula, the two natures, human and divine, are united in the Monothelete doctrine formerly accepted by Sergius, patriarch of Constantinople, and Honorius, pope of Rome, as well as the Councils of Constantinople held in 638 and 639. The immediate successors of Honorius, Severianus (638–640) and John IV (640–642), on the contrary affirmed the rejection pronounced by Heraclius.

AZIZ S. ATIYA

EDUCATION, COPTIC. The origins of Coptic education may be traced to the period of the introduction of Christianity in the second half of the first century, when ancient educational traditions in the temples became colored with the doctrines and traditions of the new religion. According to Eusebius of Caesarea in his *Historia Ecclesiastica*, written in the fourth century, Christian dignitaries established Christian schools wherever they settled in their hierarchical dioceses. Most luminous of these educational bodies in the earliest centuries was the CATECHETICAL SCHOOL OF ALEXANDRIA. Its leaders, such as PANTAENUS, CLEMENT OF ALEXANDRIA, ORIGEN, and DIDYMUS THE BLIND, proved to be the great Christian mentors, not only of Egypt but also of the rest of the Christian world. It was here that the religious and moral culture of the Copts flourished and left its indelible influence on all future generations.

The Catechetical School began to dwindle from the fourth century, followed by the rise of Coptic MONOPHYSITISM as against Chalcedonian diophysitism from the year 451 and ending up with a wave of Byzantine persecutions in Egypt. However, Coptic educational policies were persistently retained in the native churches, and more especially in monastic institutions. In fact, the heritage of the Catechetical School was preserved or perhaps concentrated in subsequent centuries at the monastery of Saint Macarius (DAYR ANBĀ MAQĀR) in the desert of Wādī al-Naṭrūn. It was here that the Alexandrian religious traditions found a permanent home and where they flourished. In the Nile Valley, however, the educational tradition persisted near the churches in more modest institutions, the equivalent of the medieval scriptoria or writing places. These new establishments were founded by both Copts and Muslims.

While the Muslims concentrated their procedures on the Qur'ān under the leadership of a Muslim *shaykh*, generally a blind scholar who had memorized the holy book, the Coptic *kuttāb*, or scriptorium, was principally run by the church cantor, or *'arīf*, who taught the children the church liturgies while training them in the art of penmanship. Some cantors were blind, in which case the art of writing and the training in mathematics and accounting was confided to another person hired by the community of Coptic families. Coptic education in the *kuttāb* revolved primarily around religious instruction beginning with readings from the Bible, particularly the Psalms, and church hymnals. However, it was in the secular subjects such as arithmetic and accounting that the Coptic scribes later excelled; they virtually monopolized all the related activities in the Egyptian state, especially in the fields of finance and agriculture. All training in the *kuttāb* was conducted on metal plates or slate tablets owing to lack of paper material.

Parallel to the instruction practiced in the *kuttāb*, technical training in various professions played a prominent part in the educational process. Coptic artisans excelled in all manner of trades, notably those associated with the building and adornment of their churches. Exquisite woodwork, ivory inlay, and all manner of artistic accomplishments were executed by skilled laborers whose training as children must have taken place over the years in the workshops of master artisans. This kind of training extended to the fields of agriculture and commerce, where the children usually followed their parents in hereditary vocations throughout the Middle Ages.

The history of modern and contemporary education in Egypt extends from the termination of the French Expedition in 1801 to the outbreak of the revolution of July 1952. This century and a half witnessed a multitude of radical changes in education, and may be roughly divided into three periods.

The first period covers the years from the departure of the French in 1801 to the end of the reign of khedive Sa'īd, son of Muḥammad 'Alī, in 1863 (see MUḤAMMAD 'ALI DYNASTY). The year before had seen the death of the 110th patriarch, CYRIL IV, who was recognized as the father of Coptic church reform, especially in the field of education. Though the *kuttāb* or scriptorium system persisted in Cairo and the provinces, the educational reforms that took place during this period at the hands of Cyril IV were significant. It would, however, be wrong to minimize the contributions of the scriptoria, which produced some eminent personalities who occupied high ranks in the government administration. In fact, Cyril IV himself was the product of those scriptoria, as was the *hegumenos* PHILŪTHĀWUS IBRĀHĪM who first headed the CLERICAL COLLEGE at its foundation in 1893.

The fee for attending a *kuttāb* varied from five to ten piasters per month, although the teacher usually received the more substantial reward of a gold sovereign at the completion of a boy's education. There was, of course, no limit to age for acceptance in a *kuttāb*. On the subject of Arabic grammar, the Coptic *kuttāb* supplemented its activities by nominating an Islamic *shaykh* who taught children in Coptic homes for a fee. Among the notable Coptic *kuttāb*s in Cairo were those of Ḥārit al-Saqqāyīn, Ḥārit al-Naṣārā in the Azbakiyyah district, and others in Old Cairo and al-Ghuriyyah as well as in the provinces.

Around the middle of the nineteenth century, during the reign of Viceroy Sa'id, the foreign missionary schools began to emerge with an impact on the antiquated *kuttāb* system. Asyūṭ College took the lead of these institutions under the leadership of American and British missionaries. Owing, however, to Protestant doctrinal differences taught in these schools, the students began to have second thoughts about participation in their religious activities. A solution to this situation was soon found in the educational reforms carried out by Cyril IV.

In 1853, Cyril IV founded in Azbakiyyah the patriarchal primary school for boys, which was inaugurated in 1855 and later supplemented by a secondary section. Another primary school was established in Ḥārit al-Saqqāyīn and two girls' primary schools were started in both the Azbakiyyah district and Ḥārit al-Saqqāyīn. The pope made sure to introduce progressive programs and foreign languages such as English, French, Italian, and Turkish, in addition to Arabic and Coptic as major disciplines. He appointed teachers, both foreign and native, to take charge of teaching all subjects. The disappointed heads of the old *kuttāb*s were conciliated by the offer of a pension.

The pope himself took to attending some of these classes and participated in their discussions. As to girls, whose education in schools seemed a novelty at the time, he instructed the heads of girls' schools to visit Coptic homes and encourage families to enroll their daughters in their institutions. He started a boarding arrangement to accommodate students from the country. In the provinces, he established a similar school at al-Manṣūrah along the same pattern of the one he had founded at Būsh during his primacy at Saint Antony's monastery (DAYR ANBĀ ANṬŪNIYŪS). All his schools were open to Muslims as well as Copts, without distinction. Ultimately, on graduation, students were subjected to the state public examinations, which gave them the right to pursue their higher education in the high schools preparatory to the university.

On the cultural level outside of education, the great patriarch established the first Coptic printing press and secured permission to have Coptic youths receive training in the art of printing at the old government Būlāq printing press. He started with the publication of a Coptic grammar, and soon a flow of religious publications poured out of this press. He founded numerous libraries, which helped many authors in the publication of their works.

Khedive Sa'īd (1854–1863) was impressed by the patriarch's achievement and granted Cyril IV land in the al-Wādī area of the Sharqiyyah province to help him cover the expenses incurred in his schools. The pope offered free education and even paid students, both Coptic and Muslim, a stipend to help them with their living expenses. And for the first time in the history of modern Egypt, a great deal of attention was accorded to female education.

The second period dates from the accession of the khedive Ismā'īl, in 1863, and extends to the era of the establishment of the new constitution of independent Egypt in 1924.

The most significant feature of this second phase was the open discussion of the educational system in the parliamentary meetings of August 1866. Among the members who conducted the discussions was Mīkhā'īl Athanāsius, a Copt. The problem of religious education was amicably settled on a nonsectarian basis, allowing the Muslims to study the Qur'ān and the Copts the Bible under the guidance of a Coptic priest. In the end, special legislation was issued on 7 November 1867 under the minister of education, 'Ali (Pasha) Mubārak, in forty articles organizing education under three categories: primary, secondary, and higher. Candidates from Cyril IV's Coptic schools were permitted to take public examinations on a par with government school students.

Owing, however, to the British Occupation of 1882, the number of government schools became limited; they were supplemented by the emergence of national schools where the Copts displayed tremendous efforts, notably in regard to technical education both for boys and for girls. Pope CYRIL V sponsored the foundation of a technical college at Būlāq in 1903, while the Tawfīq Coptic Society founded another in the Fajjālah district in 1904. Schools for girls were opened by al-Jamʿiyyah al-Khayriyyah al-Kubrā at Azbakiyyah and the Tawfīq Society at Ẓāhir (see BENEVOLENT SOCIETIES, COPTIC). Of more permanent stature was the establishment of a secondary girls' college in 1911 in ʿAbbasiyyah by the same Tawfīq Coptic Society. Other schools followed in Alexandria, Ṭanṭā, and the Fayyūm, as well as in other cities in the valley.

The third period deals with more recent times. Apart from the continuous progress in the realm of general education, perhaps the main feature in the development of Coptic education was the fostering of the CLERICAL COLLEGE for preparing a cultured generation of priesthood. Conceived originally by Pope Cyril V in 1874, this college was developed into an institution of true religious scholarship in 1893. Its organization was entrusted to Phīlūthāwus Ibrāhīm, to Yūsuf (Bey) Manqariyūs, and to archdeacon ḤABĪB JIRJIS, who assumed its headship in 1918 and improved its stature of enrollment from primary graduates to secondary. He further adopted many progressive programs from similar institutions in Europe and founded in 1931 the Church of Our Lady at the College, where he conducted practical liturgical training. In 1945, he inaugurated special night classes for the benefit of university students and graduates who intended to take holy orders.

A parallel feature in the spread of religious education among the Coptic youth in schools was inaugurated by the Holy Synod as early as 1898. This movement was later known as the Sunday School Movement. In fact, its role expanded and its labors multiplied among Coptic children, and it became one of the landmarks of the Coptic church.

To this movement must be added the establishment of the Coptic Education Society in Giza and of the Diaconate of the Rīf (Rural Areas) in the 1950s by Bishop SAMUEL. The diaconate consisted mainly of volunteers in many segregated villages, where Coptic families had lived in complete oblivion of their church for generations and oftentimes remained unbaptized. Under the leadership of Bishop Samuel, these volunteers broke the solitude of such families and extended to them the religious education that they needed as active members of the Coptic church.

Finally, and on a secular level, mention must be made of the establishment of the Coptic College for Girls in Cairo in 1932. It provided an alternative to the numerous Catholic and Protestant foreign mission schools in the country.

After 1932, the Ministry of Education established public schools throughout Egypt. These were, of course, open to the population in general. On 21 January 1954 the Higher Institute of Coptic Studies was founded with the approval of the Community Council. Although nondenominational in enrollment, it has been for the most part sponsored and supported by the Coptic church.

BIBLIOGRAPHY

Asʿad, Maurice M. *Education in the Coptic Orthodox Church: Strategies for the Future.* New York, 1970.

Georgy Sobhy. "Education in Egypt During the Christian Period and Amongst the Copts." *Bulletin de la Société d'archéologie copte* 9 (1943):103–22.

Heyworth Dunne, J. *Introduction to the History of Education in Modern Egypt.* London, 1939; 2nd ed., 1968.

Makary al-Suryani. "Ancient and Contemporary Christian Education in the Coptic Church of Egypt." Master's thesis, Princeton Theological Seminary, 1955.

Radwan, A. A. *Old and New Forces in Egyptian Education.* New York, 1949.

Sulayman Nasim. *Tārikh al-Tarbiyyah al-Qibṭiyyah.* Cairo, 1963.

———. *Al-Aqbāṭ wal-Taʿlīm fī Miṣr al-Ḥadīthah.* Cairo, 1984.

Sulayman Nasim and Bishop Bīman. *Fī al-Tarbiyyah al-Masīḥīyyah.* Cairo, 1980.

SULAYMĀN NĀSĪM

EGERTON GOSPEL, the most important of the papyrus fragments of apocryphal gospels because of its early date, its extent, and the character of the text; acquired by the British Library in 1934. It consists of two leaves of a papyrus codex together with a small fragment. Both leaves are incomplete, but in many lines the number of missing letters is small enough for the text to be restored with confidence. It is written in a literary hand but with marked documentary features; the judgment of the original editors that it is not later than about A.D. 150 has found general acceptance. Its place of origin is unknown.

The work in question is neither a collection of logia nor a harmony of the canonical Gospels; the differences are quite as striking as the resemblances. It appears to have been a straightforward account of the life and teaching of Jesus with no theological reconsiderations and no relation to any known apocryphal gospel. Of the four incidents described, the first relates a confrontation between Jesus and the lawyers, and contains some striking verbal resemblances to the Gospel of John, although the setting of the incident is synoptic in tone. The second and third incidents contain an account of the healing of a leper and a debate on the payment of taxes, recalling passages in the synoptic Gospels with both additions and omissions. The fourth incident apparently describes a miracle on the banks of the Jordan that symbolizes the Resurrection and has no parallel elsewhere. The writer probably drew on both written and unwritten traditions. If, as is likely, his sources included the synoptic Gospels, he must have been recalling them from memory. It is possible, however, that both they and *Papyrus Egerton* may draw on a common source or sources. A scrutiny of the language in the first incident suggests that either John was using the Egerton Gospel and adapting it for his own purposes or both were relying on a common source. One or two details indicate that the author had no close knowledge of the Palestinian background and was writing for a Hellenistic audience.

BIBLIOGRAPHY

Bell, H. I., and T. C. Skeat, eds. *Fragments of an Unknown Gospel*. London, 1935.

______. *The New Gospel Fragments*. London, 1935.

Jeremias, J.; E. Hennecke; and W. Schneemelcher, eds. *New Testament Apocrypha*, trans. R. McL. Wilson, Vol. 1, pp. 94–97. London, 1963. Contains bibliography.

C. H. ROBERTS

EGYPT, ADMINISTRATIVE ORGANIZATION OF.

In pharaonic times Egypt was divided into two main parts, the Delta in the north and Upper Egypt in the south. The former was subdivided into twenty administrative units, and the latter into twenty-two. In addition to about sixty major towns, the number of villages totaled about 2,500.

Under the Ptolemies the land was divided into three main regions: Lower Egypt with thirty-three administrative units, Middle Egypt with seven, and Upper Egypt with fourteen. Each of these units was called a nome, and was governed by a nomarch. With the Roman occupation the country was reorganized into thirty-six nomes: twenty-two in Lower Egypt, six in Middle Egypt, and eight in Upper Egypt.

Later, following the division of the Roman empire into Eastern and Western halves, Egypt became part of the Eastern empire whose capital was Constantinople; the country was divided into six major sections. The Delta consisted of two major sections, Augustamnic I and II, subdivided into thirty-three units. Upper Egypt consisted of Arcadia, Lower Thebes, Middle Thebes, and Upper Thebes, and was also subdivided into thirty-three administrative units.

With the ARAB CONQUEST OF EGYPT (A.D. 641), the Delta was called Asfal al-Arḍ (low land) and Upper Egypt was called al-Ṣaʿīd (high land). The former was divided into two regions: al-Ḥawf, comprising fourteen units, each known as a *kūrah* (Arabic, from Greek *khōra*, district), and al-Rīf (rural area) comprising thirty-one *kūrahs*. The southern part of the country, al-Ṣaʿīd, was divided into thirty *kūrahs*.

In the ninth century, Lower Egypt (Asfal al-Arḍ) was reorganized into three regions: the land east of the Damietta branch of the River Nile called al-Ḥawf al-Sharqī, with the city of Bilbays as its capital, consisted of eleven *kūrahs;* the land lying between the two branches of the Nile was named Baṭn al-Rīf, and consisted of twenty *kūrahs;* and the land lying to the west of the Rosetta branch, called al-Ḥawf al-Gharbī, with Alexandria as its capital, consisted of fifteen *kūrahs*. Thus the total number of *kūrahs* in Lower Egypt was forty-six, in addition to four others: Libya, Qulzum (Suez), al-Ṭūr, and part of Ḥijāz in Arabia. The Ṣaʿīd, on the other hand, comprised thirty *kūrahs*, thus bringing the total number of *kūrahs* in the Egyptian territory to eighty, each under its own local governor.

The Fatimid caliph al-Mustanṣir (1035–1094) redistributed the *kūrahs*, grouping them into twelve in the Delta and ten in Upper Egypt. The total number of villages was 2,148, of which 1,601 were in the Delta and 547 in the Ṣaʿīd, in addition to the main cities and ports. Under the Ayyubids two more *kūrahs* were added, bringing the total to twenty-four.

In the fourteenth century, al-Nāṣir ibn Qalawūn reorganized the distribution of Egyptian provinces, replacing the term *kūrah* with *'amal* (administrative district). The land register issued by him, and known as *al-Rūk al-Nāṣirī* (land survey), included twelve *a'māl* (pl. of *'amal*), in Lower Egypt, and nine in Upper Egypt.

With the Ottoman occupation (1517) the term *'amal* was substituted by *wilāyah* (state), and the country was divided into thirteen *wilāyahs*, seven in the Delta and six in Upper Egypt, as follows: in the Delta Qalyūbiyyah, Sharqiyyah, Daqahliyyah, Garbiyyah, Minūfiyyah, Beheira, and Giza; in Upper Egypt Aṭfīḥiyyah, Fayyūmiyyah, Bahnasāwiyyah, Ashmūnayn, Manfalūṭiyyah, and Jirjā. In addition to the above *wilāyahs*, there was the capital, Cairo, and six other governorates: Alexandria, Rosetta (Rashīd), Damietta (Dumyāṭ), al-'Arīsh, al-Quṣayr, and Suez.

Under the French expedition of 1798, Bonaparte's scientists made a thorough survey of the country, and recorded the following provinces in the *Description de l'Egypte* (Jomard, 1809–1828), starting from the south to the north: I: Thebes (Luxor), Jirjā, Asyūṭ, Minyā, Banī Suef (Suwayf), al-Fayyūm, Iṭfīḥ, and Giza; and II: Qalyūb, al-Sharqiyyah, al-Manṣūrah, Damietta, al-Gharbiyyah, Minūf, Rashīd, Beheira.

In 1805 Muḥammad 'Alī reorganized the administrative division of the country into *khuṭṭs* (districts) each consisting of a number of villages under a local governor. He also subdivided Bahnasāwiyyah and Ashmūnayn each into four administrative districts or *marākiz*, and later introduced another land partition in Sharqiyyah, Daqahliyyah, Gharbiyyah, and Beheira. In 1826 he replaced the term *wilāyah* with *ma'mūriyyah* (a district run by a superintendent of police). In 1833, however, he introduced the term *mudīriyyah* (province) instead of *ma'mūriyyah*, and redistributed the country into fourteen *mudīriyyah* in Lower Egypt and ten in Upper Egypt, which is identical with the distribution of provinces under the Fatimids, the Ayyubids, and the Mamluks.

In 1871 Khedive Ismā'īl adopted the use of the term *markaz* for the subdivision of the *mudīriyyah*. According to a census carried out in 1937, the number of *marākiz* was seventy-five, including 4,188 rural units, in addition to the governorates of Cairo, Alexandria, Suez, Damietta, and the Canal.

When the Arabs conquered Egypt, they recruited a vast number of Coptic scribes and translators to draw up a comprehensive list of Egyptian towns and villages. In carrying out their task, these translators had recourse to the following methods: retaining the original Egyptian name through transliteration; translating names into Arabic; or modifying the original name into a form that could be easily pronounced in Arabic.

Throughout the following centuries various Arabic words were adopted to designate villages and hamlets of different sizes. In his *al-Qāmūs al-Jughrāfī*, Muḥammad Ramzī, who had made an extensive survey of the entire land in the course of his duties as inspector of land taxation in the early 1940s, came to the conclusion that the terms *qaryah* (village), *baldah* (small town), *nāḥiyah* (small district) had been in use since the early days of the Arab conquest. The term *kafr* (village), of Syriac derivation, was adopted during the Fatimid period (969–1171) and is used frequently by the thirteenth-century writer ABŪ ṢĀLIH THE ARMENIAN. The term *naj'* also belongs to the same period. In the sixteenth century, the term *nazlah*, also meaning a small village, was introduced during the Ottoman period.

Some of these and many others are always used dually to indicate a town or village. The first part of the name remains unchanged; the second indicates a place named after a person or persons (Abū, Awlād); a tribe (Banī Aḥmad); a location or a settlement (Maḥallat, nazlat); an establishment (Ma'ṣarat Hajjāj, probably an oil press); and Tall or Kom, designating an elevated ground (Tall Rāk, Kom al-Shahīd). A list of the constants that appear in many geographic names are: Abū (father) Būṣīr or Abūṣīr (house of or temple of); Awlād (sons); Banī (tribe); Dayr (monastery or cemetery); Ḥiṣṣat (area of); 'Izbat (farm); Jazīrat (island or peninsula); Kom, Tall, and Shubrā (hillock); Ma'ṣarat (oil press); Mīt (referring to a very ancient site); Maḥallat, Minshah, or Manshiyyah (settlement); Manyal, Minyat, or Munyā (location close to a waterway); Niẓārah (administrative location); Qaṣr (named after a palace or a temple); and Ṣafṭ (wall fortress).

In 1890 the capital of each *mudīriyyah* was separated into a city administratively independent of the smaller towns and villages. In more recent times the term *mudīriyyah* was substituted by *muḥāfaẓah* (governorate). At present, the administrative organization of Egypt is as follows:

Lower Egypt Governorates
- al-Daqahliyyah
- al-Buhayrah (Beheira)
- al-Gharbiyyah
- al-Minūfiyyah
- al-Qalyūbiyyah

al-Sharqiyyah
Dumyāṭ (Damietta)
Kafr al-Shaykh

Upper Egypt Governorates
al-Fayyūm
al-Giza
al-Minyā
Aswān
Asyūṭ
Banī Suef (Suwayf)
Qinā
Suhāj

Urban Governorates
Alexandria
al-Ismā'īliyyah
Cairo
Suez
Port Sa'īd

Frontiers Administration
Southern desert province: Khargah and Dakhlah
Western desert province: Baḥariyyah Oasis, Siwa, Maryūṭ, and Matrūh
Sinai Peninsula

BIBLIOGRAPHY

Jomard, E. H., ed. *Description de l'Egypte*, 19 vols. in 23. Paris, 1809–1818.

Muḥammad Ramzī. *Al-Qāmūs al-Jughrāfī lil Bilād al-Miṣriyyah min Ahd Qudamā' al-Miṣriyyīn ilā Sanat 1945*, Vols. 1 and 2, in 5 pts. Cairo, 1953–1963.

FUAD MEGALLY

EGYPT, ISLAMIZATION OF. Islamization, or conversion to Islam, is one of the least studied interpretative problems in Islamic history. Due to a paucity of primary documentation, notably for the early periods, why, when, and under what social and political conditions the majority of the inhabitants of Southwest Asia and North Africa became Muslim are issues that have yet to be addressed in a definitive manner. We cannot speak of a general historical process of Islamization in medieval times. The rate and intensity of conversion varied according to local and regional circumstances in the *Dār al-Islām*. In the case of Egypt, our survey will reveal two peak periods of conversion: during early Abbasid times, in particular the second half of the ninth century; and that of the Baḥrī Mamluks (1250–1390).

The Arabs pursued their campaigns in Egypt as elsewhere with two basic objectives in mind. One was imposing their authority on the formerly Byzantine and Sassanid subjects in the territories they conquered, and the other was establishing an efficient and orderly administration that would yield substantial tax revenues. We have scant evidence that they were motivated by a fierce passion to convert the peoples they encountered in their line of march. Neither Muslim nor Coptic sources indicate that religious compulsion, especially at the point of the sword, played anything more than a very minor role in the meteoric progress of the Arabs. The latter wanted to rule and profitably so, while maintaining their ethnic solidarity and privileged status. This attitude generally remained the norm under the Prophet's immediate successors, the so-called Righteous Caliphs (632–661), throughout the period of the Umayyads (661–750), and into the early decades of the Abbasids in Egypt (750–868).

However, while this attitude may have remained normative, at least theoretically, the actual circumstances of Arab-Muslim rule during the first two centuries after the conquest of Egypt rendered it increasingly obsolete. Tensions between the regime and the Arab tribesmen who settled in various parts of Egypt, especially the Delta region, the onerous tax burdens that non-Muslims had to bear, the attraction of the new Muslim urban setting—originally merely an Arab garrison town—of al-Fusṭāṭ, and the prominent role of Coptic officials in the government bureaucracy, were all influential factors in this process. Each served gradually to reduce the rigid distinctions between conqueror and conquered and to encourage a mingling process that eventually resulted in the conversion of the bulk of the Egyptian population to Islam.

Now that several general factors that contributed to the Islamization process have been identified, a more detailed interpretive analysis of the problem should be considered. Individuals, communities, and societies accept innovations—spiritual, intellectual, material, or technological—for a variety of reasons. Some embrace something new because they are spontaneously drawn to it, while others feel compelled to do so to survive. A third and quite practical reason is to preserve or even enhance one's social status. In the wake of the Arab conquest, Egyptians were undoubtedly moved to accept Islam for one or more of these reasons. The major conundrum here is that sources are rarely precise in distinguishing among them.

The well-known narratives of the early Muslim historians, Ibn 'Abd al-Ḥakam and al-Balādhurī, are concerned primarily with the events of the Arab conquest and its major figures, battles, treaties, and new fiscal arrangements. The principal Coptic sources in Arabic are two: Abū Ṣāliḥ's (early thirteenth-century) *The Churches and Monasteries of Egypt,* and Sāwīrus ibn al-Muqaffa''s (d. between 979 and 1004) *History of the Patriarchs of the Egyptian Church.* Both contain much useful information, the former on Coptic buildings and monuments, the latter on the institutional changes of the Coptic church and the relationship of the patriarchate to its Muslim overlords in medieval times. Both give us a sense of the varying fortunes of the Coptic community and discuss the effects on its members of the failure of the Nile floods, diminution of arable lands, and plagues. But neither even vaguely pinpoints the steady, collective progress of Islamization, although individual tales of conversion appear here and there throughout each work.

Of greater but still limited value are the papyri. The work of G. Frantz-Murphy (1986) and Y. Raghib (1982) has amply demonstrated the utility of these documents for the economic history of early Muslim Egypt. The papyri shed considerable light on commercial activity, land use and yield, and, most significant for our study here, arabization. Intended to record commercial and agricultural affairs of the day, the papyri teach us not about conversion to Islam as such but about the process of linguistic and hence cultural change. Whereas many of the early papyri are composed either completely in Coptic or half in Coptic and half in Arabic, the later examples are usually only in Arabic.

Arabization is, in fact, of crucial importance for the Islamization of Egypt, especially in contrast to, for example, Iran. In Iran, Islam became the majority faith *without* the arabization of everyday life. Iranians accepted the Arabic revelation contained in the Qur'ān, while developing a Perso-Islamic culture of their own making. Arab settlers in Iran were very much absorbed into the Iranian milieu, whereas in Egypt absorption also meant the arabization of the conquered society. Indeed, the early appearance of Muslim names in the papyri originating outside of al-Fusṭāṭ, especially in the Eastern Delta, are evidence of this phenomenon. As Arab tribesmen took up agriculture and lived in close proximity to the Copts, arabization acted as a catalyst to the eventual acceptance of Islam. In this regard, the arabization of the administration and coinage during the caliphate of ʿAbd al-Malik (685–705) may be seen, in the Egyptian case at least, as a harbinger of conversion. ʿAbd al-Malik's decrees were a response, in part, to the increasing arabization of the Copts, a process in no small way due to the gradual arrival of Arab tribesmen in areas once wholly Coptic and Christian.

However, the evidence from the papyri, significant as it is, is insufficient to explain the spread of Islam in Egypt. If arabization was one fundamental factor, it was so because it acted in tandem with several others, notably taxation and the attitude of the Muslim authorities toward the socio-religious integration of their subjects during the initial centuries of Muslim rule. As we shall see below, both the attitude of the government toward the conversion of the Coptic masses and the efficacy of its taxation policies changed over time.

As we noted above, the Arabs from the time of the conquest observed a strict policy of ethnic solidarity and exclusivity that precluded conversion and integration on the part of their subjects. During the Umayyad period, conversion was officially discouraged and when it was permitted, it did not always entail release from the JIZYAH (poll tax) that had been imposed by the Arabs, theoretically at least, solely on non-Muslims in the conquered territories. But Arab attitudes and the ability of the government to administer effectively a centralized taxation system do not fully explain why conversion did not occur in great numbers at this time.

It is therefore instructive to consider the growth of Muslim urbanism, namely, when and how al-Fusṭāṭ ceased to be a mere provincial Arab garrison town and became a Muslim city that would serve as a magnet for new converts from the Coptic community. In Umayyad times, al-Fusṭāṭ was not the developing Muslim urban agglomeration the sources reveal by approximately the end of the ninth century. Given Umayyad attitudes and official policies, at least until very late in the history of the dynasty, it is no wonder that al-Fusṭāṭ was not a growing Muslim town attractive to new converts from elsewhere in Egypt. It might have been so if there had been a flood, rather than a trickle, of Coptic conversions. Copts remained Christian so long as conversion was officially frowned upon and the act itself meant social isolation if not total pariah status in one's former confessional community. Al-Fusṭāṭ's size and character in Umayyad times, then, are indicative of the fact that the bulk of the Coptic community did not yet see any advantages to conversion. The growth of Muslim towns was predicated in part on the migration of new converts from their previous confessional homes. Umayyad al-Fusṭāṭ did not become a Muslim city and remained little more than an administrative outpost because mass conversion had not yet found its immediate impetus.

Under Abbasid rule, the fortunes of the Coptic community took a different turn. Copts occupied important posts in the administrative bureaucracy and not infrequently intervened on behalf of their church with the Abbasid governor. However, unlike the Umayyads, the Abbasids did not frown upon conversion to Islam and, in addition, inadvertently provided some very good mundane reasons for doing so. The fifteenth-century historian al-MAQRĪZĪ tells that the Copts converted out of belief, to improve their employment prospects, to marry, and to lower their tax burdens. Al-Maqrīzī also observes that the settlement of Arab tribes in once entirely Coptic areas and the new agricultural orientation of these newcomers hastened both the breakdown of Coptic communal solidarity and the social ostracism that had once been applied to converts, particularly in the eastern Delta. But, it is taxation that seems to have ultimately been the most pressing issue for the Copts, as well as the one that provided the most powerful motor for mass conversion and the growth of a new Muslim urban culture in al-Fusṭāṭ.

The Copts had not objected to Arab Muslim rule so much as they resented the tax burdens placed on them. In fact, unlike the Umayyads, the Abbasids taxed both Coptic farmers and the Coptic church itself. There are accounts of revolts against taxation and not Muslim political sovereignty as early as 693 and on several more occasions during the Umayyad period, usually in the western Delta and not Upper Egypt. This pattern continued with even greater intensity under the Abbasids. The Copts, while still the majority religious community in the country, balked at mass conversion and chose the alternate path of revolt as a means of preserving their identity and registering their dissatisfaction with what were often rapacious Abbasid fiscal measures.

Coptic revolts against the Abbasids reached a crescendo in the first quarter of the ninth century. These revolts must be understood within the context of larger events and trends in Abbasid history: Abbasid Egypt itself was frequently beset not only by Coptic unrest but also by a succession of governors dispatched from the imperial center in Baghdad to administer a province in which they had little beyond a financial interest. In addition, these governors often had to deal with the disobedient tendencies of the Arab tribesmen in the Delta. Like their Christian neighbors, these tribesmen bitterly resented what they considered to be the excessive tax burdens imposed by the provincial government in al-Fusṭāṭ.

Politics in and around Baghdad itself also greatly affected Egypt's stability. The *fitnah* (civil war) between al-Amīn (809–813) and al-Ma'mūn (813–833), brothers and rival claimants for the caliphal throne, had repercussions in Egypt. A source of great division within the empire, this civil war lasted for two years (811–813). Though al-Ma'mūn was victorious, he had difficulty making his writ strong in Egypt, where al-Amīn had been their favorite. This fact only exacerbated an already unstable provincial setting, leading eventually to the most serious of the Coptic revolts in 832 at Bashmūr (see BASHMURIC REVOLTS) in the western portion of the central Delta. Though the revolt was opposed by the hierarchy of the Coptic church, the Copts nevertheless fought the Abbasid troops sent against them to a standstill in the marshes and swamps which dotted their lands. At last, the caliph himself arrived to take command personally, and the revolt was put down with fire, sword, and deportation. With the failure of the revolt, according to al-Maqrīzī, the conversion of the Coptic population of the entire Delta region was assured.

Our belief that Islamization in Egypt took a decisive step in the second half of the ninth century is buttressed by two additional bodies of source material which, until recently, have not been throughly explored. These are biographical dictionaries and tombstone epitaphs, each of which preserves immensely valuable information on obituary dates and Arabic naming patterns. Though still tentative, the conclusions reached by R. Bulliet (1978) on this material indicate a striking chronological convergence between traditional narrative texts and these more unconventional sources on the problem of when Islam became the majority religion in Egypt.

It would seem obvious from our discussion thus far that the Delta was the first region of Egypt to convert. Periodic revolts since late Umayyad times and fraternization with Arab tribal elements settling in the region undoubtedly gave the Delta a head start in the process of Islamization. Though Upper Egypt remained substantially Coptic for a longer time than Lower Egypt, evidence from the tombstone epitaphs indicates that Islamization there did not really follow a much slower pace. Without more primary data, however, it still remains very difficult to ascertain definitively which region of Egypt first embraced Islam in large numbers.

An additional interpretive problem that merits brief attention here is the connection between Coptic social class and Islamization. Peasant cultivators oppressed by the *jizyah* were almost certainly the first to convert. They simply made what they thought was the best of a bad situation. Excluding the religious hierarchy, many of the upper strata of Coptic society converted in order to retain their posts in an administration in which service increasingly depended on being Muslim, though Copts did serve in important administrative capacities through Mamluk times. The fate of the Coptic bourgeoisie—the bakers, olive-oil merchants, carpenters, and goldsmiths, who were always the backbone of the Coptic community—may be indicated, once again, by the Arabic onomasticon revealed by the tombstone epitaphs: these people exchanged one past, one community, and one religious tradition for another—Islam. In so doing, they formed a new Muslim middle class in Egypt, concrete evidence of which may be found in part in the biographical dictionaries devoted to Shāfi'ī and Mālikī *'ulamā'* (religious scholars).

The bloody suppression of the Coptic revolt in the Delta in 832 and the subsequent conversion of the bulk of its native inhabitants signaled the end of one era and the beginning of another in the history of Muslim Egypt. The Copts would now permanently occupy the status of a religious minority. In a larger sense, the serious numerical reduction of the Coptic community during the latter half of the ninth century meant that Egypt had now become an Islamic society with its own regional character distinct from the Iranian orientation of the imperial capital at Baghdad. Egypt had made impressive progress as a local center for Muslim education, especially in the field of law, and a core network of *'ulamā'* had begun to establish an enviable reputation in North Africa and Spain. Taxation appears as a far less vexatious issue now in our narrative sources, almost certainly because most revenues were collected for internal uses rather than the imperial treasury in Iraq. Aḥmad ibn Ṭūlūn (868–884), Egypt's first Muslim ruler independent of the caliph and founder of a dynasty that ruled until 905, built mosques and palaces, patronized scholars, and improved the general economic well-being of the country with revenues he did not send to Baghdad.

From the Arab conquest of Egypt in the seventh century to the official end of Abbasid rule in 969, the Coptic community had undergone a remarkably rapid and enduring transformation. Historically the most ancient and celebrated of the early Christian churches, its history replete with tales of passionate faith and martyrdom, the Coptic church now ministered to a minority community, one protected by Muslim law from forcible conversion, but nevertheless subject to the circumstances of local political and economic life. Like Egyptian Jewry, the Copts had assumed the status of the Dhimmis (protected people), which permitted autonomy within the parameters of their religious law, but which left them vulnerable to the whim of a Muslim ruler or the resentment of a disgruntled, perhaps even hysterical mob representing Fusṭāṭ/Cairo's underclass. And even if not physically threatened, Dhimmi communities not infrequently labored under various discriminatory legal provisions applied specifically to them regarding dress, the construction or repair of houses of worship, the vocations they could practice, the animals they could ride, and the public observance of religious rites or festivals. It is in this context—as a minority community living in a thoroughly Muslim society—that we must understand the Islamization of the Copts under three successive dynasties: the Shī'ī Fatimids (in Egypt, 969–1171), the Ayyubids (1171–1250), and the Baḥrī Mamluks (1250–1390).

The three centuries of Fatimid and Ayyubid history in Egypt were, for the indigenous Christian and Jewish communities, an era of relative peace, prosperity, and stability. While Muslim sources do record incidents, sometimes of a serious nature, involving the lives and property of non-Muslims, we do not read of concerted efforts to convert, either through propaganda or force, entire communities. We could list several matters that did indeed lead to outbreaks by Muslims against Copts, for example, their continued prominence in several of the government services, especially finance; the turmoil that accompanied the transition from Fatimid to Ayyubid rule; and the Muslim suspicion, genuine or imagined, that the Copts were collaborating with the Crusaders (see COPTS AND THE CRUSADES). Overall, incidents were political rather than confessional in nature, and the traditional discriminatory measures were occasionally revived, but only indifferently enforced.

The sole period of sustained persecution and forced conversion to Islam suffered by the Copts under these two dynasties was during the rule of the Fatimid caliph al-Ḥākim BI-AMR-ILLĀH ABŪ 'ALĪ MANṢŪR. Variously described as paranoic, mad, or possessed by intense religious visions, al-Ḥākim ordered the destruction of churches, and in general persecuted first the Copts and then the Jews with a ferocity previously unknown. The political disorder that characterized his reign led to sectarian violence throughout Egypt and the conversion of thousands of Copts. It is only with al-Ḥākim's disappearance that tensions subsided. Given the recent research of S. D. Goitein (1967–1988) on the Geniza papers, we can no longer, however, accept A. Atiya's statement that "the real grandeur and subsequent decline of the Coptic nation in Islamic times took place under the Faṭimid Caliphs" (1980, p. 87). Though the Geniza papers deal primarily with Jewish affairs, they nonetheless reveal much about Muslim society and majority–minority relations in the period from 950 to 1250). For Goitein, the Geniza papers speak to us of the flexibility, tolerance, and vitality of Islamic society in Egypt during these two centuries rather than of a general mood of religious repression. Though prejudice and the occasional incident it provoked did operate against both Copts and Jews, they were, to use Goitein's phrase, "local and sporadic rather than general and endemic" (1971, Vol. 2, p. 283). It is no accident that the so-called Geniza period ends with the advent of the Mamluks, for political and economic conditions in Egypt under their rule imperiled the general security Copts and Jews had known under the Fatimids and Ayyubids.

However, intolerance and oppression of religious minorities did not begin and end with the Mamluk dynasty itself. In later Ayyubid times, a change can already be discerned. Slave troops of foreign origin (Mamluks) had played a role in Islamic political and military life from the middle of the ninth century. But, the recruitment and deployment of these troops in large numbers became customary under the Ayyubids in a manner unknown in prior epochs. They came to represent a military elite jealously mindful of its privileges, largely alienated from the people they ruled, and scornful of seapower and the importance of militarily innovative technology. The gradual triumph of such a mentality at the level of the state came at a time when Egyptian society was itself less inclined to be tolerant of non-Muslims. As the Mamluk era proper in Egyptian history is reached, this state of affairs became only too commonplace. The Mamluk sultans were not ardent advocates of conversion themselves. They enjoyed the efficiency and prosperity that their Coptic officials brought them, and unless coerced into doing so, did not react to individual displays of Coptic wealth and political influence. These policies enraged their Egyptian Muslim subjects, who already bitterly resented the status of the Copts and deeply mistrusted the often arbitrary nature of Mamluk rule.

We noted above that the Crusades may have conditioned Muslim attitudes and responses to the Copts. In this regard, the Mongols should be mentioned. Fierce enemies of the Mamluks, favorably disposed at one time at least to Christianity and believed to be in league with the Crusaders, the Mongols have also been identified as an element in the intensification of Egyptian hostility toward the Copts. However, by the end of the reign of the Mamluk sultan al-Manṣūr Qalāwūn (1280–1290), neither Crusaders nor Mongols represented a threat to Mamluk sovereignty. From L. Northrup's research on this problem (1974), we learn, in fact, that Muslim sources record but two instances, both in Damascus, where a linkage might be assumed between persecution of Dhimmis and the Mamluks' struggle with the Mongols and Crusaders. One was the order, on the eve of the battle of Ḥimṣ (1281), that Christian officials convert or be executed, and the other a decree that Christians in government service be dismissed as the Mamluks prepared for the siege of the Crusader stronghold at ʿAkkā in 1290–1291. As Northrup observes, in neither case is the connection explicitly stated.

The impact of external threats on Mamluk policy toward the Copts does not therefore provide us with much insight. Sultan Qalāwūn did at times take certain measures against them, but these were in response to protests against Coptic officials, often by Muslim counterparts, in certain key financial posts or in the service of Mamluk amirs. At no time did Qalāwūn apply his decrees to the entire Coptic community, nor were Muslim outcries directed at all Copts. Indeed, Qalāwūn's behavior established a paradigm for his successors. He feared social strife and sectarian violence and, to placate his Muslim subjects, was not adverse to ordering the dismissal or the conversion of individual Copts in his service. When a prominent Coptic tax official appeared overzealous and arrogant in the performance of his duties, for example, a sultan had to act against him or risk the wrath of the Muslim masses. Decrees against Copts, then, were directed against a select group within the Coptic community and not against the community itself. This state of affairs, generally typical of relations between Muslims and non-Muslims in medieval Islamic Egypt, changed radically during the half-century following the death of Sultan Qalāwūn, a change which prompted what D. Little calls "the second great transformation of Egyptian religion" (1976, p. 569), since the Arab conquest of Egypt.

This second peak in the Islamization of the Copts occurred for several related reasons. Resentment against Copts ran deep in the historical, theological, and polemical works written by Muslims in Mamluk times. At the mundane level, inflamed public feeling in Cairo, galvanized by the religious propaganda of an emboldened corps of Sunnī *ʿulamāʾ*, forced the government to pursue four different campaigns, in 1293, 1301, 1321, and 1354, designed to humble and convert Copts in government service. However, such campaigns were preceded by outbreaks of sectarian violence, the likes of which had not been seen previously in Muslim Egypt. Whether it concerned the haughty mien of a Coptic official in the street, a Coptic funeral procession, the charge that Copts were unlawfully rebuilding or repairing a church, or the suspicion that Copts were dictating orders to Muslims in their government posts, the Muslim *'āmmah* (masses) repeatedly expressed their furious discontent to the Mamluk authorities and forced them to take actions they would not ordinarily have taken.

The impetus for a general persecution of non-Muslims in this period came, therefore, from below, not above. We must also realize here that protests by the *'āmmah* against the Copts were a way of voicing their discontent with an alien regime whose policies were often roundly disliked. Compelling the Mamluk rulers to level churches, expropriate pious endowments, reenact sumptuary laws once rarely in effect regarding non-Muslims, and destroy the careers of Copts in government service, were potent ways for Muslim Egyptians to express their dissatisfaction.

The hostility evident against Copts during the rule of the Baḥrī Mamluks is matched only by that against Coptic converts (*Musālimah*) to Islam. Conversion in this period unfortunately did not remove the stigma of being a Copt. Copts converted because of physical threat or because they wanted to advance their careers in government service, but the act of conversion often did not make them any less suspect in Muslim eyes. The experience of these converts is strikingly reminiscent of that of Jewish converts to Christianity in Spain in the fourteenth and fifteenth centuries.

In both cases, it often made little difference to the majority community whether converts were sincere and cut all ties with their previous religious community or had converted for practical motives and still harbored sympathies for their former coreligionists. Given the continued proximity to converts of those who had remained steadfast in the original faith, converts in both Egypt and Spain were suspect. In both cases, once again, there are numerous examples of new Muslims and Christians wielding substantial political and economic influence in their government posts or business affairs, while acting in the interests of their old religious confreres. Other converts severed all bonds out of fear that their paths to career mobility would be blocked. In the case of the Copts, conversion became an additional factor to be weighed against them, especially for those who played a major role in the shaping of Mamluk policy for collection and distribution of tax revenues.

Despite the stigma that Muslim officials of Coptic origin experienced for some generations, we can say, nevertheless, that the Islamization process which began seven centuries earlier was completed during the period of the Baḥrī Mamluks. Whereas arabization and revolts against taxation had encouraged conversion in the middle of the ninth century, the alien, arbitrary, and frequently turbulent nature of Mamluk rule combined with a groundswell of popular sentiment against the Copts to further the process and reduce the Copts to the small minority community they remain to this day.

BIBLIOGRAPHY

The study of the general problem of conversion is best begun, especially for those interested in comparative history, with A. D. Nock, *Conversion* (Oxford, 1933). In addition, the recent work by R. L. Fox on early Christianity, *Pagans and Christians* (New York, 1987), contains a lengthy and important chapter on the social setting of conversion. A pioneering work on Islamization is R. Bulliet, *Conversion to Islam in the Medieval Period* (Cambridge, Mass., 1978). His still tentative, yet extraordinarily valuable conclusions are carefully reviewed by C. Décobert in *Studia Islamica* 57 (1983):182–87, and R. S. Humphries, *Islamic History: A Framework for Inquiry* (Minneapolis, 1988). Also useful is S. Vryonis, *The Decline of Medieval Hellenism in Asia Minor and the Process of Islamization from the Eleventh through the Fifteenth Century* (Berkeley and Los Angeles, 1971).

For conversion to Islam in Egypt up to the Fatimids, one should start with the articles by J. C. Vadet, "L''acculturation' des sud-arabiques de Fustat au lendemain de la conquête arabe," *Bulletin d'études orientales de l'Institut français au Portugal* (1969):7–14; I. Lapidus, "The Conversion of Egypt to Islam," *Israel Oriental Studies* 2 (1972):248–62; and M. Brett, "The Spread of Islam in Egypt and North Africa," in *North Africa: Islam and Modernization*, ed. M. Brett (London, 1973). Useful comments may still be found in monograph form in A. Atiya, *A History of Eastern Christianity* (London, 1980). On the papyri, see G. Frantz-Murphy, *The Agrarian Administration of Egypt from the Arabs to the Ottomans* (Cairo, 1986), and Y. Raghib, *Marchands d'étoffes du Fayyoum au IIIe/IXe siècle d'après leurs archives (actes et lettres)* (Cairo, 1982). On Arabization and the revolts in the Delta, the reader should consult the unpublished Ph.D. dissertation of M. C. Dunn, *The Struggle for Abbasid Egypt* (Georgetown University, 1975).

For the Fatimids and Ayyubids, one need go no further than S. D. Goitein's *A Mediterranean Society: The Jewish Communities of the Arab World as Portrayed in the Documents of the Cairo Geniza*, 5 vols. (Berkeley and Los Angeles, 1967–1988). For our subject here, Vol. 2, *The Community*, is of inestimable value. A Geniza study of more limited but exceedingly convincing scope is M. R. Cohen, *Jewish Self-Government in Medieval Egypt: The Origins of the Office of Head of the Jews, ca. 1065–1126* (Princeton, N.J., 1980). Cohen's work is especially valuable for its review of Coptic sources and its discussion of relations between the patriarchate and the Fatimid government.

For the Crusades, see the articles by N. Faris and P. Hitti in *The Impact of the Crusades on the Near East*, ed. N. P. Zacour and H. W. Hazard, which is Vol. 5 of *A History of the Crusades*, 5 vols., ed. Kenneth M. Setton (Madison, Wis., 1969–1985).

There has been some recent and very solid research on Islamization during the period of the Baḥrī Mamlūks by D. P. Little and L. S. Northrup. One should start with Northrup's unpublished M.A. thesis, *Muslim-Christian Relations during the Reign of the Mamlūk Sultan al-Malik al-Manṣūr Qalā'ūn* (McGill University, 1974), and Little's article, "Coptic Conversion to Islam Under the Baḥrī Mamlūks, 692–755/1293–1354," *Bulletin of the School of Oriental and African Studies* 39 (1976):552–69. Each has also contributed an article, the one by Little on the status of Coptic converts to Islam, to *Conversion and Continuity: Indigenous Christian Communities in Islamic Lands, Eighth to Eighteenth Centuries*, ed. M. Gervers and R. J. Bikhazi (Toronto, 1988). Of further interest is the work of S. Ward on juridical problems of conversion in this period. See, for example, his "Sabbath Observance and Conversion to Islam in the Fourteenth Century—a Fatwa by Taqī al-Dīn al-Subkī," in *Proceedings of the Ninth World Congress of Jewish Studies* (Jerusalem, 1986). Finally, for an understanding of the "learned classes" in Mamluk Egypt, C. F. Petry's *The Civilian Elite of Cairo in the Later Middle Ages* (Princeton, 1981) is indispensable.

SAM I. GELLENS

EGYPT, ROMAN AND BYZANTINE RULE IN. The victory of Octavian (Augustus since 27 B.C.) over Cleopatra VII, the last sovereign of Ptolemaic Egypt, and her protector Mark Antony first in Actium (2 September 31 B.C.), then in Alexandria (1 August 30 B.C.) brought Egypt under Roman rule. This new epoch, conveniently subdivided into the Roman and the Byzantine periods (respectively from Augustus to DIOCLETIAN [30 B.C.–A.D. 284/5] and from Diocletian to the Arab conquest in 641), lasted nearly seven hundred years and came to an end only in A.D. 646, when the last Byzantine soldiers left the soil of Egypt. Often depicted as a period of misery and decline and as a further step downward in the long decay of late period Egypt, the centuries of Roman and Byzantine rule deserve fairer consideration: Egypt was not only one of the economically most productive provinces of the Roman and Byzantine realm, it was also a domain of great intellectual fertility for pagan as well as for Jewish and Christian culture. Late antique Egypt not only produced a towering church leader like ATHANASIUS but also inspiring figures of monasticism such as ANTONY, PACHOMIUS, and SHENUTE. The spiritual influence of Egypt was probably never greater than in the Byzantine period, when the fathers of the desert and the Egyptian monasteries attracted visitors from all over the Mediterranean world, from the Gallic West to the Greek East. At the end of the fourth century, Alexandria, though predominantly Greek and already largely Christian, still produced an outstanding pagan poet, Claudius Claudianus, writing Greek verses but famous above all for his great works in Latin. The Egyptian *chora* (countryside) of the fifth century was home not only to a mass of toiling peasants but also to Greek poets like NONNOS OF PANOPOLIS, author of poems drawing their inspiration from both pagan and Christian traditions. By that time and under the influence of Christian teaching, the popular culture of Egypt had already asserted itself firmly, elevating the Coptic language to a literary level and thus enabling Christian thought and liturgy to survive after the departure of the Greeks. Late antiquity in Egypt is not predominantly the last phase of a long decline but in many respects a brilliant, engaging period, witnessing metamorphoses and generating new developments of long-ranging impact.

Political History

The second half of the third century A.D. was a period of crisis that brought Egypt, among other things, foreign invasion by the Palmyrenes (270–272) and a string of civil wars. Other provinces of the East and of the West, especially along the Rhine and the Danube, also witnessed inroads by "barbarians," economic disruption, and social unrest. This generalized state of disorder led to a series of usurpations by pretenders to the empire, one of the last and most successful being DIOCLETIAN (284–305). Drawing on the lessons of the past, he inaugurated a set of reforms that were to affect the empire as a whole and created new conditions especially for Egypt. These reforms were partially continued by CONSTANTINE I THE GREAT (306–337), but with some important changes, the most profound being toleration (313) and soon privileges for the Christian church. After victory over Licinius, his last rival, in 324, Constantine refounded Byzantium as a town bearing his name, Constantinople, and made it his favored residence. Constantinople rapidly became a new, a second Rome and the capital of the eastern half of the empire, displacing both Alexandria and Syrian Antioch, which had been until then the leading metropolises of the Roman East, politically, economically, and not least ecclesiastically, in the hierarchy of episcopal sees. Notwithstanding the constant drifting apart of the two halves of the Roman empire, its unity was upheld in theory and in programmatic declarations. But East and West each had their own emperors (*imperator, autokrator*) who, though forming a *collegium* (colleagueship), operated separately in their respective residences and defended their own, not seldom different or even conflicting, interests. Progressively the cohesion of the empire dissolved, the decisive blow being dealt by the Germanic invasions of the West. Rome having come under the dominance of the Teutons in 476 and the last West Roman emperor, Romulus Augustulus, having been deposed, the center of gravity and imperial authority shifted completely to the East. The Roman empire had in fact become the Byzantine empire. Constantinople was now the undisputed center of what was left of the Greco-Roman world, but that did not stop rivalry and conflict with the two other metropolises of the Orient, Alexandria and Antioch. Especially in the case of Alexandria, relations with Constantinople were tense and often acrimonious. Political as well as ecclesiastical dissent continued and grew even stronger after the Council of CHALCEDON (451), until the Arabs conquered both Antioch and Alexandria in the first half of the seventh century.

In strictly technical terms, the Byzantine period could begin only with the refoundation of Byzantium as Constantinople (starting in 324) and its establishment as the privileged imperial residence in the East. But frequently, and not least in PAPYROLOGY, the Byzantine period is reckoned retroactively from the reign of Diocletian, beginning in 284. Indeed, many of the features considered typical of the Byzantine state were created through the reforms of Diocletian and his colleagues in the tetrarchy established in 293, Galerius (with Diocletian) in the East, Maximianus and Constantius in the West.

Egypt had had its own share of the many rebellions and usurpations of the third century. In 293, Galerius had reduced a revolt that resulted in the destruction of Coptos (Qifṭ). Still more far-reaching were the consequences, some years later, of the usurpation of Lucius Domitius Domitianus, proclaimed emperor in 297. Diocletian in person reconquered Egypt and took Alexandria after a siege of eight months. He afterward proceeded to Upper Egypt, affirming his control of the situation and establishing the southern border of Egypt at Philae, which meant that Lower Nubia (Dodekaschoenus) was left to the Nobatians. As in the rest of the empire, Diocletian split the old provinces in order to establish stricter control and to marshal more efficiently economic and military resources. The *provincia Aegyptus* was thus divided into three provinces: *Aegyptus Iovia* (Alexandria and western Delta), *Aegyptus Herculia* (eastern Delta and Middle Egypt), and *Thebais*, the names of the former two provinces echoing the tutelary deities of the tetrarchical college, Jupiter and Hercules. New administrative structures, the dioceses and the prefectures, were created above the level of the provinces. Each of the latter was headed by a *praefectus praetorio* (pretorian prefect) attached to the person of one of the emperors, the *praefectus praetorio Orientis* (pretorian prefect of the East) thus being established at Constantinople. This prefecture evolved in the fourth century as the administrative headquarters of the Roman East. Each prefecture included a number of dioceses, which in turn were made up of several provinces (see PROVINCIAL ORGANIZATION OF EGYPT). At first, and probably until about 381, the provinces of Egypt were part of the *dioecesis Oriens* (eastern diocese), whose regent (*vicarius*) resided at Antioch. As a consequence of Diocletian's reforms, Egypt had thus lost its former special status. It was subdivided into several provinces and firmly inserted into the restructured administrative network of the Roman Near East. Above all, Egypt had been put into line behind Constantinople and Antioch. The arrangement of provincial territories in Egypt as conceived by Diocletian did not prove definitive and was revised several times during the fourth century.

Another important consequence of the administrative resettlement of Egypt concerned the position of the *praefectus Aegypti* (prefect of Egypt). The latter had been, during the past centuries, the direct representative of the Roman emperor and the highest ranking official in Egypt. His competence was now confined to *Aegyptus Iovia* and he lost his military attributions, as did the provincial governors (*praesides*). Military command rested now with the dukes (*duces*), whose area was not always confined to a single province. A set of Latin inscriptions in Luxor records one Aurelius Maximinus who, in 308, held the position of *dux Aegypti et Thebaidos utrarumque Libyarum* (duke of Egypt and Thebais and both Libyas). This single military command was later split, but the principle of separating civil and military authority was observed during the next two centuries until it was abrogated by Justinian (see ARMY, ROMAN). Diocletian took one further step to put an end to the special status of Egypt: the mint of Alexandria lost the right to strike its own currency and started to produce standard imperial coinage.

Before Diocletian's reforms, administrative documents in Egypt had been dated by regnal years of the emperors, but from now on they adopted the consular dating practiced in all the other provinces of the empire. The transfer of the imperial residence to Constantinople, the development of a new and strengthened bureaucracy both there and on the levels of dioceses and provinces, and a revived determination to unify the composite empire and to reaffirm Roman *disciplina* and *mos maiorum* (ancestral custom): all this gave a fresh impetus to the use of Latin in the Greek East. The army had already been, and still was, a vehicle of Latin and romanization, but much less so in the Greek East than in the Roman West. Nevertheless, Latin military terms infiltrated the Greek language and survived in Arabic. For example, the Latin *fossatum* (ditch) became the Greek *fossaton* and the Arab *fusṭaṭ*, and the Latin *castra* (camp), the Greek *kastra* and the Arab *qaṣr*.

There was, in the beginning of the fourth century, a further disruption of old traditions when the nomes were replaced by city-territories (*civitates, politeiai, poleis*), which put them on the same footing with administrative subdivisions elsewhere in the Roman empire. Many of these changes took place or were at least initiated under Diocletian, Galerius, or Licinius, that is, before Constantine the Great established himself at Byzantium/Constantinople, thus inaugurating what is traditionally called the Byzantine age. For the reasons surveyed above, it seems legitimate and even appropriate to date the beginning of the Byzantine period of Egyptian history with Diocletian.

Ecclesiastical History

These developments, though not without consequence for the everyday life of people, were mostly confined to the realm of politics and administration. But at the same time, other changes were going on that left a much deeper and lasting mark on men and society. Christian belief and church were already well entrenched in Egypt and had survived the ordeal of several persecutions during the third century. The victory of Constantine was perceived and heralded as a triumph of Christ and a new epoch for the church by such writers as Lactantius and EUSEBIUS OF CAESAREA. But it was a triumph beset with numerous difficulties, many of them arising from the very privileges now bestowed upon the Christian communities. Theological debate, hierarchical dispute, and schismatic movements were henceforth freer to develop and they often involved the imperial authority and political institutions. As head of the Egyptian church, the patriarch of Alexandria faced an extremely difficult task. On the one hand, he was expected to defend the unity of his church, which proved nearly impossible in face of opposition from Arians, Melitians, and other Christian factions both in his own country and abroad. On the other hand, the patriarch had to secure the position of his church versus the pretensions of Constantinople, though he had no intention of breaking away from the Byzantine state and from the emperor in Constantinople. The tensions and compromises of this complex relationship form an important chapter not only of the ecclesiastical but also of the political history of Egypt in late antiquity. The situation was further aggravated when Alexandria was humiliated and monophysitism banned by the Council of Chalcedon in 451.

This new development and the clashes between Melchites and Monophysites in Alexandria and Egypt have been held chiefly responsible for the alienation between Egypt and the Byzantine state and thus for the easy conquest of Egypt by the Arabs. Matters, however, were much more complicated and delineations not so clearcut. The Egyptian Monophysites had at some times strong support in Constantinople, the best-known example being Justinian's empress, Theodora. On their side, the Byzantine emperors, trying to keep together the Catholic and Monophysite parts of the empire and to maintain good relations with Italy and the bishop of Rome, were sometimes anxious not to offend

Egyptian sensibilities. This proves true at least for some emperors, for instance, Justinian (529–565). The estrangement between Egypt and the Byzantine state was a slow and sometimes violent process, but serious though it was, it never led to complete disruption and separatism.

Besides the prevailing political and dogmatic issues opposing Alexandria and Constantinople, there were other frictions often involving the relation between church and state. So the judicial functions once conceded to the bishops by Constantine the Great (see AUDENTIA EPISCOPALIS) were later sharply curtailed by a series of imperial decisions. To uphold the running of towns and to secure the implementation of fiscal obligations, the state had an interest in the continuous functioning of the municipal class and would not readily allow *curiales* (municipal officers) to enter the orders or the monasteries without due safeguards regarding curial property and obligations. When political or economic pressures boiled over, functionaries of the Byzantine state in Alexandria often had to bear the brunt of popular discontent. One famous example is the death of Theodosius (Augustan prefect) killed by the people when Dioscorus was consecrated bishop in 516.

Economy and Society

The state of Egyptian economy and society during late antiquity has often been described by modern authorities as a most desolate one and has been held partly responsible for the little prestige of the Byzantine state in Egypt and thus for the apparent ease of the Arab conquest of that country. There have been, in the past, reservations about this view of things (Johnson, 1951), and opposition to it has been growing (Winkelmann, 1979). Notwithstanding a plethora of source materials, it is extremely difficult to pass a well-documented overall judgment on the degree of disaffection with the state of social and economic conditions in Egypt. Papyri, numerous as they are, mostly give a fragmentary picture and are not without risk submitted to generalization. Laws, regulations, and other official statements are precious insofar as they give information on the sectors in which state authorities perceived difficulties and on the means applied to remedy them. But these are normative texts, whereas the papyri often give a very different picture, showing the difference between ideal and reality. Important questions therefore remain frequently without answer. For instance, was the common Egyptian of late antiquity better off than his ancestors in the preceding centuries? One cannot, of course, give a simple, undifferentiated answer, but the long-prevailing view of a constant deterioration from Roman to Byzantine times has been seriously challenged (Bowman, 1986). Did the Byzantine state effect strict rigidity, confining people to their status, making trades and professions hereditary, rendering economy and society essentially immobile? This was once the consensus of opinion, but it is no longer taken for granted (Keenan, 1975). Economic plight and the raids of the "barbarians" have often been considered as having seriously contributed to the reduction of the number of inhabitants; the depopulation observed in the fourth-century Fayyūm has frequently been adduced as proof. But gradual, not necessarily man-made desertification might also, and at least partly, offer a valid explanation. Other regions of Egypt, with the exception of Oxyrhynchus and its territory, are not nearly as well known as the Fayyūm. We are ignorant of the total number of the inhabitants of late antique Egypt. It is therefore extremely difficult to assess the effects of the social and economic conditions on the overall evolution of the population through the Byzantine age.

The taxation system introduced by Diocletian, hard as it may have been, was nonetheless meant to be fair and to reduce inequality. It evolved in a way that took account of both personnel and land. As a rule, local magnates and big landowners held at the same time state positions and were charged with tax collection; hence fraud, collusion, and strong influence was exerted on minor landholders. The latter often sought an end to their tribulations, selling their land to big possessors and becoming tenant farmers in the hope of finding protection as clients of their patrons. Whole villages and communities thus became dependent on big landowners, as, for instance, the Apions. The latter were often viewed as some sort of feudal landlords, recruiting their own troops, building private prisons to defend their authority, and challenging the interests of a declining central state. This interpretation has been nuanced or contested (Carrié, 1984; Fikhman, 1965; Gascou, 1985). Among other things, the position of big landowners has been reexamined in the light of their state obligations, which they performed, according to this new approach, well within the framework of the central administration.

Religion

The end of the persecutions of the Christians and the triumph of Constantine in 324 did not mean the end of paganism, not even the end of conflicts between pagans and Christians (cf. surveys by Maspero, 1923; Hardy, 1952; Rémondon, 1960; new approaches by Pearson and Goehring, 1986). Both coexisted, often very uncomfortably, in the society at large as well as in the army. Controversies in the Christian camp, especially between Catholics (Orthodox) and Arians during the fourth century, made it sometimes easier for pagans to survive, and the attempted restoration of paganism by the emperor Julian (361–363) showed that the cause of paganism was not yet entirely lost. In Alexandria, pagans had a strong following throughout the fourth century, as shown, for example, in the pagan vendetta in 362 and the riots preceding the destruction of the Alexandrian Serapeum in 391–392 (cf. Thelamon, 1981). Notwithstanding these pagan attempts at resistance, Christianity conquered a majority of Egyptians in the course of the fourth century. But the pace and size of this progress, and its regional differentiation, are still debated (Bagnall, 1982; Martin, 1979; Wipszycka, 1986). Even less do we know the exact and respective strength of the various conflicting Christian communities in fourth-century Egypt: Catholics, Arians, Melitians, not to speak of Gnostics and Manichaeans. It may have been opportune to become a Christian, conforming oneself to official policy and imperial preferences, be they Arian (Constans II) or Catholic (Theodosius I). But many men and women in Egypt went far beyond a formal affiliation to the church and flocked to the hardships and promises of monastic life. Social care for the poor, the sick, and the captive gave fresh impulse to new forms of community life, ruled by the love and fear of God and by strict obedience to the superiors of the monasteries (Bacht, 1984; Rousseau, 1985).

Greek civilization had certainly proved very attractive to many native Egyptians, but it never achieved in depth and extent the success of Christianity. There was a real identification of the popular masses with the new religion and an awakening of spiritual activity in the various manifestations of Coptic culture. In the fourth century, this Egyptian revival occurred under Greek-speaking Christian leadership. (For a qualification of this view and the complexities of the relationship between Alexandria and Egypt, see Krause, 1981; regarding the authenticity and interpretation of Athanasius' *Vita Antonii*, see Dörries, 1966; Barnes, 1986; and Louth, 1988).

Throughout the Byzantine period, Greek continued to be spoken and written not only in Alexandria but also in the higher strata of the population of the *chora*. Even after the Arab conquest, Greek was still used, besides Coptic and Arabic, for administrative purposes and it disappeared only in the tenth century. But Coptic was on the rise since the fourth century, evidenced first in religious writings and in private correspondence. While the Greek language maintained itself in the face of Coptic progress, Hellenic culture in the sense of pagan conviction was in decline. The *gymnasium* as the traditional focus of typically Greek formation and communal activities did not survive the crucial changes of the fourth century, nor did the famous Serapeum in Alexandria. But there held out, throughout the fifth century, some strongholds of pagan culture even deep down in the Egyptian *chora*, for example, in Panopolis, home to a succession of Greek poets such as Pamprepius, Nonnos, and Cyrus (cf. Cameron, 1965). The position of these literates between paganism and Christianity is not always easy to determine. They lived in an age of transition and each case should be examined individually. That also lesser figures could be Christian without abandoning classical Greek culture and poetry is demonstrated by the sixth-century official DIOSCORUS OF APHRODITO (MacCoull, 1989). One also can observe Greek-educated aristocrats turning away not only from paganism but also from Byzantine orthodoxy and entering the ranks of Monophysites, thereby pulling down one more barrier that could have separated them from the mainstream of the population in the *chora*. Among the victims of Coptic fervor were not only the Greek pagan cults but also the old Egyptian deities and their time-honored sanctuaries. These were abandoned, burned down, or turned into Christian churches. The temple of Isis in Philae, first closed, later became a church, and so did many venerable sanctuaries in Thebes and all over Egypt, ceding the place to Christian cults (Krause, 1966, cols. 72–78).

The End of Byzantine Rule

During the last decades of Byzantine rule (cf. Butler, 1978; Winkelmann, 1979), Egypt, while continuing to be the theater of serious internal dissensions, was also caught up in the turmoil of Byzantine and international politics. Alexandria, though being torn between Melchite and Monophysite patriarchs, was nonetheless instrumental in bringing down the emperor Phocas (602–610) and contributed much to the success of Heraclius' general, Nicetas. In 619, the Persian invasion of Egypt effectively separated the country from the Byzantine realm. But when they had to leave ten years later, the Persians had not made many friends in

Egypt. At least there are good reasons to believe that the occupiers did not accord special favors to the Monophysite church. Nor did the emperor Heraclius (610–641) when he installed the "Caucasian" Cyrus as patriarch in Alexandria (the tradition that Cyrus was also appointed *augustalis* must probably be rejected; Winkelmann, 1984, pp. 21–26). Being of Melchite observance, the new representative of the Byzantine emperor met with fierce resistance in Monophysite quarters, above all from their patriarch, BENJAMIN I, who finally had to flee from Alexandria.

In the wake of the Arab conquest, the country was thus in a state of utter confusion and agitation. Such a situation was in fact nothing new to Egypt, but under the prevailing circumstances, it surely must have facilitated the task of the invading Arabs. Nonetheless, the conquest of Egypt was not easy. The Copts were not a monolithic group welcoming wholeheartedly the Arab armies. After the fall of Pelusium in 639, the troops of ʿAmr ibn al-ʿĀṣ met strong resistance in the towns of the Delta, whereas the countryside was no match for the conquerors. The military stronghold of Babylon (Old Cairo) fell only on 6 April 641 and Alexandria even later, on 29 September 642, after the Byzantine troops had left the town. Dynastic strife in Constantinople after the death of Heraclius on 11 February 641 and the resulting confusion had greatly helped the Arab cause. When, on the other hand, dissensions in the Islamic camp led to the demise of ʿAmr, the Byzantine general Manuel availed himself of the opportunity and recovered Alexandria in 645. This in turn provoked the reinstallation of ʿAmr and the definitive occupation of Alexandria by the Arabs in 646. It was the end of an epoch that had begun, nearly a millennium before, with the conquest of Egypt by Alexander the Great in 332 B.C. But the termination of Greco-Roman rule did not bring about total disruption. Continuity can be observed in many important fields, such as the Coptic language and the Coptic church. In short, the Copts as a social and cultural group survived, as did, for a time at least, the Greek language and late Roman administration. Notwithstanding these links with the past, Egypt was now set on an entirely new course and prepared to take its place within an Arab-dominated world.

BIBLIOGRAPHY

Bacht, H. *Das Vermächtnis des Ursprungs. Studien zum frühen Mönchtum.* 2nd ed., 2 vols. Würzburg, 1984.

Bagnall, R. S. "Religious Conversion and Onomastic Change in Early Byzantine Egypt." *Bulletin of the American Society of Papyrologists* 19 (1982):105–124.

———. "Conversion and Onomastics: a Reply." *Zeitschrift für Papyrologie und Epigraphik* 69 (1987):243–50.

Barnes, T. D. "Angel of Light or Mystic Initiate? The Problem of the *Life of Antony.*" *Journal of Theological Studies,* n.s. 37 (1986):353–68 (contests Athanasius's authorship; cf. reply by Louth).

Bell, H. I. *Egypt from Alexander the Great to the Arab Conquest: A Study in the Diffusion and Decay of Hellenism,* pp. 101–134. Oxford, 1948; corr. ed., 1966.

Bowman, A. K. *Egypt after the Pharaohs: 332 B.C.–A.D. 642: From Alexander to the Arab Conquest.* London, 1986.

Butler, A. J. *The Arab Conquest of Egypt and the Last Thirty Years of the Roman Dominion.* Oxford, 1902; 2nd ed. by P. M. Fraser (Oxford, 1978), with a very useful and extensive additional bibliography on pp. xlv-lxxiii.

Cameron, A. "Wandering Poets: A Literary Movement in Byzantine Egypt." *Historia* 14 (1965): 470–509.

Carrie, J.-M. "Figures du 'colonat' dans les papyrus d'Egypte: lexique, contextes." In *Atti del XVII Congresso Internazionale di Papirologia,* Vol. 3, pp. 939–48. Naples, 1984.

Dörries, H. "Die Vita Antonii als Geschichtsquelle." In *Wort und Stunde. Gesammelte Aufsätze zur Kirchengeschichte des vierten Jahrhunderts,* ed. H. Dörries, Vol. 1, pp. 145–224. Göttingen, 1966.

El-Saghir, M., ed. *Le camp romain de Louqsor. Avec une étude des graffites gréco-romains du temple d'Amon.* Mémoires publiés par les membres de l'Institut français d'Archéologie orientale du Caire 83. Cairo, 1986.

Fikhman, I. F. *Egipet na rubeze dyuch èpoch. Remeslenniki i remeslennyi trud v IV–seredine VII v.* Moscow, 1965.

Gascou, J. "Les grands domaines, la cité et l'état en Egypte byzantine (Recherches d'histoire agraire, fiscale et administrative)." *Collège de France, Centre de recherche d'histoire et civilisation de Byzance, Travaux et Mémoires* 9 (1985):1–90.

Hardy, E. R. *Christian Egypt: Church and People. Christianity and Nationalism in the Patriarchate of Alexandria.* New York, 1952.

Johnson, A. C. *Egypt and the Roman Empire.* Ann Arbor, Mich., 1951.

Keenan, J. G. "On Law and Society in Late Roman Egypt." *Zeitschrift für Papyrologie und Epigraphik* 17 (1975):237–50.

Krause, M. "Das christliche Alexandrien und seine Beziehungen zum koptischen Ägypten." In *Alexandrien. Kulturbegegnungen dreier Jahrtausende im Schmelztiegel einer mediterranen Grossstadt,* ed. N. Hinske, pp. 53–62. Aegyptiaca Treverensia 1. Mainz, 1981.

Louth, A. "St. Athanasius and the Greek *Life of Antony.*" *Journal of Theological Studies,* n.s. 39 (1988):504–509 (reply to Barnes).

MacCoull, L. S. B. *Dioscorus of Aphrodito. His Work and His World.* The Transformation of the Classical Heritage 16. Berkeley, Calif., 1989.

Martin, A. "L'Eglise et la khôra égyptienne au IVe siècle." *Revue des études augustiniennes* 25 (1979):3–26.

Maspero, J. *Histoire des patriarches d'Alexandrie depuis la mort de l'empereur Anastase jusqu'à la réconciliation des églises jacobites (518–616).* Paris, 1923.

Munier, H. "L'Egypte byzantine de Dioclétien à la conquête arabe." In *Précis de l'histoire d'Egypte par divers historiens et archéologues,* Vol. 2, pp. 1–106. Cairo, 1932.

Pearson, B. A., and J. E. Goehring, eds. *The Roots of Egyptian Christianity.* Studies in Antiquity and Christianity. Philadelphia, 1986.

Rémondon, R. "Egypte chrétienne." In *Dictionnaire de spiritualité,* Vol. 6, pt. 1, cols. 532–48. Paris, 1960.

Rousseau, P. *Pachomius: The Making of a Community in Fourth-Century Egypt.* Berkeley and Los Angeles, 1985.

Thelamon, F. *Païens et chrétiens au IVe siècle. L'apport de l'"Histoire ecclésiastique" de Rufin d'Aquilée.* Paris, 1981.

Winkelmann, F. "Ägypten und Byzanz vor der arabischen Eroberung." *Byzantinoslavica* 40 (1979): 161–82.

______. "Die Stellung Ägyptens im oströmisch-byzantinischen Reich." In *Greco-Coptica. Griechen und Kopten im byzantinischen Ägypten,* ed. P. Nagel, pp. 11–35. Martin-Luther-Universität Halle-Wittenberg. Halle, 1984.

Wipszycha, E. "La Valeur de l'onomastique pour l'histoire de la christianisation de l'Egypte. A propos d'une étude de R. S. Bagnall." *Zeitschrift für Papyrologie und Epigraphik* 62 (1986):173–81.

______. "La christianisation de l'Egypte aux IVe-VIe siècles. Aspects sociaux et ethniques." *Aegyptus* 68 (1988):117–65.

HEINZ HEINEN

EGYPTIAN CONFERENCE OF HELIOPOLIS, conference held from 29 April to 4 May 1911, attended by two thousand delegates, to discuss issues of national significance, including demands made by Copts in their COPTIC CONGRESS OF ASYŪṬ. Muṣṭafā Riyāḍ Pasha, a former prime minister, was chairman, and Ibrahīm al-Hilbāwī was secretary. Among the speakers were Aḥmad Luṭfī al-Sayyid, ʿAbd al-ʿAziz Jawīsh, Ḥāfiẓ Ramaḍān, and ʿAli Yūsuf.

The delegates drafted the following resolutions:

1. Political rights should not be based on religious considerations.
2. No religious community may claim a national day of rest.
3. Ability should be the sole criterion for official appointments.
4. All citizens should have an equal right to vote. Highly qualified persons may, however, be accorded more votes.
5. As a community Copts should not be entitled to special financial aid for their own religious amenities.

The report was concluded by urging harmonious and tolerant coexistence.

SAMIRAH BAḤR

EGYPTIAN DEMOCRATIC PARTY. *See* Political Parties.

EGYPTIAN NATIONAL IDENTITY. A sense of their uniqueness, of their separateness from the rest of the world, has been permanent in the people of Egypt, but apart from this deeply ingrained feeling, no thoughts of national identity troubled the Egyptians until the end of the eighteenth century, when the bey ʿAlī al-Kabīr took up arms against the Turks and when General YAʿQŪB planned independence for Egypt. The question of national identity was not really broached before the French Expedition made its tremendous impact on Egypt and before Muḥammad ʿAlī became the unquestioned ruler of Egypt—after breaking the resistance of the Mamluks.

All through the nineteenth century, the history of Egypt was that of an opening up to Western influences, a gradual modernization imposed by Muḥammad ʿAlī and his successors Saʿīd and Ismāʿīl. This finally had its impact on Islamic thinkers, who were brought to ideas of reform in order to come to terms with the modernizing process. Jamāl al-Dīn al-Afghānī, Muḥammad ʿAbdū, and Qāsīm Amīn were in the forefront of a movement that aimed at reforming Islam without weakening the deep faith of its followers and its pervasive presence in everyday life.

At the same time, the vastness of the Egyptian cultural heritage and its great antiquity were opened up to a cultured minority of Egyptians through the work of informed and devoted foreigners. But the importance of this heritage only penetrated—or appeared to penetrate—the consciousness of the people during the 1919 uprising against the BRITISH OCCUPATION, when an inspirational return to the past glories of Egyptian history was in evidence; this was exemplified in the pharaonic character of the sculptor Mukhtār's monumental group of the "Awakening of Egypt." But this turned out to be only a short phase in the history of modern Egypt.

Meanwhile, the promises of Westernization were not kept, mainly because the king and the British fought so hard to reduce the power of the main party, the Wafd, which alone could have imposed the necessary adjustments. Also, the Wafd's outlook was too exclusively political, so that it did not give enough attention to social and economic problems. For these and other secondary reasons, there was a reversal in the Westernizing tendency. People remained willing to accept the West's science and technology but not its moral and intellectual values, without understanding that the West's technology could not be separated from its values.

Growing disappointment with the opening toward the West led intellectuals to turn back to the East and to Islam. Great writers disowned the Westernizing fervor of their younger days and the liberal beliefs of their mature age. Some imagined an Oriental culture opposed to Occidental culture; they advised people to resist European influences the better to preserve genuinely Oriental values. Others sought refuge in traditional notions representing religion as a sufficient font of political and social principles; they thought that Islam could supply the inspiration for remaking Egypt and restoring hope to the Egyptians.

After the failure of the liberal and democratic experiment, revolution came in 1952, fostered as always by selfishness and lack of foresight in the ruling minority. The military regime started by declaring its faith in an essentially Egyptian nationalism. As a token of this assertion, a colossal statue of Ramses II was moved from Memphis to a main square in Cairo, and an obelisk from Tanis was erected in a public garden on the banks of the Nile.

But a factor in the background of Egyptian concerns, arabism, suddenly surfaced. This new departure from Egyptian nationalism was the result partly of the Arab awakening, partly of the failure of the liberal and democratic experiment. It was also a result of the establishment of the state of Israel as an alien, West-supported body in the Arab world. This situation aroused inordinate ambitions in Egyptian leaders, who aspired to be at the head of an Arab empire.

So the Arab contribution was inflated to the point of constituting alone the whole content of the Egyptian cultural heritage. The Arabic character of Egypt was officially established as the dominant element of the Egyptian national spirit—which was therefore lost in arabism. This orientation was pushed to such a degree that the venerable name of Egypt, as well as its name in Arabic *(Miṣr)*, was struck out from the title of the state from 1958 to 1971. It was called the United Arab Republic until after the death of President Nasser.

Young and old alike became confused by these repeated changes, which were immediately implemented in school curricula as well as in the press, radio, and television. The sudden changes in orientation were reflected in the violent oscillations of policy that inflicted so much damage on Egypt in the thirty years between 1941 and 1971.

After President Sadat came to power, a more thoughtful attitude prevailed for some time in the councils of state, but since about 1978 the call for a return to Islam has come back in full force. This movement was allowed to grow by President Sadat, who was more afraid of communist subversion than of Muslim extremism. This was a grave mistake on his part, and he paid for it with his life.

Besides the importance of a stable national orientation for Egypt itself, Egyptian national orientation is of capital importance for the whole Arab world, of which Egypt is truly the hub and the axis, the center of gravity. Egypt's geographical position makes it either the link that unites the Arab world or the rift that divides it. The cultural and political orientation of the Arab community, the degree of union or disunion among its members, the form of its international institutions, all these depend on the Egyptians. This was amply proved during the furor caused by the Camp David agreements, which ended with Egypt being unconditionally invited back into the Arab fold.

Egypt's contribution to Arab civilization has been greater than any other; in turn, it was deeply marked by Arabic civilization. Egypt is thus part of the Arab world, but it retains its national identity, just as the other Arab countries retain their national identities.

BIBLIOGRAPHY

Anawati, G. C., and M. Borrmans. *Tendances et courants de l'Islam arabe contemporain*, Vol. 1,

Egypte et Afrique du nord. Munich, 1982.
Berger, M. *The Arab World Today.* New York, 1964.
Boutros Boutros Ghali. "Al Sha'b al-Wāḥid wa-Waṭan al-Wāḥid." Paper presented at Ahram Center for Political and Strategic Studies. Cairo, 1982.
Al-Fikr al-Mu'āṣir 50 (April 1969). Special issue on the Egyptian personality.
Fu' ād Ni'māt Aḥmad. *Shakhsiyāt Miṣr.* Cairo, 1978.
Ḥannā Milād. *Na'am . . . Aqbāṭ, Lākin . . . Miṣriyūn.* Cairo, 1980.
Haṣan Ṣa'b. *Taḥdīth al-'Aql al-'Arabī.* Beirut, 1969.
Jamāl A. Badawī. *Fitnah al-Ṭa'ifiyah fī Miṣr.* Cairo, 1980.
Jamāl al Dīn Maḥmūd Ḥamdān. *Shakhṣiyat Miṣr: Dirāsah fī 'Abqariyat al-Makān.* Cairo, 1970.
Kalisky, R. *Le monde arabe, le réveil et la quête de l'unité.* Verviers, 1968.
Khālid, Muḥyī al-Dīn, et al. *Al-Mas'alah al-Ṭa'īfiyyah fī Miṣr.* Beirut, 1980.
Lerner, Daniel. *The Passing of Traditional Society, Modernizing the Middle East.* New York, 1958.
Majid Khaddūrī. *Al-Ittijahāt al-Siyāsiyah fī-al 'Ālam al-'Arabī.* Beirut, 1972.
Mirrit Boutros Ghali. "The Egyptian National Consciousness." *Middle East Journal* 32, no. 1 (Winter 1978):59–77.
Muḥammad 'Abd al-Raḥmān Burj. *Dirāsah fī al-Ḥarakah al-Waṭaniyah Al-Miṣriyah.* Cairo, 1980.
Richmond, J. C. B. *Egypt 1798–1952, Her Advance Towards a Modern Identity.* London, 1977.
Safran, Nadav. *Egypt in Search of Political Community.* Cambridge, Mass., 1961.
Samīrah Baḥr. *Al-Aqbāṭ fī al-Ḥayat al-Siyāsiyyah al-Miṣriyyah.* Cairo, 1984.
Al-Sayyid, Yasīn. *Shakhṣiyah al-'Arabiyah.* Cairo, 1983.
Tāriq al-Bishri. *Al-Muslimūn wā al-Aqbāt.* Beirut, 1982.
Wendell, C. *The Evolution of the Egyptian National Image.* Berkeley, Calif., 1972.
William Sulaymān. *Al-Ḥiwār Bayna al-Adyān.* Cairo, 1976.

MIRRIT BOUTROS GHALI

EGYPTIAN NATIONAL UNITY, the great achievement of the 1919 national uprising against British Occupation. It was the highest expression of harmony and understanding between Muslims and Christians in Egypt. Expressions of this harmony were numerous and varied. Their best exemplification could be found in the speeches given by Muslim *shaykhs* in the Coptic churches and by Coptic priests in mosques.

This national understanding was more notable since it had been preceded eight years earlier by sharp exchanges between Muslims and Copts, after the murder of BOUTROS GHĀLĪ. The agitation culminated in the holding of the COPTIC CONGRESS OF ASYŪṬ in 1911, and the EGYPTIAN CONFERENCE OF HELIOPOLIS at which the demands and the allegations of the Coptic Congress were refuted.

The main body responsible for this new understanding was the Wafd party, which, from its formation in 1919, upheld a firm policy of cooperation between Muslims and Christians. When George Khayyāṭ asked SA'D ZAGHLŪL, the founder of the *Wafd*, what the future of the Copts would be after independence, the answer was "their status will be our status, they will have the same rights and the same duties, with no difference between any of us, save in personal achievement."

The *Wafd* also had a marked secular tendency and this helped to reassure the Copts on their position in the party. The success of the *Wafd* exceeded the hopes of its founders. All sections of the population, landowners, peasants, and townspeople, flocked to its membership. The *Wafd* adopted a strong nationalist attitude. This attracted the enmity of the king, who did not wish his own authority to be weakened by too strong a political party, and of the British, who had their own reasons for not having an Egyptian party with strong popular backing.

Thus the *Wafd*, in spite of being the largest and most popular party, was in power relatively few years from 1919 to 1952, as it was constantly fought by the other parties. In their fight for power, the other POLITICAL PARTIES did pay lip service to national unity, but they were often activated by different interests and paid less attention to the cause of national unity.

An important issue was that of minority rights. This question had already been broached when the Legislative Assembly was established, but it was again discussed at much greater length in the Constitution Committee in 1923. This was because the British Declaration of 28 February 1922 had mentioned minority protection as one of the reserved points. In order to invalidate the British argument for minority protection, the prime minister at the time, Ḥusayn Rushdī, tried to influence the Constitution Committee to decide for minority representation in both chambers of Parliament.

Minority protection was opposed by the *Wafd* party and the National party. The Constitution Committee finally decided against minority representation, after protracted discussion.

Despite all subsequent events, the Copts as a

whole have not regretted this decision. They stand steadfastly for a society where religion is a matter between man and his God. They understand that minority rights protection could have branded them as not being an integral part of the national community.

The call for Egyptian national unity is still at the forefront of all official declarations, but it is now being somewhat obscured by various extremist Islamic movements, the call for Islamic legislation to be applied in Egypt, the increase of Islamic pressure against the Christian minority, and the violence perpetrated by Islamic pressure groups. These last deserve special mention, because they are directed not only against Christians but also against the Muslim religious establishment, which they accuse of laxity and indifference in their call for Islamic legislation. In fact, it could be said that they are directed less against Christians than against their own establishment. Christian rights are always carefully recognized, in words if not always in deeds.

A blow to the cause of unity among Egyptians was the alliance of the *Wafd* with the Moslem Brotherhood during the electoral campaign for the People's Assembly in 1984. What Christians fear is once again to become second-class citizens in a country ruled by Islamic law, as they had been ever since the Arab conquest of Egypt up to the enlightened nineteenth century rule of Muḥammad ʿAlī and his successors.

The example of the Sudan, where Islamic law is stringently applied in the North and where it has caused a renewal of the civil war in the South, does not augur well for the future.

Early in 1985, President Numayrī of the Sudan was overthrown and a new regime came into power. Apart from the Muslim Brotherhood, most of the Sudan's political parties demanded the abolition of Islamic law. This had a strong influence in Egypt, where the People's Assembly disregarded the previous elaborate codification of Islamic law and decided that only provisions in direct contradiction to the Qur'ān would be amended. For several months following, the daily and weekly papers were full of calls for avoiding haste in applying Islamic law and for preserving good understanding between Muslims and Christians, as spelled out in the Constitution of 1923 and subsequent revisions.

MIRRIT BOUTROS GHALI

EGYPTIAN PARTY. *See* Political Parties.

EIKOSTON, one of the monasteries in the coastal strip separating Lake Mareotis from the sea, west of Alexandria. The site has not been located. Like the ENATON or the OKTOKAIDEKATON, it was so called from the number of milestones (in this case twenty) separating it from Alexandria (Raabe, 1895, pp. 64–65). According to the Life of Petrus Iberus, its monks took part in 457 in the election of the "Coptic" archbishop TIMOTHY AELURUS.

John Moschus places at the Eikoston the LAURA of Kalamon. He visited there the holy man Abbā Theodorus in company with Sophronius (*Pratum Spirituale*). This monastery is most certainly mentioned by JOHN OF NIKIOU. Timothy Aelurus is said to have been a monk there.

If we follow the Greek text of Moschus to the letter, we deduce that 2 miles (3.2 km) west of al-Qalamūn was the place called Maphora. According to the undated STELA (Lefebvre, 1907, p. 14) the Byzantine monk George, from the cenobium of Maphora, was buried at Dikhaylah, the probable site of the PEMPTON.

BIBLIOGRAPHY

Lefebvre, G. *Recueil des inscriptions grecques-chrétiennes d'Egypte*. Cairo, 1907.

Raabe, R. *S. Petrus der Iberer*. Leipzig, 1895.

Zotenberg, H. "Mémoire sur la chronique byzantine de Jean, évêque de Nikiou." *Journal asiatique*, ser. 7, 10 (1877):451–517; 12 (1878):245–347; 13 (1879):291–386.

JEAN GASCOU

ELEPHANTINE, an island at the level of Aswan, and the most southerly town in Egypt. In the pharaonic period it was the capital of the Elephant nome, but from Ptolemaic times it was reduced to a temple town and the administration was transferred to Syene, today Aswan, on the eastern river bank. The two main temples cover almost the whole of the former town area of Elephantine, and are dedicated to the god Satet (a place of worship on the same site can be traced back to the Thinite period; Kaiser, 1977, pp. 63ff.) and Khnum (Ricke, 1960).

After profanation of the temples in the Christian period, the forecourt of the temple of Khnum was converted into the barracks of an infantry cohort in the second quarter of the fifth century (Grossmann, 1979). For reasons of chronology, however, this cohort cannot be identified with the Cohort I Felix Theodosiana mentioned in the *Noticia Dignitatum Orientis* 31.64. A church inserted into the *pronaos*

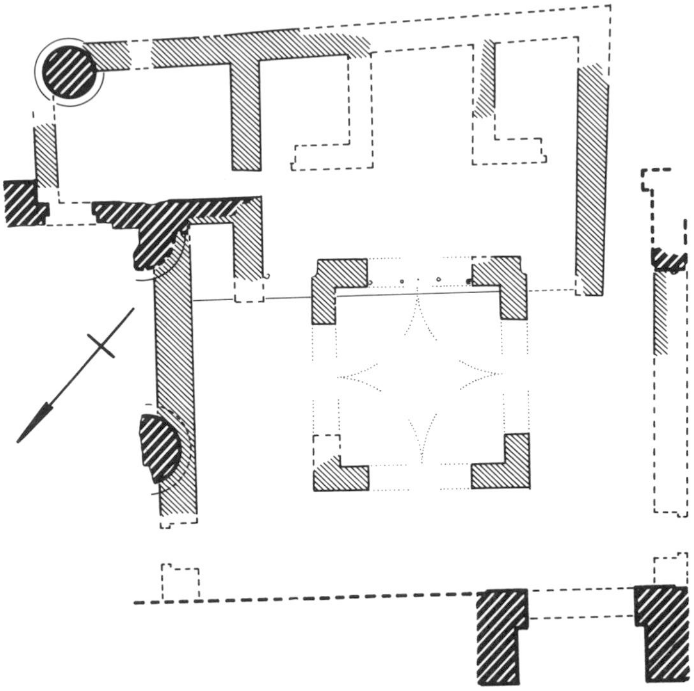

Plan of the ruins at Elephantine. *Courtesy Peter Grossmann.*

of the same temple in the late sixth century was formed as a centrally oriented building with an ambulatory and four corner pillars. Of a second church that once stood in the northwest part of the town and probably had the form of a basilica, only a few fallen column shafts and their bases have survived. The apse appears to have been provided with an inner ring of columns. The building itself was destroyed by the *sabbākhīn* (manure diggers).

BIBLIOGRAPHY

Grossmann, P. *Elephantine II, Kirche und spätantike Hausanlagen im Chnūmtempelhof.* Archäologische Veröffentlichungen 25. Mainz, 1980.

Kaiser, W., et al. "Stadt und Tempel von Elephantine." *Mitteilungen des deutschen archäologischen Instituts—Abteilung Kairo* 26 (1970):87ff.; 27 (1971):181ff.; 28 (1972):157ff.; 30 (1974):65ff.; 31 (1975):39ff.; 32 (1976):67ff; (1977):63ff.

Ricke, H. *Die Tempel Nektanebos' II in Elephantine.* Beiträge zur ägyptischen Bauforschung und Altertumskunde 6. Cairo, 1960.

PETER GROSSMANN

ELIANO, GIAMBATTISTA (1530–1589), member of Roman Catholic embassies to the Coptic and Maronite churches. He was born in Rome to a Jewish family and educated by his famous maternal grandfather, the learned Elias Levita, at Venice and at Isny, Germany. His family settled in Venice and he traveled with his father in the Middle East, where during a three-year stay in Egypt he learned to speak Arabic. A long, unsuccessful attempt by him and his family to convince his brother, Vittorio, who had become a Roman Catholic, to return to the Jewish faith, resulted instead in Eliano himself being baptized a Roman Catholic in 1551. Shortly after, he entered the Jesuit order; he became a priest in 1560. The Coptic patriarch GABRIEL VII (1525–1568) had sent a message of accommodation to Pope Paul IV (1555–1559) whose successor, Pius IV (1559–1565), sent an embassy to the patriarch in 1561. Eliano was sent as companion and interpreter for the papal legate, Christophorus Rodriquez. There were no practical results from the embassy, so Eliano returned to Rome in 1563, where he took up a professorship in Arabic and Hebrew at the Jesuit college. He founded one of the first Arabic printing establishments there. In 1578, Pope Gregory XIII (1572–1585) sent Eliano to the Maronites, and he attended the Maronite synod of 15–17 August 1580 at Qannūbīn (Kannobin) and translated the proceedings for the approval of the participants. The Coptic patriarch JOHN XIV (1570–1585) had sent a letter of allegiance in 1574, and Eliano for a second time went to Egypt (1582–1584). Again nothing toward a union of the churches was achieved.

VINCENT FREDERICK

ELIAS OF BISHWĀW, SAINT, monk who lived with exceptional austerity (feast day: 17 Kiyahk). He is known through the notice in the recension of the SYNAXARION from Upper Egypt. Two Arabic manuscripts also preserve the Life of this saint (Coptic Museum, Hist. 475, fols. 156–57 [Graf, Catalogue no. 718], and National Library, Paris, Arab. 153, fols. 112–14).

Elias was born at Iskhīm in the district of Qūṣ on the east bank of the Nile. While still young, he crossed the river and went to the mountain of Bishwāw. This site is located by the rolls of Bishop Timotheus, for the monastery of Saint VICTOR was afterward built on this spot (*cf.* Coquin, 1977, p. 145). He learned by heart thirty books of scripture. His habit, in conformity with the custom of the monks, was to read every morning, but he did not stop before he had finished the books. Then he devoted himself to manual labor. Often he recited the one hundred and fifty psalms, with his hands raised to heaven. He lived in a tomb in the midst of bones, emitting such a foul odor that his disciple John became sick and could not dwell with him.

BIBLIOGRAPHY

Coquin, R. G. "A propos des rouleaux coptes-arabes de l'évêque Timothée." *Bibliotheca Orientalis* 34 (1977):142–47.
Crum, W. E. *The Monastery of Epiphanius at Thebes,* Vol. 2. New York, 1926.
Graf, G. *Catalogue de manuscrits arabes chrétiens conservés au Caire.* Studi e Testi 63. Vatican City, 1934.
Troupeau, G. *Catalogue des manuscrits arabes,* Vol. 1. Paris, 1972.

RENÉ-GEORGES COQUIN

ELIAS OF SAMHŪD, SAINT, a sixth-century (?) monk whose birth was foretold by an angel (feastday: 13 Kiyahk). His Christian parents, who lived in the Fayyūm, held a monthly *agape* (meal) for the poor as well as widows and orphans, and were reportedly visited by the Old Testament prophets Elijah (Elias) and Elisha. Despite their prayers, his parents remained a long time without children. At last God sent the archangel MICHAEL to them, in the semblance of a monk, to announce to them the birth of a son, whom they were to call Elias and in whom the spirit of the prophet Elias would dwell. Shortly afterward his mother conceived, and after nine months gave birth to a boy. When he grew up, the child was the target of jealousy from his fellow pupils because of his success. Some of his fellows stole a gold necklet from one of the children and hid it under Elias' bed. When accused, he protested his innocence in vain. After class, one of the pupils was bitten by a serpent and died, but Elias restored him to life, which caused his holiness to shine forth in the eyes of his teacher and the other pupils.

Later he desired to become a monk, and joined a hermit who enjoined him to go into the monastery of Saint PACHOMIUS. He went to Pbow, where he received the monastic habit. After dissensions arose there he left for Djeme (west bank at Luxor), where he stayed for two years, then lived at Banhadab (west bank opposite Qifṭ) for some time. Finally he went to Hiw (Diospolis Parva), where an angel commanded him to go to Farshūṭ, north of Hiw.

The text of the Sahidic recension of the SYNAXARION, which is the sole source, has unfortunately lost its ending, and consequently the rest of his life remains unknown; but since the beginning of the notice indicates that he died "in the mountain of Samhūd," it is probable that he settled in that region. J. Doresse, like J. Muyser (1943, p. 226, n. 3), did not see that the continuation of the text after the lacuna is part of the life of the Syrian saints Banham and Sara, and that the "monastery of the vault" mentioned there is not in Egypt but in Iraq, in the neighborhood of Mosul (Coquin, 1978, p. 360).

BIBLIOGRAPHY

Coquin, R.-G. "Le synaxaire des Coptes." *Analecta Bollandiana* 96 (1978):351–65.
Doresse, J. "Elie de Samhud." *Dictionnaire d'histoire et de géographie ecclésiastiques,* Vol. 15, cols. 196–97.
Muyser, J. "Ermite Pérégrinant et Pèlerin infatigable." *Bulletin de la Société d'archéologie copte* 9 (1943):159–236.

RENÉ-GEORGES COQUIN

ELKASITES, name occurring in variant spellings in several patristic texts and referring either to an allegedly revelatory book or to a religious teacher.

Details about a book connected with the name Elchasai or Elxai are found in Hippolytus' *Refutation* and in the *Panarion* of Epiphanius. In Hippolytus, Elchasai is assigned a role in the transmission of the book, while Epiphanius states that Elxai was the author of the book. In addition, the book is briefly mentioned in Eusebius' *Ecclesiastical History* (VI.38) and in patristic texts that are dependent upon Eusebius.

From Hippolytus (*Refutation* IX.13 and IX.16), we may conclude that the book in question was written by an anonymous Jewish author in Mesopotamia during Trajan's Parthian war (114–117). On the authority of an angel of gigantic proportions and his female companion, "the Holy Spirit," the book announced that a war of much larger dimensions, a final struggle among all forces of evil, would break out within three years (*Refutation* IX.16.4). Furthermore, the book stipulated how men should act in view of the forthcoming Day of the Great Judgment. They should formally declare before seven nonhuman witnesses (heaven, water, holy spirits, angels of prayer, oil, salt, earth) that they would keep themselves free from all kinds of sins (*Refutation* IX.15.5f.). The book also indicated how certain sins (idolatry, fornication) could be avoided.

Although the book was originally written in Aramaic, the text quoted in Hippolytus and Epiphanius is that of a Greek version. In the Greek text, the eschatological features of the book were obscured while the esoteric, mysterious features were strongly emphasized. Missionary representatives of a Judeo-Christian community resident in Syria, who appeared in Christian churches in Rome and Palestine between 220 and 253, were in possession of this book and proclaimed that whoever listened to the book and believed in it would be forgiven his sins (Hippolytus *Refutation* IX.13–17; Eusebius *Ecclesiastical History* VI.38).

The leader of the above-mentioned Judeo-Christian missionaries in Rome, a certain Alcibiades, referred to Elchasai as a "righteous man" who had brought the book of revelations from Parthia to somebody called Sobiai (or, rather, to a community of *sobiai* [baptists]) in Syria (Hippolytus *Refutation* IX.13.1f.; apparently this was all Alcibiades knew about Elchasai).

In the fourth century, a syncretistic sect of Elkeseans living in trans-Jordan areas referred to Elxai as their teacher (Epiphanius *Panarion* 53.1.2). The Cologne Mani Codex includes four stories about a baptist authority, Alchasaios, supposedly told by Mani. In al-Nadīm's *Fihrist,* al Ḥasīḥ is reported to have been the head and founder of a baptist sect in Babylonia. Curiously, there are no clear indications that the trans-Jordan Elkeseans of Epiphanius' *Panarion* and the Babylonian baptists of the Cologne Mani Codex and the *Fihrist* were acquainted with or influenced by the book.

In all likelihood, the name Elchasai (*Ḥayil kesai,* Aramaic for "hidden power") originally belonged to the manlike angel who was said to have revealed the book. It is possible to conclude from Hippolytus and Epiphanius that the name of the angel was mentioned in the title of the book. Since readers of the Greek version could no longer relate the name Elchasai to the revealer-angel, this title is liable to have given rise to misunderstandings. Thus it would seem that Syrian Judeo-Christians believed that the name belonged to the one who had put the book in their possession. This may have been the basis of the idea of Elchasai as a religious teacher.

In the course of time, the book was lost and the supposed teacher became more and more a legendary figure. In the Cologne Mani Codex, Alchasaios is a precursor of Mani and the prototype of the Manichaean elect.

[*See also:* Manichaeism.]

BIBLIOGRAPHY

Brandt, W. *Elchasai. Ein Religionsstifter und sein Werk.* Amsterdam, 1971. Reprint of 1912 edition.

Cirillo, L. "La tradizione eresiologica di Elchasai." *Henoch* 1 (1979):371–95.

Henrichs, A. "The Cologne Mani Codex Reconsidered." *Harvard Studies in Classical Philology* 83 (1979):339–67.

Henrichs, A., and L. Koenen. "Ein griechischer Mani-Codex (*P. Colon.* inv. nr. 4780)." *Zeitschrift für Papyrologie und Epigraphik* 5 (1970):97–216.

______. "Der Kölner Mani-Kodex. Edition der Seiten 79, 8–99, 9." *Zeitschrift für Papyrologie und Epigraphik* 32 (1978):87–199.

Klijn, A. F. J., and G. J. Reinink. "Patristic Evidence for Jewish-Christian Sects." In *Supplements to Novum Testamentum* 36. Leiden, 1973.

______. "Elchasai and Mani." *Vigiliae Christianae* 28 (1974):277–89.

Luttikhuizen, G. P. *The Revelation of Elchasai.* Tübingen, 1985.

Strecker, G. "Elkesai." In *Reallexikon für Antike und Christentum,* Vol. 4. Stuttgart, 1959.

GERARD P. LUTTIKHUIZEN

ENATON, THE, one of the chief monastic centers of Byzantine and medieval Egypt, near Alexandria. It was called in Arabic Dayr al-Zujāj (Monastery of Glass) or Dayr al-Zajjāj (Monastery of the Glass Maker). Although the whole complex of monasteries at Enaton was completely ruined at the end of the Middle Ages, numerous Greek and Oriental sources give evidence of the high quality of its monastic life, the profundity of its religious conviction, and the distinction of many of its members.

Location

The Enaton (from the Greek *ennea* ["nine"]) derives its name from its location near the ninth milestone west of Alexandria on the coastal road to Libya. At the beginning of the twentieth century, archaeologists discovered funerary stelae, on which one of the monasteries of the complex appeared, and the remains of a church. As a consequence of those discoveries, the tendency is to locate the Enaton in the neighborhood of the present village of Dikhaylah, on the *taenia* (coastal strip) separating the sea from the western tongue of Lake Mareotis.

But nothing is less certain, and the forceful discussion of the epigraphic data by E. Schwartz in the 1920s shows that Dikhaylah is more likely to be the site of the ancient monastery of the PEMPTON, and that we must look for the Enaton on the *taenia* but some miles west of Dikhaylah on Kom al-Zujāj. Like other communities on the *taenia,* the monastery had at its disposal a sea anchorage and access to the lake. These geographical features were favorable to the vitality of economic and religious relations. We must bear them in mind in the light of human factors when we examine the historical role of the Enaton.

The Mareotis region, and the *taenia* in particular, was considerably more populated and more prosperous in late antiquity than it was only fifty years ago. Religious establishments abounded. Independently established but intimately linked with the Enaton were the Pempton, the OKTOKAIDEKATON, the EIKOSTON, and others. Travelers and monks mingled on the coastal road and occasionally made a stop at the Enaton with their beasts. The monastery provided them with appropriate quarters for the night. On crossing the lagoon, travelers arrived in the rich domain of the sanctuary of Saint MENAS (see ABŪ MĪNĀ). The devotees of the great martyr could enhance their pilgrimage with a visit to the Enaton. Farther to the south lay the monasteries of Nitria, Kellia, and Scetis, whose relations with the Enaton are well recorded. Close by, to the east was the populous civil and religious metropolis of Alexandria. Even though the monks of the Enaton did not always have permission to go to town, news as well as local and foreign visitors circulated rapidly between the city and the monastery. Finally, beyond Alexandria there flourished the METANOIA, whose monks in the 480s lent assistance to "sympathizers" of the Enaton on the occasion of an expedition against a clandestine shrine of Isis at Menouthis.

Origins

The date and circumstances of the founding of the Enaton are utterly obscure. The Passion of Serapammon, bishop of Nikiou martyred under DIOCLETIAN, says that he embraced the monastic life there (Hyvernat, 1886–1887, pp. 304–333), which would date the first attestation of the monastery at the end of the third century or the beginning of the fourth. But the Passion is unreliable, so one hesitates to accept this testimony. More creditable is the Coptic Life of Longinus, a great figure of the Enaton, the historicity of which is not in doubt. This text presents a picture of a prosperous and celebrated Enaton in the mid-fifth century that has already existed for a long time, since there is reference to monks buried in its cemetery. But this does nothing to clarify the question of its origins.

The Enaton at Its Height

The period from the mid-fifth to the mid-seventh century, in the Byzantine period, was the most animated in the history of the Enaton. During that time its organization and monastic life are best known.

Organization. The fact that the Enaton was called both a laura (a monastery in an Eastern church) and a *monasterion* ("monastery") should not mislead one into thinking of it as a single monastery. In fact, the Enaton was a conglomeration of autonomous establishments of varying size and population, sometimes no more than an isolated cell. These establishments also were called *monasteria* or above all *koinobia* (Latin, *coenobium,* or "monastery"). Each *koinobion* had its own church and holy men, who instructed disciples. The several *koinobia* of the Enaton were separately identified by a name which might recall that of a particular HEGUMENOS or PROESTOS or "father" or illustrious "cenobiarch," a personage sometimes confused with the founder himself. There were, for example, the *koinobion* of the cenobiarch Apa Gaius in the middle of the fifth century and that of Abba Salamah, known in 551 and again at the beginning of the seventh century; the eponymous head of that *koinobion* is perhaps the "great Solomon" mentioned about 482 to 489 in the Life of Severus (PO 2, 15, 24–27, 36 and 39).

A number of other components of the Enaton are known. The Three Cells (end of the fifth century) was the dwelling place of the ascetic Abba Zenon. The Monastery of the Fathers was one of the most celebrated. The Monastery of the Epiphany appears about 567 to 569. The Koinobion of Tougara appears in the beginning of the seventh century. The Monastery of the Antonians appears about 615. There was also the Monastery of Dalmatia.

Information about other monastic foundations at the Enaton is uncertain or confused. The Monastery of the Patrician founded in the reign of Justinian by the patrician lady Anastasia, friend of the theologian SEVERUS OF ANTIOCH, is placed at the Enaton by the Syriac Life of this lady and at the Pempton by the Greek versions. It is not improbable, however, that this monastery has been confused with the monastery of the patrician Caesaria, another friend of Severus, the exact location of which we do not know.

There are still more uncertainties with regard to the various *koinobia* or *monai* mentioned by epigraphic material from Dikhaylah, such as those of Abba Eustathius, Abba John, or Zaston. Except for the *koinobion* of Abba Salamah mentioned above, there is nothing to prove that these monasteries were attached to the Enaton. Moreover, the *koinobion* of Maphora is placed by one source near the Oktokaidekaton and the Eikoston.

According to the HISTORY OF THE PATRIARCHS, there were six hundred of these monasteries at the Enaton in the late sixth and early seventh centuries, but this figure is difficult to accept. According to the Arab Jacobite Synaxarion and the Ethiopian Synaxarion, this figure more likely refers to the total number of monasteries in the region of Alexandria. However that may be, the many establishments at the Enaton must have given it the appearance of a large town with irregular streets, houses with terraced roofs, and dogs running about.

The Enaton was a sort of federal institution presided over by a *hegumenos* as the supreme authority and an assembly of the community. From the beginning of the seventh century there was also an *oikonomos*, or steward, which shows that the separate monasteries had common material interests. Nevertheless, we have only a very summary idea of their form and extent. The wealth of the Enaton was in any case considerable enough to have excited the greed of the Persians under archbishop Andronicus in the early seventh century. We can just see the part taken by the offerings in its constitution.

Monastic Life. Life at the Enaton can be reconstructed with the aid of numerous edifying anecdotes. Certain features stand out. One is the large proportion of foreign-born monks. Apa Gaius, the *hegumenos* of the Enaton in the fifth century, was a Corinthian, and his disciple, the future *hegumenos* Longinus, came from Lycia (in Asia Minor), like his friend Lucius. Later there is reference to Carians and a Cilician. The strongest contingent, however, was from Syria and Palestine, which is explained by the proximity of these countries to Egypt and above all by a political and religious connection with Egypt.

A second feature is the importance accorded, alongside asceticism and prayer, to manual work. As in many other Egyptian communities, the work was chiefly the production of baskets and rope. This practice gave rise, according to the Life of Longinus, to a regular commerce, notably with the seafarers, from which the monks derived some personal profits, which they could dispense as alms.

A final feature is a high intellectual level. In the 480s the Enaton rivaled the philosophical school of Alexandria. The "great Solomon" taught there "the true philosophy" to an audience of educated disciples like the "sophist" Stephen and many students from Alexandria and elsewhere. These disciples then formed their own schools at the Enaton.

According to John Moschus, the Enaton welcomed the "philosopher" Abbā Theodorus. The theological erudition of Archbishop Damian, of Syrian origin and a former monk of the Enaton, is mentioned by several sources. One of the Enaton's finest claims to glory is to have been the setting in 615–616, at the Monastery of the Antonians, for the philological activity of two Syrians—Thomas of Harkel, bishop of Mabbug, made a collation of a Syriac translation of the New Testament with Greek manuscripts and Paul of Tella made a Syriac translation of the Septuagint after Origen's Hexapla. By a rare chance we possess several colophons of Syriac biblical manuscripts composed by these two scholars that mention the Enaton.

Religious History. The religious history of the Enaton is marked by a strong hostility to the Council of CHALCEDON (451) in its insistence on the dual nature of Christ. The monks there rallied around the energetic *hegumenos* Longinus, and took the side of DIOSCORUS, Monophysite patriarch of Alexandria, whom the council had deposed. He sent them a statement of his faith, and Longinus on the spot roused resistance against the emperor Marcian and his representative. The same Longinus played a decisive role in the election of Dioscorus' "Coptic" successor, TIMOTHY II AELURUS. Later on, at various periods, persecuted "Monophysites," notably Syro-Palestinians, took refuge or established themselves at the Enaton, either as individuals such as Thomas of Harkel or in a body such as the monastery of which John of Ephesus speaks. Notorious anti-Chalcedonians such as Zacharias Scholasticus or John of Ephesus visited the Enaton or sojourned there. The most illustrious of these guests was certainly Severus after his deposition from the archiepiscopal see of Antioch in 518. After the death of the great Monophysite theologian, his relics were returned to the Enaton and were buried there in a mausoleum. Miracles followed. Several "Monophysite" bishops came from the ranks of the Enaton, such as John of Hephaestus and Peter of Smyrna. There were also patriarchs of Alexandria: JOHN II, PETER IV, and Saint DAMIAN. Since the emperor forbade access to Alexandria to these last two pontiffs, the Enaton, where they continued to live, became practically the Holy See of the Coptic church. It was perhaps in this monastery that, in 616, the reconciliation between the Jacobite churches of Alexandria and Antioch was sealed.

Nevertheless, this presentation of an Enaton monolithic in its opposition to Chalcedon requires some emendations. At some points, a spirit of compromise seems to have prevailed. In the mid-sixth century the emperor JUSTINIAN, in a dogmatic treatise addressed to the monks, congratulates them on having returned to the communion of the "Melchite" archbishop Zoilus. To replace Zoilus, Justinian chose at the Enaton a docile archbishop, Apollinarius. John Moschus, in the course of his visits to the Enaton, does not appear to have met any "heretics." In the early seventh century the "Melchite" archbishop John the Almoner (John of Cyprus) entrusted to the steward of the Enaton a mission of confidence in Palestine, then occupied by the Persians, which implies that there was communication between them. Note also that Nicephorus Callistus implies that Theodora of Alexandria, a fifth-century saint recognized by the Greek church, lived at the Enaton.

The Enaton after the Arab Conquest

Sacked, as it seems, by the Persians in 619, the Enaton must have recovered rapidly. It passed safely through the ARAB CONQUEST OF EGYPT in 641, even benefiting on occasion from the favor of the Muslim authorities. It survived thereafter and even prospered for seven or eight centuries, perhaps a millennium. But for this period the sources are rare or mediocre. The final phase of the Enaton remains as obscure as that of its origins.

Several features of the earlier period survived for a long time, notably the federal structure of several

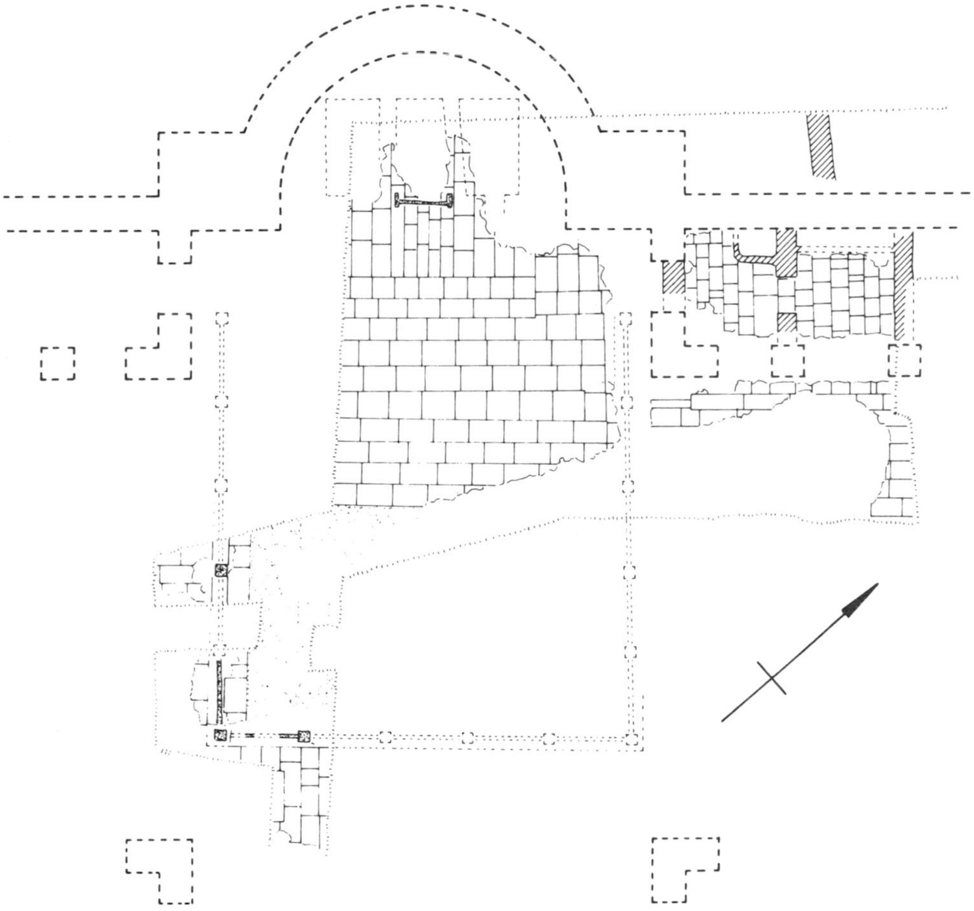

Plan of the remains discovered near Dikhaylah, presumed to form part of the Enaton. *Courtesy Peter Grossmann.*

koinobia presided over by the *hegumenos.* Nonetheless, one has the impression that from the eleventh century on, the Enaton was no longer more than a single monastery. We know that this kind of evolution is typical in medieval Egypt. The foreign element continued, however, to hold its place; there were Syro-Palestinians such as SIMON I, a former oblate of the mausoleum of Saint Severus who became patriarch of Alexandria, and even "Greeks." The monks still distinguished themselves by virtue of their "erudition" or the sanctity of their lives, despite a few black sheep.

The most notable change is the exclusive religious domination of the Jacobites, symbolized by the cult of the relics of Saint Severus, which is attested down to the eleventh century. The Enaton is placed at this period under the invocation of Severus, the great doctor. It was thus able to continue to provide the Coptic Church with patriarchs such as Simon I and ALEXANDER II. Other holy men were sounded out for the pontificate, such as the *hegumenos* Abbā John in 689, or his namesake John ibn Tīrūs in 1066. If every patriarch did not come from the Enaton, a custom attested for the first time under MARK II in the late eighth century that was extinct in the fifteenth century required that a newly elected patriarch should make a visit to or a stay at the Enaton.

Al-MAQRĪZĪ is the last author to treat of the Dayr al-Zujāj, which was then dedicated to Saint George, as if it were still active. It is true that the monastery appears in various Western maps dating from the fourteenth to the seventeenth century, but perhaps it was reduced to the status of a place name. It is, however, impossible to fix the date and circumstances of its disappearance. Perhaps it was the victim of an attack by those bedouin settled nearby in the time of the patriarchs SHENUTE II and CHRISTODOULUS in the eleventh century. At this period the Enaton numbered scarcely more than forty monks, a figure certainly much lower than that of its population in the late Roman period. Perhaps we should see at work here the most likely cause, in the long term, of its decline: the depopulation and progressive "return to nature" of the Mareotis region, as a consequence of drought and of the insecurity of the coast from the time of the Crusades.

BIBLIOGRAPHY

Cauwenbergh, P. van. *Etude sur les moines d'Egypte depuis le concile de Chalcédoine (451) jusqu'à l'invasion arabe (640).* Paris-Louvain, 1914; repr. Milan, 1973. The most exhaustive study.

Cosson, A. de. *Mareotis.* London, 1935.

Faivre, J. "Alexandrie," DHGE 2, 347–48 (valuable collection of sources).

Honigmann, E. *Evêques et évêchés monophysites d'Asie Mineure au 6e siècle,* CSCO 127, pt. 2, p. 144.

Maspero, J. *Histoire des patriarches d'Alexandrie depuis la mort de l'empereur Anastase jusqu'à la réconciliation des églises jacobites (518–616).* Paris, 1923.

JEAN GASCOU

ENCRATITE, member of an ascetic group arising in the second century that abstained from marriage, wine, and meat. The name "Encratite" is derived from the Greek word *enkrateo* (to be in control of), but it is well to distinguish at the outset between *encrateia,* which is the virtue of temperance, and an excess of it, which characterized certain heretics.

It seems clear that the Encratite texts were not the work of Egyptian authors, and that those of which CLEMENT OF ALEXANDRIA, for example, speaks (see Chadwick, cols. 358–60) were foreign; likewise, the clearly Encratite documents such as those from Nag Hammadi (in particular the EXEGESIS ON THE SOUL) existed on Egyptian soil only in translations. If the need was felt to make Coptic translations, this shows that the Egyptians had been won over to such ideas. But it remains clear that they were no more than imports.

Beyond doubt, the virtue of *encrateia* is extolled by a number of monastic writers, but they did not by any means aspire to impose upon all what appeared to them an evangelic "counsel," offered to the most perfect but not imposed as a condition sine qua non for baptism and hence for admission to the ranks of the Christians.

There is no lack of texts that express a pessimistic conception of the body, but it would appear that their authors addressed themselves to ascetics and wished to underline the necessity for a monk to hold in check all desires of the body, including the sexual, if he wished to be truly a "monk." But there are also a number of writings that display an optimistic conception of the flesh: the body must be considered an instrument willed by God. Thus EVAGRIUS PONTICUS rises up against those who disparage the body, such as the Manichaeans, and in so doing blaspheme against the Creator (*Kephalaia gnostika* IV.60). John CASSIAN, also a foreigner, but one who no doubt handed on the teaching of the desert fathers, says in reporting the precepts of Macarius that one must behave toward one's body as if one had to live with it for many a year. Evagrius reports the same remark, placing it on the lips of Macarius the Egyptian.

What characterizes the Egyptian texts, in contrast with those deriving from Cappadocia or Mesopotamia, is that they are very pragmatic and do not seek to give their teaching an anthropological basis, a particular conception of man and of his relations with God; hence the absence of what one might call ideological motivations (in contrast with writings from Syria or from Palestine). It is perhaps for this reason that we do not find any Encratites in Egypt except for those who had been won over to conceptions from outside.

BIBLIOGRAPHY

Chadwick, H. "Enkrateia." In *Reallexikon für Antike und Christentum,* Vol. 5, cols. 343–65. Stuttgart, 1962.

Coquin, R.-G. "Les Vertus ('aretai) de l'esprit en Egypte." In *Mélanges d'histoire des religions offerts à H.-Ch. Puech,* pp. 447–57. Paris, 1974.

RENÉ-GEORGES COQUIN

ENTOMBMENT. *See* Good Friday.

EPACTS. *See* Book of Epact.

EPARCHY, the equivalent of the Latin province from the time of republican Rome. Whereas most provinces of the empire were administered by senatorial governors at the beginning of the imperial period, the province of Egypt was the first to have at its head a governor of equestrian rank, the *eparchos* or *praefectus Alexandreae et Aegypti.* The administrative unity of the Egyptian province was to some extent dissolved by the reforms of Diocletian (see PROVINCIAL ORGANIZATION OF EGYPT for the details of these reforms). The newly created provinces covering the territory of late Roman Egypt (Aegyptus Iovia, Aegyptus Herculia, Thebais, and others) became now eparchies. Their civil administration was directed by a governor. In sixth-century Egypt the civil governors of the provinces were subordinated to the *duces* (the *dux* was originally the military commander of the province). The former province, or a plurality of provinces, could thus be conceived as ducal territories. But eparchy continued to be used officially as the designation of a province (see, for example, Justinian's edict XIII), whereas the frontier provinces of Thebais and Libya were termed *limites* (boundaries). Changing designations, minor rearrangements, and the random nature of our documentation must not obscure one basic feature: In the face of the fluctuating attributions of their governors and other administrators, Egypt and its territorial divisions maintained a remarkable continuity throughout late antiquity.

As far as the ecclesiastical use of eparchy is concerned, canons 4, 5, and 6 of the Council of NICAEA (325) refer to (civil) eparchies in order to delimit the jurisdictions of single churches. Canon 6 of the Council of CONSTANTINOPLE (381) and canon 9 of the Council of CHALCEDON (451) recognize and recommend the institution of provincial synods as bodies of ecclesiastical jurisdiction. That the ecclesiastical status of communities was directly linked to their political or administrative status is clearly shown by canon 17 of the Council of Chalcedon, specifying that the ecclesiastical "order" has to adapt itself to the public one. Canon 9 of the same council puts in evidence the ascending line from the bishop of the single bishopric to the synod of the province (*eparchia*), directed by the metropolitan, and from there to the exarch (patriarch) of the diocese.

BIBLIOGRAPHY

Lallemand, J. *L'Administration civile de l'Egypte de l'avènement de Dioclétien à la création du diocèse (284–382). Contribution à l'étude des rapports entre l'Egypte et l'Empire à la fin du IIIe et au IVe siècle,* pp. 41–57. Brussels, 1964.

Mason, H. J. *Greek Terms for Roman Institutions: A Lexicon and Analysis,* pp. 135f. American Studies in Papyrology 13. Toronto, 1974.

Rouillard, G. *L'Administration civile de l'Egypte byzantine,* 2nd ed. Paris, 1928.

HEINZ HEINEN

EPHESUS, FIRST COUNCIL OF (431), third ecumenical council, summoned by Emperor Theodosius II in order to settle the Nestorian controversy. The period from 381 to 431 was dominated by the efforts of the bishops of Rome and Alexandria to undo the work of the second ecumenical council, that of Constantinople I (381). The rivalry of the three sees came to a head in the conflict between CYRIL OF ALEXANDRIA (412–444) and NESTORIUS, archbishop of Constantinople (428–431).

Nestorius was a monk of Antioch strongly influenced by the principles of that city's school of theology. He acquired a considerable reputation as a preacher, and when the see of Constantinople became vacant in 428, Theodosius II appointed him archbishop, overriding the claims of local candidates. Nestorius, who had a fanatical streak and was eager to rid the city of schismatics and heretics, posed as a zealous supporter of orthodoxy. He fully supported his chaplain, Anastasius, who had preached against the use of the word *Theotokos* (Mother of God) as savoring of APOLLINARIANISM. A violent controversy arose over the use of the term, which had gained popularity with the growing devotion to the Virgin Mary. Nestorius' opponents gained the support of Cyril and the Egyptian monks.

The antipathy between Alexandrian and Antiochene theology and Cyril's love of conflict and intolerance of dissent added fuel to the flames, and led to his defending *Theotokos* in his paschal letter of 429. Cyril's agents in Constantinople spread the idea that Nestorius did not like *Theotokos* because he did not believe that Jesus was God. Excerpts from Nestorius' sermons were equated with the utterances of the third-century heretic Paul of Samosata. Cyril thus succeeded in building up an atmosphere of suspicion in Constantinople against Nestorius. He then persuaded Celestine, bishop of Rome, to summon a synod at Rome in 430; it condemned Nestorius, as did Cyril's own synod in Alexandria. Cyril then sent notice of both condemnations to Nestorius with a covering letter and twelve anathemas. The twelve anathemas condemned the "two natures" theology of Antioch—the division of the words and actions of Jesus between His divine and human natures—and required Nestorius to agree that the Word of God suffered in the flesh.

Meanwhile, Theodosius II had summoned a council, to be held at Ephesus, for Pentecost 431. Nestorius was confident that he could prove that the twelve anathemas were Apollinarian in tendency, but he underestimated the ability of Cyril to sway the proceedings to his own views, and also failed to appreciate the distress that his remarks concerning *Theotokos* had caused. Nestorius had enemies in Asia Minor who were jealous of their own liberties, and Memnon, bishop of Ephesus, became a violent opponent, throwing in his lot with Cyril. Nestorius had the support of John, bishop of Antioch, and other Syrian bishops. The scandal caused by Nestorius' remark that "God is not a baby two or three months old" continued unabated.

The third ecumenical council finally met on 22 June 431, when Cyril and his suffragans assumed control of the proceedings and deposed Nestorius. The Syrians arrived four days later, having been delayed by severe weather, and on hearing the news, held a rival synod and deposed Cyril and Memnon. Finally the legates of the bishop of Rome arrived and joined the main council in accordance with Celestine's wish. Cyril's dubious actions thus had Western ratification, and he went on to condemn PELAGIANISM, to grant Cyprus ecclesiastical independence, to appoint Juvenal patriarch of Jerusalem, and to prohibit any addition to the Nicene Creed. The two rival synods had, however, cursed each other; and the emperor, not knowing what to make of the impasse, ratified the depositions of Nestorius, Cyril, and Memnon as if these were the acts of a single council. Cyril was, however, a master of bribery of state officials, and the position of Nestorius began to weaken. His offer to return to his monastery at Antioch was accepted, and Cyril's position was strengthened by the support he received from the papal legates and by his ability to escape punishment for his overbearing behavior. At Alexandria he was greeted with triumph on his return.

The breach between John of Antioch and Cyril was healed in 433 by large concessions on both sides. However, this reconciliation was maintained only with difficulty and broke down completely after the deaths of the main protagonists. The third ecumenical council was not really influential as such in later centuries. It was subsumed under the authority of the Council of NICAEA (325) as representing an orthodoxy from which no deviation was possible. However, the formal approval that it gave to the title *Theotokos* was significant for Greek Orthodoxy. In Coptic Christianity it is accepted, unlike CHALCEDON, as an ecumenical council.

BIBLIOGRAPHY

Bathune-Baker, J. D. *Nestorius and his Teaching.* Cambridge, 1908.

Chadwick, H. *The Early Church,* pp. 194–200. Harmondsworth, 1967.

D'Alès, A. *Le Dogme d'Ephèse.* Paris, 1931.

Fliche, A., and V. Martin, eds. *Histoire de l'église,* Vol. 4, pp. 163–196. Paris, 1939.

Frend, W. H. C. *The Monophysite Movement,* pp. 1–49. Cambridge, 1972.

Hefele, C. J., and H. Leclercq. *Histoire des conciles,* Vol. 2, pt. 1, pp. 287–377. Paris, 1908.

Kraatz, W., ed. *Koptische Akten zum Ephesinischen Konzil vom Jahre 431.* Texte und Untersuchungen 26, no. 2. Leipzig, 1904.

Loofs, W. *Nestorius and his Place in the History of Christian Doctrine.* Cambridge, 1914.

LESLIE W. BARNARD

EPHESUS, SECOND COUNCIL OF, convoked on the order of Emperor Theodosius II (408–450) ostensibly to heal the rift that had developed between Flavian, patriarch of Constantinople, and the archimandrite EUTYCHES. It met at Ephesus in two sessions, 8 and 22 August 449.

Flavian had accused Eutyches of preaching a Christology that denied that Christ was true man, and asserted that the Divine Word itself participated in the sufferings of the Passion. Behind this dispute, however, was a test of strength among the four great sees of Christendom: Rome, Constantinople, Antioch, and Alexandria. Jerusalem, under its ambitious bishop Juvenal (422–458), was in the wings, seeking its own advantage wherever possible. The outcome was a triumph for Alexandria, which placed it as the foremost see in the Christian world, before the Council of CHALCEDON in 451 restored the primacy to Old and New Rome.

Eutyches had been condemned by bishops at the synod of Constantinople on 22 November 448. He was declared deposed from his position as archimandrite of an influential monastery in the capital. Immediately he appealed to what he called "the councils" of Rome, Alexandria, Jerusalem, Thessalonica, and Ravenna (the imperial residence). He received the support of Alexandria, whose patriarch, Dioscorus I, was already engaged in a growing controversy with Domnus, patriarch of Antioch (441–449), and Flavian on the issue of the alleged persistence of "Nestorianism" in the east. He was also finding support from the emperor, who had once upheld NESTORIUS but now feared Nestorianism, as though it were a reversion to paganism. In February 448, Theodosius II had ordered the burning of "Nestorian works" along with those of the anti-Christian Neoplatonist philosopher Porphyry (*Codex Justinianus* 1.1.3).

Events in the spring of 449 favored Eutyches. Dioscorus received him into his communion. The emperor expressed dissatisfaction with the manner in which Flavian had conducted the proceedings against Eutyches and demanded a confession of faith from Flavian. There were violent anti-Nestorian outbreaks in the city of Edessa, which alarmed the emperor further. On 30 March, Theodosius published a decree ordering a council of bishops to meet at Ephesus. It was to be a judicial council designed to try the single issue of the rightness or wrongness of Eutyches' condemnation. Its numbers were confined to metropolitan bishops assisted by ten other learned bishops from their own respective provinces. In order to represent monastic opinions, a supporter of Dioscorus, the Syrian monk Barsaumas, was added to the bishops' numbers; an imperial official, Count Helpidius, would represent the emperor at the proceedings. The task of convening the council and presiding over its deliberations was entrusted to Dioscorus.

The main point in doubt was the attitude of the pope. In the previous dispute involving Constantinople and Alexandria over the views of Nestorius (430–431), Pope Celestine had supported Alexandria. The question was whether Pope LEO THE GREAT would support Eutyches and Dioscorus. Flavian's tardiness in informing Leo of the decision of the Home Synod—he did not write to Leo until March (Leo, *Letters* 26)—may have cost him some sympathy at Rome, for Leo's reply on 21 May 449 (*Letters* 38) indicated no particular urgency in the matter. Leo's considered response, written on 13 June—the famous *Tome*—was not sent direct to Flavian at Constantinople but taken to Ephesus by the pope's legates. The *Tome,* while forcefully asserting the necessity of acknowledging Christ "in two natures," came too late to help Flavian.

On 8 August, about 135 bishops assembled at Ephesus. At the first session of the council, Dioscorus took every opportunity to humiliate his fellow archbishops. Flavian was accorded precedence not only below the papal legates (Bishop Julius of Puteoli and the deacon Hilarus) but also below Domnus of Antioch and even Juvenal of Jerusalem. The pope's tactical error in not addressing the *Tome* directly to Flavian became crucial, because Dioscorus could assert with some show of propriety that its discussion must take place after the main business of the council as stated by the emperor—the case of Eutyches. It was thus moved to the bottom of the agenda and never read at all.

Eutyches was able to cite documents allegedly written by Pope Julius, Gregory "the Wonderworker," and Athanasius to support his case. In fact, these were among the "Apollinarian Forgeries," but at this time they were accepted as genuine documents. Having listened to these, the council had no hesitation in acquitting Eutyches. "Two natures before the union, one afterward. Is that not what we all believe?" Dioscorus' question was answered with an enthusiastic affirmative. Eutyches was declared guiltless and restored to office.

Had the matter stopped there, Alexandria would have gained a great triumph for both its doctrine and its ecclesiastical status. Unfortunately, Dioscorus was no moderate. Disgraceful scenes ensued. Flavian found himself condemned for "causing disturbance in the holy churches" and "adding without authorization to the teaching of the creed of Nicaea." He and the fellow accuser of Eutyches, Eusebius of Dorylaeum, were declared deposed. Flavian himself was so brutally manhandled that he died soon afterward. The papal legates were insulted and fled from the assembly, vainly protesting. Bishops present were overawed by soldiers and monks, and forced to sign blank forms on which the condemnation of Flavian and his supporters could later be written.

On 22 August, the council completed its work by deposing Domnus of Antioch, Theodoret, bishop of Cyrrhus, and Ibas, bishop of Edessa. It pronounced solemnly the acceptance of CYRIL OF ALEXANDRIA'S twelve anathemas as canonical. Dioscorus gained what appeared to be a final triumph over Flavian by having his representative *(apocrisarius)*, Anatolius, consecrated archbishop in his stead. The title of patriarch now became normal for the holders of the great sees of Christendom. Juvenal of Jerusalem was admitted to the company of patriarchs. He was to oversee six provinces (three of Palestine and three of Arabia) carved out of the patriarchate of Antioch.

Ephesus II is the high-water mark of the power of the see of Alexandria. So long as THEODOSIUS II lived, its decisions were proof against protests by the papacy and a section of the imperial court. It was "the city of the orthodox." However, continued opposition of the Roman see and the innate strength of Constantinople as capital of the empire might well have prevented the consolidation of that authority. As it was, the shock of the disorderly proceedings (cf. Theodoret of Cyrrhus, *Letters* 113, PG, cols. 1319–1324), as well as the arrogance of Dioscorus, contributed to the rapid change of policy at the imperial court after the death of Theodosius II as the result of a hunting accident on 28 July 450. The revolution that then took place in the ecclesiastical policies of the east Roman world ensured that Ephesus II went down in history in Pope Leo's description (*Letters* 95) as the Latrocinium (Robber Synod).

BIBLIOGRAPHY

Camelot, T. "De Nestorius à Eutyches." In *Das Konzil von Chalcedon*, ed. A. Grillmeir and H. Bacht, Vol. 1, pp. 213–42. Würzburg, 1953.

Chadwick, H. "The Exile and Death of Flavian of Constantinople: A Prologue to the Council of Chalcedon." *Journal of Theological Studies*, n.s. 6 (1955):17–34.

Frend, W. H. C. *The Rise of the Monophysite Movement*, chap. 1. Cambridge, 1979.

Haase, F. "Patriarch Dioskur: Nach monophysistischen Quellen." *Kirchengeschichtliche Abhandlungen* 6 (1908).

Honigmann, E. "Juvenal of Jerusalem." *Dumbarton Oaks Papers* 5 (1950): 211–79.

Sellers, R. V. *The Council of Chalcedon*. chaps. 2 and 3. London, 1953.

W. H. C. FREND

EPHESUS, THIRD COUNCIL OF. A large synod of bishops from the provinces of Asia Minor, Ephesus III was presided over by TIMOTHY II AELURUS in 476, on his way from Constantinople to Alexandria, during the latter stages of the usurpation of Basiliscus (475–476). The convening of the synod was Timothy's final effort to gain the empire's acceptance of the anti-Chalcedonian views of the see of Alexandria.

The council petition was not "Eutychian," as has been suggested. It did, however, request Basiliscus to stand firm in his condemnation of the *Tome* of Pope LEO THE GREAT and the Council of CHALCEDON, as set out in the encyclical published the previous year. Chalcedon, it was declared, had caused "deaths and slaughters" and "the blood of the orthodox," and should remain condemned (Evagrius *Historia ecclesiastica* 3.5). The council also asked Basiliscus to confirm its deposition of Acacius, the patriarch of Constantinople (471–489), and, in addition, to emphasize its opposition to the policy of the see of Constantinople. It also restored to Ephesus "patriarchal rights" (meaning the right to consecrate the bishops of the province of Asia), which had been lost to Constantinople under the terms of Canon 16 of Chalcedon. It also restored Bishop Paul, who had been deposed (perhaps by Acacius), to the see of Ephesus.

The restoration of Emperor Zeno in August 476 rendered the decrees of the council invalid. By this time Timothy had returned to Alexandria, where he died under renewed threat of exile on 31 July 477.

BIBLIOGRAPHY

Frend, W. H. C. *The Rise of the Monophysite Movement*. Cambridge, 1979.

Hole, C. "Paulus (31)." In DCB, Vol. 4, p. 261. Repr. New York, 1974.

Simonetti, M. "Efesi." In *Dizionario patristico e di antichità cristiana,* Vol. 1, pp. 1099–1103. Rome, 1983.

W. H. C. FREND

EPHRAEM SYRUS, SAINT (c. 306–373), one of the most productive spiritual writers of the fourth century. Lives of Saint Ephraem (Bibliotheca Hagiographica Orientalis 269) are late and provide us with no objective information about him. His portrait can best be traced through the considerable quantity of his works. He was born at Nisibis around 306 and must still have known and been subject to the influence of James of Nisibis (303–338). The portrait he gives of the latter is that of a pastor and a saint, an ascetic and a churchman, whose relics protected the town against the Persians. Bishop Vologesus (346–361) is also the subject of the most lively eulogies. Through innumerable hymns it is possible to compile a table of the numerous doctrinal deviations on the periphery of Christianity in the fourth century in Mesopotamia. In 363 the town of Nisibis was handed over to the Persians following the defeat of JULIAN THE APOSTATE. Ephraem then went to Edessa, where he certainly taught at its famous school. He appears never to have been other than a deacon. The hymn dedicated to Julian Sabas (d. 367) bears the tone of a fervent disciple. According to the *Chronicle of Edessa,* Ephraem died in 373.

The work of Ephraem appeared at the same time in Syriac and in Greek, and it is not easy to establish the priority for his thought, which was certainly first given expression in Syriac. The theological profundity of his works resulted in his being declared a doctor of the universal church by the Roman Catholic Church in 1920. Like all prolific writers, Ephraem inspired a large number of pseudepigrapha. Other works sought the support of such a celebrated name. Sifting the authentic from the apocryphal has mainly been the labor of D. Hemmerdinger-Iliadou and J. Kirchmeyer, as published in two articles in the *Dictionnaire de spiritualité.*

In Coptic, under the name of Ephraem there remain the following eight texts:

1. An ascetic discourse (Clavis Patrum Graecorum 3909; British Museum, Manuscript, Or. 6783, written in 973 at DAYR ANBĀ MAQĀR [Monastery of Saint Macarius of Idfū], fols. 45–63). It was published by E. A. Wallis Budge in 1914. The text existed in Syriac, Greek, and Latin almost from the start.

2. Sermon on the patriarch Joseph, in the Pierpont Morgan Series (Vol. 31 of the photographic edition) and in a codex of Dayr Anbā Shinūdah (Clavis Patrum Graecorum 3938).

3. A sermon on the transfiguration (Clavis Patrum Graecorum 3939). This sermon is variously attributed in the manuscripts. It was interpolated in various ways by the Chalcedonians in Greek, whence its attribution by various patristic scholars to Ephraem of Antioch, but in Coptic it is interpolated in an anti-Chalcedonian way. As there is an extant Georgian version that is not in the service of either of the two factions, one must ask whether the homily is not prior to Ephraem of Antioch, and therefore authentic.

4. A sermon on the vain life and on penitence (Clavis Patrum Graecorum 4031; Vatican Library, Coptic manuscripts, 57, fols. 66–74 [Bohairic] under the name of John Chrysostom; also in PG 60, cols. 735–38; but it can also be found in Greek in Ephraem's name).

5. The sermon on the adulteress (Clavis Patrum Graecorum 3952; there is a Bohairic Coptic version in Vatican Library Coptic manuscripts, codex 68; this has been published by I. Guidi (1897).

6. A letter attributed to Ephraem, which exists only in Coptic (Clavis Patrum Graecorum 4135) was published by E. A. Wallis Budge (1914) from the same manuscript that contains the *Asketikon.*

7. Some fragments from the White Monastery contain the remains of *De Antichristo* (Clavis Patrum Graecorum 3944); others have the remains of the *Catecheses* (T. Orlandi, 1970, p. 118).

8. A text published among the Coptic festal letters of Saint Athanasius by L. T. Lefort (1955, pp. 121–38) corresponds to *A Doctrine for Certain Monks,* published in Georgian by I. Imnaišhvili (Clavis Patrum Graecorum 4145, item 16). Authenticity cannot be ruled out. Ephraem's influence in Egypt, though late, has been analyzed by H. J. Polotsky (1933).

BIBLIOGRAPHY

Beck, E. "Ephrem le syrien." In *Dictionnaire de spiritualité,* Vol. 4, cols. 788–800. Paris, 1958.

Budge, E. A. W. *Coptic Martyrdoms in the Dialect of Upper Egypt.* London, 1914.

Guidi, I. "La traduzione copta di un'omelia di S. Efrem." *Bessarione,* ser. 2, 4 (1897):1–21.

Hemmerdinger-Iliadou, D. "Ephrem (Les versions)." In *Dictionnaire de spiritualité,* Vol. 4, cols. 800–819. Paris, 1958.

Kirchmeyer, J. "Autres versions d'Ephrem." In *Dictionnaire de spiritualité,* Vol. 4, cols. 819–22. Paris, 1958.
Orlandi, T. *Elementi de lingua e letteratura copta.* Milan, 1970.
Polotsky, H. J. "Ephraem's Reise nach Ägypten." *Orientalia* 2 (1933):269–74.

MICHEL VAN ESBROECK

EPICLESIS, the invoking of the name of God upon a person or thing. Although in the baptismal liturgy the Holy Trinity is invoked upon the baptized person, and in the rites of confirmation and ordination the invocation is of the Holy Spirit, this article is limited to the liturgy of the Holy Eucharist. In the liturgy, the priest petitions the Father to send in the first epiclesis the Logos and in the second epiclesis the Holy Spirit upon the bread and wine to make them the Body and Blood of Christ. However, in the Coptic liturgies it is also extended to invoke the Holy Spirit upon the people and to sanctify them through the Holy Eucharist.

Whether the full consecration is accomplished through the epiclesis of the Word or the Holy Spirit or the words of institution is a point of controversy between the Oriental Orthodox and the Roman Catholic churches. The Coptic Orthodox church, being of the Oriental Orthodox family, believes that the eucharistic liturgy is one inseparable unity and that the full consecration is a process that requires all the elements of the Divine Liturgy: the ANAMNESIS, the words of consecration, and the epiclesis. The Roman Catholic church believes the words of institution are the only requirement despite the fact that reference to the epiclesis of the Holy Spirit, or rather the Logos, has been traced in its early canons of the mass. However, some prayers included there are interpreted as being forms of epiclesis.

According to the Coptic Liturgy of Saint Serapion (d. after 360), which is not in recent use, the epiclesis takes place before the words of institution, though with the invocation of the Logos (the holy word), probably to present the divine nature of the Lord Jesus Christ at the time of the Arian heresy.

The three usual Coptic divine liturgies—Saint Basil, Saint Gregory, and Saint Mark—contain explicitly a double epiclesis before and after the words of institution. The first epiclesis is inaudibly prayed by the priest and is petitioned to the Holy Logos, being the spotless Lamb, as a request for His presence on the altar and is in concurrence with the Old Testament paschal figure:

> O Lord and Master, Jesus Christ, the Co-Partner, the Logos of the undefiled Father, the Consubstantial with the Holy Spirit; Thou art the life-giving bread that came down from heaven; Thou hast made of Thyself a spotless lamb for the life of the world. We beseech and implore Thy goodness, Thou lover of mankind [pointing with his finger to the bread], to reveal Thy divine visage unto this bread [and pointing to the chalice] and this chalice; [and pointing to the Altar he says] both of them are placed on the priestly table which is Thine. [He then crosses the bread and wine thrice, saying] Bless them, sanctify them, purify, and transform them. [He then points to the bread in particular saying] So that this bread will be Thine Holy Body; [and to the wine saying] and the mixture in this chalice will be Thine Honorable Blood. [He then continues saying] May they be for us all a source of exaltation, a balsam, a redemption for our souls, our bodies and our spirits too. . . .

The second epiclesis comes right after the words of institution, when the officiating priest petitions for the invocation of the Holy Spirit not only on the bread and wine but also on the congregation:

> We beg Thee, O Lord, our God, we are Thy sinful and unworthy servants, to permit us through the pleasure of Thy Goodness to worship Thee; And that Thine Holy Spirit may descend upon us and upon these oblations; purify, transform, and manifest them in sanctity unto Thine holy people. [The priest then crosses the holy bread thrice saying] and this bread is made into His Holy Body. [Then bowing with stretched arms he says] Our Lord, God, and Savior Jesus Christ, this is given for the remission of sins; whoever partakes of it is granted eternal life. [He does the same with the chalice and says] And this chalice too hath His Honored Blood of the new covenant that is His. [Then he says while kneeling] Our Lord, God, and Savior Jesus Christ, this is given for the remission of sins; whoever partakes of it is granted eternal life.

According to the Coptic Divine Liturgies this does not mean that the mystery is at this time also made complete. After the prayer of the fraction, which follows, the priest offers the inaudible prayer that explicitly indicates the completion of the mystery.

BIBLIOGRAPHY

Atchley, E. C. *On the Epiclesis of the Eucharistic Liturgy and on the Consecration of the Font.* Oxford, 1935.

Deiss, L. *Springtime of the Liturgy: Liturgical Texts of the First Four Centuries,* trans. Matthew J. O'Connell. Collegeville, Minn., 1979.
Jasper, R. C. D., and G. J. Cuming. *Prayers of the Eucharist, Early and Reformed.* New York, 1980.
Lee, R. D. *Epiclesis and Ecumenical Dialogue.* Diakonia 9. Bronx, N.Y., 1974.

GABRIEL ABDELSAYYED

EPIGRAPHY. *See* Inscriptions.

EPIGRAPHY OF THE KELLIA. *See* Kellia.

EPIMA, SAINT, martyr in the persecutions of DIOCLETIAN (feast day: 8 Abīb). The text of his Passion has come down in a Bohairic codex (Vatican Library, Coptic manuscripts, codex 66, fols. 96–123; Balestri and Hyvernat, 1908) and a Sahidic codex (Coptic Museum, Cairo; Togo-Mina, 1937).

The beginning of the Passion is connected with the CYCLE of Basilides and forms an introduction not necessarily linked to the Passion of Epima. It tells the story of the war between Diocletian and Shapur, king of Persia, the capture of Shapur's son, Nicodemus, as a hostage, and the betrayal of Bishop Gaius, which provoked the anger of Diocletian against the Christians. The first martyr is a soldier whose name is not known (cf. Horn, 1982). Then the famous edict demanding sacrifice to pagan gods is promulgated and sent to the prefect Armenius in Alexandria.

Here begins the real Passion of Epima, who came from Pankoleus, near Pemje (Oxyrhynchus). He has a vision and goes to the *dux* Culcianus at Pemje, who orders Epima to bring the priests and sacred objects to him. Epima refuses and is imprisoned and tortured. He has a vision of the archangel MICHAEL, who heals him; he is tortured again, and then sent to Armenius in Alexandria. Here he performs various miracles in prison. Julius of Aqfahṣ visits him, and his sister is healed by Epima. In court there is a fresh argument with Armenius and also torture, miraculous healings, and visions. The *duces* Rucellianus and Sebastianus come to Alexandria, and Epima is handed over to them to be killed. Julius bids him farewell. After his martyrdom, the servants of Julius take the body to Shmum and then to Pankoleus, and return to tell Julius what has happened. Julius "signs" the text of the Passion.

This text, therefore, belongs to the Cycle of Julius of Aqfahṣ, and the lively inventiveness and the introduction would indicate that it is among the oldest in the cycle, dating to about the seventh century.

BIBLIOGRAPHY

Balestri, I., and H. Hyvernat. *Acta Martyrum,* 2 vols. CSCO 43, 44. Paris, 1908.
Horn, J. "Der erste Märtyrer. Zu einem Topos der koptischen Märtyrerliteratur (mit zwei Anhängen)." In *Studien zur spätantiken und frühchristlichen Kunst und Kultur des Orients,* ed. G. Koch. Wiesbaden, 1982.
Togo Mina (J. Muyser). *Le Martyre d'apa Epima.* Cairo, 1937.

TITO ORLANDI

EPIMACHUS OF PELUSIUM, SAINT, a martyr in the great persecutions of DIOCLETIAN about 303 (feast day: 14 Bashans). He was of considerable prominence in Christian Egypt. Sa'īd ibn al-Biṭriq (876–939) writes in his *Annals* (Cheikho, 1906, Vol. 1, p. 16): "In the days of both Diocletian and Maximian thousands of martyrs died; they tortured Mār Jirgis in all sorts of ways and put him to death in Palestine although he was of the Cappadocian nation, and these two killed Mār Menas, Mār Victor, Vincent, Epimachus and Mercurius." For an Egyptian of the ninth century, Epimachus occupied quite naturally a place close to the most renowned figures. The Oxyrhynchus papyrus calendar, dated 535–536, notes a liturgical synaxarion in honor of the martyr, in the church founded by PHOIBAMMON on 3 Hātūr. Only four mutilated papyrus leaves now preserved at Turin remain in Coptic on Saint Epimachus. They have been published by F. Rossi (1888, p. 235). The reading of the text of the first fragment of a column was improved by O. von Lemm (1910, pp. 1461–64). The Coptic fragments are particularly striking because of the large number of Egyptian toponyms and because of the date they imply. These fragments, which belong to the fifth–sixth centuries, show in their title 14 Bashans but give 3 Hātūr for the execution of the martyr.

It would hardly be possible to interpret these fragments without the help of the Arabic parallel preserved in the notice of the Arabic SYNAXARION, which summarizes in detail the contents of the longest Coptic legend. We should also consult the rare Greek Passions of which an Arabic version also exists (Esbroeck, 1966, pp. 399–442). These parallel accounts allow us to affirm that Epimachus was a weaver at Pelusium, and that he was twenty-seven years of age when he voluntarily offered himself as a witness to his faith before Polemius, the governor, who had set up his court of justice on the dried-up river near Naucratis, where the altars for pagan sacrifices were also erected. When he reached the place of torture, Epimachus comforted a girl called Eutropia, fortified the prisoners in their prison, and brought them the comfort of prayer and of faith. When he himself suffered martyrdom, a drop of his blood was responsible for cures.

The Coptic fragments also make it possible to state that he brought the Eucharist (five loaves and two fishes) to his brothers Kallinikos and Dorotheos, leaving the golden key (perhaps for the tabernacle) to them. The two latter names are in fact those of the two bishops who succeeded one another after Constantine in the see of Pelusium. The Synaxarion also speaks of a translation at Pelusium that has been completely preserved in Arabic and has been published by M. van Esbroeck. From this it appears that Epimachus was first of all placed in a convent and that because of the peace of Constantine his body was transferred to Pelusium, where, thanks to the emperor, a large church was built. There is no ground for disallowing this item of information, for the cult very soon spread beyond the frontiers of Egypt.

At Rome the cult of Saint Epimachus was later mixed with that of Saint Gordian. A Latin text places the Passions of these two saints in the reign of Julian the Apostate (*Bibliotheca hagiographica latina* 3612). However, the end of that text and the oldest topographical notices in the Latin world show that Gordian was, in fact, buried in the Church of Saint Epimachus, who therefore antedated him.

For both of them, however, the feast day has continued to be May 10, probably because of the initial commemoration of Epimachus of Pelusium. At Constantinople a relic of Epimachus was brought by Constantine and placed in his palace. According to a Greek synaxarion of the twelfth century, the saint's day was celebrated in the martyrium of Saint Stratonikos.

In Egypt itself, the cult of Saint Epimachus suffered a fate parallel to the progressive sanding up of Faramā or Pelusium. The episcopal seat gradually moved to Tinnis. The bishops finally came to be designated bishops of Tinnis and Damirah. Epimachus of Pelusium acquired a counterpart in the person of Epimachus of Arwat or of Shubra Minsīnā—a disciple of John of Arwat under the patriarch ALEXANDER II (705–730). Epimachus of Arwat seems to have been called Moses when he was at Scetis. When he became bishop of Faramā in the patriarchate of KHĀ'ĪL I (744–767) he assumed the name of Epimachus, undoubtedly because of the great martyr of his episcopal see. The HISTORY OF THE PATRIARCHS OF ALEXANDRIA records that he performed two miracles to the disadvantage of the Chalcedonians.

The location of Damirah in the Arabic translation and in the Synaxarion—halfway between Faramā (or later Tinnis) and Naucratis—corresponds to the spot where Epimachus was laid before being moved to Pelusium. It would provide a valid toponymical explanation for Miamyris, the place transcribed in the Coptic Passion, where the dried-up river was on the route from Pelusium to Naucratis.

Epimachus also has an ancient liturgical canon, preserved only in Georgian. More than one detail makes it possible to recognize in this Passion passages of the type we find in the Arabic Synaxarion. The hymn was probably composed in the Greek Palestinian period prior to the activity of the monastery of the Studium at Constantinople, when a great quantity of hymnographical literature was preserved for us in Georgian translations.

The Arabic "translation" of Epimachus tells us that the chapel of Epimachus, built by Constantine before the large church, was the work of a certain Sophronius and of Annianus. At Oxyrhynchus, too, a church was founded by one Annianus, before the persecutions ended, in honor of Saint Colluthus. There is nothing odd in the rediscovery of such ancient hints relating to Epimachus. To the north of the famous temple of Abu Simbel there is a fresco that shows Epimachus on horseback: it is a work dating from the eleventh or twelfth century (Leclant, 1965, p. 203). Finally, in the heart of Nubia a STELA has been found, dating from around the eighth century and with an inscription in Coptic that reads: "On this day the commemoration of the blessed Epimachus, the third day of Paoni [Ba'ūnah]." This is the southernmost evidence for the cult.

BIBLIOGRAPHY

Cheikho, L., ed. *Annals,* Vol. 1, by Sa'īd ibn al-Batriq. Paris and Beirut, 1906.

Esbroeck, M. van. "Saint Epimaque de Péluse, III. Les fragments coptes." Bibliotheca Hagiographica Orientalis 274. *Analecta Bollandiana* 84 (1966); II, 85 (1967); III, 100 (1982):125–45.

Leclant, J. "Fouilles et travaux en Egypte et au Soudan, 1963–64." *Orientalia* 34 (1965).

Lemm, O. von. "Koptische Miszellen XCI." *Bulletin de l'Académie Imperiale de Saint-Petersbourg* 4.2 (1910).

Mina, T. *Inscriptions coptes et grecques de Nubie.* Cairo, 1942.

Rossi, F. "I martirii Geoore, Heraei, Epimaco e Ptolomeo." *Memorie della Reale Academia delle Scienze di Torino* 38 (1888).

MICHEL VAN ESBROECK

EPIPHANIUS, CANONS OF. *See* Canons of Epiphanius.

EPIPHANY, FEAST OF THE. *See* Feasts, Major.

EPIPHANY, LITURGY OF THE. The celebration of the Epiphany, one of the seven major feasts (see FEASTS, MAJOR) of the Coptic church, takes place on the eve of 12 Ṭūbah. It commemorates the manifestation of the divinity of Jesus Christ as He was baptized in the river Jordan. There are four services on this feast.

1. In the evening prayer and the *psalmodia,* the priest conducting the service says the prayers of the raising of incense for the evening of the feast. These are followed by a hymn in glorification of Saint John the Baptist, beginning with: "A glorious name indeed is thine, O kinsman of Emmanuel."

Meanwhile a special tank, or basin, called *laqqān,* is filled with water. At the conclusion of this hymn the clergy and deacons, carrying crosses and lighted candles, proceed to the middle part of the nave of the church, and say the prayers of the office of midnight. Then the *psalmodia* is said over the *laqqān* water.

2. In the *laqqān* service, the *laqqān* basin is a symbolic representation of the river Jordan, scene of Christ's baptism. The Coptic Orthodox church in Jerusalem holds this particular service of the Epiphany festival at the riverside, while the rest of the prayers are conducted in the Monastery of Saint John the Baptist close to the river.

In some of the older churches in Egypt, the *laqqān* basin, which is made of marble, stone, or metal, is usually kept underneath the floor in the middle of the nave, covered with floor boards, marble, or flagstones. It is used only on three occasions throughout the year: for the service of the sanctification of the waters, for the footwashing on Maundy Thursday, (see FEASTS, MINOR) and for the footwashing on the feast of Saint Peter and Saint Paul.

The priest begins with the words, "Have mercy upon us O God Father almighty. All-holy Trinity, have mercy upon us. Lord God of powers, be with us, for we have no help in our tribulations and afflictions save Thee." The people say the Lord's Prayer and the prayer of thanksgiving. This is followed by lections containing relevant prophecies from the Old Testament, in this order: Habakkuk 3:2–19; Isaiah 35:1,2; 40:1–5; 9:1,2; Baruch 3:36–38; 4:1–4; Ezekiel 36:24–29; 47:1–9.

The Pauline epistle is taken from 1 Corinthians 10:1–13. The hymn of John the Baptist follows, after which the people recite the Trisagion (see MUSIC), and the priest says the intercession of the Gospel, and reads the Gospel (Mt. 3:1–17). The priest then says "O God, have mercy upon us," etcetera, after which the deacons sing *"Kyrie eleison"* twelve times. Then follow the seven great intercessions, for the sick, the travelers, the winds and the fruits, the head of state, the dormants, the oblations, and the catechumens. The priest then recites the petition and lifts up the cross of lighted tapers, and the people say *"Kyrie eleison"* one hundred times. This is followed by the three great prayers (for peace, the fathers, and the congregation) and the celebrant says the prayer for the sanctification of the waters, at the end of which he signs the water three times with the cross, saying, "Sanctify this water, impart to it the grace of the River Jordan. . . . Thou didst sanctify the streams of the Jordan, having drawn upon them Thy Holy Spirit from heaven. . . . Do Thou now sanctify this water. May it become the fountain of blessing, a gift of purification, an absolver from sin, a purger of sickness, that it may be a purification of the soul, body and spirit, for all who shall draw from it or partake of it. . . ."

The people say the Lord's Prayer, and the priest recites the three prayers of Absolution, followed by the benediction.

At the end of this service, the assistant priest takes a white napkin, called *shamlah* (see LITURGICAL VESTMENTS), dips it into the water, and signs the forehead of the chief priest with it three times, an action symbolic of the baptism of our Lord Jesus Christ by the hand of John the Baptist. After this, it is the chief priest who takes the *shamlah* and signs the priests, the deacons, and the congregation on the forehead. Meantime, the deacons sing Psalm 150 and the priest says a prayer of thanksgiving.

3. In the service of morning offering of incense, prayers are resumed from the sanctuary, and deacons go back to their usual place at the choir.

4. The Divine Liturgy, as is usually the case in all major feasts of the church, is celebrated according to the Anaphora of Saint GREGORY, with the following variations appropriate to the Epiphany: (1) following the reading from the SYNAXARION, the deacons sing the hymn of Saint John the Baptist; (2) the psalm versicle is Psalm 117: 25, 27; (3) the Gospel is from John 1: 18–34; (4) after the sermon the deacons sing the Gospel hymn for the Epiphany: "This is the Lamb of God who carries the sins of the world, He who brought a horn of salvation to save His people. Hallelujah, Hallelujah, Hallelujah, Hallelujah; Jesus Christ, the Son of God, was baptized in the Jordan"; and (5) the theme of the FRACTION prayer is regeneration of man through baptism: "Thou hast granted us the grace of filiation through the laver of the new birth and the renewal of the Holy Spirit."

ARCHBISHOP BASILIOS

EPIPHANY TANKS, relatively large basins, measuring 8¼ × 9¾ feet (2.4 × 3.0 m) in the church of Saint Mercurius at the monastery of DAYR ABŪ SAYFAYN and 5½ × 8½ feet (1.7 × 2.6 m) in the church of Saint Sergius. As a rule they are rectangular and may be 4½ feet (1.4 m) deep, as in Saint Sergius. Epiphany tanks are particularly to be found in the medieval churches of Cairo. Down to the beginning of modern times, they were used for the ceremonies of the feast of Epiphany, 11 Ṭūbah. The tanks were filled to the brim with water, and anyone who wished could plunge in. CYRIL III ibn Laqlaq (1235–1243) prohibited the visiting of a public bath on the same day. For convenience in climbing out, several steps were placed at the corners.

Originally the feast took place by night on the banks of the Nile. Since this was associated with much noise and disturbance, and probably attracted too many Muslims, it had to be transferred within the churches under AL-ḤĀKIM (996–1021). In accordance with the importance of the Epiphany feast, the Epiphany tank is placed in the vicinity of the entrance, usually in the middle of the narthex. In the church of Anbā Shinūdah of Dayr Abū Sayfayn in Cairo, it is located in a side room in the southern section of that church since that had served in the intervening period as an entrance chamber. An unusual case is the small church of Banī Majdā (south of Manfalūṭ) where the Epiphany tank is located in a side room behind the sanctuary.

BIBLIOGRAPHY

Burmester, O. H. E. *The Egyptian or Coptic Church,* pp. 250–56. Cairo, 1967.

Butler, A. J. *The Ancient Coptic Churches of Egypt,* Vol. 2, pp. 346–49. London, 1970. Reprint of 1884 edition.

Vansleb, J. M. *Nouvelle relation en forme de journal d'un voyage fait en Egypte en 1672 et 1673,* p. 342. Paris, 1677.

PETER GROSSMANN

EPISCOPACY. *See* Bishop.

EPISTOLOGRAPHY, anglicized Greek word denoting the writing (*graphe*) of a letter (*epistole*). The study of letter writing has as its goal distinguishing and classifying the various kinds of letters, analyzing the form and function of the component elements (introduction, body, conclusion) of these letters, learning of and describing the mechanisms or postal systems through which these communications moved to their destinations, and examining the theories of the ancients on the art of letter writing.

Awareness of the letter as a unique and specialized form of communication, sometimes even an art form, is evidenced in the works of ancient literati and rhetoricians. Demetrius, for example, in discussing letter writing in his work *On Style,* attributes to Artemon, the editor of Aristotle's letters, the statement that the subject of a letter should be conversational (223). An Egyptian letter from the New Kingdom with the heading "Beginning of the Lesson in Letter [writing]" attests that instruction in the art of writing letters was available to the would-be epistolographer. "Practice" letters of this sort in Greek and several Greek letter-writing handbooks are still extant. These exercises and handbooks not only show that epistolography was a matter for study and practice but also help to explain the promulgation of the formulaic phrases so evident in ancient letters.

Greek Correspondence

Inasmuch as the study of Greek epistolography is far more advanced than the study of Coptic and Arabic letters, and has given rise to an approach and a terminology that are used in the investigation of both Coptic and Arabic epistolography, an overview of letter writing in Coptic Egypt should begin with Greek correspondence. Greek letters are generally divided into four categories.

Familiar Letters. These communications are usually between relatives or friends, but other letters that employ expressions of familiarity are also included in this group. Such letters almost always have a greeting from the sender (A) to the recipient (B), with the sender's name first, such as "A-B greetings," in addition to a wish of health; these salutations often include some mention of the relationship of the two correspondents. In this function, the words "brother" and "sister" occur regularly as terms of friendship and equality, even when the correspondents have no blood relationship. "Lord" and "lady" appear as deferential terms for parents with increasing frequency during the Roman rule of Egypt. The phrase "before all things," followed by an expression such as "I pray you are well" or "I greet you," is often found in the opening of these letters. The same phrase is used in Coptic letters (see below). As a closing these letters have simply "farewell" or, more elaborately, "I pray for your health." In the first century A.D., secondary greetings to friends or relatives in the recipient's vicinity, such as those found at the end of the New Testament Pauline epistles, became common in the closing of familiar letters. In the second century and afterward, such secondary greetings became part of the opening.

Petitions/Applications. Under this heading are not only petitions and applications (usually for rental or purchase) but also other legal documents addressed to officials, such as birth and death notices, census registrations, and complaints. In documents of this class, the address formula regularly gives the name of the recipient before that of the sender. By placing the recipient's name first, the writer acknowledges his inferiority to the official he is addressing. Greetings may or may not be included with this address. Among the variations are "To B from A," "To B, A," "To B from A, greetings," and "To B, greetings, A." The designations that accompany the greetings in such letters are usually of a more formal and definitive nature than those in familiar letters, giving such information as patronymic, age, occupation, place of residence, and distinguishing physical characteristics. Petitions normally close with "farewell."

Business Letters. Many of the texts in this category are not letters at all but commercial documents drawn up in epistolary form. Their opening formulas, usually in the form "A to B, greetings," generally include much identifying detail about both the writer and the recipient, including occupation, age, physical characteristics, and names of parents, spouses, and guardians. The opening formulas sometimes contain a health wish. Many of the letters in this class have no special closing formula, but "farewell" is used frequently.

Official Letters. Administrative and business correspondence written or received by official persons comes under this rubric. The opening formula in letters of this category is usually "A to B, greetings." This opening sometimes includes some mention of the relationship between the writer and the recipient. Most of these letters end with "farewell."

In those varieties of letters that used "farewell" as a closing, the expanded formula "I pray for your health" began to supplant the simple form after the first century. In all but familiar letters, an illiteracy formula was appended to the end of the letter if the sender was unable to write and had the document drawn up by someone else. In the standard formula the scribe, after writing his own name, declared, "I wrote [this] on behalf of X since he does not know letters." In the body of letters from all four of these classes, standard phrases or clichés were common (see Steen, 1938, pp. 125–72, and White, 1981, pp. 98–102).

In the study of Greek epistolography, as well as of Latin, Coptic, and Arabic epistolography, letters from the four categories above are usually labeled "real" or "nonliterary," while letters that were intended for the public at large (though perhaps addressed to an individual), as well as treatises and essays written in epistolary form with an opening and closing, are called "nonreal," "fictitious," or "literary." Use of the letter form as a vehicle for philosophic or didactic thought has a long and rich tradition. The classical authors Plato, Aristotle, Isocrates, Demosthenes, Epicurus, Horace, Seneca, Sallust, Pliny, and Quintilian all wrote treatises in the form of epistles. The tradition was continued by Saint Paul, Saint Basil, Saint Gregory Nazianzus, Saint John Chrysostom, and Saint Shenute.

Despite the fact that most studies of ancient letters deal only with real letters or only with fictitious epistles, many of the same formulas evident in the four classes of real letters are found in literary letters. Accordingly, a number of scholars have found it suitable to apply the same kind of analytical approach to both varieties of communication (see, for instance, Betz, 1975, p. 353).

Coptic Correspondence

Only recently have Coptic letters begun to enjoy the kind of extensive and detailed analysis that has been lavished on their Greek counterparts, but Biendenkopf-Ziehner's *Untersuchungen zum koptischen Briefformular* is a significant and valuable first step.

The broad categories for Coptic correspondence are (1) private letters; (2) official letters (documents, business letters, administrative correspondence, and such); and (3) epistles (literary or nonreal letters). The Coptic letters that have survived date from the period between the third or fourth century to the tenth or eleventh century. The various parts of these letters with their component formulas are the following: polite preface (apology, introduction formula, greeting, health formula, letter reception formula, opportunity formula); body (introductory phrase); and closing (prayer formula, remembrance formula, confirmation, closing formula, date, address).

This paradigm represents diachronically the range of formulas that were available to Coptic letter writers. However, few of the formulas were in use for the entire period from which we have Coptic letters, and it is not to be expected that a writer from any given period will employ all of the formulas at his disposal. Nonetheless, with the exception of the prayer and remembrance formulas, which evince changes attributable to the advent of Islam and the decline of Greek as the administrative language, each formula remained surprisingly stable throughout the period in which it was used.

Writers used the apology when they were unable to find a piece of papyrus and were forced to pen a letter on an OSTRACON. This formula made its appearance in the sixth century and was quite common in the seventh and eighth centuries. The evidence indicates that it was used only in letters to superiors. In its simplest form it reads, "Forgive me; I found no piece of papyrus."

In its fullest form the introductory formula gives the names, occupations, and titles of sender and recipient, and the relationship of the sender to the recipient; abbreviated forms, such as "it is X, who writes to Y," leave out much of this information. Variations can include a self-abasing reference to the sender as a servant; greetings; additional verbs (e.g., "it is X, who writes [and] greets Y," "it is X, who dares it [and] writes to Y"), and preposed elements such as "before all things" and "farewell in the Lord."

The greeting usually stands in the preface of the letter, but it is sometimes found in the conclusion. Its standard form is "X greets Y." Frequently two or more verbs are combined in a single greeting. In many letters the name of the sender and/or recipient is replaced by pronouns or epithets such as "servant" (used of the sender), "son," and "holy father." To the simple greeting many writers add modifiers such as "very much" and "with my whole heart." Often greetings are sent to others in the home or vicinity of the recipient.

With the health formula the sender inquires after the wellbeing of the recipient. The simple formulation of this inquiry is "I ask about your health." Often the query is followed by an assurance that the sender himself is in good health. In many letters, the introductory and health formulas are combined; for instance, "I am X [and] I write and inquire after the welfare of Y."

The letter reception formula indicates that an earlier letter has been received; for example, "I [we] have received the letter of Y." This simple form was used mostly in official correspondence, which dealt with mundane matters and was sent between persons of equal rank. In other letters, the formula is usually expanded to include some expression of joy at the news contained in the previous letter, especially the news that its sender is well, such as "I [we] have received the letter of Y; I [we] was [were] very pleased because I [we] learned thereby that Y is well." The letter reception formula occurs in letters written between the fourth and ninth centuries.

With the opportunity formula the writer explicitly states the obvious: that he writes because he has the opportunity and/or the need to write ("I found an opportunity [and] it is a duty and a constraint for me to write"). Greetings are usually attached to this formula; for instance, "I found the opportunity, [so] I wrote, in order to greet Y." Sometimes a writer expresses this notion in negative fashion, such as "without any inducement I greet Y." The opportunity formula was used in the sixth, seventh, and eighth centuries. It occurs primarily in papyrus letters. Often the content of the letters in which it appears is a combination of business and private matters; these letters were usually sent to equals or superiors.

In some letters the body follows the preface immediately without any introduction, but in many others the actual communiqué is introduced by a formula or a formulaic expression. The various kinds of introductions fall into six classes: (1) actual introductions; (2) those which contain a request; (3) those which contain a command or a summons; (4) those which contain a protest; (5) those which contain a confirmation; and (6) those which introduce a report.

In the prayer formula, which can come at either the beginning or the end of the letter, the sender asks the recipient to pray for him. Simply formulated, it reads "pray for me," but addenda are common: "in love," "in your holiness," and "in your holy prayers." More complicated forms are also attested, such as "be so dear," "have the goodness [to] pray for me," and Saint Shenute's "we ask your spotlessness to pray for us that we may be capable of completing our way in peace as our holy brother. . . ." Most of the letters in which the prayer formula occurs are dated to the sixth, seventh, or eighth century.

The remembrance formula asks the recipient to keep the sender in his thoughts, such as "think of me." It is often prefaced by the phrase "be so dear [as to]" or followed by such phrases as "in your holy prayers" and "in the uplifting of your hands." The formula is attested between the fourth and ninth centuries from the Fayyūm to Thebes. While it appears in letters on both ostraca and papyri, and in both private and business communications, it was used primarily in correspondence with persons of ecclesiastical standing.

The confirmation formula occurs almost exclusively in papyrus letters of the seventh and eighth centuries. It is normally bipartite in form, with the first part always being "by writing these things." The second part admits of some variation. Sometimes it is a greeting, such as "I greet Y." Sometimes it is a health wish, such as "remain well in the Lord," or an expression of hope that the sender will fare well through the concern of the recipient, such as "I hope that I will be well through your prayers." Combinations of both a greeting and a health wish (either for the recipient or for the sender) are also common in the second part.

The closing formula, like the health wish, addresses the welfare of the recipient. In effect it is a parting salutation. Sometimes it is as simple as the command "be well." More often it is modified by phrases such as "until we come," "always," and "in the Lord." In the letters of Saint Athanasius and Saint Shenute the closing formula sometimes takes the form "I pray that you are well in the Lord."

In Coptic letters, the date is often given in Greek. The writer normally specifies the month, day, and the indiction year, for example, "it was written on 21 Bābah, 8th indiction year." Only rarely does one find number words instead of numerals and complete words. Instead, alphabetic symbols as numerals and abbreviations are the norm in dates.

The address is normally written on the back of the letter. If the letter itself is continued on the back, the address is usually placed above the continuation. Occasionally the address is written on the front, at the beginning of the letter. In letters on ostraca the address is often attached to the body of the letter or sometimes omitted altogether, its purpose being fulfilled by the introductory formula. The standard form of the address is "it [the writing/letter] is to be given to X from Y."

Arabic Correspondence

The study of Arabic epistolography has not advanced as far as that of Greek and Coptic letters, but several observations on the nature of Arabic correspondence are worthy of mention (see Jahn, 1937, pp. 157–73).

The preface of Arabic letters consists of either the *basmala* ("in the name of God, the Compassionate, the Merciful") and the address, to which various health wishes can be attached, or the *basmala* alone. In the address, the name of either the sender or the recipient can appear first. Writers using the former style followed the precedent established in Muḥammad's correspondence, while those who placed the recipient's name first did so in accordance with the urging of Caliph al-Walīd, who espoused the principle that the inferior ought to be subordinated to the superior. Often the name of the sender is omitted altogether. Among the formulaic wishes that appear in the preface of Arabic letters are the following: "may God protect you," "may God prolong your life," "may God make me for all evil your ransom," "may God cause your might, honor, and strength to continue." Often two or more such wishes are combined in the same preface. An especially elaborate preface from a letter of the mid tenth century reads, "In the name of God, the Compassionate, the Merciful. I am writing, O Ahmad b. Hudayy—may God prolong your life and may He cause your might and strength to continue—from Qus in safety and good health—praise and thanks be to their giver—on Thursday when eight [nights] had passed of Ragab—may God make it honoured for his favourite—and blessings on all the years to come; and praise be to God, the Lord of all created beings" (see Grohmann, 1955, text 306, pp. 66–75).

Arabic letters are often undated. In those that do bear dates, the formulas normally state the month, day, and year of the Hegira; for example, "[and] he [name missing] wrote it in the month Gumada 1, 127" (see Jahn, 1938, no. 3, pp. 177–78).

The phrase "and afterward" is often used to introduce the body of the letter.

Most of the formulas that occur in the preface of Arabic letters can appear in the conclusion. Many letters close with the phrase "hail to you" or with "my [our] sufficiency is God alone."

Like their Greek and Coptic counterparts, Arabic letters written on papyrus were folded so that the back of the papyrus sheet served as an envelope and bore the address. Occasionally the address was written on the front above the letter, and the sheet was then folded in such a way that the address was on the outside. What was said above about the form of the internal address in the preface of Arabic letters applies also to the external address. Either the sender's or the recipient's name can be given first.

In all periods, private letters in Egypt traveled mainly by messenger. Wealthy individuals were able to use slaves, servants, or employees as couriers, but the average person had to rely on caravans, friends, or strangers who happened to be going in the direction of the letter's intended destination.

Egyptian and Greek documents suggest that an organized postal system through which official letters moved between districts was in existence at least as early as the New Kingdom. This system used horses for urgent communications and camels for ordinary post. A separate system handled letters within each district. Witnesses for the Roman period are scanty, but the evidence suggests that the Romans incorporated both systems into their post, the *cursus publicus*.

In the Byzantine era, there was a *cursus velox* (swift course) and a *cursus clabularis* (transport-wagon course). The *cursus velox,* attested as early as A.D. 322, at first made use of donkeys, horses, and mules to move the mail, but after a funding cutback in the reign of Justinian it was limited to donkeys. Beginning as early as 470, large landholders, the wealthy, and the church established their own independent postal systems. Occasionally several landholders joined together to form a mail delivery service.

In Islamic states the official postal service was known as the *barīd* (from Latin *veredus*/Greek *beredos,* post horse). In Egypt, the stages (*markaz al-barīd*) were approximately 4 *farsakhs* (15 miles) apart. Horses and camels carried the mail between these stages.

BIBLIOGRAPHY

Betz, H. D. "The Literary Composition and Function of Paul's Letter to the Galatians." *New Testament Studies* 21 (1975):353–79.

Biedenkopf-Ziehner, A. *Untersuchungen zum koptischen Briefformular unter Berücksichtigung ägyptischer und griechischer Parallelen.* Koptische Studien 1. Würzburg, 1983.

Demetrius. *On Style,* ed. W. Rhys Roberts. Cambridge, 1902.

Doty, W. G. *Letters in Primitive Christianity.* Philadelphia, 1973.

Exler, F. J. *The Form of the Ancient Greek Letter of the Epistolary Papyri.* Repr. Chicago, 1976.

Grohmann, A. *Arabic Papyri in the Egyptian Library,* Vol. 5. Cairo, 1955.

Jahn, K. "Vom frühislamischen Briefwesen." *Archiv orientalni* 9 (1937):153–200.

Malherbe, A. J. "Ancient Epistolary Theorists." *Ohio Journal of Religious Studies* 5, no. 2 (1977):3–77.

Sourdel, D. "Barid." In *The Encyclopaedia of Islam,* new ed., Vol. 1. Leiden, 1960.

Steen, H. A. "Les Clichés épistolaires dans les lettres sur papyrus grecques." *Classica et Mediaevalia* 1 (1938):119–176.

White, John L. "The Greek Documentary Letter Tradition, Third Century B.C.E. to Third Century C.E." *Semeia* (1981):89–106.

RANDALL STEWART

ERA OF THE MARTYRS, or Era of DIOCLETIAN, reckoned from the accession of Emperor Diocletian in the latter part of 284. Since the seventh century the Copts have regularly called it the Era of the Martyrs, in memory of the persecution of Christians launched by Diocletian. Its use has been almost entirely confined to Egypt, where it originated, and to Christian Ethiopia, the first year of the era, *anno martyrum* (A.M.) 1, being the Alexandrian year running from the Julian 29 August 284 to 28 August 285. Isolated dating according to the era of Diocletian has been detected in the Latin West (Ambrose in Milan, Bede in Northumbria).

[*See also:* Calendar, Coptic.]

AELRED CODY, O.S.B.

ERICHSEN, WOLJA (1890–1966), Danish Egyptologist and demoticist. He studied Oriental languages but specialized in demotic and Coptic.

His most important work, a dictionary, *Demotisches Glossar,* was published in Copenhagen in 1954 and reprinted in Milan in 1972.

BIBLIOGRAPHY

Dawson, W. R., and E. P. Uphill. *Who Was Who in Egyptology,* p. 98. London, 1972.

AZIZ S. ATIYA

ERMAN, ADOLF (1854–1937), German Egyptologist. He was professor at Berlin University, a founder of the Berlin school, a teacher of W. E. CRUM, Georg STEINDORFF, and others, working in all fields of Egyptology and Coptology. He published Coptic literary and nonliterary texts.

BIBLIOGRAPHY

Dawson, W. R., and E. P. Uphill. *Who Was Who in Egyptology,* pp. 99–100. London, 1972.
Erman, A. *Mein Leben und mein Wirken.* Berlin, 1929.

MARTIN KRAUSE

ESCHATOLOGY, the study of the last things, of the destiny of individual persons, and, more broadly, of society, of the world, and of the universe. In the culture of the pagan Greco-Roman world, concern with the destiny of the individual after death received comparatively little attention outside the mystery religions, but Hellenistic speculation on successive eons of the world and on the return of all things cyclically to some sort of starting point were to have their influence in the elaboration of Christian views of history leading from one age to the next. Eschatology is also concerned with representations of future life, its conditions, the ways in which the dead can be helped by their survivors in this life and can themselves help those survivors, and whether such representations are primarily a matter of popular religious imagery or of a more sophisticated metaphysical theology.

In Judaism, eschatological expectations, usually associated with the advent of the Messiah, were centered on the future of the chosen nation or of a small group faithful to God, and were increasingly expressed in apocalyptic descriptions of radical transformation of the world in an imminent or distant future. In the earliest years of Christianity, a chronological tension arose between an eschatological moment of salvation already realized by the Incarnation and Christ's saving actions, on the one hand, and a future definitive moment to be realized at the time of Christ's return in glory, on the other. A view of the time between Christ's first and second comings as the time of the church became apparent in the Gospels of Matthew and Luke, and the resurrection of the dead (1 Cor. 15) became an integral part of Christian theology and hope.

The concept of two eons—one of the eschatological future, though present now as the condition of the heavenly realities of salvation already realized, and the other identified with the world perceptible by the senses—became evident in Christian thought. Thanks to the union of the divine and the human in the Incarnation of the Word of God and to the saving actions of Christ, already available in the church by participation in the mysteries or sacraments, the individual could gain access to the heavenly eon of supernatural realities and thus be saved. At the same time, that eon remained future; and perfect, definitive access to it was to be had only at the end of the present eon. Metaphysical interest in the last things was mingled with ethical interest, for access to the supernal world of salvation was to be had only after a judgment of the individual on the basis of his or her behavior in this life. Anthropological questions of the respective conditions of body and soul (and personal spirit) after death had to be raised, and they have been answered in different ways.

As official theologies developed, there was by the end of the fourth century relatively little that distinguished the eschatological views of one part of Christendom from those of another, if one discounts ideas rejected as more or less alien to general Christian consensus. Metaphysical minds have continued to stress the vision of God as the ultimate perfection of rational created beings. The Origenist doctrine of *apocatastasis,* that is, of the ultimate return of all rational beings to their original condition of purity and perfection (itself an extension of the Hellenistic idea of all time and history as cyclic), was rejected as incongruent with the doctrines of definitive judgment and of eternal torment of the damned, although the idea that all may finally share in the grace of salvation was proposed in other ways by CLEMENT OF ALEXANDRIA and GREGORY OF NYSSA, and traces of it have remained in subsequent Christian thought, including that of Coptic Egypt.

In the Coptic church, doctrine on the last things differs little from that of other ancient churches. Specifically Egyptian concepts of judgment and of the condition of the dead are more easily found in popular piety, evident in ancient Christian narratives and in the religious practice of more recent times, with its popular and traditional interpretation. In the acts of Egyptian martyrs, Coptic apocrypha, and popular stories, images of the otherworld from pre-Christian literature, particularly in the Eygptian *Book of the Dead*, are often found. *Amenti*, basically the West, but in pharaonic cosmology also the place to which the dead go, became the Coptic word for hell. The dark roads and the river of fire through which the dead must pass recur in Christian imagery, as do beings with animal heads, ready to devour sinners in the judgment hall of Osiris, which became the judgment hall of Christ. The pharaonic iconographic scene in which the heart of a dead person is weighed on a balance in order to see whether that person's good deeds or his evil ones weigh more, with Anubis observing Thoth announcing the results, is reflected in Coptic literature, with the pre-Christian gods replaced by Saint Michael.

As in pharaonic Egypt, the activities of the just in the other world tended in popular representations to be envisaged as similar to those of daily social life in this world. In more properly theological literature and its liturgical expressions, however, the condition of the dead is represented in imagery drawn more exclusively from the Bible. Allusions to the story of Lazarus and the rich man (Lk. 16:19–31) and to the bosom of Abraham (and Isaac and Jacob) are frequent, and so are biblical images of waters of refreshment, of a pasture, of saints singing praise with angels. In theological and liturgical texts, transference of earthly society to the world beyond is minimal, and paradise is emphatically the kingdom of heaven. While the direct vision of God, according to traditional popular literature, is enjoyed only by a few, particularly by the Mother of God, Saint Michael, Saint George, the twenty-four elders, and the four living beings of Revelation (4:4, 6), in theological literature the saints do see Christ in his glorified humanity but, with the exception of the Mother of God, Saint Michael, and perhaps some favored others, they will not perceive the divinity of Christ or the Trinity until after the Last Judgment.

In legends and canonical literature of the early Egyptian church, and also later, the opinion can be found that judgment of the individual does not take place until around forty days after death. Throughout Coptic tradition it is held that the ultimate fate of the individual is sealed only in the Last Judgment, at the end of this world, and that before the Last Judgment there is still hope for deliverance from torment. The Catholic doctrine of purgatory as a place or condition distinct from both heaven and hell, in which the individual is purified from venial sin and from the temporal punishment due to sin, is not accepted by the Coptic church. In Coptic tradition, the dead who suffer torment are considered to be in hell. Nevertheless, by the eucharistic offering and by prayer, by good works, almsgiving, and fasting, members of the church on earth can alleviate the torments of those who have suffered for Christ or have shown charity for his sake. The old popular idea that those in hell are freed temporarily between Easter and Pentecost may be related to the fact that a Coptic intercessory prayer for the release of the Orthodox believers suffering in hell is recited on Pentecost. The statement within that prayer that "we have the great hope that all who are in the depths of pain will be freed" may be the remnant of an idea of *apocatastasis*, of the ultimate salvation of all rational beings. In the theology of the Coptic church generally, however, hell with its torments is everlasting, although those who die with unforgiven sins that are not deadly (1 Jn. 5:16) still have the hope of being freed from their sins and their torment in the final judgment of the world.

BIBLIOGRAPHY

Bietenhard, H. *Die himmlische Welt im Urchristentum und Spätjudentum*. Wissenschaftliche Untersuchungen zum Neuen Testament 2. Berlin, 1951.

Bouyer, L. *Christianisme et eschatologie*. Paris, 1948.

Doresse, J. *Des hiéroglyphes à la croix*, pp. 45–56. Uitgaven van het Nederlands Historisch-Archaeologisch Instituut te Istanbul 7. Istanbul, 1960.

Florovsky, G. "Eschatology in the Patristic Age: An Introduction." In *Studia Patristica*, ed. Kurt Aland and F. L. Cross, Vol. 2, pp. 235–50. Texte und Untersuchungen zur Geschichte der altchristlichen Literatur 64. Berlin, 1957.

Kopp, C. "Glaube und Sakramente der koptischen Kirche." *Orientalia Christiana* 25, no. 1 (1932): 51–74.

Piankoff, A. "La descente aux enfers dans les textes égyptiens et dans les apocryphes coptes." *Bulletin de la Société d'archéologie copte* 7 (1941):33–46.

AELRED CODY, O.S.B.

ESDRAS. *See* Old Testament, Arabic Versions of the.

ESNA. *See* Isnā.

ETHIOPIAN ART, COPTIC INFLUENCE ON.

Coptic influence on Ethiopian art, comparable to the Coptic influence in the eighth century on Nubian art, would have been probable because of the dependence of Christian Ethiopia for more than a millennium upon the Coptic patriarchate of Alexandria. We must perhaps attribute the general absence of such an influence to the power of native traditions.

One notable exception, however, is the Bieta Mariam church at LĀLIBELLĀ in the province of Lasta between Addis Ababa and Axum. Of some ten churches of the twelfth and thirteenth centuries grouped in this provincial capital, it alone is decorated with themes and details of Coptic art of the Fatimid period on the ceilings and on the lower curves of the arches that rest on columns. On the ceilings, within quadrangular compartments divided into four and also in a band separating them, circles are occupied by rosettes of eight petals—such as are found in the mosque of Ibn Ṭulūn in Cairo and in the fabrics of the following centuries—alongside meandering patterns interrupted by a cross patté; some of these are inscribed in a Solomon's seal (du Bourguet, 1968, fig. 87; 1980, p. 240).

In the central nave, on a vertical panel adjoining a pilaster adorned with rosettes in circles, are busts of both bearded and beardless saints. They support a parchment on each shoulder with the hand of the same side. Their expression is close to that of the Coptic monks, without any relationship to the style common to representations of Ethiopian visages (Gerster, 1968, figs. 61–63).

This unusual fact confirms the tradition that under the Fatimids, some Coptic monks who had come to Ethiopia were among the counselors of King Lālibalā. This coincided with the persecution of Christians in Egypt by the sultan al-Ḥākim, a circumstance reputed to have caused the flight of Copts as far as Ethiopia.

The first known biography of Muḥammad, a travel narrative by an Arab woman, mentioned the mural paintings decorating the first cathedral of Axum. No other detail is supplied, although the first Ethiopian liturgical decoration imitated models seen by Ethiopian Christian travelers in Egypt, whence the Ethiopians took their faith (du Bourguet, 1980, pp. 240ff.)

We cannot report any other Coptic impressions on the Christian art of Ethiopia.

BIBLIOGRAPHY

Bourguet, P. du. *L'Art copte.* Paris, 1968.

______. *Peintures chrétiennes: couleurs paléochrétiennes, coptes et byzantines,* pp. 239–48. Geneva, 1980.

Gerster, G. *L'Art éthiopien.* La Pierre-qui-Vire, 1968.

Leroy, J. *L'Ethiopie. Archéologie et culture.* Paris, 1973.

PIERRE DU BOURGUET, S.J.

ETHIOPIAN CHRISTIAN LITERATURE.

The literature of Christian Ethiopia was, and still is, written in the ancient Ethiopic language called Ge'ez, which is supposed to have ceased to be a living language around the tenth or eleventh century, when it was superseded by "modern" Semitic languages. This literature is related to traditional Ethiopian culture, which was born and developed as a scion of Oriental Christianity, spread in Ethiopia from about the fourth century onward. It covers almost all aspects of social life, so its content is either strictly doctrinal and catechetical (possibly unconsciously preserving some rare vestiges of Gnostic literature) or else profane (historical, juridical, magical, etc.) but inspired by Christian principles. It began between the fourth and seventh centuries and was at first mainly a literature of translations.

Translated Literature

Translations undoubtedly began with the Bible and apocryphal and patristic works. Although other branches of Oriental Christianity (mainly Syriac) may have contributed to that activity, from the very beginning the bulk of the translation into Ethiopic apparently was done under the direct influence of the Christian church of Egypt and its literature. In fact, the Ethiopian Christian church was an offspring of the Egyptian church, under whose official leadership it survived. Until the twentieth century, the head of the Ethiopian church was selected by the Coptic patriarch from Egyptian monks and sent to Ethiopia. Paleographic evidence clearly suggests that the Ethiopians must also have learned the art of writing their manuscripts on parchment from their Christian forebears in Egypt.

Certain translations include works no longer extant in the original Oriental Christian literature.

Therefore, they preserve texts otherwise unavailable or even, at times, different versions of texts known in other Christian literatures of the Orient.

Until about the seventh century, translations came mainly from Greek, since Greek prevailed in the church of Egypt. Although no conclusive evidence exists to confirm this, some translations may have been made from Coptic, seemingly between the seventh and the twelfth centuries. When Arabic became the dominant language in the Egyptian Coptic church around the twelfth century, translations were made from Arabic. Among the works translated from Greek, besides the Bible, are books such as *Maṣḥafa Hēnok* (The Book of Enoch), *Maṣḥafa Kufālē* (The Book of Jubilees), *'Ergata Isāyiyās* (The Ascent of Isaiah), and *Hērmā Nabiy* (The Prophet Hērma). Of these the first two are preserved in their entirety only in the Ethiopic version. All four books are reckoned as part of the biblical canon of the Ethiopian church. Textual hints lead one to surmise that the translation from original texts—especially Enoch and the Jubilees—was performed in the presence of, if not upon, an Aramaic version and that some or all of the translators may have been religious men, possibly from the Monophysite church of Syria.

Most of another work of great relevance to the theological teaching of the Ethiopian church was also translated at this time. This is *Qērelos* (The Book of Cyril), a collection of homilies, mostly belonging to Saint Cyril of Alexandria. Since the first of these homilies, the "Prosphonetikos," addressed to Emperor Theodosius II, was a work by Cyril, it has provided that collection with its Ethiopic title. Still another work of high inspiration for Ethiopian monasticism is *Śer'at wate'zāz za'abbā Pākwmis* (The Rule of Pachomius). As far as is known, translations from Greek include a few lives of saints, a pious genre of paramount importance to Ethiopian literature to this day.

It appears that when Greek ceased to be the language of the Egyptian church, countless translations were made from Arabic texts of Coptic literature. The translations from Arabic are the most numerous and include a revision of the books of the Bible. The lively activity that motivated such translations went on from the twelfth century to the eighteenth. The translations of that period include several notable works. *Sēnodos* (Synodicon), is a basic collection of canonical regulations, beginning with those of different church councils (save that of Chalcedon). A work of similar contents, *Didesqelyā* (Didascalia), is the revered source of the internal regulations of the Ethiopian church. Both works might have found their way into Ethiopia in the twelfth or thirteenth century. It was apparently the thirteenth or fourteenth century that saw the translation of the *Story of Alexander*, a widely known narrative about Alexander the Great, which in Coptic literature possessed peculiarly Egyptian characteristics and in Ethiopic literature took on other features of its own. In the fourteenth century occurred the translation of some liturgical books, such as *Maṣḥafa genẓat* (Book for the Preparation of the Body of the Dead), a ritual for funerals; the widespread *Maṣḥafa sa'atāt* (Book of the Hours), the horologion of the Western church; *Gadla samā'tāt* (Contendings of the Martyrs); *Gadl* (Meritorious Acts, i.e., of saintly persons; cf. Greek *athlēsis*); *Gadla ḥawāryāt* (Contendings of the Apostles, i.e., their apocryphal acts); *Gebra ḥemāmāt* (Acts of the Passion), a lectionary for Holy Week; *Wūddāsē Māryām* (Celebration of Mary), derived from the Copto-Arabic Theotokias from the *Psalmodia*, together with some lives, or contendings (*gadl*), of Egyptian saints. Some of these works—as well as others, for example, the *Filkesyus* (Philoxenos), written by Philoxenos of Mabbug, regarding monastic life, and *Lāha Māryām* (Bewailing of Mary)—were translated directly by, or with the aid of, a highly reputed Egyptian Coptic metropolitan named Abbā Salāmā, who became the head of the Ethiopian church as Abuna Salāmā II, during the second half of the fourteenth century. He is known to have been in Ethiopia between 1348 and 1388, which was probably the year of his demise in that country, since metropolitans were supposed to stay in Ethiopia until the end of their lives. His brisk literary activity must have resulted in stimulating a lively movement in Ethiopian literature within the church.

The fourteenth century is probably the time when the translation of *Zēnā abaw qeddusān* (Stories of the Holy Fathers) was made. This contains the renowned *Apophthegmata Patrum*, a work of great resonance in the thought of Ethiopian monks. It seems likely that between the fourteenth and fifteenth centuries, another Egyptian monk undertook the translation of a different liturgical work of paramount importance to the church: the Synaxarion. In the course of the following centuries, Ethiopians made their own contributions to it by adding commemorative lives of Ethiopian holy men, who in this way began to take their place beside the foreign saints. Another addition was made in the form of short poems in honor of the saints of the day. Still another, similiar work, *Ta'ammera Māryām* (Miracles of Mary), translated in the fourteenth or fifteenth century, enjoyed an enormous diffusion in the Ethiopian church, on account of the topic to which it was devoted—namely, the Virgin Mary, whose cult has always been strong in the Ethiopian church, a trait it shared with the Egyptian church. (The materials of this work had been drawn from Oriental as well as Occidental Christian sources.) Later additions included original miracles referring to the local milieu. The translation from an Arabic original, now lost, of an apocalyptic work in the same period entitled *Rā'ya Sinodā* (The Vision of Shenute) is the only known text available.

Attributed to the fifteenth century is the translation of another revered book of juridical relevance, *Fetḥa nagaśt* (The Code of the Kings). Until modern times, this work was considered the basic legal text of Ethiopian high courts of justice. It is a version of the thirteenth-century *Majmu' al-Qawānīn* of al-As'ad IBN AL-'ASSĀL, a nomocanon written for the Christians of Egypt.

In the sixteenth century the corpus of monastic works underwent a substantial enrichment through the translation of two renowned treatises of ascetic life. The first is entitled *Aragāwi manfasāwi* (The Spiritual Elder), the Ethiopic equivalent of *Al-Shaykh al-Rūḥānī*, a work by Yuḥannā ibn Sibā'. According to Ethiopian tradition, the Egyptian metropolitan Mārqos I, who died in 1530, contributed to that translation, along with an Ethiopianized monk of foreign origin (perhaps Yemeni) named 'Enbāqom. The second work was *Mār Yīsḥaq* (Master Isaac), the reputed work of Isaac of Nineveh. Both of these works, together with *Filkesyus*, constitute a sort of a trilogy in the schools of the Ethiopian church under the collective title *Maṣāḥefta manakosāt* (Books of the Monks).

In the sixteenth and seventeenth centuries, other theological works were translated into Ethiopic, including *Haymānota abaw* (The Faith of the Fathers), which reiterated Ibn Rajā's Arabic treatise entitled *I'tirāf al-Ābā'*. This and *Qērelos* remained the most authoritative theological texts in the church. Other works deriving from Arabic are *Tilmidh* (The Pupil), Ethiopic *Talmid*, and *Maṣḥafa Ḥawi* (Book of Hāwi), the original Arabic title of which was just *Al-ḥāwī*. Another book, *Faws manfasāwi* (The Spiritual Medicament), was translated by order of Queen Sabla Wangēl in the seventeenth century.

So far, works of purely religious content have been listed. Of those more profane, or, more precisely, Christian-profane, several translations deserve mention. In the fourteenth century, the *Zēnā ayhud* (Story of the Jews), attributed in the Ethiopic translation to Yosef ben Goryon, was translated into Ethiopic from an Arabic original, possibly one from Egypt. Other nonreligious works rendered into Ethiopic include the universal history *Maṣḥafa tārik* of the Egyptian Jirjis ibn al-'Amīd al-MAKĪN, possibly translated in the second half of the thirteenth century, as well as Abū Shākir's work appearing under the Ethopic title *Maṣḥaf buruk zadarasa Abu Sāker* (Blessed Book Composed by Abū Sākīr), translated in the sixteenth century. Still more important was the translation of the chronicle of JOHN OF NIKIOU, relating to the ARAB CONQUEST OF EGYPT, a translation executed by an Egyptian cleric named Qebryāl (Ghubrīyāl) in the seventeenth century. The original of this unique work is lost, and the Ethiopic version is the only one that survives.

The bulk of Ethiopian Christian literature, it appears, is drawn from Coptic sources. It is worthwhile to recall the fact that now and then the Ethiopic translations of foreign works either offer a version of their own, different from the one extant in other literatures, or append original Ethiopian contributions to the body of the translated work, thus producing new pieces of purely local literature, as in the case of the Rule of Pachomius.

Some of these translations were made outside Ethiopia, either in Egypt or in the Holy Land, by Copts or Ethiopian monks on pilgrimage. The rest must have been done in Ethiopia by foreign monks (mostly Copts), who may have had the assistance of Ethiopians in performing their work. Yet such translators were not confined to that task and now and then became authors in Ge'ez, displaying outstanding skill and knowledge, like the already mentioned Metropolitan Salāmā or the monk 'Enbāqom.

Original Literature

The overwhelming mass of Coptic literature passing into Ethiopia stimulated a vigorous movement of purely original Ethiopic literary production. It is difficult to fix the time of its beginning. The oldest surviving works seem to date no further back than the thirteenth or fourteenth century, a period when the activity of Egyptian clerics in Ethiopia as translators and original writers in Ge'ez was at a peak.

Original Ethiopian literature emulates the parent genres of the Coptic Christian literature of Egypt. In character, it was theological (dogmatic and pastoral), didactic and monastic, as well as apocalyptic, eschatological, and hagiographic (*gadl* is the typical Ethiopic term for such narratives), mainly concentrating on Ethiopian "saints" and historical material (based on Christian principles and telling about events in the life of the rulers of Ethiopian society, such as kings, high officials, and dignitaries of the church). Other topics included in this prolific literature were grammar, magic, and chronology. The contents, as a rule, drew on the models offered by the Christian literature of Egypt. Even so, the Ethiopic writers developed an impressive degree of originality. Noteworthy are the grammatical works, called *sawāsǔw* (ladder), derived from the Coptic works known as *scalae* (Arabic, *sullam*), which developed a peculiar art of their own and seem to have emerged in the course of the fifteenth century. No one knows why it is called ladder or, more precisely, why Bishop Yoḥannes of Samannud (Egypt) called it ecclesiastical ladder (Graf, 1947, p. 372). In this connection, it is worthwhile to mention an original and thriving method of commentary on the Scriptures and patristic texts, which developed in the traditional oral teaching in church schools, where the *sawāsǔw* was taught. The language was the living one, called Amharic, employed also as a teaching language. This art of commentaries is usually called *andemtā,* or enumeration in succession, one after another, of the various interpretations.

All the literature so far taken into account was written in prose, but poetry was also widely cultivated. Although there is no direct evidence of Coptic poetry translated into Ethiopic (the rhymed liturgical texts constitute a special case), the Ethiopians eventually developed a flourishing poetic literature of original stock, some types of which are thought to have been inspired by Coptic models. Such is the poetic form called *malke'* (effigy, image), a composition made of stanzas, each of them praising, with symbolic language, the physical parts as well as moral qualities of a saintly person (Christ, the Virgin Mary, etc.). Sometimes it dealt with sacred items. The earliest of these poetic compositions may be traced to the fifteenth century. The same may be said of another type of poetry, similar in form and content to the *malke'*, which is used to praise holy persons; such poems are called *salām* (peace, equal to the greeting "hail"), taken from the word with which they begin. The *salām* also seems to date from the beginning of the fifteenth century. Another typical poetic genre is the *qenē*, which is metaphorical and possesses a hidden meaning. This type of original composition may have been inspired by Coptic models. It has a high degree of elaborateness and is considered by Ethiopians the highest genre of poetry. All these compositional forms and styles seem to go back for their beginning to the fifteenth century, so it may be that grammar and poetry were introduced into Ethiopia at the same time, the schools being the place where they were studied and practiced.

In conclusion, a final case deserves mention. Sometimes original works of Ethiopian literature appear to have been translated into Arabic, seemingly for the use of the Christian church of Egypt. A certain Arabic narrative ascribed to the sixteenth century deals with the widespread legend of the queen of Sheba. It is allegedly a translation of a portion of a famous work written in Ethiopia in the fourteenth century, bearing the title *Kebra nagaśt* (The Nobility of the Kings). Also in the sixteenth century there was made a translation, or redrafting, from Ethiopic into Arabic of the life of one of the most important (politically and religiously) saints, Takla Hāymānot. Again in the twentieth century, an Ethiopian monk whose name had been Arabicized to Yūḥannā al-Mutawaḥḥid al-Ḥabashī published a new Arabic version of the miracles of the saint. The monk died in 1955 in Egypt, after living in the convent of DAYR AL-MUḤARRAQ, where a copy of that publication is to be found. One wonders if he himself executed the translation.

BIBLIOGRAPHY

Comprehensive Treatises

Cerulli, E. *La letterature etiopica,* 3rd ed. Florence and Milan, 1968.

Colin, G. *La Profession de foi christologique du Talmud: Mélanges linguistiques offerts à Maxime Rodinson,* ed. Christian Robin, pp. 161–163. Paris, 1985.

Doresse, J. *Les Anciens monastères coptes de la Moyenne Egypte et leurs influences sur l'Ethiopie chrétienne médiévale: Documents pour servir à l'histoire des civilisations éthiopiennes* 1. Paris, 1970.

Guidi, I. *Storia della letteratura etiopica.* Rome, 1932.

Harden, J. M. *An Introduction to Ethiopic Christian Literature.* London, 1926.

Littmann, E. "Geschichte der äthiopischen Literatur." In *Geschichte der christlichen Literaturen des Orients,* ed. C. Brockelmann, 2nd ed. Leipzig, 1909.

Ricci, L. "Letterature dell'Etiopia." In *Storia delle letterature d'Oriente.* Milan, 1969.

Rossini, C. *Note per la storia letteraria abissina.* Rome, 1900.

Monographs and Articles on Special Topics

Cerulli, E. *Il libro etiopico dei Miracoli di Maria e le sue fonti nelle letterature del Medio Evo latino.* Rome, 1943.

———. *Etiopi in Palestina,* 2 vols. Rome, 1943–1947.

———. *Scritti teologici etiopici dei secoli XVI–XVII,* Vol. 1, *Tre opuscoli Mikaeliti.* Vatican City, 1958.

———. *Storia dei Quattro Concili.* Rome, 1960.

Chojnacki, S. *Major Themes in Ethiopian Painting.* Wiesbaden, 1983.

Cowley, R. W. *The Traditional Interpretation of the Apocalypse of St. John in the Ethiopian Orthodox Church.* Cambridge, 1983.

Devos, P. "Les Miracles de saint Ménas en éthiopien." In *Atti del Convegno Internazionale dei Studi Etiopici,* pp. 335–43. Rome, 1960.

Donzel, E. van. *Enbāqom—Anqaṣa amin (La Porte de la Foi): Apologie éthiopienne du christianisme contre l'Islam à partir du Coran.* Leiden, 1969.

Fusella, L. "Libro dei Giubilei-Libro di Enoc." *Apocrifi dell'Antico Testamento.* Turin, 1981.

Getatchew Haile. *The Different Collections of Nägś Hymns in Ethiopic Literature and Their Contributions.* Oikonomia 19. Erlangen, 1983.

Imbakon Kalewold. *Traditional Ethiopian Church Education,* trans. Mengestu Lemma, pp. 33–38. New York, 1970 (contains an appendix by translator on *Ethiopian Classical Poetry).*

Knibb, M. A., and E. Ullendorff. *The Ethiopic Book of Enoch,* 2 vols. Oxford, 1978.

Lantschoot, A. van. *Abbā Salāmā métropolite d'Ethiopie (1348–1388) et son rôle de traducteur.* Atti del Convegno Internazionale dei Studi Etiopici, pp. 397–401. Rome, 1960.

Meinardus, O. F. A. "Ecclesiastic Aethiopica in Aegypto." *Journal of Ethiopian Studies* 3, ser. 1 (1965):23–35.

Metzger, B. M. *The Early Versions of the New Testament: Their Origin, Transmission and Limitations.* Oxford, 1977.

Moreno, M. M. *Struttura e terminologia del Sawāsew.* Rassegna di studi etiopici VIII–1949. Rome, 1950.

Murad Kamil. *Das Josef Ben Gorion (Josippos): Geschichte der Juden—Zēnā ayhud.* New York, 1938.

———. "Translations from Arabic in Ethiopic Literature." *Bulletin de la Société d'archéologie copte.* Cairo, 1942.

———. *Al-Qinī: Lawn min al-Shi'r al Ḥabashī.* Majallat Kulliyyat al-Adāb. Cairo, 1948.

Rodinson, M. "Notes sur le texte de Jean de Nikiou." In *IV Congresso Internazionale di Studi Etiopici,* Vol. 2. Rome, 1974.

Sauget, S. M. "Un Exemple typique des relations culturelles entre l'arabe-chrétien et l'éthiopien: Un Patericon récemment publié." In *IV Congresso Internazionale di Studi Etiopici,* Vol. 1. Rome, 1974.

Schall, A. *Zur äthiopischen Verskunst: Eine Studie über die Metra des Qenē auf Grund der Abhandlung "al-qenē laun min as-si'r al-ḥabasī" von Dr. Murad Kamil.* Wiesbaden, 1961.

Uhlig, S. *Das äthiopische Henochbuch.* Gütersloh, 1984.

Ullendorff, E. *Ethiopia and the Bible.* London, 1968.

———. "Hebrew, Aramaic, and Greek: The Version Underlying Ethiopic Translations of the Bible and Intertestamental Literature." In *The Bible World: Essays in Honor of Cyrus H. Gordon,* ed. G. Rensburg, R. Adler, M. Arfa, and N. H. Winter. New York, 1980.

Vergote, J. *La Littérature copte et sa diffusion en Orient.* Atti del Convegno Internazionale sul tema L'Oriente Cristiano nella storia della civiltà. Rome, 1964.

Weischer, B. M. "Der Dialog 'Dass Christus Einer ist' des Cyrill von Alexandrien," pt. I, *Oriens Christianus* 51 (1967):130–85; pt. II, *Oriens Christianus* 52 (1968):92–137.

———. "Die äthiopischen Psalmen und Qērlosfragmente in Erevan/Armenien." *Oriens Christianus* 53 (1969):113–58.

———. *Qērellos I: Der Prosphonetikos 'Über den rechten Glauben' des Kyrillos von Alexandrien an Theodosius II,* ed. J. Lukas. Afrikanische Forschungen 7. Glückstadt, 1973.

———. *Qērellos III: Der Dialog "Dass Christus Einer ist" des Kyrillos von Alexandrien.* ed. E. Hammerschmidt. Äthiopistische Forschungen 2. Wiesbaden, 1977.

———. *Qērellos IV 1: Homilien und Briefe zum Konzil von Ephesos,* ed. E. Hammerschmidt. Äthiopistische Forschungen 4. Wiesbaden, 1979.

———. *Qērellos IV 2: Traktate des Epiphanios von Zypern und des Proklos von Kyzikos,* ed. E. Hammerschmidt. Äthiopistische Forschungen 6. Wiesbaden, 1979.

———. *Qērellos IV 3: Traktate des Severianos von Gabala, Gregorios Thaumaturgos und Kyrillos von Alexandrien,* ed. E. Hammerschmidt. Äthiopistische Forschungen 7. Wiesbaden, 1979.

LANFRANCO RICCI

ETHIOPIAN CHURCH AUTOCEPHALY.

In the middle of the fourth century, Saint ATHANASIUS, the twentieth patriarch of Alexandria, appointed Frumentius (Salāmā I) to be the first primate (ABUN) of Ethiopia. From then until the nineteenth century, negotiations between the two churches were generally restricted to Ethiopian requests for a new *abun* to be consecrated and sent to Ethiopia by the Coptic patriarch after the death of the previous *abun*. These requests were usually made through an embassy sent to Egypt with presents for the Coptic patriarch and the Muslim ruler of Egypt, without whose approval the new *abun* could not travel to Ethiopia.

The question of providing a greater number of bishops than the one *abun* for the Ethiopian see is reported to have been broached as early as the twelfth century, when Emperor Haile of the Zāgwē dynasty asked for ten bishops to assist Abuna Mikā'ēl. Patriarch GABRIEL II (1131–1165) considered the request to be justified, but the ruler of Egypt is reported to have prevented the appointment of additional bishops, in order to keep the church of Ethiopia under the church of Egypt and consequently under the ruler of Egypt.

Whatever the truth of this report, it was not until the latter part of the nineteenth century, after the death of Atnātēwos, the 108th archbishop of Ethiopia, that Emperor Yoḥannes asked the patriarch of Alexandria, CYRIL V, to appoint three Coptic bishops to assist the new *abun*. In 1881 the synod of the Coptic church decreed that an archbishop and three bishops would be appointed for Ethiopia. One of these bishops was Mātēwos who was appointed bishop of Shewa province. When Emperor Menelik II acceded to the throne as King of Kings, he requested the patriarch to appoint Mātēwos as the *abun* of Ethiopia. Abuna Mātēwos died in 1926.

Rās Tafari Makonnen (then regent of Ethiopia, later Emperor Haile Selassie I) asked Patriarch Cyril V to choose a new archbishop and to appoint several Ethiopian bishops to assist him in his spiritual mission. But the death of Cyril V in 1927 left the question in suspense until the election of Patriarch JOHN XIX (Yu'annis) in 1928. The synod in 1929 appointed Archbishop Qērelos to be the 111th *abun* of Ethiopia, together with four Ethiopian bishops. When Patriarch John XIX visited Ethiopia in 1930, a fifth Ethiopian bishop, the EČČAGE, was appointed. This was the first time that Ethiopian bishops were appointed by the church of Egypt.

Before leaving Ethiopia after the Italian occupation in 1935, Emperor Haile Selassie asked Abuna Qērelos to stay in Ethiopia to take care of the church. The Italians tried to persuade him to declare the church of Ethiopia independent from the church of Egypt. This Abuna Qērelos naturally refused to do, despite threats, blandishments, and a stormy interview with Mussolini in Rome. He was then brought back to Egypt, and the Italian authorities proceeded with their plan to detach the church of Ethiopia from its parent church. Abraham, the Ethiopian bishop of Gojam, was appointed patriarch of the Ethiopian church, with three archbishops and three bishops to assist him. By a decree dated 28 December 1937, the Coptic synod excommunicated Abraham and his assistants, with the approval of the emperor, who was then in exile in England.

After the emperor's return to Ethiopia, Abuna Qērelos traveled to Addis Ababa in May 1942, accompanied by a mission of three Coptic layman to discuss church matters and political questions (notably the resumption of diplomatic relations between the two countries). A formula was found to validate sacraments performed by the illegal patriarch and bishops "as if they had been performed by legally appointed ecclesiastical authorities." Abuna Qērelos stayed in Ethiopia, and the three laymen returned to Egypt on the day following the death of Patriarch John XIX. They bore with them new requests from the Ethiopian church that an Ethiopian be appointed as *abun* after the death of the incumbent and that authority be immediately granted to him to consecrate bishops for the Ethiopian church.

By a decree dated 26 June 1942, the Coptic synod lifted the excommunication, but made no mention of the Ethiopian requests. Because of this, the decree was not published in Ethiopia and the Ethiopian church proclaimed that the *eččagē* would henceforth be entitled to consecrate priests. The Coptic *abun* was practically set aside. When Patriarch MACARIUS III was elected on 12 February 1944, his name was not mentioned in Ethiopian church services, as required by tradition.

A new mission was sent to Ethiopia in June 1944. It conferred with an Ethiopian committee, which made known the Ethiopian church's wishes in a letter to the patriarch dated 28 June 1944. The wishes were the following: (1) that His Holiness choose from among his sons of the Ethiopian clergy a man of merit and consecrate him archbishop of Ethiopia; (2) that an Ethiopian synod be established as counterpart to the synod of the Alexandrian church, this synod to have the right to choose the bishops to be consecrated by the archbishop appointed by the patriarch; (3) that the Egyptian synod welcome representatives of the Ethiopian church to take part in the election of the patriarch of the See of Saint Mark, Alexandria; (4) that the Ethiopian synod have a permanent seat in the Alexandrian synod and be invited to attend all its meetings; (5) that the excommunication be lifted from the bishops whom the Ethiopian church was forced to choose under the Italian occupation, to save the faith when the church had to break its relation with the church of Alexandria; (6) that an ecclesiastical college be founded at Addis Ababa and be placed under the high authority of the patriarch, and that an exchange of missions be established between Egypt and Ethiopia.

An argument often used by the Ethiopians in their discussions with the Egyptians was that their number was much greater than that of the Copts in Egypt and that, moreover, they were not a minority in their country, as are the Copts in Egypt, but a majority in a state that officially proclaimed Christianity the state religion.

A delicate question was that of the patriarch's position as head of the whole See of Saint Mark and, at the same time, as direct head of the church of Egypt. At one time, the idea was broached that a position similar to that of the ecumenical patriarch of Constantinople could be established, whereby the patriarch would retain the title pope of Alexandria and become the superior of a patriarch of Egypt and a patriarch of Ethiopia, and perhaps later, a patriarch of the Sudan and other regions.

The idea never had much success, mainly because of the long historical identification of the Copts of Egypt with the head of their church and the difficulty of imagining that this head could become two persons. Also the idea smacked too much of Greek usage and could not be accepted by the Egyptians.

Patriarch Macarius called the synod on 29 January 1945, and a committee was entrusted with the study of the requests formulated by the Ethiopian church. On 16 June 1945 the synod approved the committee's findings, which (1) refused to give the *abun* the right to consecrate bishops; (2) refused to appoint an Ethiopian *abun;* (3) approved of Ethiopian participation in the election of the patriarch; (4) approved of Ethiopian representation in the Egyptian synod; (5) confirmed the lifting of the excommunication; and (6) approved of an exchange of missions and of the establishment of an ecclesiastical college in Addis Ababa.

Negotiations stopped at this point. Patriarch Macarius III died on 31 August 1945, and Athanasius, archbishop of Banī Suef, was appointed as locum tenens. In December 1945 a congress of Ethiopian church representatives made several decisions, including one to send delegates to Egypt for further discussion of the Ethiopian demands. The work and decisions of this congress were published in the Amharic-language *Ethiopian Church Review* in its first issue, dated 10 Khedār 1938/19 November 1945 and its second issue dated 30 Tākhśāś 1938/8 January 1946. It was stated therein that the Ethiopian church would be forced to separate from the Coptic church if its demands were not met.

The mission brought a letter from the emperor to Athanasius, the locum tenens, urging that the demands be accepted for the good of the two churches. Eight demands were formulated. The synod, in its meeting of 31 January 1946, with the locum tenens presiding, answered that (1) it accepted that the next archbishop of Ethiopia should be an Ethiopian; (2) it denied the archbishop of Ethiopia authorization to consecrate bishops; (3) it approved increasing the number of bishops for Ethiopia; (4) it would permit delegates of the Ethiopian church to take part in the election of the patriarch; (5) it would permit the church of Ethiopia to be represented at the meetings of the synod at the patriarchate; (6) it approved exchanges of missions between the churches; (7) it would allow a seminary to be founded at Addis Ababa; (8) it refused to let the Ethiopian church have a special synod at Addis Ababa, but allowed the archbishop to call a regional congregation of bishops.

The Ethiopian church sent five monks to Egypt, asking that they be consecrated as bishops. During their presence in Cairo, Patriarch YŪSĀB II was elected on 26 May 1946. He called the synod on 20 June 1946 to examine once again the Ethiopian demands. The most important, that of the archbishop's right to consecrate bishops, was again refused. In addition, the conditions put forward by the patriarch for consecrating the five Ethiopian monks as bishops (namely, that they should formally undertake a solemn oath never to consecrate a patriarch, an archbishop, or a bishop) was refused by the Ethiopians, as this would have precluded any possibility for the Ethiopian archbishop to consecrate bishops in future.

On 30 June 1946, Rās Asrate Kassa proposed mediation to end the conflict. He asked the Coptic church to send a mission to Addis Ababa in order to resume the talks on the following bases: (1) the patriarch would ordain the bishops proposed by the Ethiopian church, and the bishops would individually take an oath of allegiance to the Coptic church; and (2) the patriarch would examine with paternal benevolence the other requests of the Ethiopian church, and any decision taken would have a retroactive effect and thus apply to the bishops already ordained. The Coptic mission left for Addis Ababa on 23 July and returned on 3 August without having obtained a result. The Ethiopian ecclesiastics returned to Addis Ababa on 4 August 1946.

In June 1947 the emperor told the patriarch that he desired to end the disagreement. The patriarch appointed a committee, the report of which was approved by the synod on 24 July 1947. The Ethiopian archbishop would have the right to ordain bishops by special delegation from the patriarch. A delegation would be given for each individual candidate. Furthermore, a Coptic bishop would be appointed as "patriarchal delegate for African questions," with residence at Addis Ababa. He would carry the delegations from the patriarch to the *abun* for ordaining the bishops. On 29 March 1948 the patriarch sanctioned the Ethiopian acceptance of the synod's decisions, except for the patriarchal delegate, who was absolutely refused by the Ethiopians.

On 25 July 1948 five Ethiopian bishops were ordained by the patriarch. They were Bāslyos of Shewa, Mikā'ēl of Gonder, Tēwoflos of Harar, Yā'qob of Leqemt, and Ṭimotēwos of Yerga Alem. On 22 October 1950, Abuna Qērelos, the last Coptic archbishop, died in Cairo after a long illness. The bishop of Shewa was ordained as archbishop of Ethiopia by the patriarch on 28 June 1959 and thus became the first Ethiopian *abun*. On 2 September 1951 five other Ethiopian bishops were ordained by the *abun* by virtue of a delegation for this purpose from the patriarch. They were Mārqos of Eritrea, Fileppos of Jerusalem, Gorgoryos of Jimma, Tādēwos of Gore, and Gabre'ēl of Wollo.

In 1956 the Coptic church faced a crisis brought about by the weakness of the patriarch and the reported acts of simony committed by his secretary, Melek. The patriarch was first abducted by a group of young fanatics called Group of the Coptic Nation. Later, at the request of part of the Community Council and of Coptic public opinion, he was forced by the Egyptian government to retire to a monastery in Upper Egypt. This drastic measure was carried out despite the protests of other members of the Community Council, who believed that asking government help in setting aside a patriarch would constitute a dangerous precedent. The folly of such an action was amply proved by subsequent events connected with Patriarch SHENOUDA III twenty-five years later.

From the DAYR AL-MUḤARRAQ, to which he had been relegated, the patriarch, in a letter to Emperor Haile Selassie, asked for the mediation of the church of Ethiopia. In June 1956 a delegation of seven Ethiopian bishops left for Cairo and visited the patriarch at the monastery. It proved unable to resolve the crisis and returned to Ethiopia. The patriarch then became ill and was taken to the Coptic Hospital in Cairo, where he remained for about five months. He died on 13 November 1956, at the age of eighty-two, and was buried in the Church of Saint Mark at Cairo. Anbā Athanasius was again appointed locum tenens by the synod.

On the patriarch's death, the question of Ethiopian participation in the election of his successor arose again, complicated by the fact that on 3 November 1957 a new law had been issued by presidential decree, at the request of the Synod and the Community Council, regulating the procedure for the election of the patriarch. As the patriarch is a public official, the procedure for his election is regulated by law and supervised by the Office of Elections at the Ministry of Interior. The same applies to the elections of the Coptic Community Council.

The new law fixed the representation of the Ethiopian church and people in the election of the patriarch, with votes to be given either in person or by proxy. The representatives of Ethiopia were to be (1) the archbishop, the bishops, and the *eč̣č̣agē* (2) the delegate of the emperor; and (3) twenty-four notables of the empire to be chosen by the emperor.

In November 1957, Anbā Yu'annis (John), archbishop of Giza and secretary of the synod, was delegated to Addis Ababa to invite the Ethiopian representatives to participate in the election, but the Ethiopian church replied that "since the place of the Ethiopian Church in this matter has apparently not been clearly stipulated in the order of procedure, and in view of the fact that the legitimate rights and privileges of the Ethiopian Church were not accorded her in the decision made concerning the previous patriarch, it has become necessary that this breach of our privilege be discussed and a decision reached before we can participate in the election. If it would be your pleasure to discuss this matter with us, we shall be happy to send our delegates for this purpose."

The patriarchate made another effort to persuade the Ethiopian church to participate in the election procedure. Anbā Yu'annis again went to Ethiopia for this purpose, but to no avail. It was finally agreed that negotiations with the Ethiopian church would be carried on concurrently with the electoral procedure. An Ethiopian mission composed of two bishops and three laymen arrived in Cairo on 24 May 1958, and after protracted negotiations, a protocol was signed on 21 July and approved by the synod on 23 July.

This was an unusual document in church history. Its main clause was that the patriarch, who would always be an Egyptian orthodox Copt, would be elected by an equal number of voters on the same day in Egypt and in Ethiopia (about seven hundred voters in each country). Accessory clauses were that the archbishop of Ethiopia would be granted the rank of vice-patriarch at the first opportunity after the election of the patriarch and that the patriarch would make a state visit to Ethiopia after his consecration.

This protocol, had it been implemented, would have greatly enhanced the stature of the Coptic patriarch and ensured him a practically unassailable position. The Egyptian government naturally did not want the position of the Coptic patriarch to be strengthened to such a degree, and it refused to implement the protocol (i.e., to modify the newly issued electoral law in accordance with the clauses of the protocol). The Ethiopian delegates to the negotiations, who were to stay on in order to take part in the electoral proceedings, returned to Ethiopia at the end of October 1958.

Patriarch CYRIL VI was finally elected on 19 April 1959, two and a half years after the death of Patriarch Yūsāb II, and consecrated on 10 May. The Ethiopian church and government abstained from attending the consecration. On 7 May and again on 16 May, the new patriarch wrote to the emperor and sent a mission of bishops and laymen to Addis Ababa to invite an Ethiopian delegation to resume discussions in Cairo. This was accepted, and the Ethiopian delegation arrived in Cairo on 11 June.

A new protocol was quickly drafted, and after arduous discussion, it was signed by the two delegations on 25 June. Its main clause is the provision for the elevation of the Ethiopian archbishop, the *abun*, to the rank of patriarch. His investiture and consecration shall be performed "by the Pope and patriarch who occupies the chair [throne] of Saint Mark of Alexandria." He is authorized to ordain archbishops and bishops.

This was the first time in Christian history that a church granted independence (to use a political term) to another church. Otherwise, the Ethiopians threatened to go to Armenia or Syria to be consecrated. This protocol remains the basic document that has since then governed the relations between the two churches. On 26 June the emperor informed Patriarch Cyril VI that Abuna Bāslyos, archbishop of Ethiopia, had been chosen as the first patriarch of Ethiopia. He was consecrated in the presence of the emperor at the Coptic Cathedral of Saint Mark in Cairo on Sunday, 28 June 1959.

Patriarch Cyril VI made a state visit to Ethiopia in October 1960. He again visited Ethiopia in January 1965 to attend the Conference of Oriental Orthodox Churches.

Patriarch Bāslyos of Ethiopia died on 12 October 1970. Patriarch Cyril sent a delegation to convey the condolences of the Coptic church, as he could not attend the funeral himself because of his illness. Tēwoflos, the bishop of Harar, was chosen to be the second patriarch of Ethiopia. Meanwhile, Patriarch Cyril VI died in Cairo on 9 March 1971. The question then arose as to whether the locum tenens of the Coptic patriarch, Archbishop Anṭuniyus of Suhāj, could take the place of the patriarch at the consecration of the patriarch of Ethiopia. The question was quickly resolved, and the locum tenens traveled to Addis Ababa for the investiture and consecration of the new Ethiopian patriarch on 9 May 1971.

On 29 October 1971, Patriarch Shenouda III was among the three candidates elected to the See of Saint Mark. The lot was drawn two days later, and he was consecrated on 14 November 1971. In September 1973 he made a state visit to Ethiopia.

After the Ethiopian revolution of 1974, Patriarch Tēwoflos continued to direct the affairs of the Ethiopian church until he was arrested and imprisoned by the government in 1975. His fate is unknown. The Ethiopian church elected Patriarch Takla Hāymānot to replace him, but this election was not recognized by Patriarch Shenouda III. A decision of the Coptic synod dated 14 August 1976 condemned the arrest of the previous patriarch of Ethiopia and the election of a new patriarch as illegal, because it did not respect canon law, by which a patriarch can be removed only by a synodal decision after he has been allowed to present his defense.

The revolutionary government of Ethiopia disestablished the church of Ethiopia and confiscated all its properties. It organized indoctrination classes and campaigned against religious practice, both Christian and Muslim. The older archbishops in Ethiopia were put "on pension" in 1980, and younger ecclesiastics were chosen to take their place, presumably in order to be more in tune with the government's views. An ecclesiastical opposition led by some Ethiopian bishops outside Ethiopia took shape, with the aim of informing public opinion of the situation of the church in Ethiopia.

BIBLIOGRAPHY

Edict of Excommunication, dated 28 December 1937 (in Arabic and Amharic). Government Press, Cairo, 1938.

Murād Kāmil. "La Dernière phase des relations historiques entre l'église copte d'Egypte et celle d'Ethiopie (jusqu'en 1952)." *Bulletin of the Society of Coptic Archeology* 14 (1957):1–22.

———. "Al-'Ilāqāt Bayn al-Kanīsah al-Miṣriyyah wa-al-Ithyūpiyyah." *Al-Siyāsah al-Dawliīyyah,* 3, no. 8 (April–June 1968).

Yolande, M. *The Church of Ethiopia: The National Church in the Making.* Asmara, 1972.

MIRRIT BOUTROS GHALI

ETHIOPIAN HERESIES AND THEOLOGICAL CONTROVERSIES. Although isolated from the Christian world until the twentieth century, Ethiopia has had knowledge, and even followers, of the major heresies that caused schism and created ecclesiastical minorities in the early history of the Christian church. A letter from the emperor Constantius II (337–361) (Athanasius, 1857, cols. 636–37) shows a reasonable line of communication between Ethiopia and the outside world. The Arian emperor wrote to the rulers of Ethiopia to demand that Frumentius, or Abuna Salāmā I (cf. ETHIOPIAN PRELATES), the first metropolitan bishop of Ethiopia, be sent to Egypt to be instructed in the Arian faith by Gregory, who was made patriarch of Alexandria when Saint ATHANASIUS (326–373), the legitimate patriarch, was in forced exile because of his refusal to embrace Arianism. Constantius thought that Athanasius himself was hiding in Ethiopia.

Church history during the reign of the Zāgwē dynasty (1137–1270) and the period preceding it is too sketchy to include the controversies, since the parties involved destroyed each other's evidence. A scholar, Giyorgis of Saglā, who died around 1420, has left a voluminous work, *Maṣeḥafa Mesṭir* (The Book of the Mystery), refuting heresies such as those of ORIGEN, ARIUS, EUTYCHES, Bitu (a local theologian), and NESTORIUS, and even the religion of Islam. The heresies refuted must have had relevance to Ethiopia. Indications are that practices by Christians, such as celebrating certain religious holy days in the form of orgy, taking advice from sorcerers, or praying with magic words, created conflict in the church. However, this treatise deals with conflicts of Christological or theological importance.

The Esṭifānosites

The earliest recorded heresy of the Ethiopian church stemmed from the extreme reverence accorded the icon of the Madonna and Child and the cross by the established church. Sources do not name leaders or state whether the objection was related to the ICONOCLASM of the eighth and ninth centuries in the Mediterranean world. In Ethiopia it started during the reign of Yāgbe'a Ṣeyon (1285–1294), when a group of clergy maintained that the icon was mere slate and the cross a mere piece of wood from Golgotha. These dissidents created great schism in the church.

Since Ethiopian leaders suppressed dissidence, another such movement did not appear in the records until the fifteenth century. At this time a monk named Esṭifānos (Stephen) from the Monastery of Qwayyaṣā in Tigre questioned the worship of icons, crosses, and worldly rulers, especially the monarch. It is not clear whether the movement was a continuation of the earlier one or not. At first Esṭifānos' criticism was directed against lax ascetic rules in monasteries. His defiance of established monastic life and his decision to establish his own monastery attracted many who preferred strict asceticism and was a threat to the church. Failing to dissuade Esṭifānos from his views, the authorities brought him before the royal court with accusations of disobedience.

His experience at court strengthened his position, since the king expected his subjects to prostrate themselves whenever they saw him or heard his name mentioned, even in his absence. Esṭifānos and his followers held that Christians should prostrate themselves only before God the Father, God the Son, and God the Holy Spirit.

It was during the reign of Zar'a Yā'qob (1434–1468) that the Blessed Virgin was worshiped through her icon. Many miracles that she worked in Spain, France, Italy, Syria, and Egypt were translated into Ge'ez, the church language of Ethiopia. At that time, the rule from Mu'allaqa, *Maṣeḥafa śer'at,* ordaining thirty-three holidays in honor of the Virgin, was brought to Ethiopia. The Esṭifānosites honored her as the Mother of God, but they considered the reverence the king demanded for the icon, the cross, and himself excessive.

They suffered severe persecution, including mass

arrest, execution, amputation (especially of hands and tongues), and isolation. Metropolitans Mikā'ēl III (Michael) and Gabre'ēl (Gabriel), both of whom lived near the middle of the fifteenth century, were sympathetic, but the political leaders were concerned with unity of the nation through conformity. Little more is known about the Esṭifānosites before the war with Grāññ (1527–1543), but their center, the Monastery of Dabra Garzēn, in Tigre, is still an important holy place of Ethiopia. Although its monks still revere their founding father, the monastery has been under the church of Ethiopia since the middle of the sixteenth century.

The Ēwosṭātēwosites

Probably since its beginning, the Ethiopian church has observed Saturday as the first Sabbath and Sunday as the Christian Sabbath. As one of the Ten Commandments, the observance of Saturday Sabbath should be practiced by any people whose book is the Bible, they believed. Furthermore, the Synodicon, one of the canonical works of the Ethiopian church, states that Peter and Paul directed that these two days be observed as holy days. During the reign of ʿAmda Ṣeyon (1314–1344) a controversy arose on the question of observing the Jewish Sabbath. The Coptic church in Egypt had objected to Jewish customs practiced by Ethiopian Christians and decreed the abolition of Saturday observance. Abolishing an ages-old religious custom was, however, difficult, although the decree had come from spiritual and political authorities. The choice in the monasteries was to obey temporal authorities or to follow the Scriptures.

Ēwosṭātēwos (Eustathius), a highly revered monk, led the opposition. His appeal in person to the patriarch in Cairo did not bring results. His followers at home withdrew from the church to live in organizations strictly controlled by the leadership. Some attempted to convert the Falasha, who are called Jews and who are an Ethiopian community, and who, judging from their literature, confuse Judaism and Christianity. When Zar'a Yāʿqob ascended the throne, he decided to end the controversy. Before that time, he himself did not keep the Sabbath, but he saw no harm in allowing Christians to observe Saturday if that could unify his kingdom. At the famous Council of Dabra Meṭmāq (1450), or Dayr al-Maghṭas, the king questioned metropolitans Michael and Gabriel about the grounds for abolishing the first Sabbath: they were not found in the Scriptures, in the Octateuch, in the books of the Prophets, in the Gospels, or in the writings of the apostles. He reminded them that Peter and Paul, the head of the apostles, handed down their reckoning in the Synodicon, that being to work for five days and not to perform any work on Saturday and Sunday. The metropolitans reversed the decree of their predecessors Salāmā II (1348–1388) and Bartalomēwos (1398–1436), and abandoned the position decreed by the church in Egypt. In the Ethiopian church, observance of the two Sabbaths starts at sunset on Friday and ends at sunset on Sunday.

The Zamikā'ēlites

The writings of the emperor Zar'a Yāʿqob (1434–1468) refer to scholars who objected to his religious views. The most serious controversy dealt with the unity and trinity of God. Since Dāwit (1382–1413), or even before, the church had taught that each Person in the Trinity has an image resembling man, who was created according to the image of God (Gn. 1:27). Sources maintain that when the Son was incarnated, he appeared as before the Incarnation and that after his Resurrection he sat on the right side of his Father in the same image. For the Last Judgment the Son will join the Father and the Holy Spirit, each one appearing to all nations in his human-divine image. Zar'a Yāʿqob compared the unity and trinity of God with three suns whose lights are united when they appear side by side, three suns (persons) with one light (divinity).

The opponents of this view, the Zamikā'ēlites, so called after Zamikā'ēl, an articulate monastic leader, proposed instead, as Fre Mākhebar did, one sun with a disk (God the Father), light (God the Son), and heat (God the Holy Spirit). Furthermore, the Zamikā'ēlites rejected the view that the Father and the Holy Spirit will appear with the Son at his second coming. They opposed the emperor's promotion of translated and newly composed versions of the miracles of the Blessed Virgin and opposed the dedication of so many days to her. They also disagreed with the constitution of the canonical books of the church.

Controversy Concerning the Preexistence of Souls

During the reign of Galāwdēwos (1540–1559), after the war with Grāññ, there arose a group who taught that there is a store for the supply of souls. According to its views, when a child is conceived, a soul is infused into the embryo; only the body descends from parents to child. The controversy may have been related to the teachings of Origen, but sources make no mention of other groups espousing this variety of Neoplatonism before this time. It does not seem to have made a lasting impression in Ethiopia.

The Jesuits and the Controversy Concerning the Unction of Christ

This was a more lasting controversy, also started during the reign of Galāwdēwos. When Islamic pressure threatened the extinction of Christianity in Ethiopia, the rulers of Ethiopia turned to Portugal for help. The Portuguese responded favorably, believing that the Ethiopian church would come under the sway of the Roman Catholic church when the war ended. Emperor Galāwdēwos, seeing no other way to save his country, favored such a religious alliance. The Portuguese, who fought the enemies of his country and the church, proved the importance of such an alliance. Nevertheless, the Ethiopian clergy was firmly committed to Alexandria. The Portuguese were finally either dismissed from the country or settled in a non-Christian region.

The desire of the Catholic church to have the Ethiopian church submit to the authority of the Roman pope has a long history, beginning with Pope Julius III (1487–1555), or even before. Jesuit missionaries finally succeeded in converting Emperor Zadengel (1603–1604). The impact of royal conversion was greater when Emperor Suseneyos (1607–1632) officially embraced Catholicism and issued a decree that his subjects follow. The arrival of Alfonso Mendez, the Catholic patriarch, in Ethiopia and his decree that the people abandon their religious culture and adopt the Latin rite caused social unrest and disruption. Metropolitan Sem'on (Simon or Simeon) was among thousands martyred in witness to the Alexandrian faith.

Stiff resistance and the fact that the king had suffered a stroke caused him to abdicate in favor of his son Fāsiladas (1632–1667). Thereafter, the Catholics left, leaving behind a theological controversy that gave a local color to Catholicism in Ethiopia and to the teaching of the two natures in Christ. This expresses itself in the theological meaning of *qeb'at,* or unction (Acts 10:38), and *bakwr,* or firstborn (Rom. 8:29), when applied to Jesus, the Christ, or Messiah (*masiḥ*) who is the only Son of God. Raising these questions was meant to show to the Monophysites the inferior human nature of Christ compared to his divine nature.

The controversy divided the local church into three sects: (1) the Unionists, or Tawāḥedo; (2) the Unctionists, or Qebātočč; and (3) the Adoptionists, or Ṣaggočč or Ya-Ṣaggā Lejočč. The Tawāḥedo taught that "by the union [of the two natures, Christ] became the Only Son of God and, by the anointment, he became King, Messiah, Prophet, and Priest." The Qebātočč believe that God the Father is the anointer; God the Son, the anointed; and God the Holy Spirit, the ointment. For a time they interpreted "He made himself poor" (2 Cor. 8:9) to mean that Christ at a given time was solely human. Through unction or the anointing of the Holy Spirit, he became a natural Son, this time in his humanity as well. The Ṣaggočč, claiming to be successors of the Tawāḥedo (as did all these schools) of the Monastery of Dabra Libānos, accept "the only Son by union" of the Tawāḥedo. In interpreting this formula and in an effort to explain the place of the human flesh of the Word Incarnate in his Sonship, they teach a third birth for Christ—after the eternal birth from the Father and the temporal birth from the Blessed Virgin—at which time, in his humanity, he was adopted as the Son of God by the unction of the Holy Spirit. In opposition to this pro-Nestorian heresy or crypto-Catholicism, the Tawāḥedo (later called Karročč after Kārrā, the leader of the movement) developed their formula of faith, which recognized Christ as the natural son of God by the union of his humanity and divinity. In answer to the inferior role they thought the other schools gave to the Son in the process of unction, they developed the formula *wald qeb'* (the Son is the ointment). In this, Christ actually becomes "the anointer, the anointed, and the ointment." Together with the Qebātočč, the Kārročč reject the Ṣaggočč's idea of speaking about Christ's divinity and humanity separately, because after the union of the two natures there is only one Christ of one nature.

The Qebātočč, who occasionally held the political upper hand during the Gonderite dynasty, are now disappearing. The Ṣaggočč were influential in Shewa until the late nineteenth century, but lost ground at the Council of Boru Mēdā (Wallo), which was summoned by Emperor Yoḥannes IV (1872–1889), a Tawāḥedo zealot, to decide the number of births of Christ. The decision against the Ṣaggočč was made after a letter from the Coptic patriarch CYRIL V (1874–1927) was read, although the translation of the Arabic into Ge'ez was questioned. Another important theological decision made by this council was that the sentence "Worship and prostration are meet to her [Mary] together with her

Son" be changed to "Worship and prostration are meet to her Son."

The Kārročč and the Ṣaggočč have both contributed something toward widening their differences, the Kārročč accusing the Ṣaggočč of Nestorianism and the Ṣaggočč accusing the Kārročč of Eutychianism. Today the number of the Qebātočč and Ṣaggočč is insignificant.

BIBLIOGRAPHY

Athanasius. *Ad imperatorem Constantium apologia.* In PG 25, cols. 595–642. Paris, 1857.

Cerulli, E. *Il libro etiopico dei miracoli di Maria e le sue fonti nelle letterature del Medio Evo latino.* Rome, 1943.

———. *Scritti teologici etiopici dei secoli XVI–XVII.* Studi e testi 198. Rome, 1958.

Crummey, D. *Priests and Politicians: Protestant and Catholic Missions in Orthodox Ethiopia, 1830–1868.* Oxford, 1972.

Dillmann, A. *Über die Regierung, insbesondere die Kirchenordnung des Königs Zar'a-Jacob.* Abhandlungen der Königlichen Akademie der Wissenschaften zu Berlin, Philosophisch-historische Klasse 2. Berlin, 1885.

Getatchew Haile. "The Letter of Archbishops Mika'el and Gäbr'el Concerning the Observance of Saturday." *Journal of Semitic Studies* 16, ser. 1 (1981):73–78.

———. "Religious Controversies and the Growth of Ethiopic Literature in the Fourteenth and Fifteenth Centuries." *Oriens Christianus* 65 (1981):102–136.

———. "The Homily of Aṣe Zär'a Ya'qob of Ethiopia in Honour of Saturday." *Orientalia Lovaniensia Periodica* 13 (1982):185–231.

———. "The Homily of Zär'a Ya'qob in Honour of St. John the Evangelist." *Oriens Christianus* 67 (1983):144–66.

———. "The Cause of the Esṭifānosites: A Fundamentalist Sect in the Church of Ethiopia." *Paideuma* 19 (1983):93–119.

Giyorgis of Saglā. *Maṣeḥafa Mesṭir.* Unedited; see, for example, Eth. MS 113, H. Zotenberg, *Catalogue des manuscrits ethiopiens (Gheez et Amharique de la Bibliothèque Nationale),* pp. 127–31. Paris, 1877.

Guidi, I. "Di due frammenti relativi alla storia di Abissinia." *Rendiconti della Accademia Nazionale dei Lincei, Classe di scienze morali* 2 (1893):579–605.

Hammerschmidt, E. *Stellung und Bedeutung des Sabbats in Äthiopien.* Stuttgart, 1963.

Heyer, F. *Die Kirche Äthiopiens: Eine Bestandsaufnahme.* Berlin and New York, 1971.

Murad Kamil. "Letters to Ethiopia from the Coptic Patriarchs Yo'annas XVIII (1770–1796) and Morqos VIII (1796–1809)." *Bulletin de la Sociéte d'archéologie copte* 8 (1942):89–143.

Rossini, C. and L. Ricci. *Il libro della luce del Negus Zar'a Yā'qob (Maṣḥafa Berhān).* In CSCO 250–51, 261–62, *Scriptores Aethiopici* 47–48, 51–52. Louvain, 1964–1965.

Taddesse Tamrat. "Some Notes on the Fifteenth-Century Stephanite 'Heresy' in the Ethiopian Church." *Rassegna di studie etiopici* 22 (1966):103–115.

Ullendorff, E. "Hebraic-Jewish Elements in Abyssinian (Monophysite) Christianity." *Journal of Semitic Studies* 1 (1956):216–56.

Wendt, K. "Die theologischen Auseinandersetzungen in der äthiopischen Kirche zur Zeit der Reformen des XV. Jahrhunderts." *Atti del Convegno Internazionale di Studi Etiopici,* pp. 137–46. Rome, 1960.

———. *Das Maṣḥafa Milād (Liber Nativitatis) und Maṣḥafa Sellāsē (Liber Trinitatis) des Kaisers Zar'a Yā'qob.* In CSCO 221–222, 235–236, *Scriptores Aethiopici* 41–44. Louvain, 1962–1963.

———. "Der Kampf um den Kanon Heiliger Schriften in der äthiopischen Kirche der Reformen des XV. Jahrhunderts." *Journal of Semitic Studies* 9 (1964):107–113.

Yacob Beyene. *L'unzione di Cristo nella teologia etiopica.* Orientalia Christiana Analecta 215. Rome, 1981.

GETATCHEW HAILE

ETHIOPIAN LITURGY. One of the key factors in the history of the Ethiopian Orthodox Church has been its ecclesiastical dependence on the Coptic church of Alexandria. This has been so great that for most of its known history, it has been headed by a bishop of Egyptian birth and education chosen by the Coptic patriarch. This dependence has inevitably been a powerful force, tending to maintain the conformity of the Ethiopian liturgy with that of the mother church of Alexandria. A closer look at the liturgies of the two churches, however, reveals that the conformity is by no means complete. It turns out, in fact, to be notably less than the liturgical conformity to be found in the daughter churches of the churches of Rome, Constantinople and Seleucia-Ctesiphon.

The explanation of this curious paradox may lie in the fact that the Egyptian metropolitans who headed the church of Ethiopia, being foreigners at the time of their appointment, had little knowledge of Ethiopia, its people, and their language. It required, therefore, metropolitans of more than ordinary force of character and ability to exercise much influence over the church confided to them. Some such metropolitans there were during the course of history, such as Salāmā II and III (see ETHIOPIAN PRELATES), but the impression one gleans from the chronicles of Ethiopia is that these were relatively rare exceptions. The strongest influence on the church of Ethiopia was clearly exercised by the emperors and their ecclesiastical advisers who came from the world of Ethiopian monasticism.

It must be noted that knowledge of the history of the Ethiopian liturgy is severely limited by an almost complete absence of documents antedating the fifteenth century and by a lack of in-depth studies of the material that is available, by scholars with a competency in comparative liturgy. The collection and description of materials is still, for the most part, in its preliminary stage. Any conclusions that may be drawn as to the significance of these materials is therefore merely tentative at this time.

In general, the conformity between the Coptic and Ethiopian liturgies is greatest in sacerdotal ceremonies and least in offices of prayer and chant. This is what one might have anticipated. Priests, of necessity, could be ordained by the Egyptian metropolitan alone, and he would be in a position to insist that candidates for ordination first learn the ceremonies that he judged proper. Offices, on the other hand, consist largely of chant that would to a great extent be governed by the exigencies of Geʿez, the liturgical language, and of Ethiopian music and would be executed by clergymen, called *dabtarās* or scribes, who, as such, would not receive ordination and whose education was obtained in certain monasteries, without reference to, or control by, the metropolitan.

Turning to particular ceremonies, one finds a substantial conformity with the Coptic liturgy in the *qeddāsē*, the eucharistic service or mass, but rather surprising differences in detail. The principal ceremonies found in the Coptic Ordinary recur in the Ethiopian; for example, the preparation of the altar, the preparation procession and blessing of the gifts, the absolution, the incensing, the reading of the four scriptural lessons, the prayers, the recitation of the Creed, the washing of hands, the kiss of peace, the use of the eucharistic anaphora, and so on. Similarly, one finds all the properly sacerdotal prayers of the Coptic liturgy faithfully repeated in the Ethiopian liturgy and in the same order, such as the prayers before and after the preparation of the altar, prayer of thanksgiving and offertory, the Absolution to the Son, the prayers for the different readings, and so on. Nevertheless, the differences to be found in the Ordinary are confined to secondary prayers or ceremonies that the Ethiopian liturgy has but the Coptic lacks, or much less frequently, the Coptic has and the Ethiopian lacks, or to minor variations of order. Some points deserve particular mention. At each mass the Ethiopians bless the material objects that come in direct contact with the Eucharist—that is, the paten, the chalice, and the spoon—and have even added in recent times at the very beginning of their missals the prayers by which Coptic bishops consecrate these instruments. For the procession with the gifts, the Ethiopians also have a chant not found in the Coptic liturgy, "How dread is this place," which is chanted by both Syrian and Chaldean deacons at the solemn epiclesis (petition for the consecration of the bread and wine) of their liturgies. Did Ethiopian pilgrims to Jerusalem encounter this chant and bring it back with them to Ethiopia? Again, the prayers precede the scriptural lessons in the Ethiopian liturgy, but follow them in the Coptic. If one may judge from the texts of these prayers, which are the same in both churches, they were originally composed to prepare the hearers to profit from the lessons, so that the Ethiopian order would seem to be more ancient. The same is clearly also true of the formula for dismissing catechumens, which the Ethiopian liturgy has preserved but the Coptic has long since discarded.

When one turns to the anaphora, the central prayer of the eucharistic service, the differences seem astonishingly great. Whereas the Coptic church today has only three anaphoras, the Ethiopian church has in its printed missal no less than fourteen, only one of which, the Anaphora of Saint BASIL THE GREAT, is found with the Copts. Six other anaphoras can be found in manuscripts (including the Anaphora of Saint MARK, used by the Copts), but with the exception of the Anaphora of Saint Mary *(Maʿazā qeddāsē)* they are not commonly used by present-day orthodox churches. The Ethiopian Catholics, on the contrary, have adopted three of them in their missal, the anaphoras of Saints Mary, Mark, and James.

The anaphora most frequently used in Ethiopia is the short Anaphora of the Apostles, which is the one found in the *Traditio apostolica* of Saint Hippolytus (Duensing, 1946, pp. 20–30; Quasten, 1935, pp. 26–33), expanded somewhat to provide intercessions and adapted to conform to the Ethiopian liturgical order. This is the anaphora that is always incorporated in missals, both manuscript and printed, in the Ordinary. It is usually assumed, therefore, that this is the original anaphora of the Ethiopian church, much as Mark's is the anaphora of Alexandria and James's that of Jerusalem, but the assumption seems rather dubious. It simply does not suit the characteristic order of the Ethiopian anaphora, which has at least two notable peculiarities. The order of the second and third exchanges between the celebrant and the people in the prefatory dialogue is the opposite of what is observed in other churches ("Let us give thanks to the Lord." "It is right and just." "Lift up your hearts." "We have to the Lord"), and the anaphoral prayer is divided into three parts. If the Anaphora of the Apostles were the original Ethiopian anaphora, one would expect that its opening words would refer to the last exchange ("Lift up your hearts." "We have to the Lord"), but they actually refer to the previous exchange. This suggests that the actual order of the Ethiopian prefatory dialogue was intended to introduce not the Anaphora of the Apostles but some other. Furthermore, this anaphora is so short that dividing it into three parts makes little sense, and the divisions occur at points that awkwardly interrupt the flow of ideas. One is led by this to the conclusion that the anaphora has been made to conform to a preexisting pattern.

The church of Ethiopia has two anaphoras to which these objections do not apply, the anaphoras of Saints John, Son of Thunder, and Cyril. Their incipits ("To thee, Lord, we have lifted up our eyes," and "To thee, Lord, God of gods") refer to the final exchange of the Ethiopian prefatory dialogue, and the two breaks in these anaphoras occur at natural pauses in the thought. It would be tempting to think, therefore, that one of these was the original anaphora of Ethiopia. However, Getatchew Haile has pointed out (1981, pp. 116–33) that both anaphoras reflect doctrinal controversies that were rife in Ethiopia during the fourteenth century. Perhaps, then, both of these anaphoras were composed in the pattern of another anaphora now lost; perhaps one of them is the ancient anaphora, but its text has been reworked; or possibly the fourteenth-century controversies merely continue or repeat much earlier controversies of a time when the ancient anaphora would have been composed.

This raises the question of the origin of the Ethiopian anaphoras. Clearly the anaphoras of the Apostles, the Lord, and Saints Basil, Mark, and James are translations of anaphoras derived from other churches, presumably all through the Coptic church. All the others seem to be of Ethiopian authorship. This is true even of the popular Anaphora of Saint Mary, which is attributed in the manuscripts to Cyriacus, bishop of al-Bahnasā, for, as Getatchew Haile has again pointed out (1983, pp. 376–89), it, like the two anaphoras mentioned above, reflects strictly Ethiopian theological debates of the Middle Ages and may with probability be ascribed to Abba Samuel of Wali. The liturgical structure of these anaphoras is remarkably varied. Some include unusual elements, such as exhortations and eschatological contemplations; in others, the anamnesis does not explicitly mention the Passion and Resurrection of Christ; and in still others, the epiclesis does not petition the transformation of the gifts into the Body and Blood of Christ.

The Ethiopian liturgies of the other sacraments have been much less studied than that of the Eucharist. However, the close relationship between them and their Coptic counterparts is obvious from even the most casual comparison. This is especially true of the rite of ordination, which was translated from Coptic into Geʿez only in very recent times when the church of Ethiopia was at last granted an indigenous hierarchy. Similarly, the *Maṣeḥafa qēder,* the rite of penitential baptism for apostates, seems to be a direct translation from the Coptic church. With the rite of baptism, on the other hand, one finds at least two noteworthy differences. The Coptic rite, which Ethiopian Catholics follow, has three oils that are used to anoint the baptized and to mix with the baptismal waters. The Ethiopian Orthodox, on the contrary, now use only two oils, they do not anoint the baptized after their confession of Christ (formerly, according to manuscripts, they did), and do not pour oil into the baptismal water before the scriptural lessons. The other peculiarity of Ethiopian baptism is that the neophytes, after communion in the Eucharist, are given milk and honey, following the prescription of Saint Hippolytus in his *Traditio apostolica.*

Ethiopian chant and the composition of the Ethiopian antiphonary, or *Deggwā,* are attributed to Saint Yārēd, who is supposed to have lived at the time of King Gabra Masqal in the seventh century. Unfortunately, the relationship between the Ethiopian *Deggwā* and the Coptic DIFNĀR has not been studied. Velat has done valiant spadework on the *Meʿrāf,* the Ethiopian Ordinary, but its relationship to its Coptic counterpart is again unclear. The Coptic horologion, on the other hand, was translated into Geʿez and, judging from surviving manuscripts, seems to have been extensively used during the

Middle Ages (the Ethiopian Catholics have revived its use in recent times); but it was supplanted by an indigenous horologion composed around 1400 by Giyorgis of Saglā. Getatchew Haile has analyzed both (e.g., 1982, pp. 4–10, 176–83), but a casual comparison of the two reveals almost nothing in common. At least the sistrum that Ethiopian clergymen use while chanting their divine office is clearly derived from Egypt. One suspects a priori that the influence of the Coptic on the Ethiopian divine office must be vastly greater than just that, but unfortunately, the studies that will identify the elements of that influence have yet to be made. On the other hand, the stately liturgical dance that the Ethiopians perform during their festive offices seems to be a strictly indigenous creation.

BIBLIOGRAPHY

Colin, G. *Vie de Georges de Saglā*. In CSCO 492, *Scriptores Aethiopici* 81; CSCO 493, *Scriptores Aethiopici* 82. Louvain, 1987.

Daoud, M., and M. Hazen. *The Liturgy of the Ethiopian Church.* Cairo, 1959.

Denzinger, H. *Ritus Orientalium, Coptorum, Syrorum et Armenorum, in Administrandis Sacramentis,* Vol. 1, pp. 222–33, 411–14. Würzburg, 1863.

Duensing, H., ed. *Der aethiopische Text der Kirchenordnung des Hippolyt.* Abhandlungen der Akademie der Wissenschaften in Göttingen, Philologisch-Historische Klasse, Vol. 3, no. 32, pp. 20–30. Göttingen, 1946.

Getatchew Haile. "Religious Controversies and the Growth of Ethiopic Literature in the Fourteenth and Fifteenth Centuries." *Oriens Christianus* 65 (1981):102–136.

———. *A Catalogue of Ethiopian Manuscripts Microfilmed for the Ethiopian Manuscript Microfilm Library . . . ,* Vol. 6. Collegeville, Minn., 1982.

———. "On the Identity of Silondis and the Composition of the Anaphora of Mary Ascribed to Hereyaqos of Behensa." *Orientalia Christiana Periodica* 49 (1983):366–89.

Hammerschmidt, E. "Zur Bibliographie äthiopischer Anaphoren." *Ostkirchliche Studien* 5 (1956):285–90.

———. *Studies in the Ethiopic Anaphoras.* Berliner Byzantinische Arbeiten 25. Berlin, 1961.

Mercer, S. A. B. *The Ethiopic Liturgy: Its Sources, Development, and Present Form.* London, 1915.

Quasten, J., ed. *Monumenta eucharistica et liturgica vetustissima,* pt. 1, pp. 26–33. Bonn, 1935.

Raes, A. *Introductio in Liturgiam Orientalem.* Rome, 1947.

———. "Il rito etiopico." In *Enciclopedia Cattolica,* Vol. 5, cols. 701f. Vatican City, 1950.

Sauget, J. M. *Bibliographie des liturgies orientales (1900–1960),* pp. 94–101. Rome, 1962.

Tecle Mariam, Semharay Selam. *De SS. Sacramentis Secundum Ritum Aethiopicum.* Rome, 1931.

Velat, B. *Etudes sur le Meʿerāf, commun de l'office éthiopien.* In PO 33. Paris, 1966.

———. *Meʿerāf, commun de l'office divin éthiopien pour toute l'année.* In PO 34, pp. 59–160. Paris, 1966.

———. *Soma Deggua, antiphonaire du carême, quatre premières semaines.* In PO 32. Paris, 1966.

WILLIAM MACOMBER

ETHIOPIAN MONASTICISM. Perhaps the most important aspect of Ethiopian Christianity is its monasticism. Introduced into the country probably at the time when Christianity itself was first preached, its centers, the monasteries, have set the rule of conduct for the domestic and foreign policy of the Christian kingdom up to the twentieth century. The monks were the voice of the church, and the monasteries were the heart of the church. Risking their lives and frequently suffering martyrdom, the monks openly castigated political leaders when they behaved in an un-Christian manner. The monks dictated their views to the leaders of the nation by various means, including excommunication. The monasteries, headed sometimes by abbots appointed by the political head of the country, were small empires, building daughter churches in their territories and collecting large revenues. They were also places of banishment to which disgraced dignitaries were exiled after being condemned to be clothed in the monastic garb. Most important, the spread of Christianity into the interior and to the furthest frontiers of Ethiopia was the accomplishment solely of the monks. Both solitary eremitism, based on the Rule of Saint ANTONY, and communal cenobitism, based on the Rule of Saint PACHOMIUS, became part of Ethiopian monasticism. The Rule of Pachomius was among the first books translated into Geʿez, or Ethiopic.

Early Period

Tradition ascribes the introduction of monasticism into Ethiopia to monks who entered the country between the fourth and sixth centuries. Their number, origin, motive, and even the time of migration into the highlands of East Africa have been points of speculation. Broadly speaking, they came from the Mediterranean or Hellenistic world, more specifically from Egypt and Syria. Internal sources indicate that most of them had connections with the Monastery of Apa Pachomius in Egypt. Tradition has it that Abba Yoḥannes Kāmā (JOHN KAMA) and Abba Libānos, or Maṭṭā', were ordered, at different times, by Pachomius (d. 346) to go to Ethiopia to teach. If this is a historical fact, it must have taken place on the occasion of Frumentius' consecration by ATHANASIUS as the first bishop of Axum in 340 (see ETHIOPIAN PRELATES: SALĀMĀ I). In any event, each of these two monks taught and established monasteries that, although their ancient churches have become victims of time, are still centers of pilgrimage, Dabra Sinā by Yoḥannes Kāmā and Dabra Libānos by Libānos, both in the province of Eritrea. Of the monks who are said to have migrated to Ethiopia in groups, the so-called Nine Saints are the most celebrated fathers of monasticism. These are Aragāwi or Zamikā'ēl of Dabra Dāmo, Panṭalēwon of Asbo or Bēta Panṭalēwon, Garimā or Yesḥaq of Madarā, Afṣē or Afāṣim of Yēha, Gubbā (whose monastery seems not to have survived), Alēf of Aḥse'a or Beḥzā or Allēlo, Yem'atā of Guḥ, Liqānos of Dabra Qwanāṣel, and Seḥmā of Sideyā. It is not certain whether Oṣ or Oẓ is a name of either Alēf or Seḥmā, as several sources suggest, or of another monk, Oṣ of Dabra Kwerāzā.

The tradition, whether written or oral, is firm in asserting that the hundreds of monasteries that have flourished in the course of the history of the Ethiopian church were founded by individual monks who traced their monastic genealogy to one of these eleven or twelve saints. But it is quite possible that there were from time to time other monastic fathers who received their monastic habits in one of the Egyptian monasteries and went to Ethiopia, where they founded new monasteries. Abuna Gabra Manfas Qeddus of Zeqwālā (d. c. 1382), for example, went to Ethiopia from a monastery in Neḥisā (Egypt) and taught in the regions of Medra Kabd before he settled on the summit of Mount Zeqwālā, where his monastery is still a center of pilgrimage. As in all aspects of Ethiopian history, it is very difficult to trace the history of the spread of Ethiopian monasticism from the time of its beginning in the fourth century to the fall of the Zāgwē dynasty in 1270. But many of the monasteries known only in the literature (e.g., Kadiḥ, Akwrēn, Awḥezi, Waṣif, Dabra Tabāydā, Dabra Harasā, Bēta Danāgel in or near Axum, Dabra Barāh, and Ṣi'at) must have been famous centers of worship established by the first, second, and third generations following the founders of Ethiopian monasticism.

Late and Postmedieval Periods

The founders of Ethiopian monasticism as it is known today are Abba Yoḥanni, Abuna Iyyasus Mo'a, Abuna Takla Hāymānot, and Abuna Madkhānina Egzi'.

No reliable historical source is known to exist on Abba Yoḥanni. The *gadl*, or acts, of Abuna Iyyasus Mo'a, his spiritual son, describes him as the seventh abbot of Dabra Dāmo, the monastery founded by Abba Zamikā'ēl, one of the Nine Saints. Genealogically, this fits into the picture of another source that makes him the seventh abbot beginning with Zamikā'ēl (Zamikā'ēl, Māteyās, Yosēf, Masqal Bēzāna, Madkhānina Egzi', Masqal Mo'a, Yoḥanni). The chronological problem with this genealogy, that Yoḥanni, flourishing in the twelfth century, is only six generations from Abba Zamikā'ēl, who is said to have arrived in Ethiopia in the sixth century, may be related to the time when Zamikā'ēl and the rest of the Nine Saints arrived in Ethiopia rather than the time when Abba Yoḥanni lived. Yoḥanni left the comfortable life at the royal court of the Zāgwē dynasty to lead an ascetic life in Dabra Dāmo. In the church tradition, Yoḥanni is remembered as one who never left his hermitage from the time he entered it, and he became the spiritual father of two influential monks of the Ethiopian church, Abuna Iyyasus Mo'a and Abuna Takla Hāymānot.

Abuna Iyyasus Mo'a was the founder of the famous monastery Dabra Ḥayq Esṭifānos, in Amhara (now Wollo). He successfully stood the harsh monastic test under Abba Yoḥanni of Dabra Dāmo, who eventually clothed him in monastic garb. An insignificant spot before Iyyasus Mo'a, Ḥayq became a center of education and pilgrimage even during the lifetime of its founder. There is a tradition that Yekunno Amlāk, the founder of the so-called Solomonic dynasty in 1270, studied there under Iyyasus Mo'a before moving to Qawat and Tagwelat in the south. According to a tradition of Ḥayq, it must be assumed that Abuna Iyyasus Mo'a must be credited with helping the future king to seize power from the Zāgwē, though historically this controversy remains unresolved. As a result of this, the abbots of Ḥayq Esṭifānos became the *'aqqābē sa'āt* (administrative heads) of the Ethiopian church from that time to the rise of Dabra Libānos in Shewa. Like the *eččagē* (high church dignitary) of Dabra Libānos from the sixteenth century onward, the *'aqqābē sa'āt* of Dabra Ḥayq was the indigenous head of the church in administrative matters. Dabra Ḥayq, which also occasionally had

Coptic monks, was a center of education and was usually an ardent supporter of the Egyptian metropolitan in any decrees he issued. The manuscript of the four gospels that Abuna Iyyasus Mo'a donated to his monastery and is still found in its library contains written references to visits to the monastery by the two most powerful Ethiopian monarchs of the day: Yekunno Amlāk (1270–1285) and ʿAmda Ṣeyon (1314–1344). Many spiritual sons of Abuna Iyyasus Mo'a established other monasteries.

Abuna Takla Hāymānot, the brightest luminary of Ethiopian monasticism, was a pupil of Abba Yoḥanni of Dabra Dāmo as well as Iyyasus Mo'a of Dabra Ḥayq before the former returned to his homeland in the south with vigor and enthusiasm to start his preaching. It is through the energetic Takla Hāymānot that Christianity and monasticism flourished in Shewa and Dāmo. Although his monastery of Dabra Asbo (later renamed Dabra Libānos) was devastated by pestilence in which many monks, including Taklā Hāymānot and his successor, Abba Ēlsā', perished, those who survived succeeded in Christianizing the south and the west and in establishing other important monasteries, such as the famous Dabra Beśrāt of Abuna Zēnā Māreqos.

Abuna Madkhānina Egzi' of Bankwal was one of the earlier disciples of Abuna Takla Hāymānot. His master left him in Tigre when he headed south. Madhānina Egzi' owes his fame to the fact that a great number of his disciples became celebrated stars, or *kawākebt,* in Ethiopian monasticism. Among them are Sāmu'ēl of Wāldebbā, Sāmu'ēl of Qwayyaṣā, Sāmu'ēl of Ṭārēṭā, Sāmu'ēl of Saqwār, Yoḥannes of Gurānqwā, Tādēwos of Bāltārewā (or Bartawā), Yassāy of Mandābbā, Yāfqeranna Egzi' of Gwegwbēn, Aron of Ketur, Marqoreyos of Hēbā, Zakkāreyās of Gēfā, Gabra Krestos of Bitāneyā, Dāne'ēl of Ṣaʿdāmbā, Endereyās of Amā'tā, Demeyānos of Dabra Sinā, Krestos Bēzāna of Ta'aminā, Hirut of Māya Sakaym, Gabr Khēr of Zān Megāgā, Gabra Krestos of Anāgśē, and Malka Ṣēdēq (of Dāginā). Most of these in turn trained other noted followers who established their own monasteries.

It should be pointed out here that, although monasteries were built in places "far from this world," they were not merely places of seclusion inhabited by anchorites who devoted their lives to prayer and worship. They were also centers of education and evangelical activity for the surrounding regions. Children came to them from far and near to learn. The monasteries were (and still are) institutions for traditional church education in literature (including poetry), music, biblical studies, and canon law. In them, books were composed, and translations of Christian literature into Geʿez were produced, and from there monks went out in bands of two or three into the neighborhood to spread Christianity. Many suffered martyrdom in the field. Metropolitan Yāʿqob (1337–1344) is remembered by tradition as one who encouraged Ethiopian monks to go and preach the Gospel in the pagan regions. He seems to have contacted the most important monasteries of his time to organize these missions efficiently. According to the sources from Dabra Libānos, for example, he chose twelve of its monks and divided Shoa and Dāmot among them. Each of the twelve monks (the Twelve Apostles) was given the title *nebura ed* (appointed by the laying on of the hand; pl. *neburāna ed*) and ordered to limit his evangelical activity to the region assigned to him. Only the abbot Fileppos, who was considered to be the counterpart of Saint Peter, was allowed to visit any region he wanted. The list of the *neburāna ed* varies slightly from one source to another. But because of their great success in their apostolic mission and the part they played in the history of the church, they became recognized among the important saints of Ethiopia. They included such names as Adkhani of Dāmot, Anorēwos (the Elder) of Warab of Dabra Ṣegāgā, Iyyoseyās of Wāg, Māteyās of Faṭagār, Yosēf of Ennāre'et, Gabra Krestos of Dembi, Tādewos of Ṣelālesh, Sāmu'ēl of Wagag, Qawesṭos of Maḥaggel, Anorēwos (the Junior, in some sources identified with the famous Zēnā Māreqos) of Morat, of Dabra Beśrāt, Tasfā Ḥeẓān of Dawwāro, and Marqorēwos of Marḥa Bētē. Metropolitan Yāʿqob and the monks could have done more if only the emperor ʿAmda Ṣeyon had been cooperative.

Ethiopian monasteries were semiautonomous institutions. The most important factor that held the monasteries together was the priesthood that was received from the metropolitan. The independence of the monasteries was a serious problem for the head of the church as well as for the monarch, both of whom saw that the strength of their authority depended on a united church and country behind them. The first test in recorded history took place when a metropolitan and the king at the time issued a decree to stop the practice of Jewish customs, especially the observance of the Saturday Sabbath. Many monasteries resisted the decree to the bitter end. One of the leaders of the opposition was Abba Ēwosṭātēwos (c. 1273–1352), who was a disciple and a relative of Dāne'ēl of Gar'altā, a spiritual descendant of Libānos. Ēwosṭātēwos left his monastery in Sarā'ē (Eritrea) and went to Egypt, accompanied by a few of his disciples, to seek support from the patriarch himself. To his disappointment, the view of patriarch BENJAMIN (1327–1339) was not different from that of his opponents. Ēwosṭātēwos died in Armenia. In Ethiopia, his followers left the church and established their own fully independent monastic communities. Ēwosṭātēwos' most important and immediate descendants founded important monasteries, including Absādi of Dabra Māryām (Qohayyen), Marqoreyos of Dabra Demāh, Bakkimos of Dabra Ṣarābi, Gabra Iyyasus of Dabsān (or Dabra Sān), Mātēwos of Barbarrē, Gabra Masqal of Māy Qwerqwer, Buruk Amlāk of Marāquz, and Ṣēwā Dengel of Bur. All these disciples became monastic leaders with many followers, including the celebrated Fileppos, the founder of Dabra Bizan (in Eritrea), which is one of the leading religious and educational centers of Ethiopia even today. Since the council of Dabra Meṭmāq (1450), at which the church accepted their position, the Ēwosṭātēwosites have again become part of the established church.

The spread of monasteries during the Solomonic dynasty can be attributed to many factors, such as the return to the fundamentals of monasticism as outlined in the ancient literature. But the kings of Ethiopia and other dignitaries felt it to be their duty to show liberality in adding new land grants to what the monasteries already possessed, and such wealth apparently became a menace to the rule of monastic asceticism. The monasteries ruled over vast territories granted to them by the rulers as *gwelt* or territory (Arabic, *awqāf*). They collected immense revenues from these territories and even ruled over their inhabitants, hearing cases, settling disputes, and punishing criminals. A closer look at the acts of the Ethiopian monastic leaders gives the impression that many of them left their mother monasteries and founded new ones in protest against the "worldly life" of their original foundations. Abuna Esṭifānos and his movement embodied this new tendency. Esṭifānos was a disciple of Abuna Sāmu'ēl of Qwayyaṣā. He left Qwayyaṣā when his critical remarks brought him into conflict with that brotherhood. The tenets of his movement included the strict adherence to the old monastic rules and principles. He spoke out against any monastery that relaxed these rules and professed the principle of the separation of state and church. He preached the rejection of the worship of the cross and the Blessed Virgin through her icon, and forbade prostration before any man, the emperor included. The rulers, especially Zar'a Yā'qob (1434–1468), used all kinds of persuasion, coercion and persecution to suppress the movement. Their father, Esṭifānos, and many of his followers died in prison or from other forms of martyrdom as leaders of a "heretical movement." Although their movement, which alarmed the entire church of Ethiopia, died out toward the beginning of the sixteenth century, their monastery of Dabra Garzēn in Gwendāgwendi (Eritrea) is still one of the important religious centers of Ethiopia. For obvious reasons, however, the calendar of the church does not recognize the fathers and brothers of Dabra Garzēn: Esṭifānos, Ferē Krestos, Abakerazun, Minās, Galāwdēwos, Ṗāwlos, Berhāna Masqal, Yesḥaq, Ezrā, Gabra Masiḥ, and many others.

Other monks who founded famous monasteries between the thirteenth and sixteenth centuries include the uncompromising Baṣalota Mikā'ēl of Dabra Gol (Amhara, now Wollo); Yoḥannes of Wifāt, the Apostle of Manz (Shewa); Giyorgis of Gāseçhā (Amhara), who made important innovations in the liturgy; Yonās of Addi Ugri (Tigre); Akāla Krestos of Dabra Mākhew (Bagēmder); Beẓu' Amlāk of Endā Śellāsē (Eritrea); Anbass of Ḥazalo (Shewa); Mother Feqerta Krestos of Emma Me'uz (Amhara); Iyyāsu of Jarr Śellāsē (Shewa); Mabā'a Ṣeyon of Endagabṭān (Shewa); Yoḥanni of Dabra 'Asā (Tigre); Mother Walatta Ṗēṭros of Qorāṣā (Gojam); Takla Ḥawāreyāt of Ṣemmonā (Shewa); Śarẓa Ṗēṭros of Dabra Warq (Gojam); Sinodā of Ṣemmonā (Gojam); Takaśta Berhān of Dimā (Gojam); and Mother Krestos Śamrā of Gwangwet Mikā'ēl (Gojam).

Asceticism

It has been suggested that some monasteries occasionally relaxed the strict rules of ascetism. This is a matter of relative degree and obviously an exception to the rule. The most important feature of Ethiopian monasticism, past and present, is the self-imposed torture of the body. The body, which is temporal, is the enemy of the soul, which is eternal, and it is necessary for the soul to be victorious over the body by tormenting it with fasting, prostration, and standing for protracted periods in one place, whether in the waters of the lakes and rivers or out of doors in exposed places where the temperature can be extremely hot or cold. Such deeds of asceticism may have been exaggerated in the *gadlāt*, or acts, of the saints, but travelers, including Alvarez in the sixteenth century, have witnessed the harsh life of monks in what they eat (leaves and bitter roots of plants) and in what they wear (rough skins, sackcloth, and iron girdles). The abodes of the hermits are so narrow that they do not lie down when they sleep.

There is the belief in the monasteries that when an ascetic reaches the extreme limit of self-torture, he will grow wings like an angel's as a sign of perfection. One finds many manuscripts depicting Abuna Takla Hāymānot with six wings, three on each side. Perfection is also measured by the number of crowns with which a saint is bedecked in heaven. An accomplished ascetic does not need to eat or drink, and if he does, the waste is disposed of miraculously from the stomach. This is the level of perfection an Ethiopian ascetic aspires to achieve. The kind of fasting practiced by ascetics is tantamount to starvation. If two monks disagree on the number of days of a given fast, the rule is "side with him who is for fasting longer." Many caves have been discovered with the mummified bodies of hermits holding crosses in their hands. A number of Ethiopian monks have lived in austerity in the monasteries in Egypt and the Holy Land, impressing the local monks. And in the New World, one of them had to be taken to a mental hospital for extending his standing in prayer into the winter snows of New York.

Modern Times

As an Islamic *jihād*, or holy warfare, the revolt of Aḥmad ibn Ibrāhīm al-Ghāzī, or Grāññ Muḥammad, the ruler of the eastern territories of Ethiopia in the sixteenth century, was primarily aimed at eradicating Christianity from Ethiopia by killing the Christians or converting them to his faith and by destroying Christian religious institutions, including churches and monasteries, which were at that time excessively rich in solid gold and silver and fine vestments. For about fifteen years, Grāññ systematically sacked the churches and monasteries and set their buildings on fire. Very few monasteries escaped his devastations. As a result, many famous monasteries, such as Dabra Karbē, are known only in the literature or as archaelogical sites. The mass migration of the pagan Galla (Oromo) at the end of the war with Grāññ, in about 1559, also had its share in the destruction of the heritage of the Christian church. One must say with emphasis that although it survived, the church never recovered fully from those two shocks. With the exception of a very few, the present monasteries are those built anew on the sites of the ruins of the old ones. Today, the sites of famous monasteries, such as Dabra Ṣegē in Boranā (Wollo), are discovered occasionally and accidentally. There is no ostensible effort for the restoration of those archaeological remains of a glorious past. And since 1974 the voices heard throughout the country are clamoring for cultural revolution and burying the past rather than digging it up.

There has been no reliable survey to determine the number and location of active monasteries. Even the criteria for determining whether a given religious center is a monastery or not are unclear. In the local language there are two terms, *gadām* and *dabr*, which can be translated as *monastery*, although in many cases *dabr* indicates the size of the center. In the church register, one finds many churches that are listed as either *gadām* or *dabr*, but lack the characteristics of a monastic community. For example, the Holy Trinity Cathedral and the Church of Saint Mary of the Patriarchate, both in Addis Ababa, are listed as *gadām*. Dabra Libānos, on the other hand, is now not registered as a *dabr*. This may be the reason why the sources on the present number of monasteries in Ethiopia differ from one another by wide margins. As far as can be determined, a church and its courtyard is called a *gadām*, or monastery, because it is (1) a monastery in fact (e.g., Dabra Libānos and Dabra Bizan); (2) a center that once had a monastic community; or (3) a church that has been designated a *gadām* by the relevant authorities, the king, and the metropolitan. The last two categories of *gadām* may not have any monks other than the heads of their churches.

The nationalization of land by the military Marxist-Leninist government that came to power in 1974 has left the monasteries without material possessions. They may have to find other means of subsistence, such as the establishment of cottage industries. But at present the future of Ethiopian monasticism is very dim.

[See *also:* Ethiopian Heresies; Ethiopian Saints.]

BIBLIOGRAPHY

Alvarez, F. *The Prester John of the Indies*, 2 vols. Trans. C. F. Beckingham and G. W. B. Huntingford. Cambridge, 1961.

Arras, V., ed. *Collectio Monastica*. In *CSCO* 238, *Scriptores Aethiopici* 45; CSCO 239, *Scriptores Aethiopici* 46. Louvain, 1963.

Basset, R. ed. *Histoire de la conquête de l'Abyssinie (XVIe siècle) par Chihab Eddin Aḥmed Ben ʿAbd El Qâder surnommé Arab-Faqih*. Vols. 1 [text] and 2 [trans.]. Paris, 1897.

Budge, E. A. W. *The Life of Takla Hâymânot in the Version of Dabra Libânos, and the Miracles of*

Takla Hâymânot in the Version of Dabra Libânos, and the Book of the Riches of the Kings. London, 1906.

———. *The Book of the Saints of the Ethiopian Church*, 4 vols. Cambridge, 1928; repr. Hildesheim and New York, 1976.

Cerulli, E. "Gli abbati di Dabra Libānos, capi del monachismo etiopico, secondo la 'lista rimata' (sec. xiv–xviii)." *Orientalia* n.s. 12 (1943):226–53; 13 (1944):137–82; 14 (1945):143–71.

———. *Etiopia in Palestina: Storia della Comunita etiopica di Gerusalemme*, 2 vols. Rome, 1943–1947.

———. "Il monachismo in Etiopia." *Orientalia Christiana Analecta* 153 (1958):259–78.

Dillmann, A. *Chrestomathia Aethiopica*, pp. 57–76. Repr. Darmstadt, 1967.

Getatchew Haile. "From Strict Observance to Royal Endowment: The Case of the Monastery of Däbrä Halle Luya." *Le Muséon* 93 (1980):163–72.

———. "The Monastic Genealogy of the Line of Täklä Haymanot of Shoa." *Rassegna di Studi Etiopici* 29 (1982–1983):7–38.

———. "The Cause of the Esṭifānosites: A Fundamentalist Sect in the Church of Ethiopia." *Paideuma* 29 (1983):93–119.

Guidi, I. "Il Gadla Aragâwî," *Memorie della Reale Accademia dei Lincei, Classe di scienze morali* 2, pt. 1, ser. 5 (1896):54–96.

Huntingford, G. W. B. *The Land Charters of Northern Ethiopia*. Monographs in Ethiopian Land Tenure 1. Addis Ababa, 1965.

———. "Saints of Mediaeval Ethiopia." *Abba Salama* 10 (1979):257–341.

Kaplan, S. B. "The Monastic Holy Man and the Christianization of Ethiopia 1270–1468." Ph.D. diss. Hebrew University, Jerusalem, 1982.

Kinefe-Rigb Zelleke. "Bibliography of the Ethiopic Hagiographical Traditions." *Journal of Ethiopian Studies* 13, pt. 2 (1975):57–102.

Kur, S. *Actes de Iyasus Mo'a abbé du couvent de St-Etienne de Ḥayq*. In CSCO 259, *Scriptores Aethiopici* 49; CSCO 260, *Scriptores Aethiopici* 50. Louvain, 1965.

Ricci, L. *Via di Walatta Pịéṭros*. In CSCO 316, *Scriptores Aethiopici* 61. Louvain, 1970.

Rossini, C. "Il Gadla Filpos e il Gadla Yohannes di Dabra Bizan." *Memorie della Reale Accademia dei Lincei, Classe di scienze morali* 8 (1903):61–170.

———. "Il convento di Tsana in Abissinia e le sue Laudi alla Vergine." *Rendiconti della Accademia nazionale dei Lincei, Classe di scienze morali* 19, ser. 5 (1910):581–621.

———. *Vitae Sanctorum Antiquiorum: Acta Yārēd et Pạnṭalēwon*. In CSCO 26, *Scriptores Aethiopici* 9; CSCO 27, *Scriptores Aethiopici* 10. Louvain, 1955.

Six, V. *Die Vita des Abuna Tādēwos von Dabra Māryām im Ṭānāsee*. Wiesbaden, 1975.

Taddesse Tamrat. "Some Notes on the Fifteenth-Century Stephanite 'Heresy' in the Ethiopian Church." *Rassegna di Studi Etiopici* 22 (1966):103–115.

———. "The Abbots of Däbrä-Hayq, 1248–1535." *Journal of Ethiopian Studies* 8, pt. 1 (1970):87–117.

———. *Church and State in Ethiopia 1270–1527*. London, 1972.

———. "A Short Note on the Traditions of Pagan Resistance to the Ethiopian Church (14th and 15th centuries)." *Journal of Ethiopian Studies* 10, pt. 1 (1972):137–50.

Turaiev, B. *Vitae Sanctorum Indiginarum: Acta S. Aaronis et Philippi*. In CSCO 30, *Scriptores Aethiopici* 13; CSCO 31, *Scriptores Aethiopici* 14. Louvain, 1955.

———. *Vitae Sanctorum Indiginarum: Acta Sancti Eustathii*. In CSCO 32, *Scriptores Aethiopici* 15. Louvain, 1955.

Ullendorff, E. "Hebraic-Jewish Elements in Abyssinian (Monophysite) Christianity." *Journal of Semitic Studies* 1 (1956):216–56.

Varenbergh, J. "Studien zur abessinischen Reichsordnung *(Sĕrʿata Mangĕst)*." *Zeitschrift für Assyriologie und verwandte Gebiete* 30 (1915–1916):1–45.

GETATCHEW HAILE

ETHIOPIAN ORTHODOX CHURCH. The Ethiopian church was the only state church in the Orient that remained intact from early times into the late twentieth century, when it was separated from the secular state by a revolutionary decree of 1974. With a membership of at least 12 million, it is still the largest single autocephalous Christian institution in Africa. In its sixteen-hundred-year history, it not only has survived devastating internal and external wars and dissensions but also has remained a citadel of spiritual resource, formal education, local culture, art, and architecture for Ethiopian society.

History

Though the church's traditions go back to the introduction of Christianity in Ethiopia in the era of the apostles, the actual establishment of the church did not occur until about the middle of the fourth century. The ground was prepared for it by the existence in the country of Judaic elements and small Christian communities consisting of foreign traders and their local associates. The pioneer was Frumentius of Tyre, whom fate led to Axum in his youth and who grew up in the palace, where he acquainted the crown prince and other members of the royal house with Christianity. Around 330, he went to Alexandria to seek a bishop for Ethiopia, and Patriarch ATHANASIUS (328–356) chose him for the purpose, thereby laying the foundations for the lasting relationship between the Coptic and Ethiopian churches. Frumentius thus became the first *abun* of Ethiopia (cf. ETHIOPIAN PRELATES), where he subsequently came to be known as Abba Salāmā I (Father Peace) and Kaśātē Berhān (Revealer of Light). As a saint, he is commemorated on 26 Ḥamlē of the Ethiopian calendar.

That Frumentius succeeded in converting the royal household and that the sovereign transferred his divine role of pre-Christian cult to the new religion facilitated immensely the peaceful establishment, expansion, and protection of the church. Throughout the centuries, the sovereign remained the protector and Alexandria the source of the faith. It was because of the cooperation of Frumentius and King 'Ēzānā (c. 327–357) that the Ethiopian Orthodox Church remained pro-Nicene, despite the attempts of Constantius (337–361) to introduce ARIANISM into the country. King Kālēb (c. 515–545) also led two military expeditions, in 523 and 525, on behalf of the Christians of Najrān in South Arabia, who were besieged by the Jews.

The expansion of Christianity in Ethiopia was further aided by an influx of its followers who had been persecuted by the pro-Chalcedonians in the Byzantine empire in the late fifth and early sixth centuries. These immigrants brought with them their priests, books, and church articles, thereby enriching the institution of the church in Ethiopia. They settled in various parts of northern Ethiopia and founded schools, churches, and monasteries, many of which still bear their names. Missionaries went out from these monasteries to spread Christianity among the pagan Amhara and Agaw peoples farther south. Their activities were encouraged, and at times required, by the sovereigns, who gradually moved their political seat to the central highlands partly because of external pressures and partly for reasons of further conquest and territorial gains. Some of the sovereigns were zealous not only to defend the faith against internal and external threats and to support the church through bountiful land grants but also to reform some of the religious practices and to impose Christianity on all areas under their rule. Among such rulers was Emperor Zar'a Yā'qob (1434–1468), who had authored several works on religious themes, introduced many reforms, and obliged pagan remnants to accept Christianity. Emperor Sarṣa Dengel (1563–1597) carried the religion farther south to the kingdom of Enāryā beyond the Gibē.

But both the church and the secular state suffered a series of setbacks in the sixteenth, seventeenth, and eighteenth centuries. Comparable in severity to the devastating war of the Falasha (Ethiopian Jews) in the tenth century was the invasion of the Muslims led by Imām Aḥmad Muḥammad al-Ghāzī of Zeila, aided by a Turkish military contingent, in 1527–1543. Numerous churches were burned, books were mutilated, and a great number of Christians perished or were forced to profess Islam. With the help of a Portuguese force, Emperor Galāwdēwos (1540–1559) succeeded in freeing the country and reestablishing the church. This success was nonetheless temporary, as a horde of pagan invaders known as the Oromo or Gāllā struck from the southeast and quickly invaded the greater part of the empire, burning churches and killing or assimilating the Christians. The Portuguese, too, demanded compensation in the form of territorial grants and the investiture of a Catholic bishop who could head the Ethiopian church. This provoked civil upheavals, and the emperor had to banish the Portuguese. Several attempts were thereafter made on the part of the Catholics to convert the Ethiopians, and missionaries were repeatedly sent to the country. The most significant of the missionaries was the Jesuit Pedro Páez, who arrived in Ethiopia shortly after 1600 and began to teach children and translate books in northern Ethiopia. He subsequently gained access to the imperial court and brought two or more princes under his influence. One of these was Susenyos, who became supreme ruler after killing his reigning cousin in a battle in 1607, in which the Coptic metropolitan also fell. Susenyos and some of his officials were secretly converted to Catholicism and entered into correspondence with the pope of Rome and the emperor of Spain. Páez died in 1621, and a bishop named Alfonso Mendez arrived in the next year.

The emperor was soon converted, and the bishop began to exercise his authority over the rights and properties of the Ethiopian Orthodox Church. In 1626 a civil war broke out that lasted about six years and led to the abdication of the emperor in favor of his son, who remained faithful to the orthodox religion. The missionaries were expelled, and Europeans were thereafter regarded with hostility for at least a hundred and fifty years. The Ethiopian Catholics were either executed or obliged to recant their new faith. Only since 1838 have European missionaries been again permitted to teach and then almost exclusively in the so-called open areas, where the Ethiopian Orthodox Church has had little or no influence, though they have also been allowed to conduct their activities in the Christian areas so long as they do not interfere with affairs of the church and render medical and educational services to the public.

After the expulsion of the Jesuits in 1633, the church could still have no peace, as Christological disputes broke out within the church itself, leading to a series of inconclusive councils and violent conflicts. In principle, the doctrine of the church was already set with the translation from the Greek of *Qērelos* (the Book of Cyril) in the sixth century, followed by other works from the Syriac and the Arabic (see ETHIOPIAN CHRISTIAN LITERATURE). But the translations were by no means standardized. Sometimes the same concept was rendered by different Ethiopic terms, and sometimes one Ethiopic term was used to translate different concepts. Time and again, disagreements broke out among the clerics on some point of teaching. Often the state settled their differences by force. In the eighteenth and early nineteenth centuries, however, the state itself suffered from dissensions and was scarcely in a position to deal with the problems of the church. The various princes allied with one or another religious faction and tried not only to assert their power but also to promote the tenets of their allies. The controversy revolved mainly around the nature of Christ—whether the inseparable union of his divinity and humanity took place at the time of his conception or on the occasion of his baptism at the river Jordan and whether Christ replaced Adam as the firstborn son of God's grace.

The church was divided into three factions, each dominating a particular region and each contemptuously nicknaming the others. Hence, a situation was created in which three denominations could have developed from the Ethiopian Orthodox Church. Emperor Yoḥannes IV (1872–1889), who believed that the union of religion and the state was as essential as that of the body and the soul, consulted the patriarch of Alexandria and summoned a national council at Boru Mēdā in 1878. The council endorsed the tenet that Christ's divinity was from eternity and that the inseparable union of his divinity and humanity took place at the time of incarnation. All those who refused to conform with the decisions of the council were declared heretics and were dealt with accordingly. The subsequent monarchs upheld the same policy, and although some differing sentiments are still discernible, the church has had no more such disputes since then.

Organizational Structure and Hierarchy

The spiritual head of the Ethiopian Orthodox Church has been the *abun*, who traditionally had to be a Copt ordained by the patriarch of Alexandria. However, an Ethiopian acceded to the metropolitanate for the first time in 1951 and was promoted to the status of patriarch in 1957, in accordance with the diplomatic arrangements made between the Ethiopian government and the See of Alexandria (see ETHIOPIAN CHURCH AUTOCEPHALY). The counterpart of the *abun* had always been an Ethiopian dignitary from one of the prominent monasteries who acted as the overseer of the general administrative affairs of the church. In the last four or five hundred years, this office was dominated by the EČČAGĒ of Dabra Libānos who acted both as liaison between the church and the state and as judge for clerical cases. His role on the national level diminished with the establishment of the Bēta Kehnat (central church administration office) in the twentieth century.

From the viewpoint of internal administration, the churches and monasteries have always been autonomous, each having belonged to the community that had founded and maintained it. Their material wealth was therefore scarcely uniform until the Provisional Military Council nationalized all landed properties by a decree of 1975. The churches were grouped under two heads. First were the *adbārāt* (sing. *dabr*), usually located in monasteries and large community centers; they were full-fledged churches enjoying rights and privileges granted to them throughout the centuries and, to a greater or lesser extent, owning land, animal stock, schools, and libraries. Often they were well staffed with priests, deacons, musicians, and teachers, at the head of which was the *alaqā* (dean), appointed by the sovereign or his representative or elected by his society. The other group consisted of the *gaṭar*, minor churches staffed by five or seven clerics and serving small communities distant from the *dabr* that had jurisdiction over the area. Any of the *gaṭar* churches could, under special circumstances, develop into a *dabr*.

Education and Literature

The church was for centuries the only Christian institution that sponsored formal education in Ethiopia. The schools were in principle open to both sexes, though the male pupils were by far the majority at all times. Basic education consisted of reading and, to a limited extent, writing, as well as reciting the Lord's Prayer, the Nicene Creed, and the Hail Mary, and chanting portions or the whole of the Psalterium. Relatively few went to the higher institutions of learning, which were organized in three faculties: the *qenē bēt* (school of poetry), in which grammar, comparative history, and various aspects of poetry could be studied; the *zēmā bēt* (school of music), where the elaborate compositions of the axumite Saint Yārēd and his successors were offered; and the *tergum bēt* (school of interpretation), where studies of the Holy Scriptures, the works of the ancient fathers, and ecclesiastical and civil laws could be pursued.

The Holy Bible of the Ethiopian Orthodox Church consists of forty-six books of the Old and thirty-five books of the New Testaments, eighty-one books in all. The various books of the Bible were translated into Ge'ez at different times before the end of the seventh century of the Christian era from the Septuagint and Syriac versions. Apart from the translations of various works from the Greek, the Syriac, the Arabic, and possibly the Coptic, a number of hagiographies, encomiums, and commentaries were also produced in the country itself. The ETHIOPIAN LITURGY is based on the Holy Scriptures and the compositions of the early fathers, and the congregation participates in all celebrations. The mass is said by a minimum of five celebrants—three priests and two deacons. In its teachings, the church lays due emphasis on the seven mysteries: baptism, the Eucharist, confession of sin, resurrection of the dead, matrimony, priesthood, and extreme unction. The last one is scarcely practiced. The fasts of Ninevah, Lent, the Apostles, the Assumption of the Virgin, and the prophets are observed, while Christ's birth, crucifixion, resurrection, and ascension, as well as Pentecost, Saint John's Day or New Year, and the Day of the Holy Cross are among the major holy days celebrated with elaborate church services.

Architecture and Paintings

The church has also been the Ethiopian institution richest in architecture and paintings. Because of the political circumstances that prevailed in the country for centuries, very few secular edifices were erected after the Axumite era. Instead, much investment went into the churches, thousands of which were built and rebuilt as well as decorated with paintings and ornaments. The majority of the church buildings are round, though some of the oldest ones have rectangular or even polyangular forms. Every church is divided into three parts, each with a specific purpose. Entering from the porch, one reaches the *qenē mākhlēt* (choir), separated from the inner circle by a wall concentric with the exterior wall. This passagelike room extends around the entire building and is devoted to the laymen as well as to the ritual dances and singing of the clergy. A few doors lead into the inner circular room known as the *maqdas* (sanctuary) where the mass is celebrated. The lay members enter it mainly to receive the Holy Communion. In the center of the *maqdas* is a square room, likewise separated by walls and known as the *qeddesta qeddusān* (holy of holies). It is accessible through a small entrance, and only the celebrant priests may enter it. The *tābot* (the ark of the Decalogue) and the holy books are deposited here. Almost all the walls are covered with paintings that depict motives from the Holy Scriptures, lives of saints and martyrs, and particulars from Ethiopian history. Many of the parchment books are also illustrated and ornamented.

BIBLIOGRAPHY

Bonk, J. *An Annotated and Classified Bibliography of English Literature Pertaining to the Ethiopian Orthodox Church.* Metuchen, N. J., 1984.

Crummey, D. "Orthodoxy and Imperial Reconstruction in Ethiopia 1854–1878." *Journal of Theological Studies* 29 (1978):427–42.

Geddes, M. *The Church-History of Ethiopia.* London, 1696.

Gerster, G., et al. *Kirchen im Fels: Entdeckungen in Äthiopien.* Zürich, 1972.

Guèbrè Sellassié. *Chronique du règne de Ménélik II: Roi des rois d'Ethiopie,* 2 vols., ed. M. Coppet. Paris, 1930–1931.

Heiler, F. *Die Ostkirchen.* Munich, 1971.

Heyer, F. *Die Kirche Äthiopiens: Eine Bestandsaufnahme.* Berlin and New York, 1971.

______. "Die orthodoxe Kirche Äthiopiens in der krisenhaften Zuspitzung der Lage des Landes." *Ökumenische Rundschau* 26 (1977):196–204.

______. "Die orthodoxe Kirche Äthiopiens im 5. Revolutionsjahr." *Ökumenische Rundschau* 28 (1979):327–33.

Hyatt, H. M. *The Church of Abyssinia.* London, 1928.

Rossini, C. *Storia d'Etiopia*, Vol. 1. Africa italiana 3. Milan, 1928.

Sergew Hable Selassie. *Ancient and Medieval Ethiopian History to 1270*. Addis Ababa, 1971.

Taddesse Tamrat. *Church and State in Ethiopia, 1270–1527*. Oxford, 1972.

Tesfazghi U. *Current Christological Positions of Ethiopian Orthodox Theologians*. Rome, 1973.

Weischer, B. M. *Qērellos III: Der Dialog "Dass Christus Einer Ist" des Kyrillos von Alexandria*, ed. E. Hammerschmidt. Äthiopistische Forschungen 2. Wiesbaden, 1977.

Yocob Beyene. *L'unzione di Cristo nella teologia etiopica*. Rome, 1981.

BAIRU TAFLA

ETHIOPIAN PRELATES. The *abun* (metropolitan bishop) was a Coptic monk chosen by the patriarch of Alexandria to head the Ethiopian church. The metropolitanate started in the middle of the fourth century when Pope ATHANASIUS appointed Frumentius as the first metropolitan, with the name of Abuna Salāmā. This custom remained in force until the agreement reached in July 1948 gave the Ethiopian church full autonomy.

SALĀMĀ I (c. 300–c. 380)

More commonly known as Frumentius (Ethiopian, Frēmnāṭos), he is considered a saint in the Ethiopian church (festal date 26 Ḥamlē [Abīb]), as well as in the Roman Catholic and Greek Orthodox churches. He is said to have been born at Tyre. After his consecration as bishop, he took (or was attributed) the name Salāmā (peace), a term probably derived from Syriac. In Ethiopia, he is often referred to as Abba Salāmā Kaśātē Berhān (Father Salāmā, Revealer of Light), for he is credited, in both historical and religious records, with having officially introduced Christianity into the country.

Details of the historic event were first written around 410 by Rufinus Tyrannius, bishop of Aquilea, who heard the tale directly from the aged Aedesius, companion or brother of Frumentius. The story has since been recorded, with minor variations, by other writers such as Socrates Scholasticus, Theodoret, and Sozomen in the fifth century and Nicephoras Callistus in the fourteenth century, all of whom depend entirely on Rufinus' text.

According to this account, a certain Meropius, a citizen of Tyre, undertook a trip to "India" (actually the empire of Axum, but called India because of its location on the long sea route linking the Egyptian ports on the Red Sea to the markets of India). It was essentially a cultural voyage because Meropius took with him Frumentius and Aedesius, two children for whose education he was responsible. On the return trip, they stopped at an "Indian" port (probably Adulis, near present-day Zula), where, because of a breakdown in relations between Axum on one side and Byzantium and its allies on the other, the ship was pillaged, and Meropius and his crew massacred. Only the two boys were spared and handed over to the king of the country (unnamed by Rufinus), who made Aedesius his cupbearer and Frumentius his secretary.

Upon the king's death, the queen regent asked the two young men to aid her in the duties of state while her son was still a minor, and thus, Frumentius was able to have some churches constructed for Christian merchants trading in Axumite lands. When the young prince came of age, he allowed the two foreigners to leave Axum. Aedesius returned to his relatives in Tyre, where he became a priest, and Frumentius journeyed to Alexandria to request that a bishop be named for the Christians in Ethiopia. Upon receiving Frumentius' petition, Saint ATHANASIUS, twentieth patriarch of Alexandria (who, according to Rufinus, had recently been consecrated to this position), ordained Frumentius a priest and then consecrated him as bishop and sent him back "to the land whence he had come." Once again in Ethiopia, Frumentius was able to convert a great number of pagans, and thereby the Christian church made its beginnings in "India."

According to Rufinus, Bishop Salāmā, as Frumentius was now known, must have arrived in Ethiopia between 328 (Athanasius' election to the See of Saint Mark) and 335 (Council of Tyre; i.e., the beginning of Athanasius' first exile). This date may be further confirmed in the Ethiopian traditions, for, according to the abridged chronicle of Ethiopian kings (Béguinot, 1901, p. 2), Salāmā is supposed to have come to the country 333 years after the birth of Christ (333 of the Ethiopian calendar corresponds to A.D. 340–341). This same chronicle notes that during this time, the ruling kings in Ethiopia were Abreha and Aṣbaḥa, names that modern Ethiopian specialists consider to be the crown names or surnames of the Axumite king ʿĒzānā (well known through pagan and Christian coins) and of his brother and coregent, Šeʿazānā.

Precise knowledge is lacking concerning Salāmā's religious activities in the Axumite territories. However, his name appears twice in relation to an episode important in the early history of Christianity, as follows: Emperor Constantius II (337–361), son of Constantine I, who favored the heretical doctrines of ARIUS, wrote a letter to Aezanus and Sazanas (i.e., king ʿĒzānā and his brother Šeʿazānā), rulers of Axum, wherein he severely criticized the doctrines of Athanasius and his fight against ARIANISM, and called upon the two Axumite princes to send Frumentius (Salāmā) back to Egypt for severe judgment and rectification of his faith. This missive, dated 356 and probably never answered, shows that Abuna Salāmā I was still alive at this time, that he had preserved the church from Arianism, and had kept it close to the orthodox dogma championed so brilliantly by Athanasius.

The names of the immediate successors to Salāmā I remain unknown. After him the first *abun* mentioned in historical documents as metropolitan in Ethiopia is Yoḥannes I, who held the episcopacy toward the middle of the ninth century. However, the Ethiopian tradition lists a bishop by the name of Minās as the immediate successor of Salāmā, and attributes to the former the authorship of a number of homilies.

BIBLIOGRAPHY

Altheim, F. *Geschichte der Hunnen*, Vol. 5, pp. 157–80. Berlin, 1962.

Athanasius. *Ad imperatorem Constantium apologia*. In PG 25, cols. 635–638. Paris, 1857.

Basset, R. "Etudes sur l'histoire d'Ethiopie." *Journal asiatique* ser. 7, 17 (1881):411, 421–22, n. 30.

Béguinot, F. *La cronaca abbreviata d'Abissinia*, p. 2. Rome, 1901.

Bettini, G. "Per la storia del cristianesimo in Etiopia: S. Frumenzio." *Nuova Rivista Storica* 21 (1937):359–65.

Budge, E. A. W., trans. *The Book of the Saints of the Ethiopian Church*, Vol. 4, pp. 1164–65.

Dombrowski, B. W. W., and F. A. Dombrowski. "Frumentius/Abbā Salāmā: Zu den Nachrichten über die Anfänge des Christentums in Äthiopien." *Oriens Christianus* 68 (1984):114–69.

Getatchew Haile. "The Homily in Honour of St. Frumentius Bishop of Axum (EMML 1763, ff. 84ᵛ–86ʳ)." *Analecta Bollandiana* 97 (1979):309–318.

Monneret de Villard, U. "Perche la chiesa abissina dipendeva dal patriarcato d'Alessandria." *Oriente moderno* 23 (1943):308–311.

Rossini, C. *Storia d'Etiopia*, pp. 146–54. Bergamo, 1928.

Sergew Hable Sellassie. *Ancient and Medieval Ethiopian History to 1270*, pp. 98–104. Addis Ababa, 1972.

Ullendorff, E. "Note on the Introduction of Christianity into Ethiopia." *Africa* 19 (1949):61–62.

[The next section on Minās was written not by Salvatore Tedeschi but by Getatchew Haile. We place it here, rather than at the end of this entry or as a separate entry, to maintain the chronological order of the Ethiopian prelates.—Ed.]

MINĀS (fl. sixth century)

Ethiopian sources list Bishop Minās (Menas) as the successor of the first Ethiopian metropolitan bishop, Salāmā or Frumentius, and call him Salāmā II. He flourished, according to tradition, during the reign of Anbasā Wedem, before the Arab conquest of Egypt. However, in the chronologies of Axumite kings, no less than twenty-five kings are listed between the king who ruled during Frumentius' metropolitanate and the reign of Anbasā Wedem (his dates are uncertain). This may indicate that the chair of the metropolitanate was vacant for a long time after Frumentius or his immediate successors. Minās's designation as "the second Salāmā" could simply mean a fresh start of vigorous Christian activities in Ethiopia with Bishop Minās as its leader. The literary heritage he left seems to support this explanation.

Although the information on Minās is sketchy, he did enrich the literary tradition of the Ethiopian church with a number of homilies. At least six of these are extant and are read in Ethiopian monasteries at designated times in the year. They include the homilies on the apostles, dormition of the Virgin Mary, the holy cross, season of spring, the seventy disciples and the 318 Orthodox fathers of the Council of Nicaea, and Abbā Yoḥanni. The translation of the book of Revelation into Ethiopic or Geʿez is also ascribed to Minās. It is also possible that the translation into Geʿez of Rufinus' work on Frumentius, "The Story of How the Interiors of Ethiopia Came to Christianity," is this bishop's achievement.

BIBLIOGRAPHY

Cowley, R. W. *The Traditional Interpretation of the Apocalypse of St. John in the Ethiopian Orthodox Church*. Cambridge, 1983.

Getatchew Haile. "The Homily in Honour of St. Frumentius, Bishop of Axum (EMML 1763, ff. 84ᵛ–86ʳ)." *Analecta Bollandiana* 97 (1979):309–318.

Getatchew Haile and William F. Macomber. *A Catalogue of Ethiopian Manuscripts Microfilmed for the Ethiopian Manuscript Microfilm Library, Addis Ababa, and for the Hill Monastic Manuscript Library, Collegeville,* Vol. 5. Collegeville, Minn., 1981.
Guidi, I. "Le liste dei metropoliti d'Abissinia." *Bessarione* 6 (1899):2–16.

GETATCHEW HAILE

YOḤANNES I (fl. second quarter ninth century)

This is the first metropolitan whose name is recorded after that of Salāmā I (Frumentius), evangelist of Ethiopia. According to the HISTORY OF THE PATRIARCHS OF ALEXANDRIA, the only source to mention him, Yoḥannes I was named to this position by Patriarch Jacob (819–830) and served during the patriarchates of SIMON II (830) and YŪSĀB I (831–849). During the latter period, Yoḥannes I was obliged to leave Ethiopia and return to Egypt, where he withdrew to DAYR AL-BARĀMŪS. It was the queen of Ethiopia who expelled him, and in order to do so, she had had to wait for the king to absent himself from the court, on this occasion to lead his troops into battle. (The names of the king and queen are not mentioned in the Arabic version of the *History of the Patriarchs.*) With Yoḥannes out of the country, another prelate, chosen and appointed in Ethiopia against all canon law, replaced him. Ethiopia then suffered many disasters, epidemics, and military defeats, which induced the Ethiopian sovereign to write to Patriarch Yūsāb, renewing his allegiance to Alexandria and requesting the return of Yoḥannes to his country. Thereupon, Yoḥannes left his retreat in the desert, and in the company of a few fellow clergymen, returned to Ethiopia and reoccupied his episcopal throne. Prosperity then reigned anew in the land.

Later, however, Yoḥannes had to face another difficulty. In 838, certain Ethiopian factions claimed that the bishop was uncircumcised and insisted that he submit to this operation or be banished again to Egypt. But, upon examining him, they discovered that he had already been circumcised. The *History of the Patriarchs* treats this event as a miracle. However, it may rather be explained by the progressive spread of circumcision among the Copts after the ARAB CONQUEST OF EGYPT and by the fact that in Ethiopia this practice had been followed since the most ancient times, even before the introduction of Christianity.

The immediate successor to Yoḥannes I remains unknown. The next person listed as holding this office is Abuna Pēṭros I in the tenth century.

BIBLIOGRAPHY

Budge, E. A. W., ed. and trans. *The Book of the Saints of the Ethiopian Church,* 4 vols. Cambridge, 1928.
Renaudot, E. *Historia Patriarcharum Alexandrinorum Jacobitarum,* pp. 283–87. Paris, 1713.
Rossini, C. *Storia d'Etiopia,* p. 284. Bergamo, 1928.
Tedeschi, S. "L'Etiopia nella storia dei patriarchi alessandrini." *Rassegna di studi etiopici* 23 (1967–1968):262–69.

PĒṬROS I (fl. first half tenth century)

According to the *History of the Patriarchs,* Pēṭros (Buṭrus in Arabic) was chosen and consecrated by Patriarch Quzma, or Cosmas III (920–932), during the reign of an Ethiopian sovereign whose name is not mentioned in the Arabic text. As metropolitan, Pēṭros stood at the very center of an episode important in the history of ancient Ethiopia. Before his death, the king confided his two sons to Pēṭros, asking the *abun* to choose whichever one would be the better ruler. Pēṭros selected the younger brother and placed him on the throne. However, at this time, a monk by the name of Minās (Mīnā) came forth from the Monastery of Saint Antony (DAYR ANBĀ ANṬŪNIYŪS) with another Coptic monk known as Victor (Buqṭur). The two approached Pēṭros and asked him for money but were refused, whereupon they began to plot against the prelate. The angry monks succeeded in forging a letter, purportedly written by Patriarch Cosmas, in which the pontiff declared that Pēṭros was an imposter and should be replaced by Menas and that the election and crowning of the younger brother as king were illegal and he should be dethroned and replaced by the elder son. The latter, upon seeing the false missive, immediately assembled an army, conquered and eliminated his younger brother, and occupied the throne. The new king then deposed Pēṭros, relegated him to a distant place, and gave the see to Menas. However, soon thereafter, Menas quarreled with his old friend, Victor, who then pillaged the bishop's headquarters, fled Ethiopia, and converted to Islam.

When Patriarch Cosmas learned of the conspiracy, he excommunicated Menas, whereupon the king executed the false pretender and hastened to find Pēṭros, who had already died in exile. Meanwhile, the patriarch, still greatly offended by the usurper king's ill treatment of Ṗēṭros, refused to name a new metropolitan bishop for Ethiopia. Thereupon, the Ethiopian sovereign commanded the coadjutor to assume the functions of metropolitan ad interim, which he did to an advanced age. Because the king was afraid to let his country be without a bishop to perform the necessary ordinations and blessings, he never allowed this man, who remains unnamed in the *History of the Patriarchs of Alexandria*, to journey to Egypt for his official consecration.

The four patriarchs who succeeded Cosmas—MACARIUS I, THEOPHANES, MĪNĀ II, and ABRAHAM—also refused to name a metropolitan bishop for this region. Not until the patriarchate of PHILOTHEUS (979–1003) did Ethiopia receive a properly consecrated bishop, Dān'ēl.

BIBLIOGRAPHY

Budge, E. A. W., trans. *The Book of the Saints of the Ethiopian Church,* Vol. 1, pp. 233–34; Vol. 3, pp. 666–69. Cambridge, 1928.

Perruchon, J. "Vie de Cosmas, patriarche d'Alexandrie de 923 à 934." *Revue sémitique* 2 (1894):78–93.

Renaudot, E. *Historia Patriarcharum Alexandrinorum Jacobitarum,* pp. 339–41. Paris, 1713.

Rossini, C. *Storia d'Etiopia,* p. 285. Bergamo, 1928.

Sergew Hable Sellassie. *Ancient and Medieval Ethiopian History to 1270,* pp. 215–18. Addis Ababa, 1972.

DĀN'ĒL (fl. late tenth century)

Dān'ēl is considered to be the direct successor to Ṗēṭros I, despite the decades that separate their episcopates. According to the *History of the Patriarchs,* an unnamed Ethiopian ruler wrote a letter to King George II of Nubia (who acceded to the throne around 969), informing him of grave conditions rampant in Ethiopia. His kingdom had been invaded by rebels led by the queen of Banū al-Hamūyah, who brought ruin and desolation everywhere while pursuing him from place to place. The Ethiopian sovereign attributed all these calamities to divine wrath incurred by the ill treatment of Abuna Ṗēṭros I by one of the kings who preceded him. Since then the church in Ethiopia had remained without a metropolitan. The king pleaded with George II to intercede with the Coptic patriarch, requesting his pardon and the appointment of a new *abun* for Ethiopia. George II did indeed write to Patriarch PHILOTHEUS (979–1003), whereupon the latter consented to name a bishop for Ethiopia, a monk from DAYR ABŪ MAQĀR by the name of Dān'ēl (Dānyāl in Arabic).

Ethiopia received the new metropolitan bishop with great joy, and "God then brought an end to the actions of that woman who had so severely afflicted the land" *(History of the Patriarchs).* There is no other information extant about this *abun.*

However, the episode concerning his appointment to Ethiopia has given rise to many interpretations, with the preferred hypothesis being that of Carlo Conti Rossini. This scholar suggests that the invasion of Ethiopia was probably a reaction or revolt against the Christian dynasty by the queen of Damot, an independent pagan kingdom; he proposed that Banū al-Hamūyah in the Arabic text should be corrected to read Banū al-Damūtah.

The Christian kingdom then suffered a serious crisis that was overcome only by the arrival of Abuna Dān'ēl, who succeeded in consolidating the Christian Ethiopian dynasty.

The immediate successor to Dān'ēl is unknown. The next metropolitan bishop of Ethiopia named in history is Abuna Fiqṭor.

BIBLIOGRAPHY

Budge, E. A. W., trans. *The Book of the Saints of the Ethiopian Church,* Vol. 1, pp. 233–34. Cambridge, 1928.

______. *Storia d'Etiopia,* pp. 285–86. Bergamo, 1928.

Monneret de Villard, U. *Storia della Nubia cristiana,* pp. 125–26. Rome, 1938.

Perruchon, J. "Lettre adressée par le roi d'Ethiopie au roi Georges de Nubie sous le patriarcat de Philotée." *Revue sémitique* 1 (1893):71–79; 359–72.

Renaudot, E. *Historia Patriarcharum Alexandrinorum Jacobitarum,* pp. 381–82. Paris, 1713.

Rossini, C. "I manoscritti etiopici della Missione cattolica di Cheren." *Rendiconti della Reale Accademia dei Lincei* 13, ser. 5 (1904):266.

Sergew Hable Sellassie. *Ancient and Medieval Ethiopian History to 1270,* pp. 223–25, 229–30. Addis Ababa, 1972.

Taddesse Tamrat. *Church and State in Ethiopia 1270–1527,* pp. 38–41. Oxford, 1972.

FIQṬOR (fl. second half eleventh century)

Fiqṭor (Victor; Arabic, Buqṭur) is the first metropolitan bishop mentioned in the *History of the Patriarchs* after Dān'ēl, who had been consecrated near the end of the tenth century, thus indicating a hiatus in the succession. According to the above-mentioned *History,* Fiqṭor was bishop of the Ethiopian church just before his nephew Sāwiros occupied the same position. Since the latter was consecrated by Patriarch CYRIL II (1078–1092), it may be deduced that Abuna Fiqṭor was consecrated toward the middle of the eleventh century by Patriarch CHRISTODOULUS (1047–1077). At any rate, it is certain that Fiqṭor's metropolitanate occurred during the pontificate of Christodoulus.

Renaudot (1713, p. 47) doubted the existence of this particular Ethiopian bishop and proposed that he was probably confused with a certain Buqṭur who, at about this time, was metropolitan bishop for the church in Nubia. However, there is no proof of such a supposed confusion. The Ethiopian Synaxarion (Budge, 1928, Vol. 4, p. 995) does mention that Fiqṭor was the brother (not uncle) of his successor, but it is obvious that priority must be given to the Arabic text, for the Ethiopian text is based thereon.

During Fiqṭor's metropolitanate there was a Coptic monk in Ethiopia, by name of ʿAbdūn, who himself assumed the title of bishop and the name Qūrīl (Cyril), and then plotted to have Fiqṭor deposed so that he might usurp the episcopal throne. Using a certain ʿAlī al-Qifṭī as intermediary, ʿAbdūn began his intrigues before the all-powerful Amīr al-Juyūsh, Badr al-Jamālī, who was vizier (1074–1094) of the Fatimid caliph al-Mustanṣir. Claiming Fiqṭor to be a ruthless enemy of the Ethiopian Muslims, ʿAlī al-Qifṭī suggested to Badr al-Jamālī that Christodoulus should be forced to depose this bishop and replace him with ʿAbdūn. Ceding to the vizier's heavy pressure, Christodoulus decided to send to Ethiopia a delegation led by a bishop and charged with consecrating ʿAbdūn in place of Fiqṭor. However, before the delegation could depart, ʿAlī al-Qifṭī fell into disgrace and was executed after confessing his treachery. This, of course, ended all plans for the delegation. Although he failed in his first attempt to become bishop, ʿAbdūn merely postponed his plans, which he renewed during the episcopate of Sāwiros, Fiqṭor's successor.

The *History of the Patriarchs* gives no other information concerning Abuna Fiqṭor, who seems to have died during the pontificate of Christodoulus.

BIBLIOGRAPHY

Budge, E. A. W., trans. *The Book of the Saints of the Ethiopian Church,* Vol. 4, p. 995. Cambridge, 1928.

Renaudot, E. *Historia Patriarcharum Alexandrinorum Jacobitarum,* p. 47. Paris, 1713.

Rossini, C. *Storia d'Etiopia,* p. 287. Bergamo, 1928.

Taddesse Tamrat. *Church and State in Ethiopia 1270–1527,* p. 47. Oxford, 1972.

[This article continues in Volume 4.]